Politics and the Media

To Dale, Emily, and Sanda

CQ Press, *an imprint of SAGE, is the leading publisher of books, periodicals, and electronic products on American government and international affairs. CQ Press consistently ranks among the top commercial publishers in terms of quality, as evidenced by the numerous awards its products have won over the years. CQ Press owes its existence to Nelson Poynter, former publisher of the* St. Petersburg Times, *and his wife Henrietta, with whom he founded Congressional Quarterly in 1945. Poynter established CQ with the mission of promoting democracy through education and in 1975 founded the Modern Media Institute, renamed The Poynter Institute for Media Studies after his death. The Poynter Institute (www.poynter.org) is a nonprofit organization dedicated to training journalists and media leaders.*

In 2008, CQ Press was acquired by SAGE, a leading international publisher of journals, books, and electronic media for academic, educational, and professional markets. Since 1965, SAGE has helped inform and educate a global community of scholars, practitioners, researchers, and students spanning a wide range of subject areas, including business, humanities, social sciences, and science, technology, and medicine. A privately owned corporation, SAGE has offices in Los Angeles, London, New Delhi, and Singapore, in addition to the Washington DC office of CQ Press.

Politics and the Media
Intersections and New Directions

Jane Hall
American University

FOR INFORMATION:

CQ Press
An imprint of SAGE Publications, Inc.
2455 Teller Road
Thousand Oaks, California 91320
E-mail: order@sagepub.com

SAGE Publications Ltd.
1 Oliver's Yard
55 City Road
London, EC1Y 1SP
United Kingdom

SAGE Publications India Pvt. Ltd.
B 1/I 1 Mohan Cooperative Industrial Area
Mathura Road, New Delhi 110 044
India

SAGE Publications Asia-Pacific Pte. Ltd.
18 Cross Street #10-10/11/12
China Square Central
Singapore 048423

Printed in Canada

ISBN: 9781544385143

This book is printed on acid-free paper.

Acquisitions Editor: Scott Greenan
Editorial Assistant: Lauren Younker
Production Editor: Astha Jaiswal
Copy Editor: Megan Markanich
Typesetter: Hurix Digital
Indexer: Integra
Cover Designer: Candice Harman
Marketing Manager: Jennifer Jones

21 22 23 24 25 10 9 8 7 6 5 4 3 2 1

Brief Table of Contents

Preface   xii

Biography of the Author   xiv

Acknowledgments   xvi

Chapter 1   The Landscape of Media and Politics Today   1

Chapter 2   Underlying Concepts and Historical Foundations   38

Chapter 3   Political Advertising: Persuasion and Deception   66

Chapter 4   Reporting the News: Cultural Bias, Trust, and Accountability   96

Chapter 5   Politicians, the Media, and Social Media: The Push-Pull Relationship   137

Chapter 6   Race and Immigration in Media and Politics: Protests, Policies, and Reform   182

Chapter 7   Global Media: The International Influencer   213

Chapter 8   The Media and Women in Politics   251

References   284

Annotated Media Resources   356

Detailed Table of Contents

Preface   xii

Biography of the Author   xiv

Acknowledgments   xvi

Chapter 1   The Landscape of Media and Politics Today   1

The 2016 Presidential Election   1
   Donald Trump   1
   Hillary Clinton   3
   The Role of Identity Politics   4
   Impeachment   6
   The 2020 Presidential Campaign and Election   7
   The COVID-19 Pandemic   8

Media-Centered Politics   10
   The Landscape   11
   The First Amendment   13
   Public Opinion on Media Credibility   15
   Perceptions of Media Bias and Political Polarization   16
   The Economics of News   18
   Federal Communications Commission and
   Deregulation of Media Ownership   19
   Who Owns What in the Media   20

The Roles Media Play   26
   Gains for the *Washington Post* and the *New York Times*   28
   Declining Local News and Civic Engagement   28
   The Importance of Cable TV News   30
   The Internet and Democratizing Information   31

The Goals for This Book   32
   Media and Politics Research Tool Kit   33

Chapter 2   Underlying Concepts and Historical Foundations   38

Media-Effects Theory   39
   Walter Lippmann and the Nature of News   39
   The Episodic Nature of News Coverage   40

Agenda-Setting Theory   42
   Civil Rights and the History of Agenda-Setting   43

Agenda-Setting in Major Media Today   44
The Role of Elites   45
Agenda-Building   46
Reverse Agenda-Setting   47
Agenda-Setting on Social Media   48

Priming Theory   49
Priming Presidential Campaigns   50
Priming Personal Presidential Traits   51
Priming Presidential Spouses   52

Framing   53
Framing Language and Issue Frames   54
■ Case Study: Framing and Counter-Framing Obamacare   55
Visual Framing   57
Framing and Reframing Same-Sex Marriage   59

The Power of the Senses   61
Debate over Symbols   62
The Power of Sound   63

Summary   63
■ End-of-Chapter Assignment: Agenda-Setting and Framing   65

Chapter 3 Political Advertising: Persuasion
and Deception   66

Spending on Political Advertising   67
Citizens United and Beyond   67
The Impact of Political Ads   70
Public Attitudes toward Money in Politics   71
Ads Alone Can't Win It   72

Persuasive Techniques: From Classical Rhetoric
to Product Advertising   73
Code Words and Distortion   73
Running against "Washington": "Make 'Em Squeal"   75
Heroism and the Plain Folks: "Eisenhower
Answers America"   76
Positive Messaging and the Association Technique:
"Morning in America"   77
Provoking Fear: The "Daisy" Ad   79
Code Words and Stereotyping: Willie Horton   79
■ Case Study: Swift Boat Campaign   80

Advertisements in Recent Campaigns   85
The 2008 Presidential Election   85
The 2012 Presidential Election   86

The 2016 Presidential Election   87
The 2018 Congressional Midterm Elections   90
The 2020 Presidential Election   91

Summary   93
■ **End-of-Chapter Assignment:** Political Ad Analysis   94

Chapter 4   Reporting the News: Cultural Bias, Trust, and Accountability   **96**

Bias toward Immediacy across Media   97
The Early Days of "Immediacy"   97
The Internet Redefines Immediacy   98
Social Media Changes the Game   99
■ **Timeline:** History of Media and Technology   100

Bias toward Conflict and Narrow Debate   104
Moderating Presidential Debates   104

Bias toward Insiderism   106
Revolving Door in Media and Politics   106
What's Wrong with Politics as an Insiders' Game   108

Bias toward Horse-Race Coverage   109
Defense of Horse-Race Coverage   109

Bias toward Establishment Candidates and
    Perceived Front-Runners   110
Interview with Senator Bernie Sanders   110
Critiquing Media Coverage of Sanders   112

Bias toward Official Sources   113

Bias toward Media Narratives   115
Media Narrative in the 2000 Presidential Campaign   117
Access Counts   119

Bias toward Objectivity in Journalism   120
■ **Case Study:** Climate Change and "False Equivalence"
    in Reporting   121

Where Do We Go from Here?   125
The Need for Greater Diversity in Media   125
Trust and Accountability in the Media   126
Building Trust and Accountability   129
Future Directions and Tips   130

Summary   131
■ **End-of-Chapter Assignment:** Book Analysis   132

Chapter 5 Politicians, the Media, and Social Media: The Push-Pull Relationship   137

Congress: Divided and Gridlocked   138
    Senator Susan Collins on Congressional Gridlock   138
    Gridlock Example: Impasse over Gun Control Legislation   139
    The High Cost of Running for Office   140
    Public Support for Limiting Campaign Spending   143
    All Politics Is No Longer Local   144
    Donald Trump and the Republican Party   144
    Covering Congress versus Covering the Presidency   147

The Presidency and the Media   148
    Ronald Reagan and George W. Bush   149
    Barack Obama   150
    Donald Trump   151

Covering Trump   153
    Changes in the White House Press Briefing   154

Changes in Coverage of Party Conventions   157

Outreach on Social Media—Messaging and Mobilizing   158
    Impact of Twitter   158
    @realDonaldTrump and @POTUS   160
    Alexandria Ocasio-Cortez and Social Media   161
    Social Media in the 2020 Presidential Campaign   163

Fake News/Disinformation   164
    The Role of Fake News and Disinformation in the 2016 Election   165

The 2020 Campaign and Moving Forward   167
    Tips for How to Spot Fake News/Disinformation in Your
    Social Media Feed   168
    ■ **Case Study:** Late-Night Comedy   171

Critiques and Self-Critiques of 2016   177

Summary   178
    ■ **End-of Chapter Assignment:** Analyzing Depictions of Politicians
    and Journalists in Popular TV Shows and Classic Movies   179

Chapter 6 Race and Immigration in Media and Politics: Protests, Policies, and Reform   182

Death of George Floyd   182

Coverage of Race and Ethnicity in the Media   185
    The Civil Rights Movement   185

#BlackLivesMatter and Digital Activism   186
The Power of the Social Media Hashtag   190

The Obama Presidency   191
Framing Obama as "the Other"   193
Obama's Discussion of Race   195
Obama's Reelection and Presidency   197
Public Opinion on Racial Discrimination in 2016   197

Immigration   199
Immigration Policy Historically in the U.S.   199
Impact of Media Coverage of Immigration   200
Framing Immigrants and Immigration   200
Interview with Univision Anchor Maria Elena Salinas   201
Republican Party and Immigration   202
Trump Policies on Immigration and on Race   203
■ **Case Study:** Building "the Wall" and Framing Dreamers   205
Latino Voters and the Latino Vote in 2020   208
Kamala Harris as Vice President, and Voters in 2020   209

Summary   212
■ **End-of-Chapter Assignment:** Framing Race and Immigration   212

Chapter 7   Global Media: The International Influencer   **213**

American Exceptionalism and Global Public Opinion   216
Global Public Opinion on the Role of the U.S.   218

The Coronavirus Pandemic   219
International versus Domestic   219
President Trump's Response   222
Role of Fox News Channel and Conservative Media   223
Coronavirus and the 2020 Campaign   226

Climate Change   228
Trends in Public Opinion and Coverage   228
The Environment in the 2020 Presidential Campaign   229

Humanitarian Crises   230
What Gets Covered and Why   230
Shining a Light: The Importance of International News   232
The Syrian Civil War   233

Terrorism   235
The Fear Frame   236
Islamophobia in Media Coverage and Politics   238

Far-Right Domestic Terrorism   239
■ **Case Study:** The War in Iraq   241

Wartime Coverage 245
    Dissent and Wartime Propaganda 245
    Media-Military Relationship 246
    Future of War and War Reporting 248

Summary 249
    ■ **End-of-Chapter Assignment:** Comparing U.S. and International
    Newscasts 250

Chapter 8   The Media and Women in Politics   251

Gender Dynamics in Running for President 254
    Gender and Media in the 2016 Presidential Campaign 254
    Milestones in History of Women in Office 255
    Elizabeth Warren's Presidential Campaign in 2020 256

"Hair, Hemlines, and Husbands": Sexist Coverage
    and Impact 257
    The "Double Bind" for Women in Politics 258
    The "Likeability" Factor 260
    ■ **Case Study:** Elizabeth Dole's 2000 Presidential Campaign 262

Women World Leaders and Structural Barriers to
    Women Running in the U.S. 265
    Women's Suffrage and the History of Women in Office 267
    Why Haven't More Women Run for Office? 269
    Hillary Clinton in the 2008 and 2016 Presidential Campaigns 270
    Critiquing Media Coverage of Clinton in 2016 272
    Donald Trump and Comments about Women 273

Identity Politics and Voters in 2016 275
    The Women's March, the #MeToo Movement, and the 2018
    "Year of the Woman" in Congress 276
    The Gender Gap in Voting and Women Candidates 278

Gender in Media and Politics in the 2020
    Presidential Campaign 279

Kamala Harris 280

Summary 281
    ■ **End-of-Chapter Assignment:** Women Candidates in
    Announcement Videos and Debates 282

References 284

Annotated Media Resources 356

Index 364

Preface

"Hello and welcome to Politics and the Media." If you were a student in my longtime course in politics and the media at American University in Washington, D.C., that's how I would introduce my class. I have been developing, teaching, and learning from my students in political communication, political science, journalism, and media studies in this course since I came to American University more than twenty years ago. I came to full-time teaching, scholarly research, and writing as well as continued work in media criticism from a career as a journalist covering the news media, politics, and policy for many years—most recently as a national correspondent for the *Los Angeles Times* in New York. This book is a culmination of my professional, scholarly, and teaching experience.

I hope that this book will help you understand, examine, and analyze the forces that come together at the important intersection of politics and the media today.

From the roles of race and gender in American politics and society to the 2020 election and from the coronavirus pandemic and the shocking storming of the U.S. Capitol to the inauguration of a new administration, what Americans are facing today is an extraordinary moment for politicians, the news media, and the democracy itself. The 2018 congressional midterm elections and the 2020 presidential election brought historic new diversity and representation to political office—and, at the same time, the country has an electorate that some historians say is as polarized as during the Civil War. The Internet has proven to be a powerful force for communication and organization, for good and for ill, while the loyalty of viewers of major news organizations begins to split along party lines. Major news organizations have seen attacks on their credibility and even their right to report, and yet the public continues to support and call for the news media to fulfill their watchdog role under the First Amendment.

The goal of this book is to help readers understand these seemingly dichotomous forces in politics and the media, how we got here, what is happening today, and what may be future directions. We will look at the intersection of media and politics and how that impacts the candidates we choose, the issues we focus on, and the outcomes in politics and policies that affect people's lives.

Chapter 1 begins with an introduction to the current media landscape and the interplay of politics and media in the most recent national elections. We will discuss the First Amendment, media ownership, economics of news and the impact of deregulation, along with perceptions of media bias. Chapter 2 explores basic concepts such as framing and agenda-setting and how they apply today. Chapter 3 examines political advertising and persuasive techniques, with "classic" and contemporary examples, while Chapters 4 and 5 describe the push-pull relationship between journalists and politicians, including operational and cultural biases in news-gathering, coverage of Congress and the presidency, "fake news" and disinformation, and the role of the Internet and social media in political campaigns and social movements. Chapter 6 examines the important topic of depictions of race and ethnicity in American media and politics (from both an historical and contemporary perspective)—from media coverage of the civil rights movement and the election of Barack Obama to the impact of racist, anti-immigrant rhetoric and widespread protests sparked by video of the death of George Floyd, an unarmed Black man, in police custody. Chapter 7 looks at international news, including comparing U.S. and global news coverage of climate change and the coronavirus pandemic and discussing issues in covering war and humanitarian crises. The insurrection and mob violence at the U.S. Capitol took place days after this book went into production, but the roots and rise of far-right domestic terrorism and mobilization over the Internet are discussed in Chapter 7 as well. And, finally, Chapter 8 examines gender in media and politics—how the ways that women are depicted and perceived have impact on their credibility and viability as candidates—from the suffrage movement to Shirley Chisholm, Elizabeth Dole, Hillary Clinton, and Kamala Harris, just to name a few.

In each chapter you'll hear from prominent figures in media and politics—from senators and members of Congress to journalists, political strategists, activists, and media critics—via interviews that I have conducted for the book, privately and publicly, always with my students and this book in mind. A list of the interviewees is included in Chapter 1. They offer important perspective, as do the many scholars and studies that are quoted and included here. A guide for researching and writing your own case study analysis is in Chapter 1 as well. After the introductory Chapter 1, each additional chapter includes a reading, writing, and/or viewing assignment to enhance your understanding of the topic in addition to a topical case study. I look forward to hearing from you in your explorations of politics and media; you are the next generation.

Biography of the Author

Jane Hall is an associate professor in the School of Communication at American University in Washington, D.C., specializing in researching, writing, and teaching about the intersection of media and politics and journalism. Before joining American University, Hall was a journalist covering the news media, politics, and policy for national publications, including nine years as the media correspondent for the *Los Angeles Times* in New York. She was a finalist for the Pulitzer Prize and winner of the Los Angeles Times Editor's Award and the Los Angeles Press Club Award.

Hall is moderator and executive producer for the long-running American Forum events series in Washington, D.C., interviewing prominent journalists and politicians with college students on TV, public radio, and online. Professor Hall has been a regular contributor to *Columbia Journalism Review*, the *Harvard International Journal of Press/Politics*, and the Freedom Forum *Media Studies Journal*. She has written for other publications from *Rolling Stone* to the *Wall Street Journal*. Her *New York Times* op-ed essay about the impact of Fox News Channel on politics and journalism was widely quoted. Hall is frequently interviewed about issues in media and politics by the *New York Times*, *Washington Post*, AP, National Public Radio (NPR), *Politico*, and numerous other outlets. A former media commentator on Fox News Channel, she has regularly appeared as a media expert on CNN's media analysis program *Reliable Sources* as well as *PBS NewsHour*, MSNBC, C-SPAN, and other networks.

Hall has specialized in writing and teaching about the depiction of women in politics and media, including a chapter on the status of women in TV and print journalism for *Gender and Women's Leadership: A Reference Handbook* (SAGE); she also focuses on writing and teaching about young people and news and politics as well as media ethics. Hall coauthored a survey and analysis of more than two hundred journalists regarding self-censorship of imagery from the Iraq War that was praised as an important study by *Columbia Journalism Review*. Professor Hall teaches a popular interdisciplinary course, Politics and the Media, that attracts majors from political science, political communication, and journalism. She also teaches courses in reporting on the federal government and on understanding media and popular culture.

Hall has collaborated with news organizations and students on numerous student-centered editorial and national polling projects, including a yearlong series with the *Washington Post* around the 2008 presidential election as well as a yearlong project about the 2018 congressional midterm elections that culminated in a live town hall on WAMU public radio in

Washington, D.C. Hall has twice been chosen Professor of the Year by student government at American University for her work with student groups.

A native of Abilene, Texas, Professor Hall earned her undergraduate degree from the University of Texas at Austin and her master's from the Columbia University Graduate School of Journalism. She is a member of Phi Beta Kappa.

Acknowledgments

This book would not have been possible without the continuing support, personally and professionally, of my family, friends, colleagues, and editors. I am indebted to Chris Martin, who began this project as my teaching assistant a number of years ago and has continued to provide editorial assistance ever since. Over the past tumultuous year in media and politics, Matt Thibault, also a former assistant, has provided important research in my quest to write a book that aims to be both timeless and contemporary.

Sarah Welch, my current assistant, has provided invaluable editorial assistance.

Scott Greenan, the editor of this book, has ably guided me through editing and throughout the publication process at CQ Press/SAGE, and I am grateful also for the work of Lauren Younker, senior editorial assistant; Astha Jaiswal, production editor; and Megan Markanich, copy editor.

I have not known the anonymous reviewers until now; I appreciate their suggestions and feedback—and I know that everyone involved has made this a better book. Jerry Higgins and Ashley Dodge have been early supporters. And I am grateful also to the many journalists, political leaders, political strategists, academic researchers, and media critics who agreed to be interviewed by me for a real-world, critical perspective about their work and the role of media and politics in the health of our democracy.

American University has provided an academic and professional home for me for more than twenty years, and I want to acknowledge the encouragement and support for all my work and teaching over the years from School of Communication deans Larry Kirkman, Jeff Rutenbeck, and Laura DeNardis; university president Sylvia Burwell; Matt Bennett; Women and Politics Institute founder and professor Karen O'Connor; Professors Amy Eisman, Wendy Swallow, and Kathy Fitzpatrick; Jeffrey Madison; and librarians Derrick Jefferson and Robin Chin Roemer, along with Jason Hacker and Claire Savage. Conrad Rippy has been my adviser and friend throughout my professional and academic career. Sanda Bragman Lewis has been an extraordinary teacher and mentor. Carol Slatkin, Melissa Torgovitsky, Skaidra Waggoner, Lindsay Minter and Bill Minter; my sister, Carol, and brother-in-law, Leonard Majzlin; Elizabeth Clay, Gail Ionescu, and numerous other family and friends have been supportive—and grounding.

Finally, I want to express my deepest appreciation and love for my lifetime partner, Dale Anderson, and our wonderful daughter, Emily. Dale cheered me on or left the room—whichever I needed, or both—so that I could work. Emily has been the joy of our lives, soaring in her own accomplishments and loving nature and delighting her late-in-life parents since she was a child circling the dining table helping compile packets for tenure. Dale's three older daughters, Ariel, Lucky, and Chicky, were and are a great advertisement for what a fine father he is. It has been difficult—and poignant—to bring this book to publication without Dale's daily presence. But he is here with us in every meaningful way.

I would also like to acknowledge the following reviewers for their work in helping me to shape this text:

- Jeffrey N. Carroll, *Chestnut Hill College*
- Rod Carveth, *Morgan State University*
- Darlena Cunha, *University of Florida*
- Donna Halper, *Lesley University*
- Ken Hicks, *Rogers State University*
- Dann L. Pierce, *University of Portland*
- Ivy Shen, *Southeast Missouri State University*
- Jason Sides, *Southeast Missouri State University*
- Zachary Taylor, *University of Wyoming*
- Robert Velez, *University of Texas Rio Grande Valley*
- Ken J. Ward, *Lamar University*
- Aaron Weinschenk, *University of Wisconsin–Green Bay*
- Diane Winston, *University of Southern California*

CHAPTER 1

The Landscape of Media and Politics Today

The 2016 Presidential Election

In the tumultuous 2016 presidential campaign, Donald Trump rode a wave of economic discontent, anti-Washington anger, and nativist blame of "the Other" to one of the most stunning political upsets in recent American history. The Manhattan real estate mogul and reality TV star had no experience in government. But he defeated Hillary Clinton—one of the most prominent and experienced politicians in the country—in her bid to become the first female president of the U.S. by fashioning himself as the friend of the forgotten "common man" who would "drain the swamp" in Washington, D.C., and fight for voters, particularly those who felt displaced and unheard through lost jobs, multiculturalism, and globalization.

Hillary Clinton won the popular vote by nearly 2.9 million votes,[1] but Trump's surge in voters in previously Democratic Rust Belt states as well as in rural areas was missed by almost every major poll, including the candidates' own internal polling. Pollsters and pundits had confidently predicted a Clinton win on the night of the election, missing the surge and calling their research methods into question.[2]

After the election, many in the news media and political capitals of Washington, D.C., and New York questioned if they had missed the Trump phenomenon by living in a blue state, urban bubble. "To put it bluntly, the media missed the story," *Washington Post* media columnist Margaret Sullivan wrote the day after the election.[3]

Donald Trump

Trump—who announced his candidacy in 2015 with a speech that characterized Mexican immigrants to the U.S. as "rapists" and "drug-dealers"[4]—received huge free media attention for his incendiary remarks and promises to build a wall across Mexico, deport eleven million immigrants living in the U.S. illegally, and temporarily ban Muslims from entering the country.[5] His comments about women—from Fox News Channel anchor Megyn Kelly to Republican primary opponent Carly Fiorina—were capped in the final month of the campaign with the release of a 2005 *Access*

Hollywood off-camera video in which Trump was heard making vulgar comments and boasting about groping women.[6]

Trump—whose rhetoric was condemned, including by Republican House Speaker Paul Ryan, during the primaries[7] for fanning the flames of racism, misogyny, and fear of immigrants—won the white vote by record margins. According to exit polls, Trump won 71 percent of non-college-educated white men but also 61 percent of non-college-educated white women.[8] Clinton won overwhelmingly among nonwhite voters as well as winning among women overall.[9] But an expected big increase in voting by Latinos did not occur, and the level of support for Clinton among African Americans, Hispanics, and Asian Americans was less for Clinton than their support for Barack Obama, the nation's first African American president, in his 2012 reelection.[10] Many women, in particular, were dismayed that Trump's misogynistic remarks about women did not lead to a higher turnout and higher margin for Clinton among women overall, and there were protests among college students and other young people who expressed fears about Trump's campaign promises and their future.[11]

There were several contradictory messages in the exit poll election results. Clinton won voters who thought the economy was the most important issue; a majority of voters said they disagreed with Trump's plans on immigration, but his stances on immigration, along with criticism of U.S. trade policy, were decisive issues for his supporters.[12] Clinton and Trump were both historically unpopular nominees,[13] and voters who expressed serious reservations about Trump's qualifications and temperament still voted for him.[14] In an interview with the author, one Democratic strategist who worked on Clinton's campaign said, "We did not account for cognitive dissonance in our focus groups."[15] Four in ten voters said a candidate who "can bring needed change" was the most important character trait, with "has the right experience" (Clinton's strong suit) second.

One need only look at the extraordinary amount of free news media coverage—and high ratings—that Donald Trump received in the 2016 Republican presidential primaries and the general election to see that his canny understanding of the live cable TV news environment, the bias of the news media toward conflict and outrageous remarks, and the commercial needs of the news media all helped fuel his rise to the Republican nomination and the ardent support he built among millions of supporters.

According to an analysis by mediaQuant, a firm that tracks media coverage of candidates and assigns a dollar value to media coverage, based on source, for comparable paid advertising, Trump earned $2 billion worth of *earned media, unpaid media coverage and commentary*, across print, broadcast, and other sources as well as online-only sources such as Facebook, Twitter, and Reddit over the course of the Republican primary campaign and into the important Super Tuesday primaries. Trump, who did not have a super PAC and was spending little on TV advertising or ground organization

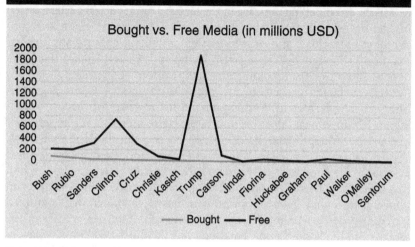

Figure 1.1 Bought versus Free Media

Bought vs. Free Media (in millions USD)

Bush, Rubio, Sanders, Clinton, Cruz, Christie, Kasich, Trump, Carson, Jindal, Fiorina, Huckabee, Graham, Paul, Walker, O'Malley, Santorum

―― Bought ―― Free

Note: **As of February 2016

Sources: Data from mediaQuant, SMG Delta, and the *New York Times*.

during the primaries, had in media coverage, as the *New York Times* put it, earned "about twice the all-in price of the most expensive presidential campaign in history" as well as twice the estimated $746 million of earned media for Hillary Clinton.[16]

At the same time, the then-insurgent Democratic primary campaign of Vermont senator Bernie Sanders and his support, particularly among young people, for proposals regarding income inequality, the cost of college, and campaign finance reform was initially dismissively covered—and under-covered—for many months, including by the *New York Times* and the *Washington Post*. The initial coverage, TV punditry, and attitude of officials in the Democratic Party about Sanders reflected a bias toward establishment candidates and the two-party system as well as the inside-the-Beltway media-politics echo chamber that for several months missed Sanders' appeal and his significant fundraising among small-dollar donors online. The ratio of minutes of coverage of Senator Sanders' campaign compared to Donald Trump's—on the three broadcast evening newscasts on ABC, CBS, and NBC—was a startling eighty-one to one in 2015, according to the Tyndall Report, a long-running analysis of the per-topic minutes on the broadcast evening news.[17]

Hillary Clinton

In postmortems among Democrats, Clinton and her team were criticized for not campaigning and reaching out more to working-class and blue-collar voters in swing states who had lost jobs and wages through factory closings and a slow economic recovery and also for not clearly articulating how she would help voters in the economy.[18] Clinton struggled to present a compelling message in the face of Trump's attacks. She focused instead on using Trump's own words—where he was mocking and condemning individuals and groups as well as talking about using nuclear weapons in foreign policy—against Trump in TV commercials that were designed to prove Trump temperamentally unfit to be president.[19]

It is difficult to separate the possible impacts of Clinton's gender from her long history in Washington and her own controversies, including an FBI investigation of her use of a private email server as secretary of state. An in-depth analysis of election coverage in the *New York Times*, *Washington Post*, *USA Today*, *Wall Street Journal*, and the *Los Angeles Times* as well as the broadcast networks, CNN and Fox News Channel found that coverage of both Clinton and Trump was "overwhelmingly negative in tone and extremely light on policy" in a "nasty" campaign that continued a trend decried by political scientist Thomas E. Patterson, author of the report from the Shorenstein Center on Media, Politics and Public Policy, at Harvard University. "A healthy dose of negativity is unquestionably a good thing," Patterson wrote. "Yet an incessant stream of criticism has a corrosive effect. It needlessly erodes trust in political leaders and institutions and undermines confidence in government and policy," resulting in a media environment with many false equivalencies that can mislead voters about the choices they make.[20]

One such false equivalence, Patterson wrote, may have been coverage of Clinton's use of a private email server. Coverage of the two candidates, he said, was "virtually identical" in terms of the negative tone. "Were the allegations surrounding Clinton of the same order of magnitude as those surrounding Trump?" Patterson asked. "It's a question that political reporters made no serious effort to answer during the campaign."[21]

The FBI in 2016 found Clinton's use of a private email server while secretary of state "extremely careless" but recommended that no charges be filed against her.[22] A government investigation completed in 2019 found no deliberate mishandling of private information by Clinton.[23] But the email server story was cited by voters in focus groups as evidence of Clinton's untrustworthiness and allowed Trump to repeat his label for her—"crooked Hillary"—to supporters who chanted "Lock her up!"[24] After the election, many voters at the time expressed disgust with politics and the 2016 campaign as well as skepticism about whether either nominee could unite the country.[25]

The Role of Identity Politics

The Republican establishment—which initially had backed former Florida Governor Jeb Bush as the presumptive nominee and then saw Trump emerge among a crowded field of seventeen presidential candidates during the primaries and TV debates—missed the anger at the establishment (including the Republican establishment) and disaffection over lost jobs and changing demographics that Donald Trump tapped into and stoked. Ronald F. Inglehart of the University of Michigan and Pippa Norris of Harvard, along with other researchers and scholars, have linked Trump's election to the surprising Brexit vote by British voters to leave the European Union and the growth of right-wing populism worldwide, attributing these forces not only to lost jobs and globalization but also to changing demographics and a "cultural backlash" among some against rapid social change.[26]

At the same time, the second media narrative that emerged—that Trump voters were overwhelmingly "working class" and even poor in terms of income—was belied in 2017 by analysis of the long-running American National Election Studies, which found that only 35 percent of people who said they voted for Donald Trump in 2016 had incomes below $50,000 per year.[27]

In 2016 President Trump was accused of using what are called "dog whistle politics," which political scientist Ian Haney Lopez defined as "sending a message about racial minorities inaudible on one level, but clearly heard on another."[28] Dog whistle appeals have a history in American politics. Trump was overt in his characterizations of people of color and immigrants as taking over the country and responsible for the problems faced by the white working class. And his slogan "Make America Great Again" strongly implies that America today is no longer great because, as he asserted in his 2015 announcement speech, Mexican immigrants were "rapists and murderers" "bringing drugs" and their problems while America was "laughed at" by the Chinese.[29]

In their 2018 book *Identity Crisis, The 2016 Presidential Campaign and the Battle for the Meaning of America*, coauthors John Sides of George Washington University, Michael Tesler of the University of California, Irvine, and Lynn Vavreck of the University of California, Los Angeles analyzed extensive voting and polling data and concluded that, to a degree not seen in the 2008 and 2012 Republican primaries, it was issues of *identity*— race, religion, gender, and ethnicity—*not* economics—that determined how people voted, particularly voters who were white.[30]

"What made this election distinctive was *how much* those identities mattered to voters," the authors wrote. "During Trump's unexpected rise to the nomination, support for Trump or one of his many rivals was strongly linked to how Republican voters felt about blacks, immigrants, and Muslims, and how much discrimination Republican voters believed that whites themselves faced. . . . These same factors helped voters choose between Trump or Hillary Clinton in the general election—and again, these factors mattered even more in 2016 than they had in recent presidential elections. More strikingly still, group identities came to matter even on issues that did not have to be about identity, such as the simple question of whether one was doing okay economically."[31]

In what was viewed as a backlash against the Trump presidency and the 2016 election, Democrats dramatically shifted the balance of power in the House of Representatives in the 2018 midterm elections, gaining control of the House. Voters eighteen to twenty-nine years old increased their percentage of voting, while women, particularly white college-educated women, increased the gender gap between the Republican and Democratic Parties in the voting.[32] A record number of women were elected or appointed to Congress, with 102 women, including 43 women of color, serving in the House, and 24 women, including four women of color, in the U.S. Senate.[33] Republicans made gains in the Senate, reflecting a divided country, including between cities and suburbs and rural communities.[34]

Impeachment

In 2019 President Trump became only the third president in U.S. history to be impeached,[35] on charges of abuse of power and obstruction of Congress. Democrats charged that the U.S. president had pressured the president of Ukraine to investigate the business dealings of former vice president Joe Biden and his son in Ukraine by withholding nearly $400 million in military aid approved by Congress to help Ukraine defend itself against Russian military intervention; the president, they said, had endangered U.S. national security interests in an attempt to influence the 2020 election and later to obstruct the congressional investigation.[36]

President Trump and his defense team repeatedly denounced the Democrats, the impeachment inquiry, and trial, which began with a White House whistleblower's official complaint expressing concerns about the president's phone call to the president of Ukraine, as a "witch hunt" and a "hoax" and a "brazen" attempt to reverse the results of the 2016 election.[37] Rep. Adam Schiff, the California Democrat who chaired the House Intelligence Committee, was a frequent guest on MSNBC's *The Rachel Maddow Show*, and she and other MSNBC hosts emphasized the testimony of diplomats and White House national security officials during the House inquiry. Covering the testimony from witnesses in the House and then the debate in the Senate impeachment trial, host Sean Hannity and other prime-time hosts on Fox News Channel praised President Trump and repeated the president's criticisms of the motives of the Democrats and the diplomats and White House national security officials who testified in the House inquiry.[38]

While CNN, MSNBC, and National Public Radio (NPR) covered the Senate trial live in its entirety, including the defense of the president's actions by his lawyers, Fox News Channel turned away from the House Democratic leaders' arguments to air their prime-time hosts criticizing the trial instead.[39] "The goal of this entire process is not to remove the president from office, it's simply to remove certain Republican senators," Republican senator Tim Scott of South Carolina told reporters.[40]

Representative Schiff, the California Democrat who led the Democrats making the case during the Senate impeachment trial, made an emotional closing argument that went viral, urging the Republican-majority Senate to vote to remove the president from office.[41] In the end, a divided Senate, as expected, voted to acquit the president of the charges against him in a vote that split along party lines, with only one Republican senator, Mitt Romney, the 2012 Republican presidential nominee, voting guilty on the charge that the president abused his power for political gain in his dealings with Ukraine.[42] President Trump retweeted an attack ad that called Romney a "Democrat secret asset" and declared what he called "our Country's VICTORY on the Impeachment Hoax."[43]

A Gallup poll of Americans taken amid the Senate impeachment trial found 52 percent of respondents favoring acquitting the president, with 46 percent in favor of convicting and removing him from office.[44] The president's approval rating overall had risen to 49 percent, his highest since he took office, with nearly 50 percent of respondents disapproving of his performance. Trump had increased his approval rating among independents several points, to 42 percent, while his support among Democrats had dropped from 10 percent to 7 percent in recent months. The president's approval rating among Republicans in the Gallup poll was 94 percent, resulting in the biggest gap in approval measured to date by Gallup, higher than the previous record, between Barack Obama and Trump.[45] In the same poll, 63 percent approved of Trump's handling of the economy.[46]

The 2020 Presidential Campaign and Election

In the 2020 presidential campaign, the initial field of Democratic candidates was both historically large and historically diverse. The field included a record six women running to be the first female president of the U.S.: Massachusetts senator Elizabeth Warren, California senator Kamala Harris, Minnesota senator Amy Klobuchar, New York senator Kirsten Gillibrand, Hawaii representative and military veteran Tulsi Gabbard, and author Marianne Williamson. There were two African American candidates, New Jersey senator Cory Booker along with Kamala Harris. Also running was Julián Castro, who is Latino and a former cabinet official in the Obama administration.[47]

Another candidate, businessman Andrew Yang, is Asian American. Former South Bend, Indiana, mayor and Afghanistan War veteran Pete Buttigieg was the first openly gay presidential candidate—and, running at thirty-seven, Buttigieg would have been the youngest president if elected.[48]

Joe Biden, the seventy-seven-year-old former senator and vice president under Barack Obama, had entered his third campaign for president with some hesitation, he said, but a determination to defeat Donald Trump.[49] Vermont senator Bernie Sanders, seventy-eight, who had mounted an insurgent campaign and done well against Hillary Clinton in several 2016 primaries, emerged as a front-runner in 2020, raising millions of dollars online and attracting a loyal following among young people, in particular, with his calls for "Medicare for All" and reforming income inequality and "corporate greed" on Wall Street. Warren, an Oklahoma-born Harvard law professor who had built the Consumer Financial Protection Bureau under President Obama,[50] linked her family's personal story to her plans for "structural change" in health care and taxes on Wall Street. Billionaire businessman and former New York City mayor Michael Bloomberg entered the race well into the campaign, spending more than $500 million on advertising in states where he planned to compete in the March multistate Super Tuesday primaries.[51]

As we know now, after highly watched debates, intense campaigning and media coverage, and strong shifts in the standing of candidates in polling and voting in primaries, the race for the Democratic nomination came down to a two-person contest between Biden and Sanders. Biden—who had faltered in TV debates and with voters in early contests in Iowa and New Hampshire—scored a major victory in South Carolina, particularly among African American voters, after winning the important endorsement of longtime South Carolina Representative Jim Clyburn. In dramatic moments carried live on television, Klobuchar and Buttigieg ended their campaigns and endorsed Biden on the eve of the Super Tuesday primaries as the more moderate wing of the Democratic Party sought to consolidate support for the candidate they and many voters viewed as a safer choice who was more electable against Donald Trump. For Democrats, "what set the tone and template for 2020 . . . wasn't the DNC [Democratic National Committee] or the primary calendar," wrote Amy Walter, national political editor of the *Cook Political Report*. "It was the single-minded focus on 'electability.'"[52]

The COVID-19 Pandemic

The coronavirus pandemic that swept around the world in the spring of 2020 upended world economies and plans for the 2020 presidential election. The U.S. was ill-prepared for the pandemic—and President Trump faced severe criticism for his downplaying of the disease and his administration's handling of the crisis, especially from the time the virus emerged in China in late December[53] until the beginning of May.[54] Economies around the world were shut down—and devastated—in a global economic depression. Among the 3.8 million cases reported between January and May 2020, the U.S. alone registered 1.7 million cases of COVID-19, the illness caused by the new virus.[55] More than seventy-five thousand people in the U.S. had died, with the government predicting nearly a doubling of that total by August at the same time that President Trump was pressing states to reopen.[56]

The stock market crashed as businesses and the economy were shut down in measures to curb the spread of the highly contagious disease. In April, 20.5 million Americans suddenly lost their jobs, according to the Labor Department, creating an unemployment rate of 14.7 percent, which was the highest since the 25.5 percent of the Great Depression in 1932.[57]

The coronavirus crisis revealed, reflected, and *amplified* both an economic divide and a partisan divide in politics and the media in this country, with Fox News Channel prime-time hosts dismissing the risks and blaming Democrats and the news media for allegedly exaggerating the crisis. As we will discuss in Chapter 7 on international news, the divides had significant impact on how the pandemic has been perceived—and experienced—and how voters viewed the president during the 2020 campaign.

In the 2020 election, President Trump reportedly had hoped to run on a strong economy and profits on Wall Street, despite criticism from Bernie Sanders and Elizabeth Warren that tax cuts under Trump had widened economic disparities overall. If Bernie Sanders, a self-described Democratic socialist, or Elizabeth Warren, had won the Democratic nomination, Trump and the Republicans would have been able to more successfully attack the candidate and down-ballot Democrats as tax-and-spend, "nondemocratic" socialists who would ruin the American economy with excessive regulation. "Americans of all political beliefs are sick and tired of the radical, rage-filled, left socialists," Trump told supporters at a campaign rally in January 2020. "Really, the Democrat Party is the socialist party and maybe worse."[58]

Trump and Vice President Mike Pence tried to make that argument first against the more moderate Joe Biden and senator Harris, the Democrats' vice presidential nominee. In the wake of widespread protests and calls for police reform after the death of George Floyd, Trump doubled down on racial appeals in 2020, emulating the 1968 presidential campaign of Alabama governor George Wallace in portraying himself as the "law-and-order" president protecting voters against "lawless" protesters and anarchists.[59] Trump was widely criticized for his refusal to disavow white supremacists in the first presidential debate and, on the eve of the election, was losing support among white suburban women and seniors who had supported him in 2016. Harris, the first woman of color and only the second woman (after Geraldine Ferraro) to win the vice presidential nomination of a major party, dubbed Trump's appeals "a dog-whistle through a bull-horn."[60]

With the stock market collapse and record unemployment claims, along with more than 210,000 deaths by October in the coronavirus pandemic, Biden and the Democrats made the election a referendum on President Trump and his handling of the pandemic.

Media-Centered Politics

It is hard to imagine today, but American politics once reflected the stereo-typical "smoke-filled room" where strong parties and party bosses picked candidates, and the public once had direct access to candidates and even to the president within the White House. Today, national politics is conducted primarily through the media, including the *media primary*, where the media, in effect, vet potential candidates.

"The United States is the only democracy that organizes its national election campaigns around the news media," Thomas E. Patterson wrote in his book *Out of Order*. Patterson called the news media "the miscast institution" for their role in the democracy. "Even if the media did not want the responsibility for organizing the campaign, it is theirs by virtue of an election system built upon entrepreneurial candidates, floating voters, freewheeling interest groups, and weak political parties."[61] Many journalists take very seriously their role in the democracy and in today's media-centered politics, often providing more context and analysis in reporting than in political reporting in years past. Yet, the nature and practices of news-gathering—what we will call here the *conventions of news-gathering*—along with economic pressures often create a disconnect between the commercial imperatives of the media and the public interest needs of the democracy.

There has always been a tension for major news media between giving the public *what they need to know* versus *what they want to know*, as former CBS News president Richard Salant memorably described it in an interview with the author.[62] But today, news media that traditionally have played a major role in the democracy are under twin pressures—from the growth of Internet advertising sapping their advertiser-supported business model to increasing concentration of ownership of the media by a few major corporations that bring layoffs, cutbacks in coverage, and increased pressure for short-term profits.

It is difficult for serious work in journalism to even break in to the cacophony of today's media environment, in which all kinds of communication across all kinds of platforms are considered "the media" and "the news" by the public. Ratings and readership of the news since the 2016 election are up on cable TV and online on the sites of the *New York Times*, *Washington Post* and some other national news sites and publications, but many local newspapers are struggling.

U.S. voter participation remains relatively low compared to other developed countries, especially during nonpresidential years, with more motivated voters affecting party primaries while others stay home. In the 2016 presidential election, nearly one hundred million Americans—representing 43 percent of the eligible voting-age population—did not cast a vote for president.[63]

Many people are simply not paying attention to news—or politics—today. A landmark study of nonvoters, published by the Knight Foundation in 2020, found nonvoters reporting feeling variously overwhelmed, confused, and skeptical of the contemporary media environment as well as the state of politics and the political system.[64] A year before the 2020 presidential election, in a survey by the nonpartisan Pew Research Center, some 46 percent of social media users said they were feeling "worn out" by the number of political posts and discussion they were seeing on their social media—a 9 percent increase in the response from the summer of 2016.[65]

The Landscape

Today we live in challenging times for media, politics, and the democracy—and it is more important than ever to examine the intersection and impact of these forces. Faith in the democracy—and democratic institutions—has declined in the U.S. and globally. President Trump's attacks on the news media, labeling journalism he disagreed with "fake news" and even, ominously, calling journalists "treasonous" and "the enemy of the people,"[66] have alarmed First Amendment scholars and media critics from a range of political perspectives who have raised concerns about the long-lasting impacts of undermining the important role of the news media in the democracy.

The contemporary media-political environment has been redrawing the lines of credibility and authority in news media and changing the ways that politicians, journalists, and members of the public interact with each other, with impact on politics, policy, and the media. Describing what had emerged as "one of the most frustrating challenges faced by candidates Barack Obama and John McCain" as far back as the 2008 presidential campaign, *New York Times* political reporter Adam Nagourney wrote, "The proliferation of communications channels, the fracturing of mass media and the relentless political competition to own each news cycle are combining to reorder the ways voters follow campaigns and decide how to vote. It has reached a point where senior campaign aides say they are no longer sure what works, as they stumble through what has become a daily campaign fog, struggling to figure out what voters are paying attention to, and not incidentally, what they are believing."[67]

These trends have only accelerated in recent years, with the growth of the Internet and social media, a bifurcated cable news environment, and an assault on the very notion of agreed-upon facts. It was Trump adviser Kellyanne Conway who coined the phrase "alternative facts" to defend then-press secretary Sean Spicer's false statement about the number of people who attended the president's inauguration,[68] and the president himself tweeted and retweeted conspiracy theories and outright falsehoods to his millions of Twitter followers in ways that traditional media were hard-pressed to keep up with. President Trump frequently set the agenda for news media, particularly on cable and online, via his Twitter feed, announcing foreign policies that surprised his own advisers or railing against his opponents in provocative ways that cable TV shows and other media found irresistible to report.

At the end of 2019, a team of fact-checkers at the *Washington Post*, using a database to categorize and analyze the president's statements, counted that the president had made 15,413 false or misleading statements from 2017 to the end of 2019—many of them repeated multiple times on Twitter, on subjects from immigration and the impeachment inquiry to his assertion on the eve of the 2020 presidential election that the strong U.S. economy was the best in U.S. history.[69]

President Trump presented a conundrum for major media in the U.S., which have for many years promoted an ideal of objectivity and separating facts from opinion in their news coverage—a concept that also has been criticized as *false objectivity*, as we will discuss in Chapter 4. The *New York Times* and the *Washington Post*, in particular, along with CNN, have been targeted as "failing," liberal, and even "treasonous" by Donald Trump for their reporting on him and his administration.[70] "We're not at war with the administration—we're at work," *Washington Post* executive editor Martin Baron said in 2017.[71]

With President Trump's attacks on specific news organizations and journalists, the distinction between facts and opinion—already blurred on cable television shows mixing journalists and political strategists—became even more strained as prime-time cable TV hosts on CNN, MSNBC, and Fox News Channel readily stated their opinions about the president.

Where Americans get their news today is a significant factor in determining what people believe. In a poll published after the midterm elections in 2018, the *Washington Post* found that "even as Trump's fact-free statements proliferate, there is evidence that his approach is failing," with "fewer than 3 in 10 Americans—including 4 in 10 Republicans" in the poll believing "his most-common false statements."[72] Yet, in that same poll, "a pool of strong Trump approvers—about 1 in 6 adults"—accepted "several, although not all," of the president's falsehoods as true.[73] Respondents who listed Fox News Channel as one of their top news sources were more likely to believe the false statements tested in the 2018 *Post* poll than those saying Fox News Channel was not a main news source.[74] Along with these disparities in media consumption and belief, today's politics and political structure also rewards polarization, in primaries and in Congress. A simple but important truth is that it is difficult for citizens and political leaders to work together—and to consider outcomes to be legitimate—if they cannot agree on a basis set of facts.

The First Amendment

The First Amendment to the Constitution gives news media protections against government interference because the framers of the Constitution believed that a free press provided a vital check against abuse by the government. This is known as the *watchdog role of the media* in the democracy, an ideal that the public traditionally has supported, despite criticism of the media—that the news media deserve protection, as they have under the First Amendment, in order to serve the public interest as an independent watch on corruption and government abuse.

The First Amendment is part of the Bill of Rights that was added to the Constitution in 1791 to protect civil liberties.[75] It states that "Congress shall make no law respecting an establishment of religion, or prohibiting the free exercise thereof; or abridging the freedom of speech, or of the press; or the right of the people peaceably to assemble, and to petition the Government for a redress of grievances."[76] As many observers have noted, this is the *first amendment* in the Bill of Rights because of the importance attached to these civil liberties.

Thomas Jefferson famously wrote this in a letter in 1787, "The basis of our governments being the opinion of the people, the very first object should be to keep that right. And if it were left to me to decide whether we should have a government without newspapers, or newspapers without a government, I should not hesitate a moment to prefer the latter."[77]

As historians have noted, Jefferson did not anticipate the highly partisan press that followed; as president and like other presidents, he was critical of the media and even moved to curb a critical press at one point.[78] Still, he remained a champion of the First Amendment, writing in 1823 that "the only security of all is in a free press."[79]

The infamous Alien and Sedition Acts of 1798 may have proved his point. These acts, passed by a Federalist-controlled Congress in anticipation of an expected war with France, passed restrictions on immigration and prohibited any criticism of the Federalist government by opposing Democratic-Republican publications but did not extend to publications that supported the Democratic-Republicans. When he was elected president in 1800, Jefferson pardoned the journalists for Democratic-Republican publications who had been convicted by Federalist judges under these laws, which flew in the face of the First Amendment.[80]

U.S. governments have regularly curbed freedom of the press and limited journalists' access in wartime—from Abraham Lincoln's unconstitutional attempts to prosecute journalists who criticized his conduct of the Civil War[81] to the Office of War Information that restricted images of the war during World War II.[82] The Obama administration and the Trump administration both have pursued prosecutions against government sources for allegedly leaking information to journalists that the government said compromised national security.[83]

Two modern-day landmark U.S. Supreme Court cases have helped define freedom of the press: In the first case, *New York Times Co. v. Sullivan* in 1964, a Montgomery, Alabama, city commissioner sued the *New York Times* and four Black clergymen for an ad the *Times* published from supporters of Dr. Martin Luther King that Sullivan said was false and defamatory against him. The U.S. Supreme Court ruled that in the case of a government official or a person running for office, in addition to proving that the statements were false and defamatory, the government official or candidate must prove "actual malice" and "reckless disregard for the truth" by the publication in publishing the account.[84]

In what is known as the *Pentagon Papers* case, in 1971, first the *New York Times* and then the *Washington Post* began publishing classified documents from a Vietnam War–era government history of U.S. involvement in Indochina from World War II to 1968 in the Vietnam War. Leaked to the newspapers by Daniel Ellsberg, who had worked on the report, the documents proved that the John F. Kennedy and Lyndon Johnson administrations had expanded the war in Vietnam and told the American public as well as the news media that the war was being won when intelligence and military officials were saying for years that the war was not being won by the U.S.—and that it was effectively unwinnable, for many reasons.[85]

The Nixon administration, citing "immediate and irreparable harm" to national security, obtained a restraining order enjoining the *Times* and the *Post* from publishing. The case, *New York Times Co. v. United States*, went to the U.S. Supreme Court, with the editors and publishers under pressure from stockholders and business interests as well as under threat of criminal prosecution. The Supreme Court ruled in favor of the news organizations, saying that the government had failed to justify prior restraint of publication.[86]

At the end of 2019, the *Washington Post* published a groundbreaking, six-part series based on classified interviews with military commanders and others conducted at the time by the U.S. government and obtained by the *Post* through yearslong Freedom of Information Act (FOIA) public record requests and a legal battle about the U.S. war in Afghanistan. The documents and interviews starkly revealed that in the George W. Bush administration and, later, the Obama administration, "senior U.S. officials failed to tell the truth about the war in Afghanistan throughout the eighteen-year campaign, making rosy pronouncements they knew to be false and hiding unmistakable evidence the war had become unwinnable."[87] The war in Afghanistan, launched to fight terrorism by the Bush administration after the terrorist attacks on September 11, 2001, was the longest armed conflict in U.S. history. The *Post* investigation has been dubbed this generation's *Pentagon Papers* case.

Public Opinion on Media Credibility

The credibility of the news media overall has declined in recent years, as has the credibility of other major institutions, not only in Congress, the presidency, and TV news but also big business, the criminal justice system, and organized religion, according to Gallup and other polling.[88] "The story of the past half-century is the steady degradation of trust in the institutions and gatekeepers of American life," Ben Domenech, cofounder of the Federalist, a conservative news site, told the *New York Times* at the end of 2019. "Everything from politics to faith to sports has been revealed as corrupted or corruptible."[89]

Yet, in this atmosphere, the public has continued to say that they want the news media to fulfill their role as a watchdog in the democracy. Despite criticisms of accuracy, fairness, and independence of the news media, "broad majorities of Americans continue to say the press acts as a watchdog by preventing political leaders from doing things that should not be done, a view that is as widely held today as at any point in the past three decades," Pew researchers found, with support for the media's watchdog role rising ten points from 58 percent to 68 percent, from 2011 to 2013 "in the wake of revelations [in the news media] about government activities, including the NSA [National Security Agency] surveillance program and the IRS [Internal Revenue Service] targeting of political groups."[90] In 2018, in the annual nonpartisan Freedom Forum survey of public attitudes toward the First Amendment, 74 percent of respondents agreed with the statement that "it is important for our democracy that the news media act as a watchdog on government," a slight uptick from 68 percent in 2017.[91]

Most recently, trust in news media during the Trump era was showing an increased partisan divide amid strong tensions between Donald Trump and major news organizations and amid the president's repeated attacks on the media. Trust in media dropped to an all-time low of 32 percent saying they had a "great deal of confidence" in the media in 2016 in Gallup polling, which Gallup researchers attributed at least in part to Donald Trump's attacks on the news media.[92] In 2018, the percentage of those who said they had "a great deal of confidence" had increased to 45 percent. That number was the highest since 2009 overall, with Democrats trusting the media more than Republicans but trust also increasing among Republicans and independents.[93]

At the end of 2019, however, the Pew Research Center was finding that partisan dynamics and political party affiliation were "overshadow[ing] other factors in Americans' evaluation of the news media."[94] The researchers found Trump's strongest supporters expressing the lowest confidence in journalism and journalists' ethics.[95]

Declining—and partisan—trust or mistrust in the news media did not begin with Donald Trump, however; and some media ethics groups as well as news organizations are exploring ways to improve trust, including through greater transparency about news-gathering as well as promoting the First Amendment and the value of a free press to the public. "Trust in media is a vital and urgent problem," Indira Lakshmanan, the former ethics chair of the Poynter Institute for Media Studies, said in an interview with the author.[96]

Perceptions of Media Bias and Political Polarization

Many people today believe charges from some Republicans and conservative media critics over the years that the news media have a liberal bias in their reporting. More recently, supporters of Sen. Bernie Sanders and liberal media critics have accused the news media of having a "corporate" bias in their reporting on progressive candidates and proposals that they say challenge the corporate status quo. The allegations of liberal bias in the media were prominent in critiques from the Nixon administration during the Watergate era—and they have been a daily feature on Fox News Channel and conservative talk radio for many years.

Survey results over the years have indicated that journalists are more liberal than the population overall.[97] In their long-running study, journalism professors Lars Willnat, David Weaver and G. Cleveland Wilhoit wrote in 2013 that they found a majority of full-time journalists identifying themselves as independents, while those who said they were Democrats had dropped since 2002 to about 28 percent, "moving this figure closer to the overall population percentage of 30 percent," according to a 2013 ABC News/*Washington Post* national poll. "This is the lowest percentage of journalists saying they are Democrats since 1971," the authors wrote. "An even larger drop was observed among journalists who said they were Republicans in 2013 (7.1 percent) than in 2002 (18 percent), but the 2013 figure is still notably lower than the percentage of U.S. adults who identified with the Republican Party (24 percent according to the poll mentioned previously)."[98]

Journalists for mainstream news organizations dispute the notion of liberal bias in major media, for example, citing critical coverage of Democrats and criticism of their coverage from both the Left and the Right as proof of evenhandedness. (Friendly coverage of Ronald Reagan, for example, belies the "liberal" charge, as do critiques of media coverage in the 2016 election.)

Journalists rightly draw a distinction between how one may vote as a private citizen versus one's role as a fair reporter, and mainstream news media in the U.S. today have a journalistic process and culture that values objectivity and balance to such a degree that they have been criticized for an overreliance on officialdom and objectivity that has led to false equivalences.

Despite anecdotal allegations of liberal bias, researchers in multiple studies have not found systematic liberal bias in mainstream media. Instead, they have found that, as Jonathan M. Ladd wrote in *Why Americans Hate the Media and How It Matters*, to emphasize *being told* the media are biased has impact on people's perception.[99]

"Despite research to the contrary, the general public and a significant number of politicians are convinced the U.S. news media have a liberal and pro-Democratic bias," Tien-Tsung Lee wrote in one study.[100] "Findings based on two large national surveys suggest that audiences' ideologies and partisanships affect how they view the media. Strong conservatives and Republicans are more likely to distrust the news media."[101] Researchers for Pew Research Center have found similar partisan divides.

While charges of liberal, conservative, or corporate bias in the media are important to consider here, there are *operational and cultural biases* in the way that news is determined, gathered, and distributed that happen *every day*. In Chapter 4 we will decode these often-unspoken cultural norms of journalism—from a bias toward immediacy to groupthink and an inside-the-Beltway punditocracy—and how they affect what the public sees and reads.

There is debate about the causes of political polarization in politics and the media today, including whether polarization in Congress came before polarization in the public as well as the impact of polarized media outlets on politics. But, according to several major studies and surveys, both the major political parties and voters are more polarized ideologically than in the past twenty years. Political scientists Keith Poole and Howard Rosenthal have developed a metric that they have used to calculate votes by both Democrats and Republicans in Congress; they have found that, after decades of relatively little political polarization in Congress, ideological polarization began to rise and increase rapidly since the 1970s. Today, Congress "is more polarized than at any time since the end of Reconstruction."[102]

In their book *It's Even Worse Than It Looks: How the American Constitutional System Collided with the New Politics of Extremism*, Thomas Mann and Norman Ornstein, who had traced recent historical trends in dysfunction in Congress, declared that the two major sources of dysfunction were (1) "the serious mismatch between the political parties, which have become as vehemently adversarial as parliamentary parties, and a governing system that, unlike a parliamentary democracy, makes it extremely difficult for majorities to act" and (2) a move to the right and "away from the center of American politics" by some in the Republican Party.[103]

An article by Princeton University professor Nolan McCarty, titled "What We Know and Don't Know about Our Polarized Politics" and published in the *Washington Post*, summarized points of agreement from a task force on political polarization and its impacts on negotiation and governance convened by the American Political Science Association. McCarty said that "evidence points to a major partisan asymmetry in polarization" in Congress. McCarty added, "Despite the widespread belief that both parties have moved to the extremes . . . each new cohort of Republicans . . . has taken more conservative positions on legislation than the cohorts before them" and "any movement to the left by the Democrats can be accounted for by a decline in white representatives from the South and an increase in African-American and Latino representation."[104]

At the same time, a yearlong survey of ten thousand adults in the U.S. in 2014 by the Pew Research Center found that Republicans and Democrats were "further apart ideologically than at any point in recent history," with the center getting smaller, growing numbers of Americans expressing consistently conservative or consistently liberal opinions, and Democrats and Republicans expressing more negative views about the other party than before. "Political polarization is the defining feature of early 21st century American politics, both among the public and elected officials," the author of the report, Carroll Doherty, concluded.[105] "The most ideologically oriented Americans" among Democrats and Republicans "make their voices heard through greater participation in every stage of the political process," from self-reported voting rates to political donations.[106] Appealing to Americans who may be somewhat in the middle and not easily classified—for example, young people who may be liberal on social issues but conservative on government—remains a challenge to political parties and voter turnout, especially in non–presidential election years.[107]

The Economics of News

In order to understand the interplay of politics and media and how that impacts the role of the media in a democracy, it is important first of all to understand how the business of American media works. Major American media are almost exclusively commercially owned, with the exception of National Public Radio (NPR) and the Public Broadcasting Service (PBS). NPR and PBS are nonprofit public media underwritten by foundations, corporate and individual contributions, and some government funding.

Ownership of the media today is increasingly concentrated in the hands of a few huge entertainment and media corporations. Major news organizations that historically have played a significant role in exposing abuse, wrongdoing, and neglect are under pressure. The broadcast TV network news divisions of CBS News, NBC News, and ABC News—which focused national attention on the civil rights movement, the Vietnam War, and other important stories of the 1960s and 1970s—had been somewhat exempt from financial pressure in news-gathering, according to interviews with news executives and journalists who were there at the time.[108] This was because the prime-time entertainment shows on the so-called Big Three broadcast networks were making tremendous profits, while their news divisions, which were also making money, were touted to Congress and the public as fulfilling their public interest obligations in exchange for operating on the public's airwaves.

Today, TV news, particularly cable TV news, is a major profit center for the corporations that own them; but news is one brand among many required to make profits. Newspapers, in particular, are in crisis as they face serious challenges: first, to their advertiser-supported business model with advertising going to the Internet and second, from cutbacks, layoffs, and even closure with consolidation under large corporations and hedge funds.

Federal Communications Commission and Deregulation of Media Ownership

According to the Communications Act of 1934, local TV stations, the largest of which are owned by the national broadcast TV networks, are licensed by the Federal Communications Commission (FCC) to operate in the "public interest, convenience and necessity" in exchange for operating for free on the airwaves, which are owned by the public.[109] The fact that the public owns the airwaves, as a scarce resource, appears to be little known by the public today, especially as station license renewals have become much less rigorous and license challenges much more rare. Cable television is not regulated by the FCC, although cable TV networks, along with Hollywood studios, have reacted to pressure from Congress. In the late 1990s, for example, under bipartisan pressure from Congress, the White House, children's television advocates, and the FCC, the TV networks and entertainment companies agreed to voluntarily institute a movie-style TV ratings system for children's programming[110] and to require three hours of educational programming each week for children.[111]

The head of the FCC and the commissioners are political appointees—and which party, Republican or Democratic, is in the White House and thus has the majority on the FCC, impacts rulemaking at the FCC. The Internet has traditionally not been subject to government regulation because it has been seen as a "common carrier"—a carrier like the telephone, not a publisher. But that could change in the future—or lead to further self-regulation by Facebook, Twitter, and other Internet giants—with public concerns about privacy and evidence of fake news and disinformation on the sites.

Deregulation of media ownership began under the Ronald Reagan administration, with corporations arguing that consolidation was needed to compete locally and that the marketplace would decide which media enterprises should survive. The lifting of restrictions, for example, on the same company owning both the local newspaper and the local TV station—and caps on how much of the national TV station market one corporation can control—led to an era of approved media mergers in the 1990s that led to rapidly increased concentration of media ownership. CBS, ABC, and NBC all merged with or were acquired by larger entertainment-based global corporations, Viacom, Disney, and Universal, respectively,[112] while Time Inc. (which owned *Time*, *People*, and other magazines) merged with Ted Turner's CNN and other cable networks as well as AOL.com before becoming Time Warner with the Warner Bros. entertainment company. In 2016, telecommunications company AT&T agreed to buy Time Warner, the home of CNN and HBO, for about $85.4 billion in a merger that would create a giant for creating content and distributing it, from phones to satellite television.[113] As Table 1.1 indicates, even great consolidation and bigger mergers are continuing today.

Table 1.1 Who Owns What in the Media

National Amusements	Major Holdings
	• ViacomCBS
	o BET
	o CBS All Access
	o CBS Entertainment
	o CBS Interactive
	o CBS News
	o CBS Sports
	o CBS Television Studios
	o Comedy Central
	o MTV
	o Nickelodeon
	o Paramount Network
	o Paramount Pictures
	o Paramount Television Studios
	o Pluto TV
	o Showtime Networks
	o Awesomeness
	o Bellator
	o CBS Sports Network
	o CBS Television Distribution
	o CBS Television Stations
	o Channel 5
	o CMT
	o Colors
	o Network 10 Australia
	o Pop TV
	o Simon & Schuster
	o Smithsonian Channel
	o Telefe
	o The CW

	o TV Land
	o VH1
	o ViacomCBS Global Distribution Group
	o VidCon
	• Showcase Cinemas
The Walt Disney Company	**Major Holdings**
	• Disney Channel
	• ABC
	• Freeform
	• ESPN
	• FX
	• National Geographic
	• Disney Parks, Experiences and Products, Inc.
	• The Walt Disney Studios
	• Walt Disney Animation Studios
	• Pixar Animation Studies
	• Marvel Studios
	• Disneynature
	• LucasFilm Ltd.
	• Disney Music Group
	• Disney Theatrical Group
	• Blue Sky Studios
	• 20th Century Studios
	• Searchlight Pictures
	• Disney+
	• ESPN+
	• Hulu
	• Hotstar
AT&T	**Major Holdings**
	• AT&T Communications
	• WarnerMedia
	o Home Box Office (HBO)
	o Cinemax
	o TNT
	o TBS
	o truTV
	o Otter Media
	o CNN
	o HLN
	o Turner Sports
	o Bleacher Report
	o DC Entertainment

(Continued)

Table 1.1 (Continued)

	o Cartoon Network o Adult Swim o Boomerang o Turner Classic Movies o Warner Bros. business units • AT&T Latin America • Xandr

Comcast Corporation	**Major Holdings**
	• Xfinity
	• NBCUniversal Media
	  o Universal Television Alternative Studios
	  o Universal Parks & Resorts
	  o Bravo
	  o E!
	  o Olympic Channel
	  o Oxygen
	  o Syfy
	  o Universal Kids
	  o USA Network
	  o Universal Cable Productions
	  o NBC News
	  o MSNBC
	  o CNBC
	  o NBC Sports
	  o NBC Golf
	  o Peacock
	  o Fandango
	  o GolfNow
	  o Hulu
	  o SportsEngine
	  o NBCUniversal Telemundo Enterprises
	  o Cozi TV
	  o TeleXitos
	  o NBCUniversal Owned Television Stations
	  o hayu
	  o DreamWorks Animation
	  o Universal Studios
	  o Universal Pictures Home Entertainment
	• Sky
	• Comcast Business
	  o Focus Features

Fox Corporation	**Major Holdings** • Fox News Media • Fox Sports • Fox Entertainment • Fox Television Stations

Newspapers and Local TV Stations

News Corp	**Major Holdings**
	• News Corp Australia
	  o *The Australian*
	  o *Daily Telegraph*
	  o *Herald Sun*
	  o *Courier-Mail*
	  o *The Advertiser* (Adelaide)
	  o *The Mercury* (Hobart)
	  o *Northern Territory News*
	  o *Townsville Bulletin*
	  o *Cairns Post*
	  o *Gold Coast Bulletin*
	  o *Geelong Advertiser*
	  o *Weekly Times*
	  o *Vogue Australia*
	  o *Vogue Living*
	  o *GQ Australia*
	  o Taste.com.au
	  o Fox Sports
	  o Foxtel
	  o Sky News Australia
	  o REA Group Ltd
	• News UK
	  o *The Times*
	  o *Sunday Times*
	  o *The Sun*
	• Dow Jones
	  o *Wall Street Journal*
	  o *Barron's*
	  o MarketWatch
	  o Factiva
	  o *Financial News*
	  o DJX
	  o Dow Jones Risk & Compliance
	  o Dow Jones Newswires
	  o Dow Jones VentureSource
	• *New York Post*
	• HarperCollins Publishers

(Continued)

Table 1.1 (Continued)

	• News America Marketing • Move, Inc. • Storyful
Sinclair Broadcast Group	**Major Holdings** • Owns 191 stations

Gannett	**Major Holdings**
	• *USA Today*
	  o ReachLocal digital marketing
	    company
	• 261 local daily brands
	• United Kingdom-based Newsquest
	  Media Group manages more than
	  165 news brands and more than fifty
	  magazines online and in print

Tegna	**Major Holdings**
	• Operates sixty-two television stations
	  (including those serviced by Tegna) and
	  four radio stations, including ABC, CBS,
	  NBC, and Fox affiliates

Sources: investors.cbscorporation.com; viacom.com; viacbs.com; thewaltdisneycompany .com; investors.att.com; cmcsa.com; foxcorporation.com; newscorp.com; sec.gov; gannett .com; investors.gannett.com; investors.tegna.com; cnn.com; indiewire.com; nytimes.com; wsj.com; focusfeatures.com; newsquest.co.uk (May 2020).

One concern about consolidation of ownership is that it limits the voices and views audiences hear and see, providing not real choice but an illusion of choice among media. The dominance of Sinclair Broadcast Group in TV station ownership and what they were revealed to be doing with it is one example of what can happen. With the lifting of regulatory caps, Sinclair, by 2016, owned 173 local TV stations covering 40 percent of TV station ownership.[114] Sinclair has been criticized for promoting a conservative news agenda and commentary among its stations. In 2018 the company was revealed to be dictating that its ostensibly local TV anchors deliver identical anti–news media attacks in on-air promos that seemed drawn from Donald Trump's talking points. A compilation video published by the sports website *Deadspin* showed dozens of anchors at Sinclair-owned stations repeating identical statements that the media were "extremely dangerous for democracy," and some irresponsible "members of the media" were using their platforms to publish "biased and false news" to "control exactly what people think."[115]

Sinclair anchors had told CNN media reporter Brian Stelter that they were extremely uncomfortable with the corporation's requirement, with which nearly fifty anchors complied.[116] The compilation tape went viral and caused an uproar, with the head of the Republican-controlled FCC and advocacy groups objecting to Sinclair's proposed acquisition of another large TV station group in 2018. The proposed $3.9 billion deal subsequently was terminated by the corporations.[117]

In music, Clear Channel Communications (now called iHeartMedia) controls the airplay of music across a coast-to-coast commercial radio network.[118] As Table 1.2 indicates, ownership on the Internet has also grown increasingly more concentrated, with Facebook acquiring Instagram and other properties, and Google buying YouTube. Google alone owns many properties, from Gmail to Google Maps, that can provide advertisers with detailed analytics about customers' online activities and that have raised concerns about preferential treatment of allied companies and the recreation of a "walled garden" invisibly limiting choice, even on what seem to be the wide-open spaces of the Internet.

Table 1.2   Two Internet Giants

Facebook, Inc.	Major Holdings
	• Facebook (social network)
	○ Facebook Messenger
	○ Facebook Blueprint
	○ Facebook IQ
	• Instagram
	• WhatsApp
	• Oculus
	• Facebook Audience Network
Alphabet Inc.	Major Holdings
	• Google
	• YouTube
	• Android
	• Google Maps
	• X Development LLC
	• Google Fiber
	• Verily Life Sciences LLC
	• Sidewalk Labs
	• Calico
	• GV
	• CapitalG
	• Jigsaw

(Continued)

Table 1.2 (Continued)

	• DeepMind Technologies
	• Waymo
	• AdMob
	• Google Marketing Platform
	• Google AdSense
	• Google Nest
	• Advanced Technology & Projects
	• Google Cloud
	• Loon LLC
	• Wing Aviation LLC

Sources: facebook.com; oculus.com; x.company; abc.xyz; verily.com; boards.greenhouse.io/
sidewalklabs; googlepress.blogspot.com; jigsaw.google.com; deepmind.com; waymo
.com; marketingplatform.google.com; admob.google.com; android.com; google.com; nest
.com; atap.google.com; cloud.google.com; youtube.com; businessinsider.com; loon.com
(May 2020).

The Roles Media Play

According to the annual survey by the American Society of News Editors, there were thirty-eight thousand full-time newsroom jobs at newspapers in 2012, a decrease from more than fifty-fix thousand jobs a decade ear-lier.[119] Newspapers employed 62 percent of U.S. newsroom employees in 2008; a decade later, that figure was less than half, at 40 percent in 2018.[120] Newspapers, many of which had large staffs of reporters in the days when newspapers were making large profit margins and had a monopoly on news and advertising, have seen their profit margins and their staffs shrink in recent years, as they have lost circulation and advertising to the Internet.

Many of these previously family-owned media companies were bought by larger corporations and hedge fund companies. The longtime business model of newspapers—that advertising revenue and circulation support and finance reporters and staff doing journalism—has been upended with cutbacks, layoffs, and consolidation.

Major newspapers have innovated online, but ads online bring in much less revenue—and newspapers that have given their content away for free online, including via Facebook and social media, are now warily negotiating with Facebook to share revenue and erecting paywalls and sub-scriptions online to get readers to pay to help finance the journalism they're used to getting for free.

At the same time, with deregulation, increased concentration of own-ership, and short-term financial goals set to please investors and Wall

Street, there have been tremendous layoffs and cutbacks in newspaper employment. Digital media jobs are growing in some cities, especially on both coasts of the U.S., and digital subscriptions at the *New York Times*, *Washington Post*, and *Wall Street Journal* are increasing. But in local newspapers in major cities as well as smaller ones, there is a decline in newspapers that concerned critics are calling a crisis in local journalism that has serious implications for media and the democracy.[121]

"The persistent financial demands of Wall Street have trumped the informational needs of Main Street," media critic David Carr wrote about such moves in the *New York Times*.[122]

Behind the statistics that were just provided, here are some examples: The *Times-Picayune*, which had won many awards for its investigations of local New Orleans and Louisiana state governments as well as its coverage of Hurricane Katrina in 2005, announced in 2012 that its new owners were ceasing daily publication after two hundred years as a daily presence in the community, despite strong circulation and protests from the community.[123] The *Los Angeles Times*, once a family-owned newspaper with a large staff including national and international correspondents as well as local reporters, had rounds of staff and budget cuts under the Tribune company.[124] Alden Global Capital, a hedge fund, has been buying local newspapers, from the *Denver Post* to the *Orange County Register*, instituting deep cuts in staff and local coverage over public protests and resignations—even by their editors.[125] "There's no long-term strategy other than milking and continuing to cut," said *Newsonomics* expert Ken Doctor.[126] In 2020, Alden began pursuing the Tribune company, owner of the *Baltimore Sun* and the *Chicago Tribune*.

Also in 2020, the respected McClatchy newspapers, the nation's second largest newspaper chain and owner of the *Miami Herald*, the *Sacramento Bee*, and other award-winning newspapers, declared bankruptcy, with a hedge fund becoming their majority stockholder and their national news editor tweeting out some of the many impactful local news investigations McClatchy journalists were working on.[127]

Gannett, which owns *USA Today* as well as newspapers, trade publications, and local TV stations, announced plans to eliminated 1,000 positions in 2008; in 2011 the company laid off about seven hundred employees.[128] At the end of 2019, shareholders at Gannett, which owned over one hundred newspapers, and GateHouse Media, whose parent company owned nearly 400 newspapers in 39 states, voted to approve a merger that would have one in six newspapers in the U.S. owned by the same new company.[129] Both Gannett and GateHouse have a reputation for cutting staff—and many observers expressed concerns that the up to $300 million in cost savings the two companies said the new merger would bring inevitably would mean new rounds of layoffs and cutbacks in coverage. "The GateHouse-Gannett merger is another nail in the coffin for the state of our news and information system," former FCC Chairman Michael Copps said.[130]

Gains for the *Washington Post* and the *New York Times*

In a significant departure from trends under new corporate owners, Jeff Bezos, the founder of Amazon, personally purchased the *Washington Post* for $250 million in 2013 from the Graham family, the longtime family owners. Rather than cut staff and resources, the *Washington Post* has been able to invest in additional reporters and resources for reporting and has successfully moved the *Post* from a print and largely local publication losing advertising revenue to a profitable business with digital subscriptions and national and international readership online.[131] The *New York Times*—which has remained primarily family owned by the descendants of Adolph Ochs, who bought the newspaper in 1896—also has faced declining advertising revenue, in print and digital. But the New York Times Company, in 2019, had a record-breaking year in terms of digital-only subscribers, adding one million new digital subscribers to end the year with a record 5.25 million total subscriptions across all of their print and digital products.[132] Because of the subscription revenue, one newspaper analyst wrote, "The paper now sits well above its national newspaper peers and breathes an entirely different atmosphere than its local newspaper brethren."[133] The *Wall Street Journal* has been a national newspaper, with a paywall and subscriptions, for a number of years. Other newspapers, including the *Los Angeles Times*, which was bought by a new owner in 2018, have struggled to compete digitally.[134]

The *Washington Post* has won numerous Pulitzer prizes for investigative reporting in recent years under executive editor Martin Baron, who, as editor of the *Boston Globe*, led the Pulitzer Prize–winning investigation into child sexual abuse in the Catholic Church that is depicted in the Oscar-winning movie *Spotlight*. In an interview with the author in 2016, Baron said that serious reporting is essential to journalism: "There is an essence to who we are—I like to call it our soul; the businesspeople call it the brand; I'll call it the soul. People need to have confidence that you will work on their behalf. They may not like the results, but they need to have confidence that you will be working on their behalf. . . . There's a lot of talk these days about the responsibility of the press. I believe the single most irresponsible thing we could do would be to abandon this kind of work [investigative reporting] and to stop holding powerful interests accountable."[135]

Declining Local News and Civic Engagement

The local news crisis was not immediately obvious; today, in addition to the changes described here, there are towns and areas across the country known as "news deserts," where the local newspaper has ceased publication, leaving the city and region without a vital source of news and information.

Continuing deep cuts in staff and coverage, of course, means less attention to events and issues in local and regional government as well as less possibility for deeper reporting and investigative journalism. In addition, researchers in new research are finding surprising impacts on politics and policy from the decline of local newspapers. In a report for the Brookings Institution,[136] research analyst Clara Hendrickson and other Brookings researchers have found that, as Hendrickson wrote, "places that have seen local news sources and reporters disappear are more likely to see an increase in the costs of municipal bonds."[137] In other studies, political scientists have found fewer candidates running for mayor and evidence suggesting a decline in voter participation in state and local elections as newspapers have declined.[138]

Hendrickson noted, "The decline in local journalism is a national concern, too. Voters in communities that experience a newspaper closure are more likely to vote for the same party for president and senator compared to voters in communities that did not lose a local newspaper, exacerbating national political polarization. Meanwhile, the poor health of local newspapers means national newspapers have fewer local outlets to turn to and fewer sources on the ground to inform national coverage."[139]

The coronavirus pandemic brought praise to many local and national news organization for their coverage of their communities—but it also led to many further layoffs and even closures in local news. A coalition of public interest groups, authors, journalists, and public officials called for $5 million in aid to local news outlets as part of the economic stimulus aid to small businesses being provided by Congress despite many journalists' traditional resistance to government involvement in news-gathering.[140]

There has been a decline in the number of Washington, D.C.-based reporting by local newspapers on their congressional delegations.[141] Local TV news, which remains a primary source of news for many Americans, already was devoting little time to stories about politics and government (3 percent, according to a study of sample local newscasts, in 2012, compared to 40 percent for traffic, weather, and sports—plus interesting videos of accidents and disasters, reflecting many TV consultants' business advice that local TV viewers don't care about politics and government).[142]

In a study of more than ten thousand stories on House races in the 2010 and 2014 midterm elections, political scientists Jennifer Lawless and Danny Hayes found decreases in coverage in both numbers and substance in stories from one midterm to the next. Then, in a survey of nine thousand five hundred respondents testing knowledge of the 2010 and 2014 races before each election, they found what they determined was a correlation between political knowledge and political engagement and the substance and amount of the political coverage.[143]

The Importance of Cable TV News

Cable news has shown real growth—in profits, ratings, and influence—in politics over the past several years. Not only primary debates but also town halls on cable with Pete Buttigieg and other, lesser-known candidates in 2020 boosted their name recognition and polling, aides said. "Aides to every major Democratic presidential campaign have told *The Daily Beast* that they've been stunned by the degree to which the conversation taking place on cable and national news has impacted the trajectory of the race," Sam Stein and Maxwell Tani wrote. Although cable news was not the only factor, they reported that "at a time when the party is trying to utilize new mediums to expand its reach beyond the traditional electorate, it's been the old, stodgy TV press—fed by print reporters-turned-pundits—that has had the biggest tangible impact."[144]

The growth of Fox News Channel as the highest-rated cable news network created an ideologically bifurcated cable news landscape. Fox News Channel was created in 1996 by media mogul Rupert Murdoch and former Republican strategist Roger Ailes after Ted Turner's founding of CNN as the first global, twenty-four-hour news channel. Fox News Channel did not invent polarization in politics and in Congress—but it has abetted and amplified it, playing a major role in shaping the media landscape and political discourse today. Fox News Channel—which has been the largest cable TV network for many years in terms of viewers and profits estimated at $1 billion annually—is watched by many more Republicans than Democrats.

MSNBC, the third cable news network, is watched by many more Democrats than Republicans and has fashioned itself as the "anti-Fox," with Rachel Maddow and other liberal prime-time hosts. CNN—the first twenty-four-hour cable news network—had struggled in recent years in the ratings on a slow news day and against Fox News Channel's highly rated prime-time opinion shows and hosts like Bill O'Reilly, Sean Hannity, and Tucker Carlson. But since the 2016 election, CNN gained, in ratings and in profits, by focusing on political news and punditry in prime-time. CNN had its most-watched month ever in January 2021 and was the highest-rated cable news network during this period. Fox News Channel dipped in the ratings as some viewers, angry over the network's election-night news coverage, turned to conspiracy theories about the election on the small Newsmax and OAN networks. But Fox News Channel finished 2020 first in cable news ratings for the nineteenth consecutive year.[145] And the network moved a more traditional news program with anchor Martha McCallum out of its 7:00 p.m. time slot to make way for a new prime-time opinion show, with rotating hosts.[146]

Local news and the broadcast TV evening newscasts (which still reach a combined audience of some 22.5 million per night)[147] attract the largest audiences in terms of numbers—and have actually shown growth in over-all audience in recent years. But it is the three cable TV news networks—Fox News Channel, CNN, and MSNBC—that command the most attention from their viewers.

Cable news viewers, particularly those loyal to Fox News Channel, are older (as are many party primary voters), loyal, and engaged with what they're hearing. "On average, the cable-news audience devotes twice as much time to that news source as local and network news viewers spend on those platforms," a 2013 Pew ratings analysis found. "And the heaviest cable users are far more immersed in that coverage—watching for more than an hour a day—than the most loyal viewers of broadcast television news." Reflecting on these viewers' engagement, the researchers added, "The deeper level of viewer engagement with cable news may help to explain why cable television—despite a more limited audience—seems to have an outsized ability to influence the national debate and news agenda" as prime-time hosts on Fox News Channel and MSNBC "tend to hammer away at a somewhat narrow news agenda that magnifies the day's more polarizing and ideological issues," with the TV ratings data showing that "cable's audience is staying for a healthy help-ing of that content."[148]

The Internet and Democratizing Information

The Internet has been a tremendous force for democratizing infor-mation and communication, empowering individuals, building social movements, and creating "the global village" once envisioned by media guru Marshall McLuhan. And yet, as Internet scholar David Karpf put it, in exploring the role of the Internet in politics, it depends on which Internet you're talking about. "The Internet itself is a still-developing cluster of technologies, many of which can be used to countervailing political ends," he wrote. "The Internet can be used to empower dis-sidents, or to track and suppress them. It can be used to the benefit of disenfranchised communities or to reassert existing power dynamics. It can be used to strengthen or to erode public discourse."[149] The 2010 "Arab Spring" uprising against authoritarian regimes and a low stan-dard of living in the Middle East, and the 2019 and 2020 protests against Chinese rule of Hong Kong, are two prominent international examples of this dichotomy. In Hong Kong student protesters wore face masks to thwart the government's facial-recognition software.

We will discuss the role of the Internet in politics, media, and social movements throughout this book.

The Goals for This Book

In this book we will examine and analyze the intersection of politics and the media—and the impact of that interaction on the following:

1. The candidates who are chosen

2. The issues that are focused on

3. The outcome of elections and public policy

4. The public's attitude toward government and media

5. The future of media and politics—and the democracy

We'll talk about the intersection and impact of politics and the media in political campaigns, policy discussions, and cultural debates—from the impact of President Trump via Twitter to debates over the role of the "media primary" and punditry in promoting candidates and issues. We'll look at the role of race and gender in American politics, and we'll study how framing language can affect attitudes and policy from immigration to health care and foreign policy. We'll examine how consolidation and cutbacks in media ownership are affecting news coverage and civic engagement—and we'll pull back the curtain on why politicians and journalists today do what they do. We'll look at the role of the Internet in politics, media, and social movements and suggested reforms in the political and media system.

You'll learn important concepts such as *framing, agenda-setting, and persuasive techniques* in media and politics, and we will apply those techniques to examining case studies and specific episodes. Our focus will be primarily on media and politics in the U.S., but we will also look at international news and media coverage of the war in Iraq, Syria, and other conflicts as well as coverage of the coronavirus pandemic and climate change. The history of developments and changes in media and politics over the past sixty years are included here to help us put today's events in context. We'll look also at popular culture—for example, the role of late-night comedy shows—and you'll have an assignment to examine the portrayals of politicians in TV series and classic movies for what they reveal about attitudes toward politicians at the time.

The goal of this book is to enable you to subject both media and politics to informed analysis that is neither pro- nor anti-media or politics but that holds both journalists and politicians accountable for their roles in the democracy.

A key element of our approach will be to analyze media and political communication thematically, in primary-source form and in case studies—tracing, for example, how climate change has been framed in the media and how that has impacted policy. We will learn about—and apply—important scholarly research and concepts to contemporary media coverage. You'll hear targeted quotes from interviews conducted by the author as well as from some presentations with important figures in media and politics and critics of both fields. Among those are 2020 Democratic presidential candidate and Sen. Bernie Sanders, 2004 Democratic presidential candidate Howard Dean, Sen. Susan Collins, and former representatives Martin Frost and Tom Davis; TV anchors Chuck Todd, Maria Elena Salinas, Cecilia Vega, Jake Tapper, Anderson Cooper, and Christiane Amanpour; Republican and Democratic strategists, including David Winston, Ryan Williams, Ana Navarro, and Celinda Lake; civil rights leader Julian Bond; *Washington Post* executive editor Martin Baron and White House and congressional reporters, including Yamiche Alcindor of PBS and Ed O'Keefe of CBS News; experts on Internet activism; immigration activist Jose Antonio Vargas; Islamic studies scholar Akbar Ahmed; researchers and other experts on race and gender in media and politics; Pentagon officials and war correspondents; and critics of media and politics from a range of perspectives.

Media and Politics Research Tool Kit

Here at the end of this chapter is a media analysis tool kit that was developed by the author over the past several years.

The tool kit contains a guide for researching and developing your own media analysis case study and rubric for analyzing politics and the media. There is also a section at the end of this book with annotated links and descriptions of resources for your research.

This tool kit will be helpful for what is a major focus of this book: reading, examining, and analyzing media coverage and political media in primary source form—that is, related articles in print or online, TV news transcripts, websites, social media, online videos, political ads, and other pieces of political communication as they appear, in primary source form, in the media. You will then develop a thesis grounded in your research and proving it with evidence and examples while applying and incorporating scholarly research and the concepts we will be discussing here in this book. You can access and research these sources online and for free through databases at your college library.

The idea here is an approach developed in many years of teaching an interdisciplinary course in politics and the media: that it is important—and even vital—to stand back from the media environment in which we are all participants in order to examine media coverage and political communication from some distance and with fresh eyes.

There are also viewing and writing assignments at the end of each chapter to build on—and enhance—what is covered in the chapters.

How to Do Your Own Media Analysis Case Study

Our goal with this book is to be "media archaeologists," standing back from the media-politics environment we are surrounded by to examine a *variety of media*—the newscasts, the online pages, the videos, the ads, the tweets—in *primary source form* as if we are *archaeologists* examining the artifacts of a civilization other than our own. As media archaeologists, we are examining what specific artifacts and episodes in media-politics *reveal* about the underlying values, social forces, and interplay among politics, media, and culture in this not-so-ancient civilization of our own.

To develop, research, and write a case study in media politics based on content analysis, your first task is to determine what's your research question—what are you trying to answer? That will guide everything else you do. To do a media content analysis, you will need to read and watch a range of media to discern patterns and trends, develop a thesis or hypothesis, examine fully, then analyze and evaluate. You need to examine your subject in the media in primary source form—i.e., the newspaper articles, the TV newscasts, the pundit shows, the Twitter feed—to be able to develop your thesis and support it with examples.

In order to speak with authority, you need to look at more media than you will quote in your paper. It is tempting—but not enough—to look at three newscasts or a handful of stories and decide that a news outlet has been biased or unfair. If you find an example of alleged bias on a partisan website, you must read, watch, and analyze the complete video or story independently. Partisan "mediawatch" sites, on the left and right, cherry-pick from media, data, and time frames to "prove" their points. They can be a jumping-off point for how an organization may contend there has been bias—but they are not an end point.

Picking a specific episode from recent or contemporary media and politics gives you a specific time frame and a way to set your "search terms," giving you the opportunity for specificity and some depth so that your topic is not too vague—or overly broad.

You will want to be *specific in the focus* of your research and written analysis—for example, comparing coverage of an episode in two different media outlets or examining how framing and coverage of an issue has changed, over a specific time frame. You must offer *specific examples* from media from your research that are illustrative and representative and that provide evidence for your thesis.

How do you find what you're looking for? Use this guide as well as the annotated resource pages provided at the end of the book. These materials have been developed over time for students, and they are designed to help you in researching and studying politics and the media. Most of the resources here are readily available online; some are academic databases that many colleges and universities commonly have. Consult your librarian about which your school has.

If you're looking at how a topic was covered in newspapers, setting search terms and doing several keyword searches on a database such as LexisNexis will help you gather articles one newspaper or several newspapers have done on the topic. LexisNexis also has TV news and news talk-show transcripts. If you're looking at websites, you can search on Google News or search via the website. YouTube has many famous historical and contemporary videos from politics and media. If you're looking for press releases or video material an organization took down because they later proved to be embarrassing, you might find that on a website called ShadowTV or the Internet Archive, which has extensive video cataloged. In their studies of media content, the human coders at Pew Research Center search closed-captioning text on cable and broadcast TV.[150] These and other resources are included in your media analysis tool kit.

The annotated resource pages with links includes the following items:

- Background information for understanding politics and the media

- Primary sources for analysis

- Secondary sources for scholarship on media coverage and political communication

- Sources for researching political ads

- Useful links for further understanding the topic

The rubric for research and analysis (below) can apply to all of your work, whether you are developing and researching a case study episode in media and politics, researching and analyzing a political ad campaign, or developing a more thematic paper on how the framing of a particular issue has developed and changed over time. Take a look at the case studies in this book to give you some ideas.

(Continued)

(Continued)

Ideas for Topics

One good approach is to compare how two different media outlets covered a specific episode or topic during the same time period. Another idea is to study how media coverage of a particular topic has changed and evolved. Depictions of gender and race in specific episodes or between comparative media are important topics for inquiry. You may want to look at how selected publications and platforms cover a political leader's speeches, press conferences, or policy initiative. You might trace the movement and veracity of a controversial video through the media and into politics or even a congressional investigation—and back again. You may want to look at the logos and slogans among political candidates in a major race, comparing them for their intended messaging and approach. You may want to look at how a particular social movement or opposing candidates in a race use Twitter and social media and what their key messages there are. You may want to look at the uses—and misuses—of polling in media in specific campaigns. There are many interesting and exciting possibilities.

You should research and be mindful of the historical context in which your subject was taking place. And, in all cases, you should be mindful of—and apply and cite—some of the concepts such as agenda-setting, framing, priming, visual appeals, emotional appeals, persuasive techniques, and the conventions of news-gathering and politics that you have been learning about in this book.

Your papers should include academic citations, and you should include hard copies of several of the articles, TV transcripts, or other primary materials you consulted when you turn in your paper. As mentioned in the next section, also be prepared to present your main findings, with some primary source media examples to show to your colleagues in the class.

Rubric for Research and Analysis

1. **Research:** Read, read, read—and watch, watch, watch. Read and watch across media genres and platforms on a subject you're interested in or something you've noticed.

2. **Description:** Take notes on what you see as you look at primary source media, and describe what you see. Set search terms and time frame, and look for key words or phrases. What do the media look like? What patterns emerge? If it's political communication, what do you think is the intended messaging?

3. **Development of a thesis/hypothesis:** Based on what you've seen, what's your working thesis/hypothesis about the way an episode in politics-media is covered and depicted? As said, it can be useful to pick two different outlets or two different platforms and compare or set a time frame of important plot points—events in a campaign or recent history—and see how a movement or a subject developed and the depiction of it changed over time or among media.

4. **Examination:** Examine your subject and your hypothesis fully—and consider alternative evidence. Research the historical context and public opinion at the time. Think which concepts we've discussed apply—and how.

5. **Written analysis:** Write a thoroughly researched, well-written paper that synthesizes your research and states and supports your thesis, with specific examples from the media and politics, historical context, and application of the relevant concepts we have discussed. Your paper must reflect the most important step: evaluation.

6. **Evaluation:** What does the episode or topic *reveal* about the nature and practices of news-gathering and politics, the interplay of politics, and the media or the impact of one field upon the other?

7. **Presentation:** Be prepared to share your key findings—and show some of the media you have examined—with your colleagues in class.

2

Underlying Concepts and Historical Foundations

M edia scholars and regular consumers of media have been trying to figure out how—and how much—influence the media have on public opinion and policy practically since the creation of mass media. No one likes to think that they're influenced by an unseen hand, and yet we know from the billions of dollars that are spent on product advertising that exposure to persuasive techniques in advertising and marketing can lead to changes in behavior and buying habits. We will talk about these techniques and how they apply to politics and political messaging in Chapter 3. In the 1920s and 1930s, the emergence of radio and other mass media news networks, the success of wartime propaganda, and a new interest in psychological perception all combined to raise fears about the power of mass media. The concern at the time was that mass media could singularly and easily sway the public, injecting messages like a hypodermic needle into a passive mass audience.[1]

Today, the media landscape is more fractionalized and polarized than in recent years. The hegemony of a few big media has been undermined by the Internet and the creation of cable, digital, and online news and opinion. And yet, as we saw in Chapter 1 and will discuss further here, media ownership is increasingly concentrated among a few global corporations, and there can be an illusion of choice across media platforms owned by the same company. Elite opinion is still a force in what motivates politicians, while the decline of local newspapers arguably has placed even more pressure—and influence—in the hands of a few national newspapers in terms of what they highlight in their media coverage and what gets the attention of the public and politicians. At the same time, the loyalty of Fox News Channel viewers to the views of the networks' prime-time hosts during the coronavirus pandemic had demonstrable impacts on their views on the seriousness of the coronavirus epidemic and misinformation about it, according to several studies.[2]

While people are not petri dishes and it can be difficult to isolate a precise cause and effect between a single media exposure and opinion, the effects are there, especially cumulatively, and can be analyzed. The traditional concepts and historical foundations for studying the media still apply and can be adapted to include today's media environment, including visual media. Along with more recent work on the role of emotion and "your brain on politics," the concepts here provide an important framework for being "media archaeologists" analyzing the impact of media on politics and public opinion.

Media-Effects Theory

Media-effects theory is the concept that exposure to media affects people's attitudes and perceptions. News inevitably involves selection. Not everything that happens gets covered, and the news media thus play a gatekeeper role. The prominence and display of stories connotes significance. Big headlines and photos on the front page, web page, or lead story on the newscast are all ways that the news media signal to the reader or viewer that this is what the media outlet considers most important today and at the moment. Issues compete for attention from the media, from political actors, and from the public. And coverage in one major news outlet often generates coverage—and commentary—in other media outlets, adding to the issue's salience, its perceived importance. Conversely, an event or an issue that does *not* get covered by the media may not be considered important or even known by the public and political leaders.

When political scientists in the 1940s began measuring whether exposure to media led to actual changes in voting behavior, using that standard for a specific impact—on voting—led them to conclude that the media had what was called minimal effects. More recent research has tracked media effects more broadly, focusing more on the cumulative effects and influence of media coverage on learning, opinion formation, and public opinion.

Walter Lippmann and the Nature of News

In his 1922 book *Public Opinion*, author Walter Lippmann effectively anticipated today's twenty-four-hour news environment; he came up with concepts about the nature of news that are helpful and relevant today. Lippmann was a journalist who had worked for the Allies during World War I, and he was one of the first to explore how the ways that journalists gather the news have impact on what gets covered and how coverage, in turn, affects perceptions of events and people in the news. In this book we'll call these journalistic practices and culture the conventions of news-gathering.

Lippmann observed early on that the public was increasingly perceiving the world around them not through direct experience but through the reflected, distorted reality of the world as published in what was then called "the press." Lippmann likened the public to the cave dwellers in

Plato's *Republic*, people who see the world above them not through direct experience but through the shadows of the world above on the walls of the cave—i.e., through the media.[3]

Lippmann recognized that the news media are not ideally suited for their role in the democracy—in part because of the commercial demands of the media and the ways news is gathered and disseminated. "The press is no substitute for institutions," he wrote. "It is like the beam of a searchlight that moves restlessly about, bringing one episode and then another out of darkness into vision. Men cannot do the work of the world by this light alone. They cannot govern society by episodes, incidents, and eruptions. It is only when they work by a steady light of their own, that the press, when it is turned upon them, reveals a situation intelligible enough for a popular decision."[4]

The image of the news media as a *restless searchlight*, focusing intently on one person or story in a glaring spotlight before moving on to another, brilliantly describes the excesses of some coverage on television, particularly on twenty-four-hour cable news. The death of a celebrity, a celebrity scandal, or a highly publicized criminal trial that has other cultural resonances can become what cultural critic Neal Gabler has called real-life movies, making public figures and even celebrities out of previously unknown people and drawing viewers in for incremental updates in a seemingly real-life soap opera that conforms to the norms of TV entertainment—and, for good and for ill, is entertaining.[5]

The Episodic Nature of News Coverage

The image of the moving spotlight is an excellent metaphor for describing and examining another important concept: *the episodic nature of news coverage*. On television and in online video, it is easier for the news media to cover a single incident than an ongoing situation or an in-depth investigation. The single, breaking news event has immediacy and drama—and a defined time and place—to draw viewers and readers.

Lippmann compared an ongoing situation to a seed growing in the ground. The news, he maintained, is not likely to tell you about the situation until the seed visibly bursts through the ground, as what we today call a breaking news story.[6] This episodic nature of news coverage, media critics and researchers say, makes the public less likely to connect individual episodes to the larger issues—whether it's food safety or the environment. Political scientists have found that episodic news coverage leads people to assign individual causes and responsibility to such events, rather than holding public officials accountable.[7]

The example Lippmann gave from his day was the difference in coverage between a miners' strike and the conditions that might have led to the strike. To cite an example on the same subject from more recent media, TV networks devoted many hours of coverage in 2010 to an explosion in a coal mine in West Virginia that led to the deaths of some thirty miners and a criminal investigation against the owner. Government inspectors' reports of multiple safety violations and fines levied against the mine had gone largely uncovered until the widely covered disaster, as had mine safety experts' concerns over independent oversight by the federal Mine Safety and Health Administration.[8]

The West Virginia disaster was what journalists call the *news peg* for reporting that, in the days afterward, found national journalists using the incident to write about previous problems at the plant and in mining inspections overall.[9] Similar trends can be found in other recent stories of disasters and death among consumers. But it appears to have taken the seed bursting through, the mining disaster, to bring national attention to the issue germinating on the ground.

Aware of television's—and the government's—bad habit of turning off the cameras and moving on once the compelling drama and video from a disaster have subsided, major TV news anchors have kept their promise to come back to stories such as rebuilding after Hurricane Sandy and Hurricane Katrina, often doing so on anniversaries, which is another convention of news-gathering. But the rebuilding of Puerto Rico after disastrous hurricanes virtually disappeared from the news after a time, which officials there said affected their ability to get ongoing federal aid. And, except in crises, there can be little ongoing coverage of whole continents internationally on network television, which reflects both cutbacks in international reporting as well as a presumed lack of interest on the part of Americans until Americans and American interests are involved.

In a distinguishing counter trend, a few major news organizations today are devoting significant resources to reporting on the seeds in the ground, through multiplatform packages that combine in-depth investigative reporting and interviews with people affected by an issue, along with data analysis, still photography, online video, documents display, and other reporting tools. Here are some examples: the *New York Times* revealing documents that showed a pharmaceutical company knew about the addictive uses of its popular opioid drug;[10] the *Wall Street Journal* investigating Medicare billing;[11] the Associated Press investigating severe labor practices in the seafood industry that led to the freeing of two thousand slave workers, criminal trials, and reforms;[12] the *Washington Post* reporting on the lives of low-wage workers;[13] the *Los Angeles Times* investigating a corrupt city government in a small California town;[14] and the staffs of the *Arizona Republic* and USA Today Network combining text, podcasts, video, and virtual reality to provide a variety of perspectives on building a wall across the U.S. border with Mexico.[15]

Online, *Vox* has pioneered in "explainers" that lay out the facts and data on policy topics.[16] On broadcast television, *Frontline* and *POV* on the

Public Broadcasting Service (PBS) continue award-winning investigative and independent filmmakers' documentaries in a medium where the one-hour investigative documentary was once a public interest staple on all the broadcast networks.

In contrast to these examples are the stories—from local government meetings to investigative reporting—that undoubtedly are going uncovered due to cutbacks and layoffs with media consolidation in local news. In 2015, to cite one example, reporter Rob Kuznia was in the news when it was reported that he had left the *Daily Breeze* of Torrance, California, by the time he and two other journalists had won the Pulitzer Prize for local reporting on a corrupt local school district. Kuznia and one of his coauthors, who has also since left the newspaper, cited cutbacks in staffing and an increasingly stressful work environment as reasons for leaving journalism for public relations.[17]

Agenda-Setting Theory

In 1963, Bernard Cohen made an important observation that the press "may not be successful much of the time in telling people what to think, but it is stunningly successful in telling its readers what to think about . . . The world will look different to different people, depending . . . on the map that is drawn for them by writers, editors, and publishers of the papers they read."[18] That distinction between telling people what to think versus what to think about is an important aspect of agenda-setting in the media. *Agenda-setting theory* describes, and seeks to measure how media content influences the relative salience that the public attaches to different topics and issues.

In 1968, Maxwell McCombs and Donald Shaw, two professors at the University of North Carolina, noticing that "more than ever before, candidates go before the people through the mass media rather than in person," tested their hypothesis that "while the mass media may have little influence on the direction or intensity of attitudes, it is hypothesized that *the mass media set the agenda for each political campaign, influencing the salience* of attitudes toward the political issues."[19]

Building on the concept of *cognitive mapping* in psychology, McCombs and Shaw described what they called a *need for orientation*. "Each individual will strive to 'map' his world, to fill in enough detail to orient himself, to intellectually find his way around," they wrote.[20] Two factors, they said, help determine the strength of a person's need for orientation via the media: (1) relevance (Is the issue being written about relevant personally?) and (2) uncertainty (Does the reader/viewer feel that he or she has enough information on the topic?).

Studying voters in one community—Chapel Hill, North Carolina—and their attitudes about the issues in the 1968 presidential campaign, McCombs and Shaw attempted to match what these voters who were registered but undecided said were the key issues in the campaign with the actual content of the mass media used by these voters, including their local newspapers, *Time* magazine, and the evening newscasts on CBS and NBC.

The 1968 presidential race between Republican Richard Nixon and Democrat Hubert Humphrey, Lyndon Johnson's vice president, took place during a tumultuous time, with the Vietnam War and anti-war protests, the civil rights movement, and a Republican platform calling for law and order. Segregationist Alabama governor George Wallace was running as a third-party candidate. In their research, McCombs and Shaw found that although the news media devoted "a considerable amount of campaign coverage to . . . *analysis of the campaign itself* . . . i.e., horserace coverage about a candidate's chances or tactics, there was a very strong correlation (+.967) between the relative rankings of issues by the news media (in terms of amount of coverage and prominence of coverage) that these respondents consumed and the issues they said they were most concerned about and thought the government should do something about."[21]

The media, McCombs and Shaw found, reflected the emphasis by candidates to a considerable degree—but "while the three presidential candidates placed widely different emphasis on different issues, the judgment of the voters seem to reflect the *composite* of the mass media coverage."[22] In other words, as David H. Weaver wrote in an article describing the history of agenda-setting research, McCombs and Shaw had found that "the public learns not only about a given issue but also how much importance to attach to that issue by the amount of information in news reports and its position."[23]

Civil Rights and the History of Agenda-Setting

National media coverage of the civil rights movement in America in the 1960s is an outstanding example of agenda-setting by national media. At a time when the broadcast TV networks' nightly newscasts were seen by virtually everyone tuned in to television, national TV reporters' and print reporters' accounts of nonviolent civil rights protests and brutal, racist responses in the South helped Dr. Martin Luther King and other civil rights leaders put their movement and conditions in the South on the national agenda. "The news media played an enormous role in mobilizing public opinion," civil rights leader Julian Bond said in an interview with the author, "saying to the country, to the world really, 'Here's this movement. It's about this: X-Y-Z. It's very simple: here are these people who can't do something because of the color of their skin and they ought to be allowed to.'"[24]

Bond, who later became a Georgia state representative and senator as well as chairman of the NAACP, cofounded the Student Nonviolent Coordinating Committee (SNCC), a group of young civil rights activists, when he was twenty years old. SNCC led lunch counter sit-ins and other protests against segregation in the South. "An important part of my job with SNCC was to get media coverage of what we were doing," Bond recalled.[25]

As Bond noted, media coverage, including on TV and in memorable still photographs, shone a national spotlight on racism and violent reaction to nonviolent protest in the South. In 1963, for example, images of policemen in Birmingham, Alabama, turning dogs and powerful water hoses against peaceful young civil rights demonstrators affected public opinion and helped move President John F. Kennedy to push for important civil rights legislation. "President Kennedy watched the TV pictures from Birmingham, and he said, 'It makes me sick,'" Bond recalled. "Here's the president of the United States watching this happen, and if it made him sick, what do you think other people felt, too? It made them sick and made them say, 'This has got to stop.'"[26] Kennedy, who had been reluctant to push civil rights legislation, later gave a televised speech to put forth broad civil rights legislation that was enacted under President Lyndon Johnson after Kennedy's assassination in 1963.[27]

Agenda-Setting in Major Media Today

Since the original studies of agenda-setting, there have been hundreds of studies using Shaw and McCombs' methodology to compare content of news media with rankings of issues and public opinion, including online and in social media. In their book *News That Matters: Television & American Opinion*, Shanto Iyengar and Donald R. Kinder compared news agendas with the public's agenda. They concluded that issues that receive broad coverage in national media are perceived as important, while those that are not covered lose credibility. They and other researchers have found these connections continuing over time, with significant media attention to inflation or to energy, for example, being reflected in national polls of the public about the most important issues of the day.[28]

The wide range of what people consider "the media," plus polarization in politics and partisan media, have led some researchers to ask how strongly agenda-setting applies today.[29] We live in an era of increased *selective exposure*, where many people may seek out specific outlets to reinforce their beliefs. The credence people give to stories also, interestingly, has been linked to whether the subject is something they feel they already know about—or not. Media coverage and the response of politicians and the public interrelate, and the impact of media coverage may vary according to what is being discussed—and where—and how politicians and the public respond.

But while there is need for a more nuanced view of agenda-setting and related concepts in today's media-politics culture, researchers are finding that it still applies, including in experiments attempting to measure exposure to news on Facebook and news organizations' websites. "Overall, the evidence in support of the agenda-setting function is overwhelming," Iyengar wrote. "One-shot surveys, time-series analysis of public opinion, and laboratory experiments all agree that the issues in the news *are* the issues that people care about."[30]

Citing congressional hearings on tobacco and public health risks that came after major media coverage of the issue, Iyengar continued, "Policy-makers know that when the media spotlight is on a particular issue, they are likely to have greater success in promoting or moving along legislation [over opposition] because the public is clamoring for action."[31]

The reporting of the *New York Times*, the *Washington Post*, and the *Wall Street Journal*, in particular, had a major agenda-setting function in contemporary media and politics during the Trump administration, with these publications regularly breaking news, including from sources within the Trump administration, that had members of Congress citing news organizations reporting—positively and negatively—as evidence in congressional hearings and investigations, including impeachment. President Trump and his allies in Congress and among prime-time hosts on Fox News Channel and conservative talk radio quoted their reporting to attack them and their journalists. The reporting of these publications and others from *Politico* to *USA Today* has been amplified by debriefs of their reporters on cable television.

Violence in children's television, the practices of tobacco companies, and government health care for military veterans are among the many issues where investigative reporting by major media have led to public outcry—and then to congressional hearings and legislation.

The revelation in the *New York Times* and *New Yorker* magazine of women's allegations of sexual assault by Hollywood entertainment mogul Harvey Weinstein ultimately led to more women telling their stories with the #MeToo hashtag (based on the original Me Too movement founded by activist Tarana Burke), a national conversation, and ultimately a criminal conviction of Weinstein for rape.[32] Other investigations by the *New York Times* and *Washington Post* of allegations of sexual harassment and even sexual assault led to the resignations of powerful figures in the media from NBC *Today* show host Matt Lauer to PBS's Charlie Rose.

The Role of Elites

People vary in their attention to politics and exposure to political information, and many remain uninformed or scarcely informed, while others view being informed as important and even a civic duty. In his book *The Nature and Origins of Mass Opinion*, John R. Zaller argued that political elites—politicians, government officials, activists, experts and policy specialists—play a key role in how the world is portrayed and understood by citizens overall.[33] Public opinion, he wrote, is largely shaped by exposure through the media to elite discourse on issues.

Creating a model of public opinion, Zaller theorized that, rather than holding one attitude or a single opinion about an issue, people's stated opinions reflect their responses to considerations (what they have heard or read about), what they have accepted (if the message is consistent with their own prior beliefs), and what they have sampled from (which ideas from a mix of opinions and ideas are salient—and can be reached for, or top of mind—at the time).[34] He found, somewhat surprisingly, that the more closely people follow the news, the more their opinions reflect those of elites in government and in politics. Elite media affect elite opinion, which impacts on what politicians and policymakers view as important—and believe they need to respond to.

One might think that the seemingly endless frontier of the Internet would undermine the hegemony of political elites and mainstream media in determining agenda-setting—and it has. But, even online, readers tend to favor a few brand-name outlets and voices they trust from major news organizations. And, while political TV talk show producers are on the look-out for younger, more diverse voices, these influential programs still tend to book traditional elites—from journalism, government, and political strategy.

In his important book *The Myth of Digital Democracy*, political scientist Matthew Hindman analyzed data about readership online and found that online news audiences are concentrated among the top twenty outlets. He also found a concentration in online fundraising and organizing among major interest groups. Finally, his data showed that, contrary to what had been commonly believed, the Internet also is dominated by political discussion among elites.[35]

Agenda-Building

In their work on what moves public opinion, Everett M. Rogers and James Dearing argued that communications scholars should look also at the interrelation among the media agenda, the public agenda, and the policy agenda, including what political elites such as the president and members of Congress are reading and seeing in news coverage and how that affects the policy agenda. They talked about the importance of agenda-building as well as agenda-setting, defining *agenda-building* as "a process through which the policy agendas of political elites are influenced by a variety of factors, including media agendas and public agendas."[36] The media, in other words, do not operate in a vacuum and are influenced by what political elites and other political actors highlight as important—and vice versa—with impact on policy and public opinion. In later research, political scientists have used other phrases to describe agenda-setting today, including *intermediate agenda-setting*—major news media setting the agenda for other news media via their coverage[37]—and *network agenda-setting*, which is how the media's linking of attributes or elements in a story can influence the audience themselves to see the elements as interconnected in their own minds.[38]

On MSNBC, Rachel Maddow and other hosts agenda-set by focusing intensely on the investigation into special counsel Robert Mueller's investigation into Russian interference in the 2016 election, the impeachment trial, and—later—on criticism of the Trump administration's response to the coronavirus.

The loyalty of Fox News Channel viewers and the interconnectedness between the channel and the Trump administration, with a number of senior Trump officials being hired from positions as prominent commentators on Fox News Channel, is an example of the concept of agenda-building.

In previous years what some journalists called a "Fox News story" used to be ignored by other major media, but that is much less likely to be the case today. In 2014, for example, the story of a Nevada cattle rancher leading a protest against paying grazing fees on federal public lands fit a Fox narrative about the government taking away freedoms and received repeated airplay on Fox, conservative talk radio and online media and light coverage elsewhere—until the dispute led to a tense, armed standoff between the rancher and his supporters and law enforcement officials.[39] The network repeatedly aired disputedly edited "undercover sting" videos by two anti-abortion activists that appeared to show a Planned Parenthood official discussing selling fetal tissue for medical research. Planned Parenthood said that it did not sell fetal tissue for medical research and that the edited video was unrepresentative of their work. But, in the debate over abortion, the videos led to repeated proposals by Republican lawmakers to defund Planned Parenthood.[40]

Reverse Agenda-Setting

Reverse agenda-setting is the term that has been used to describe how user-generated content, from blogs to popular memes and Twitter posts, can help set the agenda of what have been called major "legacy" media. Today, it works both ways, especially when it comes to news coverage and politicians' social media, with politicians quoting major media and major media focusing on politicians' social media in their news coverage.

YouTube video and social media have accelerated the way that a compelling photo or video shot at the scene of an event can personalize a story from around the world, go viral on the Internet; be picked up as online video news; and set the agenda for discussion on TV, in print, and online. A Turkish photographer's picture of a small Syrian child drowned on the beach in 2015 went viral; news organizations reported on the identity of the child and his family as the image, however fleetingly, became a symbol for the crisis of desperate refugees fleeing the Syrian civil war.[41] The #BlackLives Matter movement started in 2013 as a hashtag by three women reacting to an acquittal in the death of Trayvon Martin, the unarmed Black teenager who was shot and killed in Florida by a neighborhood watch volunteer.[42] Citizen journalists exposed unsafe drinking water in Flint, Michigan, and forced the attention of the public—and local officials—to the problem through their videos and subsequent news coverage in other media.[43]

Agenda-Setting on Social Media

Despite the highly contentious relationship between Donald Trump and major media, his tweets were featured in—and often dominated—the contemporary news agenda to a remarkable degree. Trump—who began his presidency with what he called his "war with the media"—stepped up making the media an enemy, on Twitter and in his political rallies, in 2019 and throughout the 2020 presidential campaign. The nonpartisan Freedom of the Press Foundation in January 2020 found that over the previous year, "Trump tweeted negatively [himself, not including retweets] about the media 548 times—almost as many as his first two years in office combined . . . That means that more than 11% of the presidents original tweets focused on delegitimizing and insulting the U.S. media."[44] The foundation's database analysis found that the frequency and rate of the president's anti-media tweets "ramped up" with his 2019 announcement of his reelection campaign and reporting on his administration and congressional investigations, shifting his attention also to attacking Democrats in Congress with the opening of the official impeachment inquiry.[45]

In the 2020 presidential race, Sen. Bernie Sanders criticized what he called "the corporate media," which he said reflected corporate interests opposed to his proposals. Sanders supporters and several media critics also were critical of commentary by some MSNBC hosts that they maintained reflected bias against Sanders by the Democratic National Committee. We'll discuss news coverage of Sanders as well as how politicians, political leaders, and social movements overall aim to influence and drive the news agenda.

Facebook, Twitter, and other social media present challenges to measuring their impact overall on politics and policy. But scholars today are adding big data analysis to more traditional surveys, coded content analyses of media coverage, and experiments where, as researchers have done for many years with traditional media, they research agenda-setting by altering parts of a mock-up—for example, changing the race or gender or the news outlet in a mock-up story. In one experiment, Jessica T. Feezell found agenda-setting and issue salience of news stories distributed on Facebook feeds among a group of college students.[46] In another 2018 study, the authors harvested and analyzed thematically millions of tweets on what are called Black Twitter, Asian American Twitter, and Feminist Twitter and interviewed members of these Twitter subgroups to see how these groups use digital media and their perceptions of media coverage of their communities.[47] In her research on the implications of consuming news on mobile devices such as tablets and smartphones versus reading news on a computer, Johanna Dunaway and her colleagues used eye-tracking software to watch how the people in their experimental studies read and engaged with news stories.[48]

Priming Theory

The media, including entertainment and news media, provide important cultural role models for what is considered masculine and what is feminine—and what is heroic. Our view of what we want in a president is influenced by what is emphasized and portrayed in the media as "presidential." Researchers have found that the relative emphasis the news media place on a president's programs and policies—for example, his or her handling of the economy versus foreign policy—has impact on what the public considers important in evaluating presidential performance. This concept is called *priming*.

Iyengar and Kinder, who advanced the theory of media priming, defined it as "changes in the standards that people use to make political evaluations," with the focus of the media having influence over the benchmarks by which a president, a candidate or a government might be judged.[49] Priming can be seen as an extension of agenda-setting. People cannot and do not pay attention to everything. Rather, we are what researchers call "cognitive misers"; we ordinarily rely on a few heuristics—intuitive shortcuts and rules of thumb, with one such heuristic being relying on information that is most accessible. Iyengar and Kinder theorized that the standards by which people judge a president, while likely having several sources, were strongly influenced by which stories were covered on TV news.[50] They and other researchers have found that voters tend to vote for the presidential candidate they think can do the best job on the issue they think is most important; extensive media coverage conveys importance and can help move one issue to the foreground while another less favorable to the candidate recedes.

In their research on presidents and priming, Iyengar and Kinder found that voters' views on the then president Jimmy Carter's overall competence in his reelection bid in 1980 against California governor Ronald Reagan were influenced by the daily coverage of the protracted negotiations to free American hostages captured and held by followers of Ayatollah Khomeini in Iran.[51]

If you look at news coverage from this period, you will see pictures of American hostages in blindfolds and the U.S. embassy occupied dominating the news.

On a new ABC News daily late-night program created to follow the crisis, *America Held Hostage* (later, *Nightline*), influential news anchor Ted Koppel quizzed government officials and experts about the failure of the Carter administration to free the hostages. On screen was a count of the ultimately 444-day crisis that called attention to the Carter administration's failures and—as the title of the show said—sent the message to millions of viewers that the U.S. itself was being held hostage.[52] That was not the only issue on which voters judged President Carter's competence; the economy was also key. But the hostage crisis—and the coverage of it—had impact on how voters reacted and viewed the competence of President Carter and his administration to deal with it.

President Richard Nixon was defined by the Watergate scandal, impeachment, and his resignation from office, while public opinion about President Bill Clinton's impeachment led by Republicans in Congress over the Monica Lewinsky scandal ultimately did not appear to matter to voters at the time as much as the economic performance of the Clinton administration. The Gallup poll at the time showed that Clinton's approval ratings actually went *up*, not down, during the Monica Lewinsky scandal, perhaps in response to the strong economy or perhaps, it was thought at the time, in a "sympathy vote" for the president in reaction to the twenty-four seven coverage and more partisan-led impeachment charges.[53] (In recent years, however, Bill Clinton's standing with the public is being reexamined in media and politics through the prism of media revelations of sexual misconduct by prominent figures in media and politics and the #MeToo movement.)

Priming Presidential Campaigns

Former Texas governor George W. Bush (the son of forty-first president George H. W. Bush) defeated Al Gore, Bill Clinton's vice president, in 2000 in a contested election that ultimately was decided by the U.S. Supreme Court. (We'll discuss media and politics in that election in Chapter 4.) President Bush's approval ratings were strongly linked to his handling of the September 11, 2001, terrorist attacks: His approval ratings surged from 35 percent to a record 90 percent, the highest in Gallup polling history, with his September 20, 2001, speech to a joint session of Congress rallying the country and outlining a fight against global terrorism seen as a defining moment with the public, according to Gallup polling that was done before and immediately after the speech.[54] "Almost three-quarters of all

Americans say they saw the address live, and another 14% saw rebroadcasts or excerpts of the speech," Gallup reported at the time.[55] Bush's popularity declined in the aftermath of the U.S. invasion of Iraq in 2003 and the Iraq War, but national security and fighting terrorism remained key issues as Bush won reelection against Sen. John Kerry, the Democratic nominee, in a contest we'll discuss further in Chapter 3.

In the 2008 presidential election between Barack Obama and Sen. John McCain, the Republican nominee, the public was concerned about the global financial crisis known in the U.S. as the Great Recession. The news media were covering the crisis extensively, while coverage of other issues such as terrorism and immigration were less prominent. In 2008 exit polls, voters in the general election overwhelmingly named the economy as the most important issue—62 percent in exit polls, a very high percentage for exit polls historically—compared to the war in Iraq (10 percent), health care (9 percent), and terrorism (9 percent).[56] Sen. McCain, a Vietnam War hero and longtime supporter of the war in Iraq, received 86 percent of the votes of those who listed terrorism as the top issue, but those voters accounted for only 10 percent of the electorate. Barack Obama had voted against the war in Iraq, and he and the Democrats were seen as better able to deal with the economy than Senator McCain.[57]

Priming Personal Presidential Traits

The media—both in news and in popular entertainment—also have an impact in priming what personal traits are considered "presidential" and relatable.

And soft-focus, personal coverage of candidates' and presidents' families helps make the public feel connected to presidents, members of Congress, candidates, and other elected officials. Jacques Lowe, President John F. Kennedy's personal White House photographer, took the photographs of the president and Jacqueline Kennedy with their young children, Caroline and John Jr., that, published in *Life* magazine and other publications, constitute many people's memories of the Kennedy presidency—even among those born long after Kennedy was president.[58] A close-up color photo of a genial, rugged-looking Ronald Reagan smiling in a cowboy hat at his California ranch, taken by Reagan's

Photo 2.1 White House photos of the Obamas on Flickr created new intimacy with the First Family and the public.
Obama White House/Flickr

personal photographer, has been widely used and published for many years because it conveys what has been perceived and portrayed as Reagan's trademark optimism and the mythic "Western individualism." that has roots in America's history and self-image and still has appeal to many today.[59]

Many of the engaging, intimate photos of President Obama; First Lady Michelle Obama, and their daughters Malia and Sasha as well as the president's frequent interactions with children came from the extensive access granted to official White House photographer Pete Souza, who also took the famous dramatic photo of the president and advisers in the "war room" monitoring the capture of Osama bin Laden.[60] These photos were widely distributed to the news media—and to the public–via the Obama administration's then new and sophisticated social media operation, including an active White House Flickr photo account and Instagram.[61] By contrast, in the first few years of Donald Trump's presidency, there were few official intimate White House family photos.

Photos of the president participating in cabinet meetings, signing bills and showing his signature, and meeting with world leaders became the staples of a more limited official White House photography operation.[62]

In 2013 the White House Correspondents' Association and thirty-seven news organizations submitted a letter to then Obama press secretary Jay Carney protesting Souza's exclusive access to what the journalists said were newsworthy events. "The way they exclude us is to say that this is a very private moment," said Doug Mills, a *New York Times* photographer covering the White House since Ronald Reagan. "But they're making private moments very public."[63] The Obama administration argued that photographers couldn't be at every event and that they were simply making use of new tools in social media to give the public new behind-the-scenes access to the presidency.

Priming Presidential Spouses

The appeal of these images, along with the Obamas' ease on popular talk shows—including President Obama on the daytime talk show *The View*[64] and Michelle Obama's "Carpool Karaoke" in the White House driveway with CBS *Late Late Show* host James Corden[65]—could help explain President Obama's personal popularity in office and beyond.[66] (We'll discuss how and why politicians and political leaders go on talk shows and late-night comedy programs in a case study in Chapter 5.) Michelle Obama's popularity consistently ranked higher than her husband's in office, and Laura Bush (the wife of George W. Bush) was one of the most popular First Ladies ever. Both women championed important causes such as health and education; but, as with other First Ladies in office, these were portrayed and viewed as less "political" initiatives.[67]

At the same time, when it comes to having a woman elected as president, as we will discuss in Chapter 8, researchers and candidates for many years have found that perceived likeability—defined in gendered terms and reflected in media coverage and candidates' focus groups—has been a long-standing criterion by which the public has been primed to judge female candidates for office, especially for president of the U.S. When Hillary Clinton was first running for president in 2008, there were real questions and humorous asides about how that would work and what the former president should be called—First Gentleman? First Dude?—although other countries have been led by female presidents. With the nomination of Biden and Harris in 2020, their marriages and their roles in the marriages were portrayed as both traditional and contemporary by the Democrats.

Framing

How something is framed in news media and by political groups has real impact on how an issue is perceived, according to many studies. The simplest way to think about it is as a frame around a picture, with the frame defining the picture. In media and politics, framing attempts to define the subject—and influence perception—by emphasizing certain elements of the subject while excluding other elements. "*Framing essentially involves selection and salience*," Robert Entman wrote. "To frame is to *select some aspects of a perceived reality and make them more salient in a communicating text, in such a way as to promote a particular problem definition, causal interpretation, moral evaluation and/or treatment recommendation* for the item described."[68]

Entman and other researchers have studied, for example, how the Cold War frame of the Soviet Union versus America dominated U.S. foreign policy—and U.S. media coverage of foreign affairs—for many years. In addition, as Entman and other researchers have noted, what is *not* included as a choice in a frame is significant. Tax cuts, for example, can be framed as promoting economic growth—or adding to income inequality. Entman and others have argued that, in the buildup to the war in Iraq post–9/11, the option *not* to go to war in Iraq was not sufficiently considered or included in the frame of lost lives and fighting a war on terrorism.

Psychologists Daniel Kahneman and Amos Tversky won the Nobel Prize in Economic Sciences for their work challenging the rational model of decision-making and the effects of cognitive biases in thinking and framing risk and decision-making. They found that presenting the same information in different ways has an impact on the choices people make. To cite one simple example, stores have sales that offer "buy one, get one free" because that is more appealing psychologically. Kahneman wrote in his book *Thinking, Fast and Slow* that if you say "Italy won" or "France lost" the World Cup in soccer in 2006, for "the purposes of logical reasoning," the two outcomes are interchangeable—but "there is another sense of *meaning*" in which the two sentences do not mean the same thing if the meaning is what happens in your associative memory while you understand it. . . . The fact that logically equivalent statements evoke different reactions makes it impossible for Humans to be as reliably rational as Econs" (humans studied in the abstract by economists).[69]

In one famous experiment about the outbreak of a fictional, dangerous new disease, Kahneman and Tversky posed questions about possible actions that had identical outcomes as to how many people would die if different courses of action were followed. There were different results because of the way the questions and risks were framed in terms of lives saved or lives lost.[70] Their work, which relates to people's loss aversion—in the stock market and in life—helped set the stage for other framing research.

Framing Language and Issue Frames

There are two categories of framing to consider here: (1) framing language and (2) issue frames. In terms of framing language, message creators hope to trigger associations that are positive or negative in the mind of the receiver of the message, depending on their side of the issue. This fight over whose language prevails is called *framing* and *counter-framing*, and it relates particularly to framing political and policy issues about which people may feel deeply. Advocacy and political groups work hard to have their own, positive descriptions of themselves used in news stories and political discourse. In the debate over abortion, for example, one side describes themselves as pro-life, while the other describes themselves as pro-choice not "pro-abortion," as some opponents have aimed to characterize them.

Words matter, and researchers have found that, rather than offering and responding to purely rational appeals, people respond to and politicians may deal in code words and stereotypes—bra-burning feminists, corrupt politicians, tax-and-spend liberals, hard-hearted capitalists, welfare queens, and worse—that appeal to and amplify often unconscious fears and other negative emotions about "the (unknown) Other."

There are real consequences to which *framing language* and *issue frames* prevail in political and advocacy campaigns as well as media coverage—in terms of public perceptions and opinion and even legal action and funding for solutions. There was a strong debate in 2016, for example, over the framing of the mass shooting in which a gunman pledging allegiance to ISIS killed fifty people and wounded many others at an Orlando, Florida, nightclub: Was it an act of terror, an antigay hate crime, new evidence of the need for gun control legislation, as many Democrats and some Republicans in Congress said?

Or was it an act of "radical Islamic terrorism" and evidence of what then presidential nominee Donald Trump claimed was President Obama's timidity about using that term?[71]

In 2019, there were back-to-back mass shootings in Dayton, Ohio, and El Paso, Texas. A young, white gunman drove ten hours to El Paso after writing an online "manifesto" against the "invasion" of the U.S. by "Mexicans" at the U.S.-Mexico border, with President Trump himself and Fox News Channel prime-time hosts having used the word *invasion*.[72] After the shootings, there were renewed calls for gun control legislation to be passed in Congress. There were also debates over whether political leaders should call out President Trump over the similarities in language,[73] along with questions about whether the government—and the news media—had done enough to label and investigate the rise of white supremacy and anti-Semitism, online and in mass shootings in the U.S. and abroad.[74]

Case Study: Framing and Counter-Framing Obamacare

Politics and media in the passage of the Patient Protection and Affordable Care Act, or Affordable Care Act, is an example of the power of framing—and counter-framing—including the importance of the *timing* of framing language, the repetition of competing frames in powerful language from politicians and the media, and the involvement of the president in the debate.

In his first year in office as president, Barack Obama made comprehensive health-care reform—an important but complex topic—a top priority. With insurance premiums rising dramatically in recent years and health-care costs accounting for one-sixth of the economy and forty-seven million Americans uninsured,[75] many Americans were concerned about the affordability of their health care. In a Pew Research Center poll released in June 2009, 41 percent of respondents said that the health-care system needed to be "completely rebuilt," and an additional 30 percent said the system "needs fundamental change," while only 24 percent said the health-care system "works pretty well and needs only minor changes."[76] Unlike in 1993, when the health insurance industry opposed health-care reform put forth by the Bill Clinton administration, this time the industry, and doctors and hospitals, was expressing support for fixing the health-care system.

(Continued)

(Continued)

In this context and with Obama's popularity with the public as a new president, there appeared to be an argument to be made that reforming health care was an economic necessity for the future as well as a social good.

Republicans in Congress mounted a powerful, frightening, and repeated framing campaign against what came to be known as "Obamacare." Soon, angry citizens were confronting legislators at local town halls—with dramatic moments videotaped and broadcast on YouTube—that had been intended to discuss and promote the benefits of Obama's proposals.[77] Jokes about the irony of senior citizens who had benefited from a major government health-care program, Medicare, shouting for the government to "take your hands off my health care" were no laughing matter for advocates for Obamacare.

Former 2008 Republican vice presidential candidate Sarah Palin, who remained a popular political figure among conservatives and Tea Party members, made personal the false notion that Obamacare would include "death panels," who would decide whether the elderly and infirm would receive health care. Referring to her own child who was born with Down syndrome, Palin wrote this on her Facebook page: "The America I know and love is not one in which my parents or my baby with Down Syndrome will have to stand in front of Obama's 'death panel' so his bureaucrats can decide, based on a subjective judgment of their 'level of productivity in society,' whether they are worthy of health care. Such a system is downright evil."[78]

The idea of death panels was not true, and many fact-checking organizations—including FactCheck.org from the Annenberg Public Policy Center of the University of Pennsylvania—said it was untrue.[79] But polls showed that many Americans *believed* it to be true. And, more importantly, the framing of Obamacare as a dangerous government takeover dominated the political narrative—and the media narrative as well. Republican legislators repeated "government takeover" not only in Congress but also on the influential Sunday morning newsmaker talk shows—and conservative prime-time hosts on Fox News Channel and talk radio repeatedly used exactly the same language—dangerous "government takeover"—as well.[80]

Winning the Message War on Obamacare

"An analysis . . . of the language used re: Obamacare" across the board by opponents in "those crucial months in the media reveals that opponents of the reform won the 'messaging war' in the coverage," researchers for the nonpartisan Project for Excellence in Journalism concluded in a study of key terms used in more than 5,500 health-care stories in the mainstream media between June 2009 and March 2010.[81] The researchers found that "opponents' leading terms appeared almost twice as frequently (about 18,000 times) as the supporters' top terms (about 11,000 times)."[82]

There were media stories that attempted to explain the complicated proposals, but congressional coverage shifted to horse-race coverage of politics and strategy. Meantime, ideological debates on cable news and radio talk shows were the most prominent venue for discussion of Obamacare, the researchers found, with the health-care proposals the number one story by far in the talk-show sector, accounting for 31 percent of the airtime during the period studied, compared to 10 percent of the new coverage in newspapers and on network news and 9 percent of coverage in the online sector.[83]

The economy and president Obama's work to deal with the recession received far less attention on cable and radio talk shows than in other media; President Obama, the researchers found, was a "fluctuating" presence in the health-care story, while positive coverage of the proposals and negative commentary about "greedy" insurance companies by liberal hosts on MSNBC were overshadowed by negative portrayals by Republicans and prime-time hosts on Fox News Channel. A Gallup poll in 2010 found that "government involvement in health care" had emerged as a top concern, cited by 10 percent of respondents as the number one health-care problem facing the country.[84]

By the time the Affordable Care Act won approval in Congress in March of 2010, it passed without a single Republican vote. Democrats proclaimed the sweeping legislation a singular legislative victory for President Obama and the American people; Republican House Speaker John Boehner said the legislation was an example of out-of-control big government.[85]

In the 2010 midterm elections in Congress, Democrats up for election downplayed their support for Obamacare, while Republicans running against Obamacare returned the House of Representatives to Republican control for the first time in forty years.[86] Voters cited health care as their second most important concern, after the economy, in exit polls after the midterms.[87] Meantime, throughout the debate, the public consistently reported being confused about the proposals and the programs enacted.[88]

Visual Framing

In her autobiography, longtime CBS News *60 Minutes* anchor Lesley Stahl wrote that she was surprised by the positive reaction of Richard Darman, Ronald Reagan's deputy chief of staff, to a story she had done on the then new video stagecraft techniques that critics of Reagan said were being employed to distract attention from cuts in social spending: Reagan being cheered by supporters waving small American flags, cutting a ribbon at a nursing home, giving medals to disabled athletes. Expecting criticism from the White House, as she recounted it, Stahl instead received a congratulatory call from Darman, who loved the emotional visuals in the piece and told her that nobody would remember her conflicting audio narrative.[89]

President Reagan, who had been a movie actor in Hollywood before he was elected governor of California, was called "The Great Communicator" as president, and he and his media advisers recognized the often unconscious power of visuals and stagecraft techniques in political communication on television. In their book *Image Bite Politics: News and the Visual Framing of Elections*, Maria Elizabeth Grabe and Erik Page Bucy argued for more scholarly research into the audiovisual elements of TV news and Internet sites. "Ignoring the visuals of a televised news report means overlooking much of the meaning that viewers derive from the viewing experience," they contended.[90] As we will discuss further in Chapter 3 on political advertising and persuasive techniques, the visual techniques, including editing, lighting, camera angles, and who and what is seen in the background in ads or public addresses, all are designed to put the candidate or elected official in a favorable light—literally and figuratively.

We should not forget also the power of eloquent language in presidential speeches. Ronald Reagan, like John F. Kennedy, had eloquent speechwriters: Still remembered are today Ted Sorenson for Kennedy's inaugural speech urging a new generation of Americans to "ask not what your country can do for you" and Peggy Noonan's quoting from a poem about flying to "slip the surly bonds of earth" in Reagan's speech to the nation after the *Challenger* space shuttle disaster.[91][92]

During the 2008 Democratic primary, Hillary Clinton's emotional response to a question from a sympathetic questioner at a small gathering in New Hampshire became almost a *tabula rasa* for voters' views on Clinton. After the questioner asked her why she was running for president when doing so was obviously exhausting, a teary-eyed Hillary Clinton replied that she was running because "the stakes for our country are so high." In a clear reference to Barack Obama's relative inexperience in government, she added that "some of us are ready, and some of us are not." The fact that Clinton became emotional and teary-eyed when speaking about the country, a departure from her usual demeanor in formal campaigning, made the "Hillary gets emotional" video not only prominent in the news but also prominent online and on YouTube, where it was downloaded and viewed millions of times.[93]

The Clinton video is an example not only of the power of emotional video but also how their meaning can be in the eye of the beholder. That

Hillary Clinton video moment is an example of *confirmation bias*—the tendency for people to believe something in the media if it confirms what they already believe. Reactions to the video were split between Clinton supporters and opponents, with some supporters saying it humanized her when she seemingly let down her guard, others saying it was a cynical move on her part at a time when she was down in the polls, and others debating how the video would have been received if the man running for commander in chief had grown emotional and teary-eyed.

Framing and Reframing Same-Sex Marriage

In the case of changes in the courts and public opinion about same-sex marriage that led to the five-to-four Supreme Court decision legalizing same-sex marriage across the U.S.,[94] there were multiple factors at work, including political and legal campaigns by LGBTQ rights activists to oppose state bans and build political support for first civil unions and then same-sex marriage. But the activists who led this campaign and other observers have said that the campaign was significantly helped by successfully reframing "same-sex marriage" in the minds of many Americans, especially young people, as a new civil rights issue—for couples to marry—as well as an issue that potential allies could relate to: the desire to marry someone you love.[95]

"An advantage we have is that we are in every family," Marc Solomon, national campaign director for Freedom to Marry, one of the lead groups in the campaign, said in an interview with Molly Ball of the *Atlantic*.[96] As Solomon noted, former Republican vice president Dick Cheney and his wife, Lynne, have a daughter, Mary Cheney, a political consultant, who is a lesbian. (Their second daughter, Liz Cheney, the Republican congresswoman from Wyoming, said that she opposed same-sex marriage.[97])

During the 2000 presidential campaign, Dick Cheney took the stance that, as the Associated Press reported, "states should decide legal issues about personal relationships and that people should be free to enter relationships of their choosing."[98] In 2004, as vice president to George W. Bush, Cheney opposed President Bush's proposal for a constitutional ban on same-sex marriage. "Lynne and I have a gay daughter, so it's an issue our family is very familiar with," Cheney told an audience in Iowa. "With the respect to the question of relationships, my general view is freedom means freedom for everyone. . . . People ought to be free to enter into any kind of relationship they want to."[99]

Public support for same-sex marriage changed dramatically from 2004 to 2019. In Pew Research Center polling in 2004, Americans opposed same-sex marriage by a margin of 60 percent to 31 percent. In 2019, that support had flipped, with a majority of Americans (61 percent) supporting same-sex marriage and 31 percent opposing it.[100]

Conservative critics have said that entertainment and news media "endorsed the homosexual lifestyle," as they described it, with positive coverage, while advocates have said that the media are reflecting changes in public attitudes with more inclusive coverage—and should be doing more to cover the LGBTQ community and issues. An estimated forty-four million people watched the 1997 episode of the Ellen DeGeneres sitcom *Ellen*, accompanied by a *Time* magazine cover story ("Yep, I'm Gay"), in which DeGeneres came out as gay after many years of being closeted.[101] But in her 2019 HBO comedy special, "Relatable," DeGeneres, who became a popular daytime talk-show host, said that coming out on her sitcom had hurt her professionally.

Her sitcom was canceled by ABC one year after the famous episode and, she said, several years of difficulty in returning to television until she was offered the opportunity to host a syndicated talk show in 2003.[102]

As public opinion shifted in favor of same-sex marriage, political leaders—and corporations—endorsed what had been considered a controversial stance and still is opposed by many. President Obama did not endorse same-sex marriage until 2012.[103] More recently, an analysis by NBC News in 2020 found outdated state same-sex marriage bans still on the books of numerous state legislatures. Some local officials refused to perform such marriages immediately after the 2015 Supreme Court decision overturned the state bans, and some state legislatures have subsequently introduced new state laws to limit same-sex-marriage, including on religious liberty grounds.[104]

In 2018, the U.S. Supreme Court ruled in favor of a baker in Colorado who had refused to create a wedding cake for a gay couple, citing his religious beliefs that define marriage as being between a man and a woman. The narrow ruling reaffirmed the legality of same-sex marriage but found that the Colorado Civil Rights Commission had shown animus toward the baker by suggesting that his claims of religious freedom were being used to justify discrimination.[105] The decision, Adam Liptak wrote, "left open the larger question of whether a business can discriminate against gay men and lesbians based on rights protected by the First Amendment."[106]

As the chart from the Gallup polling organization shows (see Table 2.1), public support for same-sex marriage has remained stable—at 63 percent as of 2019, with Democrats, independents, and young people showing the strongest support for legal same-sex marriage and Republicans, at 44 percent in 2019, having doubled their support from 2009.

Table 2.1 Support for Legal Same-Sex Marriage, by Group: 1999 vs. 2009 vs. 2019

	1999	2009	2019	Change, 1999–2019
	% Should be valid	% Should be valid	% Should be valid	(pct. pts.)
National adults	35	40	63	+28
Party ID				
Republicans	22	20	44	+22
Independents	38	45	68	+30
Democrats	42	55	79	+37
Age				
18-29	52	59	83	+31
30-49	39	40	68	+29
50-64	31	37	55	+24
65+	11	25	47	+36
Gender				
Men	31	37	61	+30
Women	39	43	66	+27
Region				
East	43	47	66	+23
Midwest	34	41	68	+34
South	27	31	57	+30
West	39	46	67	+28

Source: Justin McCarthy, "U.S. Support for Gay Marriage Stable, at 63%," Gallup, May 22, 2019, https://news.gallup.com/poll/257705/support-gay-marriage-stable.aspx.

The Power of the Senses

Print and online news media also can frame—and editorialize—visually, especially in magazine covers. A *Time* magazine cover favorably linked President Obama in 2008 with Franklin Delano Roosevelt leading America through the Great Depression. The cover humorously had a superimposed

Photo 2.2 *Newsweek* magazine's cover headline unfairly labeled Michele Bachmann "The Queen of Rage."

smiling Obama on a famous photograph of a jaunty FDR, cigarette holder in hand in an open car, with the headline "The New New Deal: What Obama Can Learn from FDR."[107] In a strongly criticized *Newsweek* cover story in 2011, the magazine used a photo from their cover shoot in which Minnesota senator Michele Bachmann, a Tea Party supporter and 2012 candidate in the Republican presidential primary, stares into the lights in a way that makes her look crazed. The headline on the cover story was "The Queen of Rage." Again, thinking about language, the word *queen* itself sounds sexist and demeaning. The story itself, interestingly, did not mention the word *rage*, although it did talk about the anger of Tea Party supporters.[108]

Debate over Symbols

As a former TV producer and star, Donald Trump has been keenly aware of the impact of visual images, including his own camera angles as well as the imagery behind him at his rallies and public events. During the summer of 2019, President Trump's insistence on a Fourth of July celebration that included a demonstration of American military strength by the Lincoln Memorial, with armored tanks and dramatic plane flyovers, prompted a fierce debate, with critics saying that the president was politicizing a previously apolitical national celebration that had not been attended by presidents in the past.

"Put troops out there so we can thank them—leave tanks for Red Square," said Gen. Anthony C. Zinni, a retired four-star Marine general and former head of U.S. Central Command, who had served as a special envoy to the Trump administration.[109] Architecture critic Philip Kennicott contended that the imagery of tanks at the Lincoln Memorial, the site of many peaceful rallies, was discomfiting to many because it was turning a civic space into a military one.[110] The president ultimately gave a speech in which he saluted U.S. troops against his desired backdrop, and *USA Today* reported that the celebration was a tale of three events, with Trump supporters eager to cheer for his 2020 election, some protesters, and others there who said they just wanted to see the traditional concert and fireworks without the politics.[111]

The Power of Sound

One striking example of how audio can be used to characterize a candidate is the infamous "Dean scream" in the 2004 presidential campaign. Vermont governor Howard Dean—who pioneered in Internet fundraising and Meetups with young supporters—had shown surprising strength among some voters as an anti-war candidate. When Dean lost in the Iowa caucus, he gave a speech to his young supporters in which he appeared to be screaming, almost maniacally, about how his campaign was going to go on to other primaries. The sound bite was played hundreds of times on cable TV and broadcast news and framed Dean as angry and irrational. In fact, Dean said in an interview with the author for *Columbia Journalism Review* that the speech was very different in the room. "I was in front of 1,200 screaming kids who couldn't hear the speech, and the cable networks ran it as a speech with a directional mic—no crowd noise and no pictures of the crowd. So it didn't happen at all the way it was on television," Dean said.[112]

The Dean scream fit opponents' narrative of Dean's temperament as angry. Dean and other reporters who were in the room at the time said that they did not think the moment was important until their editors asked them, "Did you see that?" "The editors said, 'How come you didn't say anything about this?' The reporters were in the room; they didn't think it was a big deal," Dean maintained.[113] The video without the ambient sound was played countless times on TV, online, and on YouTube, becoming the defining image of Dean and his campaign.

SUMMARY

In this chapter we have looked at the key concepts for examining the impact of media coverage. News-gathering and publication involves selection, and what is covered—or not covered, and how—connotes significance. Media-effects study of that influence began with the emergence of mass media in in the 1920s and 1930s after World War I, when critics were fearful about the power of the media and propaganda to influence the public. More recently, researchers have studied media effects more broadly, in terms of cumulative media effects on learning and public opinion. Walter Lippmann in the 1920s devised concepts about the conventions of news-gathering—the media as "restless searchlight" and a social condition not being covered as a seed germinating in the ground—that are even more relevant in today's twenty-four seven, breaking news environment.

Agenda-setting is the theory that media coverage has a significant influence on what the public considers important and the relative importance—salience—of issues. In 1968 Maxwell McCombs and Donald Shaw researched what voters in the presidential election considered important compared to the issues that were being covered in major media. They found a very strong correlation—and agenda-setting function for the news media—between coverage and perceived importance.

In the decades since, there have been hundreds of studies using their methodology. Two other researchers, Shanto Iyengar and Donald Kinder, compared news agendas with the public's agenda and found that the issues that received broad news coverage in major media were perceived as important, while those not covered lost credibility. Today's media environment, with broad definitions of what people think of as "the media" and chosen, selective exposure by some to news outlets they agree with, have led to more nuanced, related concepts for agenda-setting. But research in new and old media show the concepts still apply.

Agenda-building is a related concept that finds that media and politics and policy interrelate, with each influencing the other. Reverse agenda-setting refers to the ability of social media, from a Twitter-related social movement to a memorable photo that goes viral to influence attention and coverage in major media—and vice versa. Donald Trump's use of Twitter is a skillful example of reverse agenda-setting, talking directly to his millions of supporters while his tweets often dominated the news coverage of the day.

The media, both news and entertainment, provide important cultural cues about what is considered masculine or feminine (in gendered terms), what is heroic and admirable. The news media have a priming effect on what traits are "presidential" and by what standards a president should be judged, by highlighting some personal traits over others, in presidents and their spouses. In addition, the news media with their coverage and commentary prime the public and have influence over how a president should be judged—for example, about his or her performance on the economy or in international affairs.

Framing is another key concept in media and politics. How something is framed—characterized and discussed—in the media and in politics has significant impact on perception and public opinion. There are language frames and issue frames, and opposing sides strive to have their frame predominate. The framing of Obamacare is an important case study, as is the framing—and reframing—of same-sex marriage. Visual framing affects people emotionally, as does framing in sound.

End-of-Chapter Assignment:
Agenda-Setting and Framing

This assignment is designed to get you thinking about—and applying—two of the key concepts in this chapter: agenda-setting and framing. It's a precursor to your doing your own formal case study of an episode or theme in recent media coverage—and its impact. Be sure to look at the Annotated Media Resources at the end of the book for how to access news articles and TV transcripts free online and through your library. Reread "How to Do Your Own Media Analysis Case Study" at the end of Chapter 1. That will be your guide for a formal paper—but it's applicable here. Our goal with each assignment or paper with this book is to be "media archaeologists," studying media coverage and applying key concepts for analysis.

For this assignment, pick a recent newsmaking story, based on original reporting, that has been on the front page (including online) in the *New York Times* or the *Washington Post*—and look at how the topic is framed there as well as what sources are referenced in the article. Then look through the transcripts for prime-time shows on CNN, MSNBC, and Fox News Channel that evening and over the following week. Answer the following questions. Bring your notes to class, and come prepared to discuss.

1. Did these shows reference the original news story—and how?

2. Did they frame it the same way—or not?

3. Did government officials respond or not—and how?

4. Are officials, other journalists, and the public talking about the story on Twitter and other social media?

5. What about the nightly newscasts on ABC, CBS, NBC, and PBS? The Sunday pundit shows on broadcast and cable?

6. If they don't specifically credit the original story, as is often the case, do you see other media picking up the topic, positively or negatively?

7. What does your study tell you about agenda-setting and framing?

CHAPTER 3

Political Advertising

Persuasion and Deception

Presidential campaigns today are like a Cold War nuclear arms race: The costs of the weaponry are enormous and escalating, and each side is afraid not to stockpile an increasing arsenal of political advertising against their opponent. Each recent presidential race has cost more than the previous one, and the 2018 congressional midterm election saw record spending totals as well. By October of 2020, the total cost of the 2020 election was projected to be nearly $11 billion—$5.2 billion of that on the presidential campaign.[1] That total—which would be the highest ever—was "obliterating" previous spending records, according to the Center for Responsive Politics, a nonpartisan group that tallies campaign expenditures. The $11 billion price tag—which included increased, lower-cost digital ads as well as TV and radio ad buys—was more than 50 percent higher than the 2016 campaign, adjusting for inflation.[2]

With House and Senate races today costing multimillions, candidates have to spend much of their time raising money in nonstop campaigns, often from big-money donors and outside groups. Many groups are outside super PACS that operate seemingly independent of the candidate. And the tone of political ads, especially these, has grown increasingly negative, according to the Wesleyan Media Project, a project of political scientists at Wesleyan University that has been tracking and analyzing national commercial data on political ad buying since 2010.[3]

Political pundits "follow the money" in terms of which presidential candidates have raised the most money, and candidates from George W. Bush to Hillary Clinton have sought to appear as the "inevitable" nominee in their party's primaries in part by building up a huge financial war chest from big-money donors from Wall Street to unions and trial lawyers.

Since the controversial *Citizens United v. FEC* decision before the Supreme Court regarding campaign contributions in 2010, the airwaves—and voters—have been flooded with millions of dollars of ads from these often-unknown sources in endless campaigns that have many observers worried about the costs—in public perception and the health of the democracy.

Whether promoting a consumer product or a presidential candidate, campaigns and advertisers use similar persuasive techniques—including visual, emotional, and rhetorical appeals—to drive home their message and differentiate their product, which is the candidate or the cause. In both politics and consumer marketing, many of the most powerful ads are those that work *outside* the viewers' conscious awareness.

As analysts of media and politics, it is important to understand the role of money in current American politics and be able to deconstruct how political ads work through persuasive techniques. In this chapter we will look at the history, techniques, and impact of political advertising as well as the role of outside money in the increasingly negative tone of ads. You will also be given an assignment to research your own case study on a recent political ad, using the resources for research about ads provided in the resource pages that accompany this book and analyzing the ad in terms of its persuasive techniques.

Rhetorical appeals that go all the way back to Aristotle—*logos, pathos, and ethos*—can inform our analysis, as can recent research on perception and the brain. Political ad makers also use other persuasive techniques we'll talk about here, including association and disassociation, juxtaposition and false inferences along with techniques from film, such as lighting and camera angles, to make their point.

Spending on Political Advertising

American federal election campaigns are privately funded, with no major presidential candidate since the 2012 presidential campaigns taking advantage of the minimal public funding alternative established for presidential campaigns in 1974, although there are proposals for a larger public funding system, and no established public funding system for congressional races in the U.S.[4]

Citizens United and Beyond

American presidential and even congressional campaigns today are beginning years in advance, and political advertising is considered key by strategists and campaigns. Political advertising on television is the largest expenditure in major campaigns, and the money spent on political ads has skyrocketed since the controversial 2010 *Citizens United v. Federal Election Commission* decision in which the U.S. Supreme Court held that political spending by corporations could not be prohibited by the government under the First Amendment provisions regarding free speech. The *Citizens United* decision, which struck down campaign finance laws that previously had been passed in Congress with bipartisan support—has led to a tidal wave of unrestricted campaign spending by outside groups, known as super PACs.

Super PACs are a relatively new kind of political action committee that can raise unlimited amounts of money from corporations, unions, and other groups as well as from wealthy individuals. Super PACs, which usually have patriotic-sounding names like Americans for a Better America, operate independently of candidates and political parties, and they can produce ads whose funding is obscured and whose harsh attacks the candidate can be separated from.

The Wesleyan Media Project has found a dramatic jump in spending on ads and an increasingly negative tone in recent campaigns.[5] At the same time, the percentage of spending on advertising by outside political groups, relative to the major political parties, has also grown significantly, according to analysis by the Wesleyan researchers and the Center for Responsive Politics, which analyzes FEC data on political contributions.[6]

Within these outside groups, many are what are called "dark-money" groups because the source of the money is not disclosed. The Center for Responsive Politics has noted that dark money makes its way into campaigns through "politically active non-profits . . . that are generally under no legal obligation to disclose their donors even if they spend to influence elections" and through "opaque nonprofits and shell companies [that] may give unlimited amounts of money to Super-PACs. While Super-PACs are legally required to disclose their donors, some of these groups are effectively dark-money outlets when the bulk of their funding cannot be traced back to the original donor."[7]

An analysis of donors in 2018 by USA Today found that "secret donors financed more than four out of 10 television ads that outside groups broadcast this year to influence November's high-stakes Congressional elections," with two groups affiliated with conservative billionaire industrialist Charles Koch—Americans for Prosperity and Concerned Veterans for America—"training their fire" on five Democratic senators up for reelection in "five red or purple states." Missouri senator Claire McCaskill, for example, was targeted with ads from Koch-affiliated groups that attacked her for "letting Missouri down" by voting with fellow Democrats against the Republican tax cut bill passed in Congress.[8]

A common tactic of such negative ads is to credit the ad and claims to sponsorship from an unknown group whose name sounds like a grassroots organization but actually is funded by big donors. Research shows that viewers give more credence to groups with official-sounding, grassroots-sounding names than from a candidate or a party.[9]

Such ad blitzes today are not limited to election years: Koch-affiliated groups announced that they were planning to spend more than $2 million in ads designed to pressure members of Congress to support the nomination of Judge Brett Kavanaugh to the U.S. Supreme Court in 2018, while NARAL Pro-Choice America, an abortion rights group, targeted Maine Republican senator Susan Collins and other members of Congress in ads in their states, pressuring them to vote against Kavanaugh.[10]

The 2012 election was the then most expensive in history. With Barack Obama and Mitt Romney raising millions, additional spending by the parties and outside groups, the price tag for the 2012 election was projected to be $5.8 billion, according to data from the Federal Election Commission (FEC).[11] The increase in spending on campaigns was largely driven by rapidly increased spending among super PACs.[12]

In the 2014 congressional midterm elections, where Republicans gained control of the Senate as well as the House of Representatives, Republican candidates' ads and campaigns linked Democratic candidates to President Obama's then low approval ratings, Obamacare (the Affordable Care Act), and new threats from terrorism. Spending on close races continued to escalate, the Wesleyan researchers found, with spending on federal and gubernatorial races in the 2013–2014 cycle more than $1 billion near the end of the campaign, with 2.2 million ad airings and nearly 40 percent from groups whose donors were not disclosed.[13]

The 2016 presidential election was an anomaly, with Donald Trump receiving an extraordinary amount of free media—about $6 million[14]—which meant that Trump and groups backing him were able to spend less on buying expensive paid airtime. Hillary Clinton's campaign dramatically outspent Trump in paid advertising, spending $258 million in broadcast TV ads.[15]

At the same time, the price tag on the 2018 congressional midterm elections was a record-breaker, with $5.25 billion spent on advertising on local broadcast TV stations, local cable and digital, according to data from Kantar Media/CMG.[16] The 2018 congressional midterm elections were "the most lucrative midterms in history," as the trade publication *Adweek* described it, with total expenditures 78 percent higher than the 2014 midterm elections. In the 2018 midterm elections, Democrats elected record numbers of women to Congress and won back control of the House of Representatives two years into Donald Trump's presidency and eight years after the 2010 midterms, in which Republicans won control of the House from the Democrats, in part with ads that linked candidates negatively to President Obama, Obamacare, gun control, and terrorism. Democrats outspent Republicans by a margin of 53 to 46 percent in 2018,[17] with "defending" health care and the Affordable Care Act as the top theme of the ads for the Democrats, according to an analysis of the Kantar data by Erika Franklin Fowler, Michael Franz, and Travis Ridout, codirectors of the Wesleyan Media Project.[18] The sheer number of ads increased by 58 percent, from 2.5 million to nearly 4 million airings, from the 2014 to the 2018 midterms.[19]

The Impact of Political Ads

There has been debate among political scientists and others about the precise impact of political advertising on actual voter turnout, a difficult outcome to measure, with contradictory studies using different methodologies finding that the flood of ads may suppress voter turnout and others finding that negative advertising may stimulate voter turnout.[20] There is general agreement that the timing of ads is important, especially during primaries, with the timing of ads being important because the effects of ads fade quickly over time.[21] In an article headlined "Yes, Political Ads Are Still Important, Even for Donald Trump," Lynn Vavreck, who has written several books about campaigns and political advertising, summarized several academic studies of the effects of political ads, writing, "The evidence suggests that campaign ads have small effects that decay rapidly—very rapidly—but just enough of the impact accumulates to make running more advertising than your opponent seem a necessity. . . . Even though the effects from an ad imbalance are small and go away fast, candidates cannot allow them to pile up."[22]

Other researchers have found that voters, especially those who might not seek out the information otherwise, "learn" about candidates' positions through comparative ads. And, as political scientist Darrell M. West, who has studied political advertising in elections for many years, wrote in his book *Air Wars*, impressions about candidates that viewers take away from today's more affective ads is important. "Recent studies have found that voters form many impressions during the course of election campaigns, from views about candidates' issue positions and personal characteristics to feelings about the electoral prospects of specific candidates, and those views are decisive," West wrote. "As ads have become more gripping emotionally, *affective models* that describe feelings are crucial to evaluations of candidates' fortunes."[23]

Free media coverage of political ads, including showing and commenting on stealth ones that originally air only online, often dominates political punditry on TV. And, at the same time, the flood of outside money from unidentified dark money groups that do not have to disclose who they are, coupled with an increased role for contributions from individual millionaire donors since 2010, has reached such heights that many observers are concerned about the health of the democracy overall—and the public perception of whom the government is working for.

"This surge in campaign spending is striking," Richard Briffault, professor of legislation at Columbia University, wrote in 2018, "but I believe the volume of campaign spending is not the only problem with our campaign-finance system. The real challenge is where so much of this money comes from." Instead, he argued, the deeper issue is that "elected officials are often reluctant to take positions that are at odds with the interests of their large donors, and what gets on—or stays off—the legislative agenda can be driven by donor concerns."[24]

Public Attitudes toward Money in Politics

In the 2016 presidential race, journalists wrote about the "wealth primary" and candidates' courting of individual wealthy donors who were deciding, as some pundits put it—distressingly, without any irony—on which candidate in whom to "invest." In 2015 an analysis by the *New York Times* of FEC reports and Internal Revenue Service records showed that fewer than four hundred families were responsible for almost half of the $388 million raised to support presidential candidates by August 2015, "a concentration of political donors that is unprecedented in the modern era," with a greater concentration of donors on the Republican side and the "vast majority" of the money channeled to super PACs that can raise money in a fraction of the time it would take the candidate.[25] The trend toward the top 0.01 percent of top campaign donors giving higher percentages of total campaign spending increased dramatically from the 2012 to the 2016 presidential election, according to OpenSecrets.org,[26] and advanced further with the 2018 midterms toward an even smaller number of wealthy donors paying for a higher percentage of ads.[27]

With the 2016 presidential campaign on track to break records for campaign spending, the Pew Research Center in 2015 found that 76 percent of Americans—including identical percentages of Republicans and Democrats—believe that money is playing a bigger role in politics than in the past. "Large majorities of both Democrats (84%) and Republicans (72%) favor limiting the amount of money individuals and organizations can spend on campaigns and issues," the Pew researchers found.[28] At the same time, only 19 percent of those surveyed by Pew one year before the 2016 election said that "elected officials in Washington try hard to stay in touch with voters back home," while 74 percent said that most elected officials "don't care what people like me think."[29]

These trends in public opinion, of course, may have been reflected in the 2016 presidential primaries and the election. Although negative views of politicians are not new, the Pew researchers found that "the sense that politicians don't care what people think is more widely held in recent years," up to 76 percent in 2015 from 55 percent in 2000.[30]

In the 2016 presidential campaign, Sen. Bernie Sanders made campaign finance reform a key tenet of his insurgent campaign, raising millions online through small contributions and calling for a constitutional amendment to overturn *Citizens United* and voters to take back control of the government from "Wall Street," big corporations, and billionaires.[31] Sanders strongly criticized Hillary Clinton, who also endorsed campaign finance reform, saying that, having raised multimillions from corporations and big-money donors and personally having earned millions for speaking to Wall Street firms and other corporate clients, she would not be able to properly regulate Wall Street. And Donald Trump told his supporters that his Republican-primary rivals—and Hillary Clinton—were strongly influenced by their big-money contributors, with Trump making the case that he knew this was true because, he said, he had bought influence with his own campaign contributions in the past.[32]

In 2020, after months of being dramatically out-fundraised and out-spent on political advertising by Donald Trump, Joe Biden and the Democrats raised a formidable financial war chest, including millions with the nomination of Kamala Harris and millions after the chaotic first presidential debate. In the closing month of the campaign, the Trump campaign withdrew spending on ads in several key states[33] while Biden surged in spending across media, including Facebook. By mid-October Biden had spent over $500 million on TV, digital, and radio ads in 2020. The ads included ad buys targeting voters in key states such as Ohio, Iowa, Pennsylvania, Michigan, Florida, Wisconsin, and Texas.[34]

Ads Alone Can't Win It

Ads must be considered in the overall context of campaigns and the strengths of a candidate—Jeb Bush had multimillions of dollars from super PACs lined up in the Republican primary before Trump's performance dominated the crowded stage in debates. In 2020, billionaire and former New York City mayor Michael Bloomberg, who had spent millions in primaries, dropped out after a disastrous, unprepared performance against Elizabeth Warren's critique in a primary debate. But strategists are loath not to spend money on advertising. Importantly, in today's media climate, the "talking points" and negative assertions of ads are playing a significant role in coverage and commentary, especially in TV commentary and punditry, where conflict is catnip and independent verification can be hard to pursue. A Pew Research Center study of 2012 presidential campaign coverage found that statements from the candidates themselves—with ads being a part of those statements—accounted for 48 percent of political coverage, a big increase from 37 percent in 2000, which the researchers attributed in part to cutbacks in news coverage and the ability to verify information independently.[35]

FactCheck.org, a long-standing nonpartisan website that investigates deceptive claims in political advertising at the Annenberg Public Policy Center of the University of Pennsylvania;[36] PolitiFact, a project of The Poynter Institute;[37] and journalists at major newspapers such as Glenn Kessler at the Washington Post (who gives ads a number of "Pinocchios" based on their level of inaccuracies)[38] have responded to the tide of negative ads and deceptive claims with "ad-watch" columns and investigations that investigate the claims and determine their veracity—or falsehoods. The challenge to such efforts regarding ads is that they do not usually occur in real time while the ad is airing on local television. In fact, political scientist John Geer argues that journalists' focus on ads in news coverage has *escalated* the tendency for campaigns to create negative advertising.[39]

Persuasive Techniques: From Classical Rhetoric to Product Advertising

Beginning in 350 BC the Greek philosopher Aristotle outlined a framework for political persuasion that is still relevant today. Aristotle described three kinds of appeals he said an orator must use: *pathos* (an appeal to the audience's heart and emotions), *ethos* (an ethical appeal to credibility and authority of the speaker, which can include citing the speaker's credentials and quoting experts), and *logos* (an appeal to the audience's ability to reason, including using logic, statistics, facts and anecdotes).[40] You can see each of these appeals still used today, in both product advertising and political advertising, whether it's a heart-tugging story (*pathos*) that connects the politician or the product to images of happy families and prosperity or ads that cite experts or statistics as evidence that the claims of the ad are true (*logos*). One common—and deceptive—technique in contemporary political advertising to look out for is the use of a news organization's logo on-screen to add credibility in a negative ad. This implies that the negative quotation was reported on by the news organization when, in fact, if you look up the article after it whizzes by on TV, the ad usually is quoting an opinion piece from a partisan published in the opinion pages, not a news story.

Code Words and Distortion

Political ad makers and consumer advertisers both seek to associate the product or their candidate with powerful positive symbols and cultural values that resonate—in the case of political ads and political communication, this is the "Mom, flag, and apple pie" symbolism that predominate in ads and messaging that are positive. A common tactic of negative ads is to demonize the opponent with code words and stereotyping. In the 2012 presidential campaign, for example, the Obama campaign sought to portray Mitt Romney—early and often—as a heartless capitalist whose former venture capital firm had bought companies only to lay off employees and ship jobs overseas.[41] The infamous Willie Horton ad we will discuss later in this chapter is a powerful example of racist imagery, linkage, and stereotyping.

Another common technique is distorting the candidate's record and taking his or her remarks out of context. Opposition researchers for campaigns look for gaffes by the other candidate, in news stories and speeches on the trail that seem to confirm the stereotype of the other candidate and can be turned into ads—for example, Obama's dismissing of ISIS as "junior varsity" terrorism in an interview that, along with frightening video of ISIS, was used against Obama *and* Democrats in congressional races in 2014[42] or Mitt Romney, in secretly recorded video of his speaking before an audience of donors in 2012, criticizing the "47 percent of Americans" who he said were dependent on government and would vote for Obama. (The Romney video—which was published online by *Mother Jones* magazine—caused a sensation and was used in ads, including one where people reacted and asked Romney on camera if they were part of the lazy 47 percent.[43]) A campaign appearance in which Obama had talked about government and business, saying, "If you own a business, you didn't build that," was used in attack ads in 2012 and continues to be used by conservative commentators as proof that Obama values big government over individual effort, although Obama and fact-checkers said he had been taken out of context.[44]

A negative corollary to *association* is *disassociation*, in which a candidate tries to disassociate himself or herself from an unpopular president while the opposition is eager to link that candidate—visually and in sound—to guilt by association and the "failed policies" of that president. Alison Lundergan Grimes' disassociating herself from Obama's unpopular policies on coal pollution and guns among many voters in Kentucky—in her unsuccessful 2014 race to unseat longtime senator and Senate majority leader Mitch McConnell—is a classic attempt at disassociation. "Mitch McConnell wants you to think I'm Barack Obama," says Grimes, who is seen with a shotgun, shooting skeet. "I'm not Barack Obama. I disagree with him on guns, coal, and the EPA."[45]

Juxtaposition and *visual and auditory linking* of information in ads, including deceptively putting audio of a candidate's remarks with imagery that makes him or her appear callous or indifferent, create what Kathleen Hall Jamieson, a longtime scholar of political advertising, has called "*false inferences*" in the mind of the viewer that two elements that are edited together are related.[46] The Swift boat ad campaign against Sen. John Kerry in the 2004 presidential campaign—which we will look at as a case study in this chapter—is a prime progenitor of this technique.

"The visual aspect of campaign advertising is important because it is the one with the most impact on viewers," wrote Darrell M. West. "The reason is simple—people remember visuals longer than they do spoken words. Images also have the advantage of creating an emotional response much more powerful than that which results from hearing the spoken word."[47] Deceptive imagery also may be less easily fact-checked—by journalists and in the mind of viewers—than deceptive scripts. At the same time, giant visual text pronouncing the opponent "too liberal" or "too extreme" for the state or "not ready" for office in all capital letters is another common technique. Dark lighting and ominous music, coupled with quotations from the opponent taken out of context, are designed to instill fear and foreboding about the consequences of electing this candidate. Finally, ads may attack a candidate over a vote or policy that is widely held, even by the candidate's opponent, with the idea that simply attacking means the candidate must have done something wrong. Let's explore a few examples of advertisements.

Running against "Washington": "Make 'Em Squeal"

Running against "Washington" has a long tradition in American populism—and political advertising. Some campaigns and ads took a humorous approach about Washington before the angrier tone of ads railing against the federal government in more recent years. In 1992 millionaire businessman Ross Perot ran the most successful third-party candidacy since Theodore Roosevelt, winning nineteen million votes and a place in the presidential debates against George H. W. Bush and Bill Clinton.[48] Perot used appealingly low-tech flip charts about fiscal conservatism and the economy in thirty-minute TV infomercials that he bought—and he made a memorable promise to put all the lobbyists in the Smithsonian Museum because they would be extinct if he were elected.

Iowa state legislator Joni Ernst's 2014 "Make 'Em Squeal" ad in her bid to become an Iowa senator takes advantage of Ernst's considerable on-air abilities and her history. The low-cost ad—which helped newcomer Ernst win the election—was born, Republican political strategist Todd Harris, who produced the ad, said, when Ernst, an officer in the National Guard, mentioned that her family had been pig farmers.[49]

Threes are important in the way people remember—if you look for that, you'll often see a list of three items in a political ad. This ad highlights Ernst's three roles—mom, conservative, and soldier. It also associates Washington politicians with hogs at the trough and people who—unlike Ernst's parents, she

Photo 3.1 This ad for Joni Ernst used humor to attack "pork."

Captioning For Everyone, "2014, Joni Ernst - Squeal - political ad - closed captioned", YouTube video, 0:30, October 1, 2014, https://www.youtube.com/watch?v=zc8uLuHsNw0.

says—do not know how to live within their means. "Make 'em squeal," of course, is a reference to castrating hogs—and, by inference, Washington politicians, which manages to be funny. The ad set the tone for how Ernst was favorably covered as a down-home fresh face in the national media.

Heroism and the Plain Folks: "Eisenhower Answers America"

The first presidential campaign to use TV advertising was the "Eisenhower Answers America" series of ads in 1952. These ads are a wonderful example of combining Eisenhower's heroism and credibility as the commander of Allied troops in World War II with what advertisers call the "plain-folks appeal" of a vaunted hero talking with ordinary Americans. Rosser Reeves, an elegant Virginian who is said to be the professional model for the Don Draper character in the TV series *Mad Men*,[50] made millions as a pioneer in TV advertising in the 1950s. Reeves—who is said to have held two silver dollars in his hand and told staffers that the business of advertising was to convince people that the silver dollar in his left hand was superior to the silver dollar in his right hand—used simple words and phrases, along with a few images, and literally hammered home the message of what he called the "unique selling proposition" of the product. In one famous and highly successful ad for Anacin pain reliever, Reeves showed a hammer bashing a cartoon image of a person's cerebellum repeatedly before—voila—the solution to the problem that had been created by the ad: Anacin, which promised "fast, fast, fast relief" for headaches.[51] (Again, notice the tricolon [three words], the ancient rhetorical technique that has since been found to be pleasing and memorable to the brain.) It's a slogan that Baby Boomers can repeat to this day.

In an interview with TV journalist Bill Moyers in the 1980s, Reeves recounted those early days: "Television hit after World War II; everyone in the advertising business was absolutely terrified. . . . It was almost impossible to tell the difference between a good ad and a bad commercial, and it was a very exciting era, naturally, because we were all discovering. We were all Christopher Columbuses, you see. . . . We did not know what a thing we had, what a powerful medium we were working with." The evidence? "We were in packaged goods. We knew almost instantly when things were working because we could see the goods move right off the shelves."[52]

Photo 3.2 Eisenhower's "Eisenhower Answers America" ads pioneered depicting presidents as "just plain folks."

BNA Photographic/Alamy Stock Photo

After many years of Democrats in office and an unresolved Korean War, the Republicans' nominee was a war hero who was a newcomer to politics, Gen. Dwight D. Eisenhower, the leader of the Allied troops in World War II. A group of wealthy Republicans asked Reeves to propose a series of TV commercials for Eisenhower. After listening to Eisenhower's speeches and other materials, Reeves felt that the campaign had many points but no consistent or memorable message. Rather than conduct a focus group or commission a poll to find out what issues and opposition points would work, as today's campaigns often do, Reeves simply asked George Gallup (the creator of the Gallup poll) what one issue was of the most concern to the American people.[53] Rather than answering with one, Gallup listed three: corruption, rising taxes, and inflation. Reeves commissioned several scripts, using Eisenhower's own statements, and he insisted that the general appear in the commercials.[54]

What's remarkable about the ads is that the questions and answers were filmed separately, with ordinary citizens asking Eisenhower questions and Eisenhower answering the questions separately in a TV studio.[55] The citizens—who were recruited among tourists who were visiting Radio City Music Hall in New York—are looking up at Eisenhower, literally and figuratively, a camera angle (part of the grammar of film) that conveys admiration of the hero above. In the ad, Eisenhower, who was plainspoken in real life, speaks colloquially of his wife Mamie "getting after" him about the high price of food (under the Democrats). The commercials cleverly combine the need for heroes with the "plain folks" technique in advertising, associating the candidate with simplicity and ordinary people. Eisenhower was a natural, Reeves told Moyers, filming some thirty-five short spots, including one he wrote himself in a day and joking afterward, "To think an old soldier has come to this."[56]

Adlai Stephenson—the self-described "egghead" intellectual governor of Illinois who was the liberal Democratic candidate for president against Eisenhower—attacked the idea of selling presidents like soap, saying, "I don't think the American people want politics and the presidency to become the plaything of the high-pressure men, of the ghostwriters, of the public relations men."[57] Even some network TV executives said the ads were beneath the dignity of the presidency, but they ran in some forty states. Eisenhower likely would have won without the ads, but they set a precedent for years to come.

Positive Messaging and the Association Technique: "Morning in America"

> "It's morning again in America. Today, more men and women will go to work than ever before in our country's history. With interest rates at about half the record highs of 1980, nearly 2,000

Photo 3.3 Ronald Reagan's ads invoked symbols of patriotism and optimism in America.

Courtesy of the Ronald Reagan Presidential Library & Museum

families today will buy new homes, more than at any time in the past four years. This afternoon, 6,500 young men and women will be married. And with inflation at less than half of what it was just four years ago, they can look forward with confidence to the future. It's "Morning again in America". And, under the leadership of President Reagan, our country is prouder and stronger and better. Why would we ever want to return to where we were less than four short years ago?"[58]

The 1984 ad known as "Morning in America" is considered one of the most effective ads in recent political history—and it is a great example of the association technique in advertising and political communication.[59] People rarely acknowledge that they have been influenced by such techniques, but they are used because they can be powerful, especially when they connect with deep human needs. The most effective political leaders—from Martin Luther King to Ronald Reagan—appeal to our emotions as well as to our capacity for reason, psychologist Drew Westen argued in his book *The Political Brain*. "Campaign strategists would do well to think in evolutionary terms [and in terms of emotion] as they craft messages and select images, since nothing is as potent as a message about the welfare of our children, followed by our extended family, local community, and nation," Westen wrote.[60]

"Morning in America," created by the same advertising team that very successfully associated Maxwell House coffee with morning and happiness, was in keeping with the upbeat tone of President Reagan's campaign—and his presidency—as Westen and other political scientists have noted, with an appeal to optimism and the idea of American exceptionalism (America as "a shining city on a hill").

"Morning in America" skillfully links the promise of morning, images and themes of family and work, and specific statistics, from one, relatable day. The upbeat ad associates Reagan with a return to national pride and prosperity, linking the Democratic candidate, Vice President Walter Mondale, to inflation and the Iran hostage crisis under President Jimmy Carter and presaging the slogan for Reagan's campaign: "Are you better off now than you were four years ago?"[61]

Provoking Fear: The "Daisy" Ad

Fear is a powerful motivator of human emotions, and provoking fear about what might happen to you or your loved ones if a candidate or a party wins is a common technique in many negative ads—from those that provoke fear about the loss of a government program to those that say a candidate is going to take away individual rights. Although it aired on television only once after protests against it, the "Daisy" ad for Lyndon Johnson against Barry Goldwater in 1964 is still discussed today as an

Photo 3.4 The "Daisy" ad combined childhood innocence with fears of nuclear war.

Library of Congress, Motion Picture, Broadcasting, and Recorded Sound Division

example of using sights and sounds to powerfully evoke fear and the fear frame. A little girl innocently pulls flower petals and counts in what turns ominously into a nuclear countdown. The ad, which played to comments from Sen. Barry Goldwater, the Republican nominees, and fears over his nuclear policies, never mentions Goldwater, with the ad "filling in the fear," as creator Tony Schwartz described it to journalist Bill Moyers.[62] Moyers, who was LBJ's press secretary at the time, said in the documentary that he was "haunted to this day" that, while the nuclear arms race was undoubtedly important, LBJ's plans for the Vietnam War were scarcely mentioned in the campaign. The "Daisy" ad was a powerful priming of what was important—and how the candidates should be judged.

Code Words and Stereotyping: Willie Horton

The 1988 Willie Horton ad was run by an independent political committee in George H. W. Bush's campaign against the Democratic candidate, Massachusetts governor Michael Dukakis. The ad used racist appeals and association principle in ugly, powerful ways. The ad linked Dukakis to his veto of the death penalty and a weekend prison furlough program under which a convicted murderer, Horton, was freed to rape and shoot victims again. The ad has two messages, Drew Westen wrote in *The Political Brain*: an explicit message that "Dukakis is soft on crime" and an implicit message that "Dukakis lets scary black men endanger your safety."[63] The close-up mug shot of Horton, which plays to the brain's responsiveness to "both facial expressions and fear-invoking stimuli," Westen wrote, communicates that all Black men are criminal and dangerous, especially to white women, a long-standing racist appeal. A similar ad from the Bush campaign, which was led by then Republican strategist (and future Fox

News Channel chairman) Roger Ailes, made a similar case against Dukakis. The governor—a self-described intellectual technocrat who was not well known outside of Massachusetts—had begun the summer before the election with a seventeen-point lead against George H. W. Bush. The Dukakis campaign, according to several accounts, failed to recognize as important and did not respond adequately to the ad, which received wide exposure. Dukakis's lead disappeared.[64]

Case Study: Swift Boat Campaign

The Swift boat ad campaign against Sen. John Kerry in the 2004 presidential campaign became a verb—*swiftboating*—to describe an effective, unfair assault on a candidate's record—and is a progenitor for other darkly lit, attack-ad campaigns from obscure outside groups that have had significant impact through free media—far beyond a small, paid ad buy. It is also an example of how the failure of not understanding the cable news landscape—and not responding to attacks—can be harmful.

During the 2004 campaign between president George W. Bush and John Kerry, a liberal Democrat from Massachusetts, one sixty-second TV commercial from Swift Boat Veterans for Truth, a previously unknown group, dominated the political news for weeks.[65] The Swift Boat Veterans for Truth were a small group of Vietnam War veterans who had remained angry about Senator Kerry's s controversial 1971 testimony in Congress, where, as the leader of a group of Vietnam veterans who had turned against the war, Kerry testified that American soldiers had seen or committed atrocities in Vietnam. In the first presidential race since the terrorist attacks on September 11, 2001, national security, the war in Iraq, and the war on terrorism were important issues, with national security a traditional strength for Republicans among voters.

To portray their nominee as a strong commander in chief, Kerry and the Democrats were making the senator's record as a Swift boat commander in Vietnam and his three Purple Heart medals a centerpiece of Kerry's campaign. The Swift Boat Veterans' first attack ad initially aired in only three battleground states, shortly after the Democratic National Convention. The ad charged that Kerry was lying about his record as a Swift boat commander in the Navy in Vietnam.[66] The ad segued from Senator Kerry's running mate, North Carolina senator John Edwards, urging voters who had any questions about John Kerry as president to "spend three minutes with the men who served with him"—to the several speakers in the ad, who said, "I served with John Kerry" and "John Kerry is not telling the truth about what happened in Vietnam." This first attack ad was followed by others, including one that attempted to link Kerry's congressional testimony about the war to the torture of U.S. soldiers by the North Vietnamese during the war.[67]

The allegations in the Swift Boat Veterans for Truth campaign were largely discredited several weeks after they began running through independent investigations by the *Washington Post, New York Times*, and other publications.[68] It was also later revealed that funding for the campaign came from three prominent Republican donors from Texas. As FactCheck.org, the nonpartisan political ad watch project at the Annenberg Public Policy Center of the University of Pennsylvania, noted in its extensive analysis of the ads' claims, "None of those in the attack ad by the Swift Boat group actually served on Kerry's boat, and their statements are contrary to the accounts of Kerry and those who served under him."[69] Several soldiers who had served with Senator Kerry came forward to support the official accounts of Kerry's service, including a former Army Special Forces lieutenant who wrote an article in the *Wall Street Journal* describing how Kerry had rescued him from enemy fire.[70] Republican senator John McCain—a supporter of President George W. Bush in his 2004 bid for reelection—condemned the attacks on Kerry's record with the credibility of a former Navy commander who had been tortured for years as a prisoner of war in the Vietnam War. "I deplore this kind of politics," McCain said. "I think the ad is dishonest and deplorable . . . [and] it reopens all the old wounds of the Vietnam War, which I have spent the last thirty-five years trying to heal."[71] But the Bush campaign, while stating that the president would not question Kerry's service, declined to specifically criticize the Swift Boat Veterans ads until one week after they had stopped running.[72]

Like Michael Dukakis with the infamous "Willie Horton" ad in the 1988 campaign alleging that Dukakis had freed rapists and murderers as governor of Massachusetts, Senator Kerry did not respond—and strongly—to the ads against him. In fact, Kerry did not respond for several weeks while the ad was replayed over and over as part of news stories on cable news networks, the Internet, conservative talk radio, and other venues. The ads were particularly prominent on Fox News Channel and conservative talk radio, where they ran repeatedly—and virtually unchallenged—with prime-time hosts endorsing the ads and praising the Swift boat campaign.[73]

(Continued)

(Continued)

The Swift boat ads are an important example of the ability of a small, anonymously funded group to mount a negative ad campaign relatively inexpensively with a website and a few TV ad buys, relying instead on the allegations being replayed through news coverage that may be uncritical or even, in partisan media, an outright endorsement. "[W]hat we do know from analysis of how communication functions with audiences is that if you have extended discussion about whether or not someone earned something, you're creating doubt," Kathleen Hall Jamieson, director of the Annenberg Public Policy Center and author of numerous books about political advertising and the democracy, said in discussing the impact of the Swift boat ads on the 2004 presidential election.[74] "So, for example, if we say let's have a discussion about whether Kathleen Jamieson is a murderer and [someone] goes on television and says she's definitely not. We have absolutely no proof. The fact that we've had that discussion, let's say repeatedly over cable . . . and political talk radio, might make you more wary the next time you see me with a paring knife."[75]

Adding to the impact of the ads was the fact that major news organizations were either slow to see the importance of the ads building or struggled, their editors later said, with how to report on the claims.[76]

Techniques of the Ads

The Swift boat ads use several techniques of rhetoric and political advertising that have become prevalent in attack ads, including the following:

- Your opponent's words used against him of her

- Repeated, unsubstantiated charges that demonize your opponent while seeming to establish your credibility

- Juxtaposition, linking disparate elements through visuals and sound to create linkage and false inferences among the images and assertions in the viewer's mind

- Low-tech cinematic presentation, dark lighting, ominous music, and the use of black-and-white photos to communicate to the viewer unconsciously that these charges are not slickly produced Hollywood tales but are real and historically accurate

- An official-sounding and nonpartisan-sounding group that appears to represent many people when, in fact, it may be only a few people funded by wealthy individuals

- Factual-sounding sourcing for the charges that, in fact, do not prove the ad's allegations and sources for the funding of the group that are deliberately—and legally—obscured and unknown to the viewer

Impact of the Ad Campaign

Senator Kerry and the Democrats had primed the public to judge him as a commander in chief, and the Swift boat ads, coupled with Senator Kerry's inconsistencies in his vote in Congress to authorize the war in Iraq (saying that he had "voted for" the authorization "before I voted against it"), cast doubt on Senator Kerry's integrity and ability to lead. The ads kept the Swift Boat Veterans story alive—practically until Election Day in November. Meanwhile, Democrats were not seen by voters as making the case for Kerry on the economy, an issue on which President Bush was viewed as vulnerable.

What was the impact of the campaign? In August 2004 the ongoing national election survey by the Annenberg School for Communication found that the Swift boat ads were a "powerful example of the power of free media to assist an independent group in getting its message out." More than half of the people in the Annenberg survey had either seen or heard about the Swift boat ads; those who had seen the ads or heard about them were more likely than those who had not seen the ads to believe that Senator Kerry did not deserve all of his medals.[77]

Furthermore, the researchers found that "media exposure was clearly related to opinions about the ads' sponsorship and Kerry's record in and after Vietnam" with people who watch cable news more than four times a week being much more likely than others to disapprove of Kerry's Vietnam-era anti-war statements (60 percent) and to believe that he had not earned all of his medals (31 percent).[78] A *New York Times*/CBS News survey and article two months before the election found that Bush had widened his lead, despite voters' concerns about the economy under him, and voters saying that Kerry was spending too much time talking about the past and had not made a strong enough case for unseating Bush. Three-quarters of respondents said they were aware of the Swift boat ads, with more than 60 percent saying that Kerry was either "hiding something" or "mostly lying" about his service in Vietnam.[79]

After the reelection of President George W. Bush in 2004, Senator Kerry, in little-reported-on remarks before an audience at the John F. Kennedy

(Continued)

(Continued)

Presidential Library in Boston, spoke darkly of a "sub-media" that, he maintained, had failed to check the accuracy of political claims and were responsible for the fact that many Americans erroneously believed that weapons of mass destruction (WMDs) had been found in Iraq.[80]

"Sour grapes," said the conservative talk show host Rush Limbaugh. "So, the decision-making of the American electorate is not all that great anyway," Limbaugh said sarcastically to his listeners. "They're stupid, actually stupid. So, a bunch of 'sub-media' types can [as Kerry put it] 'undermine our great mainstream media.' No wonder he thinks this. . . . The mainstream media and their allies in the Democratic Party all feel put upon, but there's an interesting term, 'sub-media.' They still don't get it. [The Democrats] are not willing to examine themselves—and that's the real thing."[81]

Mary Beth Cahill, Kerry's campaign manager, speaking to an audience at Harvard University's Kennedy School after the election, acknowledged that Kerry's advisers had underestimated the impact of the Swift boat campaign, which, she said, they thought would have no play because it was a small TV ad buy. And she said that they should have put Kerry out there in the media, as he reportedly had wanted to be, to respond personally sooner than he did, weeks into the campaign.[82]

David Winston, a Republican strategist who conducts focus groups and polling for the Republicans in Congress, believes that Kerry's advisers misjudged the impact of cable news and conservative talk radio because they were focused on traditional broadcast TV news. In an interview with the author in 2005, Winston said, "They looked at the broadcast evening news, which had not done a lot on the Swift boat story, and decided that they needed to introduce John Kerry to the American people as a strong leader at the Democratic National Convention in July. That's how you got the acceptance speech where Kerry began by saluting and saying, 'John Kerry, reporting for duty.' In fact, the Republicans had already mounted a flip-flop ad using Kerry's own words about the congressional vote to authorize the use of force in Iraq—and the Swift Boat Veterans had already held their initial press conference and were beginning to get airplay and news stories on their views. Meantime, President Bush's image as a leader was being reinforced, particularly with an effective ad that showed the president holding a little girl whose parent had died in [the terrorist attacks of] 9/11. . . . According to what my polling numbers and focus groups at the time were telling me, John Kerry did not need to be introduced to the American people at the Democratic convention—his image was pretty well set. What he needed to do at the convention, in my opinion, was to address questions about his positions on Iraq and national security, his military service in Vietnam, and charges that he was a liberal who was going to raise taxes." Winston added, "They fundamentally misread the impact that cable news had versus broadcast news."[83]

Advertisements in Recent Campaigns

The 2008 Presidential Election

Barack Obama, then a forty-six-year-old Illinois senator, came almost out of nowhere in 2007 to challenge then New York senator Hillary Clinton, the candidate who had been dubbed the "nominee-in-waiting" by political journalists and political strategists. Obama galvanized young voters, in particular, with his soaring message of hope and reconciliation and his own personal story as the biracial son of a Black father from Kenya and a young, single mother from Kansas, becoming the first African American president in U.S. history. Obama's soaring oratory and sophisticated Internet-based fundraising and organizing among young voters and others was well-matched by his slogan of "Yes We Can" in light of the unpopularity of the Iraq War and concerns about the economy. The Obama-Biden flag logo, the designers said, was intended to communicate a new perspective on the flag and a new day in politics.[84]

Senator Clinton's campaign also was historic as the former first lady won eighteen million votes against Obama and became the first woman to have a serious chance of becoming president of the U.S. Clinton complained—with some justification—that reporters were in thrall to the Obama phenomenon. Her campaign touted her long political resume—and attempted to raise fears about possible world crises and Obama's relative lack of experience to be president. In the ad called "3 A.M.," an anxious mother's checking on her child at 3:00 a.m. is equated with a president's need to respond from experience in a 3:00 a.m. call about an international crisis.[85] But the 2008 Clinton campaign did not succeed against the Obama juggernaut.

Arizona senator John McCain, a Vietnam War hero and longtime senator, along with his vice presidential running mate, Alaska governor Sarah Palin, attempted to puncture Obama's appeal, even using the *association technique* to negatively compare Obama's celebrity to Paris Hilton's in an ad that also showed footage of masses of adoring crowds in Europe on an Obama world tour.

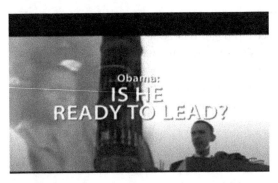

Photo 3.5 John McCain's ad used Barack Obama's celebrity against him.

John McCain, "Celeb," YouTube video, 0:31, July 30, 2008, https://youtu.be/oHXYsw_ZDXg.

As we will discuss in the chapter on race and immigration in media and politics (Chapter 6), McCain declined to use an ad that had been prepared for his campaign—one that highlighted incendiary remarks about race in America from Rev. Jeremiah Wright, Obama's former Chicago pastor, that had circulated widely on Fox News Channel and the Internet in 2008.[86] Ultimately, the 2008 campaign was about change—and which candidate would deal best with the economy.

The economy was the issue most often cited by 2008 voters in exit polls and one on which Obama was viewed more favorably than McCain—and Obama swept to victory over McCain.[87]

The 2012 Presidential Election

In contrast to the often-soaring rhetoric of Obama in the 2008 campaign, groups promoting President Obama for reelection after four bruising years in office sought to portray Mitt Romney—early and often—as a heartless capitalist whose venture capital firm had caused harm to workers by buying distressed companies and laying off workers. One ad from a pro-Obama super PAC, Priorities USA, caused an outcry from Romney and his supporters because it appeared to imply that Romney was directly responsible for the death from cancer of a woman whose husband said in the ad that he and his family had lost their health insurance when Romney's firm took over and closed a factory. The Obama camp denied that the ad said Romney caused the woman's death, but the inference was clearly there.[88] Ads by groups representing Romney in 2012 aimed to paint Obama as ineffectual at creating jobs and even dangerous in government big spending. "Each of the candidates took statements out of context, twisted the facts, and denied making claims that they actually had uttered," Darrell M. West wrote of the 2012 presidential campaign. "The decline of the mainstream media, the emergence of new communications channels, and the weakness of oversight organizations enabled campaigners to present themselves (or their opponents) in deceptive ways."[89]

The 2016 Presidential Election

In the 2016 presidential campaign, Vermont senator Bernie Sanders mounted an insurgent campaign—like Obama in 2008—with strong appeal among young people, a sophisticated Internet fundraising operation, and a message about standing together in the face of powerful interests that resonated with

Photo 3.6 Bernie Sanders supporters helped create the imagery for this ad about a diverse America.

Bernie Sanders, "Vote Together I Bernie 2016," YouTube video, 1:00, February 25, 2016, https://youtu.be/C0wsUIzMBro.

many voters. In an ad called "Vote Together" that used images submitted by Sanders supporters, headshot photos of people of many different ages and, apparently, many different backgrounds, flash rapidly by, some of them torn, until they are rematched and put back together. The voice-over is Sanders calling for unity and standing together against an unnamed "them" who would divide the country by race, gender, sexual orientation, ethnicity, or other factors.

Announcing a campaign for office online, with an accompanying announcement video with a candidate's bio and opening argument, is a relatively recent phenomenon in presidential politics that allows the candidate to speak directly to a potentially large audience. Hillary Clinton's online announcement for president in 2016 is an example of positive messaging—plus a strategy to reintroduce a well-known candidate who, like Donald Trump, was already unpopular with many people. Clinton's announcement came after many months, including an interview in which Clinton said that she and her husband were "dead broke" when they left office, although major stories in both the *Washington Post* and the *New York Times* that summer confirmed that the Clintons had later became millionaires from speaking engagements.[90]

The announcement video sought to associate Hillary Clinton with the dreams of ordinary Americans and frustration over income inequality, an emerging theme in the country and in the campaign.

After a series of vignettes with a diverse group of people talking about their dreams and pursuing new goals, such as opening a business or having a baby, Clinton says, "I'm starting something too. I'm running for president, and I want to be the champion of ordinary Americans particularly beleaguered in a growing income gap in this country." The ad also

Photo 3.7 Hillary Clinton's announcement video associated her with people starting fresh.

Hillary Clinton, "Getting Started I Hillary Clinton," YouTube video, 2:18, April 12, 2015, https://youtu.be/OuY7gLZDmn4.

represents the rollout of a candidate online on the candidate's website, where supporters and others can view it, journalists write about it and link to it on their publications' websites—and the candidate does not have to take any questions from reporters at a press conference.

In his upbeat logo and slogan ("A New American Century") in the 2016 Republican primaries, Florida senator Marco Rubio, like other Republican candidates, sought to associate himself with the remembered optimism and policies of Ronald Reagan among Republicans, citing his own rise and success as the son of Cuban immigrants as an American success story. Rubio's campaign also sought to make a generational appeal of his youth (as opposed to his relative lack of experience) against the sixty-nine-year-old Clinton. Donald Trump, however, emerged from a crowd of seventeen Republican candidates by capturing the mood of many angry voters with his anti-immigration stances and his narrative that America was no longer a winner with the powerful slogan (borrowed by Trump from Ronald Reagan and used as a negative to which Trump was the proposed solution): "Make America Great Again."

In the 2016 general election, Clinton used Trump's own remarks—and his Republican primary opponents' criticisms of him—to paint him as an inexperienced bigot who would be harmful to women, immigrants, Muslims, and others and who was, in her words, "temperamentally unfit" to be president. Trump, who benefited from unprecedented free media news coverage, as noted, repeatedly characterized Clinton as "crooked Hillary," as he had used the classical epithet in his names for his Republican primary challengers, calling them "low-energy Jeb," "little Marco," and other memorable and demeaning handles. He also used the scandal over her use of a private email server, the deaths of an ambassador and others in an attack in Benghazi, Libya, and Clinton's lucrative speaking career to stoke voters' concerns about Clinton's honesty and trustworthiness. Trump amplified his attacks via online and TV ads as well as his Twitter account.[91]

In the last months before the election, the Clinton campaign found what they believed was a possible way to break through the demonizing and nastiness of the campaign and Trump's continued popularity with his supporters despite criticism of his rhetoric by some prominent Republicans as well as Democrats. "We were all trying to pick the lock on someone who is so outrageous in so much of what they say," Jim Margolis of one of the advertising firms working on the Clinton campaign's advertising, GMMB, told the *New York Times*. "How do you communicate it in a way that feels both different but has the impact that his words should have."[92]

The result included two ads—one called "Role Models" with young children watching TV and hearing some of Trump's most profane and outrageous comments and a second, "Mirrors," with adolescent girls looking at themselves in the mirror while Trump's many comments about women play. "I'd look her right in that fat, ugly face of hers," Trump says. "She's a slob. She ate like a pig."[93] The Clinton campaign spent millions on the ads, which the campaign considered effective—and which resonated with many voters and, along with other factors, may have helped Democrats in galvanizing female Democrats and winning more suburban Republicans and independents in some 2018 congressional races.

Clinton herself gave Trump and his camp ammunition against her with her own unguarded (and recorded) remarks at a fundraiser. Clinton told her audience that half of Trump supporters were what she called "a basket of deplorables . . . The racist, sexist, homophobic, xenophobic, Islamophobic—you name it. And unfortunately there are people like that. And he has lifted them up."[94] The hashtag #BasketofDeplorables began trending with the release of the remarks—and the Trump campaign quickly produced an ad about it.

Clinton was later criticized for not making campaign appearances in industrial swing states in the last days of the campaign. The National Rifle Association (NRA), a major supporter of Trump, threw $21 million worth of ads against Clinton, including in swing states, distorting her position on the Second Amendment and telling voters that she would nominate Supreme Court justices and support laws that would take away their guns and leave them defenseless against criminals.[95]

The ad— "Don't Let Hillary Clinton Leave You Defenseless"—provokes fear as a woman searches in vain for a disappearing gun safe and is apparently murdered by an intruder because, the narrator makes clear, Clinton would take away everyone's gun if she were elected.[96]

The Clinton campaign's ad buying strategy and the content of her ads was criticized in analyses of the campaign. In their analysis of advertising in the campaign, Fowler, Franz, and Ridout found that, in addition to all other factors, Clinton's ads were, in their view "surprisingly devoid of discussions of policy." In retrospect, they wrote, "Team Clinton's message that Trump was unfit for the office of the presidency may not have been enough."[97]

The 2018 Congressional Midterm Elections

In the 2018 midterm elections, depending upon whether their state was red, blue, or purple, some moderate Democrats and Republican candidates had to decide how closely to align and associate themselves for or against the controversial incumbent president, whose favorability ratings were low overall with the American people but who had strong support among many Republicans. In the Republican primary for governor of Florida, the campaign of Rep. Ron DeSantis, who was endorsed by Trump for his stances on immigration and other topics, created a humorous ad in which DeSantis is portrayed as so close to Trump's views that he reads Trump's book *Trump: The Art of the Deal* as a bedtime story to his infant daughter. "And then Mr. Trump says, 'You're fired,'" he reads. "I love that part." DeSantis, also shows his son how to "build a wall" with building blocks in the ad, which is narrated by DeSantis's wife, Casey.[98] According to the *Orlando Sentinel*, DeSantis shot up in the polls in a tight primary race after Trump endorsed him—and after the ad, which went viral, Trump came to a DeSantis rally in person to endorse him. DeSantis won the nomination and went on to beat the Democratic nominee, Tallahassee mayor Andrew Gillum, the first African American candidate for governor in Florida.[99]

In New York's Fourteenth Congressional District in the Bronx, Alexandria Ocasio-Cortez, an activist and community organizer, scored a stunning upset in the primary against ten-term incumbent Joe Crowley, who was chairman of the House Democratic Caucus and had been thought to be in line to be House Speaker. Ocasio-Cortez's campaign included grassroots organizing and knocking on doors, and Crowley, who was supported by big-money ads and corporate donors, was vulnerable in part because he did not live primarily in the largely Hispanic Bronx neighborhood he represented. But Ocasio-Cortez became a national household name—and later a media-generating, controversial figure in the new House of Representatives—with a powerfully written and shot ad called "The Courage to Change."[100] This AOC ad is perhaps the most successful of a newer, more filmlike introduction to a new candidate

Photo 3.8 This documentary-style ad helped Alexandria Ocasio-Cortez unseat an "absent" incumbent.

Alexandria Ocasio-Cortez, "The Courage to Change | Alexandria Ocasio-Cortez," YouTube video, 0:14, May 30, 2018, https://youtu.be/rq3QXlVRObs.

that uses the techniques of intimate, documentary filmmaking and narrative to put him or her in relatable context. As the ad shows Ocasio-Cortez in her neighborhood and riding the subway, she says that as the daughter of a Puerto Rican mother and a father from the South Bronx, "people like us aren't supposed to run for office in a neighborhood where your zip code determines your destiny." She uses *us* and *we*, saying, "We've got people, they've got money," and maintaining that Crowley "cannot possibly represent us" because he "doesn't send his kids to our schools, doesn't drink our water or breathe our air." Ocasio-Cortez said that she wrote the script and used campaign volunteers in the film, which was shot, they said, for less than $10,000 by two independent filmmakers who contacted her about working with her after reading about her campaign.[101]

The 2020 Presidential Election

Joe Biden

In his 2019 ad launching his 2020 presidential campaign after months of speculation and consideration, Joe Biden said that he had decided to run after seeing President Trump's response to the neo-Nazi marches in Charlottesville, Virginia. "We are living through a battle for the soul of this nation," Biden says, contrasting the presidencies of Obama and Trump and striking the major theme of his campaign. The ad shows footage of marchers who chanted racist, anti-Semitic slogans in the march, in which one young woman was killed when a driver plowed into a crowd of peaceful counter-protesters. "The president of the United States . . . said there were quote 'some very fine people on both sides.' 'Very fine people,'" Biden repeats. "The president of the United States assigned a moral equivalence between those spreading hate and those with the courage to stand against it."[102]

Focusing beyond the election, Biden calls the Trump presidency "an abhorrent moment in time" and a "threat to this nation" that must not be repeated with Trump's reelection.[103]

Like Hillary Clinton's 2016 anti-Trump ad "Mirrors," the ad from the Democratic super PAC Priorities USA uses President

Photo 3.9 Joe Biden's campaign theme was that he was in a "fight for the soul of America" against Donald Trump.

Joe Biden, "Soul of America I Joe Biden for President," YouTube video, 0:58, December 17, 2019, https://youtu.be/HFUgU1v-Xil.

Trump's own words against him. This time, though, the subject is the coronavirus pandemic—and a timeline with audio of the president's downplaying of the threat and then praising the job his administration had done, which is overlaid with the rising death toll.[104]

Donald Trump

As the *New York Times* noted, the Trump campaign aired multiple ads that "depicted a lawless country in chaos and empty police stations" as the result of the "defund the police movement."[105] Of the $32 million the campaign spent over one month in the summer of 2020, more than $20 million was spent on ads about the police, with $16 million for ads showing an empty 911 call center and victims of crime unable to get help. In digital ads, the campaign was running what the *New York Times* called a "torrent" of ads saying that "Dangerous MOBS of far-left groups are running through our streets" and "They are DESTROYING our cities and rioting."[106] Trump himself said repeatedly that suburban women—a group he was losing support with—and others "won't be safe in Joe Biden's America."

The ad "Break In" targets another group Trump had lost support with from 2016 to 2020 with the coronavirus pandemic: seniors. The ad shows an older woman being attacked by an intruder in her home, unable to get help from the police. Although Biden had repeatedly said that he did not support defunding the police, the ad falsely and deceptively, with an altered voice, says that he did.[107]

The ad "Mourning in America 2020" provokes fear and is an ironic homage and contrast drawn between the Reagan-era "Morning in America" and Donald Trump's America, in the eyes of the creators. The ad was created by The Lincoln Project, a group of Republican strategists and other Republicans opposed to Trump. Take a look at this script: It mirrors the original, and the low-key voice here is also very similar.[108]

Photo 3.10 This Trump ad deceptively played on fears that Joe Biden and congressional Democrats would "defund the police."

Donald J. Trump, "Break In," YouTube video, 0:30, July 20, 2020, https://youtu.be/moZOrq0qL3Q.

"There's Mourning in America". Today more than 175,000 Americans have died from a deadly virus Donald Trump ignored, praising China's response instead of heeding the warnings, then blaming them to cover his own failures. With the economy in shambles, more than 30 million Americans are out of work, the worst economy in decades. This afternoon, millions of Americans will apply for unemployment and with their savings run out, many are giving up hope, millions worry that a loved one won't survive COVID-19. There's "Mourning in America" ad and under the leadership of Donald Trump, our country is weaker and sicker and poor. And now Americans are asking, if we have another four years like this, will there even be "an America"?[109]

Military Veterans

In recent years both Democratic and Republican candidates—women and men—have been military veterans who have emphasized their military experience as important qualifications for office. In the three-and-a-half-minute ad "Texas Reloaded," humorously subtitled "Greatest Joint Campaign Ad in History," Republican Texas congressman Dan Crenshaw promotes himself and a group of Republican candidates with an elaborate, humorous takeoff on a *Mission Impossible*-style spy movie. The ad, which features skydiving and other military feats by the cast, demonstrates their prowess, associates them with each other, and portrays them as superheroes. Crenshaw is credited with the concept for the mini movie, which went viral after initially playing in Texas.[110]

SUMMARY

Political advertising has been a force in U.S. campaigns and elections since advertising executive Rosser Reeves put General Dwight D. Eisenhower on camera for "Eisenhower Answers America" in the 1950s. As we have discussed, campaign ads use techniques from classical rhetoric to visual grammar and the association principle from product advertising to "sell" the candidate and influence perceptions about the candidate—and the opponent. Campaign advertising is the single largest expenditure in campaigns and the cost of presidential and congressional campaigns has skyrocketed—especially since the controversial *Citizens United* Supreme Court decision.

The level of advertising—much of it negative—concerns many critics, who fear that public confidence in politics and politicians is being undermined by the flood of ads and the increased concentration of donations from individual billionaires and super PACs. There is debate about the precise impact of ads—which is hard to measure—but most researchers and political strategists believe that they do have impact, especially in the last days of campaigns. Campaigns are loathe not to spend big on ads as their opponents and groups against them do; and, with more affective ads and ads being replayed and analyzed repeatedly by journalists and commentators on TV, ads today are seen as shaping viewers'—and voters'—important impressions. A breakout ad such as the striking spot for Alexandria Ocasio-Cortez, along with her surprise victory, can go viral, in media and politics, attracting lasting national attention.

End-of-Chapter Assignment:
Political Ad Analysis

Plan to write a seven-to-eight-page, double-spaced analysis of a recent political ad of your choice. One page in the total page count is a short "works cited" listing at the end of your paper showing what you consulted for your paper, including articles, campaign websites, or YouTube videos, for example.

The ad can be any ad for a candidate from a national political campaign since 2016, including the congressional midterm elections and governor's races as well as the 2016 and 2020 presidential campaigns. Whatever ad you pick, it needs to be a campaign ad for (or against) a candidate.

You may not write about an ad we've examined in this book.

The paper should be in the form of a memo to your professor. You should go through and answer each of the questions in order here.

You should first research the ad and the context of the campaign in which it aired. Be sure to research the funding of the ad and its factual accuracy as well as what role the ad may have played in the campaign. Use the government data and nonpartisan websites that analyze campaign spending and sources that are listed on the resource pages. You should use the concepts and persuasive techniques we have discussed in Chapter 2 and here in Chapter 3 for your research and primary-source analysis of the ad.

Your memo should include the following:

1. Describe the ad. What happens in the ad, and what is said or depicted? Quote directly from the ad, and describe what happens in the ad.

2. How does it work visually? Describe the lighting and how it looks and what that communicates to the viewer.

3. What's the goal of the ad, from your expert analysis? What is the ad trying to do?

4. In your opinion, is the ad effective? Does it succeed in what it's trying to do? If your answer is yes, how does the ad succeed? If not, how does the ad fail? Be specific.

5. What idea or theory does your ad illustrate from what we have read about how we perceive political communication and appeals to reason versus emotional appeals.

6. Pick either a rhetorical appeal from Aristotle (*logos, pathos, ethos*) or one of the persuasive techniques from commercial product advertising we have discussed. Discuss how your ad illustrates that technique. Be specific.

7. Is the ad factually accurate—and what sources, if any, does it cite? To answer this question, you will need to fact-check the claims in the ad and the sources of the information. Look up the claims on the ad, and look up some information about the claims independently. Be sure that you are quoting from a reputable, nonpartisan publication in your fact-checking—and cite your source or sources.

8. What is the source of funding for the ad? Go deeper than the listing for Citizens for Good Government—find as much as you can about who's actually behind the ad—and say what you've found out about the funders and your source of information. To find this information, you can consult the FEC website or the nonpartisan websites on your resource pages that analyze the FEC data and study the funding of political ads.

9. Discuss the ad in the context of the campaign. Was it controversial? Did the opposing candidate respond? How was the ad received, and can you find any research or reporting done that discusses possible impacts of the ad on the campaigns or voting? Cite your sources on this, in the paper ("according to . . .) as well as in your works cited.

10. Provide a works-cited brief listing at the end of your paper where you list the sources you consulted for information on the ad.

11. Along with your paper, come to class with a simple PowerPoint presentation with the highlights of your conclusions or findings—and a link to the ad—to present to your colleagues.

CHAPTER 4

Reporting the News

Cultural Bias, Trust, and Accountability

B oth cultural anthropologists and media historians have found that there appears to be an inherent human instinct for seeing, hearing, and watching the news, whether that news comes from the ancient one-to-one communication of the spoken word, the one-to-many communication of radio and television, or the Internet, which offers both the possibility of endless multiplicity of voices talking as well as the ability to customize your own personal version of the news. Media historian Mitchell Stephens has called the need for news a "hunger for human awareness"; he has noted also that the definition of the English word *news* as tidings—something new, fresh, and compelling—has been in common use for at least five hundred years.[1]

"As anthropologists began comparing notes on the world's few remaining primitive cultures," Bill Kovach and Tom Rosenstiel wrote in *The Elements of Journalism*, "they discovered something unexpected. From the most isolated tribal societies to the most distant islands in the Pacific, people shared essentially the same definition of what is news. They shared the same kind of gossip. They even looked for the same qualities in the messengers they picked to gather and deliver their news. They wanted people who could run swiftly over the next hill, accurately gather information, and engagingly retell it."[2]

That messenger coming over the hill today has ways of gathering the news and commercial pressures that influence the message. The *conventions of news-gathering*—what journalists and news organizations consider to be news and how news is gathered and distributed—all have impact on what gets covered and how. This lending of significance, as we have noted in our discussion of agenda-setting and agenda-building in Chapter 2, puts some stories and people out front and on the nation's agenda, while other stories and issues may remain in the dark. The sources on stories (whom reporters talk to) and how independently they verify what they're being told— also have serious consequences in how an issue is perceived and acted upon. The commercial nature and ownership of the U.S. media system is an important factor in how news is covered with a bias toward immediacy. Technology and media are intertwined in history, and the Internet and social media have challenged and changed the media ecosystem. Most recently, the concept of objectivity—the idea of presenting "both sides" of the story fairly and accurately—has both served the public in a time of attacks on the very nature of facts and truth and been challenged as presenting false equivalence between two unequal assertions, for example, in early media framing and reporting of "both sides" of climate change.

In this chapter we will look at the history of the news, trust in news, the need for greater diversity among journalists—and where we go from here. You will also have a writing assignment that gives you the opportunity to read and analyze a classic book choosing from a number of engaging memoirs from both politicians and political journalists, for what your book reveals about how journalists and politicians interact.

Bias toward Immediacy across Media

The human need for news and the desire for a quick messenger leads to our first cultural and operational bias in the news media: a *bias toward immediacy*—that is, a bias toward reporting on what is happening *now*. This one is key—and structural. Generations of journalists have been taught—and still are being taught today—that timeliness is the most important element of the news. The other elements of news, journalists are taught, are proximity (How close by did the event happen?), relevance to the lives of the reader, human interest aspects (Can people relate?), and prominence (Are the people involved prominent and important?)—or, as an old joke goes, if the president of the U.S. gets a cold, it's news.[3]

The bias toward immediacy comes straight from the commercial nature of news media and the presumed short attention span of the public—and it is deeply ingrained in the culture of journalism as well as the traditional view of many editors: If it happened yesterday, it's not as interesting—or salable—as what's happening today, now. "Hot off the press" was how print publications trumpeted their scoops in the days when newspapers were set in hot type. Major cities once had competing newspapers and "press wars" between rival publishers Joseph Pulitzer and Randolph Hearst, with morning and evening editions hawked by children on street corners and even an occasional "Extra!" special edition on historic days.[4]

The Early Days of "Immediacy"

The telegraph, developed in the 1840s, revolutionized communication by freeing the media from transportation on land. The transmitting of electronic signals long distance via telegraph wire enabled the creation in 1846 of the Associated Press wire service, which transmitted stories to subscriber newspapers.[5] The technology of the telegraph led to what is called the inverted pyramid style of journalistic writing, which is still prominently in use across media platforms today. Writing a story in the inverted pyramid style means that, like an upside-down pyramid, the story begins with what is called the lead—the most important facts at the top—telling what happened and when and emphasizing the element of timeliness, action, and active verbs to connote excitement and importance. The idea is that this answers the question "What happened?" right away—and the story could be cut from the bottom to fit the newspaper page.

Radio news in the 1920s, broadcast TV news beginning in the 1950s, cable TV starting in the 1980s and 1990s, and online news today all have this bias toward immediacy, from the headline to the text and the relative prominence of stories, whether it's a sports score or a vote in Congress. During the late 1960s and 1970s, the three broadcast evening newscasts on CBS, NBC, and ABC combined commanded huge audiences every night, and the three broadcast TV anchors and their programs played an influential, agenda-setting role with their coverage of politics and an era of social upheaval marked by the civil rights movement, the war in Vietnam, the anti-war movement, and modern-day feminism.

When Atlanta, Georgia, cable TV entrepreneur Ted Turner launched CNN in 1980, he created the world's first twenty-four-hour news network, with the ability to go live worldwide, including CNN correspondents reporting live from Baghdad in the first Gulf War in 1991 as the U.S. dropped bombs on the city in a multination campaign against Saddam Hussein.[6] "Breaking news" sells—and keeps—viewers and readers tuned in, which is why twenty-four-hour cable news uses this phrase all the time, even when nothing new is happening.

This media bias toward immediacy and going live communicates the narrative excitement of uncertainty and seeing events unfold, seemingly before your eyes. The problem, of course, is that some stories are exciting and compelling without having any greater significance beyond the individuals involved, whereas some stories that are highly significant may not be easily dramatized or compelling.

Despite changes in technology, content, and distribution, this valuing of the urgent now has only grown—in the layout of stories on online news sites, in customized news feeds on Facebook and Twitter, and in user-generated content, from selfies and Snapchat to TikTok.

The Internet Redefines Immediacy

The development of the Internet—which began in the late 1960s as a government-military project for time-sharing and protecting communication among academic researchers and the military[7]—was a revolutionary step in the history of communication. In contrast to top-down mass media, the Internet has brought an exchange of information that, as political scientist Bruce Bimber described it, is abundant and inexpensive to produce and distribute across the Web.[8]

For major media, the interactivity, user-generated content, and momentum-building of these newer media have changed the power relationship between formerly closed-system mass media and their readers and viewers. "News is now a conversation," as new-media guru Jeff Jarvis put it in an interview with the author.[9] Traditional media today ignore or dismiss feedback—reporting and media criticism from bloggers and social media—at their peril.

The explosion of choices of information across the Internet and social media has given major traditional news media new outlets for their work, but it has upended newspapers' business model of lucrative local advertising supporting their journalism. This, coupled with the deregulation of the media and the devaluing of the public interest obligations of corporations that own news organizations, has led to the largely unchecked concentration of ownership—and inevitable layoffs and cutbacks—we saw in Chapter 1.

In a classic cycle of innovation and commercialization, established media and political actors all have sought to harness the energy and excitement of newer forms of customized content and technology, whether by literally buying them, as Facebook did with Instagram and Google did with YouTube, or adding their own *BuzzFeed*-style "listicals," online video, podcasts, and social media accounts for their news organizations and their individual journalists.

The timeline in Figure 4.1 shows how recently—and how rapidly—invention and change have come to the media.

Social Media Changes the Game

Facebook and Twitter, in particular, have become major forces in contemporary politics and media. Twitter, which saw journalists as early adapters, has changed the nature of political reporting and political discourse, with journalists, commentators, and anybody else with a Twitter account scrambling to share and forward articles and post attention-getting, pithy tweets. President Trump effectively created his own news channel with his Twitter account, speaking directly to his supporters, sharing even proven falsehoods and conspiracy theories to frame issues in his own image and agenda-build by regularly setting the daily news agenda of mainstream media with his tweets.

YouTube has created a whole new world of shared online news video as well as a generation of content-creating YouTubers and influencers.[10] YouTube was reporting two billion unique visits monthly by 2020, attracting the eighteen-to-forty-nine-year-old demographic prized by advertisers. YouTube has added an important new market for broadcast TV excerpts, in news and entertainment, along with an extraordinary volume of user-produced and commercial content from around the world.

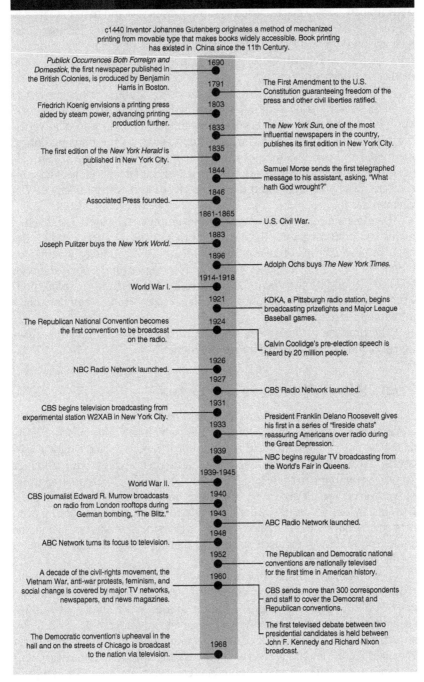

Figure 4.1 Timeline: History of Media and Technology

c1440 Inventor Johannes Gutenberg originates a method of mechanized printing from movable type that makes books widely accessible. Book printing has existed in China since the 11th Century.

1690 — *Publick Occurrences Both Foreign and Domestick*, the first newspaper published in the British Colonies, is produced by Benjamin Harris in Boston.

1791 — The First Amendment to the U.S. Constitution guaranteeing freedom of the press and other civil liberties ratified.

1803 — Friedrich Koenig envisions a printing press aided by steam power, advancing printing production further.

1833 — The *New York Sun*, one of the most influential newspapers in the country, publishes its first edition in New York City.

1835 — The first edition of the *New York Herald* is published in New York City.

1844 — Samuel Morse sends the first telegraphed message to his assistant, asking, "What hath God wrought?"

1846 — Associated Press founded.

1861-1865 — U.S. Civil War.

1883 — Joseph Pulitzer buys the *New York World*.

1896 — Adolph Ochs buys *The New York Times*.

1914-1918 — World War I.

1921 — KDKA, a Pittsburgh radio station, begins broadcasting prizefights and Major League Baseball games.

1924 — The Republican National Convention becomes the first convention to be broadcast on the radio. Calvin Coolidge's pre-election speech is heard by 20 million people.

1926 — NBC Radio Network launched.

1927 — CBS Radio Network launched.

1931 — CBS begins television broadcasting from experimental station W2XAB in New York City.

1933 — President Franklin Delano Roosevelt gives his first in a series of "fireside chats" reassuring Americans over radio during the Great Depression.

1939 — NBC begins regular TV broadcasting from the World's Fair in Queens.

1939-1945 — World War II.

1940 — CBS journalist Edward R. Murrow broadcasts on radio from London rooftops during German bombing, "The Blitz."

1943 — ABC Radio Network launched.

1948 — ABC Network turns its focus to television.

1952 — The Republican and Democratic national conventions are nationally televised for the first time in American history.

1960 — A decade of the civil-rights movement, the Vietnam War, anti-war protests, feminism, and social change is covered by major TV networks, newspapers, and news magazines. CBS sends more than 300 correspondents and staff to cover the Democrat and Republican conventions. The first televised debate between two presidential candidates is held between John F. Kennedy and Richard Nixon broadcast.

1968 — The Democratic convention's upheaval in the hall and on the streets of Chicago is broadcast to the nation via television.

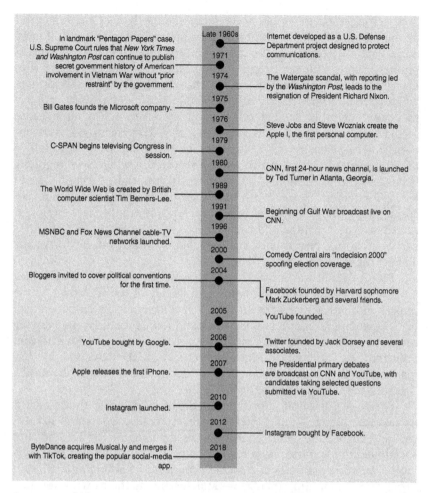

Late 1960s — Internet developed as a U.S. Defense Department project designed to protect communications.

In landmark "Pentagon Papers" case, U.S. Supreme Court rules that *New York Times and Washington Post* can continue to publish secret government history of American involvement in Vietnam War without "prior restraint" by the government. — 1971

1974 — The Watergate scandal, with reporting led by the *Washington Post*, leads to the resignation of President Richard Nixon.

1975

Bill Gates founds the Microsoft company. — 1975

1976 — Steve Jobs and Steve Wozniak create the Apple I, the first personal computer.

1979

C-SPAN begins televising Congress in session. — 1979

1980 — CNN, first 24-hour news channel, is launched by Ted Turner in Atlanta, Georgia.

The World Wide Web is created by British computer scientist Tim Berners-Lee. — 1989

1991 — Beginning of Gulf War broadcast live on CNN.

MSNBC and Fox News Channel cable-TV networks launched. — 1996

2000 — Comedy Central airs "Indecision 2000" spoofing election coverage.

2004

Bloggers invited to cover political conventions for the first time. — 2004

Facebook founded by Harvard sophomore Mark Zuckerberg and several friends.

2005 — YouTube founded.

2006 — Twitter founded by Jack Dorsey and several associates.

YouTube bought by Google. — 2006

2007 — The Presidential primary debates are broadcast on CNN and YouTube, with candidates taking selected questions submitted via YouTube.

Apple releases the first iPhone. — 2007

2010

Instagram launched. — 2010

2012 — Instagram bought by Facebook.

ByteDance acquires Musical.ly and merges it with TikTok, creating the popular social-media app. — 2018

Sources: www.history.com, www.massmoments.org, www.britannica.com, www.library.illinois .edu, www.eh.net, www.newsweek.com, www.vtdigger.org, www.nbcuniversal.com, www .npr.org, www.senate.gov, www.mac-history.net, www.cspan.org, https://ballotpedia.org, www.warnermediagroup.com, www.businessinsider.com, https://mashable.com, https:// medium.com, https://vox.com, www.youtube.com, www.cnn.com.

The ability for a user-produced YouTube video, cell phone video, or photograph to "go viral," which we take as a given today, has galvanized public opinion and even social movements by making millions of people worldwide witnesses at the scene.

Some good news for the future of traditional news media is that news consumption is not a zero-sum game: More Americans today are now getting their news often via social media than often from print media.[11] But people today report grazing among different kinds of news outlets and other sources of news and information, including on smartphones,[12] with younger people leading older people in engaging with newer forms of social media—and in the idea that news will find them when it's really important.[13] Young people and older people both say they want credible, factual information: In a recent Common Sense Media survey of teenagers, a large majority—78 percent—of thirteen-to-seventeen-year-olds in the U.S. said it's important for them to follow current events.[14] Teens in this survey reported getting news regularly from news organizations—but, indirectly, through Facebook news feeds, Twitter, and YouTube. Despite their hours spent on YouTube and social media, they expressed more confidence in traditional news organizations than YouTube and social media, with seven in ten teenagers surveyed saying they trusted traditional news organizations to "generally get the facts straight."[15]

People overall are embracing getting news via social media—but they are also expressing concerns about the accuracy of social media and the impact on political discourse. In a 2019 Pew Research Center survey, half of U.S. adults said that one-sided news and inaccurate news are very big problems with news on social media.[16] As we know now, the Russian government used Facebook and Instagram to spread fake news and disinformation aimed at disrupting the 2016 election, and U.S. officials warned that similar efforts were underway in 2020.

Each new communication medium has been greeted with fears about its possible impact—and hopeful idealism about its potential to educate and engage the whole country in the democracy. The Internet and social media, of course, have revolutionized the relationship and overlap between media users and media producers, enabling an explosion of new voices curating their news and serving as their own publisher. But, in an examination of the role of new, digital media in politics, Richard Davis and Diana Owen found that the idealistic vision of an electronic town hall and a democracy of voices has been undercut by the same commercializing forces and economic imperatives that affect "old" media.[17]

The launching of Fox News Channel, followed by MSNBC, has led to ideological bifurcation in cable news, with Fox viewers intensely loyal to the network and mistrustful of other media. Despite the long-standing drumbeat alleging liberal bias in the media from President Trump and Fox News Channel, the landscape of talk radio for many years has been overwhelmingly dominated by conservative hosts from Rush Limbaugh to Sean Hannity and Laura Ingraham; despite complaints from President Trump and some others that Facebook was censoring conservatives, data for one month in 2020 compiled by CrowdTangle, a data analytics firm owned by Facebook, found that the Fox News Channel Facebook page dominated among U.S. news organizations in engagements by a wide margin, accounting for 13 percent of all the interactions on Facebook from these news organizations, with the right-wing website Breitbart second in engagements, followed by ABC News and National Public Radio (NPR).[18] Conservative commentator Ben Shapiro led a list of top ten sites dominated by conservative voices, with the liberal Young Turks generating a small percentage of Shapiro's likes, comments, and shares.[19]

The public is very critical of the state of political discourse, with 85 percent of the people in the Pew poll in Figure 4.2 saying that political debate has become less respectful and less fact-based and 60 percent saying the debate has become less substantive. Fifty-five percent said Donald Trump had changed the tone of debate for the worse—and 78 percent said "heated" or aggressive language used by politicians against some groups made violence against them more likely.[20]

Figure 4.2 Americans' Opinions on Political Debate

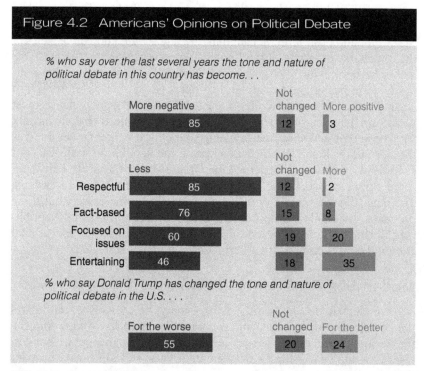

% who say over the last several years the tone and nature of political debate in this country has become. . .

	More negative	Not changed	More positive
	85	12	3

	Less	Not changed	More
Respectful	85	12	2
Fact-based	76	15	8
Focused on issues	60	19	20
Entertaining	46	18	35

% who say Donald Trump has changed the tone and nature of political debate in the U.S. . . . .

	For the worse	Not changed	For the better
	55	20	24

Sources: Survey of U.S. adults conducted April 29, 2019–May 13, 2019, Pew Research Center.
Note: No answer responses not shown.

Bias toward Conflict and Narrow Debate

Bias toward conflict and narrow debate is one of the defining characteristics of the many political talk shows and election-night "mega-panels" on cable TV that play an outsized role in contemporary politics and media. CNN's *Crossfire*, which ran for fourteen years from the beginnings of CNN, is the progenitor of this form. The creators of *Crossfire* cast Patrick Buchanan, a conservative commentator who had been a speechwriter for Richard Nixon, and other conservative commentators and former Republican lawmakers and strategists, as being "on the right," against liberal commentators, former Democratic lawmakers, and strategists such as former Democratic vice presidential candidate Geraldine Ferraro, as being "on the left." The format—widely emulated—frames the two major political parties as combatants always opposed to each other. The casting shows a narrow definition of what actually constitutes the Left and the Right in politics today. The show was promoted like a political prizefight—and it was popular for many years. A more extreme version—also long-running and satirized on late-night comedy—is the syndicated pundit show *The McLaughlin Group*. The show has come back in a mellower form; but for many years, the creator and host, John McLaughlin, literally shouted down the views of the roundtable of journalists and political strategists.[21]

In his book *Why Americans Hate Politics*, E. J. Dionne argued that politicians were pushing important and complex issues such as abortion into what are called false dichotomies of the Left versus the Right, whereas most Americans have more nuanced views on many subjects.[22] Political talk shows still typically have a narrow range of political parties and opinion as the Left and the Right, featuring Democratic and Republican strategists, not candidates or strategists from the Libertarian Party or the Green Party, and not political activists from the Left or the Right, except on rare occasions. The range of voices and groups has broadened to some degree, but these programs, especially on election nights, feature Democrats and Republicans, including former elected officials and heads of the parties' national committees, reflecting the two-part focus of much of political coverage.

Moderating Presidential Debates

Presidential debates—and party primary debates—give candidates the opportunity to be seen and compared by millions of viewers. The public still considers the debates important, according to public opinion research—and viewership to presidential debates, and some party primary debates remains strong. In 2012, an estimated sixty-seven million viewers across several networks watched President Obama debate the Republican nominee for president, Sen. Mitt Romney.[23] The first presidential debate between Hillary Clinton and Donald Trump in 2016 was the most-watched presidential debate in history, seen by an estimated eighty-four million viewers watching on TV, with millions more watching live online.[24]

The debates provide the opportunity for a candidate to have a breakout moment that can be replayed and analyzed for its significance. In 1984, incumbent Ronald Reagan had fumbled badly in a previous debate against the Democratic nominee, former vice president Walter Mondale—and questions were raised about whether, at seventy-three, Reagan was too old to be president. Reagan was ready with a humorous response in the next debate. Asked if he was too old to be president, Reagan brought down the house by saying, "I am not going to exploit, for political purposes, the youth and inexperience of my opponent," the fifty-six-year-old Mondale. Mondale laughed—and the question didn't get answered.[25]

Another moment that is often replayed came when veteran Texas senator Lloyd Bentsen, the Democrat nominee for vice president, debated a young-looking, relatively inexperienced Indiana senator, Dan Quayle, who was George H. W. Bush's running mate in 1988. When Quayle compared himself to a young president Kennedy, Bentsen pounced, using the tool of repetition from classical rhetoric. "Senator," Bentsen said, staring down at Quayle, "I served with Jack Kennedy, I knew Jack Kennedy, Jack Kennedy was a friend of mine. . . . Senator . . . you're no Jack Kennedy."[26]

The 2016 Republican primary debates were, as ABC News said after the first one, "the Donald Trump Show."[27] Trump broke the norms of the debates and political discourse, dominating a crowded field of seventeen candidates with mocking personal attacks on "Lyin'" Ted Cruz, "Little" Marco Rubio, and "Low-Energy" Jeb Bush, along with outrageous rhetoric and even references to the size of his penis.[28] Trump was rarely challenged head-on by his Republican opponents. And for all the criticism of Trump at the time, the bias of the media toward conflict led to some moderators quoting Trump's remarks, including in other interviews, and asking the candidate to respond to the awful thing Trump had just said about them. It made for interesting, ratings-getting television, including putting Trump and the other candidate side by side in a split-screen image on TV. But, although Trump began to be questioned more closely, policy was largely overwhelmed by combat and shocking theatrics. Trump was declared the winner of the first several debates, likely adding to his momentum in the primaries and appealing to supporters who wanted to disrupt the establishment political process.

The 2020 Democratic primaries also had a crowded field of entrants, and candidates had strict time limits that they didn't always observe but that left them straining for sound bites while some moderators seemed almost solely focused on differences among the candidates on "Medicare for all," to the exclusion of other topics. Joe Biden's faltering performances initially were a factor in his standing as the presumed front-runner, and Sen. Amy Klobuchar and Mayor Pete Buttigieg both built name recognition and praise for their debating skills. There were moments of genuine, sub-stantive drama—including, notably, Kamala Harris' personal story of being bused to school as a child, coupled with her criticism of Biden's previous stance on school busing and working with segregationists in Congress in the past.[29] In the early debates, the Democrats appeared to be aiming not to go after each other, but that changed over time as the lower-polling candi-dates were looking for a standout moment that would be replayed. Debates shouldn't be canned speeches. But it is striking how seeing a candidate in an interview or an informal campaign appearance, with more time and a less gladiatorial setting, almost inevitably makes them and their views more understandable and even appealing.

Bias toward Insiderism

When Pat Buchanan, the cohost of CNN's highly rated *Crossfire*, ran for president as a social conservative against George H. W. Bush in 1992, it was a new trend that raised concerns in media ethics. CNN was criticized for welcoming Buchanan back on the air after a leave of absence for his campaign on the theory that the network was only adding to his fame for another possible run for office. Chris Matthews, host of *Hardball*, and *Meet the Press* host Tim Russert both previously had worked for Democratic senators (House Speaker "Tip" O'Neill and Sen. Daniel Patrick Moynihan, respectively). But the generally accepted idea then was, as Russert put it in an interview with the author, the revolving door between politics and the media swung one way—i.e., once someone had left politics for a high-profile job in the media or vice versa, it would not be appropriate for them to go back through the door the other way.[30]

Revolving Door in Media and Politics

In recent years, the revolving door between politics and the media has been spinning so fast that it has practically come off its hinges. The cable news airwaves mix strategists and former elected officials with com-mentators and political reporters, with some once-and-likely-future politi-cal candidates, to comment on current politics, on shows and on election nights. These panels inevitably blur the lines between reporting, commen-tary, and political strategy. The prevalence of popular talk shows and elec-tion-night "mega-panels" that have both former strategists and journalists at the same desk talking about campaigns has been dubbed the media-politics punditocracy. This inside-the-Beltway world, critics say, creates an echo chamber of groupthink that confirms conventional wisdom and establishment bias from Washington, D.C.

Fox News Channel has had a lineup of hosts and paid contributors that has included numerous future and former presidential and vice presidential candidates on the air between campaigns, including Mike Huckabee, Sarah Palin, and Newt Gingrich. MSNBC has featured former Vermont governor and presidential candidate Howard Dean in his role as former chairman of the Democratic National Committee alongside former Republican National Committee chairman Michael Steele. In 2019, in a further sign of how narrow the space between politician and TV pundit has become, NBC and MSNBC hired former senator Claire McCaskill[31] and CNN hired former Florida gubernatorial candidate Andrew Gillum soon after they lost their races in the 2018 midterm elections.[32]

Also in 2019, CNN, whose political analysts include former Michigan governor Jennifer Granholm, a Democrat, and former Republican senator Rick Santorum of Pennsylvania, was criticized for giving a prominent political contributor role to former Ohio governor John Kasich, a 2016 Republican presidential candidate and critic of Donald Trump who had said that he was mulling a run for the Republican nomination in 2020. CNN's political journalists reportedly were upset about the Kasich hire, but network executives acknowledged no concerns.[33] Granholm was later confirmed as Secretary of Energy in the Biden administration.

CNN and MSNBC reference their analysts' previous campaigns. But, on Fox News Channel, Karl Rove, a prominent Republican strategist and fundraiser as well as a longtime Fox News Channel analyst, was providing negative election-year commentary on President Obama in 2012 while a super PAC Rove cofounded was raising an estimated $84.5 million against the president in his reelection campaign.[34] In one famous episode that helped build her reputation as a journalist, Fox News Channel anchor Megyn Kelly walked over to the in-house polling experts at Fox on election night in 2012 to independently confirm that what Rove was continuing to say on the air on election night was not true: Obama *had* won Ohio—and the election.[35]

In the 2016 presidential campaign, CNN—which had a banner year in terms of ratings and profits with its coverage and multiple panels around the election—was criticized for giving a paid political platform to Corey Lewandowski, Trump's former campaign manager, days after Lewandowski, who was openly hostile to the news media, had been fired from the Trump campaign. It was known at the time he was hired that Lewandowski had signed a nondisclosure agreement with the Trump campaign that presumably would make it difficult for him to comment candidly.[36] And it was later revealed that Lewandowski also had been receiving a severance from the Trump campaign while he was on the air.[37] CNN president Jeff Zucker defended the hiring, saying that the networks had too few pro-Trump voices on their political panels. Days after being spotted at Trump

Tower after the election, Lewandowski resigned from CNN to take a job in the Trump administration.[38]

During the 2016 campaign, several Republican conservative commentators across the three cable networks prominently took sides in the debate within the Republican Party over Donald Trump. Charles Krauthammer, a conservative columnist for the *Washington Post* as well as a longtime Fox News Channel pundit, said that Trump simply was not a conservative, while on MSNBC and NBC's *Meet the Press*, Steve Schmidt, former campaign adviser to Sen. John McCain, condemned Republican presidential candidates now backing Trump as putting "their party ahead of their country."[39] Republican strategist Ana Navarro, on CNN, regularly blasted Trump and her own party for Trump's stances on immigrants and women.

News organizations in previous years were more strict about having their journalists appear on television to discuss their stories on the theory that journalists should not state their opinion about the people or stories they're writing about. Today, opinion columnists from the *Daily Beast*, the *Washington Post*, the *New York Times*, the *National Journal*, and other publications are regular contributors on CNN and MSNBC, while columnists from *National Review* and other conservative publications are contributors on Fox News Channel. During the Trump administration, reporters from *Politico*, the *New York Times*, *Wall Street Journal*, and *Washington Post* were regularly debriefed about their investigative stories, clearly treading the line between talking about their reporting and stating their opinion.

What's Wrong with Politics as an Insiders' Game

In addition to blurring the lines between journalists and political strategists, all this TV punditry turns political journalists into sportscasters and the public into spectators, watching but not playing the game. "When journalists define politics as a game played by the insiders," media critic Jay Rosen wrote, "their job description becomes: find out what the insiders are doing to 'win.'"[40]

In an opinion piece in the *New York Times*, former CNN president Jonathan Klein argued that the cable TV networks should throw all the paid campaign surrogates, whom he termed "campaign mouthpieces," off the air. "It's not bad journalism; it isn't journalism at all," Klein wrote, calling cable news panels "ritualized cage matches—the WWE in loafers." Klein—who canceled *Crossfire* in favor of other news programming—noted the strong ratings for quieter CNN programming as well as the expanding audience for NPR (thirty-six million listeners weekly in 2016 for its political reporting and analysis) as evidence that cable news should resist what he called "predictable paid flunkies" in a trend that, he maintained, is contributing to declining credibility of the news media.[41]

During the Trump era, political talk shows on cable news and commentary on Twitter amplified headline-making scoops and investigative reports on the Trump administration, as said, from major newspapers, in particular. But the cacophony of commentary and partisanship in the contemporary media-politics ecosystem may also be drowning out other serious but less headline-making work by journalists to cover the daily and incremental processes of government and policymaking. "It's very hard for serious work to get attention today," observed Tom Rosenstiel, who is now executive director of the American Press Institute. "It just gets drowned out" with all the other news and noise.[42]

Bias toward Horse-Race Coverage

Many media critics have noted that political coverage during election years has an overreliance on quoting polls, who's up and who's down, at that moment in time. There are differences, of course, among polls in their accuracy, methodology, margin of error, and what was going on at the time they were taken—and polling over time and comparing is different from a snapshot poll. We know now that an apparent surge in voters for Trump in the key swing states of Michigan, Wisconsin, and Pennsylvania in 2016 was not predicted. And, most importantly, what is often missed is that state-by-state polls are much less reliable than national surveys—but they are quoted anyway. "Hopefully most Americans have figured out that both the primary elections to choose a presidential nominee and the general election to choose the president are state-by-state contests," wrote former CNBC producer Jake Novak. "Yet most stories about the Democratic primary race focus on Joe Biden's enduring lead in national polls and not on how the Democrats are faring in early voting states like Iowa and New Hampshire. It's as if we're intentionally blinding ourselves to the most pertinent facts every time anyone talks about national polls."[43]

Defense of Horse-Race Coverage

One factor cited in defense of horse-race coverage of strategy and winners or losers in political campaigns is that it's exciting—and it sells. In one study before the 2000 election in which participants were given a CD-ROM with a variety of media coverage and had their news consumption, including time spent and calculated, the researchers concluded, "Given access to a wide variety of news reports about the presidential campaign in the weeks immediately preceding the 2000 election, we find that voters were drawn to reports on the horserace and strategy. Strategy reports proved far more popular than reports about the issues."[44]

Jack Shafer, media critic for *Slate* magazine, defended horse-race coverage in an essay, writing, "You can no more divorce [horse-race] coverage from campaign coverage than you can divorce [horse-race coverage] from the coverage of horse races. Why else would they call political contests 'races'? Or their leading contestants' 'front-runners'? . . . Beyond the issues, voters need to know why a candidate is (or isn't) performing well in the polls, is (or isn't) raising money, is (or isn't) drawing crowds of supporters, or is (or isn't) keeping his cool. Candidates win or lose for a reason, reasons that have to do with issue papers but also with how they carry themselves and present their positions. Candidates appreciate this fact, which is why they commission private polls so they can construct their own horse-race results and act on them."[45]

Bias toward Establishment Candidates and Perceived Front-Runners

The focus on quoting and reflecting the establishment view from political insiders—including which candidates have raised the most money and which are viewed by the party establishment as the most viable—has led national media and pundits to miss the beginnings and growth of both the Tea Party and Occupy Wall Street movements as well as the outsider candidacies of both Bernie Sanders and Donald Trump in 2016.

Interview with Senator Bernie Sanders

"What I am going to talk about for a while is something that we don't do enough as a nation: have a serious discussion about the serious problems facing America," Senator Sanders told an audience of students at American University in the spring of 2015. "To a large degree, especially if you turn on TV, what politics appears to be is a game: what does somebody need to win, how much money do you need, where are you standing in the polls, what kind of dumb thing did somebody say last month that is played over and over again. That is media politics. That is not real politics."[46]

In his remarks and an interview with this author as moderator, Sanders outlined what he said were the most pressing problems facing the country: student debt, climate change, income inequality, and the dominance of wealthy donors in campaigns post–*Citizens United* that he said threatened to turn the U.S. into an "oligarchy" unless ordinary Americans organized, voted, and made their voices heard. "If you want to move in the direction to make college tuition-free or lower the interest rates on student debt, you can absolutely win that fight. All you have to do is bring a million of your friends to Washington, support the legislation that will do those things—and tell people what they don't believe—they believe that young people don't vote, so who cares what you think?"[47]

Hillary Clinton had announced that she was running for president the day before, in a video that talked about a "stacked deck" against ordinary Americans, and many political observers were noting that the idea of income inequality had become mainstream. "I am proud that . . . I have been one of a relatively few of us over the years" raising the issue of wealth and "income inequality," Sanders said.[48]

If he decided to run for president, he was asked by this author, was raising these issues part of the reason he would enter the race? "No, I would like to run to win, actually," Sanders responded, to laughter and huge applause from the young audience.[49]

As we know now, Sanders, appealing especially to young voters and others dissatisfied with Hillary Clinton as the anointed front-runner for the Democratic Party nomination, later mounted a strong challenge to Hillary Clinton in 2016—and was a front-runner for the nomination in 2020.

In the 2016 election, Sanders supporters charged, with some evidence, that the Democratic National Committee was seeking to limit Clinton's exposure to Sanders by limiting the number of primary debates and scheduling them on nights when they were competing with sports and entertainment programming expected to draw large audiences.[50]

Media coverage of Bernie Sanders' insurgent candidacy in 2016 missed his initial appeal among many liberal voters, young and old. Many reporters and commentators were left surprised by the size of his rallies, his standing in the polls in early primaries, and his online-based fundraising among small donors that raised $26 million—more money than Hillary Clinton—in the first months of the campaign. Journalists from major media missed the growth of the Sanders phenomenon in 2016, giving his candidacy short shrift compared to the airtime and print and online space given to other candidates—a ratio of eighty-one to one in news minutes on the three broadcast evening newscasts compared to Donald Trump in 2015.[51]

In their early stories, reporters wrote dismissively and even humorously about Sanders. "He seems an unlikely presidential candidate—an ex-hippie, septuagenarian socialist from the liberal reaches of Vermont who rails, in his thick Brooklyn accent, rumpled suit and frizzy pile of white hair, against the 'billionaire class,'" Paul Kane and Philip Rucker wrote in the *Washington Post*.[52]

The *New York Times* buried Senator Sanders' announcement in a brief story on page A21,[53] although the newspaper had run front-page announcements on multiple Republican candidates' announcements. The *New York Times* was later criticized by its own ombudswoman as well as by Sanders supporters for an article in which, after the piece about Sanders' legislative accomplishments had been published online, an editor added several new paragraphs that said that there was no indication that Sanders' "modest" victories presaged success in scaling-up his programs if he were elected.[54]

Critiquing Media Coverage of Sanders

As Steve Hendricks pointed out in a *Columbia Journalism Review* article early in the campaign called "Bernie Sanders Can't Win: Why the Press Loves to Hate Underdogs," even stories by opinion columnists writing favorably about Sanders had headlines such as "Bernie Sanders Won't Win. But His Ideas Might."[55] As it turned out, of course, Sanders' ideas about trade treaties and lost jobs were similar to Donald Trump's, and Sanders' message of economic inequality and criticisms of Clinton's speeches on Wall Street and support from big donors resonated with many voters.

The coverage of Sanders illustrates several cultural biases of the mainstream media in covering politics, especially a bias toward anointed frontrunners in the two major political parties. The invisible "media primary" of vetting and winnowing out candidates has been joined by what could be called the "wealth primary" of who has raised the most money. And journalists, pundits, and political operatives tend to anoint establishment candidates and to follow the money, not as in the famous line from the Watergate investigation movie *All the President's Men* but echoing the high value political consultants and others place on the ability to raise money and name recognition.

Outsider, insurgent movements—from the Left and from the Right— almost always seem to take both pundits and political parties by surprise, while lower-rated candidates or third-party candidates have a difficult time gaining attention and are often framed as quixotic or even quaint. Yet, as Steve Hendricks pointed out in *Columbia Journalism Review*, relatively unknown long shots from Jimmy Carter to Bill Clinton and Barack Obama have been elected president. "For not going with the flow, and for challenging Hillary Clinton, the big fish many elites have tagged as their own, Sanders' entry into the race was greeted with story after story whose message—stated or understated, depending upon the decorum of the messenger—was 'This crank can't win.' . . . 'This crank actually *could* win' [was] nearer the mark."[56]

In coverage of Sanders and other liberal or third-party candidates and protest movements such as Occupy Wall Street and Fight for $15 that have challenged the status quo in media, politics, and big business, some media critics on the left see not liberal bias in the media, as is often alleged by Fox News Channel and conservative media critics, but corporate bias in the media. These critics maintain that the commercial nature and concentrated ownership of major media as one part of huge corporations causes news organizations not to seek alternative voices or to question sufficiently the economic system of which they are part. Several critics of the coverage of Sanders versus Hillary Clinton in 2016, for example, contended Hillary Clinton's more "corporate" stances on trade and income inequality as well as her ties to big banks on Wall Street, issues that Sanders and Trump were raising, made her the more favored candidate—in the Democratic Party and in political punditry about the primary, before Sanders' surge.[57]

In 2020, Sanders received far more coverage and far more favorable coverage as he emerged as a potential front-runner. But some Sanders supporters began calling MSNBC "MSDNC" (for Democratic National Committee), citing dismissive and disbelieving commentary by *Hardball* host Chris Matthews and Democratic strategists as evidence of DNC-based corporate bias against their candidate. "The now daily MSNBC and CNN discussions of the Democratic 2020 race—which usually include mainstream print reporters and Democratic operatives singing the same tune—feature a chorus of corporate Democratic talking points (standards like 'go moderate'), while the progressive wing of the party is often alluded to but rarely heard from," Jeff Cohen, founder of the liberal media watchdog group Fairness & Accuracy in Reporting (FAIR), wrote. "If genuinely progressive pundits were present in mainstream media, they'd argue that anticorporate, populist candidates are often better positioned to win a large portion of swing voters. . . . When it comes to assessing which Democrat is 'electable' in a general election, the last group I'd rely on would be the current narrow array of mainstream pundits who dominate the TV networks. If they were reliable, we'd now be awaiting Hillary Clinton's second State of the Union address."[58]

Bias toward Official Sources

One of the most serious criticisms of journalism is that journalists rely far too heavily on government officials and other official sources in their work, sometimes with tragic results, especially in wartime. (We will discuss the failures of media reporting in the lead-up to the war in Iraq in detail in a case study in Chapter 7.) As Michael Schudson, Herbert J. Gans, W. Lance Bennett, and other political scientists have noted, journalists' focus on quoting government officials and others presumed to have credibility limits the public's knowledge of alternative voices and information. "The press is presumably the bastion of free expression in a democracy, but too often it has been one of the institutions that limits the range of expression, especially expression that is critical of leading centers of power in society," Schudson wrote. "Almost all social scientific studies of the news reveal that journalists themselves, of their own volition, limit the range of opinion present in the news."[59]

Schudson cited three significant factors for how this happens: (1) source dependence, reporters relying on the views of their primary sources, who, he maintained, "tend to be high-ranking government officials" and, even when they're outside experts, people with experience in government due to a perceived obligation to report government affairs; (2) journalists' operating within a set of professional norms that "are themselves constraints on expression"; and (3) journalists' operating, he said, "within conventional bounds of opinion, opinions common among a largely secular, college-educated, upper middle class." Interestingly, after listing these characteristics in an essay called "Why Democracies Need an Unlovable Press," Schudson argued that while, for many reasons, media discourse in the U.S. "fails to approximate an ideal of robust and wide-open discussion," "journalism as it functions today is still a practice that offends powerful groups, speaks truth to power, and provides access for a diversity of opinion," with departures from the constraints, in Schudson's view, being the exceptions that prove the rule. In fact, he lauded breaking news on unanticipated events as one-way journalists can break away from officialdom to challenge authorities from the ground.[60]

Although there were many flaws in media reporting—not to mention the government's response—during Hurricane Katrina in Louisiana, Anderson Cooper's aggressive, disbelieving questioning of both Louisiana Democratic senator Mary Landrieu and Michael Brown, head of the Federal Emergency Management Agency (FEMA), from Cooper's vantage point on the ground amid suffering and death in New Orleans and Mississippi, was an example of reporting that dramatically pointed out the difference between official-speak and the reality on the ground.

When Senator Landrieu began an interview thanking Bill Clinton and President George W. Bush for their support and congratulating Congress for voting for billions of dollars in additional funding to help FEMA and the Red Cross in their efforts, Cooper stopped her by saying, "Excuse me, senator, I'm sorry for interrupting. I haven't heard that, because, for the last four days, I've been seeing dead bodies in the streets here in Mississippi. And to listen to politicians thanking each other and complimenting each other, you know, I got to tell you, there are a lot of people here who are very upset, and very angry, and very frustrated."[61]

The long-running Washington, D.C.-based broadcast TV "Sunday shows"—NBC's *Meet the Press*, CBS's *Face the Nation*, and ABC's *This Week*—have been hugely successful financially for many years at reaching an audience of opinion makers and viewers outside of Washington, D.C., who are interested in hearing interviews with high-ranking government officials and discussion about political issues of the day. These shows—and their cable news progeny—are influential in agenda-setting beyond their on-air audience, not only with online video today but also with a long-standing tradition of the *New York Times*, *Washington Post*, and other publications quoting from their interviews in their own front-page Monday morning stories when the interview makes news, whether signaling a change in government policy or a candidate revealing himself or herself in a way that makes news.

These Sunday shows reflect the journalistic bias toward officialdom, and they have long been criticized for giving a platform to a narrow range of guests—i.e., high-ranking government officials who themselves have reflected the largely white, male power structure in Congress and the federal government that has prevailed in government until very recently in American history.

Chuck Todd, the NBC News political director who has been the moderator of *Meet the Press* since 2014, noted in an interview with the author in 2015 that he and his producers had been broadening the focus of the program. "I still believe that it's important to find out what official Washington is up to," Todd said. "At the same time, there is a lot of change happening outside of Washington, and we need to reflect that. I have probably had fewer sitting U.S. Senators on my show than any time in the history of *Meet the Press* and other Sunday programs."[62] During the coronavirus pandemic, governors from both political parties spoke directly to the Trump administration as well as viewers on *Meet the Press* and other Sunday shows several headline-making interviews about their needs and differences in policy in combatting the pandemic.

Bias toward Media Narratives

In a search for metaphors from the campaign, veteran political reporter Karen Tumulty noted wryly in an interview with the author, "If your campaign plane gets a flat tire, and you're doing well, it's a flat tire. If your campaign plane gets a flat tire and you're doing poorly, it becomes a metaphor for the campaign."[63] With the growth of online video, sound bites are distributed to potentially huge audiences online by the networks—and they're also seized upon (and repeatedly played) by commentators and a politician's opponents as confirming some greater truth about a campaign or a candidate.

Politicians today rightfully complain that a serious policy speech may get less attention from the public than a brief gaffe on the campaign trail or in a debate that is written about and circulated in video, memes, and social media. With access to presidential candidates today often highly controlled and scripted, journalists—and, presumably, the public—crave revealing, unscripted moments from the candidate. In 2013, to cite one example, Sen. Marco Rubio's repeatedly reaching for a water bottle during a live TV response to President Obama's State of the Union became a GIF that went viral.[64] There is no way that Senator Rubio's thirst met the traditional standards of newsworthy importance—except that the moment burst through the controlled imagery of a formal speech and showed Rubio to be vulnerable and human.

During the 2004 presidential campaign, for example, vice presidential candidate John Edwards' two $400 haircuts in Beverly Hills, uncovered by journalists among campaign finance expenditures, was widely repeated as a sign of Edwards's out-of-touch ego and vanity.[65] President George H. W. Bush's reportedly being overly impressed at a trade show with the then new bar-code technology for scanning groceries was a disputed story that was published in 1992 and has been invoked by Bush's critics ever since as "proof" that Bush did not know how to buy groceries and was an out-of-touch patrician in the White House.[66]

During the 2008 presidential race, John F. Harris and Jim VandeHei, the founders of *Politico*, wrote a critique of the presidential campaign coverage, including their own, after most establishment media missed that Hillary Clinton—not Barack Obama—would win the New Hampshire primary. The authors listed other "bogus narratives" in 2008, including the story that John McCain's campaign was "dead" or that the Iowa primary was "all about organization" when the winner proved to be Mike Huckabee, who did not have a strong organization in Iowa. Such errors came in part because that's what polls were showing and in part because journalists and campaigns were talking to each other.[67] "*Politico* did its part in promoting several of these flimsy story lines," they wrote. "We used predictive language in stories. We amplified certain trends and muffled the caveat, which perhaps should be printed with every story, like a surgeon general's warning: 'We don't know what will happen until voters vote.'"[68]

Coverage of presidential candidates also reflects a *bias toward the new*, with fresh faces embraced in positive coverage that can turn into a media narrative asking why the candidate hasn't lived up to expectations. This arc correctly reflects increased scrutiny of a candidate. But the buildup can seem like jaded celebrity journalism in which the media en masse "discover" a politician and then turn against them. In the 2020 Democratic primaries former Texas representative Beto O'Rourke, who had come close to staging a surprising victory in a Senate race against incumbent Republican senator Ted Cruz, received glowing coverage of his announcement to run for president that turned sour. "Since announcing his campaign for president in mid-March, just two months ago, O'Rourke has gone from the media darling who almost beat Ted Cruz in Texas to the designated punching bag of the pundit class," *Vanity Fair* media critic Peter Hamby wrote. Hamby was critical of the rise-and-fall commentary. But he added, "It's a media mess of O'Rourke's own doing, not just because he entered the campaign without a clear Reason Why, but also because he assumed that his seat-of-the-pants, D.I.Y.-style campaigning in Texas would translate neatly into the hothouse of a national campaign, against a different set of opponents and an always-on press corps."[69]

Media Narrative in the 2000 Presidential Campaign

The comparative coverage of Al Gore versus George W. Bush in the 2000 presidential campaign is an example of how reporters' groupthink and attitudes about access can harden into a media narrative about a campaign that can result in disparate language and disparate treatment of candidates and campaigns.

Reporters on the campaign trail talk to each other—and to a candidate's opposing political strategists—and they are not immune to how they're treated in terms of access or to finding a seemingly fresh face in politics more interesting than someone with whom they have already had dealings.

For an article that was published in *Columbia Journalism Review*, this author examined more than one hundred news stories in the *Washington Post, New York Times,* and the Associated Press, along with other newspapers and features in *Time* and *Newsweek.* The research also included looking at a small sampling of cable talk shows and some network evening newscasts.[70]

Major journalists covering Vice President Al Gore and former Texas governor George W. Bush in the months before the conventions and election were often wrapping their seemingly "straight-news" stories about Gore in cynical language and editorializing characterizations. Numerous news stories similarly signaled in the lead that Gore was a phony and political opportunist.[71] By comparison, coverage of then Texas governor George W. Bush seemed to not only take him at his word but also to write approvingly about his Texas roots and demeanor while endorsing the appeal of a possible political dynasty in the making if Bush succeeded his father George H. W. Bush as the Republican nominee and president. "Rising Son" was an early *Newsweek* cover that put out a positive story about Bush.[72]

On cable TV, Howard Fineman wrote in *Newsweek* magazine and reiterated on MSNBC's *The News with Brian Williams,* "Gore's handlers are plotting yet another rollout of their candidate. By my count we're on about the fifth or sixth Al Gore now. I covered his first presidential campaign—that was Bible Belt Al, followed by Environmental Al."[73]

The underlying message of all of these stories was clear: Al Gore was a lying politician who will do anything to get elected—a theme echoed by the Bush-Cheney campaign.

In contrast, Bush's proposals were not only treated straight, as they should be, in straight news stories. He was often given the benefit of the doubt on subjects where he could be vulnerable.

When the *Columbia Journalism Review* article was published, there was a strong reaction among journalists and media critics. The ombudsman of the *Washington Post* wrote an article agreeing with the criticisms in the article. "*Post* editors will deny that they have a mission to promote or destroy any candidacy in the news pages, but the analyses in *CJR*—and readers' complaints—should convince them that the question of fairness needs to be taken even more seriously story by story, page by page," ombudsman E. R. Shipp wrote.[74]

Quoting from the *Post's* own stated commitment to fairness, Shipp added, "While arguments about objectivity are endless, the concept of fairness is something that editors and reporters can easily understand and pursue. . . . No story is fair if it omits facts or major importance or significance. No story is fair if it includes essentially irrelevant information at the expense of significant facts. . . . No story is fair if reporters hide their biases or emotions behind such subtly pejorative words as 'refused,' 'despite,' 'quietly,' 'admit' and 'massive.' Fairness requires straightforwardness ahead of flashiness."[75]

Researchers at the Pew Research Center also noticed a seeming discrepancy in the coverage, and they published an extensive survey of coverage of Gore and Bush that confirmed the conclusions from *Columbia Journalism Review* about coverage of Gore and Bush.

The study by the Pew Research Center and the Project for Excellence in Journalism underscores this.[76] Examining 2,400 newspaper, TV, and Internet stories in five different weeks between February and June, researchers found that a whopping 76 percent of the coverage included one of two themes: that Gore lies and exaggerates or is marred by scandal. The most common theme about Bush, the study found, is that he is a "different kind of Republican."

The survey (which included editorials and news stories) focused on the *Washington Post*, the *New York Times*, the *Boston Globe*, the *Atlanta Journal-Constitution*, the *Indianapolis Star*, the *San Francisco Chronicle*, and the *Seattle Times*. It also included the evening newscasts of the major broadcast networks and talk shows such as *Hardball*, which alone accounted for 17 percent of the negative characterizations about scandal.[77]

Many cable talk shows were, as the Pew study found, extremely negative in their characterization of Gore. The evening newscasts on ABC, CBS, and NBC, on the other hand, appeared to play it straighter.[78]

Overall, the Pew researchers wrote, "The press has been far more likely to convey that Bush is a different kind of Republican—a compassionate conservative/a reformer, bipartisan—than to discuss Al Gore's themes of experience, knowledge, or readiness for the office."[79]

Comparing the sourcing on stories, the Pew researchers found something that also was evident in the research for *Columbia Journalism Review*: "Journalists' assertions about Bush's character were more than twice as likely than Gore's to be unsupported by any evidence. In other words, they were pure opinion, rather than journalistic analysis."[80]

Access Counts

Gore likely suffered from what some journalists readily called at the time "Clinton fatigue," his association with Bill and Hillary Clinton as Clinton's vice president and reporters' years of covering the Clintons. Gore also appeared to be struggling with the way he presented himself as a candidate, and he handed his critics ammunition with a wardrobe makeover and the hiring of an "alpha male" expert to make him look stronger. More seriously, Gore used Clintonian legalisms such as "no controlling legal authority" to say that he had done nothing illegal in making some fundraising calls for Democrats from the White House during his years as Bill Clinton's vice president.

One of the possible reasons for the differences on reporting on Bush and Gore is understandable—but also disturbing in terms of fair coverage: access. After he defeated Sen. John McCain for the nomination, Bush took a page from McCain's strategy of wide-open accessibility to the media for his maverick campaign, on a bus called the "Straight-Talk Express." Frank Bruni, who was covering Bush for the *New York Times*, wrote at the time that Bush "not only slaps reporters' backs but also rubs the tops of their heads and, in a few instances, pinches their cheeks. It is the tactile equivalent of the nicknames he doles out to many of them and belongs to a teasing style of interpersonal relationships that undoubtedly harks back to his fraternity days."[81]

In a front-page article in the *Washington Post* headlined "Chatter at 40,000 Feet: Next to Bush, a First-Class Schmoozer, Gore's in Coach," media reporter Howard Kurtz observed, "Bush makes the reporters feel that they each have a personal relationship with him."[82] Noting Gore's stiff style and lack of access, with only a handful of press conferences in the previous three months, Kurtz offered a possible explanation for the way the two candidates have been covered: "Most reporters insist their daily coverage is not influenced by whether a candidate is friendly or distant. But these sharply divergent views of the presidential contenders from the rear of their campaign planes help explain why Bush is consistently portrayed as relaxed and confident and Gore as someone who often fails to connect with people."[83]

Even as the coverage on Bush turned somewhat more skeptical with the Republican convention, a *Time* magazine cover story, titled "Republican Convention: The Quiet Dynasty," contained the following: "By every appearance, they lack the Roosevelts' intensity or the Kennedys' unembarrassed ambition. Yet they are poised to surpass them all. Theirs is the Quiet Dynasty. . . . The Bush code is not really about power; it is about winning and achieving, doing your best, better than the other guy. . . ."[84]

Bias toward Objectivity in Journalism

As analysts of media and politics, it is important to know that the idea of objectivity in journalism is a relatively new concept in American media history. American publications from colonial times forward had been openly partisan, and the idea of "just the facts" journalism arose in part through the invention of the telegraph and the creation of the Associated Press wire service, where "straight news" reporting that did not favor one side or the other was seen as having commercial value. As Michael Schudson wrote in *Discovering the News*, the rise of the *New York Times* in the 1890s in an era of tabloid journalism "took the path to factuality" and journalism as information rather than "journalism as entertainment."[85]

In recent years many critics, including journalists themselves, have pointed out the flaws in the idea of on-the-one-hand and on-the-other-hand journalism, calling out what author Brent Cunningham dubbed "the cult of objectivity"[86] as producing stories that give false equivalence and false balance on an issue where the two sides are not of equal weight factually or where there are multiple sides to a story. In the case of climate change, journalists and talk-show bookers gave equal weight to climate change deniers and climate-change-is-real speakers for many years while the preponderance of scientists and scientific opinion was heavily weighted among scientists that climate change was a real threat in need of real measures to deal with it.

In *The Elements of Journalism*, a widely read response to a "crisis of conscience, confidence and purpose" in journalism and public trust, Bill Kovach and Tom Rosenstiel laid out what they saw as several enduring values for doing journalism, the first of which was that journalism should serve the public interest. They contended that the idea of objectivity has been confused between the *method* of reporting and the *person* doing the reporting. Instead, they and other journalists said that what is most important is for reporters to be accurate, fair, and complete as possible,[87] providing what Watergate-era *Washington Post* editor Ben Bradlee called "the best obtainable version of the truth" at the time.[88] Rather than simply reporting what people say and calling that objective, Kovach and Rosenstiel argued, journalists need to be not stenographers but independent verifiers of information on behalf of the public.[89]

The conventions of objective journalism and respect for authority have made journalists reluctant to call the president of the U.S. or other high-ranking officials a liar, a convention that some media critics have said leads to false objectivity and balance, with journalists not fulfilling their role as independent watchdogs for the public. The presidency of Donald Trump presented the news media with tremendous challenges, including a debate among journalists about whether this was a time for journalists to inject more outright opinion and analysis in their stories—or whether there was more of a need for journalists to double down on the idea of providing a common set of facts, dispassionately reported. With President Trump giving voice to conspiracy theories and discredited false claims from Internet sites on his Twitter account, journalists at major news organizations from the *New York Times* to CNN began to characterize some of Trump's statements in real time as falsehoods, escalating what President Trump on his first day in office called his "running war with the media."[90] We will discuss the debate among journalists over responding to the president's attacks on the media in the next chapter.

Case Study: Climate Change and "False Equivalence" in Reporting

The depiction of the dangers of climate change and the need for policies to address it is an important case study in how unacknowledged corporate funding of on-air "climate skeptics," combined with the traditional convention of on-the-one-hand and on-the-other-hand reporting (getting "both sides" of the story) helped lead to confusion and delay in the U.S. in dealing with what is now recognized as one of the world's most pressing global concerns. Scientists have been warning for more than twenty years about the potentially disastrous impact of global warming, a recent rise in the earth's temperature due to greenhouse gas emissions.[91] A stark report in 2014 from the Intergovernmental Panel on Climate Change, a United Nations panel of scientists from around the world who periodically review climate science, shows that—as the *New York Times* reporter covering the report summarized—"decades of foot-dragging by political leaders had propelled humanity into a critical situation," with greenhouse emissions rising faster than ever, ice caps melting, water and food supplies coming under stress, heat waves and heavy rains intensifying, rising ocean waters endangering coastal communities and species migrating "or in some cases going extinct."[92]

The only good news, said the UN panel, which had issued less dire reports in the past, was that there appeared to be more political will globally today to deal with the problem. But, they warned, decisive action to reduce pollution and curb global warming must be taken within the next fifteen years—or risk unknown costs and catastrophes.[93] "We cannot afford to lose

(*Continued*)

(Continued)

another decade," said Ottmar Edenhofer, a German economist who was cochairman of the committee.[94]

Climate scientists for many years have had an overwhelming consensus—97 percent or more, according to numerous surveys and reviews of academic literature—that global warming is happening and has been caused by man-made pollution from greenhouse gas emissions.[95] Yet, while global climate change was the top-rated threat (above international financial stability and Islamic extremist groups) in the Pew Research Center's 2013 annual survey of *global* public opinion in thirty-nine countries,[96] in a second, *U.S.-based* survey conducted by Pew during the 2013 government shutdown of Congress, regarding what Americans wanted Congress and the president to prioritize, a slight majority of Americans (52 percent) named protecting the environment as a top priority, with only 28 percent naming global warming as a top priority, well below strengthening the economy (86 percent) and improving the job situation (79) percent.[97] Environmental legislation has often been portrayed by opponents as hurting the economy and jobs, and the Pew researchers and others in the past have found a consistent partisan split on the environment and global warming as priorities, with more Democrats than Republicans listing the two issues higher as concerns.[98]

The Yale Program on Climate Change Communication has found what they call widespread, persistent misunderstanding of the scientific consensus on the man-made causes of global warming among Americans. In 2013, according to a national survey conducted by the Yale researchers, "only 42 percent of American adults said that 'most scientists think global warming is happening,' 33 percent said 'there is a lot of disagreement among scientists about whether global warming is happening,' 20 percent said they 'don't know enough to say,' and 6 percent said 'most scientists think global warming is not happening.'"[99]

Asked to estimate what proportion of climate scientists are convinced that human-caused climate change is happening, only 22 percent of Americans correctly guessed (among choices) that the percentage was 81 to 100 percent.[100] Anthony Leiserowitz, the director of the Yale project, and his colleagues who coauthored an analysis of their findings, wrote, "This misunderstanding among Americans is not only pervasive—it is highly consequential," with people who don't understand the scientific consensus "less likely to believe that climate change is happening, [is] human-caused, will have serious consequences and . . . can be mitigated through concerted action."[101] The pervasiveness of this attitude, the Yale authors contended, was "not an accident" but was, instead the result of a "disinformation campaign" by organizations and corporations who opposed government action to reduce carbon emissions.[102]

False Objectivity

In an analysis of news stories about global warming published in the *New York Times*, *Los Angeles Times*, *Washington Post*, and *Wall Street Journal* between 1988 and 2002, Jules Boykoff and Maxwell Boykoff found that what has been called *false objectivity*—or "he said/she said" reporting—had greatly amplified the voices of a small group of global warming skeptics, many of them funded by carbon-based industry interests, pitting what "some scientists believe," to cite one story, against "skeptics contend," and seemingly giving equal weight to both views. "When it comes to U.S. media coverage of global warming," they wrote, "superficial balance—telling 'both' sides of the story"—without verifying the claims or indicating which side was more representative of scientific consensus—"can actually be a form of informational bias."[103]

With more evidence of the impacts of global warming and climate change as well as more scientific associations taking a public stance, the "consensus" narrative began to emerge more strongly in coverage of climate change, including in several of the major newspapers studied by Maxwell Boykoff, with an increase in reporting scientists' consensus.[104] But confusion among the public remained—and among the three cable news networks, there have been significant differences in coverage. A content analysis in 2007 and 2008 of coverage on CNN, MSNBC, and Fox News Channel by communication scholar Lauren Feldman and colleagues found that Fox News Channel "takes a more dismissive tone toward climate change than CNN and MSNBC" and "also interviews a greater ratio of climate-change doubters to believers."[105]

Subsequent studies have found that this trend has continued to today—and that Fox News Channel guests and hosts also are more alarmist about what they say would be a disastrous cost to the economy to dealing with global warming. Analyzing data from survey data from a representative sample of U.S. adults, Feldman found a strong correlation between Republicans viewing Fox News Channel and their acceptance of global warming—much stronger than a correlation between Democrats watching Fox News

(Continued)

(Continued)

Channel or CNN and their acceptance of global warming. "I don't believe that this global-warming nonsense is real," prime-time Fox News Channel host Sean Hannity said in one typical remark on his show in 2013.[106] When the 2014 UN report was released, Bill O'Reilly accused climate change activists of wanting to "destroy [the] economy or allow villains like Putin to blackmail with his fossil fuels."[107]

Funding for Messaging on Climate Change

National environmental groups spent considerable funds on general messaging about the environment, and many lobbied for "cap-and-trade" proposals, defeated in Congress in 2010, to have corporations "trade" carbon emissions. But industry groups and corporations representing the fossil fuel industry outspent environmentalists for many years, supporting candidates, lobbying, and spreading a message of climate change skepticism and concerns about government regulation. In a report titled "Pro-Environment Groups Outmatched, Outspent in Battle over Climate-Change Legislation," the Center for Responsive Politics, the nonpartisan group that analyzes Federal Election Commission data in reports on money in politics, noted that even when environmental groups spent a record $22.4 million on federal lobbying efforts in support of cap-and-trade legislation (which was not universally supported by environment groups), the oil and gas industry "unleased a fury of lobbying expenditures" at the same time, spending $175 million—"easily an industry record"—and outpacing the environmental groups' contributions by a margin of nearly eight to one.[108] The oil and gas industry has continued to be among the top contributors, primarily to Republican candidates, according to the Center for Responsive Politics.[109]

Funding Climate Skeptics

In 2007 a report by the Union of Concerned Scientists reported that ExxonMobil, a staunch opponent of climate change regulations, had given at least $16 million between 1998 and 2005 to a network of more than forty think tanks and advocacy groups that cast doubt about the science and seriousness of climate change and its causes.[110] Comparing the oil company's efforts to Big Tobacco companies' successful campaign to deny links between smoking and cancer, the authors of the report found that Exxon-Mobil had given sizable donations to both well-known conservative think tanks and to lesser-known groups, representing more than 10 percent of many group's budgets, according to a *New York Times* analysis.[111]

In opinion pieces, TV debates, and print interviews, spokespeople who were often called "climate-change skeptics" have actually been part of think tanks that received significant funding from Koch Industries and Exxon-Mobil, although they were rarely identified in terms of their funding, and think tank titles are rarely informative. "The network ExxonMobil created masqueraded as a credible scientific alternative," the 2007 report said, "but it publicized discredited studies and cherry-picked information to present misleading conclusions."[112]

A 2013 study by environmental sociologist Robert Brulle and others subsequently have found funding to deny climate change continuing.[113] At the same time, some scientists who took a strong stance regarding their belief in climate change found themselves and their science attacked while, in general, rather than having a scientific discussion about climate change, most TV media outlets at the time had political opponents debating the subject.[114]

In 2015, a federal government assessment of the effects of climate change, based on a study by experts from the government and academia around the U.S., found that every region of the country was being affected by climate change, from drought and wildfires to rising sea levels and flooding.[115] "For a long time, we have perceived climate change as an issue that's distant, affecting just polar bears or something that matters to our kids," Katharine Hayhoe, a Texas Tech professor and coauthor of the U.S. report, told the *Washington Post*. "This shows it's not just in the future; it matters today."[116]

Where Do We Go from Here?

The Need for Greater Diversity in Media

Major media organizations overall do not reflect the diversity of the country, especially in terms of management and high-profile positions, although that has been changing in recent years with a greater focus on recruitment and retention. According to the 2018 annual survey of local TV newsrooms by the Radio Television Digital News Association and Hofstra University, "the percentage of women and people of color in TV newsrooms and in TV news management [were] at the highest levels ever measured" by the survey, with the percentage of people of color in local TV news rising to 24.8 percent in 2017. Yet, as the authors of the report acknowledged, "still, the bigger picture remains unchanged," with the percentage of people of color rising 12.4 points in the U.S. overall, to 38.8 percent, in the previous twenty-eight years while the percentage in TV newsrooms rose 7 percent, to 24.8 percent. Nearly half of the people (44 percent) in local TV newsrooms in 2017 were women, and the percentage of women holding the top local news job—news director—was 34.3 percent for women overall and 14.3 percent for people of color (not counting the news directors at Spanish-language TV stations).[117]

In daily newspapers, the 2018 annual survey of newsrooms by the American Society of News Editors found increased diversity despite a net loss of several hundred jobs. "In 2018, people of color comprised 22.6 percent of employees reported by all newsrooms in our survey, compared to 16.5 percent in 2017," the author of the 2018 report wrote. "Among daily newspapers, about 22.2 percent of employees were racial minorities (compared to 16.3 percent in 2017), and 25.6 percent of employees at online-only news websites were minorities (compared to 24.3 percent in 2017)."[118] These statistics are important, both in terms of the value of better representation—and better journalism—that can come from reflecting and reporting on a more diverse country.[119] We will discuss this further in subsequent chapters on gender and race in the media and in politics.

These anchor-host roles in TV are symbolic of authority and power. With the exceptions of CNN's Candy Crowley and Christiane Amanpour, who briefly hosted ABC's Sunday show *This Week*, the influential D.C.-based Sunday morning talk shows have largely been hosted by white men until very recently; and women—and men—of color have been particularly underrepresented as hosts on broadcast TV and cable TV networks. In 2019 Margaret Brennan, CBS's White House correspondent, was named host of CBS's long-running *Face the Nation* Sunday show. It was not until 2008 that Katie Couric became the first woman to be solo anchor of a nightly broadcast evening newscast,[120] and not until 2013 that Judy Woodruff and the late Gwen Ifill, a pioneering African American journalist, became the first two women to coanchor a nightly broadcast TV newscast, *The PBS NewsHour*, on the Public Broadcasting Service (PBS).[121] And it was 2018 before CBS News named its first female president, longtime CBS News producer Susan Zirinsky.

Trust and Accountability in the Media

In the fall of 2018, the Gallup polling organization released a poll that showed Americans' trust and confidence in the mass media "to report the news fully, accurately and fairly" was "continuing to recover" from 2016, when it had fallen to its lowest level since at least 1972, when Gallup began asking the question. Asked this question—"In general, how much trust and confidence do you have in the mass media—such as newspapers, TV and radio—when it comes to reporting the news fully, accurately and fairly—a great deal, a fair amount, not very much or none at all," 45 percent of Americans in 2018 said they had a great deal or fair amount of trust in the media to report the news fully, fairly, and accurately, up from only 32 percent of respondents in 2016. (Americans' confidence in the media, as expressed in the Gallup poll, was at its highest—at 72 percent—in 1976, following the Watergate investigation and reporting on the Vietnam War, and stayed "in the low to mid-50s through the late 1990s and into the early years of the new century," Gallup noted, but has been declining slowly over the past decade.[122] From 2015 to 2016 trust in the media had declined among respondents who identified themselves as Democrats, with Democrats' trust dropping to 51 percent from 55 percent the previous year.

But it was a precipitous drop in trust that was especially striking: Republicans reporting a "great deal" or a "fair amount" of trust in the media plummeted, from 32 percent in 2015 to only 14 percent in 2016. At that time, the Gallup researchers speculated that the sharp year-to-year decline among Republicans might be attributable in part to the 2016 election, criticisms of media coverage from Republican leaders and conservative pundits, and Donald Trump's "sharp criticism of the press."[123] By 2018, Gallup found that "media trust is now the highest it has been since 2009," with increased trust among Republicans as well as Democrats and independents since 2016 but a continued discrepancy among these groups, with trust among Democrats surging to 76 percent, the highest since 1997, independents' trust rising to 42 percent, their highest level since 2005—and Republicans at only 21 percent of respondents, up from 14 percent in 2016.[124] (When Gallup asked the same question in 1972, 68 percent of Americans said they trusted the media.[125))

In addition to this continuing partisan split, which found Republicans "agreeing with [Donald Trump's] assertions that the media unfairly covers his administration, while Democrats may see the media as the institution primarily checking the president's power," the Gallup researchers wrote, they also found a new trend among an age group that traditionally leans liberal: eighteen-to-twenty-nine-year-olds. Whereas 53 percent of those sixty-five and older trust in the media, just 33 percent of those under thirty did, in the 2018 survey. "Younger adults have come of an age marked by partisan media and fake news," the Gallup report said, "while older Americans' trust may have been established long ago in an era of widely read daily newspapers and trusted television news anchors."[126]

In a 2014 survey about political polarization and media habits, the Pew Research Center had begun to pick up differences among media outlets in terms of viewers' ideology and a more intense loyalty to Fox News

Channel as a single source of news among many conservatives. "Overall, when respondents were asked what outlet they turn to most often for news about government and politics, the most frequent mentions are two cable networks: CNN (named by 16%) and Fox News (14%)," the Pew researchers wrote. "But wide ideological differences exist both in the sources that top the list for those among readers and viewers on the left and on the right and in the degree to which there is reliance on a single source".

Those with consistently conservative political values were oriented around a single news outlet—Fox News—to a much greater degree than those in any other ideological group" with about half (47 percent) of those who are consistently conservative naming Fox News Channel as their main source for news about government and politics, 11 percent naming local TV news, and "no single outlet" predominating "on the left of the political spectrum," with 15 percent for CNN and 10 percent for the New York Times. Respondents with a roughly equal mix of liberal and conservative views also had "a diffuse mix of news providers," with CNN (20 percent) and local TV news (16 percent) the most frequently mentioned followed by a long list of other sources and mentioned and by fewer than one in ten people.[127]

Overall, the Pew researchers found more trust than distrust of the media, with at least 50 percent of respondents answering when asked that they trusted CNN, ABC News, and NBC News. But, while about two-thirds of those with consistently liberal views said they trusted these networks, there was a stark ideological divide in trust and loyalty among conservatives toward Fox News Channel: "Among those with mostly conservative values, Fox is the only source trusted by a majority (72%). And among those who are consistently conservative, nearly nine-in-ten (88%) trust it as a source—by far the highest level of trust of any ideological group of any single source."[128]

Conservative and right-wing critics of the news media as well as Republican politicians appear to have been much more successful so far than left-wing critics of the media at convincing many people that there is bias in the media against their point of view—in part perhaps because of the content and loyalty of viewers to Fox News Channel as their one exclusive news source.

Excoriating the news media as liberal in segments that cherry-picked and often misreported on the reporting has been a daily drumbeat on Fox News Channel since Roger Ailes and Rupert Murdoch founded Fox News Channel in 1996.[129] Roger Ailes' slogan of "fair and balanced" for Fox News Channel was a brilliant signal to communicate to viewers, especially those outside the media capitals of New York and Washington, that the elitist media were *not* fair and balanced but were, in fact, according to Ailes, liberal, elitist, and not balanced. Ailes, a former Republican strategist and talk-show producer, had taught candidate Richard Nixon how to use television in 1968 and was linked to the infamous, racist "Willie Horton" ads against Michael Dukakis on behalf of George H. W. Bush in 1988.[130]

The pugilistic network that Ailes created has given a powerful platform, disproportionately, to Republican Party talking points, Republican candidates, including, of course, Donald Trump, as numerous analyses have shown, on its highly rated prime-time shows. Donald Trump's unprecedented attacks on the *New York Times*, *Washington Post*, CNN, and other major news organizations as "fake news," "failing," and even—ominously—"enemy of the people," coupled with the president's personal media channel on Twitter, clearly has had an impact among his supporters. While certainly not the only force in political polarization today, Fox News Channel has had real impact on the tone of political discourse as, per Ailes' directives, Fox News Channel over the past several years has emphasized repeated, negative characterizations of Democrats, government bureaucrats, and their alleged abettors—the "liberal media."[131]

It is difficult to imagine the success of Donald Trump without, first, Roger Ailes' successful vision for Fox News Channel.[132] Before Donald Trump convinced many voters that he was their champion in the Washington, D.C., "swamp" and the "fake media" were out to get him, Roger Ailes and Fox News Channel had convinced millions of viewers who felt they weren't being heard in the media that Fox News Channel was their "corner man" in the boxing ring, as Ailes put it in an early interview with the author,[133] and not only a needed conservative alternative but, for many, the *only* fair and credible source for news. Fox News Channel was the number one source for election news among voters in the 2016 presidential campaign and remained the most-watched cable news network during the 2020 presidential campaign.

Building Trust and Accountability

Declining—and partisan—trust or mistrust in the news media did not begin with Donald Trump, and some media ethics groups as well as news organizations are looking at public opinion—and possible ways to improve trust, including through greater transparency about news-gathering, Indira Lakshmanan, the former chair of journalism ethics for the Poynter Institute, said, "I personally trace this back to the 1980s with the end of the Fairness Doctrine [which required equal time for political candidates to respond to attacks from their opponents on TV] and the deregulation of the media by the FCC [Federal Communications Commission], which led to the rise of talk radio and Fox News on cable, where you suddenly had a whole ecosystem saying, 'They're not telling you the truth—we're the only ones telling you the truth; make us your sole source of news.'"[134]

To dig more deeply into trust and news consumption habits, Poynter commissioned three political scientists to create a national survey.[135] "What they found was stunning," Lakshmanan said. "Almost half of [the respondents] believe that the media fabricate stories about Donald Trump more than once in a while. . . . One third agreed with Donald Trump's claim that the media are the 'enemy of the people,' and . . . here's the scariest of all, one in four Americans surveyed endorsed limits on press freedom such as allowing the government to block stories it doesn't like."[136]

One year later, however, coauthors Jason Reifler of the University of Exeter in the United Kingdom, Brendan Nyhan of the University of Michigan, and Andrew Guess of Princeton found that "trust in all forms of news media across the political spectrum" had risen since the 2017 survey, "suggesting that the president's attempts to discredit the news may be having less effect a year and a half into his presidency."[137] Fifty-four percent of respondents "expressed 'a great deal' or 'fair amount' of trust" in 2018, compared to 49 percent eight months earlier. And, while a partisan gap remained, trust was also up among Republicans.[138] These results suggested that there might be a boomerang effect to Trump's attacks, although they continued and were even stepped up, as were the attacks on mainstream media on Fox News Channel, portraying journalists as dangerous, lying, and in league with the Democrats, on Fox News Channel, through the coronavirus pandemic and the 2020 presidential election.

Future Directions and Tips

Questions of bias, trust, and accountability are issues that will continue to be raised in media—and in politics. It is difficult to imagine an equal counterweight in the media to the drumbeat and power of Fox News Channel, although, of course, Sean Hannity, Tucker Carlson, Laura Ingraham, and conservative critics of the news media would likely counter, falsely, that they're outgunned in a liberal media system. In their commentary and their punditry as well as their reporting, news organizations do need to get out more from their geographic and cultural bubbles to reflect and represent a greater diversity of voices. News organizations need to do a better job of telling the public how journalists work and responding to the concerns of their communities. "Accountability and transparency are critical," said Indira Lakshmanan. Especially in today's media climate, she said, "It's so important to be correct, to be factual. But if you make a mistake, admit it and explain why."[139]

The popularity of podcasts and other new media suggest that longer forms of media, delivered how and where people live, are appealing. The presidency of Donald Trump, in fact, produced some of the best policy journalism by major news organizations in many years. And as media critics Chris Hamby, Margaret Sullivan, and others have pointed out, whatever your views of her and her views, the popularity and social media engagement of Rep. Alexandria Ocasio-Cortez is about personality *and* policy—and TV viewers and the public are likely ready for livelier, responsible debate and voices than the bland one-from-column A and one-from-column B they're often seeing and hearing.

As consumers, analysts, and producers of media, read widely, including news and opinion you personally disagree with. Consider the source—and what sources are cited. (We'll talk about spotting fake news and disinformation on the Internet in the next chapter.) If you're doing reporting, look for stories, communities, and voices that aren't being reported; reach beyond officialdom and "the usual suspects." If you're analyzing the media, research thoroughly, in primary sources, the whole story or transcript—and many stories, transcripts, and tweets, looking for patterns, taking notes, and applying the concepts and frameworks we're discussing here. Try to see your own cultural and political biases—and how they affect what you read and see.

SUMMARY

The human need for news, the development of media technology, and the commercial nature of the American media system have led to operational and journalistic-cultural biases—conventions of news-gathering—that affect what stories get covered and how. The influence of television—particularly, cable TV—has led to an emphasis and increasing influence of punditizing over reporting, further blurring the lines between journalism and political strategists, reporter and advocate, for inside-the-Beltway analysis that prizes horse-race coverage over reporting on policy. Investigative reporting is being amplified, but it is also difficult for serious work about the processes of government and other important stories that don't make headlines to be noticed or to gain a foothold in today's media, talk-show environment. The credibility of the news media has been declining in recent years, with attacks on the news media as liberal a drumbeat for years on Fox News Channel before the heightened presidential, with attacks from Donald Trump. There is evidence in more recent polling that public confidence and support for the role of the news media has grown during the Trump administration, although a partisan divide remains.

The goal of this assignment is to let you in on some wonderful memoirs and other important books from politicians and political journalists that, perhaps because of the "churn" in our culture, may not be known to you. These books are revealing about politics and the media behind the scenes, and this assignment has been popular with the students in my class who have appreciated the description and recommendation of books they can choose, from the professor's bookcase. Pick a book to read from this approved list—no substitutions, first come, first served, and no more than two people in the class can read the same book. You may not write about a book you've already read, of course. To get your book, try your college library—and you can also order online.

Assignment Guidelines

Read your assigned book, and write a seven-to-eight-page (double-spaced) analysis of the book that includes your discussion and answers to the prompts and questions that appear in the following list. Answer the questions in order. Include a brief "works cited" page that lists whatever you consulted as part of your research; this page is *not* part of your seven-to-eight pages of text—it's an additional page. In addition to writing your paper, as with the ad analysis paper, you'll present a simple PowerPoint about your book and your analysis to your colleagues in class.

1. Read the book. You can look up a bit about it beforehand, but don't do too much of that—I want you to read the book with fresh eyes. Take notes on important and relevant quotes—and their page numbers.

2. What was your personal reaction to the book? What did you think of it as a reader? What impressed you or surprised you about it? Discuss.

3. In your opinion, what are some strengths and weaknesses of the book? For example, does it draw you in with great anecdotes? Is it well-written (or poorly written)—or somewhere in between?

4. Look up some reviews of the book *after* you have read it. These should be reviews by book reviewers assigned to write about the book for newspapers and magazines, not customer reviews on Amazon. Discuss

briefly how the book was received by book reviewers and political analysts/observers at the time, including whether the book was seen as factually accurate—or not. This will be particularly important if it's an autobiography by a politician.

5. What are the two most important insights, observations, or anecdotes in the book, in your opinion, as a student of politics and the media? To answer this question, you need to quote directly from the book, including the page numbers of the passage in your works-cited page from the book. Also reference as a journalist would, within your paper, as in "in the section on . . . the author talks about . . ."

Book List

- *Show Time: The American Political Circus and the Race for the White House* by Roger Simon

- *The Boys on the Bus* by Timothy Crouse

- *Cooking with Grease: Stirring the Pots in America* by Donna Brazile

- *All Too Human* by George Stephanopoulos

- *Big Girls Don't Cry: The Election That Changed Everything for American Women* by Rebecca Traister

- *Becoming* by Michelle Obama

- *Notes from the Cracked Ceiling: Hillary Clinton, Sarah Palin, and What It Will Take for Women to Win* by Anne Kornblut

- *Between the World and Me* by Ta-Nehisi Coates

- *All the King's Men* by Robert Penn Warren

- *Boiling Mad: Behind the Lines in Tea Party America* by Kate Zernike

- *All the President's Men* by Bob Woodward and Carl Bernstein

- *March: Book Three* by John Lewis, Andrew Aydin, and Nate Powell (illustrator)

- *Trump: the Art of the Deal* by Donald Trump with Tony Schwartz

- *What It Takes: The Way to the White House* by Richard Ben Cramer

- *Hillbilly Elegy: A Memoir of a Family and Culture in Crisis* by J. D. Vance

(Continued)

(Continued)

- *Personal History* by Katharine Graham

- *Culture Warrior* by Bill O'Reilly

- *The Loudest Voice in the Room: How the Brilliant, Bombastic Roger Ailes Built Fox News—and Divided a Country* by Gabriel Sherman

- *The Making of the President 1960* by Theodore H. White

- *One-Car Caravan: On the Road with the 2004 Democrats before America Tunes In* by Walter Shapiro

- *Front Row at the White House: My Life and Times* by Helen Thomas

- *The Fight in the Fields: Cesar Chavez and the Farmworkers Movement* by Susan Ferriss and Ricardo Sandoval

- *The Selfie Vote: Where Millennials Are Leading America (and How Republicans Can Keep Up)* by Kristen Soltis Anderson

- *The Highest Glass Ceiling: Women's Quest for the American Presidency* by Ellen Fitzpatrick

- *The World as It Is: A Memoir of the Obama White House* by Ben Rhodes

- *Walking with the Wind: A Memoir of the Movement* by John Lewis with Michael D'Orso

- *Down and Dirty: The Plot to Steal the Presidency* by Jake Tapper

- *Listen, Liberal: Or, What Ever Happened to the Party of the People?* by Thomas Frank

- *Master of the Senate: The Years of Lyndon Johnson* by Robert Caro

- *Shattered: Inside Hillary Clinton's Doomed Campaign* by Jonathan Allen and Amie Parnes

- *The Powers That Be* by David Halberstam

- *What It Takes: The Way to the White House* by Richard Ben Cramer

- *The Way Things Ought to Be* by Rush Limbaugh

- *Game Change: Obama and the Clintons, McCain and Palin, and the Race of a Lifetime* by John Heilemann and Mark Halperin

- *An American Life* by Ronald Reagan
- *Dark Money: The Hidden History of the Billionaires behind the Rise of the Radical Right* by Jane Mayer
- *Faith of My Fathers: A Family Memoir* by John McCain with Mark Salter
- *Off the Sidelines: Raise Your Voice, Change the World* by Kirsten Gillibrand
- *My Life on the Road* by Gloria Steinem
- *Waiting for Prime Time: The Women of Television News* by Marlene Sanders and Marcia Rock
- *Dreams from My Father: A Story of Race and Inheritance* by Barack Obama
- *My Life* by Bill Clinton
- *Living History* by Hillary Rodham Clinton
- *Dispatches from the Edge: A Memoir of War, Disasters, and Survival* by Anderson Cooper
- *My Beloved World* by Sonia Sotomayor
- *Breathing the Fire: Fighting to Survive, and Get Back to the Fight* by Kimberly Dozier
- *Hold on, Mr. President* by Sam Donaldson
- *Reading Lolita in Tehran: A Memoir in Books* by Azar Nafisi
- *And the Band Played On: Politics, People, and the AIDS Epidemic* by Randy Shilts
- *The Feminine Mystique* by Betty Friedan
- *Feeding the Beast: The White House versus the Press* by Kenneth Walsh
- *Spoken from the Heart* by Laura Bush
- *A Long Time Coming: The Inspiring, Combative 2008 Campaign and the Historic Election of Barack Obama* by Evan Thomas and the staff of *Newsweek*

(Continued)

(Continued)

- *Against All Enemies: Inside America's War on Terror* by Richard Clarke
- *Showdown: The Inside Story of How Obama Fought Back against Boehner, Cantor, and the Tea Party* by David Corn
- *Blinded by the Right: The Conscience of an Ex-Conservative* by David Brock
- *The Senator Next Door: A Memoir from the Heartland* by Amy Klobuchar
- *Shortest Way Home: One Mayor's Challenge and a Model for America's Future* by Pete Buttigieg
- *An American Son* by Marco Rubio
- *Promise Me, Dad: A Year of Hope, Hardship, and Purpose* by Joe Biden
- *A Time to Die* by Tom Wicker
- *A Very Stable Genius: Donald J. Trump's Testing of America* by Philip Rucker and Carol Leonnig
- *American Carnage: On the Front Lines of the Republican Civil War and the Rise of President Trump* by Tim Alberta

* * * * * * * * * * * * * * * * * *

5

Politicians, the Media, and Social Media

The Push-Pull Relationship

The relationship between politicians and journalists is a push-pull: Politicians want to control the message as much as possible so that they and their policies are depicted favorably; journalists want unfettered access to information and unscripted moments with politicians and government officials so they can tell the public the story. With the growth of public relations and a proliferation of news outlets, the interactions between the president and the White House press corps have become more stage-managed in recent years, as have party conventions and national campaigns—and that leads to cynicism among journalists and the public about these events. Ronald Reagan and his advisers used Reagan's communications skills so well that he was dubbed "The Great Communicator" and the "Teflon president," earning coverage, especially on TV, that was criticized as uncritical and adding stagecraft and public relations techniques that have been used by every president since.

At the same time that the presidency has grown in power compared to Congress, the increased polarization in politics and in media, coupled with the high cost of running for office, has led to dysfunction in Congress, with more one-party votes and less cooperation between Democrats and Republicans.

This chapter looks at the presidency and the media—from Reagan to today. We will look at how Donald Trump went from being spurned by Republican Party leaders to being embraced by them and staging what was described as a "hostile takeover" of the GOP through the coronavirus pandemic and the 2020 election. We'll hear from senators from both major political parties discussing how constant fundraising pressures, along with political polarization and partisanship, have led to gridlock on issues on which the general public has had some consensus. We'll hear from journalists about covering President Trump, Congress, and the 2016 and 2020 presidential campaigns. And we will talk about the continuing impact of "Trumpism" on politics and political discourse beyond the 2020 election.

Campaigns today use direct mail, internal polling, focus groups, data analytics, microtargeting of messages online, and outreach through social media to try to find, target, and persuade voters. Facebook, Twitter, and

YouTube allow candidates and elected officials to speak directly to voters and the public overall, putting out campaign videos or video position papers at little or no cost and bypassing what politicians and political strategists call "the media filter" of being interviewed by journalists while also saving on the costs for paid advertising in mass media. The Internet has also proven to be a remarkable tool for fundraising and political organizing not only for candidates but also for social movements.

At the same, time the Internet and social media are also disruptive new forces in politics and the media that challenge the political and media systems, from charges of "fake news" to disinformation campaigns, internally and from Russia and other foreign actors, in attempts to heighten divisions and undermine credibility in U.S. elections. We'll look at the role of social media here—and we'll talk also about a humorous but important entertainment force in media and politics: late-night comedy and popular TV series depicting politicians and journalists.

Congress: Divided and Gridlocked

Senator Susan Collins on congressional gridlock

Maine senator Susan Collins, a self-described moderate Republican, has been known for her independence and her record of reaching across the aisle to Democrats to work on legislation. The daughter of a mother and a father who each had been the mayor of Caribou, Maine, in a family that included several generations of state legislators,[1] Collins had been rated almost equally "liberal" and "conservative" in her votes in congressional rankings by the *National Journal* in 2013.[2] Collins, a pro-choice Republican, in 2017[3] was one of the influential Republicans whose announced opposition to Republican plans to "repeal and replace" the Affordable Care Act led to an embarrassing defeat for Republicans in the Senate.[4] Collins and Alaska senator Lisa Murkowski, who, along with John McCain, voted against repealing Obamacare, were targeted online as "traitorous Republicans" (and worse) in misogynistic attacks.[5]

And Collins was criticized by conservative GOP members and groups for her votes siding with the Obama administration, which she did more than 70 percent of the time, according to a CQ Roll Call analysis.[6]

The Maine senator dramatically announced that she would not be voting for Trump for president in 2016, writing in an op-ed, "My conclusion about Mr. Trump's unsuitability for office is based on his disregard for the precept of treating others with respect, an idea that should transcend politics."[7]

She joined five other Republicans in opposing President Trump's temporary travel ban on immigration from seven Muslim-majority countries[8] and opposed the administration on other policies. But she voted with the Trump administration 87 percent of the time in 2017, according to a CNN analysis, which, in increasingly one-party partisan votes in Congress, still made her the Republican most likely to vote with Democrats.[9] In 2020 Collins was targeted by Democrats nationally for defeat after twenty-four years in the Senate after her vote to approve Trump's nomination of Judge Brett Kavanaugh to the Supreme Court and her vote to acquit Trump in the Senate impeachment trial.[10] Collins prevailed against her Democratic challenger in the 2020 election.

Speaking to an audience of college students in 2016, Collins lamented what she described as hyperpartisanship and gridlock in Congress.[11] She cited gerrymandering of districts (with the party in power drawing "safe" districts for their party when they control the state legislature), voluntary "residential sorting" leading to isolation of voters along liberal/conservative rural/urban lines, along with a decline in civil discourse, as contributing factors.[12] She was not alone in her concern. In an article for *Esquire* magazine in 2014, author Mark Warren interviewed ninety members of the House and Senate and found almost all of them—across a broad spectrum of backgrounds and beliefs—expressing discouragement and dismay about their ability to do what they were elected to do.[13]

"We can do better than this," said Sen. John McCain, who dramatically cast the deciding vote in the Senate on a House-passed bill to repeal Obamacare in 2017, shortly after McCain had been diagnosed with brain cancer. In a passionate speech on the Senate floor days before, the eighty-year-old McCain, who had served thirty-five years in the Senate, called for a return to the comity and compromise that, he said, despite disagreements had ruled Congress in the past.[14] "Our deliberations can still be important and useful, but I think we all agree they haven't been overburdened by greatness lately," McCain said. "And right now, they aren't producing much for the American people. . . . We're getting nothing done, my friends. We're getting nothing done."[15]

Gridlock Example: Impasse over Gun Control Legislation

In her talk with students in 2016, Senator Collins lamented the failure of Congress to pass gun control legislation despite public support for some bipartisan measures and multiple shootings as an example. "Every mass killing seems like a recurring nightmare," Collins told students, "like living in [the movie] *Groundhog Day*, where the same thing kept happening over and over again. Each failure by Congress to address this crisis is a replay of the hyperpartisanship that prevents progress."[16]

In the wake of the shootings of children and their teachers at Sandy Hook Elementary School in Connecticut in 2012, President Obama promised to make gun control a central part of his second term.[17] (The president had been criticized by some gun control advocates for not pushing more forcefully for gun control, a hotly contested issue, during his popular first term.[18])

Sen. Joe Manchin of West Virginia, a conservative Democrat with a high positive rating from the National Rifle Association (NRA), joined with Republican senator Pat Toomey of Pennsylvania in a bipartisan amendment to proposed legislation that would expand background checks on gun purchases at gun shows and on the Internet. The NRA, the powerful lobbying organization of gun manufacturers and gun owners, portrayed the legislation as a dangerous big-government intrusion that violated the Second Amendment and would not prevent gun violence. The bill—which needed sixty votes in the Senate to pass under recently passed Senate rules—was defeated by a 54–46 vote, with four GOP senators, including Collins, crossing party lines to support the measure, as five Democrats, mostly from red states where gun ownership is high, voting with forty-one Republicans.[19] Flanked by several families who had lost their children at Sandy Hook, a visibly angry Obama said after the vote that "it came down to politics—the worry that the vocal minority of gun owners would come after them in future elections . . . All in all, this was a pretty shameful day for Washington."[20]

The background check measure was defeated again in 2016, after the worst mass shooting to date on U.S. soil, at a gay nightclub in Orlando, Florida.[21] At that time, Collins and several other Republicans and Democrats introduced a measure to prevent people listed on the government's "no-fly" list for airplane passengers from purchasing a gun.[22] Manchin, who had described himself as a "law-abiding gun owner" and "card-carrying life member of the NRA,"[23] was vilified for his support of some gun safety legislation by the NRA,[24] which has spent multimillions in campaign contributions and ads for—and against—legislators and candidates over gun rights and gun control legislation.

In the 2016 presidential campaign, Hillary Clinton made gun violence and attacking the power of the NRA a focus of her campaign. Candidate Donald Trump won the enthusiastic endorsement of the NRA, saying at their convention, "Hillary Clinton wants to abolish the Second Amendment. . . . We're not going to allow that to happen."[25] As noted in Chapter 1, the NRA spent an estimated $21 million during the campaign in attack ads against Clinton, especially in swing states, saying she wanted to take away gun-ownership rights: charges she denied.[26]

The High Cost of Running for Office

The stakes involved in which party controls Congress, the presidency, and state legislatures and governorships has coupled with the flood of money allowed from super PACs, corporations, unions, and special interest groups since the *Citizens United* Supreme Court decision in 2010 to make running for office a hugely expensive—some would say obscenely expensive—proposition. "The recent growth of SuperPACS . . . illustrates the effects of a system that combines unlimited amounts of money with a limited number of ways to [legally] spend it," wrote Adam Sheingate, a political scientist who is the author of a book about the rise of political consulting in American democracy.[27] Although direct mail, data analytics, polling, social media, and digital advertising are all growing, television advertising remains the top expenditure of campaigns despite the fact that the results of TV ads are uncertain and many observers are worried that the tide of negative ads turns voters off not only to candidates but politics in general. Candidates today remain locked in a kind of mutually assured destruction, with increasingly expensive campaigns financed by outside groups spending in important races for negative, often misleading ads—and more ads seen as needed to match your opponent and break through the clutter.

Crunching the data in required filings to the Federal Election Commission (FEC), Sheingate found in December 2015 that Jeb Bush had spent $52.5 million, largely to political consultants for an onslaught of television advertising, making him first among Republican primary candidates in spending while he stood at 3 percent in the polls. Hillary Clinton by that time had spent $18.5 million on a variety of services, including polling, fundraising, television advertising, and digital and data analytics—and the election was a year away. Donald Trump was ninth among the Republican candidates in spending, at 39 percent in the polls as he benefited from millions of dollars of earned media (free media coverage and commentary) as opposed to advertising and other media the campaign pays for. But Trump's campaign eventually also spent on paid advertising, fundraising, and outreach, including data mining and microtargeting. See Figure 5.1.

Despite a candidate's, officeholder's, or consultant's wishes to run a positive campaign, the onslaught of money and the quest for a perceived small pool of undecided voters today has seen an increase in negative and misleading attack ads, during primaries and the general election,[28] from undisclosed groups that are designed to spark fear about an opponent, drive down his or her favorables, and even dampen the voters' enthusiasm for going to the polls.

Political consultants consistently rank the ability to raise money as a key factor in their appraisal of a candidate's viability, with related factors such as incumbency and name recognition also having major impact on who runs for office and who wins. Legislators are legally prohibited from making fundraising calls from their offices—but they can and do make fundraising calls from party call centers down the street in Washington, D.C., and state and local venues. Making phone calls to donors in support of candidates and determining which candidates should be funded from party coffers is an important part of the work of national party leaders and their national committees.

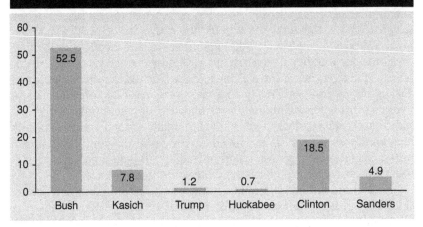

Figure 5.1   Spending on 2016 Presidential Campaign Consultants (Millions USD)

Source: Data from Federal Election Commission; CNN, and *The New York Times.* Data analysis by Adam Sheingate

Note: *Through September 30, 2015.

Once elected, members of Congress spend hours on the phone soliciting money for themselves and their party in what has become nonstop fundraising for nonstop campaigns. In a segment titled "Dialing for Dollars," CBS's *60 Minutes* in 2016 interviewed David Jolly, former Republican member of Congress (now an independent) about the pressures to fundraise, including for the national party.[29]

After winning a special election in 2014, Rep. Jolly said he sought the advice of national party leadership and was surprised by what he learned. "We sat behind closed doors at one of the party headquarter back rooms in front of a white board where the equation was drawn out," Jolly said. "You have six months until the election. Break that down to having to raise $2 million in the next six months. And your job, new member of Congress, is to raise $18,000 a day [not working in Congress] but by cold-calling a list that fund-raisers put in front of you. . . . It is a cult-like boiler room on Capitol Hill where members of Congress, frankly, are compromising the dignity of the office they hold by sitting in these sweatshop phone booths calling people asking them for money."[30]

David Boling, who ran unsuccessfully in a Democratic primary for Congress from Arkansas in 2010, related spending "70 percent to 80 percent" of his time "on the phone asking people for money," making some ninety calls in one day and being pushed by his campaign staff to shorten the calls to two minutes rather than talking longer. Although fundraising, he wrote, can be considered a measure of "hustle" (and popularity), it troubled him to think that to get elected to Congress (and then reelected) "under our current laws, one's skill at raising money has become more important than one's skill at mastering policy issues, giving a good old stemwinder or having a firm handshake. . . . Is this the kind of democracy that we really want?"[31]

Public Support for Limiting Campaign Spending

Several polls from Gallup and other organizations have found public support for setting limits on campaign fundraising after several years of a deluge of money post–*Citizens United* in 2010 and decisions by both Republican and Democratic Parties not to accept public financing in presidential elections in lieu of private money. In 2015, the *New York Times* reported that a *New York Times*/CBS News poll had found that "Americans of both parties fundamentally reject the regime of untrammeled money in elections made possible"—by *Citizens United* under a conservative majority on the Supreme Court and other court decisions—"and now favor a sweeping overhaul of how political campaigns are financed."[32] Eighty-four percent of respondents said that money has too much influence in elections. Three-quarters of self-identified Republicans in the poll supported "requiring more disclosure by outside spending organizations, which do not have to reveal the names of their donors."[33]

Most respondents in the *New York Times*/CBS News poll said that Democrats and Republicans both benefited equally from the current system. Yet, despite their views on the need for reform, a majority of those surveyed were pessimistic (as opposed to optimistic) about the prospects for change; and the *Times* reported that "virtually no one in the poll ranked campaign financing as the most important issue facing the country."[34] Finally, in a disconnect that likely was a factor in the appeal of both Bernie Sanders and Donald Trump in 2016, when asked this how wealth influences the election process, 75 percent said that wealthy Americans have more of a chance to influence the elections.[35]

Research by political scientists analyzing the congruence between what politicians do and what their constituents of differing economic backgrounds support has found that the public's perception today is correct: The wealthy do have more impact than the middle class and certainly much more than the poor in what Jacob S. Hacker and Paul Pierson in 2010 dubbed "Winner-Take-All Politics."[36] Reporting on their extensive research, Martin Gilens and Benjamin I. Page in 2014 wrote, "The central point that emerges from our research is that economic elites and organized groups representing business interests have substantial independent impacts on U.S. government policy, while mass-based interest groups and average citizens have little or no independent influence."[37]

All Politics Is No Longer Local

"Tip" O'Neill, the legendary House Speaker, many years ago famously said that "all politics is local," meaning that politicians ignore their local constituents at their peril. Today, as Tom Davis, a former House GOP chairman, wrote in *The Partisan Divide: Congress in Crisis*, a book coauthored by Martin Frost, former chair of the Democratic Congressional Campaign Committee, and Richard Cohen, "Two 'new normals' in electoral behavior have emerged over the past 20 years. The first is the tendency of the electorate to divide government between the parties. The second is the evolution of the American voters' thought from 'all politics is local' to 'all politics is national,' with less ticket-splitting and more straight-party behavior on the part of the electorate. Although these two tendencies may seem incongruent to the casual observer (straight-ticket voting equals divided government), they are indeed highly compatible and engrained in recent trends."[38]

As Davis, a former Virginia member of Congress, noted, he was the beneficiary of this trend in 1994 when he and dozens of other new Republicans were elected to the House of Representatives "as a protest to the leftward drift of the Democratic Party and the Clinton administration." From 1980 to 2014, he wrote, twenty-four of those thirty-six years "have seen divided government and only eight have witnessed one party controlling both the House and the Senate as well as the presidency." At the same time, Davis' coauthor Martin Frost maintained in a 2016 presentation with Davis about their book that "members of Congress today live in fear of being 'primaried,' challenged as not sufficiently ideological or partisan in a primary."[39]

Donald Trump and the Republican Party

In what more than one commentator described as Donald Trump's "hostile takeover" of the Republican party, one of the factors in Trump's success is that many in the Republican establishment and the media did not take him seriously in the beginning. "Trump is a master at marketing, and he was judged by a completely different standard," said Republican strategist Ana Navarro, a Nicaraguan American Republican strategist and CNN political commentator who was cochair of the Hispanic Advisory Council for John McCain in 2008 and supported Jeb Bush in 2016. Asked by the author what she thinks of Trump, Navarro responded,

"I feel about Donald Trump that he is a bigot, hostile, sexist bad human being who doesn't represent Republican values. . . . He has attacked Hispanics, immigrants, women. . . . He brings out the worst in us and preys on fear."[40]

After the Republican primaries in 2016, Sen. Marco Rubio asserted to CNN's Jake Tapper that "Donald Trump took one of the most important elections and turned it into a circus." Rubio added, "I think that all the gates of civility have been blown apart. We've now reached a point where everyone on both sides everyone is just saying or doing whatever they want, and you know, you can't just say or do whatever you want. This is not about political correctness. This is about rules of civility and the way a society talks to each other."[41]

Like many prominent Republicans, Rubio endorsed Trump for president, telling Jake Tapper that he had wrestled with the choice but decided to endorse the party's nominee.[42] When the *Washington Post* published the *Access Hollywood* videotape in which Trump boasted openly about groping women, Republican House Speaker Paul Ryan put out a statement that he was "sickened" by the tape and called off a planned joint appearance with Trump the next day.[43] Ryan opposed Trump's nomination but endorsed him, even though the House Speaker had also previously condemned Trump's remarks about an American-born judge of Mexican descent as "a textbook example of a racist comment."[44] Ryan, who had been Mitt Romney's vice presidential running mate in 2012, later worked with President Trump and congressional Republicans to pass a $1.5 trillion tax cut in 2017[45] before deciding not to run for reelection in 2018.

In his six hundred plus-page book *American Carnage: On the Front Lines of the Republican Civil War and the Rise of President Trump*, author Tim Alberta detailed how the leadership of the Republican Party and many prominent Republicans in Congress went from spurning Trump to embracing him. As Alberta noted, despite Trump's personal behavior, voters who identified themselves as evangelicals were an important voting bloc in 2016 for Trump, who promised to appoint "pro-life" judges, chose conservative evangelical Indiana governor Mike Pence as his running mate—and strongly backed the controversial appointment of Judge Brett Kavanaugh to the U.S. Supreme Court despite accusations of sexual assault against Kavanaugh years earlier by Professor Christine Blasey Ford. "I had no idea how important Supreme Court judges were to a voter," President Trump told Alberta in an interview for the book.[46]

"Evangelicals had been used over and over by Republicans," Tony Perkins, head of the conservative Family Research Council, told Alberta. "You could describe it as transactional. He wanted our votes, and he made promises that most Christian candidates would not make."[47]

Prominent Republicans from former president George W. Bush to John McCain ultimately spoke out against Trump's bullying and anti-immigrant rhetoric. But, for several Republican members of Congress who publicly opposed Trump, from Arizona senator Jeff Flake to Tennessee senator Bob Corker, the price for doing so in the face of his strong support from his base and his tweetstorms was steep. Both men decided not to run in 2018 after publicly criticizing Trump and incurring his wrath and anger from his supporters.

In a dramatic speech from the floor of the Senate in 2017, Flake announced that he would not be seeking reelection, where he faced an insurgent primary challenger from the right who was backed by Trump. Flake—who had supported Trump's judicial appointees and other parts of Trump's agenda[48]—declared in 2017 that he would "no longer be complicit or silent" in response to the personal attacks and "casual undermining of our democratic ideals" under Trump.[49]

In February 2020, before the coronavirus pandemic and economic collapse and in the midst of his impeachment trial in Congress, Trump's approval rating among Americans was 49 percent overall, his highest since taking office, according to Gallup polling.[50] His approval rating among Republicans was a stunning 94 percent, with the highest ever recorded gap—87 percentage points—ever measured by Gallup.[51]

In his book *The Great Alignment: Race, Party Transformation, and the Rise of Donald Trump*, political scientist Alan I. Abramowitz argued that "the deep partisan divide that exists among the politically engaged segment of the American public as well as among political elites and activists is, fundamentally, a disagreement over the dramatic changes that have transformed American society and culture since the end of World War II, and that continue to have huge effects in the twenty-first century."[52] The contemporary political landscape, he wrote, is marked by the following:

- A sharply polarized electorate

- Low-population rural (primarily Republican) districts numerically overrepresented in the Senate and the Electoral College while more diverse urban areas skew Democratic

- Nationalized, sub-presidential contests and "relatively small shifts in party allegiance or turnout [producing] different outcomes and dramatic swings in the direction of public policy"

Abramowitz added, "Perhaps the most important and potentially dangerous long-term consequence of the great alignment has been the increasing centrality of race and ethnicity in American politics."[53]

Supporters of the two major parties are increasingly divided by race and ethnicity and their "attitudes on race and ethnicity." Later national polling analysis released in 2017 showed that many white Republicans with incomes over $50,000 had voted for Trump in 2016.[54] But while scholars and journalists debated whether it was economic grievance or racial attitudes that predominated among Trump's base of white voters without a college degree in 2016, Abramowitz, like other scholars,[55] concluded that the two were connected and that "how these voters are faring seems to matter less in shaping their political attitudes than whom they blame for their problems."[56]

As we will discuss further in Chapter 6, on race and immigration in politics and media, Trump in 2020 doubled down on his appeal to grievance, anger, and racial resentment. Responding to the rise of protests by #BlackLivesMatter and others across the country in response to the videotaped death of George Floyd and other unarmed Black men and women by police officers, Trump portrayed himself as a "law-and-order" president, echoing Richard Nixon in 1968. Rather than "dog whistle" appeals to racism and demonizing "the Other," Trump used overtly racist language borrowed from segregationist governor George Wallace and an infamous southern sheriff in the 1960s, calling the protesters "thugs" and tweeting "when the looting starts, the shooting starts."[57]

"I don't know anyone who thinks this is the future of the Republican party," Jeff Flake said of his former congressional colleagues and Trump in an interview in 2020. "This is a demographic cul-de-sac . . . not a governing philosophy."[58]

Covering Congress versus Covering the Presidency

With recent presidents asserting the powers of the executive branch in what historian Arthur Schlesinger called "the imperial presidency,"[59] and with the compelling nature and power of a single occupant and the White House, recent presidents, in particular, have been the focus of tremendous media attention, compared to the 435 voting members of the House of Representatives and even many of the 100 U.S. senators. Political scientist Karen Kedrowski, analyzing media coverage of Congress, found that, beyond well-known party leaders, to gain media attention, members of Congress must be what she called "media entrepreneurs," interesting and quotable around an issue.[60]

The 2018 congressional midterm elections, congressional investigations and hearings, and the ultimate impeachment of president Trump in 2019 changed all that, of course, with historic conflict and compelling narratives. In the 2018 midterms, Democrats regained control of the House of Representatives, and a record number of women, including women of color, were elected. The "freshman class" photo of a newly diverse body on the steps of Congress was widely published, and news organizations rushed to interview and profile engaging newcomers including Alexandria Ocasio-Cortez, who at twenty-nine was the youngest person elected to Congress.

House Speaker Nancy Pelosi's challenges to President Trump and their relationship was widely covered and dissected, while Congress itself was divided between the Republican-controlled Senate under Senate majority leader Mitch McConnell and the Democratic-controlled House under Pelosi. The Democratic and Republican leadership, along with the chairs of important committees, drew enormous attention from the media for their battles with President Trump and with each other, from congressional hearings on Russian interference in the 2016 election to the confirmation of Judge Brett Kavanaugh to the U.S. Supreme Court and the impeachment of President Trump.

Ed O'Keefe, a political journalist for CBS News, has covered both Congress and the 2016 and 2020 presidential elections, and he says there are definite advantages to covering Congress, where the legislators are more accessible and there are many stories to be covered. "On any given day, you could go in seven different directions, from political coverage to slice-of-life stories on how the place works," O'Keefe said in an interview with the author. "You're covering immigration, health care and, now, of course, Congressional investigations. It all comes across their radar and thus across yours."[61]

The Presidency and the Media

American presidents and the White House press corps have always had a push-pull relationship between reporters' desire for access and information and presidents' and their advisers' desire for controlling the message. But since the Vietnam War and the Watergate scandal, there has been an erosion of confidence in the truthfulness of the government, on the part of journalists as well as the public.[62] That distrust in recent years has been met by the growth of public relations and increasingly sophisticated media relations operations—at the White House as well as other major institutions. At the same time, the growth of big media, the proliferation of news outlets, and the demands of a twenty-four-hour news cycle have added to the challenges for both journalists and media advisers to do their job: informing the public.

Ronald Reagan and George W. Bush

Relations between the president and the White House press corps have become much more stage-managed in recent years, and many observers say this evolution of "media management" began during Ronald Reagan's presidency. The telegenic Reagan was a former Hollywood actor with a gift for humor, and his staff included sophisticated media advisers. Reagan was dubbed "The Great Communicator" for his skills and personality. Reagan also had a wonderful speechwriter in Peggy Noonan. Reagan and his media advisers pioneered in their visual framing in backdrops for TV news stories we discussed in Chapter 2 as well as their invocation of powerful mythic symbols of "mom, flag, and apple pie" and "rugged Western individualism" in their campaign ads and political communication.

Lesley Stahl—the CBS News White House correspondent who told the story of stage-managed positive visuals overwhelming her tough script about government cutbacks under Reagan—reportedly had fights over some of her scripts with news executives who wanted to be sure that their coverage of Reagan's conservative agenda did not fit the stereotype of liberal bias in the news.[63] Reagan was called, admiringly, the "Teflon president" because seemingly nothing negative stuck to him, including the Iran-Contra scandal over the illegal sale of arms to Contra rebels in Nicaragua. Many Democrats were reluctant to criticize Reagan's foreign policy, depriving journalists of opposition to quote. But, in addition to many voters embracing Reagan's "Republican revolution," Reagan undoubtedly benefited from friendly coverage and his team's skills, particularly on television. "A lot of the Teflon came because the press was holding back," said David Gergen, former White House adviser to Reagan, Nixon, Gerald Ford, and Bill Clinton. "I don't think they wanted to go after him that toughly," Gergen added.[64]

Despite George W. Bush's friendly manner and nicknames like "Stretch" for NBC's tall David Gregory, President Bush reportedly did not trust reporters and valued a "disciplined" administration without leaks from White House officials.[65] In an article written by Ken Auletta for the *New Yorker* magazine in 2004 about media relations in the Bush White House, journalists complained that the administration focused on a set of "talking points" repeated by top officials. Auletta was disturbed by what he saw as an attitude toward the media as just another interest group. Andrew Card, Bush's chief of staff, said that it was not the job of administration officials to brief the media beyond the White House press office. Card said of journalists, "They don't represent the public any more than other people do. In our democracy, the people who represent the public stood for election. . . . I don't believe you have a check-and-balance function."[66] As we will discuss in Chapter 7 on war reporting and international news, the news media, under post-9/11 patriotic pressures, largely failed to report independently on the Bush administration's evidence for weapons of mass destruction (WMDs) in Iraq before the Iraq War. This is considered one of the most serious failures of the news media in modern times.

"What has happened over the years is that White House officials have seemed ever more devoted to spin rather than a straightforward presentation of information," said Ken Walsh, who has covered presidents from Ronald Reagan forward for *U.S. News & World Report* and is author of a book, *Feeding the Beast*, about presidents and the press corps. Walsh added that "the White House may benefit from this perpetual PR campaign, but to my mind everyone else loses because the flow of information becomes so limited. And in the end, perpetual spin also erodes the credibility of the administration itself."[67]

Barack Obama

As a presidential candidate Barack Obama promised to make government more transparent. But, according to a 2013 report from the Committee to Protect Journalists (CPJ), the international press freedom organization, the Obama administration pursued the "most aggressive" strategy since the Nixon administration to silence government officials and the media. "Six government employees, plus two contractors including Edward Snowden, have been the subject of felony criminal investigations since 2009 under the 1917 Espionage Act, accused of leaking classified information to the press—compared with a total of three such prosecutions in all previous U.S. administrations," according to the CPJ report, which was written by Leonard Downie Jr., the executive editor of the *Washington Post* during the Watergate era.[68]

In 2013, the *Washington Post*, along with independent journalist Glenn Greenwald, revealed widespread electronic surveillance by the National Security Agency (NSA) that had begun after 9/11 under the Bush administration and continued under President Obama. The leaking of classified documents from NSA contractor Edward Snowden and the government's response, the CPJ report said, had led to government officials being reluctant to discuss even unclassified information with reporters—and reporters being concerned about whether they could protect their national-security sources.[69]

In a survey of White House correspondents conducted by *Politico* magazine in 2014, nearly half said that the administration of George W. Bush had been more forthcoming than the Obama administration.[70] In interviews by the author for this book as well as the *Politico* survey and CPJ report, journalists covering the Obama White House said that their phone calls for comment were regularly not returned and that administration officials were often dismissive of reporters in general, controlling access to the president and challenging the premise of stories while not commenting on the record on them.[71]

White House press secretary Jay Carney, a former White House correspondent for *Time* magazine, responded to the *Politico* survey by saying that journalists "being yelled at" by administration officials was par for the course.[72] At the same time, the White House objected to the CPJ report, saying that President Obama "has given more interviews than his two predecessors combined, has placed online more government data, and has moved to limit the amount of classified government secrets."[73]

While "his political opponents—and even some allies" considered "President Obama to be aloof" and media critics "chafed at his administrations' many attempts to control access to the president, circumvent reporters, and chastise journalists and news outlets they deem to be unfriendly," author Martha Joynt Kumar wrote in 2015 that "no other president . . . has conducted as many interviews as Barack Obama. Not even close."[74] Kumar, an expert on the White House and the media, counted that Obama had given 872 interviews to a broad range of journalists, columnists, local TV anchors, and reporters by the end of his sixth year in office. By the end of their sixth years in office, Bill Clinton and George W. Bush combined had given 572 interviews.[75]

What was different from before? Obama was doing more interviews about a specific topic or initiative—and he was appearing on a much broader range of venues, from satellite interviews with local TV anchors to a yearly pre–Super Bowl interview on TV. Obama's media team built on their social media success during his campaign, innovating with White House-produced video, still photographs, and blog posts.[76] But, as *Washington Post* media critic Margaret Sullivan noted, many of the chosen venues were friendly and targeted to his topics, while hard-news interviews with government reporters were relatively rare. Remarkably, Sullivan wrote in 2016, President Obama had not done an individual interview with *Washington Post* news reporters since late 2009. "Think about that. The *Post* is, after all, perhaps the leading news outlet on national government and politics, with no in-depth, on-the-record access to the president of the United States for almost all of his two terms."[77]

Donald Trump

The news media have been a primary target for Donald Trump from his campaigns through his presidency. From the first days of his campaign, Trump labeled the news media as "scum" and "fake news," attacking individual reporters as well as major news organizations from the *New York Times* to the *Washington Post* and CNN at his rallies, presidential press conferences, and public appearances. Trump repeatedly told his supporters that the media were against him—and them—and that news organizations were in league with Democrats in investigations and impeachment in an effort to undermine his presidency and overturn the results of the 2016 election—and, later, the 2020 election.

"No president has been as unremittingly hostile" to the role of the media in the democracy, Floyd Abrams, the noted constitutional lawyer, said in 2018.[78] Abrams, who argued the *Pentagon Papers* case during the Nixon administration, said that Trump's goal was to undermine the media and the very nature of verifiable facts. "If news is 'fake' not because it is untrue but because it is insufficiently supportive of him, the very relevance of truth-telling becomes at risk," Abrams said. "Cynical or repeatedly false criticism [of the free press] ultimately leads to an ill-informed and ultimately ill-led people. . . . This is especially true since he has now moved from exclamations about 'fake news' to assertions that the lives of Americans are threatened by his journalistic critics."[79]

Shortly after Trump took office, Trump adviser Kellyanne Conway told NBC's Chuck Todd that there was such a thing as "alternative facts."[80] CNN's Brian Stelter wrote in response that "the presentation of 'alternative facts' undermines the media's reporting of reality in a way that decreases public trust in the media—and in facts."[81]

At rallies for his supporters, which he continued as president, Trump singled out "fake news" reporters in the press area by name, and several reporters were verbally attacked as "traitors" by some Trump supporters.[82] NBC's Katy Tur was singled out repeatedly by name as "dishonest" by Trump at rallies carried on live television. At one rally, she wrote, after Trump pointed her out and said she was "lying," the crowd turned on her, and Secret Service agents took the unusual step of escorting her to her car. "The wave of insults, harassment, and threats, via various social-media feeds, hasn't stopped since," Tur wrote.[83]

Numerous other reporters and columnists who wrote negatively about Trump reported receiving anti-Semitic, racist, and sexist comments and threats online from people who identified themselves as Trump supporters. During the coronavirus pandemic, journalists were harassed and even physically attacked by protesters who said the journalists were "lying" about coronavirus as the journalists covered pro-Trump protesters rallying against Democratic governors' stay-at-home measures.[84] Numerous journalists covering protests over the death of George Floyd in 2020 were arrested and even seriously injured, although the journalists said they had clearly identified themselves to police as reporters. Press freedom organizations were alarmed at what they saw as a dangerous new trend in the U.S.[85]

Covering Trump

Ken Walsh, the longtime White House correspondent and author, believes that President Trump's attacks on the news media are different from any of his predecessors. "Donald Trump's dealing with the media is more dangerous for the Fourth Estate and for the country than any presidential relationship with journalists in the modern era," Walsh said in an interview with the author. "He has gone beyond the customary adversarial relationship and has openly declared war on the 'fake' media. He says the media are the 'enemy of the people.' He is attempting to undermine journalism's credibility as an institution. His goal is to make as many Americans as possible believe him in his constant battles with journalists and he wants as many Americans as possible to automatically discount or ignore stories that are critical of him."[86]

White House reporters and news organizations debated how to cover President Trump, who regularly attacked reporters who challenged him for asking what he called "nasty" questions at press conferences. "There is an ongoing argument in the news media about how to respond to Trump," Ken Walsh added. "Some editors and reporters believe the media should band together and act collectively to oppose Trump. I have problems with this. Banding together and acting collectively in a sustained way would reinforce Trump's accusation that the media are conspiring against him, and this is likely to more deeply undermine media credibility. The answer is for each news organization to do its best to find the truth and point out Trump's mistakes and deceptions and let the chips fall where they may."[87]

With few Republicans willing to publicly criticize Trump or even acknowledge his tweets, journalists struggled with the traditional on-the-one-hand/on-the-other-hand concept of objectivity we discussed in Chapter 4. The *New York Times* and *Washington Post* began to count—and verify—his falsehoods, stopping short of calling them "lies," while prime-time CNN hosts, such as Don Lemon, regularly and strongly criticized the president and called him a liar.

In 2018 the president denigrated ABC News White House correspondent Cecilia Vega, as Josh Hafner wrote in *USA Today*, "telling her she 'never thinks before asking a question,' one of several slights to female journalists during a sprawling press conference."[88]

After calling on Vega, Trump said, "She's shocked that I picked her. She's, like, in a state of shock."

"I'm not," Vega said, rising from her seat. "Thank you, Mr. President."

Trump, apparently mishearing "thank you" as "thinking," responded, "I know you're not thinking. You never do."

"Sorry?" Vega responded, before Trump told her to go ahead and ask her question.[89]

"I've been asked if I thought this was misogynistic . . . or racist because I'm Mexican American," Vega said later. "I actually don't think it was. He just doesn't like us, and he doesn't respect what we do. . . . It was surreal. My whole thing was I'm not going to sit down and cede this territory to you. I have colleagues who get down and dirty [with the president]—but that's not my style. My style is to get answers, and I'm not doing anybody any good by duking it out with the president of the United States, other than to say [in effect], 'You don't get to just disrespect me,' which I think I did."[90]

Yamiche Alcindor, White House correspondent for *PBS NewsHour*, in an interview with the author and students in the fall of 2020, said that covering Donald Trump was "like covering a hurricane," which she has done, "very chaotic, and every day is different."[91]

Alcindor, like Vega and other female journalists of color, faced particular ire from President Trump for asking tough questions but was praised by media critics and others for respectfully standing her ground. The daughter of Haitian immigrants and a previously *New York Times* reporter, Alcindor said that she felt a responsibility to bring important issues facing the country during the coronavirus pandemic into her White House reporting. "People are dying, people are out of work, people are stressed out, people are grieving," she said. "So I think about that. I take to heart that I have the privilege to question the president of the United States and hold people accountable."[92]

NBC's *Meet the Press* host Chuck Todd was criticized—and praised—for his tough questioning of Trump officials and Republican lawmakers—and, for a rare editorializing monologue on his MSNBC program in 2019. After the president called on China to investigate Joe Biden on the eve of impeachment, Todd told viewers, "I will not say this lightly, but let's be frank: the national nightmare is upon us. The basic rules of our democracy are under attack from the president."[93]

In an interview with the author, Todd said, "I don't ever think I should be news. But I do believe we are having a debate about what kind of democracy we are going to have—that is the 'nightmare scenario' I described."[94]

Changes in the White House Press Briefing

When Mike McCurry became Bill Clinton's press secretary, he brought with him from his job as State Department spokesman the idea of a daily press briefing that could be televised. During the Monica Lewinsky scandal, those press briefings became ratings-getting TV on CNN, then the only cable news network. "They looked at themselves and said, 'Hey, we've got this live feed of this guy Mike McCurry getting the crap beat out of him every day and that's pretty entertaining,'" McCurry recalled, laughing, in an interview with the author. "After the first few days, I called Tom Johnson, the president of CNN, and said 'I just want you to know I'm not going to be saying anything new about sex scandals today.' He said, 'Mike, we get 175,000 more households the minute you come on.'"[95]

Press secretaries for both Republican and Democratic presidents have had contentious moments as they threaded the needle between informing and "spinning." But Trump's first press secretary, Sean Spicer, had a highly contentious relationship with reporters at the White House from Trump's first day in office, when Spicer berated reporters and echoed Trump's false claim that the crowds for the president's inauguration were the largest ever to witness an inauguration. In moves that were protested by journalists' organizations, the Trump White House "imposed some of the most draconian restrictions on the news media in recent memory, from banning TV cameras during its daily briefings to cutting back the length and frequency of its sessions with reporters," the *Washington Post* reported.[96] After that time, the daily White House press briefing by the White House press secretary under Trump all but disappeared under subsequent Trump press secretaries.

These changes in media relations extended to federal agencies. The Pentagon and the State Department made similar cutbacks, and, in another first, Secretary of State Rex Tillerson traveled with only one online U.S. journalist, a writer for a conservative news site, on his first trip to Asia, giving no other interviews and taking no other questions from reporters for months.[97]

Shortly after Trump took office, journalists from several news organizations reported that information about climate change and other topics in regulation was being removed from government websites and that scientists at the Environmental Protection Agency, the U.S. Department of Agriculture, the National Institutes of Health, and other agencies were being ordered not to talk about their research, at least temporarily.[98] The moves alarmed many scientists in light of President Trump's views on climate change, and they were adamantly objected to by the nonpartisan Sunlight Foundation and by scientists[99] and advocates for scientific research who participated in a "March for Science" in Washington, D.C.[100]

The president threatened to "open up" long-standing libel laws, and he reportedly said that both government officials and journalists should be prosecuted for leaks, including those that were apparently coming from White House officials about chaos and infighting in the administration.

Trump's comments about the judiciary, his powers as president, and his attacks on the news media as "treasonous" were condemned by conservative, libertarian, and First Amendment scholars as well as by journalists' organizations. "Donald J. Trump's . . . attacks on the press, complaints about the judicial system and bold claims of presidential power collectively sketch out a constitutional worldview that shows contempt for the First Amendment, the separation of powers and the rule of law, legal experts across the political spectrum say," wrote Adam Liptak in an article quoting a range of legal experts.[101]

Journalists and media critics saw in Trump's attacks and characterization on Twitter of the news media as not his enemy but "the enemy of the American people"[102] a calculated attempt to undermine and delegitimize factual reporting and the role of the media in a democratic society. At an event of the international CPJ, Christiane Amanpour said that she had been "chilled" when Trump's first tweet as president said that protesters against the election had been "incited by the media." Amanpour said, "As all the international journalists we honor in this room tonight and every year know only too well: First the media is accused of inciting, then sympathizing, then associating—until they suddenly find themselves accused of being full-fledged terrorists and subversives. . . . A great America requires a great and free and safe press."[103]

The *Washington Post*, the *New York Times*, and the *Wall Street Journal* all regularly published major scoops during the Trump presidency. The *Washington Post* reported that the president had revealed highly classified information about counterterrorism to the Russian foreign minister and the ambassador during a White House visit from which U.S. media were excluded.[104] The *New York Times* reported that former FBI director James Comey had prepared a contemporaneous memo saying that President Trump had urged him to drop the investigation of contacts between fired national security adviser Michael Flynn and Russian ambassador Sergey Kislyak.[105] The *Wall Street Journal* reported that U.S. intelligence officials were withholding intelligence information from Trump out of concern that it might be leaked or compromised.[106] Trump even gave a surprising interview to *New York Times* White House reporters in which the president said he should never have hired Attorney General Jeff Sessions and also discussed the *Times'* previous revelation that his son Don Jr. and his campaign manager had met in Trump Tower with Russians who had promised damaging information about Hillary Clinton.[107]

Subsequent books from inside the Trump administration, including one by former national security adviser John Bolton in 2020,[108] confirmed many previous accounts in the media and the impeachment inquiry, in which, in a near party-line partisan vote, the president was charged by the Democratic-controlled House but acquitted in the trial in the Republican-controlled Senate, with one Republican, Sen. Mitt Romney, voting to impeach.[109]

With his understanding of live television Donald Trump as candidate had used the conventions, values, and commercial needs of cable TV news, in particular, to his advantage. He made himself accessible for interviews, calling in to friendly talk shows; cable news outlets carried many of his early rallies live and unfiltered.

Trump's repetition of known falsehoods such as the notion that "thousands and thousands" of Muslims were "dancing in the streets of New Jersey to celebrate 9/11" or that president Obama had wiretapped his phone were fact-checked and contradicted by news media—and on cable and broadcast TV as well as in print and online.

CNN's Anderson Cooper and Jake Tapper, NBC's Chuck Todd, MSNBC's Chris Matthews, and others had contentious interviews with Trump where they provided simultaneous fact-checking and labeled falsehood lies, later taking to on-air chyrons (basically TV's subtitles) to label falsehoods as lies.

"Politicians lie—that didn't start on January 20," CNN anchor Jake Tapper said in an interview with the author in 2017. "But the number of falsehoods and the sheer audacity of falsehoods that have come from the White House is something that I haven't seen. . . . It's important for the press to stand up. There is an attempt by some to blur what is real and not real."[110]

Despite Trump's vilifying of the news media, *New York Times* political reporter Maggie Haberman, who covered Trump, writing several of the *Times'* headline-making stories about him as president, said at one point, "Look, I think that he loves the press. I think he lives, at least loosely, by the theory that, if not all press is good press, that most press is good press. I think you find the press has been his nurturer and validator for thirty to forty years. This is a person who courted the tabloids aggressively in New York City in the nineteen-eighties. He found a way to make himself a commodity for the gossip pages and play the tabloids off each other. He likes attention, and he likes media. He loves to manipulate the media. He's a master at it."[111]

Changes in Coverage of Party Conventions

When the Republican National Convention convened in 1992, an astonishing fifteen thousand print and TV journalists were credentialed to spend hours in the Houston Astrodome, covering a story that has changed drastically since the days the presidential nominee was actually chosen at the convention. The broadcast TV networks spent millions to broadcast the event and speeches in prime time over four days—and there was a big debate at the time about whether they were newsworthy or not—and what was the networks' public service obligation to cover.[112] Today, cable TV provides more coverage than the broadcast networks, which still show major speeches in prime time. Some recent political party conventions have seen dramatic moments and oratory: Barack Obama's 2004 speech at the Democratic National Convention, where he said, "There is not a liberal America and a conservative America—there is the United States of America,"[113] put the little-known senator on the national stage, while Donald Trump signaled his vision and appeal to his supporters the night he was nominated with a reality show–style entrance. In his dark speech that night, Trump proclaimed that only he could save America amidst delegates' chants of "lock her up" about Hillary Clinton.[114]

But in most conventions today, both parties carefully manage the speakers, the signs, and the invited guests to promote their images. Changes in the primary and nominating system have meant that it is rare to have a political convention that determines the nominee. And, while the broadcast TV networks still cover the conventions, they no longer cover them gavel to gavel as they did in the pre-cable days and the tumultuous 1960s when there were fights over seating delegates and the nominee might be determined on the convention floor. In the famous 1968 Democratic National Convention in Chicago during the Vietnam War, the three major broadcast TV networks alternated between coverage of an army of protesters and police throwing tear-gas outside the hall with the contentious, emotional nomination of Vice President Hubert Humphrey inside the hall. The coverage was viewed as having helped Richard Nixon portray himself as the "law-and-order" candidate via their party's orderly convention and control of protesters in Miami.[115]

Outreach on Social Media—Messaging and Mobilizing

In his study of Barack Obama's use of digital media in his two presidential campaigns, political scientist Bruce Bimber wrote that there were differences between the two campaigns—and digital media were part of a disciplined, centralized campaign. In 2008, "Barack Obama made the most sophisticated and intentional use of digital media of any major candidate for office in the U.S." In a new environment for political communication, Bimber said, Obama embraced "social-movement-like enthusiasm and personalized among his supporters while also running a highly disciplined, centrally organized campaign."[116] In contrast, in 2012, "in the context of lowered voter turnout and dissipated enthusiasm, the Obama campaign exploited data analytics to engage in an unprecedented level of personalized message-targeting to a handful of states, in order to win a closer election with highly honed state-by-state tactics."[117]

Impact of Twitter

The growth of Twitter and social media platforms has given politicians, political leaders, and even a social media–savvy Pope Francis[118] a way to instantly share their views around the world, connect with supporters, and respond to critics. From the standpoint of political journalists, Twitter today is their news feed where they follow other journalists and are expected to report, write, and tweet about their stories to gain attention in a crowded news environment. Most people in the country are *not* on Twitter, but what candidates and elected officials are saying—and responding to—on Twitter and social media is increasingly quoted and discussed and even driving campaign coverage as well as the national political conversation. Social media platforms were a factor in the 2012 presidential election, but 2016 accelerated the changes and impact. What was new, Jill Abramson, former editor of the *New York Times*, said, "[was] the brutality of minute-by-minute competition and coverage. There's this wild chase for scooplets. News breaks that no one remembers two days afterwards."[119]

In an interview with the author, Ryan Williams, who was deputy national press secretary for Massachusetts governor Mitt Romney in the 2012 presidential race, maintained that the relative inexperience of some young reporters who were "embeds" tracking the campaigns, combined with the speed of Twitter, has led to a tone of snark, potential for errors—and more wariness of reporters by candidates and campaigns.[120] Williams said that during the 2012 campaign, one reporter on the campaign trail tweeted out erroneously that Romney had been critical of candidate Newt Gingrich for tearing up in public over his mother's death before another reporter tweeted out that this was not what happened.[121]

"Twitter has dramatically changed the relationship between campaigns and reporters," Williams said. "It's very problematic for dealing with reporters" in terms of access "because you have to be on your guard at all times" for any gaffes that may be tweeted out by journalists and also picked up by opponents.[122]

The campaign press corps of today is younger and more diverse than "the boys on the bus" depicted in Tim Crouse's famous 1972 campaign book of the same name.[123] The "boys" were almost all older white men—and Crouse's book actually paints a critical portrait of some of them as lazy, cynical, and too focused on horse-race coverage. Many political reporters, of course, get *off* the bus—or out of the briefing room—or don't go at all, preferring to report on the issues and concerns of the public outside the campaign bubble. But, as Jonathan Martin, the *New York Times* national political reporter who opted not to be on the bus in 2012, said of the presidential candidates on the campaign trail, "We are just isolated from these folks. The layers and layers of staff, and the caution, is something that I think is detrimental to the process."[124]

@realDonaldTrump and @POTUS

Donald Trump defied—and changed—the norms of political discourse, campaigning, and leadership, and his unprecedented use of Twitter was a major factor in that disruption. Trump (with millions of Twitter and Facebook followers) turned his Twitter account into a highly effective—and highly controversial—means of speaking directly to his supporters, amplifying his speeches and rallies. As we discussed in Chapter 2, Trump used Twitter for reverse agenda-setting and direct agenda-setting. Trump's tweets regularly became the news of the day and allowed him to disrupt the news of the day when news events were negative against him. Trump's Twitter channel allowed him to spread discredited conspiracy theories and proven untruths from fringe websites and his own view of reality. He attacked his opponents and even his own administration officials with memorable incendiary epithets, proven untruths, and a level of narcissism that had Trump putting himself at the center of world events on behalf of his supporters. It is striking to note that, in addition to millions of dollars of free media in the 2016 campaign, in two months in 2015 on Twitter alone, Trump was mentioned in 6.3 million Twitter conversations, eight times as many as Republican rivals Marco Rubio, Carly Fiorina, and Ben Carson—and three times as many times as Hillary Clinton.[125]

"Mr. Trump has mastered Twitter in a way no candidate for president ever has," a reporter for the *New York Times* wrote in 2015, "unleashing and redefining its power as a tool of political promotion, distraction, score-settling and attack—and turning a 140-character task that other candidates farm out to young staff members into a centerpiece of his campaign."[126] As reporter Michael Barbaro reported, in his interview with Trump, the candidate "compared his Twitter feed to a newspaper with a single, glorious voice: his own . . . Suddenly, he said of his foes, 'I have more power than they do.'"[127]

"Conventional practices for reaching out to political constituencies have been redefined by Donald Trump's unconventional social-media practices," political scientist Diana Owens wrote in a study she conducted interviewing Trump supporters about their use of social media and political engagement, first in 2016 and then again in 2018.[128] "As a presidential candidate, Trump effectively engaged Twitter to publicize his words and actions, attack his long list of enemies, and highjack political discourse. His aggressive Twitter pronouncements . . . often sideline discussion of important policy issues, distract from embarrassing personal scandals, and attempt to camouflage the mishaps of his administration. . . . He has also exploited the mainstream media, which widely broadcasts his Twitter outbursts, as a mouthpiece for his vitriol."[129]

As Owens noted, "his use of social media, while amateurish, conveys authenticity that appeals to his base" and was "consistent with perceptions of the de-professionalization of his campaign, an illusion that was a selling point with his supporters, and which further validated his credentials as the ultimate political outsider."[130]

Trump stepped up his tweetstorms as president, especially after his agenda hit roadblocks legislatively and legally and in light of investigations into possible ties between the Trump campaign and the Russians in the election. In the spring of 2017, FBI director James Comey confirmed to the House Intelligence Committee that the FBI and other government agencies were investigating possible ties between Trump associates and Russia during the campaign that might have helped the Russians in their effort to undermine the U.S. election.[131]

Trump used Twitter to attack U.S. intelligence agencies and to label the Russian investigation and revelations about the investigation in the *New York Times*, *Washington Post*, and on broadcast news all "fake news."[132] The president fired FBI director James Comey in a move he later told NBC anchor Lester Holt was related to Comey's pursuit of the Russia investigation. Trump told Holt, "And in fact when I decided to just do it, I said to myself, I said, 'You know, this Russia thing with Trump and Russia is a made-up story, it's an excuse by the Democrats for having lost an election that they should have won.'"[133]

Alexandria Ocasio-Cortez and Social Media

New York City congresswoman Alexandria Ocasio-Cortez—who scored a stunning upset against an entrenched Democratic member of Congress in the 2018 midterms—represents generational change in politics as well as in politicians' use of social media. She has millions of followers on Twitter and Instagram; and she is engaging personally and around policy with progressives, millennials, and her opponents in fresh ways. At the same time, she has attracted tremendous attention from the mainstream media. "Ocasio-Cortez has done more than any politician since Donald Trump to usher policy debates into the

Alexandria Ocasio-Cortez @
@AOC

1. Aspirational Goals: Push the limits of what's possible.
2. Nuts + Bolts: Our lives are on the line. We shouldn't let the planet be destroyed because it's "too expensive" to save.
3. Supporters: Many
4. Opponents: Fossil fuel industry
5. Beyond Energy: A Federal Jobs Guarantee

The Hill @ @thehill · Nov 25, 2018
Five things to know about Ocasio-Cortez's "Green New Deal" hill.cm/bLVcM9v

12:10 PM · Nov 25, 2018 · Twitter for iPhone

Photo 5.1 Alexandria Ocasio-Cortez tweeted about the "Green New Deal" proposal.

Alexandria Ocasio-Cortez via Twitter, 2018

elite media conversation," media critic Peter Hamby wrote.[134] "Leveraging the Washington media's addiction to Twitter, she has opened up debates about a 'Green New Deal,' boosting the minimum wage, and raising the marginal tax rate on the wealthiest Americans to 70 percent—all proposals that are supported in polls by a bipartisan majority, but are often treated in Washington as controversial."[135]

Ocasio-Cortez has been compared to Donald Trump, according to Hamby, because "they both understand that policy proposals are mostly irrelevant to the media unless you have previously established the ability to generate attention." Hamby continued, "Ocasio-Cortez didn't get booked on *60 Minutes* because Anderson Cooper was eager to talk about her ideas on taxes. She got booked on *60 Minutes* because she's a telegenic 29-year-old working-class Hispanic female ratings-magnet with big ideas and a fearlessness rarely seen among politicians. She has earned attention because—like the Parkland students and unlike her boring colleagues in Congress—she intuits that power in 2019 is derived from social media, specifically Twitter, the drunk airline pilot of political coverage."[136]

When she arrived in Congress in 2019, Ocasio-Cortez was tapped by House Democrats to give a social media session to her older colleagues. Here were her top tips:

> "Be yourself and write your own tweets so that people know it's you talking."

> "The way we grow our presence is being there."[137]

Following up on the compelling campaign video narrative that connected her personal story in her Bronx neighborhood to what she said was neglect of people's problems by politicians, including her opponent, Ocasio-Cortez uses her Instagram account in ways that are familiar to Instagram influencers but relatively new in politics. Ocasio-Cortez, who had been a teacher and a community organizer for Bernie Sanders, built her insurgent campaign (against an inattentive opponent) from the ground up, going door to door to voters' homes.

She uses her Instagram account to give her followers a behind-the-scenes look at her new job in Congress—*and* what she's having at home for dinner.[138] It's that policy plus personality combination, now added to with her being a famous celebrity letting you in on her life, that is engaging and appealing to her supporters. One Instagram commenter wrote this: "okay Alexandria Ocasio-Cortez is literally eating instant mac and cheese with a coffee stirrer while breaking down congressional committees and answering our political questions!!! @Ocasio2018 your authenticity is truly ICONIC."[139] Near the end of the 2020 presidential election, Ocasio-Cortez and Rep. Ilhan Omar played the popular video game *Among Us* live on the streaming platform Twitch while encouraging young people to register to vote; the event was seen live by more than 400,000 viewers and more than five million viewers in aggregate.[140]

Social Media in the 2020 Presidential Campaign

You do not have to be young to attract a large following as a politician on social media: Bernie Sanders was a popular presence on Twitter for years before he ran for president, and Sen. Cory Booker was known for reaching out to his constituents—and beyond—via social media when he was mayor of Newark, New Jersey. But the elements of perceived authenticity and personal narrative seem to be key. And there are some risks in outreach on social media, especially given the media's focus on gaffes as well as the price to be paid in appearing awkward and uncool on social media to a generation that grew up speaking social media. Sen. Elizabeth Warren is a skilled speaker and campaigner who made a campaign signature of selfies with her supporters, especially "pinkie swear" photos with girls over her bid to be the first female president, in the 2020 presidential campaign. But, talking about her campaign in the beginning on Instagram, Warren's awkward reach for a beer in her kitchen on Instagram was cringeworthy to some supporters—and made fun of by some opponents. Texas congressman Beto O'Rourke, who ran unsuccessfully for president in 2020, built a following in Texas— and nationally—with a low-tech

Photo 5.2 Donald Trump campaigned at rallies with his supporters throughout his presidency.

Scott Olson/Getty Images

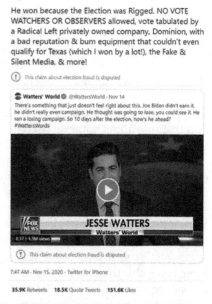

Photo 5.3 After months, Twitter began to label Trump's false tweets about the 2020 election.

Donald Trump via Twitter, 2020

videotaped "road trip" across Texas with Will Hurd, a Republican congress-man from Texas. O'Rourke nearly unseated Republican senator Ted Cruz in a Senate race and became a passionate supporter for gun control in Democratic debates after the shootings in El Paso, Texas. But, in the initial days of a national campaign and O'Rourke's performance that were said to be not ready for prime time, O'Rourke's Instagrammed trip to the dentist was also focused upon with humor in the kind of emerging media narrative we discussed in Chapter 4.

As with President Obama's campaigns, social media is important but not the only factor in a successful campaign. In the 2020 Demo-cratic primaries, Bernie Sanders continued his innovative Internet-based fundraising and mobilizing from 2016 to raise millions of dollars from small donors and bring supporters to his events. Elizabeth Warren also raised millions online from small donors. Kamala Harris sought the online endorsements of YouTube stars. Former Indiana mayor Pete Buttigieg effectively used social media plus a strategy of all-out availability for inter-views by the broadcast TV Sunday shows and cable news to build his recognition and profile.

Fake News/Disinformation

Fake news and disinformation via social media have become alarming forces in politics and the democracy in recent years, coming into focus in the U.S. after the 2016 election and continuing today. Facebook and other social media provide the selective exposure of chosen news, albeit passively chosen. We know already from research on confirmation bias that people tend to believe—and search for—information that confirms what they already believe to be true. People also tend to be hospitable to informa-tion that they think comes from their friends and others in their in-group, which is the definition of sharing and forwarding on social media. And when you add in the potential for almost instantaneous, multiplying spread of falsehoods and disinformation across the Internet from trusted sources and people and groups with large followings, with no time or perhaps no inclination, for fact-checking on the Internet, you've got a powerful force for communication—and disinformation and conspiracy theories—in a polarized political and cultural climate.

Several studies have found that repetition of false information makes it more believable to people—and more likely for them to share and forward. In one experiment, led by Professor Lisa Fazio of Vanderbilt University, participants who had correctly answered that the name for a pleated Scot-tish skirt is a kilt later increased their chances of agreeing with the false statement that "a sari is the name of a short, pleated skirt worn by Scots" the more times they reread the false statement.[141]

The Role of Fake News and Disinformation in the 2016 Election

Several months before the 2016 presidential election, *BuzzFeed* media editor Craig Silverman noticed many fabricated stories about U.S. politics on the Internet that seemed to be coming from one small town in Macedonia. Silverman and a colleague began investigating, and days before the election in November, *BuzzFeed* published a story that identified at least 140 U.S. politics websites, almost all of them "aggressively pro-Trump and aimed at conservatives and Trump supporters," that were generating real-looking news stories that were almost all false or misleading.[142] The fake stories on the websites—which had been created with American-style names by young people in the town of Veles—were being seen, shared, and commented on by huge numbers of people on the sites' Facebook pages, the largest of which had hundreds of thousands of followers. One story was headlined "Pope Francis Shocks World, Endorses Donald Trump for President"[143] while another was "FBI Agent Suspected in Hillary Email Leaks Found Dead in Apparent Murder-Suicide."[144] Neither story was true.

BuzzFeed found that the most successful stories from the Macedonian-made sites were nearly all false or misleading—and that most of the content had been derived and further sensationalized from fringe and right-wing sites in the U.S.[145] The teenaged creators told reporters that their motive was purely profit: to make money from digital Facebook advertising with fake pro-Trump content that attracted readers. But a subsequent investigation by *BuzzFeed* and partners revealed that "the fake news sites that flourished in Macedonia in 2016 weren't just the work of local teens—and that security agencies [were] probing possible connections to Russia."[146]

During the campaign, real news stories from major outlets had "easily outpaced" fake election news on Facebook, an analysis by *BuzzFeed* found. But in the final three months, the outpouring of fake news accelerated dramatically. During that crucial time, the twenty top-performing *fake* election news stories on Facebook generated more engagement than the twenty top-performing *real* news stories among nineteen major news outlets such as the *New York Times*, *Washington Post*, *HuffPost*, NBC News, and others. The fake news engagement totaled 8.7 million shares, reactions, and comments; the real news stories on the major news outlets counted were 7.36 million shares, reactions, and comments.[147]

Facebook founder and CEO Mark Zuckerberg initially was dismissive of concerns about Russian interference in the election via social media, saying in comments which he later said he regretted that it was "a pretty crazy idea" to think that false posts and disinformation on Facebook might have influenced the 2016 vote.[148] As we know now, the Russian government, in fact, used Facebook, Instagram, and other social media in a multifaceted cyber campaign that was designed to inflame social divisions and mistrust, suppress voter turnout, and elect Donald Trump.[149]

In January 2017 multiple U.S. intelligence agencies shared with the public their formal assessment that Vladimir Putin had ordered cyberattacks to hurt Hillary Clinton and help Donald Trump. The report said the following: "We assess Russian President Vladimir Putin ordered an influence campaign in 2016 aimed at the US presidential election. Russia's goals were to undermine public faith in the US democratic process, denigrate Secretary Clinton, and harm her electability and potentially presidency. We further assess Putin and the Russian government developed a clear preference for President-elect Trump."[150] President Obama had previously said, in July 2016, that government experts believed that the Russians were behind the hacking of emails at the Democratic National Committee, some of them embarrassing about doubts and conflicts within the Hillary Clinton campaign, that were leaked and published on WikiLeaks.[151]

The intelligence agencies in their 2017 report found that Putin had a personal grudge against Clinton, who was expected to win, over her criticism of Russia's human rights record when she was secretary of state. In addition to influencing the election in favor of Trump, the intelligence agencies found, the disinformation campaign was also aimed at undermining confidence in American democracy, in the U.S. and abroad.[152]

On Facebook alone, imposters had millions of interactions with people who thought they were talking to fellow Americans, according to an analysis by Jonathan Albright of the Tow Center for Digital Journalism at Columbia University.[153] Facebook received the most public attention for the spreading of fake news and disinformation about the 2016 election, and the social media giant has been criticized for not doing enough, then or today, to curb fake news and disinformation. But later reports indicate that Instagram, which is owned by Facebook, may have played a greater role in disinformation in the 2016 election than Facebook acknowledged or that was understood at the time. Instagram memes offer engaging visual framing of photos with bold captions—and, as with fake news, on Facebook.[154]— and such visual information can look especially "real" even when it is not.

Analysis of social media data in studies released in 2018 by the Senate Intelligence Committee and independent researchers found that, while Facebook had reached more people with Russian-generated fake news and disinformation, Instagram had generated more engagement.[155] The Russian government–backed Internet Research Agency (IRA) in 2016 was found to have operated a huge network of fake Instagram accounts that targeted specific groups—including African Americans, conservative Christians, gun rights supporters, and anti-immigration activists—with false, divisive content and accusations of voter fraud that appeared to be designed in part to convince Black voters that their votes didn't matter.[156]

Moreover, the use of Instagram to spread fake news and disinformation through real-looking photos and captions had accelerated in 2017, *after*

Facebook instituted some security measures following the 2016 election.[157] One 2017 meme, for example, posted by the IRA's "Blacktivist" account showed an illustration of a police officer half-clad in a Ku Klux Klan hood and sheet over the caption "The Ku Klux Klan has infiltrated police departments for years."[158] Researchers at Oxford University wrote that "over 30 million users, between 2015 and 2017, shared the IRA's Facebook and Instagram posts with their friends and family, liking, reacting to, and commenting on them along the way."[159]

It is difficult to measure the precise impact of the Russian influence campaign on the 2016 election. A 2016 Pew Research survey found that 23 percent of Americans had shared fake news—wittingly or unwittingly—and Americans are saying that they consider fake news and disinformation a serious problem. Sixty-four percent of Americans said in 2016 that fake news and disinformation were sowing "a great deal of confusion" about the basic facts of current events.[160] It is that confusion about facts and mistrust of news and government that can be so damaging to both institutions.

The 2020 Campaign and Moving Forward

With President Trump appropriating the term *fake news* for his own purpose and a multiplicity of false content on the Internet, researchers today prefer the term *information disorder* to describe fabricated stories, disinformation, and influence campaigns on the Internet. "This is a whole lot worse than" the young people making fake accounts in Macedonia, said Claire Wardle, executive director of First Draft, a nonprofit consortium of scholars and news organizations researching disinformation on the Web.[161] Wardle and Hossein Derakhshan of the Massachusetts Institute of Technology have differentiated among three different types of misinformation and disinformation. "Much of the discourse on 'fake news' conflates three notions: mis-information, disinformation and mal-information," they wrote. "But it's important to distinguish messages that are true from those that are false, and messages that are created, produced or distributed by 'agents' who intend to do harm from those that are not."[162]

They described three categories:

- "Dis-information. Information that is false and deliberately created to harm a person, social group, organization or country."

- "Mis-information. Information that is false, but not created with the intention of causing harm."

- "Mal-information. Information that is based on reality, used to inflict harm on a person, organization or country."[163]

Tips for How to Spot Fake News/Disinformation in Your Social Media Feed

First Draft and FactCheck.org both offer tips for spotting fake news and disinformation in your social media feed. An article and video on ABC-News.com also provide tips. Here are some of them:

1. Take a minute before you retweet or share, especially if what you have just seen provokes an emotional reaction—that's what moves people to share without looking.

2. Consider the source—look up the name of the site. Many fake news accounts fool people by creating a URL that is close to the name of a real news organization or simply reads like one. Look for misspellings and odd grammar that could be the sign of being written by someone outside the U.S.

3. Look up the author: Who posted it? Who are they? What is their social media history and profile? Is this a real person or a bot?

4. Read beyond the headline to see if the content supports the headline. See if you can independently verify the claim.

5. Look up the content posted on the account—there are reverse image tools that allow you to see if the image was previously used in a real account.[164]

In the 2020 election, intelligence officials in classified briefings warned Donald Trump, Bernie Sanders, and lawmakers that the Russians were again using social media, first to make Sanders the Democratic nominee and then to get Trump reelected.[165] Kamala Harris, Elizabeth Warren, Bernie Sanders, and Beto O'Rourke all were targeted with divisive memes and tweets that attacked their backgrounds and distorted their positions, *Politico* reported in an independent analysis—and there were signs that foreign actors as well as people opposed to them were behind the barrage.[166] Experts urged presidential campaigns to be proactive in fighting disinformation. "This is one of the biggest threats facing our democratic institutions, our economic institutions, our way of life," said Lisa Kaplan, an expert on digital strategy.[167] One important tool for candidates, Kaplan said, is to fight back immediately against false information so that a false narrative does not take hold. "You don't want to wait for it to come to you because by then it's too late."[168]

Experts in 2020 said that, in addition to more sophisticated disinformation attempts to influence the election and suppress voter turnout through spreading falsehoods via social media, the American electorate faced threats from within the U.S. NPR reported that "social media companies and outside experts say in 2020, the biggest threats to the election may be coming from Americans in the form of possible violence, mistruths about mail-in balloting, and misinformation in the wake of possibly delayed election results—not to mention a president who has repeatedly questioned the legitimacy of the vote."[169] Yoel Roth, Twitter's head of site integrity, told NPR that "in some ways, the people who know the most about how to mislead Americans are other Americans."[170]

In his rallies and his Twitter account, President Trump repeatedly said that the 2020 election was being "rigged," falsely claiming that mail-in voting, which was favored by Democrats, was perpetrating massive voter fraud that would delegitimize the results of the election. Voter fraud in mail-in voting and all voting, is, in fact, rare, according to numerous studies. But in addition to circulating to millions of supporters on social media, Trump's charges were repeated, although usually rebutted, in mainstream media.

In a report called "Mail-in Voter Fraud: Anatomy of a Disinformation Campaign," researchers at Harvard University's Berkman Klein Center for Internet & Society found that Trump had "harnessed" the journalistic bias and conventions of objectivity and balance we have talked about, "bending over backwards" to be fair, and blasting out Trump's false claims in the news organizations' headlines, tweets, and other social media.[171] "If Biden wins clearly by mail-in voting and not in-person voting, you may well have tens of millions of people persuaded that the election was stolen," Yochai Benkler, the center's codirector, correctly predicted to the *Washington Post*.[172] Experts call such beliefs, despite evidence, a *"perception hack."*

Internationally, researchers at Cornell University analyzed thirty-eight million articles about the pandemic globally, in English-language traditional and online media.[173] They reached a startling conclusion: "The president of the United States was the single largest driver of misinformation around Covid," Sarah Evanega, director of the Cornell Alliance for Science and lead author on the study, said. "That's concerning in that there are real-world dire health implications" to spreading misinformation and disinformation about the disease.[174]

The transition to mail-in voting during the coronavirus pandemic led to opportunities for greater disinformation about the election. In the closing weeks and days before the election, voters were inundated with a flood of robocalls, rumors, and emails—many of them aimed at minority voters. In one high-profile case, robocalls went to thousands of minority voters in Michigan, Pennsylvania, Ohio, Illinois, and New York. The calls falsely claimed that voting by mail could be used by the government to harm voters. "Mail-in voting sounds great," a woman's voice said in the call. "But did you know that if you vote by mail your personal information will be part of a public database that will be used by police departments to track down old warrants and be used by credit companies to collect outstanding debts?"[175] The woman also said—falsely—that the government also could use the information to track people down for mandatory vaccines. "Don't be finessed into giving your private information to the man," she said. "Stay safe and beware of vote-by-mail." Two right-wing operatives, were charged with voter intimidation, a felony, with these calls.[176] There were reports of other such targeted robocall operations in the days before the election.

With the 2020 election, the Cybersecurity and Infrastructure Security Agency within the Department of Homeland Security conducted an extensive election security initiative that was designed to prevent foreign interference and voter fraud. In an announcement after assessing the voting and the 2020 election, Christopher Krebs, the director of the agency, said that the 2020 election was the most secure in the history of the U.S. "There is no evidence that any voting system deleted or lost votes, changed votes, or was in any way compromised," Krebs declared in an assessment that was signed by the National Association of State Election Directors and other voting security groups. "All of the states with close results in the 2020 presidential race have paper records of each vote, allowing the ability to go back and count each ballot if necessary. This is an added benefit for security and resilience. This process allows for the identification and correction of any mistakes or errors."[177]

Days later, Trump said that he had fired Krebs for making the announcement.

The firing of Krebs was condemned by many. Rep. Adam Schiff, chairman of the House Intelligence Committee, said Krebs and his staff had "worked diligently to safeguard our elections, provide vital support to state and local election officials, and inform the American people about what was true and what was not." Rather than reward their service in keeping the nation's "institutions safe," Schiff said, "President Trump is retaliating against Director Krebs and other officials who did their duty."[178]

Trump's claims of election fraud continued to be labeled baseless—by the courts, by mainstream news media, and by state election officials, some of whom reported being targeted online and receiving death threats against themselves and

Donald J. Trump @
@realDonaldTrump

The recent statement by Chris Krebs on the security of the 2020 Election was highly inaccurate, in that there were massive improprieties and fraud - including dead people voting, Poll Watchers not allowed into polling locations, "glitches" in the voting machines which changed...

(!) This claim about election fraud is disputed

7:07 PM · Nov 17, 2020 · Twitter for iPhone

50.4K Retweets   **8.2K** Quote Tweets   **226.5K** Likes

Donald J. Trump @ @realDonaldTrump · Nov 17
Replying to @realDonaldTrump
...votes from Trump to Biden, late voting, and many more. Therefore, effective immediately, Chris Krebs has been terminated as Director of the Cybersecurity and Infrastructure Security Agency.

(!) This claim about election fraud is disputed

○ 31.1K   ↻ 42.1K   ♡ 173.9K   ⬆

Photo 5.4 Another example of Twitter labeling Trump's false tweets.

Donald Trump via Twitter, 2020

even poll workers.[179] Twitter finally labeled Trump's tweets and others about election fraud "disputed." But that did not stop the repetition, forwarding—and believing—of the claims.

Case Study: Late-Night Comedy

In the 1992 presidential campaign, Arkansas governor Bill Clinton—young, inexperienced, and not well known compared to his opponent, President George H. W. Bush—reached out to younger voters by playing a saxophone solo, wearing sunglasses, on *The Arsenio Hall Show*.[180] Clinton also answered questions of young viewers in town halls on MTV News, including, in one memorable exchange, answering whether he wore "boxers or briefs" in his underwear choices.[181] That might have seemed undignified to some viewers at the time, but both appearances helped associate Clinton with youth and irreverence on television, especially compared to the older, patrician Bush, just as, in the association technique in advertising, marketers seek to associate their products with what's considered young, hip, and cool at the moment.

The ability to be self-deprecating and to laugh at one's self has traditionally been prized by Americans about their presidents—it's part of what people expect—and appearing on late-night comedy talk shows from *The Tonight Show* to *Late Night* has been a contemporary version of the great politicians' humor at their own expense. Mixing it up on late-night TV is perceived as humanizing leaders and candidates as "one of us," allowing them to show they're game, to counteract a "stuffy" image, or be more personal in a nonthreatening interview with the late-night host.

There is research that suggests that late-night humor has some priming effects, with the potential to make a politician more likeable or an issue more salient after it has been covered in a comedy venue.[182] In a cluttered, fragmented media environment marked by distrust of both traditional media and politicians, late-night comedy humor, from James Corden's "Carpool Karaoke" to satirical sketches on *Saturday Night Live*, are considered cool—and even truth-telling—by hard-to-reach younger viewers. (In daytime talk, *The View* and *The Ellen DeGeneres Show* have allowed politicians and presidents to reach a primarily female audience.) Doing an interview on late-night allows the candidate or political leader to avoid an interview

(Continued)

(Continued)

or press conference with traditional journalists in favor of a usually (but not always) softer interview from the talk TV hosts. And the reach of the late-night shows, in particular, is significantly amplified via excerpts on YouTube videos, our contemporary watercooler, with the segments shared and commented upon by viewers, news organizations, and pundits critiquing the politician's performance or depiction, all the while embedding and linking the videos across multiple platforms.

Many Republican and Democratic presidents and presidential candidates have appeared on the broadcast TV networks' long-running *Tonight Show*, *Late Show*, and other programs, where the humor and hosts' monologues traditionally have been gently topical. Politicians from Sarah Palin to and Hillary Clinton as well as Donald Trump before he was elected president have all played themselves on NBC's *SNL*, even appearing alongside their *SNL* doppelgangers.

In what was at the time considered a radical move, independent presidential candidate Ross Perot in 1992 announced his campaign on the highly rated CNN news talk show, *Larry King Live*. Today, appearing on late-night comedy shows is part of a candidates' communications strategy, whether it's Republican presidential candidate Jeb Bush in 2016[183] or 2020 Democratic contenders Pete Buttigieg and Sen. Kamala Harris in 2020 "slow-jamming" the news with Jimmy Fallon on *The Tonight Show with Jimmy Fallon*.[184] Joe Biden in 2015 gave his first interview about the death of his son Beau to Stephen Colbert on CBS's *Late Show with Stephen Colbert* and said at the time that he was not sure he could commit to running for president.[185] As mentioned in Chapter 2, Michelle Obama did "Carpool Karaoke" in the White House driveway with James Corden (with seventy-four million views by 2020)[186] on CBS's *Late Late Show with James Corden*. She also promoted her physical fitness and healthy-eating campaigns on *The Ellen DeGeneres Show* and other talk shows. President Obama and his advisers agreed to have the president go on the edgy *Between Two Ferns* from Funny or Die to try to get more young people to sign up for the Affordable Care Act. And while host Zach Galifianakis was criticized for asking Obama "How does it feel to be the last Black president?" the segment had tens of millions of views, while HealthCare.gov saw a 40 percent increase in traffic the day the segment aired and Funny or Die became the top referrer to the government's website. "The video certainly helped drive signups," Obama speechwriter Cody Keenan said later. "The media environment had changed so much so quickly that people were no longer getting their trusted information solely from the legacy news outlets, but from all sorts of places. And so we were trying to go everywhere to reach people where they were."[187]

In the 2020 elections, Kamala Harris announced her candidacy on the early-morning *Good Morning America*, with sharp questions from host George Stephanopoulos, while Kirsten Gillibrand announced hers to Stephen Colbert on CBS's *Late Show with Stephen Colbert*. These announcements were timed with the release of campaign videos on the candidates' websites, and all the other major media covered the TV interviews, with online video—and critiqued the candidates' performance.[188]

"Soft news" and entertainment programming are part of the mediated political experience. As Michael X. Delli Carpini and Bruce A. Williams noted in an influential 2001 article, "Let Us Infotain You: Politics in the New Media Age," politics is not "a distinct and self-contained part of public life, and *citizen* is one role among many played by individuals."[189] Instead, they argued that "people, politics and the media are far more complex than this. Individuals are simultaneously citizens, consumers, audiences, family members, workers and so forth. Politics is built on deep-seated cultural values and beliefs that are embedded in the seemingly nonpolitical aspects of public and private life. Entertainment media often provide factual information, stimulate social and political debate, and critique government, while public affairs media are all too often diversionary, contextless, and politically irrelevant."[190]

Jon Stewart and *The Daily Show*

Jon Stewart—who hosted *The Daily Show with Jon Stewart* on the Comedy Central cable TV network from 1999 to 2015—regularly mocked the conventions of TV news-gathering and punditry with his "comedy correspondents" and sharp monologues. Stewart jokingly called *The Daily Show* "the most trusted name in fake news" before "fake news" took on a different meaning; he attracted a large, admiring audience, particularly among young people but also among journalists. Stewart was a serious critic of the media off camera as well as on, for many years, decrying what he called "the Great Conflictinator" of cable TV punditry.[191]

What Is the Impact of Late-Night Comedy?

There is a dispute over how much information these shows impart—and how much knowledge of politics and current affairs they require. Stewart

(Continued)

(Continued)

said that some knowledge of the news was required to get the joke but that *The Daily Show* was no substitute for reading and watching major, traditional news outlets. John Oliver, the host of HBO's *Last Week Tonight with John Oliver*, and his staff have done lengthy (thirteen-to-twenty-minute) segments on serious subjects, from net neutrality on the Internet to bail bond practices for indigent defendants in New York City.

Several researchers have found evidence that exposure to late-night comedy—particularly *The Daily Show* at its height under Jon Stewart—has what Matthew Baum has called a "gateway effect," an entry point for consumption of other media, especially by people who are otherwise politically inattentive.[192] In a 2006 study analyzing the 2004 Pew Research Center Political Communications Study and the 2004 National Annenberg Election Survey, Dannagal G. Young and Russell M. Tisinger found a positive correlation between exposure to late-night comedy programming and traditional news exposure. The authors concluded that there is not one monolithic late-night audience and that the data they examined provide evidence "illustrating that young people are tuning in to late-night comedy in addition to—rather than in the place of—news."[193]

In a 2008 study analyzing the national Annenberg data during the 2004 presidential primary season, Lauren Feldman and Young found that viewers of Jay Leno, the host of NBC's long-running *Tonight Show with Jay Leno*, David Letterman's *Late Show with David Letterman* on CBS, and *The Daily Show with Jon Stewart*, were paying *more*—not *less*—attention to traditional news about the election than nonviewers and that the greatest increase in attention to news about the election came with viewers to Letterman and Leno.[194] Their successors—especially John Oliver and Seth Myers—have focused even more on politics and policy.[195]

Saturday Night Live

The producers of NBC's *SNL* have satirized the foibles of both Republican and Democratic presidents and presidential candidates for many years, with politicians from Donald Trump accompanied by multiple *SNL* Trump impersonators in 2015,[196] to Elizabeth Warren after she ended her candidacy in 2020[197] being seen by millions on the air and online on YouTube. There is some anecdotal evidence that *SNL* characterizations have had impact on public perception. Dana Carvey's portrayal of George H. W. Bush was so affectionate that the real Bush embraced it by inviting Carvey to do his impression at a White House holiday party.[198] But, while President Gerald Ford was a gifted athlete who had stumbled once coming down the stairway from Air Force One, comedian Chevy Chase consistently played him as clumsy on *SNL*.[199]

Perhaps the strongest anecdotal evidence of impact comes from the 2008 presidential campaign. Tina Fey's dead-on impersonation of the Republican vice presidential nominee, Alaska governor Sarah Palin, on *SNL*, coupled with Palin's poor awareness of domestic and foreign policy in interviews with broadcast news anchors Katie Couric and Charles Gibson, helped cement the image of Palin as an inexperienced naif in the eyes of many voters. "I can see Russia from my house" was the answer Tina Fey as Palin—not Palin herself—gave in response to Gibson's question about her qualifications for dealing with Russia. But the line—which was close to what Palin said—has stuck as real in the minds of many.[200]

In the 2016 and 2020 presidential campaigns, *Seinfeld* creator Larry David memorably played a shouting Bernie Sanders, while Maya Rudolph played Kamala Harris, who was gleeful at Joe Biden's (played by Jason Sudeikis, Woody Harrelson, John Mulaney, and Jim Carrey at different times) gaffes during the Democratic primary debates.[201] The producers of *SNL* have said that they are equal opportunity satirists across political party lines, and there is evidence to make that case, including the show's satirizing all the Democratic candidates and the Democratic debates in the 2020 presidential race. Interestingly, Amy Poehler's portrayal of Hillary Clinton as an unemotional "careerist" in 2008 morphed into a frankly sympathetic portrayal of Clinton by Kate McKinnon in the 2016 campaign as a highly qualified woman who just wanted to be president *so much*. In the 2008 presidential campaign, *SNL* satirized some journalists' swooning over candidate Barack Obama; in one skit, the show's presidential debate "anchors" were gaga over the show's Obama (Fred Armisen) while barely letting Amy Poehler as Clinton speak.[202] In a real presidential debate in 2008, Clinton complained about the tough questions to her by saying, "And if anybody saw *Saturday Night Live*, maybe we should ask Barack if he's comfortable and needs another pillow."[203]

But, of course, it is Alec Baldwin's impression of Donald Trump on *SNL* that generated millions of views on *SNL*. Trump—who had been a ratings-getter for *SNL* and other late-night comedy talk shows—as a

(Continued)

(Continued)

reality TV star—has had a love-hate relationship with the show, appearing as a guest host and portraying himself alongside multiple Trump impersonators on *SNL* as a presidential candidate in 2015, prompting complaints that the show had given unfair and unequal time to an announced candidate.[204]

After the 2016 election, Trump limited his talk show appearances to friendly venues like Fox News Channel's *Fox and Friends* morning show. He condemned Alec Baldwin's portrayal of him as overwhelmed and unqualified to be president, saying that it was a "hit job" and calling in a tweet for "retribution" and investigations of late-night comedy shows."[205]

In a critique of the angry tone of some of the anti-Trump commentary on late-night comedy shows during the 2016 election and after Trump's election, from John Oliver on *Last Week Tonight with John Oliver* to Samantha Bee on *Full Frontal with Samantha Bee* and Trevor Noah on *The Daily Show with Trevor Noah*, author Caitlin Flanagan argued in the *Atlantic* that "though aimed at blue-state sophisticates," these show are "an unintended but powerful form of propaganda for conservatives," reinforcing the view that the media were smug elites who dismissed the rest of the country."[206] As Flanagan noted, on her show *Full Frontal*, host Samantha Bee had to apologize for describing a young man attending the Conservative Political Action Conference (CPAC) as having "Nazi hair" after it was reported that he was suffering from stage 4 brain cancer. "Somewhere along the way, the hosts of the late-night shows decided that they had carte-blanche to insult not just the people within this administration, but also the ordinary citizens who support Trump, and even those who merely identify as conservatives," Flanagan contended.[207]

In their defense, talk show hosts who became overtly partisan against Trump have said that President Trump's own provocative remarks and policies had made him fair game. After a backlash over crude joking remarks about Trump having sex with Vladimir Putin, Stephen Colbert apologized on the air for the graphic nature of his comments. But he did not apologize for insulting the president. "I don't regret that," said Colbert, who had seen his ratings for CBS's *Late Show with Stephen Colbert* grow after he began doing more biting political commentary about Trump. "I believe he can take care of himself. I have jokes, he has the launch codes. So it's a fair fight."[208]

Critiques and Self-Critiques of 2016

For more than a year before the 2016 election, Harvard Kennedy School's Shorenstein Center on Media, Politics and Public Policy analyzed the main newscasts on ABC, CBS, NBC, CNN, and Fox News Channel and election stories in the *Los Angeles Times*, *New York Times*, *USA Today*, *Wall Street Journal*, and *Washington Post*, using data provided by Media Tenor, a firm that specializes in collecting and coding news content. Network talk shows were not included in the four-part series. The report, written by Thomas E. Patterson of Harvard, was sharply critical of the media coverage, as we noted in Chapter 1.[209] Here were some of the conclusions: Media coverage had elevated Trump during the important "invisible primary," when "the usual indicators for coverage—being a leader in the polls or in fundraising—did not apply . . . Upon entering the race, he stood much taller in the news than he stood in the polls. By the end of the invisible primary, he was high enough in the polls to get the coverage expected of a front-runner."[210] Measuring coverage as either "neutral" or "positive" all of the media outlets studied gave Trump "positive" or "neutral" during this time.[211]

Patterson cited journalistic bias toward what journalists consider a good story as responsible for the amount and tenor of Trump's coverage—and he slammed the argument from some journalists and news executives[212] that Trump got so much coverage because he made himself highly accessible to the press. "Availability has never been the standard of candidate coverage," said Patterson. "If that were so, third-party candidates and also-rans would dominate coverage. They hunger for news exposure. Trump's dominant presence in the news stemmed from the fact that his words and actions were ideally suited to journalists' story needs. The news is not about what's ordinary or expected. It's about what's new and different, better yet when laced with conflict and outrage. Trump delivered that type of material by the cart load. Both nominees tweeted heavily during the campaign, but journalists monitored his tweets more closely. Both nominees delivered speech after speech on the campaign trail, but journalists followed his speeches more intently. Trump met journalists' story needs as no other presidential nominee in modern times."[213]

Emily Ramshaw, editor of the *Texas Tribune*, said after the election that media organizations failed to hear and reflect the views of everyday people. "It's easy to sit in our ivory towers and make 'educated' guesses about who the frontrunners are," Ramshaw said. "It's another thing entirely to step out of D.C. and New York—to step off of the campaign buses and out of the debate halls—and absorb the frustration and resentment of the underprivileged, the uneducated, in the South, in the Rust Belt, in the American heartland."[214]

Phil Boas, editorial page editor of the *Arizona Republic*, said that he would give a range of grades to the 2016 reporting. "We've seen great reporting. We've seen lousy reporting," he said. "But if I were to give an overall grade to news media, it would have to be an 'F.' Not because the media made Trump, but because the media never saw him coming. Virtually everyone in news media, including myself, expected Trump to flit around the primary a bit, provide some comic relief and then hit the zapper."[215]

"Our great failure these past two years was our blindness," Boas continued. "A gathering wave a popular angst was building on our horizon and we missed it. In fact, I don't believe we even understand it to this day. It will take years of reporting and academic research before we comprehend the full range of elements that fed Trump's ascent. I hear the complaints that we saturated viewers with what amounted to billions in free ads for Brand Trump. But we had to cover him. He's the most radical major-party candidate to run for president in our lifetime."[216]

SUMMARY

Politicians have a push-pull relationship, with politicians and their advisers wanting to control the message and have it presented directly and favorably, without the media filter, and journalists wanting direct access to information and politicians so they can report and tell the story independently. The growth of public relations and modern-day stage-managing at the White House and political events began with Ronald Reagan and has continued with presidents from George W. Bush to Barack Obama.

The relationship between the media and Donald Trump has been marked by Trump's attacks on the media as "fake news" and even "treasonous," and White House TV reporters and news organizations continued to struggle with how to respond and fact-check in real time. Political polarization and the high cost of running for office have led to dysfunction and gridlock in Congress, with members of Congress from both major parties lamenting the lack of compromise and getting something done.

Late-night comedy and talk shows play an influential role in satirizing—and shaping—attitudes about politicians, while popular TV series depicting fictional politicians and journalists reflect their time and cultural attitudes, from the romantic view of *The West Wing* to the dark cynicism of *House of Cards* and *The Politician*.

The Internet and social media are powerful tools for mobilizing, fundraising, and targeted messaging, from candidates to social movements, and skillful social media outreach has helped propel new voices to political prominence. At the same time, the instant circulation of falsehoods, altered imagery, conspiracy theories, and organized disinformation campaigns on social media are powerful new disrupters that challenge the political and media systems.

End-of-Chapter Assignment:
Analyzing Depictions of Politicians and Journalists in Popular TV Shows and Classic Movies

Part I

Read these two articles for background only:

- Chuck Tryon, "10 Fantastic Political TV Shows You Can Stream Right Now," Mental Floss, August 25, 2016, http://mentalfloss .com/article/84667/10-fantastic-political-tv-shows-you-can-stream-right-now.

- Zachary Pincus-Roth, "'It's the President We All Want': The Melancholy World of Liberals Watching the 'West Wing' on TV," Washington Post, July 20, 2018, https://www.washingtonpost.com/entertainment/ tv/in-the-trump-era-some-find-escapism-in-the-west-wing-its-the-president-we-all-want/2018/07/19/05c40fd4-89bb-11e8-85ae-511bc1146b0b_story.html.

Part II

Watch either two episodes from the list of TV shows below *or* watch one of the following theatrical films in its entirety.

Do some research on the shows you're watching if you're unfamiliar with them. It's OK to watch a TV series you're already watching; in that case, though, watch two episodes you haven't seen before. Indicate which episode and what season you're discussing.

Take notes on what you are watching, including what happens in *each* TV episode you watch or the one theatrical film you watch—the show, who the characters are, and some lines of dialogue that you think are reflective of the show's attitude toward politicians and politics. Be thinking how these

(Continued)

(Continued)

pieces of popular entertainment reflect underlying attitudes toward politics or the media, women and men in politics, or other themes you pick up that relate to the subject of this book. Write a five-to-six-page paper with specific examples in your paper about what these shows "say" about attitudes toward politics and media. Include direct quotations from the show and/or what happens plotwise or characterwise to support your thesis. For example, you might say that *The West Wing* reflects an idealized version of the White House—and here's how and why it does that, with your evidence being what happens in the show and quotes from it. If you pick one of the movies, you'll want to discuss the movie's depiction of politics and media—and why critics have compared them to politics today.

- Theatrical Films
  - *A Face in the Crowd*, a classic film about a politician who's an entertainer and a demagogue. From Wikipedia: "Ambitious young radio producer Marcia Jeffries (Patricia Neal) finds a charming rogue named Larry 'Lonesome' Rhodes (Andy Griffith) in an Arkansas [jail] and puts him on the air. Soon, Rhodes' local popularity gets him an appearance on television in Memphis, which he parlays into national network stardom that he uses to endorse a presidential candidate for personal gain. But the increasingly petulant star's ego, arrogance and womanizing threaten his rise to the top."
  - *Mr. Smith Goes to Washington*, a classic 1930s Frank Capra film starring Jimmy Stewart as an idealistic politician
  - *The Candidate*, a 1972 film starring Robert Redford
  - *The American President*, a romantic movie with Michael Douglas as president and Annette Bening as an environmental activist he falls in love with; Rob Reiner directed
  - *The Manchurian Candidate*, a classic—and frightening—thriller about politics. Watch the 1962 original, not the remake. From Wikipedia: "Near the end of the Korean War, a platoon of U.S. soldiers is captured by communists and brainwashed. Following the war, the platoon is returned home, and Sergeant Raymond Shaw (Laurence Harvey) is lauded as a hero by the rest of his platoon. However, the platoon commander,

Captain Bennett Marco (Frank Sinatra), finds himself plagued by strange nightmares and, together with fellow soldier Allen Melvin (James Edwards), races to uncover a terrible plot."

- TV Series
  - *The West Wing*
  - *House of Cards* (older and later season would be an interesting comparison)
  - *Mrs. America*
  - *Scandal*
  - *Veep*
  - *The Crown*
  - *The Good Wife*
  - *Madam Secretary*
  - *Parks and Recreation*
  - *The Politician*
  - *The Newsroom*

Race and Immigration in Media and Politics

Protests, Policies, and Reform

Death of George Floyd

The protests and reckoning over individual and institutional racism in the U.S. in 2020 was sparked by the horrifying cell phone video of the death of George Floyd, an unarmed, forty-six-year-old Black man, in police custody. The video shows Floyd, pinned facedown, gasping for air and saying repeatedly "I can't breathe" while a Minneapolis police officer holds his knee on Floyd's neck for more than nine minutes despite pleas for help from Floyd and bystanders.[1]

Floyd was arrested, pinned down, and showed no signs of life seventeen minutes after the first police car arrived in response to a 911 call from a convenience store employee who said that Floyd had paid for cigarettes with a counterfeit $20 bill. An analysis of witness- and security-camera video showed that Derek Chauvin, the white police officer who had his knee on Floyd's neck, did not remove his knee even after Floyd lost consciousness and for one minute and twenty seconds after medics came to the scene.[2] The four officers involved were fired the next day, and after a public outcry, Chauvin was charged first with third-degree murder and then with second-degree murder, while the three other officers were charged with aiding and abetting second-degree murder.[3]

The video of Floyd's death—which was shot by seventeen-year-old Darnella Frazier and posted on her Facebook page[4]—went viral in the midst of the coronavirus pandemic. The pandemic left millions of people unemployed and revealed racial and ethnic disparities in exposure, illness, and death from COVID-19 among Black and Latino people.[5] The killing of George Floyd followed the deaths of Breonna Taylor, a twenty-six-year-old emergency medical technician who was shot dead in her apartment by Louisville, Kentucky, police in a no-knock raid,[6] and the death of a Black jogger, Ahmaud Arbery, who allegedly was murdered by a father and son who videotaped his death.[7]

The video of George Floyd was by no means the first highly publicized video of unarmed Black men and women who were shot and died in encounters with the police. But coming as it did in the midst of the pandemic and the rhetoric of Donald Trump, the videotape of Floyd, which is hard to watch, led people to identify and empathize with him and was seen by millions of people. In the largest protests in American history, an estimated fifteen-to-twenty-six-million people, many of them young people, rallied in marches and protests across the country.[8]

The U.S. will be a majority-minority country by the year 2050, and there are indications that the country is diversifying even more rapidly than predicted, especially among young people. According to an analysis of U.S. Census data, racial and ethnic population estimates released by the Census Bureau in July 2020 in advance of the 2020 census, "nearly four in 10 Americans identify with a race or ethnic group other than white."[9] Many people, especially young people, identify as "people of color" in this country today, and they and many young white people saw themselves as allies who joined the protests over the death of George Floyd.

The video, the pandemic, and the protests, under the rallying cry of #BlackLivesMatter, prompted a wave of extensive media coverage, personal testimony, and calls not only for police reform but also an examination of systemic racism and inequality in other institutions. There were immediate changes in some police practices, and corporations announced new commitments to increase diversity and address systemic racism. The protests led to increased public support for the #Black-LivesMatter movement and resulted in accelerated changes in public attitudes about the existence of racism and racial discrimination.[10]

"Without gainsaying the reality and significance of generalized white support for the [civil rights] movement in the early 1960s, the number of whites who were active in a sustained way in the struggle were comparatively few, and certainly nothing like the percentages we

Photo 6.1 The death of George Floyd led to protests and calls for reform across the U.S.

Erik McGregor/LightRocket via Getty Images

have seen taking part in recent weeks," said Douglas McAdam, a Stanford University emeritus professor who studies social movements.[11] "It looks, for all the world, like these protests are achieving what very few do: setting in motion a period of significant, sustained, and widespread social, political change."[12]

The spring of 2020 also brought physical attacks on journalists covering the story.

There was criticism of mainstream news organizations from younger minority journalists within their ranks about the continuing lack of diversity among editors and debate over the value of the traditional concept of journalistic objectivity in what journalists of color called "reporting while Black."

Racist and anti-immigrant rhetoric and exclusionary policies have a long history at different periods in the U.S., with stereotyping language and appeals to fear and anger at "the Other," including people of color and immigrants as the cause of the problems of "real Americans." In recent years, however, a focus on issues of race, gender, and identity politics along with political polarization and negative views toward the opposite party have become defining factors in American politics. Barack Obama was not only elected but reelected, and antipathy toward Hillary Clinton personally was undoubtedly a factor in the 2016 election. But despite real progress in attitudes during Obama's two terms in office and several factors in Clinton's loss in the Electoral College, as we have discussed, many political scientists view the 2016 election and Trump's rhetoric and policies in office as a successful appeal by Trump to white voters in a backlash against rapid social change, disappearing jobs, and growing demographic diversity as well as the election of the first Black president in the U.S.

The intersection of media and politics in race, immigration, and ethnicity is one of the most important topics of our time. Media coverage, public opinion, politics, and policy around race and ethnicity have interacted and intersected in dramatic ways in the U.S. today, and it is important to understand both the most recent events and the history behind them.

In this chapter we will define and decode demagogic appeals, including the concepts of "othering" and "belonging." We'll look at the "Southern strategy" in politics that helped lead to the polarization and identity politics we have today. We'll look at immigration in media and politics, including failed attempts at bipartisan immigration reform under both Republican and Democratic presidents.

We will examine President Trump's anti-immigrant appeals and policies, public opinion, and the importance of both language frames and issue frames in media coverage from "building the Wall" to Dreamers. We'll hear important perspectives on race and immigration in media and politics—and the need for greater diversity in the media—in interviews with journalists, scholars, and activists.

Coverage of Race and Ethnicity in the Media

The Civil Rights Movement

As we discussed in Chapter 2, media coverage of the civil rights movement for equal rights for African Americans in the 1960s played a strong agenda-setting function in public opinion and policy. The movement coincided with an era in which the three major broadcast networks—CBS, NBC, and ABC—commanded huge audiences for their nightly evening newscasts and had significant influence on public opinion and policymakers in setting the news and policy agenda. The TV networks and national newspapers shone a light on racism in the South and the often-violent police response to nonviolent sit-ins and marches led by Dr. Martin Luther King and other civil rights leaders.

"The civil rights movement would have been like a bird without wings if it hadn't been for the news media," said Rep. John Lewis, the civil rights leader whose skull was fractured by police as he led the voting rights march in Selma, Alabama, in 1965 that became known as "Bloody Sunday."[13] Lewis said that civil rights leaders saw the news media as "sympathetic referees" in their struggle.[14] (In 2014 filmmaker Ava DuVernay's award-winning movie *Selma* surprised many younger audiences who had not known about the violence against voting rights marchers through Georgia, with beatings of marchers by state troopers on horseback.)

President John F. Kennedy, who had been reluctant to intervene in the South, responded to media coverage of police violence against peaceful protesters in Birmingham, Alabama, in 1963, with a televised address to the nation and a promise to send comprehensive civil rights legislation to Congress.[15] After Kennedy's assassination, civil rights leaders worked with President Lyndon Johnson to pass landmark civil rights legislation in Congress, the Civil Rights Act of 1964 and, after the march on Selma, the Voting Rights Act of 1965.

Still photography in newspapers and magazines produced images of police violence and resistance to ending school desegregation in the 1950s and 1960s that are indelible: the contorted face of a white teenage woman screaming at a young Black woman, Elizabeth Eckford, as she walked to integrate a Little Rock, Arkansas, high school in 1957;[16] Birmingham, Alabama, sheriff "Bull" Connor's police turning fire hoses and dogs on peaceful protesters in Birmingham; the March on Washington and Martin Luther King's "I Have a Dream" speech given from the steps of the Lincoln Memorial in 1963.

One earlier image that was not widely seen beyond Black readers for many years, however, was the photo of Emmett Till's mutilated body in 1955. After Till, a Black teenager from Chicago was murdered by white racists while visiting in Mississippi in 1955, his mother decided to leave his casket open. "Let the people see what they did to my boy," she said. Some 100,000 mourners, most of them African Americans, filed past Till's casket as it lay in state in Chicago. *Jet* magazine published a photo of Till's body in the open casket that was seen in *Jet* and other African American publications. But, according to historian Elliott Gorn, the photo was not published in mainstream media until many years later, when the groundbreaking Public Broadcasting Service (PBS) series *Eyes on the Prize* began with Till's story in 1987.[17]

Eyes on the Prize, along with filmmaker Stanley Nelson's 2010 documentary *Freedom Riders*, documents the long history of segregation and the civil rights movement in the South. But, in recent years, as Julian Bond, who narrated *Eyes on the Prize*, noted (in an interview with the author) surveys by the Southern Poverty Law Center at the time had found that high-school students were not being taught about the movement in a deep way. "They found that in almost every state, high-school students know two names—Martin Luther King and Rosa Parks—and four words: 'I Have a Dream,'" Bond said. "I've taught at excellent colleges, and I find that my students are ill-equipped to talk about the movement. If you don't know about the history of this great movement, you can't know what role you might play."[18]

Bond, who worked with Dr. King, cofounded the student-led Student Nonviolent Coordinating Committee (SNCC) when he was twenty years old, leading lunch counter sit-ins and voter registration drives and later running successfully for the Georgia legislature at twenty-five. As Bond noted, women also played an important role in the movement, although they have not been as well known as other leaders. One such leader is Diane Nash, then a college student, who risked her life to lead the dangerous "Freedom Rider" voter registration campaign on buses throughout the South, where Freedom Riders were attacked and one bus was burned.[19]

#BlackLivesMatter and Digital Activism

In contrast to the marriage of mainstream media coverage and the African American civil rights movement of the 1960s, contemporary social media and social media–based movements have given marginalized and disenfranchised people and groups direct access to telling their own stories and building support online. The #MeToo movement and the Women's March, about sexual assault and policies toward women; the Fight for $15 campaign for a $15 minimum wage, which was led by unions and food service workers; and the conservative Tea Party movement that elected conservative Republican candidates to office all have benefited from the narrative power—and the organizing power—of social media activism through digital media.

In the case of #BlackLivesMatter and protests over deadly police treatment of unarmed Black people, the widespread availability of cell phone video, coupled with the practically instantaneous distribution power of Twitter and Facebook, has allowed viewers to witness scenes that they might not have otherwise believed.

The first video to bring widespread public attention to racist treatment of Black men in police custody came in 1991. In that year, amateur video of a group of Los Angeles police officers brutally beating Rodney King, a Black motorist, after a high-speed car chase was shown repeatedly, first on local and then on network television.[20] The incident led to an investigation of the Los Angeles Police Department (LAPD) by an independent commission, which found a pervasive pattern of tolerating excessive force and outright racism among Los Angeles police officers.[21]

When the four white police officers were found not guilty of criminal charges against them in the case by a largely white suburban jury in 1992, Los Angeles erupted in several days of riots that left more than fifty people dead, more than two thousand injured, and many buildings destroyed or damaged.[22] (King himself called for calm, famously asking, "People, I just want to say, can we all get along?"[23]) Reforms were made in the LAPD, and the Rodney King story led to a national conversation and debate about racism in law enforcement, rioting, and poverty in cities.

Over the past several years there have been several highly publicized videos and controversies over police shootings of unarmed Black men, usually by white police officers, focusing public attention on the relationship between police departments and African American communities in cities across the U.S. The #BlackLivesMatter movement began in 2013 with a Facebook post and then a Twitter hashtag, started by three Black women, community activists Alicia Garza, Patrisse Kahn-Cullors, and Opal Tometi, who shared their dismay online over the verdict in the Trayvon Martin case.[24]

The acquittal of "neighborhood watch" volunteer George Zimmerman in the fatal shooting of Trayvon Martin, an unarmed seventeen-year-old teenager, led to national attention to the story and the trial. Photographs of Martin in a hoodie sweatshirt with "I Am Trayvon" slogans were duplicated and displayed in protests. Media coverage of the case and the trial was intense. The federal prosecutor contended that Martin, who was visiting family and had gone out to buy candy and a soda, had been presumed to be a criminal.[25] Fox News Channel star Bill O'Reilly infamously said that Trayvon Martin was killed because wearing a hoodie made him look like a "gangsta."[26] Jurors said that Florida's controversial "stand your ground" laws led them to find that Zimmerman had shot the teenager in self-defense.[27]

Martin's parents said that the verdict came as a "complete shock" that "the system . . . didn't work for us."[28] They later formed a nonprofit foundation to combat gun violence.[29]

"In the wake of the acquittal of Trayvon Martin's killer," Kahn-Cullors wrote in her autobiography, "we [had] to change the conversation. We have to talk very specifically about the anti-black racism that stalks us until it kills us. . . . There is something quite basic that has to be addressed in the culture, in the hearts and minds of people who have benefitted from, and were raised up on, the notion that black people are not fully human."[30]

In 2014 the fatal shooting of another unarmed Black teenager, Michael Brown, by a white police officer who said he acted in self-defense led to widespread protests and media coverage in Ferguson, Missouri, after the officer was not indicted.[31] The differing photos of Michael Brown that were published in media coverage led to another hashtag, #IfTheyGunnedMe-Down. On the Twitter feed young Black men posted positive-looking—and negative-looking—photos of themselves, asking, critically and rhetorically, which photo would be used by the media.[32] Later, the relative lack of attention to the deaths of the case of Sandra Bland and other Black women who died after encounters with the police led to another hashtag, #SayHerName.[33]

In other cases that gained national attention, in 2014, a bystander video showed a New York City police officer putting Eric Garner in a prohibited choke hold while arresting him for selling untaxed cigarettes. Before the video of George Floyd, Garner's last words—"I can't breathe"—became a rallying cry for marching protesters and the growing BlackLives Matter movement.[34] In Cleveland, Tamir Rice, a twelve-year-old child playing with a toy gun, was seen on video being fatally shot by a police officer within seconds of arriving on the scene.[35] In 2017 an investigation by the U.S. Department of Justice was prompted by the disclosure by an independent journalist of police video showing another unarmed teenager, Laquan McDonald, being shot sixteen times by a Chicago police officer.[36] The federal investigation found that Chicago police regularly violated the civil rights of poor Black people and Latinos and that police officers themselves were poorly trained and isolated from their communities.[37] Finally, in one of the most shocking videos in terms of live social media, the fatal shooting of Philando Castile, a thirty-two-year-old school cafeteria manager in Minnesota, after he was stopped for having an expired license plate, was livestreamed and narrated on Facebook Live by his girlfriend, who was in the car with her four-year-old daughter.[38]

Such videos have provided "corroboration of what African Americans have been saying for years" about racial profiling by law enforcement, Paul Butler, Georgetown University Law School professor and a former prosecutor, said.[39]

Police officials have said that these incidents represent a small fraction of police behavior.[40] "Every time I think maybe we're past this and we can start rebuilding, it seems another incident occurs that inflames public outrage," James Pasco, the executive director of the Fraternal Order of Police, said. "Police officers literally have millions of contacts with citizens every day, and in the vast majority of those interactions, there is no claim of wrongdoing, but that's not news."[41]

Before George Floyd and Breonna Taylor, public opinion on #BlackLivesMatter and its long-term impact was more divided. Supporters have seen it as an important voice via social media; detractors have said that #BlackLivesMatter protesters were anti-police and even anti- the value of other people's lives, a criticism that the founders and supporters have maintained is a deliberate misreading of the slogan.[42]

The founders of #BlackLivesMatter have said that they believe that it is significant and important that #BlackLivesMatter was started by three Black women and as a decentralized movement. They have also emphasized that their activities have included not only protests but working with local police and community organizations.[43]

The police officers involved in these highly publicized incidents have rarely been charged and even more rarely convicted on criminal charges, as the officers have said in their defense that they felt their lives were threatened, despite contradictory video evidence in several cases that has shown the officer shooting within seconds in some cases.[44] Even in cases when police officers have been disciplined, many have been returned to the force, and the soaring overall cost to taxpayers from multimillion dollar civil settlements for victims' families have not been reported to the public.[45] Such stories and legal outcomes, often years later, have sparked anger and racial differences about the outcome. They have also raised questions not only about racial disparities in law enforcement and the diversity of police departments but also about stereotyped fears of young Black men.

After covering several high-profile cases of fatal police shootings of civilians in 2014, *Washington Post* reporter Wesley Lowery (now with CBS News) was surprised to find that there were no official statistics on the subject. "I was shocked in some ways . . . that we didn't know the answer," Lowery said later. "We're a country that counts everything."[46]

Lowery proposed to his editors that the *Washington Post* collect the data and look for patterns; in 2016 the *Post* won the Pulitzer Prize for Public Service for reporting and compiling the first national, real-time data base of police shootings of unarmed people.[47] The data included the "threat level" of each person in encounters with the police, and the data were analyzed by a team of independent criminal researchers. The researchers found that in 2015 "unarmed black men were shot and killed last year at disproportionately high rates and that officers involved may be biased in how they perceive threats."[48]

Among 990 documented fatal shootings in 2015 by police, 93 of which involved people who were unarmed, "black men accounted for about 40 percent of the unarmed people fatally shot by police and, when adjusted by population, were seven times as likely as unarmed white men to die from police gunfire," researchers concluded.[49]

The videos in several high-profile incidents, including from police dashboard cameras that police departments increasingly have installed, led to federal investigations of local police departments by the Department of Justice in the Obama administration. Reforms in diversity of hiring and community police practices have been made in police departments around the country.[50] But critics have continued to say that the pace of change is too slow, while President Trump decried what he called a dangerous "war on police" and "anti-police atmosphere."[51]

After the deaths of George Floyd and Breonna Taylor, the phrase "defund the police" became a controversial rallying cry—and frame/counter-frame—for police reform that was used against the Democrats by President Trump in the 2020 election. Advocates define the phrase as meaning reallocating or redirecting funding away from the police department to other local government agencies, such as social services, which they said could better deal with many situations the police are called on; opponents have characterized the phrase as meaning advocating abolishing policing itself.[52]

In the weeks after the 2020 protests, local governments in New York, Los Angeles, Austin, Washington, D.C., and at least nine other U.S. cities made significant cuts to law enforcement budgets to reallocate funds to mental health services, homelessness, violence prevention, and other services. But the moves were controversial, including among police unions and some residents in local minority communities.[53] In the 2020 campaign Donald Trump said falsely (including in a deceptively edited campaign ad) that Joe Biden "fails to stand up to the radical leftists fighting to defund and abolish the police." Biden had said—and written—that he was not in favor of defunding the police.[54]

The Power of the Social Media Hashtag

In an academic study titled "Beyond the Hashtags," the authors Deen Freelon, Charlton D. McIlwain, and Meredith D. Clark analyzed 40.8 million tweets and more than 100,000 Web links as well as conducted some forty interviews with #BlackLivesMatter activists and allies in 2014 and 2015.[55] They concluded that "social media posts were essential" in spreading the Michael Brown story nationally and that "protesters and their supporters were generally able to circulate their own narratives" of the story directly on Twitter without relying on mainstream news outlets, which picked up the story from social media initially.[56]

The authors also found that "black youth discussed police brutality frequently on Twitter during 2014 and 2015, but in ways that differed substantially from how activists discussed it."[57] Although there were expressions of outrage on what the researchers called "Young Black Twitter," the postings were less overtly political, with more "simple memorialization, e.g. RIP to the person who died," and "more dark humor," with joking a possible coping mechanism about such serious topics—"one of the best-known pastimes" on what is called "Black Twitter."[58]

Attempting to measure the impact of activists influencing others on Twitter, the researchers wrote that the "evidence exists that activists succeeded in educating casual observers on Twitter . . . in two main forms: expressions of awe and disbelief at the . . . police reactions to the Ferguson protests, and conservative admissions of police brutality in the Eric Garner and Walter Scott cases," a 2015 case with video in which another unarmed man was fatally shot fleeing a North Carolina police officer after a traffic stop.[59]

Although #BlackLivesMatter began in response to the Trayvon Martin story, the authors of this study found that it was not until widespread protests over the shooting of Michael Brown that the hashtag gained prominence and grew into a loosely organized political movement that called for police reform and that had activists confronting both Hillary Clinton and Sen. Bernie Sanders during appearances in the 2016 presidential election.

In a critique of media coverage of the Eric Garner and Michael Brown cases, National Public Radio (NPR) TV critic Eric Deggans said that such stories represent "the catch-22" of racial issues. Deggans criticized what he said was the taking of sides in the cases on cable news networks, where the Rev. Al Sharpton was criticized for being both an MSNBC host and leading rallies in support of Trayvon Martin's family.[60] Cable news networks were playing to their audiences, Deggans said, adding that "cable news has sped up the path from news reporting to punditry with disastrous results."[61] The catch-22, he said, is this: "Trying to talk about systemic racial issues during a crisis is always much harder," but that's when the public is paying attention. He added, "Real progress on racial issues happens when people thoughtfully consider perspectives different from their own—and that's much tougher in a crisis. . . . In that moment, the public debate becomes polarized."[62]

The Obama Presidency

When Barack Obama, a forty-seven-year-old first-term senator from Illinois, was elected the forty-fourth president of the U.S., journalists in the U.S. and around the world emphasized the historic nature of his victory. In a front-page story headlined "Racial Barrier Falls in Decisive Victory," Adam Nagourney wrote that Obama's "sweeping away the last racial barrier in American politics with ease as the country chose him

Photo 6.2 Newspaper headlines heralded Barack Obama's historic election as the first Black president of the U.S. in 2008.

Mark Makela/Corbis via Getty Images

as its first black chief executive amounted to a national catharsis." Nagourney also wrote that it was "a repudiation of a historically unpopular Republican president and his economic and foreign politics, and an embrace of Mr. Obama's call for a change in the direction and the tone of the country. But it was just as much a strikingly symbolic moment in the evolution of the nation's fraught racial history, a breakthrough that would have seemed unthinkable just two years ago."[63]

The biracial son of a Kenyan father and a white single mother from Kansas, Obama "rode a reformist message of change and an inspirational message of hope," as Robert Barnes and Michael Shear described it.[64] Obama's rhetoric throughout the campaign had emphasized hope and change as well as a slogan of "Yes We Can," addressing his supporters and the country as an empowered *you*.

Standing with his family before a crowd of 125,000 people in Chicago's Grant Park the night of the election, Obama told the crowd, "This is your victory. . . . If there is anyone out there who still doubts that America is a place where all things are possible, who still wonders if the dream of our founders is alive in our time, who still questions the power of our democracy, tonight is your answer."[65]

The election of Barack Obama as the nation's first Black president in 2008 led to hopes among many Americans that America had made an important step forward in its long history of slavery and racial discrimination. There was even talk among some pundits that the election of President Obama meant that the U.S. was moving toward a post-racial society. In retrospect, pinning such hopes on one man, even someone as charismatic as Obama, was undoubtedly unrealistic in light of entrenched and systematic racism from the founding of America. "Hate and ignorance have not driven the history of racist ideas in America," contended author Ibram X. Kendi in his best-selling book *Stamped from the Beginning*. "Racist policies have driven the history of racist ideas in America."[66]

Obama's message of "Yes We Can" inspired many Americans and led to optimism about race relations, but divisions were present under the surface. In a Pew survey conducted a few days after the 2008 election, more Republicans and independents said that Obama made them feel proud and hopeful than had said so several months earlier. Two-thirds of voters overall said they expected Obama to have a successful first term, although Republicans were more evenly divided on that question than Democrats and independents.[67]

Obama was given very high marks overall among voters for his qualifications and for being inspiring. At the same time, nearly half of those surveyed continued to see Obama as "risky," while more than one-third said he made them feel "uneasy." A majority of voters (52 percent) said they believed that Obama's election would lead to better race relations in the U.S., with 75 percent of African American voters saying this would be the case, compared to 49 percent of white voters.[68]

Framing Obama as "the Other"

According to the classic work on the concept of self by the philosopher George Herbert Mead, people's identities are socially constructed through interaction and over time.[69] More contemporary analysis of the relationship of race, gender, propaganda, and power has found that successfully portraying someone as "the Other"—so foreign, different from yourself, and even subhuman—can blind you to your shared humanity. That is part of what happened with Nazi propaganda in the Holocaust and "ethnic cleansing" in regimes around the world—and why it important to understand the power of dehumanizing language and negative framing in media coverage and politics when it comes to race, ethnicity, gender, religion, and class. The problem of the twenty-first century is the problem of "othering," scholars john a. powell and Stephen Menendian asserted. "In a world beset by seemingly intractable and overwhelming challenges, virtually every global, national, and regional conflict is wrapped within or organized around one or more dimension of group-based difference. Othering undergirds territorial disputes, sectarian violence, military conflict, the spread of disease, hunger and food insecurity, and even climate change."[70]

During the 2008 and 2012 campaigns, the so-called birther movement repeatedly framed Barack Obama as "foreign" and an illegitimate leader. The birther movement—note the language implying that this was a social movement with many followers—was promulgated by conspiracy theorists online and championed and then given news coverage via the then private citizen Donald Trump.

Obama—whose full name is Barack Hussein Obama—was born and raised by his white grandparents in Hawaii but had spent time as a child with his mother and her Indonesian husband as a child in the U.S.[71] The "birther" framing used his race and background to portray him as foreign and illegitimate, both literally because you have to have been born to run for president and metaphorically as a candidate and president who should not be in office and does not deserve respect.

This promotion of Obama's "foreignness," which included saying that he was Muslim, represented what columnist Peter Beinart called "the new race card."[72] Obama ultimately authorized the detailed release of his Hawaiian birth certificate to show that he had been born in the U.S. But the conspiracy theories about his birth continued well into the 2016 election, when candidate Donald Trump called a press conference to finally acknowledge that Obama was U.S.-born—and then to falsely blame Hillary Clinton for the birther movement.[73]

As we discussed in Chapter 5 regarding fake news and disinformation, repetition—and forwarding from a person's trusted sources on the Internet—is one way that such provably false information takes root and spreads. The repeated falsehoods about Obama's origins had impact. In the fall of 2015, a CNN/ORC poll found that a startling number of Americans—29 percent—believed that Obama was a Muslim, although he had made numerous references to his Protestant faith. This number in 2015 was actually *higher than* the percentage of Americans who believed that Obama was a Muslim in polls conducted previously, between 2009 and 2011, by CNN and other organizations.[74] Additionally, according to the 2015 poll, 54 percent of Trump supporters said they believed Obama was a Muslim[75] at a time when Trump and others were characterizing Muslims not as followers of a world religion but as terrorists.

As we know from our discussion of the infamous "Willie Horton" ad used against Michael Dukakis in the 1988 presidential campaign, racist stereotypes, especially about African American men, can be effective at triggering negative, fearful emotions and stereotypical associations of Black men as "dangerous."[76] During the 2008 campaign, Sen. John McCain, the Republican candidate for president, declined to play that card, publicly correcting some supporters at a town hall who said they were "scared" of an Obama presidency because he was "an Arab" and even a "terrorist."[77] McCain also declined to have his political ad makers use footage of inflammatory comments about race in America in a 2003 sermon from Rev. Jeremiah Wright, Obama's longtime former Chicago pastor.

The video of Reverend Wright, reported first by ABC News and replayed many times on Fox News Channel and other news outlets, nearly derailed Obama's campaign. Wright said of African Americans, "The government gives them the drugs, builds bigger prisons, passes a three-strike law and then wants us to sing 'God Bless America.' No, no, no, not God bless America. God damn America."[78]

"Wright's unsparing critique was at odds with both Obama's message of hope and his multiracial family history," wrote Michael Fletcher. "The discrepancy raised pointed questions—gleefully fanned by Obama's political opponents—about the true sentiments of the first African American candidate with a real shot at being elected president."[79]

Obama disavowed Wright's remarks while downplaying the controversy initially. But, as it continued, he decided to give a speech on race and politics in America. That speech, "A More Perfect Union," balanced history and hope. It was widely praised and was credited with putting his candidacy back on track.[80]

Exit polls showed that voters in the 2008 presidential campaign were worried about the economy and health care as well as the overall direction of the country in the midst of the Great Recession, and they believed that Obama would do a better job than Sen. John McCain, who had said that he was not an expert on the economy and who was linked to the now-unpopular George W. Bush and the ongoing Iraq War as well as to the recession.[81] ("Why the Economy Is Trumping Race" was a *Time* magazine cover story shortly before the election.[82]) In a concession speech on election night, McCain told his supporters, "We have had and argued our differences, and he has prevailed. . . . This is an historic election, and I recognize the special significance it has for African Americans and the special pride that must be theirs tonight."[83]

During the campaign, Obama himself was "nothing short of a phenomenon," as Adam Nagourney wrote, drawing huge crowds and enthusiastic support and innovative organizing on the ground and on social media, particularly among young people.[84] Obama drew 66 percent of the vote among under-thirty voters.[85]

What became known as the "Obama coalition" gave the Democrats a higher Election Day advantage than either of Bill Clinton's two victories— and it included not only significant gains among traditionally Democratic Hispanic and African American voters over 2004 but also winning 60 percent of those making less than $50,000 per year as well as striking gains among the most affluent voters.

Obama beat John McCain by several percentage points in this traditionally Republican demographic, 52 percent to 42 percent, and he significantly improved on John Kerry's 35 percent percentage among this high-income bracket.[86] At the same time, McCain won the support of voters sixty-five and older. And there was "a sizable gap in support for Obama among whites in the South and those living in other parts of the country."[87] Just 31 percent of white people in the South voted for him, while he won the support of about half of white voters living in other parts of the U.S.[88]

Obama's Discussion of Race

Obama had come to prominence with his soaring 2004 Democratic convention speech, saying that "there's not a liberal America and a conservative America" but instead "there's the United States of America."[89] As president he was later strongly criticized in his first term by two critics, talk show host Tavis Smiley and author Cornel West, for, they maintained, not speaking directly enough about the lives of poor people and discrimination against African Americans—criticism that other Black supporters said was unfair.[90]

Obama walked a fine line in his discussion of race, rarely talking about race explicitly, according to Sam Fulwood III, a journalist and policy analyst who has focused on race and ethnicity in America.[91] In an interview with the author, Fulwood said, "If you listen to his rhetoric about hope and change, he's saying, 'We can do it'—he never said, 'I'm going to do it.' When he came in to office, people were inevitably disappointed."[92]

In Fulwood's view, Obama "let his guard down once when his friend [Harvard professor] Henry Louis Gates was accosted and arrested after entering his own house in Cambridge, Massachusetts. This was within the first few months of Obama's presidency. Obama said the police officer had 'acted stupidly,' and white moderates who loved Obama were offended that he called a white police officer stupid. Obama invited the police officer and Gates to the White House Rose Garden for a photo-op 'beer summit,' but he lost the police. I think they never forgave him, and law enforcement thought there was something suspicious about him."[93]

Obama continued to emphasize that he was the president of all Americans. But he also began to speak more personally and directly about race and racial profiling in law enforcement, saying, "If I had a son, he would look like Trayvon," and calling for an investigation into the death of Trayvon Martin in 2012.[94] The Justice Department in the Obama administration under Eric Holder, the first African American attorney general, conducted federal investigations of patterns of racial profiling by local police, bringing the federal government to bear in such cases.[95]

In 2015 Obama surprised the audience by leading mourners in singing "Amazing Grace" after his eulogy for Rev. Clementa Pinckney, the Charleston, South Carolina, minister and state senator who was killed along with eight other parishioners in church by a young white supremacist.[96] The Charleston murders led Republican governor Nikki Haley to ban the Confederate flag from the state capital.[97] It was followed by debates and protests over the Confederate flags and monuments to the Civil War that were taken down by governments—or taken down by protesters— in 2020.

In 2016 Obama again was at a memorial service—this time to honor five Dallas police officers who died in racially motivated killings by a Black gunman as they were protecting a protest rally. "We ask the police to do too much, and we ask too little of ourselves" to deal with the ills of society, Obama said to thunderous applause from the audience in a speech that nevertheless mentioned recent police shootings and called on the country to confront its racial divide.[98]

Obama's Reelection and Presidency

Barack Obama was reelected to a second term as president in 2012 against former Massachusetts governor Mitt Romney. Obama's approval ratings had dropped—and Democrats lost control of the House of Representatives in the 2010 midterm elections, largely by Republicans running against Obamacare (the Affordable Care Act). But Obama remained personally popular with many Americans, and he ended his two terms in office with high approval ratings, a rarity among modern presidents.[99] His legislative achievements, which President Trump and Republicans worked to overturn, included the Affordable Care Act and the global Paris Agreement on climate change. He is credited with leading the U.S. economy to economic recovery from the brink of the Great Recession in 2009. At the same time, although he campaigned vigorously for Hillary Clinton in 2016, he was criticized for being aloof from Democrats in Congress and for Democratic losses and Republican dominance in governorships and statehouses.

President Obama had come into office promising immigration reform, but other issues such as reforming health care took priority; his push for comprehensive immigration reform in 2010 in the face of mid-term elections went nowhere in Congress.[100] In an issue that continued to resonate in the 2020 Democratic primaries in criticism of former vice president Joe Biden, the Obama administration was strongly criticized by Hispanic and Latino groups as well as others for its aggressive enforcement of immigration laws, deporting over 2.4 million people. This total was nearly as many as Obama's two predecessors combined.[101]

After initially being portrayed as "an angry Black woman" by some commentators on Fox News Channel and in conservative media,[102] along with racist memes online, Michelle Obama became one of the most popular First Ladies in recent history. Michelle Obama was praised for her work in childhood obesity and health and earned higher approval ratings than her husband's[103] before the publication of her best-selling autobiography, *Becoming*. President Obama reported proudly in an interview before he left office that some conservative voters who had opposed him and his agenda had written to tell him that they thought he was a good father to the couple's two daughters.[104]

Public Opinion on Racial Discrimination in 2016

In the spring of 2016, at the end of Obama's two terms, Pew researchers found Black people and white people "worlds apart" in their views on racial discrimination, barriers to progress by Black people, and the prospects for change. Researchers speculated that "a series of flashpoints," including the publicized police shootings of unarmed Black men in encounters with the police and the racially motivated killings of the parishioners in Charleston, had brought new attention to this "centuries-old" deep divide on opinions between the two groups on the lives of Black people and the need for change—while also reigniting a "national conversation" about race.[105]

Seventy-one percent of Black people the 2016 survey said they had experienced discrimination because of their race, and 84 percent said that Black people were "treated less fairly than whites in dealing with the police."[106] Eighty-eight percent of Black people said "the country needs to continue making changes for blacks to have equal civil rights with whites," while researchers found 42 percent were "skeptical that such change ever would occur."[107] Among white people, 53 percent said the country "still had work to do for blacks to achieve equal rights with whites," while only 11 percent of white people said they doubted these changes will come.[108]

There were differing perceptions about discrimination, with a difference between the two groups regarding discrimination in the workplace, for example. There were significant differences within the white population, with white Democrats and white Republicans strongly disagreeing about whether too much attention was being paid to race and racial issues currently. Finally, when asked to evaluate the specific impact on race relations that President Obama had achieved in his historic two terms as president, a majority of Americans overall gave Obama credit for trying to improve race relations, but 63 percent of white Republicans said Obama had made race relations worse, while only 5 percent of white Democrats said that.

In an interview with NPR's Steve Inskeep in 2014, President Obama expressed optimism about race relations, despite discouraging numbers in Pew polling in that year as well. In the wake of protests in Ferguson, Missouri, and other cities over police shootings of unarmed Black men, Obama said that he believed the country was "less racially divided in its day-to-day interactions than when [he] took office but that the publicity and controversy over these cases had led to a more public debate on a subject that blacks and whites experienced differently."[109] "It's understandable that the polls might say that . . . race relations have gotten worse because [the incidents of police shootings] are in the news," Obama said. "I assure you, from the perspective of African Americans or Latinos in poor communities who have been dealing with this all their lives, they wouldn't suggest somehow that it's worse than 10,15 or 20 years ago."[110]

Six years later, in a town hall on race after the deaths of George Floyd, Breonna Taylor, and others, former president Obama said, "As tragic as these past few weeks have been, as difficult and scary and uncertain as they've been, they've also been an incredible opportunity for people to be awakened to some of these underlying trends and they offer an opportunity for us to all work together to tackle them. To take them on. To change America and make it live up to its highest ideals."[111]

Immigration

Immigration Policy Historically in the U.S.

Immigration policy—including the presence of some eleven million undocumented immigrants and their children in the U.S.—has been a contentious, unresolved topic in politics and policy for many years in Congress. The U.S. has historically and proudly proclaimed that it is a nation of immigrants and immigrant success stories, saying to the world, as the famous Emma Lazarus poem engraved on the Statue of Liberty promises, "Give me your tired, your poor, Your huddled masses yearning to breathe free."[112] The U.S. has welcomed immigrants, including refugees from war, from all over the world. But the country also has regulated immigration through policy and laws since winning independence from Great Britain. Historically, there have been limits or exclusions on immigration by Catholics, Asians, and other nonwhites. Anti-immigrant sentiment has risen—and been stoked—at various times in the country's history.[113] The Chinese Exclusion Act of 1882 made it illegal for Chinese workers to come to America and prevented Chinese labourers who had left the U.S. from returning. The law—which remained in force until it was repealed in 1943—set the precedent for other laws against other groups.[114]

"The United States has always had a kind of love-hate relationship with immigration," immigration historian Alan Kraut said. "In fact, the immigrants of the 19th and early 20th centuries had a saying: 'America beckons, but Americans repel.' What they meant by that is that, on the one hand, the United States had tremendous employment opportunities for them, possibilities of education for their children, freedom of religion, political freedoms that they couldn't enjoy in their home countries. And yet at the same time, the foreign-born represented a threat to some parts of the population. . . . The fear of people who somehow pollute American culture—this fear goes back to [Thomas] Jefferson. Jefferson worried that migrants to the United States would not appreciate democratic institutions and we would degenerate into a society that would seek a monarch. This love-hate relationship—or this beckoning and repelling—is a theme that runs as a constant throughout American history."[115]

Attempts at bipartisan immigration reform have failed repeatedly in Congress and under several recent presidents, including Bill Clinton, George W. Bush, and Barack Obama. Bush, a former governor of Texas, began advocating for a guest worker program in 2004. Bush had "hoped to appeal to both business owners and Hispanic voters with a comprehensive overhaul, but he was stymied by his own party" and opposition on talk radio.[116] Rachel Weiner of the *Washington Post* wrote in an analysis, "How Immigration Reform Failed, Over and Over,"[117] that Bush tried again in 2007, with Democrats in control in Congress, to craft "a compromise that allowed a path to legal status for current immigrants and a new temporary worker program, contingent on stricter border security and employer crackdowns." But that bill was opposed by conservative media and the beginnings of the Tea Party movement, while the AFL-CIO union opposed the guest-worker provisions. "Ultimately conservative Republicans, along with several pro-labor Democrats, opposed the legislation and it died in the Senate," Weiner wrote.[118]

Impact of Media Coverage of Immigration

In an analysis based on examining media coverage of immigration over more than thirty years, from 1980 to 2007, Roberto Suro, a journalism professor at the University of Southern California's Annenberg School for Communication and Journalism, noted that debates over immigration reform coincided with the fragmenting of major media and the growth of conflict-driven debate and punditry on cable news and talk radio. "The media have mirrored developments in the political arena as well," Suro wrote. "Heightened partisanship and the proliferation of less structured, often polarized, interest groups have made it more difficult" to represent "contemporary realities and policy choices."[119]

Suro also criticized the news media for what he called "the triumph of no," covering the subject of immigration, which has many elements, only episodically, and then focusing almost exclusively on immigration as *illegal* immigration—and political conflict over the issue—as if that were the only story.[120]

A study of images of immigrants in news magazines between 2000 and 2010 found that "the press frequently portrays immigrants as undocumented, presenting images of the border as well as immigrant arrests and detentions. Moreover, when immigrants are working, they are disproportionately engaged in low-skilled activities."[121] There was, the researchers found, "a general tendency to frame immigrants in a negative light, consistent with a 'threat' narrative but inconsistent with actual immigrant demographics. Our findings are particularly important in light of research establishing that such portrayals contribute to more hostile attitudes about immigration in the U.S. as well as greater support for punitive immigration policy among whites."[122]

Framing Immigrants and Immigration

Previous the framing of immigrants and immigration became an issue in the 2016 and 2020 presidential campaigns, there was long-running framing and counter-framing in the debate over U.S. immigration policies under President George W. Bush, President Obama, and before their administrations. Think of the different images and associations imagined between immigration advocates' preferred term—*undocumented workers*—versus *illegal immigrants* or even *illegal aliens*, a once-common term in U.S. laws that has come back in to use.

Jose Antonio Vargas—a former journalist who became an immigration-rights advocate after revealing that he himself was brought to the U.S. illegally as a child from the Philippines—has lobbied news organizations to drop the use of *illegal immigrants* in favor of *undocumented workers*. "I am here illegally—I am not illegal as a person," Vargas has told audiences.[123] Vargas' statement is an echo of Elie Wiesel, the Nobel Peace Prize winner and Holocaust survivor who has said, "No human being is illegal."[124]

In 2013, the Associated Press, whose stylebook is the reference guide for editors around the country, decided to drop the use of *illegal immigrant* to describe a person but kept *illegal immigration* to describe the practice of entering the country illegally. The Associated Press declined to adopt immigration advocates' preferred term of *undocumented workers* as imprecise.[125] ABC, NBC, CNN, and the *Los Angeles Times* also banned the use of the term *illegal immigrants*[126] and the term had been diminishing, although it is still used by both Democratic and Republican government officials and has been debated in newsrooms as well as in politics.[127] When the Associated Press made the change, conservative media watch group Media Research Center accused the Associated Press of "political correctness" and taking sides in the immigration debate,[128] while the activist group Colorlines, which began a campaign in 2010 to get media organizations to "Drop the I-Word," hailed the decision as a "crucial victory" because "the deliberately divisive and willfully inaccurate term has stood in the way of real discussion for too long."[129]

Interview with Univision Anchor Maria Elena Salinas

During her thirty-seven-year career at Univision, the influential Spanish-language TV network reaching millions of viewers in the U.S. and worldwide, Univision coanchor Maria Elena Salinas has seen Spanish-language TV grow along with the growth of the Latino population in the U.S, which reached nearly fifty-six million in 2016, according to U.S. census data.[130] Salinas, an award-winning journalist who is known as the "Voice of Hispanic America," has interviewed every recent Republican and Democratic president except for Donald Trump, including George W. Bush and Barack Obama, agreeing with President Obama's answer in a 2012 election town hall she moderated that not getting immigration reform was the greatest failure of his administration.[131] "There was such a huge need for information in this community when we began—I think we were helpful," Salinas recalled in a 2017 interview with this author.[132] Salinas, who retired from Univision in 2017, said in this interview that she did not want to interview Donald Trump, saying that "there would be no benefit" in doing so.[133] "I used to say that we were welcome in every White House. . . . I don't feel that we are welcome in the White House as we were for years."[134]

During the 2016 campaign, Salinas's coanchor, Jorge Ramos, was outspoken against Trump on immigration; at one point, the president had Ramos ejected from a press conference after Ramos pressed him to answer a question, saying to Ramos, "Go back to Univision."[135] Although Ramos was criticized for being an advocate, Salinas defended Ramos advocacy: "They say of Spanish-language TV, 'You're doing advocacy journalism, you're an advocate.' What we're doing is contributing to democracy. If we were not contributing to this dialogue [today], it would be a monologue accusing immigrants of all the ills in this country."[136]

Asked what improvements she would like to see in coverage of Latinos in English-language media, Salinas said, "I would like to see Latinos as regular subjects in stories. If you're going to interview an expert on economics for an economics story or a doctor for a medical story, why can't it be a Latino? During the Obama administration, you saw more African Americans recognized as an important part of society, with experts interviewed on just about every subject. They felt strong, respected. Now what's happening is those who have the same views as the president and agree with some of the rhetoric feel emboldened. What I would say to the mainstream media today is 'Don't stereotype us. Don't talk about only gang members and the only issue that Latinos care about is immigration. We care about immigration, but we care about a lot of other things, too. We're Americans, too.'"[137]

Republican Party and Immigration

After Republican presidential candidate Mitt Romney lost to Barack Obama in 2012, the Republican National Committee in 2013 issued a one-hundred-page "autopsy" on the election and recommendations for the future, called the "Growth and Opportunity Project" report, that was based on interviews with more than 2,600 people, focus groups, and polling among Hispanic voters, former Republicans, and other groups.[138] "The GOP today is a tale of two parties," the authors wrote, with a "growing and successful" gubernatorial wing and a federal wing that was "increasingly marginalizing itself" and making it difficult to win presidential elections. The authors wrote, "The Republican Party must focus its efforts to earn new supporters and voters in the following demographic communities: Hispanic, Asian and Pacific Islanders, African Americans, Indian Americans, Native Americans, women, and youth. This priority needs to be a continual effort that affects every facet of our Party's activities, including our messaging, strategy, outreach, and budget."[139]

The report urged Republicans to "embrace and champion comprehensive immigration reform," which the authors said "is consistent with Republican economic policies that promote job growth and economic opportunity for all," or risk "our Party's appeal continu[ing] to shrink to its core constituencies only."[140] The report also urged appealing more to young people and, while not explicitly endorsing same-sex marriage, called for a more inclusive approach to LGBTQ rights and marriage for same-sex couples. "There is a generational difference within the conservative movement about issues involving the treatments and the rights of gays—and for many younger voters, these issues are a gateway into whether the Party is a place they want to be."[141]

Noting changing demographics, the authors concluded, "By the year 2050 we'll be a majority-minority country and in both 2008 and 2012 President Obama won a combined 80 percent of the votes of all minority groups."[142] RNC chairman Reince Priebus, one of the report's authors, said at a press conference, "The RNC cannot and will not write off any demographic or community or region of this country."[143]

Trump Policies on Immigration and on Race

As *Politico* wrote in a 2016 article titled "Trump Kills GOP Autopsy," Donald Trump in his presidential campaign "not only ignored the [GOP] report's conclusions—he ran a campaign that moved the party in the exact opposite direction."[144] In interviews with party elders who coauthored the 2013 report and other Republican party leaders, *Politico* found a party establishment "terrified" of Trump's "GOP takeover" and fearful that "Trump's dominance will tear the party apart before they ever get a chance to put [their recommendations] in play."[145] In a scathing speech in 2016, Mitt Romney, the 2012 presidential nominee, called Trump a "fraud" and "phony" whose words and actions were "degrading" to women and whose policies would trigger a recession, make America less safe, and foster an era of "trickle-down racism."[146] As we know now, Trump won the nomination in a crowded field of Republican primary contenders and ultimately won the support of many party leaders and Republicans in Congress.

Trump—who was accused of stoking and benefiting from nativist, racist fears of immigrants and other groups—had begun his campaign with an announcement speech that described Mexican immigrants as rapists and murderers "bringing drugs,"[147] and he promised to build a wall across the U.S.-Mexico border to keep out illegal immigrants. He also proposed in that same speech to best the Chinese, who, he said were beating the U.S. in trade.[148]

Republican presidential strategist Ana Navarro, cochair of Sen. John McCain's Hispanic Advisory Council in his 2008 presidential campaign, endorsed Florida governor Jeb Bush for president in 2016. She was outspoken in her criticism of Donald Trump as the party's nominee in 2016—and since. In an interview with the author before the 2016 election, Navarro, who was born in Nicaragua, condemned the nominee for his rhetoric on Mexicans, immigrants, Muslims, and women.

"How do I feel about Donald Trump?" Navarro said, repeating the question. "I think he is a bigot, I think he is a racist, I think he is divisive, I think he is hostile, I think he is a misogynist . . . I think he is not a Republican. He brings out the worst in us . . . and he does not represent Republican values."[149] Trump, Navarro said, had "claimed my party's nomination by some fluke of nature," with both the news media and the Republican establishment not taking him seriously in the beginning, and she said she was very worried about his rhetoric "and what he has set loose in America."[150] Navarro ultimately announced that she was voting for her first Democrat, Hillary Clinton, and against Donald Trump.[151]

Soon after taking office, President Trump, to the surprise of many, began to issue executive orders based on his campaign rhetoric. Citing concerns about terrorism, he issued an executive order halting all refugee admissions and ordering a temporary travel ban on travelers coming to the U.S. from seven Muslim-majority countries, a policy that was challenged in the courts.[152] During Trump's first year in office, government statistics showed that deportation arrests within the U.S. had soared, increasing by 40 percent, while arrests at the Mexican border had dropped dramatically.[153] "The numbers released by the government . . . show that deportation officers are taking Trump's call for an immigration crackdown to heart," the Associated Press wrote.[154] "In February, then-Homeland Security Secretary John Kelly scrapped the previous administration's instructions to limit deportations to public safety threats, convicted criminals and recent border crossers, effectively making anyone in the country illegally vulnerable."[155]

In a review of these government data as well as interviews with those being arrested and deported, the Human Rights Watch group charged that many undocumented residents with long-standing family ties in the U.S. were being deported under the new crackdown, with arrests and deportation since Trump's election among people with no criminal convictions showing the greatest increase.[156]

The Trump administration began dismantling the Temporary Protected Status humanitarian program under which immigrants from Central America, Haiti, and other countries with violent conflict or natural disasters had been granted temporary visas, saying the program was never intended to be permanent.[157] And, in a speech in 2017, the president even embraced the idea of reducing legal immigration by half within the next decade by sharply limiting the ability of legal residents and American citizens to bring family members in to the country, saying that the country had taken in too many low-skilled workers.[158]

After that August 2017 speech, Trump's critics and observers speculated that Trump might be returning to anti-immigration rhetoric in the face of declining approval ratings from the public overall. "By endorsing legal immigration cuts, a move he has long supported," wrote Peter Baker in the *New York Times*, "Mr. Trump returned to a theme that has defined his short political career and excites his conservative base at a time when his poll numbers continue to sink. Just 33 percent of Americans approved of his performance in the latest Quinnipiac University survey, the lowest rating of his presidency, and down from 40 percent a month ago."[159]

President Trump's many critics included the CEOs of several major corporations who resigned from his business advisory councils, which were ultimately disbanded. Several prominent CEOs resigned in protest over his stances and remarks, including regarding immigration, the travel ban, and his highly criticized remarks equating far-white hate groups as "good people" with peaceful protesters against them and blaming "both sides" at a white supremacist rally that turned violent and led to the death of a peaceful protester in Charlottesville, Virginia.[160]

"We don't know, and we may never know, how much President Donald Trump's rhetoric influenced the white supremacist in El Paso who allegedly killed 22 people," Peter Wehner, a former official in the Reagan and George H. W. Bush administrations, wrote in 2019. "What we do know is that Trump has done more than any politician in living memory to fan the flames of ethnic and racial antipathy and nurture a culture of bigotry. A generation from now, when historians look back at the defining features of the Trump era, among the most prominent will be his dehumanizing rhetoric—the cruelty and virulence, the pulsating hate, the incitements to violence, and the effort to portray his targets as alien invaders, unworthy of dignity and respect, even subhuman."[161]

Case Study: Building "the Wall" and Framing Dreamers

Despite the continuing unresolved issue of the status of eleven million undocumented immigrants in the U.S. and immigration policy overall, immigration advocates and experts said that Trump's rhetoric and policy did not reflect today. "Trump's description of an American overrun by illegal aliens and criminal refugees is bogus," Elaine Kamarck, an immigration expert at the liberal think tank the Brookings Institution, contended. "It is

(Continued)

(Continued)

the most glaring example of a problem created to stir up political hatred, and the numbers simply do not support it."[162]

Mexican immigration peaked in 2005, as Kamarck noted, citing Pew Research Center data, "and has nearly been outpaced by immigration from Central American countries, as well as India and China. Many of those seeking to enter the U.S. from Central America are fleeing violence—a significant difference from the economically motivated migration from Mexico that used to be the norm."[163] Regarding the powerful image of building "a beautiful wall" to keep out illegal immigrants, Kamarck wrote that "the picture painted—an open border where criminal Mexicans and terrorists crossed freely into the United States—was yet another Trump fallacy, designed to create a problem that had already been addressed effectively by the two previous American presidents."[164]

A Pew Research Center poll released as Trump took office in 2017 found that building a wall along the U.S.-Mexico border was "viewed as a less important goal for immigration policy than several other objectives, such as cracking down on visa overstays. Asked about eight possible goals for U.S. immigration policy, majorities rate each one as important, except one: Only 39 percent view building the wall as a very or somewhat important goal."[165] Fifty-eight percent said it was important to increase the number of deportations of people in the U.S. illegally, which Trump had vowed to do. The most widely supported goal—viewed as important by nearly eight in ten people—was establishing "stricter policies to prevent people from overstaying visas."[166]

Despite what many critics said was an unneeded, unfeasible project with an impossible price tag—one that Mexico would not be paying for, as Trump had promised, and that many Americans said would never be built—the symbolism of "building the wall" continued to resonate with Trump voters, 72 percent of whom, in a Fox News Channel poll in August 2017, said they wanted the wall to be built, compared to 29 percent of independents and 6 percent of Democrats in the poll.[167]

Ryan Williams, a Republican strategist and former deputy press secretary to Mitt Romney's 2012 presidential campaign (in an interview with the author in 2017) was pessimistic about the chances for bipartisan work toward immigration reform in the near term. "With numbers like those," he said, referring to the support for building the wall among Republicans in the Pew poll, "it's going to be a long time before a Republican candidate can talk about bipartisan immigration reform."[168]

"If I had told you in 2015 that the Republicans were going to have on the ticket somebody who had 60 percent unfavorables yet we were going to hold the Senate seats in Ohio, Wisconsin, and Pennsylvania, you'd never have me up here again," Republican strategist David Winston said (in an interview with the author) on the eve of the 2018 congressional midterm elections.[169] "One of the things that is unusual with him that I think everybody is still trying to work through is that he has a personality that generates unfavorables but also has a personality that has created a win. I would suggest that for a lot of folks, they've said, 'The tweets are difficult sometimes, but the bottom line is that the policies generally are in the right direction.'"[170]

Regarding immigration policy under Trump, Winston added in 2018, "Immigration is how Donald Trump perceives he won the election [in 2016]. Immigration is a base issue. . . . What you see is not a debate but an element of contradiction, the value system of immigration versus the value system of the law. Voters don't like being told which value is most important. What they want policy-makers to do is make these values work together."[171]

In 2018, the Department of Justice under President Trump implemented a policy of "zero tolerance" requiring that all migrants crossing the U.S. border without permission, including asylum seekers, be referred to the government for prosecution. Undocumented asylum seekers were imprisoned—and their accompanying children under the age of eighteen were separated from their parents and sent to shelters and other facilities often hundreds of miles away, with some parents ultimately deported and the government keeping poor records for reuniting children with families.[172] Public outrage over the policy came with heart-wrenching photos of toddlers crying while their mothers were being frisked and hundreds of people living in small holding pens in a swamped system.[173] The president and Fox News Channel host Sean Hannity continued to refer to an "invasion" of the U.S. at the Mexican border, but a negative reaction to his rhetoric and harsh policies was said to be a factor in Democratic wins in the 2018 midterm elections.

In 2012 and 2014 President Obama used his executive authority to protect some 730,0000 young people brought into the U.S. illegally and living here since, under the DREAM Act (the Development, Relief, and Education for Alien Minors Act) or DACA (Deferred Action for Childhood Arrivals).[174] President Trump had expressed support for Dreamers in the program, but Trump ended DACA in 2017, saying that Obama had made an

(Continued)

(Continued)

end run around Congress and throwing the matter to Congress to resolve.[175] DACA enjoyed strong public support in polling, with 86 percent of respondents in an ABC News/*Washington Post* poll in 2017 expressing support for allowing Dreamers who had been eligible for renewable two-year work permits under DACA to remain in the U.S.[176] In a 5–4 decision in the summer of 2020, the U.S. Supreme Court upheld DACA, rejecting the Trump administration's plan to dismantle it.[177]

As we have discussed, groups fight over the framing of a controversial topic in media and politics because differences in descriptive language and the framing of issues are believed to affect how people see themselves and others as well as policy proposals. In previous debates over immigration in Congress, there have been different frames and controversy over whether changes in policy represented *amnesty*, a term that implied unfairness or even unearned "forgiveness," or a "path to citizenship," which is a much more positive way of implying hardworking people already contributing would further work their way to the prize of U.S. citizenship.

In one experiment interchanging the terms in articles about immigration policy, the researchers concluded that "Americans had far more restrictive preferences when the policy was termed as an amnesty rather than as an opportunity to eventually become legal citizens, and the effect was similar among different partisan groups."[178] They found similar results with language describing the DREAM Act. "Including language that immigrants came over as young children led to less restrictive preferences, and even tilted support slightly in favor of the policy" at the time of their research.[179]

Latino Voters and the Latino Vote in 2020

Pundits and political strategists who talked in 2020—and before—about "the Latino vote" as a single entity were making false assumptions about the more than sixty-one million Hispanic Americans, according to experts on this rapidly growing segment of the U.S. population—and the U.S. electorate.

"The assumption is that Latinos are a monolithic group of voters, and the reality is that Latinos make up individuals hailing from more than a dozen different countries," Marisa Abrajano, a professor of political science at the University of California, San Diego, said. "The Latino vote in Florida is different from the Latino vote in California, and from Nevada,

Arizona—and so to make broad strokes, or using this pan-ethnic term, can be problematic, and the same trend was evident 10 years ago."[180]

"It's laughable that in 2020, this country still needs to be reminded, Sesame Street style, that Latinos are not a monolith & the Latino vote is a mirage," *Los Angeles Times* writer Esmeralda Bermudez said on Twitter after the election.[181]

Bermudez, who writes about the lives of Latinos, added, "This misconception comes from how little u bother knowing us, how superficially you cover us & how absent we are in newsrooms."[182]

In the weeks before the 2020 election, some readers of the *New York Times* might have been surprised to read an article headlined "The Macho Appeal of Donald Trump."[183] The article helped explain why 30 percent of Hispanic voters overall said that they supported Trump, despite his anti-immigrant policies and rhetoric. The article quoted a number of U.S.-born Mexican American men in their thirties and forties at a Trump rally in Phoenix who said that they supported Trump because he was, they said, forceful, wealthy, and unapologetic—even about wearing a mask during COVID-19—and was a successful business executive they knew first from his days as host of *Celebrity Apprentice*.[184] Hispanic women overwhelmingly supported Biden, but Biden's support among Hispanic men, at 60 percent, was lower than Biden's percentages for nonwhite voters.[185] The Trump campaign did outreach to evangelical Latinos, and Trump's message of framing Democrats as "socialists" and "radicals" resonated among older anti-Castro Cuban Americans and Venezuelans in Miami, helping Trump win Florida.

During the Democratic primaries, Bernie Sanders had drawn support from young Latino voters in Nevada and other states. Biden did well among Latino voters, helping lead to victories in the Southwest and strong showings in Texas. But critics within the Democratic Party—including former San Antonio mayor and presidential candidate Julián Castro—said that, compared to the outreach to Black voters, the outreach to Latino voters in some states had been belated and not sufficient. The party, Castro said, "needs to do much more," including "a year-long, consistent effort to turn people out, and to reach voters who are harder to get—especially in Arizona and Texas, which are so close for us now."[186]

Kamala Harris as Vice President, and Voters in 2020

Black voters played a significant role in the election of Joe Biden and Kamala Harris, just as they had played a significant role in Biden's winning the Democratic nomination. Biden had several disappointing showings against Bernie Sanders and Elizabeth Warren in early Democratic primaries—until the influential endorsement of James Clyburn, longtime

Photo 6.3 President Joe Biden and Vice President Kamala Harris at a victory celebration in Delaware on the night they were declared the winners of the 2020 election.

Andrew Harnik-Pool/Getty Images

member of Congress from South Carolina, led to a game-changing win for Biden in the South Carolina primary and several Super Tuesday primaries that followed quickly after that.

Noting the key support of Black voters and organizers, particularly Black women, for Biden and the Democratic Party for years, female Black political leaders called on the former vice president to choose a Black woman as his vice presidential nominee. After a long speculation and vetting process, in the media and in politics, that brought national attention to several Black women in Congress and statehouses, Biden chose as his running mate California senator Kamala Harris, who had run for president herself in 2020. Harris, the daughter of Indian and Jamaican immigrants, became the first female, the first Black woman, and the first woman of South Asian descent to become vice president of the U.S., thirty-six years after Geraldine Ferraro became the first vice presidential nominee, twelve years after Sarah Palin ran with John McCain, and four years after Hillary Clinton won the popular vote but lost in the Electoral College in 2016.

"While I may be the first woman in this office, I will not be the last," Harris told cheering supporters at the car rally where she and Biden claimed victory. "Because every little girl sees that this is a country of possibility. And to the children of our country, regardless of your gender, our country has sent you a clear message: dream with ambition, lead with ambition. And see yourselves in a way that others may not simply because they've never seen it before, but know that we will applaud you every step of the way."[187]

Harris, a former California attorney general, had struggled during the primaries to define her record as a former prosecutor to the satisfaction of some groups; but back in the Senate she sponsored new legislation banning police choke holds and measures supporting research on women's health-care issues and access to voting.[188] She also reached out to Black voters and voters overall, particularly women, on the campaign trail once Biden chose her as his running mate. Her personal story as the child of Haitian and Indian immigrants raised by a single mother resonated with many Americans.

"Harris has been out talking primarily to Black and Latino voters and women, reminding people who she is and that she would be making history," observed Ed O'Keefe, who covered the Biden campaign for CBS News, in an interview with the author days before the election. "Biden has been able to focus on the broader message that he is better equipped to deal with the pandemic and somebody who can unite the party and win over independents and even some disaffected Republicans. It's a good way to deploy your running mate, especially in a party where you've got to bring all these kinds of constituencies together and motivate them to vote."[189]

Many Americans were outraged when President Trump deployed National Guard troops to use tear gas to disperse peaceful protesters from Lafayette Square in Washington, D.C., and then walked from the White House to a historic church, unannounced, for a political photo op with a Bible after telling the public that military troops should "dominate" the protests. The military commander involved later apologized for his participation, and the incident was severely criticized, including by Trump's former secretary of defense, Gen. James Mattis, as undermining the apolitical tradition of the U.S. military.[190]

The protests remained largely peaceful, but there was rioting and looting in Wisconsin after another police shooting of an unarmed Black man; and public opinion grew more divided as Trump portrayed himself as a law-and-order president fighting violence in the streets. The general election largely was a referendum on Trump, including his handling of the coronavirus pandemic, which disproportionately affected minority communities, versus Trump's argument that the coronavirus crisis was ending and he was the one who could rebuild the economy.

But as part of that referendum, the social justice movement that Democrats said was on the ballot was on the minds of many voters in divided ways. According to preliminary data from one large survey of voters conducted by the Associated Press, about nine in ten voters said the protests were a factor, in their vote while nearly three-fourths said it was a major factor, and about one-fifth said it was the most important factor. Among those who said it was a major factor, 53 percent voted for Biden—and 46 percent voted for Trump.[191] Scenes of looting and "defund the police" were used in ads against Democratic candidates for Congress in 2020, and the president said repeatedly that he was protecting the suburbs from violence and "low-income housing."

"The overarching racial narrative in the country now deals with policing," Sam Fulwood said in an interview shortly before the election. "The media did almost saturation coverage of George Floyd and the protests, which became the backdrop for the presidential campaign. The question was always asked what does Joe Biden think about policing, what does Trump think, and Trump came up with this law-and-order argument. #BlackLives-Matter and the police-accountability argument has been seized on by the media as almost a proxy for race without having to deal with race specifically . . . We still need to have a conversation about race in this country."[192]

SUMMARY

In the spring of 2020, the death of George Floyd in police custody, recorded on cell phone video, led to widespread protests over the deaths of Floyd, Breonna Taylor, and other Black men and women as well as calls for police reform and a reckoning over systemic racism in the U.S. Media coverage of the civil rights movement in the 1960s played an important role in public opinion and policy. The 2008 election of Barack Obama as the nation's first Black president led to progress but also unrealistic hopes for a post-racial America.

In addition to a history of racism from the founding of the country, the U.S. has had a history of welcoming immigrants while also having exclusionary policies and stoked nativism at periods in our history. Bipartisan attempts at immigration reform have repeatedly failed, and the 2016 election is viewed in part as a reaction among many Americans against lost jobs to globalism abroad, changing demographics, and rapid social change in the U.S. President Trump doubled down on racist rhetoric and characterized himself as a law-and-order president in the 2020 election, while Joe Biden called for racial unity, appealing to Black voters and others. Kamala Harris represented many firsts in her nomination and win as vice president of the U.S.

End-of-Chapter Assignment:
Framing Race and Immigration

1. Watch President Obama's speech on race in Charleston in its entirety. Read this CNN article, take notes on the speech, and be prepared to discuss in class what we've learned about race in media and politics, the "fine line" you've read about in the interview here with Sam Fulwood—and what you've learned overall about rhetorical appeals. Be ready to discuss. https://www.cnn.com/2015/06/26/politics/obama-charleston-eulogy-pastor/.

2. Watch video of Trump's announcement speech and read the transcript: https://time.com/3923128/donald-trump-announcement-speech/. Take notes on his characterizations of immigrants and appeals to the idea that America is "not winning" and being laughed at by the Chinese. Be ready to discuss.

CHAPTER 7

Global Media

The International Influencer

In the 1990s, the rapid growth of CNN in countries around the world gave rise to hopes that the network's technologically revolutionary ability to provide simultaneous, live news coverage would lead to democratization, increasing the forces for democracy by shining a light on citizens' efforts to overthrow repressive regimes and leading nations to respond with humanitarian aid in the face of natural disasters and human rights crises. The term *CNN effect* was coined to describe how real-time media coverage of humanitarian crises at the time was playing a role in the U.S. government's decision to intervene militarily in conflicts that otherwise might have been ignored.

Christiane Amanpour's CNN coverage of war and genocide through "ethnic cleansing" in the war in Bosnia-Herzegovina in the Balkans in the 1990s is credited with helping to push the Bill Clinton administration and NATO to take action that led to NATO air strikes and a peace agreement signed in 1995 in the war in the former Yugoslavia.[1] (Also influential was *Newsday* journalist Roy Gutman's exposure of modern-day concentration camps in the war.)

At one point, Amanpour confronted President Bill Clinton about his flip-flops in U.S. policy in a headline-making global interview from Sarajevo.[2] "Bill Clinton was basically referring to the war as a humanitarian disaster—that's how the whole world was referring to it back then—and saying what a great job the United States was doing," Amanpour recalled in an interview with the author.[3] "We refused to play that game. It wasn't an earthquake or famine. It was evil. It was genocide, racial and ethnic cleansing based on racial purity."[4]

In 1989 CNN's footage of the "man with the tank" standing unarmed before a tank became an indelible worldwide image of the Chinese government's assault on pro-democracy demonstrators in Beijing's Tiananmen Square.[5] In 1992 American viewers' reaction to seeing photos of a dead U.S. soldier being dragged through the streets of Mogadishu, Somalia, on a humanitarian food mission, led President Clinton to abruptly cancel the U.S.-United Nations mission.[6]

In 2011 and 2012, Al Jazeera TV's coverage of the revolts by citizens against repressive regimes that became known as "Arab Spring" spread the news of uprisings in Egypt, Tunisia, and other countries to viewers throughout the Middle East. The Qatari-based Al Jazeera—which began during the war in Iraq and was accused of anti-West bias with its beginnings—today is considered a major force in public opinion throughout the Middle East.[7]

The CNN effect has never been uniform—or universal. Foreign policy is set by presidents and their advisers as well as Congress and is more dependent also on the input of political elites than is domestic policy.[8] At the same time, presidents and their advisers have noted that international media coverage is an important factor in their decision-making. The outpouring of public support and international aid in the face of several widely covered natural disasters abroad is another barometer of the role extensive media coverage can play.

Among the impacts of the CNN effect are political agenda-setting and a shortening of the time officials believe they have between a widely covered event and reporters' and others' questions about the country's response.[9] There is some evidence that international media coverage and, more recently, social media posts to the outside world, contributes to a "boomerang effect," where regimes may show restraint in the face of attention.[10]

Although it can be difficult to measure the precise impact of media coverage on foreign policy, a number of studies have found priming effects for both domestic and foreign policy issues in how presidents are viewed.[11] In humanitarian crises, political scientist Matthew Baum wrote, "When an issue involves contested cultural norms—such as the moral value of alleviating suffering through humanitarian intervention, weighed against the risk of casualties in a conflict lacking clear national security interest—this leaves an opening for the media to challenge the government's preferred frame. In such circumstances, the media may independently influence citizens' interpretations of a leader's foreign policy actions."[12]

In 2017 President Trump cited terrible pictures of women and children in a poison gas attack in a rebel-held village in Syria for his decision to launch a single U.S. air strike against a Syrian airfield and the regime of Syrian president Bashar al-Assad. "I tell you, the attack on children had a big impact on me—big impact," the president said about what he had been "watching and seeing" on U.S. cable TV.[13]

In 2013 President Obama had been criticized by proponents of military action in Syria for not acting militarily against al-Assad after declaring that he was drawing "a red line" over the use of chemical warfare in Syria in 2013.[14] Obama was said to believe that such strikes would not be effective despite the urgings of the then-secretary of state Hillary Clinton and others in his administration to respond to chemical weapons attacks by al-Assad, who is backed by Russia in this proxy war.[15] We will discuss policy and media coverage in the Syrian civil war, which has led to an international refugee crisis with six million Syrian refugees, later in this chapter.

In her book *Lights, Camera, War* about the role of media technology in international politics, Johanna Neuman concluded that, as in Somalia, pictures could drive diplomacy only in the absence of a clearly stated foreign policy or political leadership. "In the end, in war or peace, leadership tells," she wrote.[16]

In this chapter we will examine the interplay of media and politics in some of the most consequential events in recent times, from wars and terrorist attacks to climate change and the coronavirus pandemic. We will examine how the media's overreliance on officialdom and pressures to be patriotic in the post–9/11 environment led to insufficient questioning of the case for war in Iraq, with both the *New York Times* and the *Washington Post* issuing extraordinary mea culpas for their reporting on the administration and the existence of weapons of mass destruction (WMDs) under Saddam Hussein.

Many Americans have traditionally been uninterested in international news in general, and international news coverage on U.S. television has been Americentric.[17] Cutbacks in foreign bureaus at the broadcast TV networks diminished the "news hole" for international news on the nightly evening newscasts, where it usually represents a percentage of total coverage, according to Andrew Tyndall, who has calculated the relative minutes to topics on NBC News, CBS News, and ABC News for his *Tyndall Report* for thirty years.[18]

At the same time, however, ratings for network and cable TV news have been up in recent years, and viewership and readership have increased dramatically with the coronavirus crisis. The Internet and social media have allowed for online distribution of stories from the BBC and Al Jazeera English, while social media postings of photographs and witness videos posted online and on television have added new viewers and venues for international news.

As we noted in Chapter 4, American media have been criticized for false objectivity in giving equal weight time to scientists and phony "climate skeptics," experts funded by the fossil fuel industry in coverage that misinformed the American public and helped keep climate change off the political and news agenda for many years. While there is still criticism of insufficient coverage of climate change and insufficient attention by politicians in the U.S., the issue has moved up on the news and political agenda, and more Americans of both major political parties today see climate change as a pressing national and international concern.[19] In 2020 several U.S. and international news organizations joined forces to report more globally on climate change, in the U.S. and abroad; and the issue is receiving significant international attention.

There is some evidence that the coronavirus pandemic has forced changes in how Americans and TV news organizations view global health crises. The coronavirus crisis was the top-rated story of 2020.[20] In 2014 the outbreak of the Ebola virus in East Africa was the second most covered story on the three broadcast evening newscasts (after winter weather). But, as Tyndall noted in an interview with the author in 2014, the Ebola outbreak was largely covered for its ramifications for the U.S. and other countries. "Ebola should have been an international story," Tyndall said, "but only 9 percent [of the TV stories] had a foreign dateline, so it became a domestic scare instead."[21]

In an increasingly interconnected world that is paradoxically both more global and more tribal in many ways, it's important to study the interplay of media, politics, and policy in international news.

In this chapter we'll talk about what gets covered—and why. We will look first at the concept of American exceptionalism, how it has impact, and how American public opinion on that concept may be changing. We'll examine the war in Iraq as an important case study, and we'll look also at the media-military relationship and the future of war reporting. We'll study the importance of framing in media coverage and policy of terrorism. Finally, you'll hear from interviews with government officials and academic experts as well as CNN anchors Anderson Cooper and Christiane Amanpour on their experiences and why they think it's important to cover international news. At the end of this chapter you'll have an assignment to sample and compare coverage of international news on American broadcast TV newscasts to the BBC and Al Jazeera English TV networks.

American Exceptionalism and Global Public Opinion

The concept of American exceptionalism—the idea that America is an elect nation and an example for the world—can be traced to the founding of the U.S. In 1630, John Winthrop, the future governor of the Massachusetts Bay Colony, said this in a sermon to his fellow New England settlers before they arrived: "We shall be as a city upon a hill. The eyes of all people are upon us."[22] Puritan leaders described New England in religious terms, as a "new Eden" with a preordained destiny of greatness, fostering "a tendency to view America in religious terms," as historian Donald E. Pease wrote.[23] But, Pease added, "American exceptionalism was more decisively shaped by the ideals of the European Enlightenment. The founders imagined the United States as an unprecedentedly free, new nation based on founding documents— the Declaration of Independence and the Constitution—that announced its unique destiny to become the champion of the universal rights of all humankind."[24] In *Rights of Man* (1792), Thomas Paine asserted that the "revolution of America presented in politics what was only theory in mechanics."[25]

As we know today, this view of America as an egalitarian ideal was flawed from the beginning, in terms of slavery, the treatment of Native Americans, and the disenfranchisement of women. In his book *American Exceptionalism: A Double-Edged Sword*, Seymour Martin Lipset argued that the concept embodies contradictory values[26] leading, for example, to the magnanimity of the U.S. in the Marshall Plan to rebuild Europe after World War II and a stated, moralizing foreign policy of "nation-building" in the war in Iraq.

Richard Hofstadter said that "America is an ideology," and he argued that the founding of the country led to "an unswerving faith in national superiority and uniqueness that is deeply ingrained in the American mind."[27] More recently, British author Geoffrey Hodgson provocatively labeled American exceptionalism a dangerous myth.[28] And, yet at the same time, the declaration of human rights and individual liberty—and individual agency—expressed in the Bill of Rights and the Constitution have inspired generations, in the U.S. and internationally, in views of the U.S. and America's obligations and role in the world.

The end of the Cold War and the breakup of the former Soviet Union led to the diminishing of what is called the Cold War frame in media and in politics, with the U.S. and the democracy in an ideological battle against communism and authoritarianism and a single, powerful foe.

As a vast, prosperous country removed from the Old World of Europe, the U.S. has also had a tradition of isolationism and periods of anti-immigrant nativism. Donald Trump's stated foreign policy— "America First"—marked a return to a phrase that has been used by some politicians in several previous periods in American history.[29] President Trump's criticism of China and international trade agreements that he said had cost American jobs resonated with his supporters and other Americans, as did his campaign promise to disengage U.S. soldiers from "endless wars" after the long wars for U.S. troops in Afghanistan and Iraq.

Several months before the 2016 election, Americans were concerned about terrorism and global economic insecurity as threats to the U.S., but many Americans were focused on problems within the U.S. and wary of global engagement. In a Pew poll, 57 percent of respondents agreed with the statement that the U.S. should "deal with its own problems and let other countries deal with their own problems as best they can."[30]

In office, Trump's criticism of the post–World War II NATO military alliance was criticized by his own defense secretary, former Marine general James Mattis.[31] The president's embrace of what he described as the strengths of Soviet president Vladimir Putin and other autocratic leaders was an about-face from Ronald Reagan's policies against "the evil empire" of the Soviet Union.

Global Public Opinion on the Role of the U.S.

President Trump's withdrawal from international agreements on climate change and the Iran nuclear weapons agreement signed under President Obama were unpopular globally, as were Trump's policies on immigration. In its annual global opinion polling, the Pew Research Center found in 2017 that international confidence in the U.S. president had "plummeted" under President Trump, while favorable ratings for the United States also declined.[32]

In a survey across thirty-seven nations, researchers in 2017 found broad opposition to President Trump and his key policies, with a median of just 22 percent of respondents saying they had confidence in Trump to do the right thing in international affairs, compared to a median of 64 percent for President Obama at the end of his presidency, with concerns about President Trump and his policies strongest among traditional American allies.[33]

Subsequent surveys found similar results. In the Pew survey released in January 2020, a median of 64 percent across thirty-two countries said they did not have confidence in Trump to do the right thing when it comes to international affairs, while 29 percent expressed confidence in the president. Fifty-four percent expressed a favorable opinion about the U.S., while 38 percent were negative.[34]

In the U.S., millennials have more positive views both of other countries and international institutions than older generations in the U.S.—and it appears that those attitudes are persisting as younger Americans grow older. Pew research released in July 2020 found majorities of Americans across generations in favor of the United Nations—but U.S. millennials (defined as twenty-four to thirty-nine years old in 2020) were ten points higher in their favorable opinion of the UN than Gen X (forty-to-fifty-five-year-olds) or Boomers (fifty-six-to-seventy-four-year-olds.) The same was true for views of NATO and the European Union.

Analyzing results over time, the researchers found that "even as they grow older, younger generations [among Americans] tend to be more internationally oriented, more favorably disposed to groups, leaders and countries beyond their border, and less likely to see the U.S. as exceptional."[35]

As Figure 7.1 indicates, about four out of ten Boomers or Silent-Generation members (seventy-six-to-ninety-two-year-olds) agreed that "America stands above all other countries in the world."[36] Only about one in four Gen Xers and millennials agreed with that statement.[37] Although governments and elected officials make policy, these generational trends could have impact on public opinion and policy in the future.

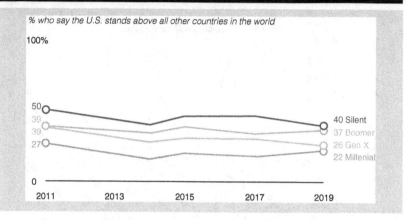

Figure 7.1 Older Generations Are More Likely to Say the U.S. "Stands above" Other Nations

% who say the U.S. stands above all other countries in the world

100%

50
39
39
27

40 Silent
37 Boomer
26 Gen X
22 Millenial

0

2011   2013   2015   2017   2019

Sources: Pew Research Center, "Older Generations More Likely to Say the U.S. 'Stands above' Other Nations," July 8, 2020. Survey of U.S. adults conducted September 5-16, 2019.

The Coronavirus Pandemic

International versus Domestic

As we noted in Chapter 1, the U.S. under Donald Trump was ill prepared for the coronavirus pandemic—and disproportionately affected in the number of cases and deaths. By the spring of 2020, the pandemic had devastated world economies and left 3.8 million people ill and 267,000 dead worldwide, from the time the virus emerged in China in late December[38] until the beginning of May.[39] The images of hospitals in New York City overrun with the dead and dying, multiple deaths in nursing homes, and nurses in need of protective masks shocked Americans—and the rest of the world.

Among the 3.8 million cases reported between January and May of 2020, the U.S. alone accounted for 1.7 million cases of COVID-19.[40] More than seventy-five thousand people in the U.S. had died. Government health officials were projecting nearly a doubling of that total by August at the same time that President Trump was pressing states to reopen.[41] As the following chart indicates (see Figure 7.2), the death toll by the spring of 2020 had surpassed U.S. military deaths in the Vietnam War and other wars and conflicts. By the end of January of 2021, the U.S. death toll had reached a grim milestone: 408,697.[42]

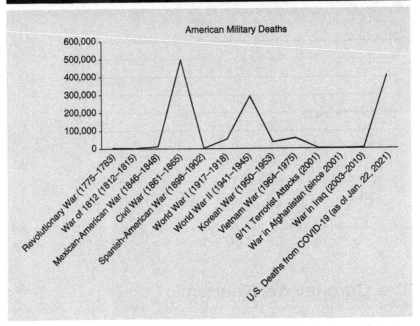

Sources: Data from the CDC, Department of Veterans Affairs, Johns Hopkins University, and National Geographic.

*War figures include military deaths in battle and in-theater deaths available.

**U.S. deaths from COVID-19 include states and territories.

With businesses and the U.S. economy shut down in measures to curb the spread of the disease, unemployment soared. With 20.5 million Americans suddenly losing their jobs in April of 2020, the Labor Department reported an unemployment rate that was the highest since the Great Depression.[43] "The United States is facing a political and economic challenge like nothing it has seen in nearly 100 years," Heather Long and Andrew Van Dam wrote with the release of the statistics.[44]

With even the recommended wearing of masks politicized, divergent responses among governors and between President Trump and his own medical advisers and no unified federal plan for testing and distributing vaccines once they could be created and made available, the U.S. response to the pandemic under Donald Trump was marred by partisanship and politicization. Fox News Channel and conservative talk radio echoed and reinforced the president's denials and downplaying of the crisis to a degree that whether viewers listened to Fox News Channel or other news sources affected perceptions—and views of the need to act, politically and personally. The economic and partisan divides that were revealed and *amplified* by the pandemic also have had significant impact on how the pandemic has been perceived—and experienced.

First is the economic divide: Although COVID-19 struck younger people as well, older people were more at risk of dying, as were people with serious underlying health conditions such as heart disease, diabetes, and lung disease.[45] Some groups, including African Americans, Hispanics, and Native Americans, have a higher prevalence of these conditions[46] while poverty, segregation, lack of health insurance and medical care, and other social conditions also contribute to health disparities, even under normal circumstances. Joe Pinsker, a writer for *Atlantic* magazine who interviewed public health researchers about the impact going forward, concluded, "While no one will be wholly untouched by the pain of the present pandemic . . . there will be stark disparities in how certain segments of the American population experience this crisis."[47]

Data reported from major cities and several states and analyzed by news organizations confirmed these startling disparities. Black Americans were bearing the brunt of the crisis, as the *New York Times* termed it, being infected and dying from the coronavirus at strikingly disproportionate rates and "highlighting what public health researchers say are entrenched inequalities in resources, health and access to care."[48]

The *Los Angeles Times* found in a separate analysis of public health data in California that older and younger Black people and Latinos aged eighteen to sixty-four were dying at higher rates relative to their percentage of the population than white people and Asian Americans.[49] In Chicago, African Americans in spring 2020 represented more than half of those who had tested positive for coronavirus and 72 percent of virus-related deaths, although African Americans were slightly less than one-third of Chicago's overall population. "This is a call-to-action moment," Chicago mayor Lori Lightfoot said. "These statistics take your breath away, they really do," said Lightfoot, who recently had been elected as the city's first Black female mayor.[50]

As the virus moved through the country, workers at meatpacking plants, nursing home residents, and prison inmates were showing high rates of infection.

Top health officials testifying warned of a second wave of cases if states moved too quickly in moves to open businesses and the economy.[51]

President Trump's Response

President Trump faced intense criticism for his handling of the crisis. As the crisis was mounting, the president repeatedly denied and downplayed the severity of the illness and the crisis for months. He variously said that the illness was "no worse than the flu,"[52] that there were just a handful of cases now recovering,[53] and that coronavirus would disappear "like a miracle" with warmer weather.[54] He reassured Americans that the situation was "totally under control"[55] even as officials from the Centers for Disease Control were warning of more cases.[56] Economically, as the stock market tumbled, Trump's economic adviser Larry Kudlow, a former Fox financial news host, said on the CNBC business network, "We have contained this. I won't say [it's] air-tight, but it's pretty close to air-tight."[57] Kudlow added that while the virus was a "human tragedy," it would not be an "economic tragedy."[58]

Although there were severe shortages of medical supplies and testing that government public health experts said were needed to treat patients and know who was infected, President Trump expressed doubt about the need for forty thousand ventilators in New York and erroneously said that the testing was "all perfect" and that anyone who wanted a test could get one.[59] In fact, the Trump administration had disbanded a White House office charged with planning for a pandemic or bioterrorism attack in 2018,[60] and the federal government had let maintenance contracts for respirators lapse, among other moves. The Centers for Disease Control did not begin sending testing kits until February; and Dr. Anthony Fauci, the country's top infectious disease expert and a member of Trump's task force, contradicted Trump, saying that the administration's early testing levels were "failing."[61]

At daily press briefings that he instituted and cable TV networks carried live, President Trump said that a vaccine would soon be available, although his own experts said it would be twelve to eighteen months. At one point during the daily press briefings he had begun, the president turned to one of his top public health experts, Dr. Deborah Birx, and mused about injecting disinfectant as a possible cure, prompting alarmed warnings from manufacturers and medical doctors about the dangers of doing so. "For months, the president has downplayed the severity of the pandemic, overstated the impact of his policies and potential treatments, blamed others and tried to rewrite the history of his response," Linda Qiu wrote in an analysis of the president's remarks.[62] David Frum, a political commentator and former speechwriter for George W. Bush, bluntly concluded, "Trump failed. He is failing. He will continue to fail. And Americans are paying for his failures."[63]

The president himself later portrayed the pandemic as a problem that "came out of nowhere." But internal documents and conversations within his administration, revealed in reports from the *Washington Post*, *New York Times*, *Los Angeles Times*, the Associated Press, and *Axios*, all showed that the president had been warned repeatedly and personally, by top economic, health, and intelligence officials, about the growing crisis as early as mid-January, although he continued to give false reassurances to the public.[64]

In September of 2020, journalist Bob Woodward's book *Rage* revealed—with audiotapes of the president talking in multiple interviews to Woodward—that Trump knew as far back as February that the coronavirus was more "deadly" than he had previously thought but that he had deliberately downplayed the severity to the public. "I wanted to always play it down. . . . I still like playing it down because I don't want to create a panic," Trump said in a call with Woodward, according to an audio clip posted on the *Washington Post* website and quoted in Woodward's book.[65]

Biden and Harris made Trump's handling of the crisis, along with health care, the centerpiece of their campaign, with Biden calling Trump's words to Woodward "a life-and-death betrayal of the American people."[66]

In the Pew Research Center poll below (see Figure 7.3) in April of 2020,[67] 65 percent of Americans said that the president was too slow to take major steps to address the crisis. In that same poll, two-thirds of Americans said they were more concerned about states lifting restrictions too quickly than not quickly enough, while 73 percent said the worst was still to come.[68]

Role of Fox News Channel and Conservative Media

For weeks before the country was shut down, President Trump repeatedly told his supporters—at rallies and on Twitter—that the Democrats, in league with the news media, were perpetrating a "hoax" about coronavirus designed to do political damage to the president in the 2020 presidential election.[69] Many people thought that Trump had called the disease itself a hoax—and, in what writer Nick Bolton called "the first true epidemic of a polarized, plugged-in era," many conspiracy theorists on YouTube and social media propagated that idea, along with the idea that the virus originated in a lab in China.[70] But when Democrats released a 2020 campaign ad to that effect, Trump tweeted this: "I never said the pandemic was a Hoax! Who would say such a thing? I said that the Do Nothing Democrats, together with their Mainstream Media partners, are the Hoax. They have been called out & embarrassed on this, even admitting they were wrong, but continue to spread the lie!"[71]

The fact-checking website *PolitiFact* backed Trump on the strict distinction while noting that the comments were confusing.[72] The remarks definitely continued the president's conflating the media with the Democrats. As *PolitiFact* noted, the president had used the word *hoax* to

Figure 7.3 Trump's Initial Response to Coronavirus Faulted

Trump's initial response to coronavirus faulted; most say 'worst is still to come'

% who say ...

Donald Trump was ___ to take major steps to address the threat of the coronavirus oubreak to the U.S.

Quick	Too slow
34	65

Greater concern is that state governments will lift restrictions on public activity ...

Not quickly enough	Too quickly
32	66

When it comes to the problems the U.S. is facing from the outbreak the ...

Worst is behind us	Worst is still to come
26	73

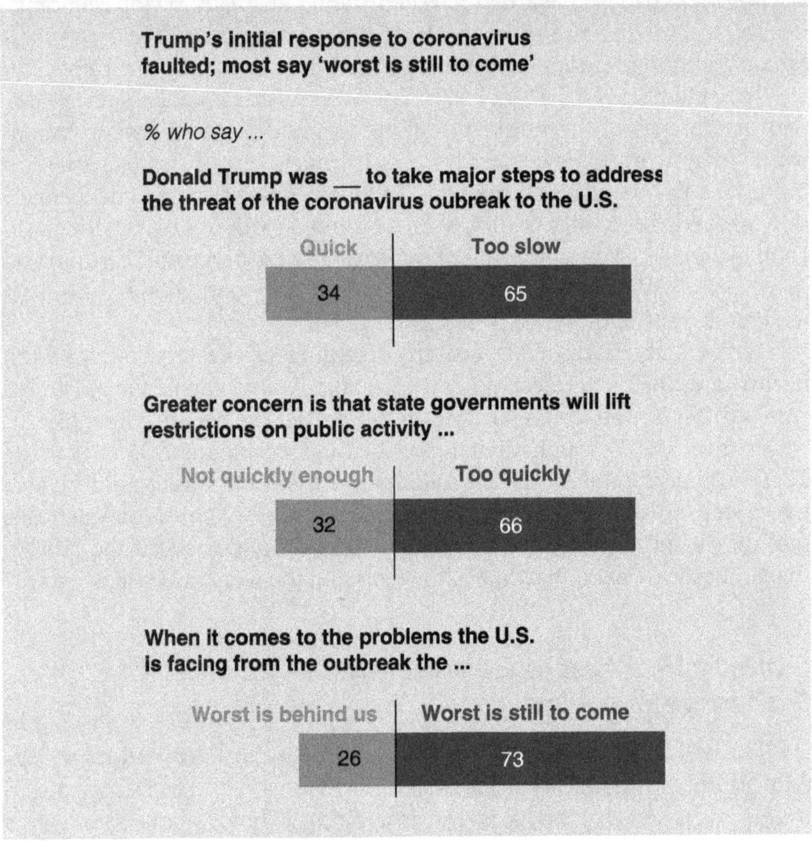

Source: "Most Americans Say Trump Was Too Slow in Initial Response to Coronavirus Threat," Pew Research Center, April 16, 2020, https://www.people-press.org/2020/04/16/most-americans-say-trump-was-too-slow-in-initial-response-to-coronavirus-threat/pp_2020-04-16_trump-and-covid-19_0-01/.

Note: No answer responses not shown.

establish his own credibility with his supporters many times before, including regarding the investigation of Russian interference in the 2016 election, global warming and the impeachment inquiry.

Matthew Kavanagh, assistant professor of global health at Georgetown University, said Trump's use of the word *hoax* regarding the coronavirus was "very dangerous" given his history of challenging the trustworthiness of the media and government officials. "Success against the pandemic depends on people believing and complying with the advice of public health officials as seen through the media," Kavanagh said.[73]

Sean Hannity, Laura Ingraham, and other prime-time hosts on Fox News Channel, along with Trish Regan on Fox Business Channel and Rush Limbaugh on talk radio, supported and amplified Trump's narrative—that coronavirus was a hoax with exaggerated claims of danger being hyped by news organizations and the Democrats.

They told this to millions of loyal viewers and listeners, many of whom are older and thus more vulnerable to COVID-19.[74] Limbaugh floated the conspiracy theory that the virus had been created in a Chinese lab. As late as March, Hannity talked about "coronavirus hysteria" and "lies, hysteria, and the media" on his highly rated prime-time Fox News Channel show. "This scaring the living hell out of people—I see it, again, as like, let's bludgeon Trump with this new hoax." During this same segment, Hannity, who had begun to take the virus more seriously, downplayed the risks except for people with compromised immune systems and older people.[75]

Public opinion polling from Gallup, Pew Research Center, and YouGov indicates that the dismissive coverage had real-world impact. As media reporter Oliver Darcy wrote, "Polls from both Gallup and Pew Research revealed that Republicans—who are largely distrustful of mainstream news organizations and primarily turn to Fox News and other right-wing sources for information on current events—were much less likely to take the coronavirus as seriously as their Democratic counterparts."[76] Gallup's poll in March found 42 percent of Republicans "very worried" or "somewhat worried" about coronavirus exposure, compared to 73 percent of Democrats.[77] A YouGov/*Economist* poll found a strong correlation between worry and media diet among Fox News Channel, CNN, and MSNBC. And Pew found at the same time that while 70 percent of the public said the news media were doing well or fairly well at covering the crisis, a majority said the news media were exaggerating the risks.[78] Within that overall figure were 76 percent of Republicans—and 79 percent of Fox News Channel viewers—who said the news media were exaggerating the risks.[79]

Commentary on Fox News Channel about the disease itself eventually turned more sober as the virus spread and the president convened a medical task force and began holding press briefings. In fact, prime-time host Tucker Carlson's news-making departure from Hannity and others to say that this crisis was real and should be taken seriously reportedly influenced the president's own approach.[80] But months had passed—and disbelief and disinformation remained. While Republicans and Democrats in Congress worked with the Trump administration to pass a massive relief bill, there was a blue state/red state divide among some Republican and Democratic governors in their safety restrictions and their plans for reopening. In demonstrations that Trump tweeted approvingly about, groups came to several state capitals in states with Democratic governors to demonstrate for "liberating" their states from quarantining measures.

Noting Fox News Channel commentary and the median age of Fox viewers at sixty-five years old, a group of seventy-four prominent journalism and communications professors in April published an open letter to Rupert Murdoch and Fox CEO Lachlan Murdoch.

They asserted that Fox News Channel coverage by Hannity and others "violated basic journalistic canons," had misinformed the public, encouraged the president's dismissiveness, "and was dangerous."[81]

"The misinformation that reaches the Fox News audience is a danger to public health," the authors wrote. "Indeed, it is not an overstatement to say that your misreporting endangers your own viewers—and not only them, for in a pandemic, individual behavior affects significant numbers of other people as well. Yet by commission as well as omission—direct, uncontested misinformation as well as failure to report the true dimensions of the crisis—Fox News has been derelict in its duty to provide clear and accurate information about COVID-19." The letter called on the network "to help protect the lives of all Americans—including your elderly viewers—by ensuring that the information you deliver is based on scientific facts."[82] Hannity, in response, told *Newsweek* magazine that he had taken the coronavirus crisis seriously.[83] Fox reportedly was preparing for numerous public interest lawsuits alleging harm from its coronavirus coverage, according to several news organizations.[84]

Several academic studies in 2020 found a direct correlation between a media diet and misinformation, with Fox News Channel viewers, who tend to be loyal to watching Fox News Channel solely, misinformed.[85]

Coronavirus and the 2020 Campaign

President Trump's approval ratings declined from March to mid-May, according to several polls. One Navigator poll in May found a majority of Americans—53 percent—approving of his handling of the coronavirus crisis, with declines in support from independents, older voters, and African American voters.[86] Numerous reports from inside Trump's reelection campaign indicated that Trump had planned to run for reelection on a booming economy along with the us-versus-them message to his base of supporters on immigration and race that helped him win in 2016.[87] By May the president had amassed a huge war chest of money—$212 million—raised by the Trump campaign and the Republican National Committee,[88] ten times more than the $20 million raised by the Democratic National Committee and Joe Biden, the presumptive nominee, who would have to raise more money virtually.[89] (These numbers were later reversed, with Biden spending nearly $500 million on advertising in the closing months of the campaign.[90])

Trump characterized himself as a "wartime president." And he blamed China, which initially had suppressed warnings from local doctors about the deadly new virus emerging there,[91] for the pandemic, repeatedly calling COVID-19 the "Chinese virus."[92]

A pro-Trump PAC for the Trump campaign, which was planning a targeted social media messaging campaign as well as regular TV, began releasing ads in several states calling the nominee Biden "Beijing Biden" and reportedly planning to link the former vice president to China, saying that his previous relationship with China was too cozy.[93] Biden disputed the attack, saying that Trump had endangered the American people by "believing the Chinese" and that he was much more capable than Trump in dealing with the Chinese and the crisis in the U.S. and abroad.[94] Trump dramatically removed his mask from the White House balcony after being treated for COVID-19 himself, further identifying not wearing a mask with being strong and dismaying public-health officials over the politicizing of mask-wearing.

President Trump's rhetoric was echoed on Fox News Channel, by Rush Limbaugh, and conspiracy theorists in social media and online. Trump blamed the Chinese for creating the crisis and perhaps even the virus itself while creating false, anti-Asian, racist associations between the coronavirus and the Asian American and Pacific Islander (AAPI) community. President Trump repeatedly called the coronavirus the "kung flu" and the "Asian" flu, although experts warned that such characterizations were inciting and dangerous. According to the Asian American Journalists Association, from spring 2020 to one year later, "violence against AAPI communities continue[d] to rise, with a 150 percent increase in reported hate crimes, according to the Center for the Study of Hate and Extremism, and 3,795 reports of anti-Asian discrimination to the Stop AAPI Hate reporting center." The journalists site added, "There is evidence to suggest that these numbers are underestimations of the surge of violence in the AAPI community."[95]

Photo 7.1 Dr. Anthony Fauci and Dr. Deborah Birx participate in a White House coronavirus press conference with President Trump in 2020.

Jabin Botsford/*The Washington Post* via Getty Images

Climate Change

Trends in Public Opinion and Coverage

In the midst of the pandemic in 2020, researchers at Yale University and George Mason University were surprised to find that Americans' acceptance of the existence of climate change—and concern about the issue—were at their highest levels ever in some categories. These findings came at a time when the health and economic crises within the pandemic had swamped the news agenda, and the researchers said that they had been concerned also about the importance of climate change in light of what psychologists call the *"finite pool of worry"* theory, which shows that when people are very concerned about one issue, their concern about others tends to diminish.[96]

In their 2020 annual report, "Climate Change in the American Mind," researchers found significant agreement that climate change is happening—and significant concern about its effects. Overall, the researchers found that two in three Americans (66 percent) say the issue of global warming is either "extremely," "very," or "somewhat" important to them personally, while one in three (33 percent) say it is either "not too" or "not at all" personally important.[97] Here are some of the report's other findings:

- Seventy-three percent of Americans believe that global warming is happening. Sixty-two percent of Americans understand that global warming is mostly caused by humans. But only 21 percent understand "how strong the level of consensus among scientists is (i.e., that more than 90% of climate scientists think human-caused global warming is happening)."

- Forty-six percent believe that their family will be harmed by global warming. Sixty-two percent believe that global warming will harm Americans overall, while 66 percent believe that people in developing countries will be harmed.

- Seventy-three percent believe that future generations will be harmed—the same percentage who believe that plant and animal species will be harmed.

Finally, the authors of the report wrote, "Many Americans think a variety of health harms, both physical and psychological, will become more common in their community as a result of global warming over the next 10 years, if nothing is done to address it."[98]

These findings suggest that climate change has "matured as an issue" and become a "durable worry" in Americans' minds, Anthony Leiserowitz, director of the Yale Program on Climate Change Communication, told the

New York Times.[99] Edward Maibach, director of the George Mason Center for Climate Change Communication, added that while Americans have accepted the reality of climate change, until recently they had seen it as a problem distant from the U.S. These latest results, Maibach said, demonstrate that "the majority of Americans see climate change as a clear and present threat to the health of their community."[100]

As we discussed in Chapter 2, for many years major media felt obliged to get "the other side" on the existence of man-made climate change from "climate skeptics" who turned out to be funded by the fossil fuel industry when, in fact, almost all scientists—more than 90 percent—believed in the existence of climate change and said that it was made by man.

The fossil fuel industry hid its own damning research, as investigative journalists later discovered, and scientists were attacked while opponents in Congress, Fox News Channel, and radio hosts such as Rush Limbaugh, operating from the same talking-points playbook, denied the existence of climate change and framed further regulation as "job-killing." Climate change became more of a partisan issue over the years: It is striking to know that Richard Nixon created the Environmental Protection Agency and that other Republicans have championed the state of the environment as an important issue. In 2013, only 42 percent of Americans believed that climate change existed and was man-made, according to the Yale survey, reflecting what Leiserowitz called a systematic "disinformation campaign" by corporations and organizations opposed to government action to reduce carbon emissions.[101]

The Environment in the 2020 Presidential Campaign

In the 2016 presidential election, according to one study, there was not a single question about global warming to Donald Trump from debate moderators.[102] The conventional wisdom among many political strategists for many years in the U.S. has been that the environment isn't a top voting issue compared to jobs and the economy. Politicians and corporations opposed to environmental regulations have often successfully framed the debate as jobs *versus* the environment, while ambitious visions of millions of jobs in a new green economy have been portrayed as gauzy futurism that threatens jobs in fossil fuels. Today, although there is still a partisan split between Republicans and Democrats on environmental issues, younger Republicans as well as young Democrats today see climate change and the environment as important issues facing their generation. While Donald Trump withdrew the U.S. from the international Paris Agreement signed by President Obama and rolled back environmental regulations that he said hurt business and the economy, Joe Biden in 2020 moved to win Democratic voters with an ambitious, $2 trillion plan to tackle climate change and rebuild infrastructure.[103] He rejoined the Paris accord as president.

Photo 7.2 Demonstrators called for international action on climate change at a rally in Italy in 2020.

Stefano Guidi/Getty Images

President Trump, who had called climate change a "hoax," had said that Biden's plans were extreme and would "kill" businesses and the energy sector on a day when he announced a "top to bottom overhaul" of a long-standing environmental policy act.[104]

Biden framed his plans as job-creating, although he walked a fine line with progressive Democrats with his continued support for fracking, and Republicans seized on his comment in the second presidential debate that a Biden administration would transition from fossil fuels. "When I think about climate change, the word I think of is 'jobs,'" Biden said, introducing his climate plans, "good-paying union jobs that will put Americans to work, making the air cleaner for our kids to breathe, restoring our crumbling roads, and bridges and ports."[105]

Humanitarian Crises

What Gets Covered and Why

As the following chart indicates, American broadcast TV networks traditionally have tended to focus on U.S.-based stories, although the global nature and U.S. effects of the coronavirus pandemic and climate change have moved these stories up in the U.S. news agenda. Wars and conflicts in which the U.S. has had troops also receive significant coverage, as have major stories in European capitals and some areas of Asia where the U.S. has economic and foreign policy interests. There are notable—and admirable—exceptions and commitment to covering important international stories, including conflicts, natural disasters, and humanitarian crises that do not directly involve Americans, on the major broadcast TV networks' newscasts and early morning programs. The nature of cable news has allowed for ongoing coverage of natural disasters and some humanitarian crises, although many stories remain uncovered and unseen on television. The media spotlight of natural disasters has led to U.S. relief efforts by the government and privately— for example, with the earthquake in Haiti in 2010 and the earthquake and tsunami in Japan in 2011.

Table 7.1　Top Twenty Stories of 2019

Mins	Total	ABC	CBS	NBC
President Trump impeachment	493	171	168	154
Ukraine-US: Zelensky-Trump call	325	112	118	95
Russia-US: election interference	298	100	100	98
Winter weather	249	118	68	63
Boeing 737 MAX fleet grounded	209	47	78	84
Hurricane Dorian in Bahamas	204	69	72	64
Syria civil war: Kurds zone, Idlib	185	49	90	46
Border controls on Mexico line	170	49	65	56
Jeffrey Epstein sex scandal	152	50	43	60
Federal budget, deficit, shutdown	149	47	55	47
College applications bribe scandal	142	48	38	56
Iran-US frictions in Persian Gulf	128	40	42	45
Tornado season	127	51	41	34
Smoking: e-cigarette vaping risks	126	23	52	50
Wild forest fires in western states	124	49	36	39
2020: Joe Biden campaign	120	41	46	34
School safety, violence prevention	110	33	28	49
TV's Jussie Smollett fake attack	109	43	31	35
Christmas holiday season	108	30	38	40
Measles outbreak: skipped shots	106	19	41	47
Total Top Twenty Stories	**3634**	**1188**	**1250**	**1195**
Total Campaign 2020 Coverage	**398**	**129**	**139**	**130**

Source: Andrew Tyndall, "Year in Review 2019," *Tyndall Report*, http://tyndallreport.com/yearinreview2019/.

In his many years of tracking news coverage on the ABC, NBC, and CBS evening newscasts, Andrew Tyndall has seen their ratings decline with the expansion of the news and entertainment universe—and then regain an audience over the past ten years, during a decade of major news. Today, the three nightly newscasts combined draw a large audience of about twenty-four-million viewers per night.

In the first six months of 2020, Tyndall said in an interview with the author, the three broadcast networks devoted about a quarter of their total news minutes to the coronavirus story, with a total of 2,289 minutes to the coronavirus story out of a "news hole" of 7,059.[106] The three networks gave 72 minutes to coverage of the implications of the crisis for U.S. foreign policy—with a separate total of 406 minutes to strictly international coverage—i.e., not U.S.-based—coverage of the pandemic. "The networks certainly geared up to cover the story from Europe and China," Tyndall said. "But the coverage accelerated and intensified once Americans started dying."[107]

The coronavirus story was overwhelmingly the most-covered story of 2020, followed by Campaign 2020 and then George Floyd as the second-most covered individual story. "Up until this year, it looked as if CNN domestically was turning in to an all-politics channel [with the Trump presidency]," Tyndall observed. "In my view, they've re-established their reputation this year as an international news channel".[108]

Major print news organizations, including the *New York Times*, *Washington Post*, *Los Angeles Times*, and *Wall Street Journal*, regularly cover international news with their foreign news bureaus. Today, courageous freelance correspondents also report at great personal risk from wars in the Middle East and other countries. But, on TV news, despite trends in international news in 2020, when it comes to ongoing coverage, many countries and even whole continents—Africa, South America, and virtually all of East Asia—go largely uncovered on a continuing basis unless the president pays a visit or there is a dramatic event or conflict.

Even then even a conflict that is viewed as internal may not get much coverage. "The TV networks' bureaus and coverage reflect the perceived foreign-policy interests of the U.S., and we've seen much more coverage of China in recent years," Tyndall said. "But there's very little ongoing coverage from India, and Mexico to me is the most egregious example of a lack of ongoing coverage."[109] When it comes to coverage of a natural disaster abroad, dramatic and compelling video is an important determinant of how much TV coverage the story receives.

Shining a Light: The Importance of International News

As data from the independent Committee to Protect Journalists (CPJ) show every year,[110] journalists and press freedom are under attack around the world today, from repressive regimes to corrupt officials as well as in wars where journalists themselves increasingly are targets. The work of jailed and murdered journalists takes place not only in wars but also under regimes in countries that often go largely uncovered on a regular basis in the U.S. Americans have been presumed to be most interested or even perhaps only interested in conflicts in which the U.S. has a direct interest—cynically described by some as "boots on the ground."

Recent surveys, as we have discussed, have found increased disengagement and skepticism about American action abroad in the face of the wars in Iraq and Afghanistan and economic problems at home. "Getting the public's attention, let alone commitment to deal with international issues is as challenging as it has ever been in the modern era," Andrew Kohut, founding director of the Pew Research Center, wrote in a 2013 report tracking American public opinion on global engagement.[111]

Christiane Amanpour and Anderson Cooper have both argued for the importance of shining a light abroad. "Some news executives say that the American public doesn't care about international coverage, but my experience has been that viewers do care about stories that are important and well told," Amanpour said in her interview with the author. "Besides, news isn't a commodity like soda or wine—it's a public service."[112]

As Amanpour and UN officials have noted, the civil wars and conflicts today are humanitarian crises. "The civil wars that have taken over," she said, "are not soldier against soldier, but soldiers against civilians and vulnerable people."[113]

Anderson Cooper—who reported from many wars and disasters as a freelance correspondent before joining CNN—has said that he feels a responsibility as a journalist to witness and report. "Anybody who has been to places where things are happening, whether it's the earthquake in Haiti, the tsunami in South Asia, or any war—you feel a responsibility to get it right and to bear witness to what people are going through," Cooper said in an interview with the author. "You know, there's nothing sadder than being in Somalia and coming upon a family who has died on the side of the road and, watching over the course of weeks as they disintegrate into nothing, literally into nothing. You know, a patch of hair is usually all that remains after several weeks in the sun. To me, you can't necessarily stop somebody from dying or being killed; you can't stop horrible things from happening.

But to know their names, to try to honor the lives they lived—I believe that is important."[114]

The Syrian Civil War

Having campaigned as an anti-war candidate who would end the wars begun under President Bush, Barack Obama ended his presidency with some American troops still in Iraq and Afghanistan eight years later.[115] President Obama was reluctant to engage in a third war in the Middle East in Syria, and 60 percent of Americans in 2012 said the U.S. did not have a responsibility to act in Syria.[116] Obama relied more heavily on drone attacks and covert operations during his presidency, and he was reluctant to back Syrian rebels in the war against Syrian dictator Bashar al-Assad, even in the face of evidence that he had used chemical weapons against his own people and hundreds of thousands of civilian casualties in the Syrian civil war. The president was criticized for not mobilizing public opinion in the U.S. toward taking action in Syria. "He has not tried to mobilize the country . . . to explain to the country what the stakes are, why these wars have gone the way they have," Eliot Cohen, a military historian who backed the war in Iraq, told the *New York Times* at the end of Obama's presidency in 2016. "For all his faults, with Bush, there was this visceral desire to win."[117]

The Syrian civil war and the humanitarian and refugee crisis caused by what has been called a "proxy war" is a case where media coverage appears not to have influenced U.S. foreign policy. International concern over whether Bashar al-Assad used chemical warfare against his own people and the Obama administration's consideration of what to do after Syria had crossed the "bright line" President Obama had set over chemical warfare made the Syrian conflict the most-covered international story on the American broadcast evening newscasts in 2013—and the fourth most-covered story overall.

By 2015 the war in Syria had dropped to the twelfth-most covered story in a year when winter weather and Donald Trump were the two most-covered stories. Syria became the most dangerous place in the world for journalists from 2012 to 2014, according to figures from CPJ,[118] with American foreign correspondent Marie Colvin and others killed in shelling, James Foley and journalists from the U.S. and other nations beheaded, and many local citizen journalists dead or silenced. Journalists who remained and advocates for greater intervention by the U.S. and other countries were frustrated by the lack of global action in the war, which had killed more than 250,000 people and displaced twelve million, according to UN estimates,[119] by 2015.

The flood of refugees fleeing the Syrian war in rafts and small boats— and the migration crisis and response in Europe and other nations—was widely covered by American and international media in 2015 and 2016, with images and interviews of families with their children. But the war in Syria—with video of children in villages where starvation was being used as a tool of war, smuggled out by citizen journalists and played on TV news—became even more perilous to report as the war dragged on. Ban Ki-moon, secretary-general of the UN, lamented the lack of global action. "The horrific war in Syria continues to worsen and bleed beyond its borders. A cold calculation seems to be taking hold: that little can be done except to arm the parties and watch the conflict rage. The international community must not abandon the people of Syria and the region to never-ending waves of cruelty and crisis."[120]

Terrorism

Before the coronavirus pandemic dominated the world's attention, terrorist attacks were the national and international story of the decade—in media and politics. One of the most widely covered attacks came in Paris in 2015. A small team of suicide bombers carried out a series of coordinated terrorist attacks and mass shootings in Paris—in a concert hall, a sports stadium, and cafes and restaurants—that seemed designed to strike at symbols of European culture and enjoyment. Eighty-nine people who were attending a rock concert were shot and killed inside the concert hall, and the death toll reached 130, with 400 wounded.[121] The Islamic State terrorist group known as ISIS, or ISIL, claimed responsibility for the attacks, which the group said were in retaliation for French participation in U.S.-led bombings of ISIS strongholds in Syria and Iraq.[122] The president of France, Francois Hollande, declared the Paris attacks an act of war and ordered further French air strikes on suspected ISIS targets in Syria.[123]

Revelations that the terrorists were Belgian- and French-born men who apparently had been trained by ISIS in Syria led to fears of further terrorist attacks and calls by right-wing populist leaders like France's Marine Le Pen to close the tide of Syrian refugees flooding into Europe.[124] Two of the terrorists had apparently gained reentry to Europe through Greece by posing as Syrian refugees.[125] There were questions about policing and lack of intelligence-sharing in the European Union, along with calls for understanding and combating alienation and radicalization to terrorism.

Extensive news coverage, including horrifying video of a pregnant woman hanging from a ledge trying to escape the concert hall, shattered wine glasses, and bodies in the street,[126] brought the Paris attacks vividly home to millions of viewers and readers.

Less than three weeks later, Syed Rizwan Farook, an American health department inspector, and Tashfeen Malik, his Pakistani-born wife, pledging loyalty to ISIS and martyrdom, killed fourteen people and seriously injured twenty-two people at a Christmas party with Farook's coworkers in Redlands, California.[127]

In a White House address, President Obama—who had been criticized by Republicans and conservative media for what they maintained was the president's unwillingness to call terrorism terrorism—defined the mass shootings as an act of terrorism as well as "a perverted interpretation of Islam."[128] The attacks were praised by ISIS, and FBI officials said that the couple appeared to have been self-radicalized over several years of consuming "poison on the Internet."[129]

American Muslim groups condemned the attacks, which they reported were leading to an increase in anti-Muslim hate crimes in the U.S.[130] Then-Republican presidential candidate Donald Trump ramped up his anti-Muslim rhetoric after these attacks, calling for a "total and complete" ban on Muslims entering the U.S. "until our country's representatives can figure out what is going on."[131] Trump's statement was widely condemned, including by the White House, Hillary Clinton, and the Pentagon, which said in a statement that "anything that bolsters ISIL's narrative and pits the United States against the Muslim faith is certainly not only contrary to our values, but contrary to our national security."[132]

The Center for Strategic and International Studies, a security think tank, has defined *terrorism* as "the deliberate use—or threat—of violence by non-state actors in order to achieve political goals and create a broad psychological impact."[133] The Paris and San Bernardino attacks and other terrorist attacks in recent years illustrate the ability of terrorists to strike fear through random violence and to recruit through sophisticated propaganda on social media. Several polls taken by the Gallup polling organization in 2015 prior to the Paris attacks found Americans increasingly worried about the possibility of attacks in the U.S., with 51 percent of respondents in 2015 expressing a great deal of concern about attacks in the U.S., an increase of 12 percentage points over 2014 measures.[134]

Terrorism in 2015 became the third-highest issue on the public's list of concerns, exceeded only by worry about health care and the economy. "Worry that oneself or a member of one's family will be a victim of terrorism has drifted up this year to the point where 49% of Americans say they are very or somewhat worried, the highest rating on this measure since 2001," the year of the 9/11 attacks in the U.S., wrote Frank Newport, Gallup's editor in chief.[135]

The Fear Frame

In several books published since the 9/11 terrorist attacks, sociologist and media scholar David Altheide found that "the use of the word *fear* is widespread in American life and, increasingly, throughout much of Europe as well."[136] Altheide, who has tracked references to fear in newspapers since the 1980s, blamed "the entertainment format, use of visuals, emerging icons of fear, slogans and especially the emphasis on the fear frame and 'evil' in the media"[137] for what he called an emerging discourse of fear that, he maintains, allows the media and politicians to play on people's innate fears of harm to themselves and their loved ones.

Sociologist Barry Glassner, in his book *The Culture of Fear: Why Americans Are Afraid of the Wrong Things,* wrote that media coverage of crime, "the war on drugs," and hyped reports, primarily on TV, about atypical threats, all treat isolated incidents as trends and misdirect attention from an ongoing situation to an alarming exception, leaving audiences fearful but not empowered to act.[138] As Sissela Bok, Brigitte Nacos, and others have noted, images of violence on TV and the Internet, including terrorist violence, are not simply reported once but rebroadcast "over and over again until they become burned in the mind's eye."[139]

The widely used phrase "war on terror"—which was first employed by the George W. Bush administration to indicate the need for a warlike response to the terrorist attacks of 9/11—is, when you think about it, an odd phrasing: It's not a war on terrorism; it's a war on terror that seems to speak to battling an unending fear. "The little secret here is that the vagueness of the phrase was deliberately (or instinctively) calculated by its sponsors," Zbigniew Brzezinski, a former national security adviser to President Jimmy Carter, later contended in an article criticizing the phrase. "Constant reference to a 'war on terror' did accomplish one major objective: It stimulated the emergence of a culture of fear. Fear obscures reason, intensifies emotions and makes it easier for . . . politicians to mobilize the public on behalf of the policies they want to pursue."[140]

The reluctance of Barack Obama and Hillary Clinton to use phrases such as "Islamic extremism" in describing terrorist attacks was characterized by Republicans as the Democrats being "soft on terrorism." That was a prominent phrase used by Republican candidates in the 2016 presidential election, and it also has been a prominent story line repeated over the years by Sean Hannity, Laura Ingraham, and other hosts on Fox News Channel as well as on conservative talk radio. In the 2014 congressional elections, several ads for Republican candidates visually linked frightening footage from ISIS videos with Democratic candidates for Congress, blaming the growth of terrorism on Obama, Clinton, and the Democrats.[141]

More than a decade after the terrorists attacks of September 11, 2001, that killed more than three thousand people on U.S. soil, 9/11 continued to have a powerful hold on the American public's collective consciousness. At the same time, the wars in Afghanistan and Iraq in response to 9/11 have made Americans more skeptical about engaging in war and "nation-building," more distressed about the government's handling of terrorism, and more divided about how to fight terrorism in the U.S. and abroad.

On the tenth anniversary of 9/11, the Pew Research Center found in polling that "virtually all adults said they remembered exactly where they were or what they were doing the moment they heard" of the stunning, tragic attacks on the World Trade Center in New York City and the Pentagon in Washington, D.C.[142] Ninety-seven percent of Americans who were alive in 2001 could recall where they were on 9/11 ten years later—and the recall was as high among Americans younger than thirty, who would have been eight to nineteen years old, as among older Americans.

Only the assassination of John F. Kennedy in 1963 and, for older Americans, the Japanese attacks on Pearl Harbor in 1941 that led to U.S. entry into World War II, had such high rates of recall.[143] Perceptions of the emotional and political impact of 9/11 were high ten years later, according to the 2011 survey, with 75 percent of respondents saying the attacks had affected them "a great deal" and 67 percent agreeing with the statement that "the country has changed in a major way" since 9/11.[144]

Before the coronavirus pandemic, analysts of foreign policy and world history noted that, compared to World War II, the Cuban missile crisis and other threats of nuclear war during the Cold War, the contemporary world, particularly the U.S., was a far less dangerous place. But, as the Pew researchers found after terrorist attacks, many people *felt* fearful. Seeking to explain the difference between perceived threat and real threat, Jonathan Rauch, quoting experts on terrorism and psychology, wrote, "People are biased to overestimate the likelihood of the sorts of events that stand out in our memory, as violence and mayhem do, and as peace and quiet do not."[145]

Islamophobia in Media Coverage and Politics

Many studies over the years have found that media coverage of Muslims in U.S. and international media is overwhelmingly negative.[146] Several recent studies have found that the word *Muslim* continues to be linked to the word *terrorism* in media coverage and political debate. Fox News Channel, in particular, has featured many commentators lambasting Democrats and the American government for what they call dangerous "political correctness" (echoing Donald Trump) in not labeling terrorist attacks "Islamic jihad," while blaming Hillary Clinton, Obama, and the Democrats for the rise of ISIS and terrorist attacks. Cable news panels convened after a terrorist attack often ask a question that implies an answer: "Does Islam Promote Violence?" as one CNN segment asked in an on-air headline. The Muslim guest on the program then is usually asked to disavow terrorism and to seemingly speak on behalf of the world's 1.6 billion Muslims.[147]

"We still see this expectation that Muslim institutions have to come out and condemn things that you wouldn't expect other groups have to condemn," maintained Corey Saylor, legislative director for the Council on American-Islamic Relations (CAIR), a Muslim advocacy group. "There's the assumption of collective responsibility. The number one victims of ISIS are Muslims; the notion that somehow we're not fully committed to combating that twisted ideology is difficult to wrap your mind around."[148]

In a 2015 study, Media Tenor International, the Swiss research group that analyzes media coverage, found that, with the rise of ISIS and other terrorist groups claiming to act in the name of Islam, media coverage of Islam had become more negative than at any time since 9/11.[149] Coding and examining 2.6 million Western news stories from ten American, British, and German news outlets from 2001 to 2014, the researchers found that most coverage depicted Islam, Muslims, and Muslim organizations as a source of violence and a security risk while seldom dealing with the lives of ordinary Muslims.[150]

In the days following the 9/11 attacks, President Bush made a point of visiting a Washington, D.C., mosque and emphasizing that jihadism and Al Qaeda were a perversion of a peaceful religion.

"Muslims [in America] are doctors, lawyers, law professors, members of the military, entrepreneurs, shopkeepers, moms and dads," Bush said. "And they need to be treated with respect. In our anger and emotion, our fellow Americans must treat each other with respect."[151] But as media coverage of Muslim Americans receded, the Media Tenor researchers found, terrorist attacks and extremist leaders had supplanted coverage of ordinary Americans who were Muslims. Looking at the "religious protagonists" in news stories on international evening news programs from 2013 to 2015, Media Tenor's research found a lack of the voices of Muslim religious leaders and very little positive coverage of Islam, compared to coverage of the leaders of other religions.[152]

When researchers Erik Bleich and A. Maurits van der Veen coded articles from 1996 to 2015 in national newspapers from the *Washington Post* and the *Wall Street Journal* to the *Denver Post* for how they portrayed Muslims, Jews, and Catholics, they found that stories that referenced Muslims were overwhelmingly negative.[153] "Given the prominence of violent Islamist terrorism and extremism since September 2001, negative stories about Muslims may simply be a result of journalists reporting the news," they wrote in 2018. "We examined this and found that U.S. newspapers associate Muslims with far more negativity than terrorism or extremism would explain. Further, articles about Muslims that have nothing to do with terrorism are substantially more negative than articles about Catholics, Jews or Hindus."[154]

In an interview with the author, Akbar Ahmed, the author of several books on contemporary Islam, decried what he saw as a "dehumanization of Muslims, a reductionism in Islam" after 9/11, "so that 19 terrorists in 9/11 became equated to the entire Muslim world." He added, "This is very counterproductive to the government's goal of winning hearts and minds in the Muslim world."[155] More recently, Ahmed, who is the former ambassador of Pakistan to Great Britain, has called for more reporting on Muslims in the U.S. and around the world.

Far-Right Domestic Terrorism

In recent years there has been an increase in far-right terrorist attacks and plots in the U.S. "Over the past decade, attackers motivated by right-wing political ideologies have committed dozens of shootings, bombings and other acts of violence, far more than any other category of domestic extremist," Wesley Lowery, Kimberly Kindy, and Andrew Ba Tran reported in 2018, analyzing data from the Global Terrorism Database, a federally funded operation that has tracked terrorist attacks in the U.S. and globally since 1970. "While the data show a decades-long drop-off in violence by left-wing groups, violence by white supremacists and other far-right attackers has been on the rise since Barack Obama's presidency—and has surged since President Trump took office."[156]

Trump was widely condemned across the political spectrum for saying that there were "some very fine people" among the far-right demonstrators chanting racist, anti-Semitic slogans in Charlottesville and for failing to disavow white supremacists in the 2020 presidential debates. He consistently denied that there was any connection between his rhetoric and the rise in hate crimes and far-right attacks such as the mass shooting by a white supremacist who gunned down Latino shoppers at a Walmart in El Paso, Texas, in 2019.[157] "If you have politicians saying things like our nation is under attack, that there are these marauding bands of immigrants coming in to this country, that plays into this right-wing narrative," said Gary LaFree, criminology professor and founding director of the organization that maintains the Global Terrorism Database. "They begin to think it's ok to use violence."[158]

In 2020 a report from the nonpartisan Center for Strategic and International Studies concluded, "Far-right terrorism has significantly outpaced terrorism from other types of perpetrators, including from far-left networks and individuals inspired by the Islamic State and al-Qaeda. Right-wing attacks and plots account for the majority of all terrorist incidents in the United States since 1994, and the total number of right-wing attacks and plots has grown significantly during the past six years."[159] The report found that "right-wing extremists perpetrated two thirds of the attacks and plots in the United States in 2019 and over 90 percent between January 1 and May 8, 2020."[160] In its annual assessment of threats to the U.S., the Department of Homeland Security said in the fall of 2020 that violent white supremacy was "the most persistent and lethal threat to the United States."[161] The agency had reached a similar conclusion in 2021. "I am particularly concerned about white supremacist violent extremists who have been exceptionally lethal in their abhorrent, targeted attacks in recent years," the acting secretary of DHS, Chad Wolf, wrote in the report, which an intelligence official had accused DHS of withholding for several weeks.[162]

Some online discussion groups and anonymous forums today have helped spread far-right extremist views—and have created a terrible sense of community in the minds of lone terrorists. The man charged in the El Paso shooting published a 2,500-word, hate-filled rant on the 8chan (now 8kun) anonymous online message board that has been frequented by white supremacists.[163] The man who allegedly murdered eleven people and injured others during a ceremony at the Tree of Life Synagogue in Pittsburgh in 2018 had regularly posted anti-Semitic rants on Gab, a small social media network that, with fewer restrictions than Facebook and Twitter, has been described as "a gathering spot for white supremacists and others in the extreme alt-right."[164] The Australian-born white supremacist who was convicted of murdering fifty-one worshippers in the mosque shootings in Christchurch, New Zealand, had posted a manifesto on his Facebook and Twitter accounts as 8chan—and even showed part of the attacks on Facebook Live.[165]

Case Study: The War in Iraq

The Iraq War—which continues to cast a long shadow over American foreign policy and American public opinion about engaging in other wars and conflicts—is a case study in how elite media, in the post–9/11 patriotic climate, failed to independently verify an administration's case for war, including reports by United Nations inspectors and debate within the U.S. intelligence community over how data were being interpreted.

As Michael Massing recounted in his book *Now They Tell Us: The American Press and Iraq*, on September 8, 2002, the *New York Times* published a disturbing front-page headline: "U.S. Says Hussein Intensifies Quest for A-Bomb Parts." "More than a decade after Saddam Hussein agreed to give up weapons of mass destruction, Iraq had stepped up its quest for nuclear weapons and has embarked on a worldwide hunt for materials to make an atomic bomb, Bush administration officials said today," the 3,600-word article began.[166] "In the last 14 months," *New York Times* reporters Michael R. Gordon and Judith Miller wrote, "Iraq has sought to buy thousands of specifically designed aluminum tubes, which American officials believe were intended as components of centrifuges to enrich uranium."[167] The specifications of these tubes, the article stated, persuaded "American intelligence officials that they were meant for Iraq's nuclear program."[168]

Quoting their own interviews with anonymous Iraqi defectors as well as information they attributed to unnamed American officials, Gordon and Miller wrote, "Iraqi defectors who once worked for the nuclear weapons establishment have told American officials that acquiring nuclear arms is again a top Iraqi priority."[169]

In an appearance that same morning on NBC's *Meet the Press*, Vice President Dick Cheney said that the *New York Times* story was public evidence for his earlier speech that there is "no doubt" that Saddam Hussein

(Continued)

(Continued)

had "weapons of mass destruction" and was preparing to use them against the U.S. In appearances that day on other network and cable TV programs, Defense Secretary Donald Rumsfeld and Secretary of State Colin Powell referenced the New York Times story, as did national security adviser Condoleezza Rice.[170] Rice quoted directly from a story attributed to "administration hard-liners" in the New York Times. Rice raised the specter of what might happen if the U.S. did not act. "[W]e don't want the smoking gun to be a mushroom cloud," she said.[171] Four days after the New York Times story was published, President Bush himself made the aluminum tubes story a key piece of evidence in the president's case for war in an important speech before the UN General Assembly.[172]

Coverage of Doubt about Weapons of Mass Destruction in Other Media

While administration officials were invoking the New York Times story to help make their case, Scott Ritter, a former U.S. Marine intelligence officer and chief weapons inspector in Iraq, was interviewed from Baghdad that same day on CNN's website, CNN.com, expressing his view that the administration had not provided any evidence to substantiate its allegations about Saddam Hussein and WMDs.[173] Chuck Hagel, Republican senator from Nebraska, said at the time that "the CIA had 'absolutely no evidence' to prove Iraq possessed or would soon possess nuclear weapons."[174] And—two days before the New York Times aluminum tubes story was published, Jonathan Landay, a Washington, D.C.-based reporter for the Knight Ridder newspaper chain, published the first of several articles that—in 2002—highlighted divisions within the U.S. intelligence community over evidence of WMDs months before the U.S. went to war against Iraq.

Headlined "Lack of Hard Evidence of Iraqi Weapons Worries Top U.S. Officials," Landay's article began with this: "Senior U.S. officials with access to top-secret intelligence on Iraq say they have detected no alarming increase in the threat that Iraqi dictator Saddam Hussein poses to American security and Middle East stability."[175] Landay's stories were carried in the Philadelphia Inquirer and other newspapers in the Knight Ridder chain—but they did not have the same impact on politicians, policy, or public opinion as the New York Times or the Washington Post. The Washington Post, in fact, had run a story by reporter Joby Warrick about challenges by "independent experts" to the claims about the tubes' potential nuclear use (as opposed to conventional rockets) and also noted reports that the administration was "trying to quiet dissent among its own experts over how to interpret the evidence."[176] But, as Michael Massing recounted in his groundbreaking account of media and the Iraq War,[177] the story was inside the newspaper, on page 18, and "caused little stir."[178]

In 2004 both the *New York Times* and *Washington Post* issued extraordinary mea culpas for their prewar reporting on the Iraq War. "We have found a number of instances of coverage that was not as rigorous as it should have been," the editors of the *Times* wrote.[179] "Looking back, we wish we had been more aggressive in re-examining the claims as new evidence emerged—or failed to emerge," they added. "Editors at several levels who should have been challenging reporters and pressing for more skepticism were perhaps too intent on rushing scoops in the paper" while the dire accounts of Iraqi defectors "were not always weighed" against their desire to have Saddam Hussein ousted.

The editors added that any misgivings about whether the aluminum tubes the Administration said were being sought were for nuclear use were "buried" as "hints" in the *Times'* article in which "Administration officials were allowed to hold forth at length," including the reference to fears that the first sign of proof that Iraq had WMDs would be a nuclear cloud.[180]

There was congressional debate and misgiving among some Republicans as well as Democrats over the 2003 vote to authorize the use of force and invade Iraq following the 2001 invasion of Afghanistan by the U.S. and allies to fight Osama bin Laden and Al Qaeda. But with strong public support, pressure to give the president what he needed, and strong insinuations from Republicans that opposition was dangerous, Congress voted for the Iraq War resolution by lopsided votes. Hillary Clinton's vote later was used against her in the 2008 election by Barack Obama, who campaigned against the by-then unpopular war and President Bush, and then again in 2016 by Sen. Bernie Sanders, who pointed out that, unlike the then-senator Hillary Clinton, he had been one of a few senators to vote against the Iraq War resolution.

We know today that this aluminum tubes story was wrong, as was much of the reporting and analysis by some of the most respected and influential news media in the so-called walk-up to the war in Iraq. The intelligence used to justify the case for war against Iraq was deeply flawed, as many articles and books have since documented. Saddam Hussein did

(Continued)

(Continued)

not have the WMDs that were feared—nor was he allied with Osama bin Laden and Al Qaeda, although officials in the Bush administration conflated the two.[181] And, in pursuit of the second goal stated by the Bush administration—liberating the Iraqi people from a dictator and "fighting the terrorists there so they don't come here," as President Bush put it—the U.S. instead was engaged for many years in a war of occupation, insurgency, and sectarian violence.

The war that led to many American and Iraqi casualties and that, as many military and civilian experts have since acknowledged, fanned anti-U.S. sentiment in the Muslim world and remains unresolved to today.

By 2013 the wars in Iraq and Afghanistan were projected to cost American taxpayers $4 to $6 trillion, according to Harvard budget expert Linda Bilmes, taking into account the medical care of wounded veterans and expensive repairs to a force depleted by more than a decade of fighting. The two wars became the most expensive wars in U.S. history and placed "significant long-term" constraints on the federal budget, particularly the national security budget.[182] The conflict divided the country and cost President Bush political capital for his domestic agenda as his popularity sank and both Republicans and Democrats questioned the administration's handling of the war.

In the post–9/11 climate, amid patriotic rhetoric and genuine fears of terrorism, the news media and political leaders did not serve the president or the American people well in the months before the war began in 2003. Many TV news hosts and commentators wore American flag pins in their lapels in the aftermath of 9/11—and if you declined to do so, you could be criticized.[183]

Cable TV—which had given the world its first live coverage of war with the Persian Gulf War in 1991—added to the drumbeat for war with unquestioning, flag-waving reporting that helped make the Bush administration's case for war. The wars in Afghanistan and Iraq both began on U.S. television with Super Bowl-style countdowns to the start of the war and TV miniseries–style titles from the military and on-air "branding" with graphics.[184] A study conducted in 2003 by Fairness & Accuracy in Reporting (FAIR) tracking the frequencies of pro-war and anti-war commentators on the major networks found that pro-war views were overwhelmingly more frequent.[185] Some corporate advertisers complained that CNN was being "un-patriotic" in showing civilian casualties and devastation in Afghanistan, the president of CNN later said.[186]

In what Robert Entman has called the *"cascading activation model,"* the ideas and feelings that support a particular frame can cascade down from an administration's expressions about an event to elites, including political leaders and journalists, who then canvas their networks of customary sources.[187] In the months preceding the war in Iraq, Entman wrote, with elite media not questioning sufficiently the administration's case for war and the need to protect the American people from danger, in the battle for frame parity between two opposing frames, the choice *not to* go to war lost resoundingly to the choice to go to war, in the media *and* in Congress.[188] "People in the media are now saying, 'We were all wrong,'" Knight Ridder reporter Jonathan Landay said in an interview with the author. "We were *not* all wrong."[189]

Wartime Coverage

Dissent and Wartime Propaganda

Dissent in wartime—in politics and in the media—has often been squelched, in the U.S. and other democracies, in what is called the "rally round the flag" phenomenon in which there is pressure on all citizens, including journalists, to be patriotic and support the country's troops, often with the argument that dissent or critical reporting is not only unpatriotic but dangerous. At the same, the U.S., as a vast, seemingly self-sufficient country, historically has had a strong isolationist tradition, a reluctance to fight in "other people's" far-off wars. This isolationist tradition has led to government propaganda efforts to *build* support for U.S. engagement and troops in both World War I and World War II.

During World War II, the U.S. government created an Office of War Information that operated from 1942 to 1945 to build support for the war effort at home and abroad. The government commissioned Hollywood filmmaker Frank Capra to produce a 1942 documentary film series, *Why We Fight*, about why it was necessary to fight the Nazis.[190] A popular song about "Rosie the Riveter," along with government newsreels, successfully promoted the idea that it was patriotic—and feminine—for real-life women to work in welding and airplane factories during the war.[191] The iconic illustration of Rosie the Riveter is still seen—and adapted—today.

During World War II, photographers from *Life* magazine, in particular, documented the battles and the lives of U.S. soldiers as well as civilians in compelling photographs that are still famous today. But, as George H. Roeder noted in his book *The Censored War: American Visual Experience During World War II*, "censors strictly prohibited visual or written depictions of atrocities by American troops or their allies," and even atrocities *against* U.S. and allied soldiers were censored in the war against Hitler's Nazi Germany, Japan, and the Holocaust.[192] At one point, however, the government released some photos of U.S. casualties to help continue support for the war.[193]

During the war in Iraq, in a survey of 210 reporters and editors reporting from Iraq and editing stories about the war in its early years, MJ Bear and this author found that many media outlets self-censored graphic imagery and content, including the hanging of bodies of American contractors killed in Fallujah, out of concerns over public reaction to graphic content. These journalists said they often put online graphic content that they did not publish in print.[194]

Media-Military Relationship

Before the Iraq War, according to interviews with several military journalists by this author, public-relations officials in the Department of Defense argued that the military should return to what had actually been common practice in the U.S. in World War II: "embedding" journalists with troops. The stated reason for keeping the media largely out of the brief Persian Gulf War in 1991 was fear over the inadvertent broadcasting of information to the enemy over the then-new twenty-four-hour satellite news channels. But another reason was the long-held belief among many in the military that the media had "lost" the Vietnam War by bringing that conflict—which was labeled the "living-room war"[195]—into American homes. Increasingly skeptical reporting by *New York Times* correspondent David Halberstam, CBS News correspondent Morley Safer, and other print and TV correspondents questioned the U.S. accounts at the daily press briefings that reporters dubbed "the five-o'clock follies" and did their own independent reporting.[196]

Daniel Hallin, in his book *The Uncensored War*, maintained that public opinion, along with an anti-war movement that attracted many young people, was shifting along with the coverage during the Vietnam War.[197] But Democratic president Lyndon Johnson, along with President John F. Kennedy before him, believed that negative reporting on Vietnam from the *New York Times* and CBS News, in particular, had affected public support. LBJ tried to get reporters from the *Times* and CBS News fired for their reporting, but their news organizations stuck by them and their reporting.[198] Following the surprising defeat of U.S.-backed South Vietnamese troops in Saigon in the Tet Offensive in 1968, CBS News anchor Walter Cronkite traveled to Vietnam to report.

In a headline-making statement, Cronkite told his audience that he believed that the U.S. was "mired in stalemate" in the long war.[199] Cronkite at the time was called "the most trusted man in America," and the CBS

News, NBC News, and ABC News prime-time newscasts commanded huge audiences every night and played a major agenda-setting role. The pronouncement by Cronkite, a then-rare step to editorialize, is considered an important moment in the interplay of coverage and public opinion in Vietnam.[200]

It's surprising to think about today, but during the Vietnam War, TV correspondents traveled freely with U.S. troops, without handlers. "We would grab a ride with soldiers on a C-130 transport plane," former CBS Vietnam correspondent Jed Duvall recalled in an interview with the author, "and our stories were shipped to CBS in New York, on film."[201]

The news media were largely excluded from the initial fighting in the war in Afghanistan against Al Qaeda in 2001, although a group of journalists from major print news organizations were allowed to cover some operations by U.S. Special Operations forces. The success of that operation, Bryan Whitman, then deputy assistant secretary of defense for media operations, said in interviews with the author in 2003 and 2004, led to the government's decision to embed six hundred journalists with troops in Iraq. "From the Defense Department's standpoint, whether countering disinformation from the enemy or giving the American people the opportunity to see their military at work, embedding seemed to work well," Whitman said. "The feedback from the large majority of journalists has been that they were able to work within the guidelines of embedding while maintaining their standards as journalists. One of our guiding principles going forward is that it's important for the American people to have a broad understanding of the U.S. military, and we have to look for ways to include journalists that don't compromise missions."[202]

"Embedding was a brilliant strategy based on a more sophisticated understanding of the role the media can play," Robert Hodierne, the former editor of *Army Times* and a veteran Vietnam War correspondent, said in an interview with the author.[203] "An objective look at the military during war shows that there are good stories to be told, with people often behaving in skillful, courageous ways," Hodierne added. "One interesting aspect of embedding is that—in contrast to the post-Vietnam era—there are now hundreds of journalists in their late 20s who have had a formative and generally positive experience with the U.S. military."[204]

John Donvan, a correspondent for ABC's *Nightline*, was one of the "unilaterals," or unembedded, reporters who covered the Iraq combat for U.S. media. Donvan believes that some significant stories were missed in the American TV networks' focus on dramatic footage of U.S. troops rolling into Iraq live and on television. "The only thing I have against embedding is that the news media itself falls in love with the glitz and glamour and whiz-bang of embedded reporting and puts so much emphasis on embedding that it lets the public forget they're not seeing the war itself, but a tiny slice of the war," Donvan said in an interview with author. "Embedded reporters were courageous and self-sacrificing, but you almost literally didn't have to breathe the air in Iraq when you traveled with U.S. troops."[205]

Donvan, whose small crew was adopted by a friendly U.S. military unit, encountered hostility from Iraqis when he came to the city of Safwan shortly after the world saw images of a just-liberated Iraqi there hitting a portrait of Saddam Hussein with his shoe. "I was surprised to find that everybody we met expressed suspicion about U.S. intentions and outrage over civilian casualties," said Donvan, who reported this and other stories about Iraqi concerns for *Nightline* during three weeks in Iraq. "The idea that Iraqis would simply greet us with dancing in the streets [as Vice President Cheney had said they would] was a skewed perception once the first soldiers came and left town."[206]

NBC's David Bloom and the *Atlantic* magazine's Michael Kelly died in the early days of the American invasion, apparently from the rigors encountered by U.S. troops. Early footage of American soldiers and tanks pouring into Iraq was dramatic and undoubtedly helped to tell the American side of the story, although such coverage was inevitably favorable to U.S. troops. But with the Pentagon initially not even keeping statistics on the numbers of Iraqi casualties, the U.S. became the subject of fiercely anti-American coverage in some other countries, and more American journalists and media critics began to question the role of the media and the war itself.

Future of War and War Reporting

An important issue facing war correspondents for the future is the changing nature of the battlefield itself. "The battlefield of the future will be much more fluid and much more rapid than ever before," Vago Muradian, editor in chief of *Defense & Aerospace Report*, an influential publication that covers worldwide defense issues, predicted in interviews with the author.[207]

"The goal of the U.S. military in a war like Iraq is to move as quickly as possible using overwhelming U.S. air superiority combined with land and sea forces to subdue the enemy as quickly and with as few casualties as possible," Muradian continued. "There is increased automation and speed in picking out targets and calling for them to be destroyed. And, at the same time, in such a war, it becomes more difficult to tell friend from foe. . . . It's possible that there may not be a safe alternative to embedding journalists" if there is another war like Iraq with U.S. ground troops in the future.[208]

Other journalists and experts say, with the nature of war itself changing, through Special Operations forces that led to the capture of Saddam Hussein and the capture and killing of Osama bin Laden, plus CIA covert operations and drone strikes, there increasingly will be action that goes largely uncovered by journalists. "We will be in a constant state of war in the future," Robert Hodierne correctly predicted in 2004, "and much of it will be secret operations that will go uncovered by the media. If six or eight Special-Ops forces are going behind enemy lines—perhaps from a landing base in a country that may not want its cooperation known—to look for Osama bin Laden or some other terrorist, they're not going to take a journalist with them. Reporters are not trained to keep secrets; they don't carry guns; and there aren't a lot of people in a newsroom who could carry 70 to 80 pounds on their back the way soldiers on a mission would do."[209]

Other veterans of Vietnam War reporting believe that journalists may be giving up their independence if embedding becomes the norm. "If Iraq is an example, the media are not going to be part of how war coverage is done in the future," said Morley Safer, the *60 Minutes* correspondent who shocked Americans with his 1965 story showing a group of Marines casually torching huts in a South Vietnamese village with cigarette lighters. "The entire agenda is being set by the Pentagon; if the media shout themselves blue, nothing's going to happen. In the post September 11th climate, the media were so hunkered down before the war that there was very little questioning of the Administration's case for war. . . ." The next time, Safer added in this interview with the author, "If it's all live, all-the-time again, no reporter is good enough to—bang—turn on a camera and tell you anything meaningful about what just happened."[210]

SUMMARY

In this chapter we have looked at U.S. media and politics in the context of international news and global events. American TV networks traditionally have reflected American exceptionalism with an Americentric approach to world affairs, with some exceptions; and cutbacks in the broadcast TV networks' international bureaus exacerbated that focus. The war in Iraq—which continues to cast a lengthy shadow over American foreign policy and public support for engaging in another long war—is an important case study for how elite media failed to independently report on and verify debate within the intelligence community about WMDs in Iraq and the administration's case for war. As in other countries, dissent and critical reporting often have been criticized as unpatriotic as the U.S. has prepared for war. News organizations in the post–9/11 climate and previously have been under pressure to support the country's troops versus fulfilling their important role in the democracy, as an independent watchdog and verifier of government claims and the truth.

Historically, during World War I and World War II, journalists, news organizations, and entertainment companies complied with government restrictions on images from combat and helped build support for America's role in World War II as American journalists were "embedded" with U.S. troops and Hollywood filmmakers helped popularize the war effort. The war in Vietnam, by contrast, divided the country, with a strong anti-war movement and ultimately independent reporting that the U.S. government had lied about the course of combat and the chances for success. The belief on the part of military officials that American media had "lost" the war in Vietnam through TV and print reporting—coupled with the new realities of live war coverage on cable TV—have led the Pentagon to strongly restrict access to the battlefield and U.S. troops, including through limited embedding with U.S. troops.

The rise of terrorism and terrorist attacks have presented new challenges to news media and governments around the world. People remember violent imagery and chaos, and terrorists aim to strike fear through random violence. Terrorists pledging allegiance to Islamist extremism have led to Islamophobia in media and politics, while coverage of Muslims as ordinary Americans has been scarce.

American media coverage—and American public opinion—are reflecting an increased concern about climate change as a global crisis. The coronavirus pandemic that caused deaths and economic crises, in the U.S. and around the world, found the U.S. strongly unprepared. The crisis revealed both an economic and a political media divide, with racial and class disparities in cases and deaths and Asian Americans falsely demonized by President Trump for the "Asian flu." The president's downplaying of the risks of COVID-19 and the government's response were strongly criticized, as was parallel coverage on Fox News Channel, for dangerously misinforming the public.

End-of-Chapter Assignment:
Comparing U.S. and International Newscasts

For this assignment, sample newscasts and news clips from one American broadcast TV nightly newscast and news organization—NBC News, ABC News, or CBS News—and then sample news clips from the BBC and Al Jazeera. Take some notes on the choice of lead stories and what countries are included, the relative prominence of U.S.-based news stories to non-U.S.-based, the overall tone of the stories and how the U.S. is featured and portrayed relative to other countries. Come to class prepared to discuss.

Here's how to sample clips: The ABC, CBS and NBC network newscasts are available on local TV stations, and some local TV stations in the U.S. also carry the BBC's nightly newscast from the U.S. nightly. The NBC Nightly News newscast is available online at https://www.nbcnews.com, and clips of other newscasts can be found online at https://abcnews.go.com, https://www.cbsnews.com, and https://www.bbc.com/news. Al Jazeera has clips on its website at https://www.aljazeera.com.

8

The Media and Women in Politics

The job of U.S. president is, as political scientist Kelly Dittmar described it, "arguably the most masculine in American politics."[1] Former Colorado congresswoman Pat Schroeder, who briefly ran for the Democratic nomination in the 1988 campaign, memorably called the U.S. presidency "the ultimate treehouse—with a 'no-girls-allowed' sign posted on it."[2] In a 2016 interview the seventy-five-year-old Schroeder maintained that stereotyping and gender-based hurdles to women in politics today are "more subtle, but it's more of the same."[3] In 2020, *Atlantic* magazine critic Megan Garber wrote that sexism was still there but "sneakier"—for example, with questions not only about Elizabeth Warren's likeability and whether "another woman" candidate could win but also a spate of stories about whether Warren was "angry," after Joe Biden said she was.[4]

Hillary Clinton's history-making run for president in 2016 coupled with Donald Trump's misogynistic attacks on Clinton, Republican candidate Carly Fiorina, Fox News Channel anchor Megyn Kelly, and other female journalists, added to the focus on gender in the campaign and media coverage in the 2016 presidential campaign. The release of an *Access Hollywood* videotape where Trump off camera bragged openly about sexually assaulting women as a celebrity,[5] led to further questions later about the role of gender and misogyny in the campaign and in media coverage.

But, as Dittmar noted, gender is always a factor in political campaigns and media coverage, particularly around the U.S. presidency, where there has yet to be a female American president, although nations around the world have been led by many women in recent years. "The presumption that previous presidential elections—without female prominent contenders—were gender-neutral is false," wrote Dittmar, a political scientist and scholar at the Center for American Women and Politics at Rutgers University. "Gender dynamics have been at play in all U.S. presidential elections to date. . . . Presidents and presidential contenders, whether male or female, are expected to meet the masculine expectations of the office through words and actions, and those around them—family, spouses, and advisors—often play a role in shaping the degree to which they are successful. In navigating American politics, candidates also face gendered treatment by opponents, voters, and media, reminding us that presidential politics is far from gender neutral."[6]

Dittmar—a lead expert on a nonpartisan project that tracked and analyzed the 2016 campaign and media coverage—has defined *gender dynamics* as referring to "the influence, operation, expression and disruption of norms of both femininity and masculinity in presidential politics for the women and men engage in them."[7] Many scholars have defined the U.S. presidency as a gendered space in which what are viewed as traditionally and stereotypically "masculine" traits are seen as normal and the ideal, with the power of the underlying beliefs "made even stronger when it goes unnoticed," as Georgia Duerst-Lahti observed in 1997.[8]

Politics and the media both reflect deep-seated—and often unrecognized and unconscious—cultural attitudes and biases about what have historically been promulgated as "appropriate" roles and behaviors for women and men, including for women and men in power. In covering female candidates and women officeholders, the news media have reflected, amplified, and even perpetuated culturally biased, sexist ideas about women and men in positions of authority. Political reporting—and especially TV political punditry—until very recently has been dominated by older white men. At the same time, some of the harshest focus on the fashion and physical attributes of female candidates in the recent past has come from some prominent female opinion columnists.

In news stories—as opposed to opinion and commentary—major news organizations have made considerable progress in recent years in their reporting on women in politics, moving away from what for many years has been an outdated focus on what has been called "hair, hemlines, and husbands" in writing about female candidates and officeholders. The 2018 congressional midterm elections saw a record number of women and women of color elected in a second "Year of the Woman"—and both the news media and political parties were forced to reckon with and describe a younger, more diverse "freshman class" in Congress, with increased political clout for women, in office and in voting.

The 2020 presidential election, with Senators Elizabeth Warren, Amy Klobuchar, Kirsten Gillibrand, and Kamala Harris, along with Rep. Tulsi Gabbard and author Marianne Williamson, running for the Democratic nomination, led to Sen. Elizabeth Warren of Massachusetts emerging as an early front-runner and the later nomination of Senator Harris as former vice president Joe Biden's running mate. Harris was the first woman of color and only the third female vice presidential nominee of a major party since Geraldine Ferraro on the Democratic ticket with Sen. Walter Mondale in 1984. As noted earlier, it took twenty-four more years after that for Alaska governor Sarah Palin to be selected as Sen. John McCain's running mate on the Republican ticket in 2008.[9] Harris represented many firsts when she was elected vice president of the U.S.

There have been significant improvements over the past twenty years in the ways that female politicians are depicted in the media. But female candidates still routinely get less attention for their campaigns and are treated less seriously than men running for office, according to several recent analyses. A Wilson Center study recently found that "the coverage of women in politics receive is still heavily biased against them, both in quantity and quality."[10]

In a study of some 1,400 news articles in major publications during 2019, authors from the Northeastern University School of Journalism found that "female candidates running for president are consistently being described in the media more negatively than their male counterparts."[11] The female candidates were much more likely to be critiqued personally and negatively than their male counterparts, while men received more attention to their policy proposals. These findings are consistent with previous studies—and the authors said they did not differ much from media coverage in the 2016 presidential campaign.[12]

Why does this matter? Because such coverage affects the impressions voters have and the way candidates are perceived. Numerous academic studies have shown that media coverage and commentary that stereotypes female candidates and officeholders has consequences, in the way campaigns are run and framed. Coverage and commentary also have been shown to affect voters' perceptions of women's viability as candidates, their strengths and weaknesses, and their capacity to lead.

As columnist Joanne Lipman, former editor-in-chief of *USA Today*, wrote in 2020, this continuing male-centered focus perhaps shouldn't be surprising. "News coverage decisions are overwhelmingly made by men, who lead the vast majority of newsrooms. Women make up two-thirds of journalism and communication grads, yet men produce 63 percent of all news coverage, according to the Women's Media Center. On television, male journalists outnumber female journalists by almost two to one. On Twitter, male political reporters ignore female reporters altogether; they retweet fellow male journalists three times more often than they retweet fellow female journalists. In other words, the female perspective is the outlier—which often translates into women simply being ignored."[13]

It is likely no accident—culturally and politically as well as in the news media—that as women have made progress being seen as and being voices of experience and authority in the news media as well as politics, the 2018 and 2020 elections saw more women running for the highest offices, more women and more diverse women covering politics, and more women and more diverse women moderating presidential and vice presidential debates.

At the same time, the growth of social media and the bitter politics in our recent elections have moved misogyny and racism against women underground. Women running for office—and women in office—are subjected to vitriol and hate speech on social media far more than male candidates and officeholders.[14]

This chapter will look at the role of women in politics and how the ways women are depicted in politics and the media influences how they are viewed, as candidates and officeholders. We'll learn about what is called the "double bind" for women in politics—and how "likeability" (culturally defined) is a hurdle that female candidates still have to clear. We'll compare the representation of women leaders internationally to the U.S. and efforts to encourage more women to run. With business executive Carly Fiorina on the ticket in the Republican primaries, Jill Stein as the Green Party nominee in 2012 and 2016, and Hillary Clinton considered poised to become the first female president of the U.S., the 2016 election attracted increased attention to gender dynamics and sexism in media coverage and politics.

We will trace differences and trends in coverage and campaigns of female candidates from the suffragettes to the 2000 race for the Republican nomination by Sen. Elizabeth Dole. We'll compare the two—1992 and 2018—"Year of the Woman" wins by women in Congress. And we'll study the role of gender and misogyny in the 2016 presidential race. Finally, we'll look at the intersection of gender, media, and politics in the historic 2020 presidential campaign.

Gender Dynamics in Running for President

Gender and Media in the 2016 Presidential Campaign

In an interview in 2017 at a conference with prominent female speakers, Hillary Clinton, making one of her first public appearances after the presidential election, was asked by *New York Times* columnist Nicholas Kristof, "This is a women's empowerment conference, so I have to ask you, fundamentally, a man who bragged about sexual assault won the election and won 53 percent of the white women's vote. How is it that in the twenty-first century—and what does it say about the challenges that one faces in women's empowerment—that, in effect, misogyny won with a lot of women voters?"[15]

"As you might guess, I've thought about it more than once," Clinton responded, "and I don't know that there is one answer. Let's be clear: In any campaign there are so many different crosscurrents and events, and some have greater impact than others. But it is fair to say, as you just did, that certainly misogyny played a role. I mean, that just has to be admitted."[16]

Disentangling misogyny and sexism from the specifics of Hillary Clinton's and Donald Trump's individual candidacies and campaigns, party identification, public anger against Washington, and other factors at work in the 2016 election is a difficult thing to do—but it's important to do.

Milestones in History of Women in Office

- **1872:** Victoria Woodhull was the first woman to run for U.S. president.

- **1916:** Jeannette Rankin was elected as the first woman to serve in Congress. A Republican representing Montana, she was a feminist and a pacifist who opposed the declaration of war against Germany in 1917. She was reelected in 1940.

- **1920:** Tennessee ratified the Nineteenth Amendment, concluding a seventy-two-year campaign by suffragettes to gain the right to vote for American women.

- **1972:** Rep. Shirley Chisholm was the first Black woman to seek the presidential nomination, running as a Democrat.

- **1981:** Sandra Day O'Connor was appointed by President Ronald Reagan as the first woman on the U.S. Supreme Court.

- **1984:** Geraldine Ferraro was selected as the first woman vice presidential running mate on a major party's national ticket—with Sen. Walter Mondale on the Democratic ticket.

- **1992:** Carol Moseley Braun was elected as the first Black woman to serve in the U.S. Senate.

- **2000:** Elizabeth Dole was the first woman to run for the Republican presidential nomination.

- **2007:** Nancy Pelosi was elected as the first woman Speaker of the U.S. House of Representatives.

- **2008:** Sen. Hillary Clinton ran for the Democratic party nomination for president.

- **2008:** Sarah Palin was selected as the first woman vice presidential nominee for the Republican Party—with Sen. John McCain for president.

- **2009:** Sonia Sotomayor was appointed by President Barack Obama as the first Hispanic and third female U.S. Supreme Court justice.

(Continued)

(Continued)

- **2016:** Business executive Carly Fiorina ran for the Republican nomination as president.

- **2016:** Hillary Clinton ran for president on the Democratic ticket; she was the first woman elected as a major party's presidential nominee.

- **2018:** A record number of women and women of color were elected to Congress.

- **2019:** Senators Elizabeth Warren, Kirsten Gillibrand, Amy Klobuchar, and Kamala Harris, along with Rep. Tulsi Gabbard and author Marianne Williamson, announced their candidacies for the Democratic presidential nomination in the most diverse slate of contenders in U.S. history.

- **2020:** Longtime Supreme Court justice Ruth Bader Ginsburg died. Judge Amy Coney Barrett was nominated by Donald Trump and confirmed.

- **2020:** Kamala Harris was elected as the vice president of the U.S. Harris was the first woman, first Black person, and first person of Asian descent to be elected vice president.

Sources: britannica.com; history.house.gov; archives.gov; womenshistory.org; supremecourt .gov; time.com; senate.gov; history.com; abcnews.go.com; womenofthehall.org; pewresearch .org; washingtonpost.com; vogue.com; nytimes.com; cnbc.com.

Elizabeth Warren's Presidential Campaign in 2020

When Elizabeth Warren announced that she was ending her presidential campaign in the spring of 2020 after a disappointing showing against Joe Biden and Bernie Sanders in the Super Tuesday primaries, she was asked if gender had played a role in the outcome that ended with two white men in their late seventies as the possible Democratic nominee. Warren, who had been a front-runner in several polls in 2019,[17] was one of the record six women running to be the first female president of the U.S. in a field that was also history-making in terms of race and ethnicity overall.

"Gender in this race, you know, that is the trap question for every woman," Warren said. "If you say, 'Yeah, there was sexism in this race,' everyone says, 'Whiner!' And if you say, 'No, there was no sexism,' about a bazillion women think, 'What planet do you live on?'"[18]

Warren, a Massachusetts senator and former Harvard law school professor who had led the creation of the Consumer Financial Protection

Bureau during the Obama administration, had drawn huge crowds, had strong organization on the ground,[19] and had raised more than $100 million to fund her campaign without holding big-dollar fundraisers.[20] She was praised for her debate performances, effectively ending the campaign of former New York City mayor Mike Bloomberg in one debate,[21] as well as her ability to connect her personal narrative from her childhood in Oklahoma to her proposals for the "big structural change" she called for to increase taxes on billionaires and corporations and make the economic system "work better for working families."

Warren was hard-pressed, including by her Democratic opponents, to put a price tag on her health-care proposal; and her later attempt to be a bridge between the progressive and more moderate wings of the party fell flat. Shane Goldmacher and Astead Herndon wrote, "She failed to attract a broader political coalition in a Democratic Party increasingly, if not singularly, focused on defeating President Trump."[22] Warren herself said that she "evidently was wrong" in not believing what she had been told from the beginning, that there was not a possible "lane" between the liberal one dominated by Bernie Sanders and the more moderate one with former vice president Joe Biden, with Biden ultimately was seen by many voters as the "safer" choice to run against Donald Trump.[23]

As tributes to Warren's candidacy and the issues she raised sprang up on a new hashtag #ThankYouElizabeth,[24] many people lamented the "message" of the outcome, especially to women and girls but also to the overall role of women in politics. As *Washington Post* journalists Annie Linskey and Amy B. Wang wrote in an analysis of questions raised by Warren's exit, "Her supporters are left to contemplate a factor that many believe contributed significantly to her loss: She's female . . . Warren was among six accomplished women who got little traction in a party that recaptured the House in 2018 with a record number of female candidates, elevated a woman as House speaker who regularly goes toe-to-toe with President Trump, and ostensibly has a new sensitivity to gender issues." The exit by Warren, they wrote, "was a reminder of four years ago, when Hillary Clinton's loss sparked a national debate over whether a woman could ever win election to the country's highest political office."[25]

"Hair, Hemlines, and Husbands": Sexist Coverage and Impact

Especially in on-air TV punditry, partisan talk shows, and online commentary, as we discussed in Chapter 4, opinion is key and media narratives get set. The accomplishments and seriousness of women in politics are still too often dismissed and diminished—through excessive focus on women politicians' physical attributes and wardrobes instead of their stances on policy; on questions and commentary about their voices, their looks, their wardrobes, their marriages, marital status, and family life; and how they are said to treat their staffs (the subject of some of the first stories on Amy Klobuchar in 2020);[26] These questions simply are not emphasized or even asked, even today, to nearly the same degree of men running for office; this is what is meant by *gendered treatment*.

Coverage of female candidates over the years has frequently had a snarky, critical tone that trivializes these women's accomplishments—and holds them to impossible standards in every area of their lives, from work to personal appearance.

Substitute a veteran male politician for a veteran female politician in the focus on their clothes or appearance—or compare the media excitement over former Texas congressman Beto O'Rourke's announcement to critiques of Sen. Kirsten Gillibrand's performance with Stephen Colbert in her campaign announcement or humorous asides about Sen. Amy Klobuchar beginning her run for the presidency in a snowstorm in her home state of Minnesota—and you can see that these differences continue.[27]

New York Times reporters raised questions in 2008 about Sarah Palin's ability to be a mother and run for vice president, when in addition to Palin's having five children, including a baby with Down syndrome, the campaign announced that Palin's seventeen-year-old daughter, Bristol, was unwed and having a baby.[28] Female candidates are still often asked how they can "balance" having children with their careers, whereas male candidates are shown with their spouses and children—and grandchildren even—with no questions from reporters about who's home taking care of the children.[29]

The "Double Bind" for Women in Politics

In her book *Beyond the Double Bind: Women and Leadership*, Kathleen Hall Jamieson described the heads I win/tails you lose binds between gendered definitions of femininity and masculinity. This double bind, she said, had been used against women by men in power for centuries.[30] Among them are "Women can exercise their wombs or their brains but not both" and "Women who are considered feminine will be judged incompetent, and women who are competent, unfeminine."[31] Hillary Clinton as the wife of candidate Bill Clinton and then as First Lady was "the Rorschach test" for the double bind in Jamieson's book.

Clinton was criticized for saying that she was "not some little woman standing by my man like Tammy Wynette," referencing a famous country-western song when she appeared with the then candidate Bill Clinton in 1992 to support him on CBS's *60 Minutes* after the campaign was rocked with a sensational tabloid story about Bill Clinton having a long-term extramarital affair.[32]

Later in the campaign, when she was asked by NBC's Andrea Mitchell about avoiding the appearance of conflict of interest between her husband's job as governor and her work as a lawyer in a Little Rock firm, Hillary Clinton's response about having an independent career—"I suppose I could have stayed home and baked cookies and had teas but what I decided to do was fulfill my profession which I entered before my husband was in public life"—was seen by many, Jamieson wrote, "not as rejection of full-time hostess for a governor but as an indictment of stay-at-home motherhood."[33]

Reviewing numerous studies of media coverage of women candidates, Diana B. Carlin and Kelly L. Winfrey wrote, "Research on media coverage of male and female candidates demonstrates important differences in coverage based on gender that go beyond sexist language or stereotypical portrayals. Differences between male and female candidates in the quantity, quality and negativity of coverage can all erode a woman candidate's credibility. Female candidates often receive less issue coverage than males, but more coverage on appearance, personality, and family. When the media does talk about women's issue positions, they tend to frame them as 'feminine' issues such as health care rather than as 'masculine' issues such as budget or employment. During general election campaigns, male candidates received more coverage on feminine issues than they did in the primary; this trend may make it difficult for voters to associate female candidates with any issue while increasing the association of both masculine and feminine issues with male candidates."[34]

Minority women face greater disparity in how they are covered. In one study examining media coverage of minority congresswomen. Sarah Gershon found that they receive less coverage and more negative coverage compared to white women and minority male congressmen.[35]

The undue focus on women's voices, wardrobe, age, and weight— think of the reams of copy over many years on Hillary Clinton's pantsuits or the descriptions of Sarah Palin as a "hottie"—has been so ingrained that it goes unquestioned. When thinking about sexism in media and politics, it's helpful to insert the name of a comparable male politician and think whether they would be subjected to the same repeated focus on their bodies, their clothes, their voices, and their perceived attractiveness—or lack thereof. Politicians, of course, can also demean women for office, as Donald Trump did repeatedly in 2016, as president and in 2020, against Hillary Clinton, Carly Fiorina, Kamala Harris, Michigan governor Gretchen Whitmer, Alexandria Ocasio-Cortez, and other women in Congress who opposed him. Speaking of Utah Republican congresswoman Mia Love, who lost in a primary in 2018, Trump said, "Mia Love gave me no love, and she lost." Love responded later at a press conference that what Trump said in the 2018 election "shines a spotlight on the problem Washington politicians have with minorities and black Americans."[36]

The "Likeability" Factor

Although Barack Obama later asked his 2008 presidential opponent, Hillary Clinton, to be secretary of state in his administration and campaigned vigorously for her in 2016, the then forty-six-year-old Illinois senator Obama in the New Hampshire Democratic primary debate dismissively told Hillary Clinton she was "likeable enough."[37] "Likeability" is a trope—and a psychological barrier for some that, researchers have found, female candidates have to overcome to a far greater degree than men.

"The whole idea of 'likeability' has to do with deep-seated, ingrained attitudes about gender roles and women in positions of power," said Celinda Lake, a Democratic strategist and expert on gender in politics who has been an adviser on many campaigns of women running for office.[38] In an interview with the author Lake noted that the question is rarely raised about male candidates and almost always raised, in gendered ways, about female candidates. "With male candidates, the focus is much more on their qualifications. People are much more willing to vote for a man they consider qualified but unlikeable than a woman," said Lake, referring to numerous experiments with voters as well as focus groups she has conducted for female candidates.[39]

As Clinton herself has noted, calling a woman "ambitious" has not necessarily been viewed as a compliment, and some pundits have reflected fears that a powerful woman is emasculating. A Hillary Clinton nutcracker was marketed during the 2008 campaign, and conservative TV commentator Tucker Carlson (now the host of a highly rated prime-time show on Fox News Channel) said of Clinton, "I cross my legs involuntarily every time she comes on the air."[40] There were far more disturbing posters depicting punishing "the bitch" Clinton, which were seen at Trump rallies in 2016.[41]

Photo 8.1 Hillary Clinton accepted her nomination as the first female nominee for president on a major-party ticket, at the Democratic National Convention in 2016.

Melina Mara/*The Washington Post* via Getty Images

Clinton was portrayed as controlled, humorless, and dying to be president on *Saturday Night Live* in 2008 and 2016. In the 2016 debates—the most-watched presidential debates in U.S. history—, Clinton emphasized her breadth of experience, compared to Trump's lack of experience, and his seat-of-the-pants approach to the debates. Clinton was widely perceived, including by Republican strategists and the public over-all, to have soundly defeated an unprepared Trump in the three presidential debates. He was also criticized for his comments about Clinton, including say-ing that she should go to jail and that she was "such a nasty woman"[42] as well as even looming closely behind her onstage.

Women in politics (and business) appear to benefit to some degree still from being perceived as more honest and trustworthy than men. But research with voters has shown that people will vote more readily for a male candidate they dislike than a female candidate they dislike—and that being portrayed and perceived as not honest and trustworthy damages a woman more than a man. In several nonpartisan studies, including one in 2016 in which voters were given descriptive words and shown photos and videos of candidates, the Barbara Lee Family Foundation, which sponsors research on women in politics, has reached this conclusion: "Women face a litmus that men do not have to pass. Voters will support a male candi-date they do not like but who they think is qualified. Men don't need to be liked to be elected. Voters are less likely to vote for a female candidate they do not like. Women have to prove they are qualified. For men, their qualification is assumed. Women face the double-bind of needing to show competence and likeability."[43]

Some of the worst coverage and commentary in the past has objectified women and undermined their credibility and discussion of their policies—and criticized them, to boot. The *Washington Post's* award-winning fashion columnist, Robin Givhan, once wrote a lengthy analysis of how Secretary of State Condoleezza Rice looked like a "dominatrix" in black boots and a long coat in her first state visit to Europe to a U.S. military base.[44] Relating the outfit to both *The Matrix* and high boots in pornography, Givhan wrote, "Rice's boots speak of sex and power—such a volatile combination."[45] (Again, imagine a parallel psychosexual analysis of what, say, previous Sec-retary of State Colin Powell's wardrobe revealed about his sex and power in his first state visit abroad.)

CNN once did an entire segment—with the network's fashion editor—on Hillary Clinton's "bottom-heaviness."[46] And it is striking how often female politicians are critically described as "strident" and "controlling," with their voice and appearance cited as evidence of these negative traits, whereas a male politician might be similarly described as "forceful" and "in charge"—with no mention of what he was wearing, his age, or his marital status.

Female politicians' voices and tone frequently are critiqued, usu-ally by male pundits, in ways that experts on gendered treatment say reflect unease and even misogynistic anger toward women in power. In 2016 TV pundits regularly negatively critiqued Hillary Clinton's voice as "strident," "annoying," or "angry. "Smile—you just had a big night," MSNBC's Joe Scarborough advised Clinton after a strong debate performance.[47] During a debate on national security, Reince Priebus, chairman of the Republican National Committee, tweeted that Clinton "was angry + defensive the entire time—no smile and uncomfortable."[48] Donald Trump gave Clinton many negative labels during the third presidential debate.[49]

Case Study: Elizabeth Dole's 2000 Presidential Campaign

The 2000 candidacy of Elizabeth Dole, who ran for the Republican nomination, provides a case study for examining ways that coverage of women has changed—and ways that it has not—in recent years. Dole, the former head of the American Red Cross and a former cabinet secretary in two administrations, ranked second (albeit a distant second) to the then Texas governor George W. Bush in early polling among a field of hopefuls. Her campaign was attracting new women voters to the Republican Party before she decided to withdraw after six months on the campaign trail.[50] She cited her inability to raise money against George W. Bush's fundraising juggernaut as the reason for her withdrawal. Despite her popularity, Dole was able to raise only $4.8 million, compared to the record-setting $56 million of Bush.[51]

Dole's candidacy generally was taken seriously in media coverage, but many articles referred snidely to Dole's pastel-colored "power suits" as if they revealed some deep, inner character flaw. Maureen Dowd, the acerbic columnist for the *New York Times*, questioned Dole's ability to be commander in chief by portraying her as a perfectionist and a control-freak who "likes to coordinate the color of her shoes with the rug on stage," and syndicated columnist Arianna Huffington wrote that Dole represented "frozen perfection."[52] (Again, whatever the level of her perfectionism, Sen. John McCain and other politicians who were running for president in 2000 also likely had perfectionist and control-freak tendencies in their quest for the presidency, but these adjectives are rarely attributed to male candidates in news stories.)

More importantly, reporters frequently asked Elizabeth Dole if she was really running for vice president. The question was not directed to John McCain or publisher Steve Forbes, and it undermined Dole's stated intent.[53] Many articles about Dole framed her as a "first woman" but also questioned her viability as a candidate in negative horse-race coverage, according to

Caroline Heldman, Susan J. Carroll, and Stephanie Olson in their study of coverage of Dole.[54]

Other articles, noting her marriage to former Republican senator (and former presidential candidate) Bob Dole, sometimes had undertones of Elizabeth Dole as a schemer who secretly had more power than her older husband. Finally, Bob Dole himself did not help his wife's candidacy with a May 1999 interview with the *New York Times*. When reporter Richard Berke asked Bob Dole to evaluate his wife's campaign, the former senator— damning with faint praise—replied, "She's getting there." Dole also allowed that he was considering giving money to the campaign of his friend and fellow war veteran John McCain.[55]

Many women who remembered Mrs. Dole's Oprah-style walk and talk on behalf of her husband at the 1996 Republican National Convention were offended, and Elizabeth Dole said that her husband had been taken to "the family woodshed" for his remarks. David Von Drehle and Dan Balz of the *Washington Post* later reported that Bob Dole was calling supporters to help raise money to keep his wife in the race, partly, as one source told the reporters, as "penance" for his earlier remarks.[56]

In an analysis of 462 newspaper stories comparing coverage of Dole's presidential campaign with that of McCain and publisher Forbes, researchers found that Dole was shortchanged in issue coverage and overcovered in personal coverage. As the sole woman in the race, she received more coverage overall than McCain or Forbes in 2000. But Dole "received significantly less issue coverage, which included descriptions of her position or record on public-policy matters," compared to McCain and Forbes, and "significantly more personal coverage, which included descriptions of her personality and attire" than did any of the male presidential candidates, researchers Sean Aday and James Devitt concluded.[57]

Before Dole left the campaign, Heldman, Carroll, and Olson found in their study of coverage of Dole that "article after article [recycled] the same adjectives: scripted, rehearsed, robotic controlled," and she was "frequently characterized as lacking substance because of deficiencies in her perceived attention to issues or her prior experience."[58]

In addition, a review of coverage in the 2000 campaign (by this author) shows that while Dole was being hit hard in news stories on her alleged lack of attention to issues, such publications as *Time* magazine and *Newsweek* magazine were publishing glowing summer cover stories on the then Texas

(Continued)

(Continued)

governor George W. Bush that helped Bush make a virtue of his supposed regular-guy lack of foreign policy experience.[59]

These stories—published more than a year before the parties' nominating conventions—noted Bush's fundraising juggernaut and linked him favorably to a new political dynasty with his father, forty-first president George H. W. Bush, in cover headlines that read "Rising Son" and "President Bush?" Also at the same time, Sen. John McCain, a favorite with the news media, was generating media coverage beyond his standing in the polls—and, initially, beyond his fundraising—by providing the press 24/7 access to his maverick campaign.[60]

In interviews with the author, political reporters said after the election that the Dole campaign made tactical errors and had organizational problems that affected the way her campaign was covered. "As a woman I was excited that a woman was perceived as a serious candidate for president," said Beth Fouhy, a political reporter who was executive producer of CNN's political unit at the time. "She had a wonderful moment [before the George W. Bush juggernaut hit] where all the talk was about how she would handle the job, not whether a woman could do it. But she gave some interviews where she was unprepared to offer her positions on Kosovo, health care and other issues a presidential candidate should be able to answer. After that, she went underground and wouldn't do interviews for months."[61]

Veteran Republican strategist Eddie Mahe agreed with these journalists' assessment of errors in Dole's campaign. "She was always a presence in every story about the Republican candidates, and the media felt good about her presence in the race . . . Elizabeth Dole's great problem with the press was her unwillingness to be part of any unscripted moment."[62]

Richard Berke, who covered Dole's campaign for the New York Times, said that Dole appears to have been ambivalent about using her gender in her campaign. "When you saw her on the stump, she would tell audiences to make history," said Berke. "But when you asked her about that, she'd say she wasn't running as a woman."[63]

Dole's concerns may have been justified at the time, although Gallup polls had shown a dramatic increase in the number of voters who say they would vote for a qualified woman (from 33 percent in 1937 to 92 percent in 1999).[64] But how voters would actually vote—vs. the self-flattering things they say to a pollster—remained untested at the time. In addition, despite the 92 percent who said in the 2001 Gallup poll that they would vote for a woman, presented with the choice between a male candidate and a female candidate, 42 percent said in 2001 that they still would prefer a male candidate to a female candidate.[65] In an interview with the author in 2000, Richard Berke said a poll of Republicans found that fully one-third of respondents said they did not think the country was ready for a female president.[66]

Women World Leaders and Structural Barriers to Women Running in the U.S.

Many countries around the world, including India, Germany, Great Britain, Chile, Israel, Liberia, and many others, have all had women leaders, although women remain underrepresented in legislatures and governments around the world. The U.S. has not yet elected a female president. Among 144 countries surveyed in the 2016 annual report on the global gender gap in health, economy, education, and politics from the World Economic Forum, the U.S. was not among the 67 countries that have had a female prime minister, a female president—or both—over the past fifty years.[67]

Experts cite a variety of factors—a number of them structural—in the American political system regarding the continuing disparity between the number of men and women attaining high elective office. "When you look at other countries, you have to wonder what do those countries do that we don't do, since, presumably, there's nothing genetic that keeps women from serving in high political office," said Laura Liswood, secretary general of the Council of Women World Leaders, in an interview with the author.[68] Liswood cofounded both the Council of Women World Leaders and The White House Project, a nonpartisan group devoted to promoting female candidates from both parties in this country. Having studied the election of women candidates both in the U.S. and abroad, Liswood cited the following factors as presenting major barriers to any out-of-power group winning elections in this country:

- The U.S. system of winner-take-all primaries, which favors candidates who are major fundraisers and well-known names

- Other countries' parliamentary systems that require coalitions in which women may have more opportunity to participate

- The extremely high costs of running for office in the U.S.[69]

In a study of press coverage of ten international women world leaders from Israel's Golda Meir to Great Britain's Margaret Thatcher, in English-language American and British-based media, Pippa Norris found that there was considerable variation in the portrayal of the women when they were first elected president or prime minister and that these stories rarely reflected "gratuitous remarks about personal appearance or simple sexism."

Many stories, including in the American media, reflected admiration for these women as world leaders. "Rather than sex-role stereotypes, the stories [in Norris' study of coverage in the 1990s] showed certain gendered news frames with common themes which proved pervasive and recurrent in early coverage of these diverse women."[70] These framing conventions, Norris wrote, "tell us something significant about what is expected from world leaders," with the most common frames revolving "around the breakthrough this appointment signified for all women, the woman leader as outsider, and the woman leader as an agent of change."[71] International women leaders have said that once a woman is not the "first" to head the country and a "critical mass" of women in government is reached, they have seen coverage become more "normalized" and more gender-neutral.[72]

The U.S., Liswood said, has drawn its political candidates from a narrower pool of professions and experience than many other countries. "In this country, we fish from a very limited pond for candidates—other countries have elected doctors, poets and academics as political leaders," Liswood noted.[73] Until Barack Obama in 2008, no U.S. senator since John F. Kennedy had been elected president, and, among the ranks of governors from whom Bill Clinton and George W. Bush came, there have until recently been only a handful of women in the job.

In addition to what were then still-small numbers, relatively, in the U.S. Congress and governorships, Eleanor Clift and Tom Brazaitis wrote in their 2000 book *Madam President*, women who were prominent at the time, from California senator Dianne Feinstein to former Republican New Jersey governor and then Environmental Protection Agency chief Christine Todd Whitman, have been eliminated over the years from consideration for a vice presidential spot on the national tickets of both parties by strategists and pundits who said they couldn't win.

The reasons given over the years for eliminating women from the ticket, Clift and Brazaitis wrote, include "too old, too inexperienced, too pro-choice on abortion, strident, coming from a small state or the wrong state to balance the ticket as a vice-presidential nominee, much less as a Presidential nominee."[74] "One by one the most promising prospects for 2000 were removed from consideration," Clift and Brazaitis, both political journalists covering the campaign, wrote in their book. "Only a few women have dared to contemplate the biggest leap in politics—to the White House. Political analysts, most of them men, put a ceiling on women's aspirations at the level of the president's helpmate, the vice-presidency. These analysts speculate about the good prospects for a woman on one or both major-party tickets, but impose stringent standards when it comes to identifying a particular person."[75]

Clift said in an interview with the author, "I would never have imagined when we wrote our book about the prospects for women as president that it would be sixteen years and counting since a woman, Geraldine Ferraro, was on the vice presidential ticket for one of the two major parties. . . . It's no longer laughable to think that a woman could be elected president. But, as Frank Luntz [the Republican pollster] has joked, the first woman president in the U.S. may have to be a combination of Jack the Ripper and Mother Teresa."[76]

Women's Suffrage and the History of Women in Office

It took women in the U.S. seventy-two years—until 1920—to secure the right to vote in a state-by-state ratification and a vote in Congress for the Nineteenth Amendment. As Rodger Streitmatter wrote in his history of American media, *Mightier Than the Sword: How the News Media Have Shaped American History*, during the era of the women's suffrage movement more than one hundred years ago, male reporters either ignored or ridiculed the movement to gain the right to vote for women. "One of the most serious impediments to the march toward gender equality was the same force that already had built a record as a highly influential institution in American history: the news media," Streitmatter wrote. "By the mid-19th Century, it had been firmly established that the Fourth Estate was a body overwhelmingly peopled by—and largely committed to serving—men. Threatened by the possibility that women might be rising from their second-class citizenship to command a share of the male power base, the men who dominated American journalism ignored the women's rights movement or, when they did cover it, did so with mockery and disdain."[77] Such treatment, Streitmatter noted, intensified with the women's suffrage movement but dates back to "the beginning of the republic, with publications of the late 18th century systematically restricting half the population to a narrow existence that had become known as the women's sphere—essentially the home."[78]

The Seneca Falls Convention, in which some three hundred women met in 1848 in Seneca Falls, New York, to declare women's rights, was derided by writers as the "Women's Wrong Convention," and men who sympathized with the women's movement were described in news articles as "Aunt Nancys": a code word for being gay.[79] James Gordon Bennett, in one of many ugly editorials from the *New York Herald* at the time, favorably compared woman's "being subject to men . . . and happier than she would be in any condition" to what Bennett said was the "natural" subjugation of African Americans.[80]

In 1992, in what was dubbed the "Year of the Woman" in Congress, a number of women including now-long-serving Democratic senators Patty Murray and Dianne Feinstein ran for office in part over their own anger—and many voters' anger—over the treatment of Anita Hill by the all-male Senate Judiciary Committee during her televised testimony alleging sexual harassment that Hill said she had experienced from then Supreme Court justice nominee Clarence Thomas.[81]

From 1992 to 2018, the number of women senators increased from two to twenty-two. Among the more recently elected women in Congress were the four senators and one congresswoman who became presidential candidates in 2020.

"When there were just seven or nine of us, we might stand in the well and talk, and the men would say, 'What are they plotting?' Nothing, of course," said Feinstein in a 2017 interview. "Now it's just well-accepted. Women in both parties have assumed responsibilities and percolated up. And with years you not only obtain experience, but you can provide more leadership."[82] The female senators gather for monthly dinners today, Republican senator Susan Collins of Maine told an audience of students at American University, adding that she believes such activities help promote bipartisanship between Republican and Democratic colleagues.[83]

Nancy Pelosi, the first female Speaker of the House of Representatives, was reelected to that role when Democrats retook the House in 2018. "Every time I get introduced as the most powerful woman in the United States, I almost cry, because I'm thinking, 'I wish that were not true,'" Pelosi told reporters. "I so wish that we had a woman president of the United States, and we came very close to doing that—[a] woman who was better qualified than so many people who have sought that office and even won it."[84]

Before the 2018 congressional midterm elections, although women had increased their numbers and influence in Congress, they remained strongly underrepresented compared to the overall population—not only in terms of gender but also in terms of race and ethnicity. In 2018, there were 110 women—81 Democrats and 29 Republicans—holding seats in the U.S. Congress; that is 20.6 percent of the total 535 members of the Senate and the House of Representatives. The twenty-three women senators represented, of course, mean 23 percent of the one-hundred-senator body. In the House of Representatives, the eighty-seven women represented 20 percent of the House. There were five women delegates including from American Samoa, and the Virgin Islands in the House of Representatives.[85]

Among the thirty-eight women of color in Congress in 2017, eighteen were Black; ten were Latina; nine were Asian American and Pacific Islander (AAPI); and one was multiracial. In 1964, Patsy Takemoto Mink of Hawaii became the first woman of color elected to the House of Representatives, while in 1992, Carol Moseley Braun, who is African American, was the first woman of color elected to the Senate. In 1998, Tammy Baldwin became the first openly gay or lesbian person elected to an initial term in Congress— later becoming the first openly gay U.S. senator.[86]

Feminist Victoria Woodhull ran for president in 1872, on a campaign for women's rights, before women could vote[87]—and New York congress- woman Shirley Chisholm, who in 1968 became the first African Ameri- can woman elected to Congress, ran for the Democratic nomination for president in 1972.[88]

Why Haven't More Women Run for Office?

Two political scientists suggest that one reason for the continued underrepresentation of women in political office is that women don't run for office in equal numbers to men. In 2001 and again in 2008, Jennifer L. Lawless and Richard L. Fox conducted surveys (with follow-up inter- views) of several thousand people they call "potential candidates"—men and women of comparable backgrounds and interests, such as lawyers, business leaders, educators, political activists, and others—to gauge and compare their interest in considering running for political office. "Despite similar levels of political activism and political interest, [potential] women candidates are dramatically less likely than men to launch an actual can- didacy," Lawless and Fox wrote in their book, *It Takes a Candidate: Why Women Don't Run for Office.*[89]

In subsequent research and writing published in 2012, the authors found the discrepancy persisting,[90] with perceived impediments to running including these factors:

- Women are "substantially more likely than men to perceive the electoral environment as highly competitive and biased against female candidates."

- "Hillary Clinton and Sarah Palin's candidacies aggravate women's perceptions of gender bias in the electoral arena."

- Women are "much less likely than men to think they are qualified to run for office"; female potential candidates are "less competitive, less confident, and more risk averse than their male counterparts."

- Women "react more negatively than men to many aspects of modern campaigns," including media coverage.

- Women are "less likely than men to receive the suggestion to run for office—from anyone," and women are "still responsible for the majority of childcare and household tasks."[91]

Lawless and Fox concluded, "Certainly, recruiting female candidates and disseminating information about the electoral environment can help narrow the gender gap in ambition [to run for office] and increase women's representation. But many barriers to women's interest in running for office can be overcome only with major cultural and political changes."[92]

In addition to cultural barriers, experts say, women candidates face issues in fundraising for their campaigns. The group EMILY's List was formed in 1985 by Ellen Malcolm to support pro-choice Democratic female candidates. EMILY is an acronym for "Early Money Is Like Yeast." The group recruits, trains, and helps raise money for pro-choice female candidates. "Research has shown that women need to be asked several times to run for office," said Karen Defilippi, vice president in charge of federal and gubernatorial campaigns for EMILY's List, in an interview with the author. "Fund-raising as a metric [of viability] has prevented women from running."[93]

Women candidates also need to be recruited—and supported—in primaries and in the general election by their national political parties. Compared to Democrats, Republican women have been outnumbered in Congress. As we will discuss, the 2018 midterms brought a new wave of female candidates on the Democratic side—and, in 2020, Republicans recruited and helped win more female candidates on the Republican side.

Hillary Clinton in the 2008 and 2016 Presidential Campaigns

In 2008 Hillary Clinton—then a U.S. senator from New York, former first lady with Bill Clinton, and one of the best-known women in the world—came closer to winning the presidential nomination of a major party than any other woman in history. In her concession speech after a closely contested race against Barack Obama for the Democratic nomination, Clinton offered a compelling metaphor to her supporters for her achievement in a hard-fought campaign against Obama for the Democratic party nomination. "Although we weren't able to shatter that highest, hardest glass ceiling this time, thanks to you, it's got about eighteen million cracks in it," Clinton said, referencing the number of votes she had received. "And the light is shining through like never before, filling us all with the hope and the sure knowledge that the path will be a little easier next time."[94]

In 2016 Trump stunned the political establishment of both major parties with his right-wing populism and promise to "Make America Great

Again" for people who felt left behind by Washington, and Vermont senator Bernie Sanders mounted a very strong challenge to Clinton for the Democrat nomination with his populist message and enthusiastic young supporters. Clinton was portrayed by Donald Trump—and seen by many voters—as a wealthy Washington insider who had benefited financially from giving several highly paid speeches to Wall Street banks and whose unauthorized use of a private email server for official communication as secretary of state was evidence of corruption or even—as Trump claimed—giving away classified information.

Trump and Clinton were two of the most unpopular presidential candidates in more than thirty years, and polling showed that Clinton's unfavorables increased significantly with renewed focus on the email scandal shortly before the election.[95] Clinton, of course, won the popular vote by nearly three million votes but lost in the Electoral College. Days before the election, the then FBI director James Comey, in a move that was widely criticized as unprecedented, told Congress that the FBI had discovered an additional cache of emails in the closed email server investigation, only to announce later that the additional emails did not change the agency's finding that, while Clinton had acted carelessly, she had not acted illegally.[96] "This changes everything!" Trump exulted[97] as he renewed his attacks on "crooked Hillary" and conflated the email story with the theft and release by WikiLeaks of embarrassing emails from the Democratic National Committee, which U.S. government officials later concluded was the work of hackers from the Russian government seeking to undermine Clinton's campaign.[98]

In addition to front-runner "complacency," gender bias, and running against Trump rather than articulating her own economic vision, polling expert Nate Silver maintains that the Comey letter "probably cost" Clinton the election.[99]

The public had strongly disapproved of Clinton's handling of the email server scandal when the story broke earlier in the campaign—and the Comey letter put Clinton's emails on the front page again just days before the election. But there is debate about the exact impact the letter may have had, with other analysts noting that Clinton's lead was narrowing before Comey's letter.[100] Clinton herself cited the Comey letter as a contributing factor to her loss in her memoir *What Happened*, along with her own mistakes, including characterizing Trump's supporters in one appearance as "deplorables." But she maintained in her book that she did not ignore the Midwest, although she did not visit key Rust Belt states she later lost in the last weeks of the campaign.

She contended that the news media ignored her policy forums and positions on issues in favor of coverage of Trump and his incendiary remarks and rallies.[101]

In an interview after the election at another women's conference, for the Women for Women International aid organization, CNN's Chris Cillizza wrote that Clinton "let it rip on Russian interference in the election, FBI Director James Comey, misogyny, the media and last, but certainly not least, Trump . . . It was a striking reversal to the measured public persona she had cultivated throughout her career. What came through loud and clear—despite her assertions that she made a number of mistakes in the course of the campaign—was that Clinton believes that the election was taken from her. And that she's still mad as hell about it."[102]

As Rebecca Traister noted in a postelection profile of Clinton in *New York Magazine*, although Clinton said that she took "absolute personal responsibility" for her loss, she was strongly criticized by several analysts and columnists from the *New York Times* to CNN and Joe Scarborough on MSNBC, who said that she was not taking enough responsibility for her defeat in the Electoral College.[103] A *New York Daily News* column by Gersh Kuntzman, who said he voted for Clinton, reacted to the interview at the women's conference and began with "Hey, Hillary Clinton, shut the f--- up and go away already. . . . No one deserves more blame for the election debacle than Hillary Rodham Clinton."[104]

Critiquing Media Coverage of Clinton in 2016

Along with complacency and polling that missed the Trump surge and Clinton's weakness in several swing states in the Electoral College, Silver and several academic studies of media coverage in the 2016 campaign—including by Harvard's Shorenstein Center[105] and *Columbia Journalism Review*—have faulted the news media for overcovering the email server scandal relative to Donald Trump's controversies as well as other important issues and policy positions in the campaign. *Columbia Journalism Review* wrote that rather than looking to right-wing media, alt-right sites such as Breitbart News and, anti-Clinton fake news on social media, much of it subsequently traced to hackers from the Russian government,[106] as key media influencers in the 2016 election, the *New York Times* and other "legacy" media should look critically at their own coverage of the scandal and the Comey letter.

"In just six days," Duncan J. Watts and David M. Rothschild wrote in *Columbia Journalism Review*, "the *New York Times* ran as many cover stories about Hillary Clinton's emails as they did about all policy issues combined in the 69 days leading up to the election (and that does not include the three additional articles on October 18, and November 6 and 7, or the two articles on the emails taken from [DNC chairman John Podesta]."[107] In retrospect, the authors said, "It seems clear that the press in general made the mistake of assuming a Clinton victory was inevitable, and were setting themselves as credible critics of the next administration."[108]

Clinton has had both strongly positive admirers and strongly negative detractors and fluctuating public approval ratings over her many years in the public eye, with a 62 percent approval rating during her first years as First Lady down to 44 percent when she and Bill Clinton left office in 2001. Her ratings rose when she made a then surprising run for the U.S. Senate from New York and also when she announced her run for president in 2007; she was widely admired as secretary of state, with a 66 percent approval rating before she ran for president again.[109] Clinton's use of the private email server and her handling of the matter during the FBI investigation appeared to hurt her standing—particularly among independents and Republicans in 2015 and again with renewed focus on the Comey letter in 2017.[110] Hillary Clinton was an early advocate for women and children's rights, both as a young woman with the Children's Defense Fund and later as secretary of state. In 2008, perhaps aiming to demonstrate her bona fides as a commander in chief, she emphasized her experience (compared to Barack Obama's relative inexperience) and her readiness to lead "from day one" in 2008. Her 2002 vote in the Senate to authorize the use of force in the invasion of Iraq under President George W. Bush, which she later said she regretted, was criticized by her Democratic opponents, first by Barack Obama in 2008 and then by Senator Sanders in 2016.[111]

Donald Trump and Comments about Women

Donald Trump's unabashed misogyny, including a focus on women as sex objects and attacks on women who challenged him, goes back decades to his days as a New York mogul, celebrated for his glamorous life and comments ranking women's physical attributes in in the New York tabloids and the popular *Howard Stern Show*.[112] Fox News Channel anchor Megyn Kelly, in the first question of the first Republican primary debate, repeated some of Trump's many derogatory characterizations of women ("fat pigs," "dogs," "disgusting animals," and someone a man would like to have "on her knees" in front of him) and asked him whether he had the "temperament" to be president in light of those comments.

Trump responded in part that he had been nice to Kelly and might not be so in the future.[113] After the debate, he was widely criticized by Republicans and Democrats for seemingly linking Kelly's debate question to menstruation. "You could see there was blood coming out of her eyes," Trump told CNN's Don Lemon. "Blood coming out of her wherever."[114] Trump later began a nine-month-long attack on Kelly on Twitter, attacking her personally as "crazy" and "sick," saying that her highly rated show *The Kelly File*, was "unwatchable" and calling for a boycott against her program.[115]

Kelly later wrote that his attacks on her were followed by death threats against her.[116] Fox News Channel stood by Kelly, calling her a first-rate journalist who was doing her job and issuing a statement that said, "Donald

Trump's vitriolic attacks against Megyn Kelly and his extreme, sick obsession with her is beneath the dignity of a presidential candidate who wants to occupy the highest office in the land."[117] More than a year later, now-president Trump denigrated Mika Brzezinski, who had said that she was concerned about Trump's mental health on MSNBC's *Morning Joe*, which she cohosts with conservative Joe Scarborough.

Before the two hosts wrote an op-ed about Trump's mental health, Trump had been a frequent favorite cable news stop for Trump. Trump's response was to tweet that he had seen "low IQ crazy Mika" recently during a social gathering at his Florida estate and she was "bleeding badly from a face-lift," although Brzezinski said she had not had a face-lift (as if that was the right focus for the discussion).[118] Republican senator Ben Sasse of Nebraska, who had opposed Trump's being the Republican nominee, tweeted "Please just stop . . . this isn't normal, and it's beneath the dignity of your office," while Republican senator Lisa Murkowski of Alaska tweeted, "Stop it! The presidential platform should be used for more than bringing people down."[119]

During the Republican primaries, Trump denigrated former CEO Carly Fiorina, the only female GOP candidate, according to an interview with *Rolling Stone*, saying as he saw Fiorina on TV, "Look at that face! Would anyone vote for that?" Can you imagine that, the face of our next president? I mean, she's a woman, and I'm not supposed to say bad things, but really, folks, come on. Are we serious?"[120]

Trump said later that he was talking about Fiorina's "persona." When CNN's Jake Tapper, in the next debate, asked Fiorina about the comments, the audience cheered when she responded coolly, "I think women all over this country heard very clearly what Mr. Trump said."[121] Fiorina told a crowd of supporters after Trump's comments, "This is the face of a sixty-one-year-old woman. I am proud of every year and every wrinkle."[122] Her campaign also made a video of women of all ages—"Look at This Face"—that was highly shared on YouTube.[123]

In October of 2016, the *Washington Post* published the 2005 "*Access Hollywood* tape" in which Trump made numerous vulgar comments about his conduct with women, including boasting off camera to host Billy Bush about "grabbing women" by the genitals just because he could, saying, "I don't even wait. When you're a star, they let you do it, you can do anything."[124] Clinton wrote on Twitter, "This is horrific. We cannot allow this man to become president."[125] Her running mate, Virginia senator Tim Kaine, told reporters, "It makes me sick to my stomach."[126] Republicans, including House Speaker Paul Ryan, condemned Trump, saying he was "sickened," with some calling for Trump to drop out of the race, which he declined to do, characterizing the *Access Hollywood* remarks as "locker-room banter."[127]

For many women, including many young women, Trump's election was seen as evidence that President Obama's agenda would be rolled back and that—at its most basic, a man who denigrated women and minorities could be elected president. Trump brought very few women (and fewer people of color) into his cabinet, and he had repeatedly vowed to nominate a Supreme Court justice who would overturn the *Roe v. Wade* decision on abortion. "His very presence in the White House excuses the kind of behavior . . . on the tape," author Jill Filipovic wrote in *Time* magazine. "It tells women and girls that we aren't valuable for our hard work, our intelligence, or our accomplishments . . . Even more dangerously, it tells men and boys the same thing."[128]

Identity Politics and Voters in 2016

At an emotional postelection session sponsored by Harvard's Kennedy School, top operatives from Clinton's campaign accused the Trump campaign of winning with "dog whistle" racism and misogyny. "I would rather lose than win the way you guys did," Clinton communications director Jennifer Palmieri said. Trump campaign manager Kellyanne Conway countered, "Do you think you could have just had a decent message for white, working-class voters?" Conway asked, "How about, it's Hillary Clinton, she doesn't connect with people? How about, they have nothing in common with her?"[129] Other researchers found that Trump voters had much higher levels of sexism—defined by their agreement with statements such as "women seek to gain power by getting control over men"—than Clinton voters and that sexism and anger over out-groups were significant factors in Trump support.[130]

In Democratic postmortems on the 2016 election, a key message was that Clinton and her campaign had failed to appeal to working-class voters with a strong message about jobs and the economy when many were feeling economic distress and anger at Washington. Only 38 percent of voters in exit polls said Trump was qualified to be president, and yet he won the Electoral College.[131] The Democratic super PAC Priorities USA, which conducted focus groups and polling on "drop-off voters"—people who voted for Obama in 2012 but did not vote in 2016—found that "Clinton and Democrats' economic message did not break through to drop-off or Obama-Trump voters [people who voted for Obama in 2012 and Trump in 2016], even though drop-off voters are decidedly anti-Trump."[132]

"Bernie Sanders' 'revolution' and attack on big money was much closer to hitting the mark than was Hillary Clinton's message, and he won millennials and white working-class voters in the primary," Democratic pollster Stanley R. Greenberg wrote. "The Democrats don't have a 'white working-class problem.' They have a 'working-class problem,' which progressives have been reluctant to address honestly or boldly."[133]

Clinton won the women's vote over Trump by among the largest gender gap—a 12 percent gap between the two candidates—in the past fifty years of exit polls[134] in an election that also found a wide educational gap in support between those who had a college degree and those who did not.[135] The majority of white women (53 percent) voted for Donald Trump, just as a majority of white women have voted for the Republican candidate since 2004.[136] That surprised—and angered—some Clinton supporters.

But political scientists noted, as Lynn Vavreck of UCLA wrote in an article titled "The Ways That the 2016 Election Was Perfectly Normal," that "the state of the nation's economy and party identification matter most in American presidential elections."[137]

As noted in Chapter 1, in their 2018 book, *Identity Crisis: The 2016 Presidential Campaign and the Battle for the Meaning of America*, Vavreck, John Sides and Michael Tesler analyzing polling data, argued that the improbable election—and the improbable candidacy of Donald Trump—turned on issues of identity in race, gender, religion, and ethnicity more than economics, particularly among white voters. They described what they called a subsequent backlash of tolerance against Trump's views and actions in office, reflecting differences in the makeup and vision of the Democratic and Republican Parties in defining who—and what—is "American."[138]

The Women's March, the #MeToo Movement, and the 2018 "Year of the Woman" in Congress

In response to the election of Donald Trump, an estimated two million people, including many women wearing pink knit hats designed to embrace Trump's crude word for women's genitals, marched the day after Trump's inauguration in protest in the Women's March in Washington, D.C., and other cities around the U.S. and the world.[139] The revelations of allegations of sexual harassment and sexual assault of women and men in entertainment, media and politics, in the *New York Times*, *Washington Post*, and other publications, in 2017 led to the firings and resignations of entertainment mogul Harvey Weinstein, Fox News Channel host Bill O'Reilly, Fox News Channel chairman Roger Ailes, *Today* show anchor Matt Lauer, and Democratic senator Al Franken.[140] The #MeToo movement—started by activist Tarana Burke more than ten years earlier[141]— went viral with women sharing their stories of sexual assault after the *New York Times* published the allegations of many women against Harvey Weinstein. The #MeToo movement spread quickly across the Internet, with news organizations, entertainment corporations, and members of Congress promising to investigate allegations of sexual harassment and sexual assault and to improve the workplace culture for women and men, including in the U.S. military. Republicans as well as Democrats said in 2018 they planned to run for office for the first time in response to Donald Trump.[142] And a Pew Research Center poll found that majorities of women and men in both political parties "believe recent sexual harassment allegations primarily reflect widespread social problems" rather than individual misconduct.[143]

In what was billed as a second "Year of the Woman" in Congress, a record number of women were elected to Congress in the 2018 midterm elections. The following statistics were compiled by the Center for American Women and Politics at Rutgers University:

- In the 116th Congress, there were 127 women, 106 Democrats and 21 Republicans serving overall, which increased the percentage of women in Congress from 20 percent to 23.7 percent, with the appointment of Martha McSally from Arizona.

- The gains by women were primarily in the House of Representatives, where the House had more than 100 women serving for the first time in U.S. history, with 102 women, 89 Democrats and 13 Republicans. Of these women in the House, there were a record number of women of color, 43, including African American, Latino and Asian American women among 42 Democrats and one Republican.

- Women in the Senate represented 25 percent of all members of the Senate, exceeding the previous percentage of 23, with four women of color, all Democrats.

- The freshman class of women in the House of Representatives in 2019 was the largest ever, with 36 (35 Democrats, one Republican) non-incumbent women elected. The previous high was 24, set in 1992.

- In states, nine women (six Democrats and three Republicans) would serve as governors in 2019, including one woman of color, a Democrat. Three states—Maine, South Dakota and Iowa—elected their first female governors in 2018. 20 U.S. states had yet to elect a female governor.

Source: Center for American Women and Politics, Rutgers University.

The 2018 candidates were among the most diverse fields ever in U.S. elections—and the winners included many firsts, including the first Muslim women, the first Native American women, and the youngest women elected to Congress. The number of LGBTQ people, women and men, in Congress rose to ten. The 2018 candidates included a number of women who had served in the U.S. military. Among members of Congress already serving in office, Rep. Tammy Duckworth, a wounded veteran of the Iraq War and an Asian American, was the first woman to give birth while serving

Photo 8.2 House Speaker Nancy Pelosi takes a selfie with new and current women in Congress after the 2018 midterm elections.

SAUL LOEB/AFP via Getty Images

in the Senate.[144] The news media broadly published photos of the freshman class, men and women, in a photo op, and Rep. Duckworth was photographed bringing her baby into Congress with her. Nancy Pelosi was reelected Speaker of the House with the new Democratic majority, having been the first woman elected Speaker in 2007, while other women in Congress moved in to more senior roles on committees and leadership.

The Gender Gap in Voting and Women Candidates

At the same time, the gains by women in 2018 were largely driven by a surge of Democratic women—many of whom had never run for office before and many of whom said they were inspired to run in reaction to Donald Trump.[145] As an article by political scientists Malliga Och and Shauna Shames titled "Year of the Woman in Congress Leaves Out Republicans" noted after the election, "the number of Republican women in Congress is actually dropping from 23 to 13," with "only 1 out of 36 freshman female representatives . . . a Republican."[146] The authors concluded, "Whether you are a progressive or a conservative, this is bad news" because "a democracy should reflect the diversity of its society."[147]

"We've seen important breakthroughs, particularly in the U.S. House," Debbie Walsh, director of the Center for American Women and Politics, said in a statement after the election, "but deepening disparities between the parties in women's representation will continue to hobble us on the path to parity. We need women elected on both sides of the aisle."[148]

With the backlash among many women against Donald Trump in the 2018 midterms, Karen Defilippi said in her interview, "Many amazing women candidates came forward and said, 'I want to run.' These were veterans, teachers, small-business owners and advocates for their community. Most of them were not politicians before they ran. But they came forward and said, 'I've got to run.'"[149]

The Republicans added only one new Republican woman to the House in 2018—and they dropped from twenty-three women in the House to thirteen. Men outnumber women in Congress—in both parties—by significant margins. But the Republican gender gap—in numbers and in leadership positions—after 2018 was enormous.

After the "blue wave" of Democratic women being elected to Congress in 2018, Republican congresswoman Elise Stefanik said that the Republican Party was facing a "crisis" in their representation of women. The 2018 results, she said, meant that "Republican women make up less than 3 percent of the House of Representatives. . . . We can and we must do better."[150] Stefanik launched a PAC called E-PAC, a political action committee to help elect more Republican women to Congress. Other new Republican groups formed to recruit and fund conservative women candidates, and the Republican National Committee also joined the effort in 2020. A record number of Republican women ran for federal office in 2020; 227 filed to run for the House, and 94 were nominated.[151]

According to statistics compiled by the Center for American Women and Politics, 126 women (91 Democrats and 35 Republicans) were elected in the 117th Congress. The number of Democrats stayed the same at 105, while the Republicans gained 16 seats in Congress overall, picking up 17 seats in the House and losing one in the Senate. After California governor Gavin Newsom appointed California secretary of state Alex Padilla as the first Latino senator from California, filling Kamala Harris' seat, the 117th Congress has 143 women overall, representing 26.7 percent of the members of Congress, an increase from the previous percentage of 23.7 percent. There were eighty-nine female Democrats and thirty Republican women in the House of Representatives—and sixteen Democrats and eight Republican women in the U.S. Senate. The number of women of color in the current Congress increased slightly from the previous Congress, from 9 percent to 9.5 percent overall. In the House of Representatives, there are forty-three Democrats and five Republicans who are women of color, representing 11 percent overall. With the appointment of Padilla, there are today three women of color, none of them Black and all of them Democrats, among one hundred U.S. Senators.[152] Several female governors played a prominent role in their states' responses to the coronavirus pandemic; but before the 2020 election, only nine states in the U.S. had female governors.[153]

Gender in Media and Politics in the 2020 Presidential Campaign

In addition to the "likeability factor," an important obstacle to the women running for president in 2020 was the "electability" question, which was raised repeatedly— (as in was the country "ready" for "another" woman presidential nominee after Hillary Clinton's loss in 2016?), and was a potential nominee somehow too much like Hillary Clinton, however that might be defined, and the high negatives she engendered among some voters in 2016. By raising the question, of course, focus—and doubt—can be created. "Democrats Puzzle Over Whether a Woman Will Beat Trump" was the headline of one *New York Times* article quoting a seventy-five-year-old former member of the Democratic National Committtee[154] who was worried about picking another woman, while the former chairwoman of the Iowa Democratic Party noted that women—candidates and voters—drove the 2018 midterms. "Obsessing over the question makes it less likely" that Americans will vote for a woman, feminist scholar Linda Hershman wrote in 2019.[155]

Sen. Kirsten Gillibrand was described by one commentator as a Hillary Clinton "Mini-Me." Gillibrand said, "The notion that all women are the same and that women should be judged on anything other than their own merit is just offensive and wrong."[156]

Perhaps because she was an early, prominent entry, Elizabeth Warren, in particular, was subject to questions about likeability, electability, and comparisons to Clinton in 2016. (Warren actually had been quite critical of Clinton's contributions from financial institutions, although she ultimately endorsed Clinton in 2016.) One early article in *Politico* that was widely criticized asked if she was "Hillary Clinton redux," a phrase that was repeated in other coverage and commentary. After Warren attacked Joe Biden during a debate for talking "Republican talking points" in his health-care proposal, Biden wrote an op-ed criticizing her "angry, unyielding" approach.[157]

In a provocative essay in the *Atlantic*, media critic Megan Garber argued that "Americans punished Elizabeth Warren for her competence."[158] Garber quoted one female supporter of Mayor Pete Buttigieg as saying of Warren, "When I hear her talk, I want to slap her, even when I agree with her," while several conservative male political columnists and TV pundits described her as variously "intensely alienating" and a "know-it-all" and "*condescending*." Such language, Garber contended, is evidence of internalized sexist animus. "*Condescending* attempts to rationalize an irrational prejudice," she wrote. "It suggests the lurchings of a zero-sum world—a physics in which the achievements of one person are insulting to everyone else."[159]

Kamala Harris

The nomination of Kamala Harris for vice president received a wave of enthusiastic media coverage in major media outlets, and public opinion polls found the public approving of the choice. But in the White House and among prominent Fox News Channel and conservative radio hosts, she was immediately greeted with misogyny—and racist tropes—that continued.

Donald Trump called her "totally unlikeable" and even "a monster," while a member of Trump's campaign advisory board was reported to have called her an "insufferable lying bitch."[160] Tucker Carlson, the highest-rated talk show host on Fox News Channel, mispronounced her name—and continued to mispronounce it mockingly after his guest corrected him.[161] Rush Limbaugh, quoting a false statement from a conservative website, used a long-standing sexualization and slur against successful women: she had "slept her way up."[162]

Harris' combination of identities is called *intersectionality*, and women of color in politics face both racist and sexist stereotypes and attacks—for example, early portrayals of Michelle Obama as "an angry Black woman" or Trump's telling four freshman representatives of color—Alexandria Ocasio-Cortez, Ilhan Omar, Rashida Tlaib and Ayanna Pressley—to "go back where they came from."[163]

Like Barack Obama and "birtherism" when he ran for president, Harris' birth and eligibility for office were immediately questioned online and on conservative talk shows, as was whether she was really African American— or African American "enough."[164] Finally, an investigation by the *Washington Post* found that sexist, false claims about Harris exploded and were shared hundreds of thousands of times on Facebook and Twitter in the days after her nomination, reflected on talk radio and by the president.[165]

Despite these characterizations and questions during the primaries from progressives about her record as California attorney general, Harris emerged as a popular figure on the campaign trail, particularly among Black and female audiences. Harris assertive, prosecutorial-style questioning of witnesses in congressional hearings had earned her fans—and critics. But when it came to the only vice presidential debate, many media critics—and snap polls as well as interviews on TV with undecided voters afterward—concluded that Harris, smiling, assertive, and refusing to be "mansplained" or interrupted, had won the debate, while she and Pence provided welcome relief from the melee of the first presidential debate.

SUMMARY

It took women seventy-two years to win the right to vote in the U.S., and the news media have reflected—and often amplified and exacerbated—the political and cultural barriers to women running for office through sexist coverage and commentary. Gender dynamics and gendered treatment of women running for office and female leaders in the U.S. reflect deep-seated fears about women in positions of author and unconscious bias that requires women to be "likeable" as well as competent. The 2018 "Year of the Woman" (which was preceded by the 1992 "Year of the Woman") saw the country electing record numbers of women and a more diverse Congress, in part in reaction to Donald Trump and the #MeToo movement. In the 2020 elections, more Republican women ran for office—and more were elected. The pipeline in Congress matters. As we have seen, after the 2008 and 2016 presidential campaigns of Hillary Clinton, having more women in the Senate helped propel four of them, plus Rep. Tulsi Gabbard, to run for president in 2020. And one of those 2020 candidates, Kamala Harris, is now vice president of the U.S.

Gender parity—and greater racial, ethnic, and economic diversity in Congress—are a long way off. But these advances in Congress and governorships—as well as the number of female candidates for president—represent real and symbolic progress. How journalists, commentators—and their opponents—cover them and run against them will be an important reflection of how far women—and men—have progressed in gender dynamics and equal treatment, in gender and in the intersectionality of gender and race, in media and politics.

End-of-Chapter Assignment:
Women Candidates in Announcement Videos and Debates

1. Look at the announcement videos, and track the initial media coverage of several of the Democratic candidates, men and women, for president in 2020. Take notes, and be ready to discuss the announcement videos in terms of what you perceive in "reading" the ad in terms of political messaging and strategy, the candidates' own choices as to what issues to discuss, what strengths to offer, and how much to discuss their personal lives and families, including, for example, being a father or a mother. Look at where—on TV—each candidate announced and be ready to discuss why, in your opinion, that venue was chosen. Then look at media coverage of each candidate's announcement, including the prominence of the coverage, critiques of the candidate's performance as well as characterizations of the candidate's perceived strengths and weaknesses and chances of winning if that is addressed. Do you perceive gendered differences in the candidate's own choices about presenting themselves based on gender and answering stereotypes about women candidates and political issues they traditionally have been associated with—or not?

Do the men and women present themselves in different ways in terms of the settings of the ads or the issues emphasized? Do you see generational differences among the way the candidates overall present themselves? In terms of the initial news coverage and the punditry on TV about their announcements, are there differences you perceive between the way some of the female candidates were covered and commented about compared to some of the men? Take notes, including quotes.

2. Watch the vice presidential debate between Kamala Harris and vice president Mike Pence—and take notes. Were there gendered differences in perception and in reality in the way the candidates responded to each other and to the moderator? How did Harris deal— if you think she did—with the "likeability" issue and stereotypes about women being "angry" or "strident"? Do you think Mike Pence did a good job defending Trump's record and attacking the Democrats? Do you think he took a different tack because he was debating a woman and there are cultural biases and gender dynamics here? If so, what's your evidence for that? Take notes, including quotes and moments in the debate—and come to class ready to discuss.

****

References

....

Chapter 1

1. Sarah Begley, "Hillary Clinton Leads by 2.8 Million in Final Popular Vote Count," *Time*, December 20, 2016, https://time.com/4608555/hillary-clinton-popular-vote-final/.

2. Nathan Bomey, "How Did Pollsters Get Trump, Clinton Election So Wrong?," *USA Today*, November 21, 2016, http://www.usatoday.com/story/news/politics/elections/2016/11/21/senate-no-rubber-stamp/94227098/.

3. Margaret Sullivan, "The Media Didn't Want to Believe Trump Could Win. So They Looked the Other Way," *Washington Post*, November 9, 2016, https://www.washingtonpost.com/lifestyle/style/the-media-didnt-want-to-believe-trump-could-win-so-they-looked-the-other-way/2016/11/09/d2ea1436-a623-11e6-8042-f4d111c862d1_story.html.

4. *Time* Staff, "Here's Donald Trump's Presidential Announcement Speech," *Time*, June 16, 2015, http://time.com/3923128/donald-trump-announcement-speech/.

5. Louis Jacobson and Amy Sherman, "Donald Trump's Pants on Fire Claim That Barack Obama 'Founded' ISIS, Hillary Clinton Was 'Cofounder,'" *PolitiFact*, August 11, 2016, https://www.politifact.com/factchecks/2016/aug/11/donald-trump/donald-trump-pants-fire-claim-obama-founded-isis-c/. Also, see Gregory Krieg, "Trump Threatens to Jail Clinton If He Wins Election," CNN, October 10, 2016, https://www.cnn.com/2016/10/09/politics/eric-holder-nixon-trump-presidential-debate.

6. David A. Fahrenthold, "Trump Recorded Having Extremely Lewd Conversation about Women in 2005," *Washington Post*, October 8, 2016, https://www.washingtonpost.com/politics/trump-recorded-having-extremely-lewd-conversation-about-women-in-2005/2016/10/07/3b9ce776-8cb4-11e6-bf8a-3d26847eeed4_story.html.

7. Heather Caygle, "Ryan: Trump's Comments 'Textbook Definition' of Racism," *Politico*, June 7, 2016, https://www.politico.com/story/2016/06/paul-ryan-trump-judge-223991.

8. "Exit Polls," CNN, November 9, 2016, http://edition.cnn.com/election/results/exit-polls.

9. Aamna Mohdin, "American Women Voted Overwhelmingly for Clinton, Except the White Ones," *Quartz* (blog), November 9, 2016, http://qz.com/833003/election-2016-all-women-voted-overwhelmingly-for-clinton-except-the-white-ones/. Also, see Jon Henley, "White and Wealthy Voters Gave Victory to Donald Trump, Exit Polls Show," *Guardian*, November 9, 2016, https://www.theguardian.com/us-news/2016/nov/09/white-voters-victory-donald-trump-exit-polls.

10. K. K. Rebecca Lai et al., "How Trump Won the Election According to Exit Polls," *New York Times*, November 8, 2016, https://www.nytimes.com/interactive/2016/11/08/us/elections/exit-poll-analysis.html.

11. Euan McKirdy, Susanna Capelouto, and Max Blau, "Thousands Take to the Streets to Protest Trump Win," CNN, November 10, 2016, http://www.cnn.com/2016/11/09/politics/election-results-reaction-streets/.

12. Jeffrey Anderson, "Trump Won on the Issues," *RealClearPolitics*, November 18, 2016, https://www.realclearpolitics

.com/articles/2016/11/18/trump_won_on_the_issues_132132.html.

13. Morning Consult Polling, "Clinton and Trump Are Historically Unpopular. Here's Why," Morning Consult, July 16, 2016, https://morningconsult.com/2016/07/16/clinton-and-trump-are-historically-unpopular-heres-why/.

14. Jeremy W. Peters, Megan Thee-Brenan, and Dalia Sussman, "Election Exit Polls Reveal a Starkly Divided Nation," New York Times, November 8, 2016, http://www.nytimes.com/2016/11/09/us/politics/election-exit-polls.html.

15. Democratic strategist source, interview with the author, November 17, 2016.

16. Nicholas Confessore and Karen Yourish, "$2 Billion Worth of Free Media for Donald Trump," Upshot (blog), New York Times, March 15, 2016, https://www.nytimes.com/2016/03/16/upshot/measuring-donald-trumps-mammoth-advantage-in-free-media.html.

17. Andrew Tyndall, "Let the Trump Circus Continue," Same Day's Blog, Tyndall Report, May 10, 2016, http://tyndallreport.com/comment/20/5776/.

18. Amy Chozick, "Hillary Clinton's Expectations, and Her Ultimate Campaign Missteps," New York Times, November 9, 2016, http://www.nytimes.com/2016/11/10/us/politics/hillary-clinton-campaign.html.

19. Nick Corasaniti, "In Visceral Ads for Hillary Clinton, Donald Trump Does All the Talking," New York Times, October 5, 2016, http://www.nytimes.com/2016/10/06/us/politics/campaign-ads.html.

20. Thomas E. Patterson, "News Coverage of the 2016 General Election: How the Press Failed the Voters" (Shorenstein Center on Media, Politics and Public Policy, December 2016), https://shorensteincenter.org/wp-content/uploads/2016/12/2016-General-Election-News-Coverage-1.pdf.

21. Ibid.

22. Mark Landler and Eric Lichtblau, "F.B.I. Director James Comey Recommends No Charges for Hillary Clinton on Email," New York Times, July 5, 2016, https://www.nytimes.com/2016/07/06/us/politics/hillary-clinton-fbi-email-comey.html.

23. Catie Edmondson, "State Dept. Inquiry Into Clinton Emails Finds No Deliberate Mishandling of Classified Information," New York Times, October 18, 2019, https://www.nytimes.com/2019/10/18/us/politics/state-dept-inquiry-clinton-emails.html.

24. Kenneth T. Walsh, "Focus Group Voters Reveal Disdain for Clinton, Trump," U.S. News & World Report, September 19, 2016, http://www.usnews.com/news/articles/2016-09-19/focus-group-voters-reveal-disdain-for-clinton-trump.

25. Jonathan Martin, Dalia Sussman, and Megan Thee-Brenan, "Voters Express Disgust Over U.S. Politics in New York Times/CBS Poll," New York Times, November 3, 2016, http://www.nytimes.com/2016/11/04/us/politics/hillary-clinton-donald-trump-poll.html.

26. Ronald F. Inglehart and Pippa Norris, "Trump, Brexit, and the Rise of Populism: Economic Have-Nots and Cultural Backlash" (working paper, Harvard Kennedy School, Harvard University, Cambridge, MA, August 2016).

27. Nicholas Carnes and Noam Lupu, "It's Time to Bust the Myth: Most Trump Voters Were Not Working Class," Monkey Cage (blog), Washington Post, June 5, 2017, https://www.washingtonpost.com/news/monkey-cage/

wp/2017/06/05/its-time-to-bust-the-myth-most-trump-voters-were-not-working-class/.

28. See Ian Haney Lopez, Dog Whistle Politics: How Coded Racial Appeals Have Reinvented Racism and Wrecked the Middle Class (New York: Oxford University Press, 2014)

29. Time Staff, "Here's Donald Trump's Presidential Announcement Speech."

30. John Sides, Michael Tesler, and Lynn Vavreck, Identity Crisis: The 2016 Presidential Campaign and the Battle for the Meaning of America (Princeton, NJ: Princeton University Press, 2018).

31. Ibid., 2–3.

32. Brian F. Schaffner, "These 5 Charts Explain Who Voted How in the 2018 Midterm Election," Monkey Cage (blog), Washington Post, November 10, 2018, https://www.washingtonpost.com/news/monkey-cage/wp/2018/11/10/these-5-charts-explain-who-voted-how-in-the-2018-midterm-election/.

33. "2018 Election Night Tally," Center for American Women and Politics, Rutgers University, http://cawp.rutgers.edu/2018-election-night-tally.

34. Jeremy W. Peters et al., "Midterm Election Results: 4 Key Takeaways," New York Times, November 7, 2018, https://www.nytimes.com/2018/11/07/us/politics/election-news.html.

35. Nicholas Fandos and Michael D. Shear, "Trump Impeached for Abuse of Power and Obstruction of Congress," New York Times, January 16, 2020, https://www.nytimes.com/2019/12/18/us/politics/trump-impeached.html.

36. Michael D. Shear, "In Impeachment Case, Schiff Accuses Trump of Trying 'to Cheat' in Election," New York Times, January 24, 2020, https://www.nytimes.com/2020/01/22/us/politics/impeachment-case-trump.html.

37. Donald J. Trump (@realDonaldTrump), "WITCH HUNT!," Twitter, December 10, 2019, https://twitter.com/realDonaldTrump/status/1204414691910410242?ref_src=twsrc%5Etfw. Also, see Tamara Keith, "Read: Trump Legal Filing Accuses Democrats of 'Dangerous Perversion' of Constitution," National Public Radio, January 20, 2020, https://www.npr.org/2020/01/20/797908079/trump-legal-team-accuses-democrats-of-dangerous-perversion-of-constitution.

38. James Rainey, "The Impeachment Show on MSNBC and Fox News: Preparing to Prosecute, or Defend, Trump," Los Angeles Times, November 13, 2019, https://www.latimes.com/politics/story/2019-11-13/msnbc-and-fox-news-girding-to-prosecute-and-defend-president-trump.

39. Rob Savillo and Nikki McCann Ramirez, "Fox News' Evening Shows Avoid Live Coverage of Trump's Senate Impeachment Trial," Media Matters for America, January 24, 2020, https://www.mediamatters.org/trump-impeachment-inquiry/fox-news-evening-shows-avoid-live-coverage-trumps-senate-impeachment.

40. Mike DeBonis and Josh Dawsey, "Trump, Democrats Keep Their Distance as GOP Moderates Face Crucial Impeachment Votes," Washington Post, January 23, 2020, https://www.washingtonpost.com/politics/trump-democrats-keep-their-distance-as-gop-moderates-face-crucial-impeachment-votes/2020/01/23/fa19f234-3e04-11ea-8872-5df698785a4e_story.html.

41. Aila Slisco, "Adam Schiff Closes Trump Impeachment Trial Argument with Plea to Republicans: 'You Are Decent.

He Is Not Who You Are,'" *Newsweek*, February 3, 2020, https://www.newsweek.com/adam-schiff-closes-trump-impeachment-trial-argument-plea-republicans-you-are-decent-he-not-1485512.

42. Nicholas Fandos, "Trump Acquitted of Two Impeachment Charges in Near Party-Line Vote," *New York Times*, February 5, 2020, https://www.nytimes.com/2020/02/05/us/politics/trump-acquitted-impeachment.html.

43. Ibid.

44. Jeffrey M. Jones, "Trump Job Approval at Personal Best 49%," *Gallup Blog*, February 4, 2020, https://news.gallup.com/poll/284156/trump-job-approval-personal-best.aspx.

45. Ibid.

46. Ibid.

47. Todd J. Gillman, "Why Is Julián Castro, the Only Latino Candidate for President, Struggling to Catch on, Even with Latinos?," *Dallas Morning News*, November 9, 2019, https://www.dallasnews.com/news/politics/2019/11/09/julian-castros-balancing-act-yet-to-pay-off-court-latinos-without-getting-pegged-as-the-brown-guy/.

48. Jeremy Hobson, "If Elected, Democratic Candidate Pete Buttigieg Would Be the Youngest President Ever," WBUR, February 19, 2019, https://www.wbur.org/hereandnow/2019/02/19/pete-buttigieg-youngest-president.

49. Joe Biden, "Joe Biden for President: America Is an Idea," April 25, 2019, video, 3:29, https://youtu.be/VbOU2fTg6cI.

50. Emily Stewart, "Elizabeth Warren Has Just One Plan," *Vox*, September 20, 2019, https://www.vox.com/policy-and-politics/2019/9/20/20867899/elizabeth-warren-cfpb-founding-plans-obama-president/.

51. Bill Allison and Mark Niquette, "Bloomberg Tops Half a Billion Dollars in Campaign Advertising," *Bloomberg*, February 24, 2020, https://www.bloomberg.com/news/articles/2020-02-24/bloomberg-tops-half-a-billion-dollars-in-campaign-advertising.

52. Amy Walter (@amyewalter), "Lotta finger pointing as to how Ds got to this place where the moderate/establish wings of party have to rally around Biden. Some blame the order of primary (IA and NH lack diversity). Or the rules for getting into debate stage. Or DNC ineptitude. Here's what I see," Twitter, March 2, 2020, 10:29 p.m., https://twitter.com/amyewalter/status/1234682381107220481. See Michelle Ruiz, "We Had the Most Diverse Group of Candidates in History. Now It's Down to Two White Guys," *Vogue*, March 4, 2020, https://www.vogue.com/article/no-longer-diverse-democratic-presidential-candidates.

53. Bethany Allen-Ebrahimian, "Timeline: The Early Days of China's Coronavirus Outbreak and Cover-Up," *Axios*, March 18, 2020, https://www.axios.com/timeline-the-early-days-of-chinas-coronavirus-outbreak-and-cover-up-ee65211a-afb6-4641-97b8-353718a5faab.html.

54. "COVID-19 Coronavirus Pandemic," Worldometer, accessed May 7, 2020, https://www.worldometers.info/coronavirus/#countries.

55. Ibid.

56. Sheryl Gay Stolberg and Eileen Sullivan, "As Trump Pushes to Reopen, Government Sees Virus Toll Nearly Doubling," *New York Times*, May 4, 2020, https://www.nytimes.com/2020/05/04/us/politics/trump-coronavirus-death-toll.html.

57. Heather Long and Andrew Van Dam, "U.S. Unemployment Rate Soars to 14.7 Percent, the Worst Since the Depression Era," *Washington Post*, May 8, 2020, https://www.washingtonpost.com/business/2020/05/08/april-2020-jobs-report/.

58. Christina Wilkie, "Trump's Argument for Reelection Is Collapsing," CNBC.com, March 19, 2020, https://www.cnbc.com/2020/03/19/coronavirus-crisis-trumps-argument-for-reelection-is-collapsing.html

59. Peter Baker, "A Half-Century after Wallace, Trump Echoes the Politic of Division," *New York Times*, July 30, 2020, https://www.nytimes.com/2020/07/30/us/politics/trump-wallace.html

60. Jennifer Amatulli, "Kamala Harris Slams Trump's Debate Rhetoric: 'A Dog Whistle Through a Bullhorn,'" *HuffPost*, September 30, 2020. https://www.huffpost.com/entry/kamala-harris-trump-biden-debate_n_5f73faeac5b6d698bb25469c.

61. Thomas E. Patterson, *Out of Order* (New York: Alfred A. Knopf, Inc., 1994), 28.

62. J. Y. Smith, "Richard S. Salant Dies," *Washington Post*, February 17, 1993, https://www.washingtonpost.com/archive/local/1993/02/17/richard-s-salant-dies/cdf0c368-8e2e-4f2b-853c-3c99d2d51dcb/. Also, Richard Salant, interview with the author, 1990.

63. See Michael P. McDonald, "United States Election Project," http://www.electproject.org/.

64. See John S. and James L. Knight Foundation, "The Untold Story of American Non-Voters," https://knightfoundation.org/reports/the-100-million-project/.

65. Monica Anderson and Dennis Quinn, "46% of U.S. Social Media Users Say They Are 'Worn Out' by Political Posts and Discussions," Pew Research Center, August 8, 2019, https://www.pewresearch.org/fact-tank/2019/08/08/46-of-u-s-social-media-users-say-they-are-worn-out-by-political-posts-and-discussions/.

66. Brett Samuels, "Trump Ramps up Rhetoric on Media, Calls Press 'the Enemy of the People,'" *The Hill*, April 5, 2019, https://thehill.com/homenews/administration/437610-trump-calls-press-the-enemy-of-the-people.

67. Adam Nagourney, "Candidates Strive to Break Through Media Fog," *New York Times*, September 15, 2008, http://www.nytimes.com/2008/09/16/us/politics/16web-nagourney.html.

68. NBC News, "Kellyanne Conway: Press Secretary Sean Spicer Gave 'Alternative Facts' | Meet The Press | NBC News," January 22, 2017, video, 3:53, https://youtu.be/VSrEEDQgFc8.

69. Glenn Kessler, Salvador Rizzo, and Meg Kelly, "President Trump Has Made 15,413 False or Misleading Claims Over 1,055 Days," *Washington Post*, December 16, 2019, https://www.washingtonpost.com/politics/2019/12/16/president-trump-has-made-false-or-misleading-claims-over-days/.

70. Katie Rogers, "As Impeachment Moves Forward, Trump's Language Turns Darker," *New York Times*, October 2, 2019, https://www.nytimes.com/2019/10/01/us/politics/trump-treason-impeachment.html.

71. Tess Townsend, "Washington Post's Marty Baron: 'We're Not at War with the Administration, We're at Work,'" *Vox*, February 14, 2017, https://www.vox.com/2017/2/14/14615824/marty-baron-not-at-war-trump.

72. Glenn Kessler and Scott Clement, "Trump Routinely Says Things That Aren't True. Few Americans Believe Him," *Washington Post*, December 14,

2018, https://www.washingtonpost.com/graphics/2018/politics/political-knowledge-poll-trump-falsehoods/.

73. Ibid.

74. Ibid.

75. U.S. Const., amend. I.

76. Ibid.

77. See the letter by Thomas Jefferson to Edward Carrington in Lindsey Bever, "Memo to Donald Trump: Thomas Jefferson Invented Hating the Media," *Washington Post*, February 18, 2017, https://www.washingtonpost.com/news/the-fix/wp/2017/02/17/trumps-war-with-the-media-isnt-new-thomas-jefferson-railed-about-newspaper-lies-too/.

78. Ibid.

79. See the quote from a letter by Thomas Jefferson to Lafayette in "Thomas Jefferson on Politics & Government," Family Guardian, https://famguardian.org/subjects/politics/thomasjefferson/jeff1600.htm.

80. See Karen O'Connor, Larry J. Sabato, and Alixandra B. Yanus, *American Government: Roots and Reform*, 12th ed. (London: Pearson, 2012), 100.

81. Harold Holzer, "Stop the Presses: Lincoln Suppresses Journalism," HistoryNet, December 2014, https://www.historynet.com/stop-the-presses-lincoln-suppresses-journalism.htm.

82. See George H. Roeder Jr., *The Censored War: American Visual Experience During World War Two* (New Haven, CT: Yale University Press, 1993).

83. Avi Asher-Schapiro, "Leak Prosecutions under Trump Chill National Security Beat," Committee to Protect Journalists, March 6, 2019, https://cpj.org/blog/2019/03/leak-prosecutions-trump-national-security-beat.php.

84. "New York Times v. Sullivan (1964)," Bill of Rights Institute, https://billofrightsinstitute.org/educate/educator-resources/lessons-plans/land-mark-supreme-court-cases-elessons/new-york-times-v-sullivan-1964/.

85. Editors of *Encyclopædia Britannica*, "Pentagon Papers" (Encyclopædia Britannica, Inc., September 18, 2017), https://www.britannica.com/topic/Pentagon-Papers.

86. Ibid.

87. Craig Whitlock, "The Afghanistan Papers, Part 1: At War with the Truth," *Washington Post*, December 9, 2019, https://www.washingtonpost.com/graphics/2019/investigations/afghanistan-papers/afghanistan-war-confidential-documents/.

88. See Lydia Saad, "Military, Small Business, Police Still Stir Most Confidence," *Gallup Blog*, June 28, 2018, https://news.gallup.com/poll/236243/military-small-business-police-stir-confidence.aspx.

89. Peter Baker, "In a Swelling Age of Tribalism, the Trust of a Country Teeters," *New York Times*, December 10, 2019, A1.

90. "Amid Criticism, Support for Media's 'Watchdog' Role Stands Out," Pew Research Center, August 8, 2013, http://www.people-press.org/2013/08/08/amid-criticism-support-for-medias-watchdog-role-stands-out/.

91. "The 2018 State of the First Amendment" (Freedom Forum Institute, 2018), https://www.freedomforuminstitute.org/wp-content/uploads/2018/06/2018_FFI_SOFA_Report.pdf.

92. Jeffrey M. Jones, "U.S. Media Trust Continues to Recover from 2016 Low," *Gallup Blog*, October 12, 2018, https://news.gallup.com/poll/243665/media-trust-continues-recover-2016-low.aspx.

93. Ibid.

94. Jeffrey Gottfried et al., "Trusting the News Media in the Trump Era," Pew Research Center, December 12, 2019, https://www.journalism.org/2019/12/12/trusting-the-news-media-in-the-trump-era/.

95. Ibid.

96. Indira Lakshmanan, interview with the author, April 4, 2018, C-SPAN.

97. See Lars Willnat, David H. Weaver, and G. Cleveland Wilhoit, "The American Journalist in the Digital Age: How Journalists and the Public Think about Journalism in the United States," *Journalism Studies* (2017).

98. Ibid.

99. For his research on sources of antipathy to the media, see, especially pages 108–30, Jonathan M. Ladd, *Why Americans Hate the Media and How It Matters* (Princeton, NJ: Princeton University Press, 2012).

100. Tien-Tsung Lee, "The Liberal Media Myth Revisited: An Examination of Factors Influencing Perceptions of Media Bias," *Journal of Broadcasting & Electronic Media* 49, no. 1 (2005).

101. Ibid.

102. Christopher Hare, Keith T. Poole, and Howard Rosenthal, "Polarization in Congress Has Risen Sharply. Where Is It Going Next?," *Monkey Cage* (blog), *Washington Post*, February 13, 2014, http://www.washingtonpost.com/blogs/monkey-cage/wp/2014/02/13/polarization-in-congress-has-risen-sharply-where-is-it-going-next/.

103. Thomas E. Mann and Norman J. Ornstein, *It's Even Worse Than It Looks: How the American Constitutional System Collided with the New Politics of Extremism* (New York: Basic Books, 2012). xxiii–xxiv

104. Nolan McCarty, "What We Know and Don't Know about Our Polarized Politics," *Monkey Cage* (blog), *Washington Post*, January 8, 2014, http://www.washingtonpost.com/blogs/monkey-cage/wp/2014/01/08/what-we-know-and-the two-know-about-our-polarized-politics/.

105. Carroll Doherty, "7 Things to Know About Polarization in America," Pew Research Center, June 12, 2014, http://www.pewresearch.org/fact-tank/2014/06/12/7-things-to-know-about-polarization-in-america/.

106. Ibid.

107. Andrew Kohut, "The Political Middle Still Matters," Pew Research Center, August 1, 2014, http://www.pewresearch.org/fact-tank/2014/08/01/the-political-middle-still-matters/.

108. This is based on interviews with the author as a journalist covering the news media from 1989 to 1998.

109. Communications Act of 1934, S. 3040, 73rd Cong. (1934), http://www.legisworks.org/congress/73/publaw-416.pdf.

110. Jane Hall, "TV Industry Reportedly OKs New Ratings," *Los Angeles Times*, July 10, 1997, A1.

111. Jane Hall, "Few Moguls Expected at Kids-TV Summit," *Los Angeles Times*, July 24, 1996, https://www.latimes.com/archives/la-xpm-1996-07-24-fi-27363-story.html.

112. Sallie Hofmeister and Jane Hall, "Disney to Buy Cap Cities/ABC for $19 Billion, Vault to No. 1," *Los Angeles Times*, August 1, 1995, http://articles.latimes.com/1995-08-01/news/mn-30178_1_walt-disney. Also, see Jane Hall, "Westinghouse Likely to Aid CBS' Moonves, Cut Elsewhere," *Los Angeles Times*, August 2, 1995, http://articles.latimes.com/1995-08-02/business/fi-30544_1_cbs-deal. Also, see Sallie Hofmeister and Jane Hall, "CBS Agrees to Buyout Bid by Westinghouse," *Los Angeles Times*, http://articles.latimes.com/1995-08-02/news/mn-30646_1_tv-station.

113. Michael J. de la Merced, "AT&T Agrees to Buy Time Warner for $85.4 Billion," *New York Times*, October 22, 2016, http://www.nytimes.com/2016/10/23/business/dealbook/att-agrees-to-buy-time-warner-for-more-than-80-billion.html.

114. "About," Sinclair Broadcasting Group, Inc., http://sbgi.net/.

115. Camila Domonoske, "Video Reveals Power of Sinclair, as Local News Anchors Recite Script in Unison," National Public Radio, April 2, 2018, https://www.npr.org/sectithe twoetwo-way/2018/04/02/598794433/video-reveals-power-of-sinclair-as-local-news-anchors-recite-script-in-unison.

116. Brian Stelter, "Sinclair's New Media-Bashing Promos Rankle Local Anchors," CNN, March 7, 2018, https://money.cnn.com/2018/03/07/media/sinclair-broadcasting-promos-media-bashing/index.html.

117. Reuters, "Tribune Media Sues Sinclair for $1 Billion in Damages after Terminating $3.9 Billion Acquisition Deal," CNBC, August 9, 2018, https://www.cnbc.com/2018/08/09/tribune-media-terminates-deal-to-be-bought-by-sinclair.html.

118. See the iHeartMedia, Inc. website, www.iheartmedia.com, for information on the company, Clear Channel Outdoor Holdings, Inc., and SEC filings.

119. American Society of News Editors, "Total Employment Declines in 2012, but Proportion of Minorities in Newsrooms Remains Stable," June 25, 2013, http://asne.org/content.asp?pl=121&sl=284&contentid=284.

120. Elizabeth Grieco, "U.S. Newsroom Employment Has Dropped by a Quarter since 2008, With Greatest Decline at Newspapers," Pew Research Center, July 9, 2019, https://www.pewresearch.org/fact-tank/2019/07/09/u-s-newsroom-employment-has-dropped-by-a-quarter-since-2008/.

121. Clara Hendrickson, "Local Journalism in Crisis: Why American Must Revive Its Local Newsrooms," *Brookings*, November 12, 2019, https://www.brookings.edu/wp-content/uploads/2019/11/Local-Journalism-in-Crisis.pdf.

122. David Carr, "Print Is Down, and Now Out," *New York Times*, August 10, 2014, http://www.nytimes.com/2014/08/11/business/media/media-companies-spin-off-newspapers-to-uncertain-futures.html.

123. David Carr, "A Doomed Romance with a New Orleans Newspaper," *New York Times*, May 27, 2012, http://www.nytimes.com/2012/05/28/business/media/the-times-picayune-new-orleans-and-a-doomed-romance.html.

124. Dylan Byers, "*Los Angeles Times* Newsroom Cuts to Begin This Week," CNN, October 5, 2015, http://money.cnn.com/2015/10/05/media/los-angeles-times-cuts-tribune/.

125. Joe Nocera, "Imagine If Gordon Gekko Bought News Empires," *Bloomberg*, March 26, 2018, https://www.bloomberg.com/opinion/articles/2018-03-26/alden-global-capital-s-business-model-destroys-newspapers-for-little-gain.

126. Ken Doctor, "Newsonomics: Six Takeaways from McClatchy's Bankruptcy," *Nieman Journalism Lab* (blog), February 14, 2020, https://www.niemanlab.org/2020/02/newsonomics-six-takeaways-from-mcclatchys-bankruptcy/.

127. Ibid.

128. For the 2008 announcement, see Robert MacMillan, "Gannett to Cut 1,000 Newspaper Jobs: Memo," Reuters, August 14, 2008, http://www.reuters.com/article/us-gannett-idUSN1427376520080814. For the 2011

announcement, see Jim Romenesko, "Gannett Lays Off 700 Newspaper Division Employees," Poynter Institute, June 21, 2011, http://www.poynter.org/2011/gannett-to-lay-off-about-700-newspaper-employees/136527/.

129. Clara Hendrickson, "How the Gannett/Gatehouse Merger Could Deepen America's Local News Crisis," *Brookings*, November 18, 2019, https://www.brookings.edu/blog/fixgov/2019/11/18/how-the-gannett-gatehouse-merger-could-deepen-americas-local-news-crisis/.

130. Jake Johnson, "'Another Nail in the Coffin' of Democracy and Journalism as US Newspaper Giants Gannett and Gatehouse Announce $1.4 Billion Merger," *Common Dreams*, August 6, 2019, https://www.commondreams.org/news/2019/08/06/another-nail-coffin-democracy-and-journalism-us-newspaper-giants-gannett-and.

131. Francesca Giuliani-Hoffman, "How the Washington Post Has Changed under Jeff Bezos," CNN, August 16, 2019, https://www.cnn.com/2019/08/16/media/jeff-bezos-donald-graham/index.html.

132. Sarah Scire, "Readers Reign Supreme, and Other Takeaways from the *New York Times* End-of-Year Earnings Report," *Nieman Journalism Lab* (blog), February 6, 2020, https://www.niemanlab.org/2020/02/readers-reign-supreme-and-other-takeaways-from-the-new-york-times-end-of-year-earnings-report/.

133. Ibid.

134. Joshua Benton, "The *L.A. Times'* Disappointing Digital Numbers Show the Game's Not Just About Drawing in Subscribers—It's About Keeping Them," *Nieman Journalism Lab* (blog), July 31, 2019, https://www.niemanlab.org/2019/07/the-l-a-times-disappointing-digital-numbers-show-the-games-not-just-about-drawing-in-subscribers-its-about-keeping-them/.

135. Martin Baron, interview with the author, February 24, 2016.

136. Pengjie Gao, Chang Lee, and Dermot Murphy, "Financing Dies in Darkness? The Impact of Newspaper Closures on Public Finance" (working paper, Hutchins Center on Fiscal & Monetary Policy, *Brookings*, September 2018), https://www.brookings.edu/wp-content/uploads/2018/09/WP44.pdf.

137. Hendrickson, "Local Journalism in Crisis."

138. Meghan E. Rubado and Jay T. Jennings, "Political Consequences of the Endangered Local Watchdog: Newspaper Decline and Mayoral Elections in the United States," *Urban Affairs Review* (April 3, 2019).

139. Hendrickson, "How the Gannett/Gatehouse Merger Could Deepen."

140. Suzanne Nossel, Craig Aaron, and Michael Copps, "Groups Call on Congress to Fund Journalism and Treat Local News as Essential Service During Pandemic," *Free Press* via *Benton Institute for Broadband & Society*, April 8, 2020, https://www.benton.org/headlines/groups-call-congress-fund-journalism-and-treat-local-news-essential-service-during.

141. Kristine Lu and Jesse Holcomb, "In 21 States, Local Newspapers Lack a Dedicated D.C. Reporter Covering Congress," Pew Research Center, January 7, 2016, http://www.pewresearch.org/fact-tank/2016/01/07/in-21-states-local-newspapers-lack-a-dedicated-reporter-keeping-tabs-on-congress/.

142. Jurkowitz et al., "The Changing TV News Landscape."

143. Danny Hayes and Jennifer L. Lawless, "The Decline of Local News and Its Effects: New Evidence from

Longitudinal Data," *The Journal of Politics* 80, no. 1 (January 2018).

144. Sam Stein and Maxwell Tani, "The 2020 Race Has Become the Cable News Primary," *Daily Beast*, February 25, 2020, https://www.thedailybeast.com/the-2020-race-has-become-the-cable-news-primary.

145. Lindsey Ellefson, "CNN Dominates January Cable News Ratings with Its Most-Watched Month Ever," *The Wrap*, February 2, 2021, http://www.thewrap.com/cnn-msnbc-fox-news-ratings-january-2021/.

146. Stephen Battaglio, "Facing Ratings Pressure, Fox News Replaces News with Opinion at 7 p.m.," *Los Angeles Times*, January 11, 2021, https://www.latimes.com/entertainment-arts/business/story/2021-01-11/fox-news-changes-daytime-schedule-martha-maccallum-afternoon.

147. Emily Guskin and Tom Rosenstiel, "Network News: The Pace of Change Accelerates," Pew Research Center, 2012, http://www.stateofthemedia.org/2012/network-news-the-pace-of-change-accelerates/.

148. Kenneth Olmstead et al., "How Americans Get TV News at Home," Pew Research Center's Journalism Project, October 11, 2013, http://www.journalism.org/2013/10/11/how-americans-get-tv-news-at-home/.

149. David Karpf, "The Internet and Politics," *Political Science* (April 28, 2016).

150. The Pew Research Center provides an overview of its processes at https://www.pewresearch.org/methods/about-content-analysis/human-coding-of-news-media/.

Chapter 2

1. See Harold D. Lasswell, *Propaganda Technique in the World War* (New York: Peter Smith, 1938).

2. See, for example, https://misinforeview.hks.harvard.edu/wp-content/uploads/2020/04/April19_FORMATTED_COVID-19-Survey.pdf

3. Walter Lippmann, *Public Opinion* (New York: Free Press Paperbacks, 1997).

4. Ibid., 229.

5. Neal Gabler, *Life: The Movie* (New York: Vintage Books, 1998).

6. Lippmann, *Public Opinion*, 216.

7. See Shanto Iyengar, *Is Anyone Responsible?* (Chicago: University of Chicago Press, 1991).

8. Gwen Ifill, "Investigators Probe Mine Disaster in West Virginia," *PBS NewsHour*, April 14, 2010, http://www.pbs.org/newshour/bb/weather-jan-june10-minesafety_04-14/.

9. Ian Urbina and Michael Cooper, "Deaths at West Virginia Mine Raise Issues about Safety," *New York Times*, April 6, 2010, http://www.nytimes.com/2010/04/07/us/07westvirginia.html. See Steven Mufson, Jerry Markon, and Ed O'Keefe, "West Virginia Mine Has Been Cited for Myriad Safety Violations," *Washington Post*, April 7, 2010, http://www.washingtonpost.com/wp-dyn/content/article/2010/04/05/AR2010040503877.html.

10. Barry Meier, "Origins of an Epidemic: Purdue Pharma Knew Its Opioids Were Widely Abused," *New York Times*, May 29, 2018, https://www.nytimes.com/2018/05/29/health/purdue-opioids-oxycontin.html.

11. "The 2015 Pulitzer Prize Winner in Investigative Reporting," The Pulitzer Prizes, https://www.pulitzer.org/winners/wall-street-journal-staff.

12. "The 2016 Pulitzer Prize Winner in Public Service," The Pulitzer Prizes, https://www.pulitzer.org/winners/associated-press.

13. Eli Saslow, "Living without a Living Wage," *Washington Post*, March 8, 2020, https://www.washingtonpost

.com/nation/2020/03/08/living-without-living-wage/.

14. "The 2011 Pulitzer Prize Winner in Public Service," The Pulitzer Prizes, https://www.pulitzer.org/winners/los-angeles-times-4.

15. "The 2018 Pulitzer Prize Winner in Explanatory Reporting," The Pulitzer Prizes, https://www.pulitzer.org/winners/staffs-arizona-republic-and-usa-today-network.

16. "Explainers," Vox, 2020, https://www.vox.com/explainers.

17. Sarah Rankin, "Pulitzer Honoree Is Latest to Win After Leaving Journalism," April 21, 2018, Associated Press, https://apnews.com/dc312a7e503f4b7b-b61a62013fea852d/Pulitzer-honoree-is-latest-to-win-after-leaving-journalism.

18. Bernard C. Cohen, *Press and Foreign Policy* (Princeton, NJ: Princeton University Press, 1963), 13.

19. For a full description of their methodology, see Maxwell E. McCombs and Donald L. Shaw, "The Agenda-Setting Function of Mass Media," *Public Opinion Quarterly* 36, no. 2 (1972): 176–187.

20. Maxwell McCombs and David Weaver, "Voters' Need for Orientation and Use of Mass Communication" (paper presented at the International Communication Association, Montreal Canada, April 25–28, 1973), quoted in Maxwell E. McCombs, Donald L. Shaw, and David H. Weaver, "New Directions in Agenda-Setting Theory and Research," *Mass Communication and Society* 17, no. 6 (2014).

21. Ibid., 180.

22. Ibid., 181.

23. David H. Weaver, "Agenda-Setting Effects," ed. Wolfgang Donsbach, *International Encyclopedia of Communication* 1 (Malden, MA: Blackwell, 2008), 145–51.

24. Julian Bond, interview with the author, October 10, 2011. See "American Forum: Julian Bond Town Hall," NBC4 Washington, October 20, 2011, http://www.nbcwashington.com/news/local/American-Forum-Julian-Bond-Town-Hall-131802173.html.

25. Ibid.

26. Ibid.

27. "The Kennedys and Civil Rights," WGBH American Experience hosted by PBS, accessed July 16, 2016, http://www.pbs.org/wgbh/american-experience/features/general-article/kennedys-and-civil-rights/.

28. Shanto Iyengar and Donald R. Kinder, *News That Matters* (Chicago: University of Chicago Press, 1987).

29. See W. Lance Bennett and Shanto Iyengar, "A New Era of Minimal Effects? The Changing Foundations of Political Communication," *Journal of Communication* 58, no. 4, 707–731 (December 2008).

30. Shanto Iyengar, *Media Politics: A Citizens Guide*, 3rd ed. (New York: W. W. Norton & Company, 2016), 246.

31. Ibid.

32. Jan Ransom, "Harvey Weinstein's Stunning Downfall: 23 Years in Prison," *New York Times*, March 11, 2020, https://www.nytimes.com/2020/03/11/nyregion/harvey-weinstein-sentencing.html.

33. John R. Zaller, *The Nature and Origins of Mass Opinion* (Cambridge: Cambridge University Press, 1992), 6.

34. Ibid.

35. Matthew Hindman, *The Myth of Digital Democracy* (Princeton, NJ: Princeton University Press, 2009).

36. Everett M. Rogers and James W. Dearing. "Agenda-Setting Research: Where Has It Been, Where Is It Going," *Communication Yearbook 11*, ed. James

A. Anderson, Newbury Park, Calif. Sage, 1988, 555–594."

37. Maxwell McCombs and Marcus Funk, "Shaping the Agenda of Local Daily Newspapers: A Methodology Merging the Agenda Setting and Community Structure Perspectives," *Mass Communication and Society* 14, no. 6 (2011).

38. Lei Guo, Hong Vu, and Maxwell McCombs, "An Expanded Perspective on Agenda-Setting Effects: Exploring Third Level Agenda Setting," *Revista de Comunicación* 11 (January 2012).

39. Michael Martinez, "Showdown on the Range: Nevada Rancher, Feds Face Off Over Cattle Grazing Rights," CNN, April 12, 2014, http://www.cnn.com/2014/04/10/us/nevada-rancher-rangers-cattle-showdown/.

40. Sandhya Somashkar and Danielle Paquette, "Undercover Video Shows Planned Parenthood Official Discussing Fetal Organs Used for Research," *Washington Post*, July 14, 2015, https://www.washingtonpost.com/politics/undercover-video-shows-planned-parenthood-exec-discussing-organ-harvesting/2015/07/14/ae330e34-2a4d-11e5-bd33-395c05608059_story.html.

41. Joe Parkinson and David George-Cosh, "Image of Drowned Syrian Boy Echoes around World," *Wall Street Journal*, September 3, 2015, http://www.wsj.com/articles/image-of-syrian-boy-washed-up-on-beach-hits-hard-1441282847.

42. See, for example, Andrea Ceron, "Internet, News, and Political Trust: The Difference between Social Media and Online Media Outlets," *Journal of Computer-Mediated Communication* 20, no. 5 (September 2015). Also, see "About the Black Lives Matter Network," #BlackLivesMatter Organization, accessed July 16, 2016, http://blacklivesmatter.com/about/.

43. Mark Peplow, "The Flint Water Crisis: How Citizen Scientists Exposed Poisonous Politics," *Nature*, July 6, 2018, https://www.nature.com/articles/d41586-018-05651-7.

44. Stephanie Sugars, "Back on the Campaign Trail, President Trump Increases His Anti-Press Tweet Offensive," *Freedom of the Press Foundation*, January 20, 2020, https://freedom.press/news/back-campaign-trail-president-trump-increases-his-anti-press-tweet-offensive/

45. Ibid.

46. Jessica T. Feezell, "Agenda Setting through Social Media: The Importance of Incidental News Exposure and Social Filtering in the Digital Era," *Political Research Quarterly* 71, no. 2 (2018).

47. Deen Freelon et. al, "How Black Twitter and Other Social Media Communities Interact with Mainstream News," John S. and James L. Knight Foundation, https://kf-site-production.s3.amazonaws.com/media_elements/files/000/000/136/original/TwitterMedia-final.pdf.

48. Johanna Dunaway, "Mobile vs. Computer: Implications for News Audiences and Outlets," Shorenstein Center, August 30, 2016, https://shorensteincenter.org/mobile-vs-computer-news-audiences-and-outlets/.

49. Iyengar and Kinder, *News That Matters*, 63.

50. Ibid.

51. Ibid, 106–111.

52. See Dylan Rosenfield, "The Portrayal of the Iranian Hostage Crisis by American Media and its Effects on the Presidential Election of 1980," *Vanderbilt Historical Review*, November 8, 2016, http://vanderbilthistoricalreview.com/iranian-hostage-crisis/.

53. Frank Newport, "Presidential Job Approval: Bill Clinton's High Ratings in the Midst of Crisis, 1998," *Gallup Blog*, June 4, 1999, http://www.gallup.com/

poll/4609/presidential-job-approval-bill-clintons-high-ratings-midst.aspx.

54. David W. Moore, "Bush Job Approval Highest in Gallup History," *Gallup Blog*, September 24, 2001, https://news.gallup.com/poll/4924/bush-job-approval-highest-gallup-history.aspx.

55. Ibid.

56. David Paul Kuhn, "Exit Polls: Economy Top Issue," *Politico*, November 5, 2008, https://www.politico.com/story/2008/11/exit-polls-economy-top-issue-015270.

57. Ibid.

58. "Creating Camelot: The Kennedy Photography of Jacques Lowe," Newseum, http://www.newseum.org/exhibits/traveling/camelot/.

59. Alex Selwyn-Holmes, "Reagan Assassination Attempt Contact Sheets," *Iconic Photos* (blog), June 28, 2012, https://iconicphotos.wordpress.com/2012/06/28/reagan-assassination-attempt-contact-sheets/.

60. Sean O'Kane, "The Photography of Trump's Presidency Is a Huge Break from Obama's," *Verge*, April 2, 2017, https://www.theverge.com/2017/4/2/15140892/trump-white-house-photographer-shealah-craighead-vs-pete-souza-obama.

61. "Obama White House," Flickr, accessed August 2019, https://www.flickr.com/photos/obamawhitehouse/.

62. O'Kane, "The Photography of Trump's Presidency."

63. Mark Landler, "Photographers Protest White House Restrictions," *New York Times*, November 21, 2013, https://www.nytimes.com/2013/11/22/us/politics/photographers-protest-white-house-restrictions.html.

64. See Associated Press, "A New 'View' for President Obama," July 29, 2019, video, 1:03, https://youtu.be/n4kqk7bg15I.

65. *The Late Late Show with James Corden*, "First Lady Michelle Obama Carpool Karaoke," July 20, 2016, video, 14:41, https://youtu.be/ln3wAdRAim4.

66. Dan Kopf, "Obama's Approval Rating from His First Day to His Last, in Charts," *Quartz* (blog), January 20, 2017, https://qz.com/889644/obamas-approval-rating-from-his-first-day-to-his-last-in-charts/.

67. Hilary Weaver, "Laura Bush, Michelle Obama, and the Soft Power of Outspoken First Ladies," *Vanity Fair*, June 20, 2018, https://www.vanityfair.com/style/2018/06/the-history-of-outspoken-first-ladies.

68. Robert M. Entman, "Framing: Towards Clarification of a Fractured Paradigm," *Journal of Communication* 43, no. 4 (1993): 51.

69. Daniel Kahneman, *Thinking, Fast and Slow* (New York: Farrar, Straus and Giroux, 2011), 363.

70. Ibid., 368.

71. Eric Bradner, "Orlando Shooting Sparks Gun Control, Language Debates," CNN, June 12, 2016, https://www.cnn.com/2016/06/12/politics/orlando-shooting-gun-control-islamic-terrorism/index.html.

72. Jeremy W. Peters et al., "How the El Paso Killer Echoed the Incendiary Words of Conservative Media Stars," *New York Times*, August 11, 2019, https://www.nytimes.com/interactive/2019/08/11/business/media/el-paso-killer-conservative-media.html.

73. Ibid.

74. Nicholas Grossman, "El Paso Was Terrorism, Dayton Wasn't, and Why That Matters," *Arc Digital*, August 7, 2019, https://arcdigital.media/el-paso-was-terrorism-dayton-wasnt-and-why-that-matters-9b01a2ed2d94.

75. Doug Gavel, "Robert Blendon Discusses Health Policy and Public Opinion," John F. Kennedy School of Government, September 29, 2009, http://www.hks.harvard.edu/index.php/news-events/news/articles/robert-blendon. Also, Carmen DeNavas-Walt, Bernadette D. Proctor, and Jessica Smith, "Income, Poverty, and Health Insurance Coverage in the United States: 2006," U.S. Census Bureau, August 2007, http://www.census.gov/prod/2007pubs/p60-233.pdf.

76. Pew Research Center, "Health Care Views Similar to '93, but Fewer Favor Rebuilding System," news release, June 18, 2009, http://www.people-press.org/files/legacy-pdf/522.pdf.

77. Pew Research Center: Journalism & Media Staff, "What Americans Learned from the Media About the Health Care Debate," Pew Research Center, June 19, 2012, http://www.journalism.org/2012/06/19/how-media-has-covered-health-care-debate/.

78. Sarah Palin's Facebook Notes, "Statement on the Current Health Care Debate," August 7, 2009, https://www.facebook.com/note.php?note_id=113851103434.

79. Justin Bank, "Palin vs. Obama: Death Panels," FactCheck.org, August 14, 2009, http://www.factcheck.org/2009/08/palin-vs-obama-death-panels/.

80. Author's research on coverage. Also, see Project for Excellence in Journalism, "Six Things to Know about Health Care Coverage: A Study of the Media and the Health Care Debate," Pew Research Center, June 21, 2010, http://www.journalism.org/files/legacy/health%20care%20report_Final.pdf.

81. Pew Research Center: Journalism & Media Staff, "What Americans Learned from the Media about the Health Care Debate," June 19, 2012, https://www.journalism.org/2012/06/19/how-media-has-covered-health-care-debate/.

82. Ibid.

83. Ibid.

84. Lydia Saad, "Access Still Top Health Concern in U.S.; Gov't Role Gains Ground," Gallup Blog, November 17, 2010, http://www.gallup.com/poll/144776/access-still-top-health-concern-u.s.-govt-role-gains-ground.aspx.

85. Sheryl Gay Stolberg and Robert Pear, "Obama Signs Health Care Overhaul Bill, with a Flourish," New York Times, March 23, 2010, http://www.nytimes.com/2010/03/24/health/policy/24health.html. Also, see Scott Wilson, "Obama Signs Health-Care Reform Bill," Fix (blog), Washington Post. March 24, 2010, http://www.washingtonpost.com/wp-dyn/content/article/2010/03/23/AR2010032301071.html.

86. Chris Cillizza, "Election 2010: Republicans Net 60 House Seats, 6 Senate Seats and 7 Governorships," Washington Post, November 3, 2010, http://voices.washingtonpost.com/thefix/morning-fix/2010-election-republican-score.html.

87. Rebecca Sinderbrand, "Exit Polls: Economy the No. 1 Issue," Political Ticker (blog), CNN, November 2, 2010, http://politicalticker.blogs.cnn.com/2010/11/02/first-exit-polls-economy/.

88. Pew Research Center, "Health Care Finale: Heavy Coverage, Huge Interest," March 23, 2010, http://www.people-press.org/2010/03/23/health-care-finale-heavy-coverage-huge-interest/.

89. Lesley Stahl, Reporting Live, Touchstone ed. (New York: Simon & Schuster, 1999).

90. Maria Elizabeth Grabe and Erik Page Bucy, Image Bite Politics: News and the Visual Framing of Elections (New York: Oxford University Press, 2009), 5.

91. "Poetry and Power—The Inaugural Address of John F. Kennedy," John F. Kennedy Presidential Library and Museum, accessed August 2019, https://www.jfklibrary.org/visit-museum/exhibits/past-exhibits/poetry-and-power-the-inaugural-address-of-john-f-kennedy.

92. Justin Wm. Moyer, "Exactly the Right Words, Exactly the Right Way: Reagan's Amazing Challenger Disaster Speech," *Washington Post*, January 28, 2016, https://www.washingtonpost.com/news/morning-mix/wp/2016/01/28/how-ronald-reagan-explained-the-challenger-disaster-to-the-world-its-all-part-of-taking-a-chance/.

93. Veracifer, "Hillary Clinton Tears up during Campaign Stop," January 7, 2008, video, 1:58, https://youtu.be/6qgWH89qWks.

94. Adam Liptak, "Supreme Court Ruling Makes Same-Sex Marriage a Right Nationwide," *New York Times*, June 26, 2015, https://www.nytimes.com/2015/06/27/us/supreme-court-same-sex-marriage.html.

95. Marc Solomon, *Winning Marriage: The Inside Story of How Same-Sex Couples Took on the Politicians and Pundits—and Won* (Lebanon, NH: ForeEdge, 2014).

96. Molly Ball, "What Other Activists Can Learn from the Fight for Gay Marriage," *Atlantic*, July 14, 2015, https://www.theatlantic.com/politics/archive/2015/07/what-other-activists-can-learn-from-the-fight-for-gay-marriage/398417/.

97. Richard Leiby, "In Cheney Family Feud Over Same-Sex Marriage, Heather Poe Isn't Holding Her Peace," *Washington Post*, December 2, 2013, https://www.washingtonpost.com/lifestyle/style/in-cheney-family-feud-over-same-sex-marriage-is-heather-poe-the-driving-force/2013/12/02/1998f294-5938-11e3-835d-e7173847c7cc_story.html.

98. Associated Press, "Cheney at Odds with Bush on Gay Marriage," NBC News, August 25, 2004, http://www.nbcnews.com/id/5817720/ns/politics/t/cheney-odds-bush-gay-marriage/#.XZKTXn97nIV.

99. Ibid.

100. "Attitudes on Same-Sex Marriage," Pew Research Center, May 14, 2019, https://www.pewforum.org/fact-sheet/changing-attitudes-on-gay-marriage/.

101. Hilary Weaver, "Ellen DeGeneres's Groundbreaking Coming Out: 20 Years Later," *Vanity Fair*, April 28, 2017, https://www.vanityfair.com/style/2017/04/20th-anniversary-of-ellen-degeneres-coming-out.

102. Joel Gallen and Tig Notaro, "Ellen DeGeneres: Relatable," Netflix, December 28, 2018.

103. Phil Gast, "Obama Announces He Supports Same-Sex Marriage," CNN, May 9, 2012, https://www.cnn.com/2012/05/09/politics/obama-same-sex-marriage/index.html.

104. Justin McCarthy, "U.S. Support for Gay Marriage Stable, at 63%," *Gallup Blog*, May 22, 2019, https://news.gallup.com/poll/257705/support-gay-marriage-stable.aspx.

105. Ariane de Vogue, "Supreme Court Rules for Colorado Baker in Same-Sex Wedding Cake Case," CNN, June 4, 2018, https://www.cnn.com/2018/06/04/politics/masterpiece-colorado-gay-marriage-cake-supreme-court/index.html.

106. Adam Liptak, "In Narrow Decision, Supreme Court Sides with Baker Who Turned Away Gay Couple," *New York Times*, June 4, 2018, https://www.nytimes.com/2018/06/04/us/politics/supreme-court-sides-with-baker-who-turned-away-gay-couple.html.

107. Arthur Hochstein and Lon Tweeten, "The New New Deal: What Obama Can Learn from FDR" *Time*, November

24, 2008, http://content.time.com/time/covers/0,16641,20081124,00.html.

108. "Newsweek's Michele Bachmann Cover Raises Eyebrows (Photo, Poll)," *Huffington Post*, October 8, 2011, http://www.huffingtonpost.com/2011/08/08/newsweeks-michele-bachman_n_920860.html.

109. Michael D. Shear and Thomas Gibbons-Neff, "Washington Prepares for a July 4 Spectacle, Starring and Produced by President Trump," *New York Times*, July 3, 2019, https://www.nytimes.com/2019/07/03/us/politics/trump-military-tanks.html.

110. Philip Kennicott, "Forget the Tanks. Trump's Violation of the Lincoln Memorial Is the Real Offense," *Washington Post*, July 3, 2019, https://www.washingtonpost.com/lifestyle/style/forget-the-tanks-trumps-violation-of-the-lincoln-memorial-is-the-real-offense/2019/07/03/23c0894c-9da9-11e9-9ed4-c9089972ad5a_story.html.

111. Christal Hayes et al., "'Are You Proud to Be an American?' Why Trump's 4th of July Was a Tale of Three Different Celebrations," *USA Today*, July 5, 2019, https://www.usatoday.com/story/news/politics/2019/07/05/4th-july-trump-put-divisions-display-protest/1653535001/.

112. Jane Hall, "Burned by the Spotlight," *Columbia Journalism Review*, September/October 2004.

113. Ibid.

Chapter 3

1. *OpenSecrets* (blog), "2020 Election to Near $11 Billion in Total Spending, Smashing Records," October 1, 2020, https://www.opensecrets.org/news/2020/10/2020-election-to-near-11-billion-in-total-spending-smashing-records/.

2. Ibid.

3. Wesleyan Media Project, accessed October 14, 2020, https://mediaproject.wesleyan.edu/.

4. Richard Briffault, "Campaign Spending Isn't the Problem—Where the Money Comes from Is," *The Conversation*, November 2, 2018, http://theconversation.com/campaign-spending-isnt-the-problem-where-the-money-comes-from-is-104093.

5. See the Wesleyan Media Project at http://mediaproject.wesleyan.edu/ for analyses of both presidential and congressional campaigns since 2010. Also, see Erika Franklin Fowler and Travis N. Ridout, "Political Advertising in 2014: The Year of the Outside Group," *The Forum* 12, no. 4 (2015).

6. Wesleyan Media Project, "More Dark Money Ads Than Any of the Past Four Cycles," news release, November 1, 2018, http://mediaproject.wesleyan.edu/releases/110118-tv/.

7. *OpenSecrets* (blog), "Dark Money Basics," https://www.opensecrets.org/dark-money/basics.

8. Fredreka Schouten, "Exclusive: Secret Money Funds More Than 40 Percent of Outside Congressional Ads," *USA Today*, July 12, 2018, https://www.usatoday.com/story/news/politics/2018/07/12/secret-money-funds-more-than-40-percent-outside-congressional-tv-ads-midterm-elections/777536002/.

9. Erika Franklin Fowler and Travis N. Ridout, "Negative, Angry, and Ubiquitous: Political Advertising in 2012," *The Forum* 10, no. 4 (2013).

10. Deirdre Shesgreen, "Pricey Ad Wars Launched in Fight over Brett Kavanaugh's Nomination to Supreme Court," *USA Today*, July 10, 2018, https://www.usatoday.com/story/news/politics/2018/07/10/

centrist-senators-brace-onslaught-ad-war-begins-over-supreme-court-nominee/770539002/.

11. Federal Election Commission, "FEC Summarizes Campaign Activity of the 2011–2012 Election Cycle," news release, April 19, 2013, http://www.fec.gov/press/press2013/20130419_2012-24m-Summary.shtml.

12. Nicholas Confessore, "Total Cost of Election Could Be $6 Billion," Caucus (blog), New York Times, October 31, 2012, http://thecaucus.blogs.nytimes.com/2012/10/31/total-cost-of-election-could-be-6-billion/.

13. Wesleyan Media Project, "Ad Spending Tops $1 Billion," news release, October 29, 2014, http://mediaproject.wesleyan.edu/releases/ad-spending-tops-1-billion/.

14. Niv M. Sultan, "Election 2016: Trump's Free Media Helped Keep Cost Down, but Fewer Donors Provided More of the Cash," OpenSecrets (blog), April 13, 2017, https://www.opensecrets.org/news/2017/04/election-2016-trump-fewer-donors-provided-more-of-the-cash/.

15. See Erika Franklin Fowler, Travis N. Ridout, and Michael M. Franz, "Political Advertising in 2016: The Presidential Election as Outlier?," The Forum 14, no. 4 (2017).

16. Jason Lynch, "Advertisers Spent $5.25 Billion on the Midterm Election, 17% More Than in 2016," Adweek, November 15, 2018, https://www.adweek.com/tv-video/advertisers-spent-5-25-billion-on-the-midterm-election-17-more-than-in-2016/.

17. Ibid.

18. See Erika Franklin Fowler, Travis N. Ridout, and Michael M. Franz, "The Big Lessons of Political Advertising in 2018," The Conversation, Dec. 3, 2018, https://theconversation.com/the-big-lessons-of-political-advertising-in-2018-107673

19. Ibid.

20. See Ken Goldstein and Paul Freedman, "Campaign Advertising and Voter Turnout: New Evidence for a Stimulation Effect," The Journal of Politics 64, no. 3 (August 2002).

21. See Alan S. Gerber et al., "How Large and Long-Lasting Are the Persuasive Effects of Televised Campaign Ads? Results from a Randomized Field Experiment," The American Political Science Review 105, no. 1 (February 2011).

22. Lynn Vavreck, "Yes, Political Ads Are Still Important, Even for Donald Trump," Upshot (blog), New York Times, June 20, 2016, http://www.nytimes.com/2016/06/21/upshot/yes-political-ads-are-still-important-even-for-donald-trump.html.

23. Darrell M. West, Air Wars: Television Advertising and Social Media in Election Campaigns, 1952–2016, 7th ed. (Thousand Oaks, CA: CQ Press, 2018), 69.

24. Briffault, "Campaign Spending Isn't the Problem."

25. Nicholas Confessore, Sarah Cohen, and Karen Yourish, "Small Pool of Rich Donors Dominates Election Giving," New York Times, August 1, 2015, http://www.nytimes.com/2015/08/02/us/small-pool-of-rich-donors-dominates-election-giving.html.

26. Sultan, "Election 2016."

27. Ibid.

28. "Beyond Distrust: How Americans View Their Government," Pew Research Center, November 23, 2015, http://www.people-press.org/files/2015/11/11-23-2015-Governance-release.pdf.

29. Ibid.

30. Ibid.

31. "Bernie Sanders for President," Bernie 2016, https://berniesanders.com/.

32. Andrew Prokop, "Donald Trump Made One Shockingly Insightful Comment during the First GOP Debate," *Vox*, August 6, 2015, http://www.vox.com/2015/8/6/9114565/donald-trump-debate-money.

33. Michael Finnegan and James Rainey, "Strapped for Cash, Trump Yanks TV Ads in Key States as Biden Spending Surges," *Los Angeles Times*, October 10, 2020. https://www.latimes.com/politics/story/2020-10-10/trump-biden-television-advertising-battleground-states.

34. Brian Schwartz, "Joe Biden Has Spent $500 Million on Ads This Year as He Seeks the Presidency," CNBC, October 9, 2020. https://www.cnbc.com/2020/10/09/joe-biden-hits-half-billion-dollar-mark-for-ads-in-trump-challenge.html.

35. "The Master Character Narratives in Campaign 2012," Pew Research Center, August 23, 2012, http://www.journalism.org/files/legacy/Character%20Narratives.pdf.2012

36. "FactCheck.org," Annenberg Public Policy Center, http://www.factcheck.org/.

37. Angie Drobnic Holan, "Who Is Politifact? Who Pays for Politifact?," *PolitiFact*, April 18, 2016, http://www.politifact.com/truth-o-meter/blog/2011/oct/06/who-pays-for-politifact/.

38. For more information, see Glenn Kessler's biography and description of the *Washington Post's* Fact Checker at Glenn Kessler, "About the Fact Checker," *Washington Post*, September 11, 2013, https://www.washingtonpost.com/news/fact-checker/about-the-fact-checker/.

39. John G. Geer, "Fanning the Flames: The News Media's Role in the Rise of Negativity in Presidential Campaigns" (working paper, Center for the Study of Democratic Institutions, Vanderbilt University, Nashville, TN, 2010), http://www.vanderbilt.edu/csdi/research/CSDI_WP_03-2010.pdf.

40. Aristotle, *The Rhetoric and the Poetics of Aristotle*, trans. W. Rhys Roberts and Ingram Bywater (New York: Modern Library, 1984).

41. Jon Greenberg, "Pro-Obama Group Blames Romney in Woman's Death," *PolitiFact*, August 9, 2012, http://www.politifact.com/truth-o-meter/statements/2012/aug/09/priorities-usa-action/pro-obama-group-blames-romney-womans-death/.

42. Eugene Kiely, "Obama Fumbles 'JV Team' Question," FactCheck.org, September 8, 2014, http://www.factcheck.org/2014/09/obama-fumbles-jv-team-question/.

43. David Corn, "The Story Behind the Percent Video," *Mother Jones*, December 31, 2012, http://www.motherjones.com/politics/2012/12/story-behind-47-video.

44. Louis Jacobson, "Putting Mitt Romney's Attacks on 'You Didn't Build That' to the Truth-O-Meter," *PolitiFact*, July 26, 2012, http://www.politifact.com/truth-o-meter/statements/2012/jul/26/mitt-romney/putting-mitt-romneys-attacks-you-the two-build-truth/.

45. Alison for Kentucky, "New Grimes Television Ad: 'Skeet Shooting,'" news release, September 15, 2014, http://alisonforkentucky.com/newsroom/press-releases/new-grimes-television-ad-skeet-shooting/. Also, see Alison for Kentucky, "Alison for Kentucky TV Ad 'Skeet Shooting,'" September 15, 2014, video, 0:32, https://youtu.be/z7Pa16JPUlY.

46. See Kathleen Hall Jamieson, *Packaging the Presidency: A History and Criticism of Presidential Campaign Advertising*, 3rd ed. (New York: Oxford University Press, 1996).

47. West, *Air Wars*, 7th ed., 16.

48. Steven A. Holmes, "The 1992 Elections: Disappointment—News Analysis an Eccentric but No Joke; Perot's Strong Showing Raises Questions on What Might Have Been, and Might Be," *New York Times*, November 5, 1992, http://www.nytimes.com/1992/11/05/us/1992-elections-disappointment-analysis-eccentric-but-no-joke-perot-s-strong.html.

49. Philip Rucker and Dan Balz, "How Joni Ernst's Ad About 'Castrating Hogs' Transformed Iowa's U.S. Senate Race," *Washington Post*, May 11, 2014, https://www.washingtonpost.com/politics/how-joni-ernsts-ad-about-castrating-hogs-transformed-iowas-us-senate-race/2014/05/11/c02d1804-d85b-11e3-95d3-3bcd77cd4e11_story.html.

50. Robert W. McChesney and John Nichols, "The Bull Market: Political Advertising," *Monthly Review* 63, no. 11 (April 2012), http://monthlyreview.org/2012/04/01/the-bull-market/.

51. Ibid.

52. Bill D. Moyers, Films Media Group, and Sunrise Media LLC, "The 30-Second President" (New York: Films Media Group, 1984).

53. Edwin Diamond and Stephen Bates, *The Spot: The Rise of Political Advertising on Television*, 3rd ed. (Cambridge, MA: MIT Press, July 1992), 54. This book is an excellent history of early political advertising on TV, including the Eisenhower ads.

54. Moyers, Films Media Group, and Sunrise Media LLC, "The 30-Second President."

55. See the videos for the then Republican presidential candidate Dwight D. Eisenhower from his 1952 campaign at "1952 Eisenhower vs. Stevenson," Living Room Candidate, last modified 2012, http://www.livingroomcandidate.org/commercials/1952.

56. Moyers, Films Media Group, and Sunrise Media LLC, "The 30-Second President."

57. Diamond and Bates, *The Spot*, 58.

58. See "Prouder, Stronger, Better," Living Room Candidate video, 1:00, 1984, for Reagan-Bush '84, made by Tuesday Team: Hal Riney, available courtesy of Ronald and Nancy Reagan/Ronald Reagan Presidential Library, http://www.livingroomcandidate.org/commercials/1984/prouder-stronger-better.

59. See *Media and Culture: Mass Communication in a Digital Age*, by Richard Campbell, Christopher R. Martin and Bettina Fabos, Bedford/St. Martins, ninth edition, Boston and New York, 2014. This book describes the association principle and other persuasive techniques included here.

60. Drew Westen, *The Political Brain: The Role of Emotion in Deciding the Fate of the Nation* (New York: PublicAffairs, 2007), 73.

61. Ibid.

62. Moyers, Films Media Group, and Sunrise Media LLC, "The 30-Second President."

63. Westen, *The Political Brain*, 65.

64. See Diamond and Bates, *The Spot*. Also, see Westen, *The Political Brain*, 63–68.

65. This statement is based on an examination of news coverage of the campaign in the *New York Times*, the *Washington Post*, and other major papers, along with TV news transcripts from May 2004, when the Swift Boat Veterans held their first press conference, through August 2004, when their first TV commercials ran, and ending with the November election.

66. "TV Ads and Videos," Swift Vets and POWs for Truth, accessed July 17, 2016, http://www.swiftvets.com/index.php?topic=Ads. Also, see Paul Farhi, "Ad Says Kerry 'Secretly' Met with Enemy; but He Told Congress of It,"

Washington Post, September 22, 2004, http://www.washingtonpost.com/wp-dyn/articles/A39744-2004Sep21.html.

67. Ibid.

68. See Kate Zernike and Jim Rutenberg, "Friendly Fire: The Birth of an Anti-Kerry Ad," *New York Times*, August 20, 2004, http://www.nytimes.com/2004/08/20/politics/campaign/20swift.html. Also, see Michael Dobbs, "Swift Boat Accounts Incomplete," *Washington Post*, August 22, 2004, http://www.washingtonpost.com/wp-dyn/articles/A21239-2004Aug21.html.

69. FactCheck.org Staff, "Republican-Funded Group Attacks Kerry's War Record," Annenberg Public Policy Center of the University of Pennsylvania, August 22, 2004, http://factcheck.bootnetworks.com/article231.html.

70. Jim Rassmann, "Shame on the Swift Boat Veterans for Bush," *Wall Street Journal*, August 10, 2004, http://www.wsj.com/articles/SB109209179651686933. Also, see Joe Strupp, "Editors Grapple with How to Cover Swift Boat Controversy," *Editor & Publisher*, August 24, 2004, http://www.editorandpublisher.com/news/editors-grapple-with-how-to-cover-swift-boat-controversy/.

71. Associated Press, "McCain Condemns Anti-Kerry Ad," *USA Today*, August 5, 2004, http://usatoday30.usatoday.com/news/politicselections/nation/president/2004-08-05-mcain-ad_x.htm. Also, see Jim Rutenberg, "Anti-Kerry Ad Is Condemned by McCain," *New York Times*, August 6, 2004, http://www.nytimes.com/2004/08/06/politics/campaign/06ads.html.

72. MSNBC.com Staff and Associated Press, "Bush Calls for Halt to Swift Boat Veterans' Ads," NBC News, August 23, 2004, http://www.nbcnews.com/id/5797164/ns/politics/t/bush-calls-halt-swift-boat-veterans-ads/.

73. These statements are based on analysis of TV shows and talk radio by the author.

74. Gwen Ifill, "Recent Accusations by Fellow Swift Boat Veterans Impact John Kerry's Campaign," *PBS NewsHour*, August 23, 2004, http://www.pbs.org/newshour/bb/politics-july-dec04-warrecord_8-23/.

75. Ibid.

76. Strupp, "Editors Grapple with How to Cover Swift Boat Controversy."

77. Annenberg Public Policy Center, "Cable and Talk Radio Boost Public Awareness of Swift Boat Ad," Annenberg Public Policy Center, August 20, 2004, http://www.annenbergpublicpolicycenter.org/cable-and-talk-radio-boost-public-awareness-of-swift-boat-ad/.

78. Ibid.

79. Adam Nagourney and Janet Elder, "Bush Opens Lead Despite Unease Voiced in Survey," *New York Times*, September 18, 2004, http://www.nytimes.com/2004/09/18/politics/campaign/bush-opens-lead-despite-unease-voiced-in-survey.html.

80. These remarks are available at on the "Forums Archive" web page of the John F. Kennedy Presidential Library and Museum under the title "A Conversation with Senator John Kerry—February 28, 2005" at http://www.jfklibrary.org/Events-and-Awards/Forums.aspx?f=all&p=3.

81. Steve Sibson, "John Kerry Coins 'Sub Media,'" *Sibby Online* (blog), March 17, 2005, http://sibbyonline.blogs.com/sibbyonline/2005/03/john_kerry_coin.html.

82. Steve LeBlanc (Associated Press), "Kerry Campaign Manager Admits Underestimating Swift Boat Ads," *SouthCoastToday.com*, December 16, 2004, http://www.southcoasttoday

.com/article/20041216/News/3121
69960.

83. David Winston, interview with the author, March 10, 2005.

84. Steven Heller, "The 'O' in Obama," *New York Times*, November 20, 2008, http://campaignstops.blogs.nytimes.com/2008/11/20/the-o-in-obama/.

85. Mark Benjamin, "It's 3 a.m. Who Do You Want Answering the Phone?," *Salon*, March 6, 2008, http://www.salon.com/2008/03/06/commander_in_chief_2/.

86. Rachel Weiner, "GOP Super PAC Rejects Plan to Invoke Jeremiah Wright," *Washington Post*, May 17, 2012, https://www.washingtonpost.com/blogs/the-fix/post/gop-super-pac-considering-jeremiah-wright-attack-on-obama/2012/05/17/gIQABYtzVU_blog.html.

87. "Inside Obama's Sweeping Victory," Pew Research Center, November 5, 2008, http://www.pewresearch.org/2008/11/05/inside-obamas-sweeping-victory/.

88. Greenberg, "Pro-Obama Group Blames Romney."

89. Darrell M. West, *Air Wars: Television Advertising and Social Media in Election Campaigns, 1952–2012*, 6th ed. (Thousand Oaks, CA: CQ Press, 2014), 152.

90. See Matea Gold, Rosalind S. Helderman, and Anne Gearan, "Clintons Have Made More Than $25 Million for Speaking Since January 2014," *Washington Post*, May 15, 2015, http://www.washingtonpost.com/politics/clintons-earn-more-than-25-million-in-speaking-fees-since-january-2014/2015/05/15/52605fbe-fb4d-11e4-9ef4-1bb7ce3b3fb7_story.html. Also, Maggie Haberman and Steve Eder, "Clintons Earned $30 Million in 16 Months, Report Shows," *New York Times*, May 15, 2015, http://www.nytimes.com/2015/05/16/us/politics/clintons-reportedly-earned-30-million-in-the-last-16-months.html.

91. See Tom LoBianco, "Trump Video Shows Clinton Laughing Over Benghazi Wreckage," CNN, November 23, 2015, https://www.cnn.com/2015/11/23/politics/donald-trump-hillary-clinton-laughing-benghazi.

92. Nick Corasaniti, "In Visceral Ads for Hillary Clinton, Donald Trump Does All the Talking," *New York Times*, October 5, 2016, https://www.nytimes.com/2016/10/06/us/politics/campaign-ads.html.

93. Hillary Clinton, "Mirrors | Hillary Clinton," September 23, 2016, video, 0:30, https://youtu.be/vHGPbl-werw.

94. Amy Chozick, "Hillary Clinton Calls Many Trump Backers 'Deplorables,' and G.O.P. Pounces," *New York Times*, September 10, 2016, https://www.nytimes.com/2016/09/11/us/politics/hillary-clinton-basket-of-deplorables.html.

95. Jon Schuppe, "NRA Sticking with Trump, Breaks Own Record for Campaign Spending," NBC News, October 12, 2016, https://www.nbcnews.com/news/us-news/nra-sticking-trump-breaks-own-record-campaign-spending-n665056.

96. NRA, "Don't Let Hillary Clinton Leave You Defenseless," September 20, 2016, video, 0:30, https://youtu.be/hPM8e_DauUw.

97. Fowler, Ridout, and Franz, "Political Advertising in 2016."

98. *Guardian News*, "Ron DeSantis Has Released an Ad Indoctrinating His Children into Trumpism," August 2, 2018, video, 0:30, https://youtu.be/z1YP_zZJFXs.

99. Gray Rohrer, "Ron Desantis Teaches Kids About Trump in New Ad," *Orlando*

Sentinel, July 30, 2018, https://www
.orlandosentinel.com/news/politics/
political-pulse/os-desantis-trump-
kids-ad-20180730-story.html.

100. Erik Sherman, "The DIY Viral Ad That
Will Change Politics Forever," *Inc.*,
June 29, 2018, https://www.inc.com/
erik-sherman/this-128-second-viral-
ad-can-teach-you-everything-you-
should-know-about-marketing.html.

101. Zaid Jilani, "How a Ragtag Group of
Socialist Filmmakers Produced One
of the Most Viral Campaign Ads of
2018," *Intercept*, June 5, 2018, https://
theintercept.com/2018/06/05/ocasio-
cortez-new-york-14th-district-demo-
cratic-primary-campaign-video/.

102. Barbie Latze Nadeau, "Biden 2020
Campaign Launch Video: 'We Are in
a Battle for the Soul of This Nation,'"
Daily Beast, April 25, 2019, https://
www.thedailybeast.com/joe-biden-
2020-video-attacks-trump-we-are-in-
a-battle-for-the-soul-of-this-nation.

103. Ibid.

104. Simon Dumenco, "The Anti-Trump
Ad That Trump Basically Made
for the Priorities USA PAC Gets a
Grim Update," *AdAge*, March 30,
2020, https://adage.com/article/
campaign-trail/anti-trump-ad-
trump-basically-made-priorities-usa-
pac-gets-grim-update/2247011.

105. Nick Corasaniti, "Trump Campaign Ads Depict His Own Lawless Dystopia," *New York Times*,
July 21, 2020, https://www.nytimes
.com/2020/07/21/us/politics/trump-
campaign-ads.html

106. Ibid.

107. Donald J. Trump, "Break In," July 20,
2020, video, 0:30, https://youtu.be/
moZOrq0qL3Q.

108. Paige Williams, "Inside the Lincoln
Project's War against Trump," *New
Yorker*, October 5, 2020, https://www
.newyorker.com/magazine/2020/10/
12/inside-the-lincoln-projects-war-
against-trump.

109. See The Lincoln Project, "Mourning
in America," May 4, 2020, video,
1:08, https://www.youtube.com/
watch?v=t_yG_-K2MDo .

110. Dan Solomon, "Dan Crenshaw's New
Campaign Ad Is a Whole Thing,"
Texas Monthly. September 25, 2020,
https://www.texasmonthly.com/poli-
tics/dan-crenshaws-new-campaign-
ad-is-a-whole-thing/.

Chapter 4

1. Mitchell Stephens, *A History of News*,
3rd ed. (New York: Oxford University
Press, 2007).

2. Bill Kovach and Tom Rosenstiel, *The
Elements of Journalism: What Newspeo-
ple Should Know and the Public Should
Expect* (New York: Three Rivers Press,
2001), 9.

3. John Bender et al., *Writing and Reporting for the Media*, 12th ed. (New York:
Oxford University Press, October
2018).

4. See Michael Schudson, *Discovering
the News: A Social History of American
Newspapers* (New York: Basic Books,
1978).

5. See Mitchell Stephens, *A History of
News*. Also, see Schudson, *Discovering
the News*.

6. Richard L. Eldredge, "Where Are
They Now? CNN's Boys of Baghdad,"
Atlanta, March 18, 2015, https://www
.atlantamagazine.com/90s/where-are-
they-now-cnns-boys-of-baghdad/.

7. History.com Staff, "The Invention
of the Internet," History.com, 2010,
http://www.history.com/topics/
inventions/invention-of-the-internet.

8. Bruce Bimber, *Information and American Democracy: Technology in the Evolution of Political Power* (Cambridge:
Cambridge University Press, 2003).

9. Jeff Jarvis, interview with the author, 2005.

10. Paige Leskin, "YouTube Is 15 Years Old. Here's a Timeline of How YouTube Was Founded, Its Rise to Video Behemoth, and Its Biggest Controversies Along Way," *Business Insider*, May 30, 2020, https://www.busines-sinsider.com/history-of-youtube-in-photos-2015-10.

11. Elisa Shearer, "Social Media Outpaces Print Newspapers in the U.S. as a News Source," Pew Research Center, December 10, 2018, https://www.pewre-search.org/fact-tank/2018/12/10/social-media-outpaces-print-newspa-pers-in-the-u-s-as-a-news-source/.

12. "How Americans Get Their News," American Press Institute, March 17, 2014, https://www.americanpressinstitute.org/pub-lications/reports/survey-research/how-americans-get-news/.

13. Ibid. This information also comes from multiple surveys by the Pew Research Center.

14. Laura Wronski, "Common Sense Media|SurveyMonkey Poll: Teen Media Literacy," SurveyMonkey, https://www.surveymonkey.com/curiosity/common-sense-media-teen-media-literacy/.

15. Ibid.

16. Elisa Shearer and Elizabeth Grieco, "Americans Are Wary of the Role Social Media Sites Play in Delivering the News," Pew Research Center, October 2, 2019, https://www.journalism.org/2019/10/02/americans-are-wary-of-the-role-social-media-sites-play-in-delivering-the-news/.

17. See Richard Davis and Diana Owen, *New Media and American Politics* (New York: Oxford University Press, 1998).

18. Oliver Darcy, "Trump Says Right-Wing Voices Are Being Censored. The Data Says Something Else," CNN, May 28, 2020, https://www.cnn.com/2020/05/28/media/trump-social-media-conservative-censorship/index.html.

19. Ibid.

20. "Public Highly Critical of State of Political Discourse in the U.S.," Pew Research Center, June 19, 2019, https://www.people-press.org/2019/06/19/public-highly-criti-cal-of-state-of-political-discourse-in-the-u-s/.

21. Erik Pedersen, "'The McLaughlin Group' Returning to PBS in January after Local Relaunch," *Deadline*, August 13, 2019, https://deadline.com/2019/08/the-mclaughlin-group-returning-to-pbs-in-janu-ary-1202667082/.

22. E. J. Dionne Jr., *Why Americans Hate Politics* (New York: Simon & Schuster, 1991).

23. "First Presidential Debate Draws 67.2 Million Viewers," Nielsen Company, October 5, 2012, https://www.nielsen.com/us/en/insights/article/2012/first-presidential-debate-draws-67-2-mil-lion-viewers/.

24. Alex Weprin, "First Trump-Clinton Debate Is the Most-Watched Debate of All Time," *Politico*, September 27, 2016, https://www.politico.com/blogs/on-media/2016/09/first-trump-clinton-debate-smashes-ratings-records-228788.

25. M. J. Stephey, "Top 10 Memorable Debate Moments: Reagan's Age-Old Wisdom," *Time*, http://content.time.com/time/specials/packages/article/0,28804,1844704_1844706_184461 2,00.html.

26. "Senator, You're No Jack Kennedy," National Public Radio, May 23, 2006, http://www.npr.org/templates/story/story.php?storyId=5425248.

27. ABC News, "First GOP Debate: Donald Trump, and Other Memorable

Moments," August 7, 2015, video, 7:23, https://youtu.be/U2zjsh5noOw.

28. Gregory Krieg, "Donald Trump Defends Size of His Penis," CNN, March 4, 2016, https://www.cnn.com/2016/03/03/politics/donald-trump-small-hands-marco-rubio.

29. Isabella Grullón Paz, "Kamala Harris and Joe Biden Clash on Race and Busing," *New York Times*, June 27, 2019, https://www.nytimes.com/2019/06/27/us/politics/kamala-harris-joe-biden-busing.html.

30. Jane Hall, "Fuzzy Lines Blur Face of TV, Politics," *Los Angeles Times*, May 30, 1997, http://articles.latimes.com/1997-05-30/news/mn-64012_1_political-campaign.

31. Dori Olmos, "Claire McCaskill Joins NBC, MSNBC as Political Analyst," *KSDK*, January 16, 2019, https://www.ksdk.com/article/news/politics/claire-mccaskill-joins-nbc-msnbc-as-political-analyst/63-1ed4c485-553e-494e-a2c8-11cd1834d790.

32. Naomi Lim, "Andrew Gillum to Become CNN Commentator After Florida Loss," *Washington Examiner*, January 29, 2019, https://www.washingtonexaminer.com/news/andrew-gillum-to-become-cnn-commentator-after-florida-loss.

33. Maxwell Tani, "Why Is CNN Paying John Kasich to Seemingly Trial-Balloon a 2020 Run?," *Daily Beast*, February 19, 2019, https://www.thedailybeast.com/why-is-cnn-paying-john-kasich-to-seemingly-trial-balloon-a-2020-run.

34. *OpenSecrets* (blog), "Independent Expenditures," Electioneering Communication and Communication Costs by Targeted Candidate as of March 02, 2018, https://www.opensecrets.org/outsidespending/recips.php?cmte=C00487363&cycle=2012

35. "Here's 5 Times Megyn Kelly Absolutely Nailed It," Rare, July 30, 2014, http://rare.us/story/heres-5-times-megyn-kelly-absolutely-nailed-it/.

36. Hadas Gold, "Corey Lewandowski to Join CNN," *Politico*, June 23, 2016, http://www.politico.com/blogs/on-media/2016/06/corey-lewandowski-to-join-cnn-224733.

37. Hadas Gold, "Trump Campaign Pays off Corey Lewandowski Contract," *Politico*, September 29, 2016, http://www.politico.com/blogs/on-media/2016/09/corey-lewandowski-no-longer-receiving-severance-from-trump-campaign-228887.

38. Alex Weprin, "Corey Lewandowski Resigns from CNN," *Politico*, November 11, 2016, http://www.politico.com/blogs/on-media/2016/11/corey-lewandowski-resigns-from-cnn-231267.

39. Chuck Todd, "Meet the Press—October 9, 2016," NBC News, October 9, 2016, http://www.nbcnews.com/meet-the-press/meet-press-october-9-2016-n662746.

40. Jay Rosen, "Why Political Coverage Is Broken," *PressThink* (blog), August 26, 2011, http://pressthink.org/2011/08/why-political-coverage-is-broken/.

41. Jonathan C. Klein, "Throw Campaign Mouthpieces off Cable News," *New York Times*, November 9, 2016, http://www.nytimes.com/2016/11/09/opinion/throw-campaign-mouthpieces-off-cable-news.html.

42. Tom Rosenstiel (presentation, Politics and Prose Bookstore, Washington, DC, February 16, 2019).

43. Jake Novak, "Why Experts Are Getting Presidential Election Polls Wrong—Again," CNBC.com, November 5, 2019, https://www.cnbc.com/2019/11/05/why-experts-are-getting-

presidential-election-polls-wrong-again.html

44. Kyu Hahn, Shanto Iyengar, and Helmut Norpoth, "Consumer Demand for Election News: The Horserace Sells," *Political Communication Lab*, August 30, 2002, https://pcl.stanford.edu/common/docs/research/iyengar/2002/APSA2002.pdf.

45. Jack Shafer, "In Praise of Horse-Race Coverage," *Slate*, January 24, 2008, http://www.slate.com/articles/news_and_politics/press_box/2008/01/in_praise_of_horserace_coverage.html.

46. Bernie Sanders, interview with the author, April 13, 2015, American University, Washington, D.C.

47. Ibid.

48. Ibid.

49. Ibid.

50. Brendan Bordelon, "Why Democrats Buried Their Debates at Times No One Will Watch," *National Review*, November 13, 2015, http://www.nationalreview.com/article/427026/why-democrats-buried-their-debates-times-no-one-will-watch-brendan-bordelon.

51. Andrew Tyndall, "Let the Trump Circus Continue," *Same Day's Blog, Tyndall Report*, May 10, 2016, http://tyndallreport.com/comment/20/5776/.

52. Paul Kane and Philip Rucker, "An Unlikely Contender, Sanders Takes on 'Billionaire Class' in 2016 Bid," *Washington Post*, April 30, 2015, https://www.washingtonpost.com/politics/sanders-takes-on-billionaire-class-in-launching-2016-bid-against-clinton/2015/04/30/4849fe32-ef3a-11e4-a55f-38924fca94f9_story.html.

53. Alan Rappeport, "Bernie Sanders, Long-Serving Independent, Enters Presidential Race as a Democrat," *New York Times*, April 29, 2015, https://www.nytimes.com/2015/04/30/us/politics/bernie-sanders-campaign-for-president.html.

54. Margaret Sullivan, "Were Changes to Sanders Article 'Stealth Editing'?," *Public Editor's Journal* (blog), *New York Times*, March 17, 2016, http://publiceditor.blogs.nytimes.com/2016/03/17/new-york-times-bernie-sanders-coverage-public-editor/.

55. Steve Hendricks, "Bernie Sanders Can't Win: Why the Press Loves to Hate Underdogs," *Columbia Journalism Review*, May 21, 2015, http://www.cjr.org/analysis/bernie_sanders_underdog.php.

56. Ibid.

57. Amy Goodman, "Robert McChesney: Mainstream Corporate Media Covering 2016 Election through Eyes of Clinton Campaign," *Democracy Now!*, May 19, 2016, https://www.democracynow.org/2016/5/19/robert_mcchesney_mainstream_corporate_media_covering.

58. Jeff Cohen, "Corporate Media Bias on 2020 Democratic Race Already in High Gear," *Common Dreams*, January 14, 2019, https://www.commondreams.org/views/2019/01/14/corporate-media-bias-2020-democratic-race-already-high-gear.

59. Michael Schudson, "Why Democracies Need an Unlovable Press," in *Freeing the Presses: The First Amendment in Action*, ed., Timothy E. Cook, (Baton Rouge: Louisiana State University Press, 2005), 73–86. Also, see its appearance in Doris A. Graber, ed., *Media Power in Politics* (Washington, DC: CQ Press, 2011).

60. Ibid.

61. Brian, "Katrina: Anderson Cooper Berates Senator Landrieu; 'There Was a Body on the Streets…Being Eaten by Rats,' He Says," TVNewser, September 1, 2005, http://www.adweek.com/tvnewser/katrina-anderson-cooper-berates-senator-landrieu-there-was-a-body-on-the-streets-being-eaten-by-rats-he-says/7543.

62. Chuck Todd, interview with the author, November 10, 2015.

63. Karen Tumulty, interview with the author, 2000.

64. Emily Feldman, "Marco Rubio's Water Grab Preserved in GIFs," NBC New York, February 13, 2013, http://www.nbcnewyork.com/news/national-international/NATL-Marco-Rubios-Water-Grab-Preserved-in-GIFs-190964571.html.

65. Associated Press, "Edwards' Haircuts Cost a Pretty Penny," NBC News, April 17, 2007, http://www.nbcnews.com/id/18157456/ns/politics-decision_08/t/edwards-haircuts-cost-pretty-penny/.

66. Brendan Nyhan, "The Bush 41 Grocery Scanner Myth," *Brendan Nyhan: Political Scientist and Media Critic* (blog), August 4, 2008, http://www.brendan-nyhan.com/blog/2008/08/the-bush-41-gro.html.

67. Jim VandeHei and John F. Harris, "Why Reporters Get It Wrong," *Politico*, January 9, 2008, http://www.politico.com/story/2008/01/why-reporters-get-it-wrong-007822.

68. Ibid.

69. Peter Hamby, "'You Have to Have a Plan to Deal with Them': How the Media Fell out of Love With Beto O'Rourke," *Vanity Fair*, May 15, 2019, https://www.vanityfair.com/news/2019/05/how-the-media-fell-out-of-love-with-beto-orourke.

70. See Jane Hall, "Gore Media Coverage—Playing Hardball," *Columbia Journalism Review*, September/October 2000, 30–32.

71. Ibid.

72. See the cover page of the "Rising Son" issue of *Newsweek* from June 21, 1999.

73. Howard Fineman, "Al Gore's Next Makeover," *Newsweek*, June 4, 2000, http://www.newsweek.com/al-gores-next-makeover-160615. Also, Bob Somerby, "Our Current Howler (Part I): E Pluribus, Unum Story," *Daily Howler* (blog), June 7, 2000, http://www.daily-howler.com/h060700_1.shtml.

74. E. R. Shipp, "In Pursuit of Fairness," *Washington Post*, September 17, 2000, http://www.washingtonpost.com/archive/opinions/2000/09/17/in-pursuit-of-fairness/00d0ef56-302c-414e-ab10-653b5af8bfc1/.

75. Ibid.

76. Project for Excellence in Journalism and Committee of Concerned Journalists, "A Question of Character: How the Media Have Handled the Issue and How the Public Has Reacted," Pew Research Center, July 27, 2000, http://www.journalism.org/files/legacy/character_0.pdf.

77. Ibid.

78. Ibid.

79. Ibid.

80. Ibid.

81. Frank Bruni, "The 2000 Campaign: Campaign Memo; for a Suddenly Accessible Bush, Everything Is on the Record," *New York Times*, April 14, 2000, http://www.nytimes.com/2000/04/14/us/2000-campaign-campaign-memo-for-suddenly-accessible-bush-everything-record.html.

82. Howard Kurtz, "Chatter at 40,000 Feet," *Washington Post*, June 15, 2000, http://www.washingtonpost.com/archive/politics/2000/06/15/chatter-at-40000-feet/872c1c8f-f344-4c45-bd25-cbccafa1b958/.

83. Ibid.

84. Michael Duffy and Nancy Gibbs, "Republican Convention: The Quiet Dynasty," *Time*, August 7, 2000, http://content.time.com/time/magazine/article/0,9171,997635,00.html.

85. Schudson, *Discovering the News.*

86. Brent Cunningham, "Re-Thinking Objectivity," *Columbia Journalism Review*, July/August 2003, http://

archives.cjr.org/feature/rethinking_objectivity.php.

87. Kovach and Rosenstiel, *The Elements of Journalism.*

88. Jennifer Calfas, "Read the Advice Bob Woodward and Carl Bernstein Gave at the White House Correspondents' Dinner," *Time,* April 30, 2017, http://time.com/4760743/white-house-correspondents-dinner-woodward-bernstein-speech-2017/.

89. Kovach and Rosenstiel, *The Elements of Journalism.*

90. Brian Stelter, "Trump Says He Has 'Running War' with Media, Gets Facts Wrong, in CIA Speech," CNN, January 21, 2017, http://money.cnn.com/2017/01/21/media/donald-trump-war-with-the-media/index.html.

91. Justin Gillis, "Panel's Warning on Climate Risk: Worst Is Yet to Come," *New York Times,* March 31, 2014, http://www.nytimes.com/2014/04/01/science/earth/climate.html.

92. Justin Gillis, "Climate Efforts Falling Short, U.N. Panel Says," *New York Times,* April 13, 2014, http://www.nytimes.com/2014/04/14/science/earth/un-climate-panel-warns-speedier-action-is-needed-to-avert-disaster.html.

93. Christopher B. Field et al., eds., *Climate Change 2014: Impacts, Adaptation, and Vulnerability: Summary for Policymakers,* Intergovernmental Panel on Climate Change, (Cambridge: Cambridge University Press, 2014), http://ipcc-wg2.gov/AR5/images/uploads/WG2AR5_SPM_FINAL.pdf.

94. Gillis, "Climate Efforts Falling Short."

95. "Consensus: 97% of Climate Scientists Agree," National Aeronautics and Space Administration, last updated July 11, 2016, http://climate.nasa.gov/scientific-consensus/. For more information, see William R. L. Anderegg et al., "Expert Credibility in Climate Change," *Proceedings of the National Academy of Sciences of the United States of America* 107, no. 27 (July 6, 2010): 12107–9, http://www.pnas.org/content/107/27/12107.full.pdf. Also, see Peter T. Doran and Maggie Kendall Zimmerman, "Examining the Scientific Consensus on Climate Change," *Eos, Transactions American Geophysical Union* 90, no. 3 (January 2009): 22–23, http://onlinelibrary.wiley.com/doi/10.1029/2009EO030002/pdf. The author also recommends the January 21, 2005, updated version of Naomi Oreskes, "The Scientific Consensus on Climate Change," *Science* 306, no. 5702 (December 3, 2004): 1,686, http://science.sciencemag.org/content/306/5702/1686.full.

96. Richard Wike, "Many Around the World See Climate Change as a Major Threat," Pew Research Center, March 31, 2014, http://www.pewresearch.org/fact-tank/2014/03/31/many-around-the-world-see-climate-change-as-a-major-threat/.

97. Pew Research Center, "Protecting the Environment Ranks in the Middle of Public's Priorities for 2013," Pew Research Center, April 22, 2013, http://www.pewresearch.org/daily-number/protecting-the-environment-ranks-in-the-middle-of-publics-priorities-for-2013/.

98. Ibid.

99. Anthony Leiserowitz et al., *Climate Change in the American Mind: Americans' Global Warming Beliefs and Attitudes in November 2013,* Yale Project on Climate Change Communication and George Mason University Center for Climate Change Communication, 2014, http://environment.yale.edu/climate-communication-OFF/files/Climate-Beliefs-November-2013.pdf.

100. Ibid.

101. Ibid.

102. Edward Maibach, Teresa Myers, and Anthony Leiserowitz, "Climate Scientists Need to Set the Record Straight: There Is a Scientific Consensus That Human-Caused Climate Change Is Happening," *Earth's Future* 2, no. 5 (May 7, 2014): 295–98, http://www.climatechangecommunication.org/wp-content/uploads/2016/03/May-2014-Climate-scientists-need-to-set-the-record-straight-There-is-Scientific-Consensus-that-Human-Caused-Climate-Change-is-happening.pdf.

103. Jules Boykoff and Maxwell Boykoff, "Journalistic Balance as Global Warming Bias: Creating Controversy Where Science Finds Consensus," Fairness & Accuracy In Reporting, Inc., November 1, 2004, http://fair.org/extra-online-articles/journalistic-balance-as-global-warming-bias/.

104. Maxwell T. Boycoff, "Flogging a Dead Norm? Newspaper coverage and anthropogenic climate change in the United States and United Kingdom from 2003 to 2006, *Area*, Vol. 39 No 2, 2007" https://rgs-ibg.onlinelibrary.wiley.com/doi/10.1111/j.1475-4762.2007.00769.x.

105. Lauren Feldman et al., "Climate on Cable: The Nature and Impact of Global Warming Coverage on Fox News, CNN, and MSNBC," Harvard *International Journal of Press/Politics* 17, no. 1 (November 2, 2011): 3–31.

106. *Hannity*, "Daryl Hannah Risks Arrest to Protest Keystone XL Pipeline," February 13, 2013, video, 4:41, http://video.foxnews.com/v/2163423203001/daryl-hannah-risks-arrest-to-protest-keystone-xl-pipeline/.

107. Bill O'Reilly, "Bill O'Reilly: The Truth about Obamacare and Global Warming," Fox News, March 31, 2014, http://www.foxnews.com/on-air/oreilly/2014/04/01/bill-oreilly-truth-about-obamacare-and-global-warming.

108. Evan Mackinder, "Pro-Environment Groups Outmatched, Outspent in Battle over Climate Change Legislation," *OpenSecrets* (blog), August 23, 2010, http://www.opensecrets.org/news/2010/08/pro-environment-groups-were-outmatc/.

109. *OpenSecrets* (blog), "Oil & Gas," https://www.opensecrets.org/industries/indus.php?ind=e01.

110. *Union of Concerned Scientists* (blog), "Smoke, Mirrors & Hot Air: How ExxonMobil Uses Big Tobacco's Tactics to Manufacture Uncertainty on Climate Science," January 2007, http://www.ucsusa.org/sites/default/files/legacy/assets/documents/global_warming/exxon_report.pdf.

111. Jennifer 8. Lee, "Exxon Backs Groups That Question Global Warming," *New York Times*, May 28, 2003, http://www.nytimes.com/2003/05/28/business/exxon-backs-groups-that-question-global-warming.html.

112. Ibid.

113. Robert J. Brulle, "Institutionalizing Delay: Foundation Funding and the Creation of U.S. Climate Change Counter-Movement Organizations," *Climatic Change* 122, no. 4 (February 2014): 681–94.

114. Aaron Huertas and Rachel Kriegsman, "Science or Spin? Assessing the Accuracy of Cable News Coverage of Climate Science," *Union of Concerned Scientists* (blog), April 2014, http://www.ucsusa.org/assets/documents/global_warming/Science-or-Spin-report.pdf.

115. Jerry M. Melillo, Terese (T.C.) Richmond, and Gary W. Yohe, eds., *2014: Climate Change Impacts in the United States: The Third National Climate Assessment*, U.S. Global Change Research Program, October 2014,

http://nca2014.globalchange.gov/downloads.

116. Darryl Fears, "U.S. Climate Report Says Global Warming Impact Already Severe," *Washington Post*, May 6, 2014, http://www.washingtonpost.com/national/health-science/us-climate-report-says-global-warming-impact-already-severe/2014/05/06/0e82cd3c-d49c-11e3-aae8-c2d44bd79778_story.html.

117. Bob Papper, "2018 Research: Women and People of Color in Local TV and Radio News," Radio Television Digital News Association, June 27, 2018, https://rtdna.org/article/2018_research_women_and_people_of_color_in_local_tv_and_radio_news.

118. American Society of News Editors, "ASNE's 2018 Diversity Survey Results Reflect Low Participation but Encouraging Shifts," Nov. 15, 2018. https://members.newsleaders.org/diversity-survey-2018.

119. Ibid.

120. See Jane Hall, "Women as Leaders in Broadcast TV News and Print Journalism," in *Gender and Women's Leadership: A Reference Handbook*, ed. Karen O'Connor, (Thousand Oaks, CA: Sage, 2010), 770–79.

121. Eyder Peralta, "Gwen Ifill, Host of *Washington Week* and PBS *News Hour*, Dies," National Public Radio, November 14, 2016, http://www.npr.org/sectthe twohetwo-way/2016/11/14/502031518/gwen-ifill-host-of-washington-week-pbs-newshour-dies.

122. Jeffrey M. Jones, "U.S. Media Trust Continues to Recover from 2016 Low," *Gallup Blog*, October 12, 2018, https://news.gallup.com/poll/243665/media-trust-continues-recover-2016-low.aspx.

123. Art Swift, "Americans' Trust in Mass Media Sinks to New Low," *Gallup Blog*, September 14, 2016, http://www.gallup.com/poll/195542/americans-trust-mass-media-sinks-new-low.aspx.

124. Jones, "U.S. Media Trust Continues to Recover from 2016 Low".

125. Ibid.

126. Ibid.

127. Amy Mitchell et al., "Section 1: Media Sources: Distinct Favorites Emerge on the Left and Right," Pew Research Center, October 21, 2014, http://www.journalism.org/2014/10/21/section-1-media-sources-distinct-favorites-emerge-on-the-left-and-right/.

128. Ibid.

129. Jane Hall, "The World Roger Ailes Created," *New York Times*, July 22, 2016, https://www.nytimes.com/2016/07/22/opinion/the-world-roger-ailes-created.html.

130. See Gabriel Sherman, *The Loudest Voice in the Room: How the Brilliant, Bombastic Roger Ailes Built Fox News—and Divided a Country* (New York: Random House, 2014). Also, see Edwin Diamond and Stephen Bates, *The Spot: The Rise of Political Advertising on Television*, 3rd ed. (Cambridge, MA: MIT Press, July 1992).

131. This is based on the author's analysis of content on Fox News Channel in articles as a journalist and media critic as well as nine years as a media analyst on Fox News Channel.

132. See Hall, "The World Roger Ailes Created."

133. Ibid.

134. Indira Lakshmanan, interview with the author, April 4, 2018, in "Press and the Presidency," C-SPAN, https://www.c-span.org/video/?443466-1/journalists-discuss-covering-trump-presidency.

135. Andrew Guess, Brendan Nyhan, and Jason Reifler, "'You're Fake News!': The 2017 Poynter Media Trust Survey" (Poynter Institute for Media Studies, November 29, 2017), https://

poyntercdn.blob.core.windows.net/files/
PoynterMediaTrustSurvey2017.pdf.

136. Lakshmanan, interview with the author.

137. Indira Lakshmanan, "Finally Some Good News: Trust in News Is up, Especially for Local Media," Poynter Institute, August 22, 2018, https://www.poynter.org/ethics-trust/2018/finally-some-good-news-trust-in-news-is-up-especially-for-local-media/.

138. Ibid.

139. Lakshmanan, interview with the author.

Chapter 5

1. "About Susan Collins," Senator Susan Collins, https://www.collins.senate.gov/about.

2. Richard E. Cohen et al., *The Almanac of American Politics* (Bethesda, MD: Columbia Books & Information Services, 2015).

3. "Roll Call Vote 111th Congress—1st Session," United States Senate, https://www.senate.gov/legislative/LIS/roll_call_lists/roll_call_vote_cfm.cfm?congress=111&session=1&vote=00396.

4. Juliet Eilperin, Sean Sullivan, and Ed O'Keefe, "Senate Republicans' Effort to 'Repeal and Replace' Obamacare All but Collapse," *Washington Post*, July 18, 2017, https://www.washingtonpost.com/powerpost/trump-suggests-republicans-will-let-aca-market-collapse-then-rewrite-health-law/2017/07/18/5e79a3ec-6bac-11e7-b9e2-2056e768a7e5_story.html.

5. Heather Timmons, "The Three Female Republican Senators Who Won't Repeal Obamacare Are Facing a Vicious Backlash," *Quartz* (blog), July 19, 2017, https://qz.com/1033358/the-republican-senators-who-are-against-a-healthcare-repeal-bill-are-facing-a-vicious-misogynist-backlash/.

6. Niels Lesniewski, "Collins, Murkowski Most Likely Republicans to Back Obama," *Roll Call*, February 4, 2014, https://www.rollcall.com/2014/02/04/collins-murkowski-most-likely-republicans-to-back-obama/.

7. Susan Collins, "GOP Senator Susan Collins: Why I Cannot Support Trump," *Washington Post*, August 8, 2016, https://www.washingtonpost.com/opinions/gop-senator-why-i-cannot-support-trump/2016/08/08/821095be-5d7e-11e6-9d2f-b1a3564181a1_story.html.

8. Steve Collins, "Maine's Senators Denounce Trump's Ban on Immigration from 7 Muslim Countries," *Sun Journal*, January 29, 2017, https://www.sunjournal.com/2017/01/29/maines-senators-denounce-trumps-ban-immigration-7-muslim-countries/.

9. Harry Enten, "Susan Collins Was a More Reliable Vote for GOP in 2017 Than Any Other Year," CNN, July 11, 2018, https://www.cnn.com/2018/07/11/politics/susan-collins-supreme-court-vote-analysis/index.html.

10. Ella Nilsen, "Why Democrats Think 2020 Is the Year They Can Defeat Susan Collins," *Vox*, June 26, 2019, https://www.vox.com/policy-and-politics/2019/6/26/18715434/susan-collins-maine-senate-race-2020.

11. Gregg Sangillo, "Susan Collins Speaks at AU," American University, September 12, 2016, http://www.american.edu/ucm/news/20160912-Collins-KPU.cfm.

12. Ibid.

13. Mark Warren, "Help, We're in a Living Hell and Don't Know How to Get Out," *Esquire*, October 15, 2014, http://www.esquire.com/news-politics/news/a23553/congress-living-hell-1114/.

14. Dana Farrington, "Watch: Sen. McCain Calls for Compromise in Return to Senate Floor," National Public Radio, July 25, 2017, https://www.npr

.org/2017/07/25/539323689/watch-sen-mccain-calls-for-compromise-in-return-to-senate-floor.

15. Ibid.

16. Sangillo, "Susan Collins Speaks at AU".

17. Alan Zarembo, "Obama Pushes to Extend Gun Background Checks to Social Security," *Los Angeles Times*, July 18, 2015, http://www.latimes.com/nation/politics/la-na-gun-law-20150718-story.html.

18. Aamer Madhani and Kevin Johnson, "Analysis: Obama Pressured to Step up on Gun Control," *USA Today*, December 15, 2012, https://www.usatoday.com/story/news/politics/2012/12/15/pressure-on-obama-gun-control/1771317/.

19. Aaron Blake, "Manchin-Toomey Gun Amendment Fails," *Washington Post*, April 17, 2013, https://www.washingtonpost.com/news/post-politics/wp/2013/04/17/manchin-toomey-gun-amendment-fails/.

20. Gregory Korte and Catalina Camia, "Obama on Senate Gun Vote: 'A Shameful Day,'" *USA Today*, April 17, 2013, https://www.usatoday.com/story/news/politics/2013/04/17/guns-background-checks-manchin-senate/2090105/.

21. Richard Cowan and John Whitesides, "Senate Rejects Gun-Control Measures after Orlando Shooting," Reuters, June 20, 2016, http://www.reuters.com/article/us-florida-shooting-guns-idUSKCN0Z61BS.

22. Ben Mathis-Lilley, "Bipartisan No-Fly-List Gun Bill Introduced in Senate," *Slate*, June 22, 2016, http://www.slate.com/blogs/the_slatest/2016/06/22/susan_collins_bipartisan_senate_group_back_no_fly_gun_control_bill.html.

23. "Manchin Statement Opposing WV Bill Eliminating Concealed Carry Permit and Training Requirements,"

news release, March 12, 2015, https://www.manchin.senate.gov/newsroom/press-releases/manchin-statement-opposing-wv-bill-eliminating-concealed-carry-permit-and-training-requirements.

24. Institute for Legislative Action, "Sen. Joe Manchin Reveals Gross Contempt for U.S. Constitution," National Rifle Association, June 16, 2016, https://www.nraila.org/articles/20160616/sen-joe-manchin-reveals-gross-contempt-for-us-constitution.

25. "Trump to NRA: 'Hillary Wants to Abolish the 2nd Amendment,'" Fox News, May 20, 2016, http://insider.foxnews.com/2016/05/20/nra-endorses-donald-trump-2016-election-national-convention-louisville-kentucky.

26. Jon Schuppe, "NRA Sticking with Trump, Breaks Own Record for Campaign Spending," NBC News, October 12, 2016, http://www.nbcnews.com/news/us-news/nra-sticking-trump-breaks-own-record-campaign-spending-n665056. Visit www.livingroomcandidate.org to see the presidential campaign commercials.

27. Adam Sheingate, "The Political Consultant Racket," *New York Times*, December 30, 2015, https://www.nytimes.com/2015/12/30/opinion/campaign-stops/the-political-consultant-racket.html. Sheingate is the author of *Building a Business of Politics: The Rise of Political Consulting and the Transformation of American Democracy*.

28. See Kenneth M. Winneg et al., "Deception in Third Party Advertising in the 2012 Presidential Campaign," *American Behavioral Scientist* 58, no. 4 (February 20, 2014).

29. Norah O'Donnell, "Are Members of Congress Becoming Telemarketers?," CBS News, April 24, 2016, http://www.cbsnews.com/news/

60-minutes-are-members-of-congress-becoming-telemarketers/.

30. Ibid.

31. David Boling, "The Ability to Raise Money Has Become a Politician's Greatest Qualification for Office," *Washington Post*, June 6, 2014, https://www.washingtonpost.com/opinions/the-ability-to-raise-money-has-become-a-politicians-greatest-qualification-for-office/2014/06/06/fd8b7a4c-dbb2-11e3-8009-71de85b9c527_story.html.

32. Nicholas Confessore and Megan Thee-Brenan, "Poll Shows Americans Favor an Overhaul of Campaign Financing," *New York Times*, June 2, 2015, https://www.nytimes.com/2015/06/03/us/politics/poll-shows-americans-favor-overhaul-of-campaign-financing.html.

33. Ibid.

34. *New York Times* and CBS News, "A *New York Times*/CBS News Poll on Money and Politics," *New York Times*, https://www.nytimes.com/interactive/2015/06/01/us/politics/document-poll-may-28-31.html.

35. Ibid.

36. See Jacob S. Hacker and Paul Pierson, *Winner-Take-All Politics: How Washington Made the Rich Richer—and Turned Its Back on the Middle Class* (New York: Simon & Schuster Paperbacks, 2010).

37. Martin Gilens and Benjamin I. Page, "Testing Theories of American Politics: Elites, Interest Groups, and Average Citizens," *American Political Science Association* 12, no. 3 (September 2014).

38. Tom Davis, Martin Frost, and Richard E. Cohen, *The Partisan Divide: Congress in Crisis* (Campbell, CA: Premiere, 2014).

39. Tom Davis and Martin Frost, presentation hosted by the American Political Science Association, Philadelphia, Pennsylvania, September 2, 2016.

40. American University School of Communication, "Countdown to Election '16: Political Persuasion'" October 10, 2016, playlist, https://www.youtube.com/playlist?list=PLZGmcfRNf0Mj7AezF-LBJc1T3ydG-kZPmc.

41. Eric Bradner, "Rubio: It's 'Harder Every Day to Justify' Backing Trump," CNN, March 13, 2016, http://www.cnn.com/2016/03/13/politics/marco-rubio-donald-trump-support/index.html.

42. Ibid.

43. Jake Sherman, "Ryan 'Sickened' by Trump, Joint Appearance Scrapped," *Politico*, October 7, 2016, https://www.politico.com/story/2016/10/paul-ryan-donald-trump-comments-women-wisconsin-229307.

44. Deirdre Walsh and Manu Raju, "Paul Ryan Rips Donald Trump Remarks as 'Textbook Definition of a Racist Comment,'" CNN, June 7, 2016, https://www.cnn.com/2016/06/07/politics/paul-ryan-donald-trump-racist-comment/index.html.

45. Benjy Sarlin, "Republican-Led Congress Passes Sweeping Tax Bill," NBC News, December 20, 2017, https://www.nbcnews.com/politics/congress/republican-tax-bill-house-senate-trump-n831161.

46. Tim Alberta, *American Carnage: On the Front Lines of the Republican Civil War and the Rise of President Trump* (New York: Harper, 2019), 328.

47. Ibid.

48. Jessica Taylor, "Jeff Flake Has Taken on Trump and the GOP, But Will It Matter?," National Public Radio, August 8, 2017, https://www.npr.org/2017/08/08/542069448/jeff-flake-has-taken-on-trump-and-the-gop-but-will-it-matter.

49. Sheryl Gay Stolberg, "Jeff Flake, a Fierce Trump Critic, Will Not Seek Re-Election for Senate," *New York Times*, October 24, 2017, https://www.nytimes.com/2017/10/24/us/politics/jeff-flake-arizona.html.

50. Jeffrey M. Jones, "Trump Job Approval at Personal Best 49%," *Gallup Blog*, February 4, 2020, https://news.gallup.com/poll/284156/trump-job-approval-personal-best.aspx.

51. Ibid.

52. Alan I. Abramowitz, *The Great Alignment: Race, Party Transformation, and the Rise of Donald Trump* (New Haven, CT: Yale University Press, 2018), x.

53. Ibid.

54. Nicholas Carnes and Noam Lupu, "It's Time to Bust the Myth: Most Trump Voters Were Not Working Class," *Monkey Cage* (blog), *Washington Post*, June 5, 2017, https://www.washingtonpost.com/news/monkey-cage/wp/2017/06/05/its-time-to-bust-the-myth-most-trump-voters-were-not-working-class/.

55. See John Sides, Michael Tesler, and Lynn Vavreck, *Identity Crisis: The 2016 Presidential Campaign and the Battle for the Meaning of America* (Princeton, NJ: Princeton University Press, 2018).

56. Abramowitz, *The Great Alignment*, xiii.

57. Michael Wines, "'Looting' Comment from Trump Dates Back to Racial Unrest of the 1960s," *New York Times*, May 29, 2020, https://www.nytimes.com/2020/05/29/us/looting-starts-shooting-starts.html.

58. KK Ottesen, "Jeff Flake on Trumpism: 'I Don't Know Anyone Who Thinks That This Is the Future of the Party,'" *Washington Post*, April 28, 2020, https://www.washingtonpost.com/lifestyle/magazine/jeff-flake-on-trumpism-i-dont-know-anyone-who-thinks-that-this-is-the-future-of-the-party/2020/04/24/60424846-622b-11ea-b3fc-7841686c5c57_story.html.

59. See Arthur M. Schlesinger Jr., The *Imperial Presidency* (Boston: Mariner Books, 2004).

60. Karen M. Kedrowski, *Media Entrepreneurs and the Media Enterprise in the U.S. Congress* (Cresskill, NJ: Hampton Press, 1996).

61. American University School of Communication, "American Forum with Ed O'Keefe," September 25, 2017, playlist, https://www.youtube.com/playlist?list=PLZGmcfRNf0MgLfUeinWiz7aJ_v3JziO9h.

62. See David Wise, *The Politics of Lying: Government Deception, Secrecy, and Power* (New York: Random House, 1973).

63. See Mark Hertsgaard, *On Bended Knee: The Press and the Reagan Presidency* (New York: Schocken, 1989).

64. Mark Hertsgaard, "Beloved by the Media," *Nation*, June 10, 2004, https://www.thenation.com/article/archive/beloved-media/.

65. Ken Auletta, "Fortress Bush," *New Yorker*, January 12, 2004, https://www.newyorker.com/magazine/2004/01/19/fortress-bush.

66. Ibid.

67. Ken Walsh, "White House and Press Relations Getting Worse," *U.S. News & World Report*, March 4, 2013, https://www.usnews.com/news/blogs/ken-walshs-washington/2013/03/04/white-house-and-press-relations-getting-worse. Also, see Kenneth T. Walsh, interview with the author, March 28, 2018.

68. Leonard Downie Jr. and Sara Rafsky, "The Obama Administration and the Press," Committee to Protect Journalists, October 10, 2013, https://cpj.org/reports/2013/10/

obama-and-the-press-us-leaks-sur-veillance-post-911.php.

69. Ibid.

70. "What the Hacks of 1600 Penn Really Think," *Politico*, May/June 2014, http://www.politico.com/magazine/story/2014/04/whca-survey-the-white-house-beat-uncovered-106071.

71. Ibid. Also, see Downie Jr. and Rafsky, "The Obama Administration and the Press." This information also comes from an interview with the author with a White House correspondent in November 2013.

72. Downie Jr. and Rafsky, "The Obama Administration and the Press."

73. David Kravets, "Obama's Efforts to Control Media Are 'Most Aggressive' Since Nixon, Report Says," *Wired*, October 10, 2013, https://www.wired.com/2013/10/obama-nixon-media-war/.

74. Martha Joynt Kumar, "Obama Meets the Press—on His Terms," *RealClear-Politics*, August 29, 2015, https://www.realclearpolitics.com/articles/2015/08/29/obama_meets_the_press_--_on_his_terms_127907.html.

75. Ibid.

76. Jim VandeHei and Mike Allen, "Obama, the Puppet Master," *Politico*, February 19, 2013, http://www.politico.com/story/2013/02/obama-the-puppet-master-087764.

77. Margaret Sullivan, "Obama Promised Transparency. But His Administration Is One of the Most Secretive," *Washington Post*, May 24, 2016, https://www.washingtonpost.com/lifestyle/style/obama-promised-transparency-but-his-administration-is-one-of-the-most-secretive/2016/05/24/5a46caba-21c1-11e6-9e7f-57890b612299_story.html.

78. Dick Polman, "Donald Trump's Unprecedented Assault on the Media," *Atlantic*, August 18, 2018.

79. Ibid.

80. Justin Green, "Today's Top Quote: Kellyanne on 'Alternative Facts,'" *Axios*, January 22, 2017, https://www.axios.com/todays-top-quote-kellyanne-on-alternative-facts-1513300040-0d8272b0-3610-46d5-98eb-ddca6ae5dba7.html.

81. Brian Stelter, "'Alternative Facts:' Why the Trump Team Is 'Planting a Flag' in War on Media," CNN, January 22, 2017, http://money.cnn.com/2017/01/22/media/alternative-facts-donald-trump/index.html.

82. CNN, "Trump Supporter Accosts Reporters at Rally," August 12, 2016, video, 2:11, https://youtu.be/-GA7EgB7KpY.

83. Katy Tur, "My Crazy Year with Trump," *Marie Claire*, August 10, 2016, https://www.marieclaire.com/politics/a21997/donald-trump-katy-tur/.

84. Marc Tracy, "Anti-Lockdown Protesters Get in Reporters' (Masked) Faces," *New York Times*, May 13, 2020, https://www.nytimes.com/2020/05/13/business/media/lockdown-protests-reporters.html.

85. Jessica Jerreat, Pete Cobus, and Eric Neugeboren, "Across US, Journalists Caught in Protest Crossfire," *Voice of America*, June 2, 2020, https://www.voanews.com/press-freedom/across-us-journalists-caught-protest-crossfire.

86. Ken Walsh, interview with the author, February 20, 2020.

87. Ibid.

88. Josh Hafner, "Trump Insults Female Reporter: 'You're Not Thinking. You Never Do,'" *USA Today*, October 2, 2018, https://www.usatoday.com/story/news/politics/onpolitics/2018/10/01/trump-insults-abc-reporter-cecilia-vega-you-never-think/1493105002/.

89. Ibid.

90. Amy Eisman, "Inside the Trump Presidency: ABC's Cecilia Vega on Covering the White House," American University, October 26, 2018, https://www.american.edu/soc/news/cecilia-vega-visits-soc.cfm.

91. American University School of Communication, "American Forum: Yamiche Alcindor," October 22, 2020, playlist, https://youtube.com/playlist?list=PLZGmcfRNf0MggKOhDT1lXkW1YB9MOcBhY.

92. Ibid.

93. Joseph A. Wulfsohn, "MSNBC's Chuck Todd Sounds the Alarm on Trump: 'The National Nightmare Is Upon Us,'" Fox News, October 3, 2019, https://www.foxnews.com/media/msnbc-chuck-todd-trump-national-nightmare.

94. Chuck Todd, interview with the author, October 2019, American Forum with Chuck Todd, American University, Oct. 10, 2019 https://www.youtube.com/watch?v=0l-tq3ZX8Vc.

95. Mike McCurry, interview with the author, October 15, 2015.

96. Paul Farhi, "Restrictions Lead to Grumbling, but No Boycotts, from White House Press," Washington Post, June 26, 2017, https://www.washingtonpost.com/lifestyle/style/restrictions-lead-to-grumbling-but-no-boycotts-from-white-house-press/2017/06/26/ee61c3c0-5a88-11e7-9fc6-c7ef4bc58d13_story.html.

97. Joshua Keating, "The Invisible Secretary," Slate, March 15, 2017, http://www.slate.com/blogs/the_slatest/2017/03/15/why_is_rex_tillerson_avoiding_the_media.html.

98. Brian Resnick and Julia Belluz, "Sudden Changes at the EPA, USDA, and CDC Under Trump, Explained," Vox, January 25, 2017, https://www.vox.com/science-and-health/2017/1/25/14370712/trump-science-gagging-explained.

99. "On Trump, Transparency and Democracy," Sunlight Foundation, July 20, 2017, https://sunlightfoundation.com/2017/07/20/trump-administration-open-government-record/.

100. Maggie Fox, "March for Science: Scientists Hit the Streets to Demand Respect, Funding," NBC News, April 21, 2017, http://www.nbcnews.com/health/health-news/march-science-scientists-hit-streets-demand-respect-funding-n749486.

101. Adam Liptak, "Donald Trump Could Threaten U.S. Rule of Law, Scholars Say," New York Times, June 3, 2016, https://www.nytimes.com/2016/06/04/us/politics/donald-trump-constitution-power.html.

102. Max Greenwood, "Trump Tweets: The Media Is the 'Enemy of the American People,'" The Hill, February 17, 2017, http://thehill.com/homenews/administration/320168-trump-the-media-is-the-enemy-of-the-american-people.

103. "Christiane Amanpour: International Press Freedom Awards," Committee to Protect Journalists, 2016, https://cpj.org/awards/2016/christiane-amanpour.php.

104. Greg Miller and Greg Jaffe, "Trump Revealed Highly Classified Information to Russian Foreign Minister and Ambassador," Washington Post, May 15, 2017, https://www.washingtonpost.com/world/national-security/trump-revealed-highly-classified-information-to-russian-foreign-minister-and-ambassador/2017/05/15/530c172a-3960-11e7-9e48-c4f199710b69_story.html.

105. Michael S. Schmidt, "Comey Memo Says Trump Asked Him to End

Flynn Investigation," *New York Times*, May 16, 2017, https://www.nytimes .com/2017/05/16/us/politics/james-comey-trump-flynn-russia-investigation.html.

106. Shane Harris and Carol E. Lee, "Spies Keep Intelligence from Donald Trump on Leak Concerns," *Wall Street Journal*, February 16, 2017, https://www.wsj .com/articles/spies-keep-intelligence-from-donald-trump-1487209351.

107. Jo Becker, Matt Apuzzo, and Adam Goldman, "Trump Team Met with Lawyer Linked to Kremlin during Campaign," *New York Times*, July 8, 2017, https://www.nytimes .com/2017/07/08/us/politics/trump-russia-kushner-manafort.html.

108. Peter Baker, "Bolton Says Trump Impeachment Inquiry Missed Other Troubling Episodes," *New York Times*, June 18, 2020, https://www.nytimes .com/2020/06/17/us/politics/bolton-book-trump-impeached.html.

109. Nicholas Fandos, "Trump Acquitted of Two Impeachment Charges in Near Party-Line Vote," *New York Times*, February 5, 2020, https://www .nytimes.com/2020/02/05/us/politics/trump-acquitted-impeachment .html.

110. Jake Tapper, interview with the author, April 4, 2017, on "American Forum" at American University, Washington, DC.

111. David Remnick, "A Conversation with Maggie Haberman, Trump's Favorite Foe," *New Yorker*, July 21, 2017, http://www.newyorker.com/ news/news-desk/a-conversation-with-maggie-haberman-trumps-favorite-foe.

112. Jane Hall, "TELEVISION: Is the Party Over?: New Realities Have Some Wondering If the Networks Need to Spend Prime Time with the Democratic and Republican Conventions," *Los Angeles Times*, August 16, 1992, https://www .latimes.com/archives/la-xpm-1992-08-16-ca-6866-story.html.

113. Mark Leibovich, "The Speech That Made Obama," *New York Times*, July 27, 2016, https://www.nytimes .com/2016/07/27/magazine/the-speech-that-made-obama.html.

114. Shane Goldmacher, "Trump Paints a Dark America Only He Can Save," *Politico*, January 20, 2017, http:// www.politico.com/story/2017/01/ trump-american-carnage-233913.

115. Haynes Johnson, "1968 Democratic Convention," *Smithsonian Magazine*, August 2008, http://www.smithsonianmag.com/history/1968-democratic-convention-931079/.

116. Bruce Bimber, "Digital Media in the Obama Campaigns of 2008 and 2012: Adaptation to the Personalized Political Communication Environment," *Journal of Information Technology & Politics* 11, no. 2 (2014).

117. Ibid.

118. Pope Francis, Twitter, https://twitter .com/Pontifex.

119. Juliet Eilperin, "To Stay Relevant, Newsrooms Rethink Campaign Coverage," *Nieman Reports*, March 23, 2016, http://niemanreports.org/ articles/to-stay-relevant-newsrooms-rethink-campaign-coverage/.

120. Ryan Williams, interview with the author, September 26, 2013.

121. Ibid.

122. *Up with Steve Kornacki*, "Changing Political Journalism, 140 Characters at a Time," September 6, 2013, video, 11:42, http://www.msnbc .com/up/watch/changing-political-journalism-140-characters-at-a-time-47226947707.

123. See Timothy Crouse, *The Boys on the Bus* (New York: Ballantine Books, 1973).

124. Peter Hamby, "Did Twitter Kill the Boys on the Bus? Searching for a Better Way to Cover a Campaign," in Discussion Paper Series (Joan Shorenstein Center on the Press, Politics and Public Policy, September 2013).

125. Michael Barbaro, "Pithy, Mean and Powerful: How Donald Trump Mastered Twitter for 2016," *New York Times*, October 5, 2015, https://www.nytimes.com/2015/10/06/us/politics/donald-trump-twitter-use-campaign-2016.html.

126. Ibid.

127. Ibid.

128. "Trump Supporters' Use of Social Media and Political Engagement," Diana Owens, Georgetown University (paper prepared for presentation and the annual meeting of the American Political Science Association, August 30–September 2, 2018).

129. Ibid.

130. Ibid.

131. Jessica Schulberg, "FBI Director Confirms Agency Is Investigating Ties between Trump and Russia," *Huffington Post*, March 20, 2017, http://www.huffingtonpost.com/entry/james-comey-confirm-investigation-trump-russia-fbi_us_58cfe036e4b0ec9d29dd728c.

132. Louis Nelson, "Trump Tweets NBC, ABC Broadcast 'Biased and Fake' Russia Stories," *Politico*, March, 23, 2017, http://www.politico.com/story/2017/03/trump-tweet-nbc-abc-russia-fake-news-236407.

133. James Griffiths, "Trump Says He Considered 'This Russia Thing' before Firing FBI Director Comey," CNN, May 12, 2017, http://www.cnn.com/2017/05/12/politics/trump-comey-russia-thing/index.html.

134. Peter Hamby, "'The News Is Dying, but Journalism Will Not': How the Media Can Prevent 2020 from Becoming 2016," *Vanity Fair*, January 24, 2019, https://www.vanityfair.com/news/2019/01/how-the-media-can-prevent-2020-from-becoming-2016.

135. Ibid.

136. Ibid.

137. Devin Dwyer, "Alexandria Ocasio-Cortez's Twitter Lesson for House Democrats," ABC News, January 17, 2019, https://abcnews.go.com/beta-story-container/Politics/alexandria-ocasio-cortezs-twitter-lesson-house-democrats/story?id=60443727.

138. Frank Dale, "Alexandria Ocasio-Cortez Is Changing the Way Politicians Use Social Media," ThinkProgress, December 4, 2018, https://archive.thinkprogress.org/alexandria-ocasio-cortez-social-media-house-democrats-twitter-instagram-stories-democratic-socialist-congress-01a76857a3d2/.

139. Ibid.

140. Joshua Rivera, "AOC Played among Us and Achieved What Most Politicians Fail at: Acting Normal," *Guardian*, October 22, 2020, https://www.theguardian.com/games/2020/oct/22/alexandria-ocasio-cortez-ilhan-omar-among-us-twitch-stream-aoc.

141. Lisa K. Fazio et al., "Knowledge Does Not Protect Against Illusory Truth," *Journal of Experimental Psychology: General* 144, no. 5 (2015).

142. Craig Silverman and Lawrence Alexander, "How Teens in The Balkans Are Duping Trump Supporters with Fake News," *BuzzFeed News*, November 3, 2016, https://www.buzzfeednews.com/article/craigsilverman/how-macedonia-became-a-global-hub-for-pro-trump-misinfo#.op95xv35M.

143. Dan Evon, "Pope Francis Shocks World, Endorses Donald Trump for President," *Snopes*, July 10, 2016, https://www.snopes.com/fact-check/pope-francis-donald-trump-endorsement/.

144. David Mikkelson, "FBI Agent Suspected in Hillary Email Leaks Found Dead in Apparent Murder-Suicide," *Snopes*, https://www.snopes.com/fact-check/fbi-agent-murder-suicide/.

145. Silverman and Alexander, "How Teens in The Balkans Are Duping Trump Supporters."

146. Ibid.

147. Craig Silverman, "This Analysis Shows How Viral Fake Election News Stories Outperformed Real News on Facebook," *BuzzFeed News*, November 16, 2016, https://www.buzzfeednews.com/article/craigsilverman/viral-fake-election-news-outperformed-real-news-on-facebook.

148. Sam Levin, "Mark Zuckerberg: I Regret Ridiculing Fears Over Facebook's Effect on Election," *Guardian*, September 27, 2017, https://www.theguardian.com/technology/2017/sep/27/mark-zuckerberg-facebook-2016-election-fake-news.

149. Scott Shane, "What Intelligence Agencies Concluded about the Russian Attack on the U.S. Election," *New York Times*, January 6, 2017, https://www.nytimes.com/2017/01/06/us/politics/russian-hack-report.html.

150. "Background to 'Assessing Russian Activities and Intentions in Recent US Elections': The Analytic Process and Cyber Incident Attribution," ed. Office of the Director of National Intelligence (United States of America, January 6, 2017).

151. Damian Paletta and Devlin Barrett, "Obama Says Experts Tie Russia to DNC Hacking," *Wall Street Journal*, July 27, 2016, https://www.wsj.com/articles/obama-says-experts-tie-russia-to-dnc-hacking-1469619650.

152. "Background to 'Assessing Russian Activities and Intentions in Recent US Elections.'" Also, see Silverman, "This Analysis Shows How Viral Fake Election News Stories Outperformed."

153. Jonathan Albright, "Facebook Must 'Follow the Money' to Uncover Extent of Russian Meddling," Center for American Progress Action Fund, October 9, 2017, https://www.americanprogressaction.org/issues/ext/2017/10/09/168826/facebook-must-follow-money-uncover-extent-russian-meddling/. Also, see https://d1gi.medium.com/data-resources-misinfo-and-media-manipulation-d4fc1d0e2b07.

154. Ibid.

155. "The Disinformation Report," *Yonder*, December 17, 2018, https://www.yonder-ai.com/resources/the-disinformation-report/.

156. Ibid.

157. Kevin Roose, "Russian Trolls Came for Instagram, Too," *New York Times*, December 18, 2018, https://www.nytimes.com/2018/12/18/technology/russian-interference-instagram.html.

158. Alex Pasternack, "It's Not Over: Russia's Divisive Instagram Memes Are Still Racking up Likes," *Fast Company*, December 19, 2018, https://www.fastcompany.com/90283167/russia-instagram-war-facebook-memes.

159. Philip N. Howard et al., "The IRA, Social Media and Political Polarization in the United States, 2012–2018," University of Oxford, https://comprop.oii.ox.ac.uk/wp-content/uploads/sites/93/2018/12/IRA-Report.pdf.

160. Michael Barthel, Amy Mitchell, and Jesse Holcomb, "Many Americans Believe Fake News Is Sowing Confusion," Pew Research Center, December 15, 2016, https://www.journalism.org/2016/12/15/many-americans-believe-fake-news-is-sowing-confusion/.

161. Claire Wardle and Hossein Derakhshan, "Information Disorder: Toward an Interdisciplinary Framework for Research and Policy Making" (Strasbourg, France: Council of Europe), September 27, 2017, https://rm.coe.int/information-disorder-report-version-august-2018/16808c9c77%2039. Also, see "Understanding and Addressing the Disinformation Ecosystem" (Annenberg School for Communication), December 15–16, 2017, https://firstdraftnews.org/wp-content/uploads/2018/03/The-Disinformation-Ecosystem-20180207-v3.pdf?x17007.

162. Ibid.

163. Ibid.

164. Ibid.; see also Erin Calabrese, "5 Ways to Spot Disinformation on Your Social Media Feeds," ABC News, May 29, 2020, https://abcnews.go.com/US/ways-spot-disinformation-social-media-feeds/story?id=67784438.

165. Adam Goldman, Julian E. Barnes, Maggie Haberman, and Nicholas Fandos, "Lawmakers Are Warned That Russia Is Meddling to Re-Elect Trump," *New York Times*, September 22, 2020, https://www.nytimes.com/2020/02/20/us/politics/russian-interference-trump-democrats.html.

166. Natasha Korecki, "'Sustained and Ongoing' Disinformation Assault Targets Dem Presidential Candidates," *Politico*, February 20, 2019, https://www.politico.com/story/2019/02/20/2020-candidates-social-media-attack-1176018.

167. Matt Holt, "Information War Underway as Democrats Line Up to Run," *National Journal*, May 21, 2019.

168. Ibid.

169. Greg Myre and Shannon Bond, "'Russia Doesn't Have to Make Fake News': Biggest Election Threat Is Closer to Home," National Public Radio, September 29, 2020, https://www.npr.org/2020/09/29/917725209/russia-doesn-t-have-to-make-fake-news-biggest-election-threat-is-closer-to-home.

170. Ibid.

171. Yochai Benkler et al., "Mail-In Voter Fraud: Anatomy of a Disinformation Campaign," Berkman Klein Center for Internet & Society at Harvard University, October 1, 2020, https://cyber.harvard.edu/publication/2020/Mail-in-Voter-Fraud-Disinformation-2020.

172. Margaret Sullivan, "Trump Doesn't Need Russian Trolls to Spread Disinformation. The Mainstream Media Does It for Him," *Washington Post*, October 7, 2020, https://www.washingtonpost.com/lifestyle/media/trump-doesnt-need-russian-trolls-to-spread-disinformation-the-mainstream-media-does-it-for-him/2020/10/06/9612d602-07da-11eb-9be6-cf25fb429f1a_story.html.

173. Sarah Evanega et al., "Coronavirus Misinformation: Quantifying Sources and Themes in the COVID-19 'Infodemic'" (Cornell University), https://allianceforscience.cornell.edu/wp-content/uploads/2020/09/Evanega-et-al-Coronavirus-misinformationFINAL.pdf.

174. Sheryl Gay Stolberg and Noah Weiland, "Study Finds 'Single Largest Driver' of Coronavirus Misinformation: Trump," *New York Times*, October 22, 2020, https://www.nytimes.com/2020/09/30/us/politics/trump-coronavirus-misinformation.html.

175. Pam Fessler, "Robocalls, Rumors and Emails: Last-Minute Election Disinformation Floods Voters," National Public Radio, October 24, 2020, https://www.npr.org/2020/10/24/927300432/

robocalls-rumors-and-emails-last-minute-election-disinformation-floods-voters.

176. Ibid.

177. Kevin Johnson and David Jackson, "Trump Ousts Homeland Security Cyber Chief Chris Krebs, who Called Election Secure," *USA Today*, November 18, 2020, https://www.usatoday.com/story/news/politics/2020/11/17/trump-ousts-homeland-security-chris-krebs-called-election-secure/6276676002/.

178. Ibid.

179. Jane C. Timm, "'This Has to Stop': Harassed and Threatened, GOP Election Officials Urge Party Leaders to Take Stand," NBC News, December 2, 2020, https://www.nbcnews.com/politics/elections/has-stop-harassed-threatened-gop-election-officials-urge-party-leaders-n1249769.

180. David Zurawik, "Bill Clinton's Sax Solo on 'Arsenio' Still Resonates Memorable Moments," *Baltimore Sun*, December 27, 1992, http://articles.baltimoresun.com/1992-12-27/features/1992362178_1_clinton-arsenio-hall-hall-show.

181. Dan Fastenberg, "Boxers or Briefs? Clinton Answers," *Time*, July 29, 2010, http://content.time.com/time/specials/packages/article/0,28804,2007228_2007230_2007258,00.html.

182. Patricia Moy, Michael A. Xenos, and Verena K. Hess, "Priming Effects of Late-Night Comedy," *International Journal of Public Opinion Research* 18, no. 2 (2006).

183. Andrew Rafferty, "2016 Candidates Flock to New Class of Late-Night Show Hosts," NBC News, September 7, 2015, http://www.nbcnews.com/politics/2016-election/despite-new-faces-2016-candidates-still-flocking-late-night-n422051.

184. Peter Bailey-Wells, "Kamala Harris, Jimmy Fallon, and The Roots 'Slow-Jammed' the News," *Boston Globe*, September 17, 2019, https://www.bostonglobe.com/news/politics/2019/09/17/kamala-harris-jimmy-fallon-and-the-roots-slow-jammed-news/St70FE73zZdd7vFZJSI3eI/story.html. See *The Tonight Show Starring Jimmy Fallon*, "Slow Jam the News with Mayor Pete Buttigieg," May 13, 2019, video, 5:44, https://youtu.be/XJ3DmxZFX6w. Also, see *The Tonight Show Starring Jimmy Fallon*, "Slow Jam the News with Senator Kamala Harris," September 16, 2019, video, 5:38, https://youtu.be/27Shqh88oYg.

185. *Late Show with Stephen Colbert*, "Biden Talks to Colbert about His Son," *New York Times*, September 11, 2015, https://www.nytimes.com/video/us/politics/100000003904591/biden-talks-to-colbert-about-his-son.html.

186. *The Late Late Show with James Corden*, "First Lady Michelle Obama Carpool Karaoke," July 20, 2016, video, 14:41, https://youtu.be/ln3wAdRAim4.

187. Matt Wilstein, "Scott Aukerman Reveals the One Joke Obama White House Wanted to Cut from 'Between Two Ferns,'" *Daily Beast*, September 25, 2019, https://www.thedailybeast.com/scott-aukerman-reveals-the-one-joke-obama-white-house-wanted-to-cut-from-between-two-ferns.

188. Jill Cowan, "Kamala Harris Steps Into the Ring," *New York Times*, January 22, 2019, https://www.nytimes.com/2019/01/22/us/california-today-kamala-harris-president-campaign.html. Also, Matt Viser and Chelsea Janes, "Kamala Harris Enters 2020 Presidential Race," *Washington Post*, January 21, 2019, https://

www.washingtonpost.com/
politics/kamala-harris-enters-
2020-presidential-race/2019/01/21/
d68d15b2-0a20-11e9-a3f0-
71c95106d96a_story.html. Also, Mel-
anie Mason, "Kamala Harris Jumps into
Presidential Campaign as First-Tier
Candidate," *Los Angeles Times*, January
21, 2019, https://www.latimes.com/
politics/la-na-pol-kamala-harris-pres-
ident-election-20190121-story.html.
See "Sen. Kamala Harris Announces
2020 Presidential Run," *Good Morning
America*, January 21, 2019, ttps://www
.goodmorningamerica.com/news/
video/sen-kamala-harris-announces-
2020-presidential-run-60518540.

189. Michael X. Delli Carpini and Bruce
A. Williams, "Let Us Infotain You:
Politics in the New Media Age," in
*Mediated Politics: Communication in
the Future of Democracy*, ed. W. Lance
Bennett and Robert M. Entman
(Cambridge: Cambridge University
Press, 2001), 160–81.

190. Ibid.

191. Craig Aaron, "Jon Stewart Versus the Perpetual Panic Conflictinator" Huffpost, Nov. 1, 2010,
https://www.huffpost.com/entry/
jon-stewart-vs-the-perpet_b_777392.

192. Matthew A. Baum, "Soft News and
Political Knowledge: Evidence of
Absence or Absence of Evidence?,"
Political Communication 20, no. 2
(2003).

193. D. G. Young and R. M. Tisinger,
"Dispelling Late-Night Myths: News
Consumption Among Late-Night
Comedy Viewers and the Predictors
of Exposure to Various Late-Night
Shows," *Harvard International Journal
of Press/Politics* 11, no. 3 (2006).

194. Lauren Feldman and Dannagal Gold-
thwaite Young, "Late-Night Comedy
as a Gateway to Traditional News:
An Analysis of Time Trends in News

Attention among Late-Night Comedy
Viewers during the 2004 Presidential Primaries," *Political Communication* 25, no. 4, November 26, 2008,
https://www.tandfonline.com/doi/
abs/10.1080/10584600802427013

195. Alissa Wilkinson, "5 Years in, HBO's
Last Week Tonight Is a Lot More Than
'Just Comedy,'" Vox, February 17,
2019, https://www.vox.com/cul-
ture/2019/2/14/18213228/last-week-
tonight-john-oliver-hbo-season-six.

196. Ali Vitali, "Donald Trump Hosts 'Saturday Night Live' Amid Protests," NBC
News, November 8, 2015, http://www
.nbcnews.com/politics/2016-elec-
tion/donald-trump-hosts-saturday-
night-live-amid-protests-n459341.

197. *Saturday Night Live*, "The Ingraham
Angle Coronavirus Cold Open—
SNL," March 8, 2020, video, 9:20,
https://youtu.be/XezLiezWN0E.

198. KellyWurx, "Dana Carvey Imper-
sonates Bush and Perot," June 2,
2012, video, 6:10, https://youtu.be/
z851sZXYq5g.

199. Adam Howard, "How 'Saturday Night
Live' Has Shaped American Politics,"
NBC News, September 30, 2016,
http://www.nbcnews.com/pop-culture/
tv/how-saturday-night-live-has-
shaped-american-politics-n656716.

200. Eoin O'Carroll, "Political Misquotes:
The 10 Most Famous Things Never
Actually Said," *Christian Science Monitor*,
June 3, 2011, https://www.csmonitor
.com/USA/Politics/2011/0603/Politi-
cal-misquotes-The-10-most-famous-
things-never-actually-said/I-can-see-
Russia-from-my-house!-Sarah-Palin.

201. Matt Wilstein, "*SNL*: Larry David's
Bernie Sanders Exposes His 'Army of
Internet Trolls,'" *Daily Beast*, February
9, 2020, https://www.thedailybeast
.com/snl-larry-david-as-bernie-sand-
ers-defends-his-army-of-internet-trolls.

202. Helena Andrews, "'SNL' Skits Raise Doubts About Neutrality," *Politico*, March 6, 2008, http://www.politico.com/story/2008/03/snl-skits-raise-doubts-about-neutrality-008888.
203. Ibid.
204. Emily Van DerWerff and Caroline Franke, "Donald Trump's Saturday Night Live episode was worse than bad--it was boring," Vox, Nov. 8, 2015 https://www.vox.com/culture/2015/11/8/9690978/saturday-night-live-donald-trump.
205. Kate Lyons, "Alec Baldwin Tweets Back as Donald Trump Talks of 'Retribution' for SNL," *Guardian*, February 18, 2019, https://www.theguardian.com/us-news/2019/feb/18/donald-trump-talks-of-retribution-after-alec-baldwin-parody-on-snl.
206. Caitlin Flanagan, "How Late-Night Comedy Fueled the Rise of Trump," *Atlantic*, May 2017, https://www.theatlantic.com/magazine/archive/2017/05/how-late-night-comedy-alienated-conservatives-made-liberals-smug-and-fueled-the-rise-of-trump/521472/.
207. Ibid.
208. Stephen Loiaconi, "Late Night Comedy's War on Trump Escalates as Ratings Rise," WJLA, May 8, 2017, http://wjla.com/news/entertainment/late-night-comedys-war-on-trump-escalates-as-ratings-rise.
209. Thomas E. Patterson, "News Coverage of the 2016 General Election: How the Press Failed the Voters" (Shorenstein Center on Media, Politics and Public Policy, December 2016).
210. Ibid.
211. Ibid.
212. Ibid.
213. Ibid.
214. Kristen Hare and Alexios Mantzarlis, "How the 2016 Campaign Changed Political Journalism," Poynter Institute, November 8, 2016, https://www.poynter.org/reporting-editing/2016/how-the-2016-election-changed-political-journalism/.
215. Ibid.
216. Ibid.

Chapter 6

1. Evan Hill et al., "How George Floyd Was Killed in Police Custody," *New York Times*, June 22, 2020, https://www.nytimes.com/2020/05/31/us/george-floyd-investigation.html.
2. Ibid.
3. Ibid.
4. Isabella Ullmann, "Justice for George Floyd: This Is the 17-Year-Old Who Filmed His Murder," *Shine Global* (blog), June 12, 2020, https://www.shineglobal.org/2020/06/12/justice-for-george-floyd-17-year-old-who-filmed-his-murder-darnella-frazier/.
5. Joe Pinsker, "The Pandemic Will Cleave America in Two," *Atlantic*, April 10, 2020, https://www.theatlantic.com/family/archive/2020/04/two-pandemics-us-coronavirus-inequality/609622/.
6. Errin Haines, "Family Seeks Answers in Fatal Police Shooting of Louisville Woman in Her Apartment," *Washington Post*, May 11, 2020, https://www.washingtonpost.com/nation/2020/05/11/family-seeks-answers-fatal-police-shooting-louisville-woman-her-apartment/.
7. Michael Brice-Saddler, Colby Itkowitz, and Cleve R. Wootson Jr., "Father and Son Charged in the Killing of Black Georgia Jogger, Ahmaud Arbery, After Footage Sparked Outrage," *Washington Post*, May 8, 2020, https://www.washingtonpost.com/politics/2020/05/07/killing-ahmaud-arbery-draws-condemnation-calls-prosecution/.

8. Larry Buchanan, Quoctrung Bui, and Jugal K. Patel, "Black Lives Matter May Be the Largest Movement in U.S. History," *New York Times*, July 3, 2020, https://www.nytimes.com/interactive/2020/07/03/us/george-floyd-protests-crowd-size.html.

9. See William H. Frey, "The Nation Is Diversifying Even Faster Than Predicted, According to New Census Data," *Brookings*, July 1, 2020, https://www.brookings.edu/research/new-census-data-shows-the-nation-is-diversifying-even-faster-than-predicted/.

10. See Michael Tesler, "The Floyd Protests Have Changed Public Opinion about Race and Policing. Here's the Data," *Washington Post*, June 9, 2020, https://www.washingtonpost.com/politics/2020/06/09/floyd-protests-have-changed-public-opinion-about-race-policing-heres-data/.

11. Buchanan, Bui, and Patel, "Black Lives Matter."

12. Ibid.

13. David Treadwell, "Journalists Discuss Coverage of Movement: Media Role in Civil Rights Era Reviewed," *Los Angeles Times*, April 5, 1987, https://www.latimes.com/archives/la-xpm-1987-04-05-mn-380-story.html.

14. Ibid.

15. "JFK and Civil Rights," PBS, accessed July 6, 2020, https://www.pbs.org/wgbh/americanexperience/features/jfk-domestic-politics/.

16. "School Photo of Elizabeth Eckford, 1957," *Facing History and Ourselves*, accessed July 6, 2020, https://www.facinghistory.org/resource-library/image/school-photo-elizabeth-eckford-1957.

17. See Elliott J. Gorn, *Let the People See* (New York: Oxford University Press, 2018). Also, see Maureen Corrigan, "'Let the People See': It Took Courage to Keep Emmett Till's Memory Alive," WBUR, October 30, 2018, https://www.wbur.org/npr/660980178/-let-the-people-see-shows-how-emmett-till-s-murder-was-nearly-forgotten.

18. Julian Bond, interview with the author, October 10, 2011, in "American Forum: Julian Bond Town Hall," NBC4, October 20, 2011, http://www.nbcwashington.com/news/local/American-Forum-Julian-Bond-Town-Hall-131802173.html.

19. Thad Morgan, "How Freedom Rider Diane Nash Risked Her Life to Desegregate the South," History.com, April 1, 2019, https://www.history.com/news/diane-nash-freedom-rider-civil-rights-movement.

20. *Los Angeles Times* Staff, "The L.A. Riots: 25 Years Later," *Los Angeles Times*, April 26, 2017, http://timelines.latimes.com/los-angeles-riots/.

21. Robert Reinhold, "Violence and Racism Are Routine in Los Angeles Police, Study Says," *New York Times*, July 10, 1991, http://www.nytimes.com/books/98/02/08/home/rodney-report.html.

22. "Los Angeles Riots Fast Facts," CNN, April 23, 2017, http://www.cnn.com/2013/09/18/us/los-angeles-riots-fast-facts/index.html.

23. *Los Angeles Times* Staff, "The L.A. Riots: 25 Years Later."

24. NPR Staff, "Black Lives Matter Founders Describe 'Paradigm Shift' in the Movement," National Public Radio, July 13, 2016, https://www.npr.org/sections/codeswitch/2016/07/13/485895828/black-lives-matter-founders-describe-paradigm-shift-in-the-movement.

25. Greg Botelho and Holly Yan, "George Zimmerman Found Not Guilty of Murder in Trayvon Martin's Death," CNN, July 14, 2013, http://www.cnn.com/2013/07/13/justice/zimmerman-trial/index.html.

26. Erin Nyren, "Bill O'Reilly's Most Shocking Quotes: The Hoodie, ACLU Terrorists and Victim-Blaming," *Variety*, April 19, 2017, http://variety.com/2017/tv/news/bill-oreilly-wildest-quotes-1202390457/.

27. Botelho and Yan, "George Zimmerman Found Not Guilty."

28. Dana Ford and Chelsea J. Carter, "Justice System 'Didn't Work for Us,' Trayvon Martin's Father Says," CNN, July 18, 2013, http://www.cnn.com/2013/07/18/justice/trayvon-martin-parents/index.html.

29. Susan Page, "Trayvon Martin's Parents, Five Years after His Shooting, Weigh Political Bids," *USA Today*, January 29, 2017, https://www.usatoday.com/story/news/politics/2017/01/29/trayvon-martins-parents-five-years-after-his-shooting-weigh-political-bids-trump-race-justice/97185846/.

30. See Patrisse Khan-Cullors and Asha Bandele, *When They Call You a Terrorist: A Black Lives Matter Memoir* (New York: St. Martin's Griffin, 2017). Also, see Charles Kaiser, "When They Call You a Terrorist Review: Black Lives Matter Memoir Convinces," *Guardian*, January 28, 2018, https://www.theguardian.com/us-news/2018/jan/28/when-they-call-you-a-terrorist-black-lives-matter-review.

31. Monica Davey and Julie Bosman, "Protests Flare after Ferguson Police Officer Is Not Indicted," *New York Times*, November 24, 2014, https://www.nytimes.com/2014/11/25/us/ferguson-darren-wilson-shooting-michael-brown-grand-jury.html.

32. Tanzina Vega, "Shooting Spurs Hashtag Effort on Stereotypes," *New York Times*, August 12, 2014, https://www.nytimes.com/2014/08/13/us/if-they-gunned-me-down-protest-on-twitter.html.

33. Lilly Workneh, "#SayHerName: Why We Should Declare That Black Women and Girls Matter, Too," *Huffington Post*, December 6, 2017, https://www.huffingtonpost.com/2015/05/21/black-women-matter_n_7363064.html.

34. Andy Newman, "The Death of Eric Garner, and the Events That Followed," *New York Times*, December 3, 2014, https://www.nytimes.com/interactive/2014/12/04/nyregion/04garner-timeline.html.

35. German Lopez, "Cleveland Just Fired the Cop Who Shot and Killed 12-Year-Old Tamir Rice More Than 2 Years Ago," *Vox*, May 30, 2017, https://www.vox.com/identities/2017/5/30/15713254/cleveland-police-tamir-rice-timothy-loehmann.

36. Jon Schuppe, "Three Chicago Cops Charged with Conspiracy to Cover up Laquan McDonald Killing," NBC News, June 27, 2017, https://www.nbcnews.com/news/us-news/three-chicago-cops-charged-conspiracy-cover-laquan-mcdonald-killing-n777306.

37. *Investigation of the Chicago Police Department*, U.S. Department of Justice Civil Rights Division and Northern District of Illinois U.S. Attorney's Office (January 13, 2017), https://www.justice.gov/opa/file/925846/download.

38. Mitch Smith, "Minnesota Officer Acquitted in Killing of Philando Castile," *New York Times*, June 16, 2017, https://www.nytimes.com/2017/06/16/us/police-shooting-trial-philando-castile.html.

39. Pérez-Peña and Williams, "Glare of Video Is Shifting Public's View of Police."

40. Ibid.

41. Ibid.

42. Ann M. Simmons and Jaweed Kaleem, "A Founder of Black Lives Matter Answers a Question on Many Minds: Where Did It Go?," *Los Angeles Times*, August 25, 2017, http://www.latimes.com/nation/la-na-patrisse-cullors-black-lives-matter-2017-htmlstory.html.

43. Ari Shapiro, "Black Lives Matter Founders Describe 'Paradigm Shift' in the Movement," National Public Radio, July 13, 2016, https://www.npr.org/sections/codeswitch/2016/07/13/485895828/black-lives-matter-founders-describe-paradigm-shift-in-the-movement.

44. Madison Park, "Police Shootings: Trials, Convictions Are Rare for Officers," CNN, June 24, 2017, http://www.cnn.com/2017/05/18/us/police-involved-shooting-cases/index.html.

45. Zusha Elinson and Dan Frosch, "Cost of Police-Misconduct Cases Soars in Big U.S. Cities," *Wall Street Journal*, July 15, 2015, https://www.wsj.com/articles/cost-of-police-misconduct-cases-soars-in-big-u-s-cities-1437013834.

46. Allyson Vasilopolos, "Pulitzer Prize Winner Wesley Lowery Talks about Police Shootings, Data Surprises," *Columbia Missourian*, April 4, 2017. https://www.columbiamissourian.com/news/local/pulitzer-prize-winner-wesley-lowery-talks-about-police-shootings-data/article_1e928b08-1996-11e7-a40d-3f428525473a.html. Also, Wesley Lowery, presentation, American University, 2017.

47. Paul Farhi, "Post Series on Police Shootings Wins Pulitzer Prize for National Reporting," *Washington Post*, April 18, 2016, https://www.washingtonpost.com/lifestyle/style/post-series-on-police-shootings-wins-pulitzer-prize-for-national-reporting/2016/04/18/a9eeeda2-055d-11e6-b283-e79d81c63c1b_story.html.

48. Wesley Lowery, "Study Finds Police Fatally Shoot Unarmed Black Men at Disproportionate Rates," *Washington Post*, April 7, 2016, https://www.washingtonpost.com/national/study-finds-police-fatally-shoot-unarmed-black-men-at-disproportionate-rates/2016/04/06/e494563e-fa74-11e5-80e4-c381214de1a3_story.html.

49. Ibid.

50. See MSNBC, "Police Supt.: Trump Narrative About Chicago Is 'Frustrating,'" December 28, 2017, video, 2:46, http://www.msnbc.com/all-in/watch/police-supt-trump-narrative-about-chicago-is-frustrating-1125633091819.

51. Dennis Robaugh, "Donald Trump Decries 'War on Police,' Says Democrats Take Blacks for Granted," *Patch*, August 17, 2016, https://patch.com/wisconsin/waukesha/donald-trump-decries-war-police-says-democrats-take-blacks-granted.

52. Rashawn Ray, "What Does Defund the Police Mean and Does It Have Merit?," *Brookings*, June 19, 2020, https://www.brookings.edu/blog/fixgov/2020/06/19/what-does-defund-the-police-mean-and-does-it-have-merit/.

53. Jemima McEvoy, "At Least 13 Cities Are Defunding Their Police Departments," *Forbes*, August 12, 2020, https://www.forbes.com/sites/jemimamcevoy/2020/08/13/at-least-13-cities-are-defunding-their-police-departments/?sh=1b78fcd029e3.

54. Rem Rieder, "Trump's Deceptive Ad on Biden and Defunding the Police," FactCheck.org, June 12, 2020, https://www.factcheck.org/2020/06/trumps-deceptive-ad-on-biden-and-defunding-the-police/.

55. Deen Freelon, Charlton D. McIlwain, and Meredith D. Clark, "Beyond the Hashtags," (American University's School of Communication: Center for Media & Social Impact, February 2016), http://cmsimpact

.org/wp-content/uploads/2016/03/beyond_the_hashtags_2016.pdf.

56. Ibid., 5. Also, see Deen Freelon, presentation, American University, October 20, 2016.

57. Freelon, McIlwain, and Clark, "Beyond the Hashtags," 76.

58. Ibid.

59. Tim Stelloh, "Sentencing Begins for Michael Slager, Ex-Cop Who Killed Walter Scott," NBC News, December 4, 2017, https://www.nbcnews.com/storyline/walter-scott-shooting/sentencing-begins-michael-slager-ex-cop-who-killed-walter-scott-n826431.

60. Scott Collins, "Al Sharpton's Ties to Trayvon Martin Case Beset MSNBC," Los Angeles Times, March 27, 2012, http://latimesblogs.latimes.com/showtracker/2012/03/al-sharptons-ties-to-trayvon-martin-case-beset-msnbc.html.

61. Eric Deggans, "Four Lessons from the Media's Conflicted Coverage of Race," National Public Radio, December 6, 2014, https://www.npr.org/sections/codeswitch/2014/12/06/368713550/four-lessons-from-the-medias-conflicted-coverage-of-race.

62. Ibid.

63. Adam Nagourney, "Racial Barrier Falls in Decisive Victory," New York Times, November 8, 2008, 1.

64. Robert Barnes and Michael D. Shear, "Obama Makes History," Washington Post, November 5, 2008, A1.

65. "Transcript: 'This Is Your Victory,' Says Obama," CNN, November 4, 2008, http://edition.cnn.com/2008/POLITICS/11/04/obama.transcript/.

66. Ibram X. Kendi, Stamped From the Beginning: The Definitive History of Racist Ideas in America (New York: Bold Type Books, 2017), 9.

67. "Section 2: The President-Elect's Image and Expectations," Pew Research Center, November 13, 2008, http://www.people-press.org/2008/11/13/section-2-the-president-elects-image-and-expectations/.

68. Ibid.

69. See George Herbert Mead, Mind, Self, and Society, ed. Charles W. Morris (Chicago: University of Chicago Press, 2015).

70. Zuleyka Zevallos, "What Is Otherness?," Other Sociologist (blog), https://othersociologist.com/otherness-resources/.

71. Alana Abramson, "How Donald Trump Perpetuated the 'Birther' Movement for Years," ABC News, September 16, 2016, http://abcnews.go.com/Politics/donald-trump-perpetuated-birther-movement-years/story?id=42138176.

72. Peter Beinart, "Why Obama's 'Foreignness' Became the New Race Card," Time, October 20, 2008.

73. Jon Greenberg and Linda Qiu, "Fact-Checking Donald Trump's Claim Hillary Clinton Started Obama Birther Movement," PolitiFact, September 16, 2016, http://www.politifact.com/truth-o-meter/statements/2016/sep/16/donald-trump/fact-checking-donald-trumps-claim-hillary-clinton-/.

74. Sarah Pulliam Bailey, "A Startling Number of Americans Still Believe President Obama Is a Muslim," Washington Post, September 14, 2015, https://www.washingtonpost.com/news/acts-of-faith/wp/2015/09/14/a-startling-number-of-americans-still-believe-president-obama-is-a-muslim/.

75. Ibid.

76. See Westen, The Political Brain.

77. Jonathan Martin and Amie Parnes, "McCain: Obama Not an Arab, Crowd Boos," Politico, October 10, 2008, https://www.politico.com/story/2008/10/mccain-obama-not-an-arab-crowd-boos-014479.

78. Michael Fletcher, "The Speech on Race That Saved Obama's Candidacy," Washington Post, April 22, 2016, https://www.washingtonpost.com/

graphics/national/obama-legacy/jere-
miah-wright-2008-philadelphia-race-
speech.html.

79. Ibid.

80. "Barack Obama's Speech on Race,"
New York Times, March 18, 2008,
http://www.nytimes.com/2008/03/18/
us/politics/18text-obama.html.

81. David Paul Kuhn, "Exit Polls:
Economy Top Issue," *Politico*,
November 5, 2008, https://www
.politico.com/story/2008/11/exit-
polls-economy-top-issue-015270.

82. Lonnie C. Major, "Why the Economy
Is Trumping Race," *Time*, October 20,
2008, cover page.

83. Barnes and Shear, "Obama Makes
History."

84. Adam Nagourney, "Obama Shatters
Barriers in a Democratic Sweep," *New
York Times*, October 5, 2008, http://
www.nytimes.com/2008/11/05/world/
americas/05iht-elect.3.17555722
.html.

85. Ibid.

86. "Inside Obama's Sweeping Victory," Pew Research Center,
November 5, 2008, http://www
.pewresearch.org/2008/11/05/inside-
obamas-sweeping-victory/.

87. Ibid.

88. Ibid.

89. Mark Leibovich, "The Speech That
Made Obama," *New York Times*,
July 27, 2016, https://www.nytimes
.com/2016/07/27/magazine/the-
speech-that-made-obama.html.

90. LZ Granderson, "What's Motivat-
ing Some of Obama's Black Critics?,"
CNN, July 26, 2013, http://www.cnn
.com/2013/07/23/opinion/grander-
son-tavis-smiley/index.html.

91. "Sam Fulwood III," Center for American Progress, accessed April 22, 2020,
https://www.americanprogress.org/
about/staff/fulwood-iii-sam/bio/.

92. Sam Fulwood III, interview with
the author and lecture by the inter-
viewee, April 9, 2020.

93. Ibid.

94. Krissah Thompson and Scott Wilson,
"Obama on Trayvon Martin: 'If I Had
a Son, He'd Look Like Trayvon,'"
Washington Post, March 23, 2012,
https://www.washingtonpost.com/
politics/obama-if-i-had-a-son-hed-
look-like-trayvon/2012/03/23/gIQA-
pKPpVS_story.html.

95. Sarah Childress, "How the DOJ
Reforms a Police Department Like
Ferguson," *Frontline*, March 4, 2015,
https://www.pbs.org/wgbh/front-
line/article/how-the-doj-reforms-a-
police-department-like-ferguson/.

96. Sarah L. Kaufman, "Why Obama's
Singing of 'Amazing Grace' Is So
Powerful," *Washington Post*, June 26,
2015, https://www.washingtonpost
.com/news/arts-and-entertainment/
wp/2015/06/26/why-obamas-sing-
ing-of-amazing-grace-is-so-powerful/.

97. David Adams, "Nikki Haley Signs
Bill into Law Banning Confederate
Flag from South Carolina Capitol
Grounds," *Huffington Post*, July 9,
2015, https://www.huffingtonpost
.com/2015/07/09/nikki-haley-con-
federate-flag_n_7765124.html.

98. Jordan Fabian, "Obama Uses Dallas
Memorial to Confront Nation on Race,"
The Hill, July 12, 2016, http://the-
hill.com/blogs/blog-briefing-room/
news/287419-in-mourning-dallas-
victims-obama-makes-plea-for-unity.

99. Justin McCarthy, "President Obama
Leaves White House with 58% Favorable Rating," *Gallup Blog*, January
16, 2017, http://news.gallup.com/
poll/202349/president-obama-leaves-
white-house-favorable-rating.aspx.

100. Ibid.

101. Kathleen Hennessey, "Obama Legacy:
Immigration Stands as Most Glaring Failure," Associated Press, June

30, 2016, https://apnews.com/898a
599f75354323bd107d49f3c4337c/
obama-legacy-immigration-stands-
most-glaring-failure.

102. Tom Allison, "O'Reilly Says of
Michelle Obama: 'She Looks Like
an Angry Woman,'" *Media Matters
for America*, September 17, 2008,
https://www.mediamatters.org/
research/2008/09/17/oreilly-says-
of-michelle-obama-she-looks-like-
a/145062.

103. McCarthy, "President Obama Leaves
White House."

104. "From 'Good Job' to 'Good Riddance':
Obama on Letters from Everyday
Americans," National Public Radio,
December 19, 2016, https://www.npr
.org/2016/12/19/505860259/from-
good-job-to-good-riddance-obama-
on-letters-from-everyday-americans.

105. "On Views of Race and Inequality, Blacks and Whites Are Worlds
Apart," Pew Research Center, June 27,
2016, http://www.pewsocialtrends
.org/2016/06/27/on-views-of-race-
and-inequality-blacks-and-whites-
are-worlds-apart/.

106. Ibid.

107. Ibid.

108. Ibid.

109. Steve Inskeep, "Transcript: President Obama's Full NPR Inter-
view," National Public Radio,
December 29, 2014, https://www
.npr.org/2014/12/29/372485968/
transcript-president-obamas-full-
npr-interview.

110. Ibid.

111. "Former President Obama Holds
Town Hall on Racial Justice &
Police Reform," C-SPAN, June 3,
2020, https://www.c-span.org/
video/?472749-1/town-hall-president-
obama-racial-justice-police-reform.

112. "Statue of Liberty National Monu-
ment," http://www.libertystatepark
.com/emma.htm.

113. See D'Vera Cohn, "How U.S. Immigration Laws and Rules Have Changed
through History," Pew Research
Center, September 30, 2015, http://
www.pewresearch.org/fact-tank/
2015/09/30/how-u-s-immigration-
laws-and-rules-have-changed-
through-history/.

114. *Encyclopædia Britannica Online*, s.v.
"Chinese Exclusion Act," by Yun-
ing Wu, accessed April 13, 2021,
https://www.britannica.com/topic/
Chinese-Exclusion-Act.

115. Priscilla Alvarez, "A Brief History of
America's 'Love-Hate Relationship'
with Immigration," *Atlantic*, February 19, 2017, https://www.theatlan-
tic.com/politics/archive/2017/02/
donald-trump-immigration/517119/.

116. Rachel Weiner, "How Immigration
Reform Failed, Over and Over," *Washington Post*, January 30, 2013, https://
www.washingtonpost.com/news/the-
fix/wp/2013/01/30/how-immigra-
tion-reform-failed-over-and-over/.

117. Ibid.

118. Ibid.

119. Roberto Suro, "The Triumph of No:
How the Media Influence the Immi-
gration Debate" (Washington, DC:
Brookings Institution, 2008).

120. Ibid.

121. Emily M. Farris and Heather Silber
Mohamed, "Picturing Immigration:
How the Media Criminalizes Immigrants," *Politics, Groups, and Identities*
6, no. 4 (2018): 814–24.

122. Ibid.

123. Jose Antonio Vargas, presentation,
October 6, 2014, American University, Washington, DC.

124. Long Island Wins, "No Human Being
Is Illegal and Elie Wiesel," Long Island
Wins, July 6, 2016, https://longisland-
wins.com/news/national/no-human-
being-is-illegal-and-elie-wiesel/, in
Isabel Johnston, "Words Matter: No
Human Being Is Illegal," *Immigration*

and Human Rights Law Review (blog), May 20, 2019, https://lawblogs.uc.edu/ihrlr/2019/05/20/words-matter-no-human-being-is-illegal/.

125. Paul Colford, "'Illegal Immigrant' No More," Associated Press, April 2, 2013, https://blog.ap.org/announcements/illegal-immigrant-no-more.

126. Tom Murse, "Is Medical Help for Illegal Immigrants Covered under Obamacare?," About, April 17, 2016, http://uspolitics.about.com/od/healthcare/a/Are-Illegal-Immigrants-Covered-Under-Obamacare.htm.

127. Rui Kaneya, "'Illegal,' 'Undocumented,' or Something Else? No Clear Consensus Yet," Columbia Journalism Review, December 23, 2014, http://www.cjr.org/united_states_project/illegal_immigrant_or_undocumented.php.

128. Tim Graham, "AP Won't Use the Term 'Illegal Immigrant' Because of Its 'Anti-Ethnic Undertones,'" NewsBusters (blog), April 3, 2013, http://newsbusters.org/blogs/nb/tim-graham/2013/04/03/ap-wont-use-term-illegal-immigrant-because-its-anti-ethnic-undertones.

129. Rinku Sen, "Why the AP's Choice to Drop the I-Word Is a Crucial Victory," Colorlines, April 3, 2013, https://www.colorlines.com/articles/why-aps-choice-drop-i-word-crucial-victory.

130. U.S. Census Bureau, "The Nation's Older Population Is Still Growing, Census Bureau Reports," news release, June 22, 2017, https://www.census.gov/newsroom/press-releases/2017/cb17-100.html.

131. White House Office of the Press Secretary, "Remarks by the President at Univision Town Hall with Jorge Ramos and Maria Elena Salinas," news release, September 20, 2012, https://obamawhitehouse.archives.gov/the-press-office/2012/09/20/remarks-president-univision-town-hall-jorge-ramos-and-maria-elena-salina.

132. See American University School of Communication, "Stories of Migration—Interview with Maria Elena Salinas," October 31, 2017, playlist, https://www.youtube.com/playlist?list=PLZGmcfRNf0MiKD4bZzyWPhl4IhymCPwF0.

133. Ibid.

134. Ibid.

135. Theodore Schleifer, "Univision Anchor Ejected from Trump News Conference," CNN, August 26, 2015, http://www.cnn.com/2015/08/25/politics/donald-trump-megyn-kelly-iowa-rally/index.html.

136. See Salinas, interview with the author, October 27, 2017.

137. Ibid.

138. Henry Barbour et al., "Growth & Opportunity Project: A One-Year Check-Up," (Republican National Committee, March 17, 2014), https://prod-static-ngop-pbl.s3.amazonaws.com/docs/RNC_Growth_Opportunity_Book_2013.pdf.

139. Ibid.

140. Ibid.

141. Jennifer Rubin, "GOP Autopsy Report Goes Bold," Washington Post, March 18, 2013, https://www.washingtonpost.com/blogs/right-turn/wp/2013/03/18/gop-autopsy-report-goes-bold/.

142. Benjy Sarlin, "6 Big Takeaways from the RNC's Incredible 2012 Autopsy," Talking Points Memo, March 18, 2013, http://talkingpointsmemo.com/dc/6-big-takeaways-from-the-rnc-s-incredible-2012-autopsy.

143. Ibid.

144. Kyle Cheney, "Trump Kills GOP Autopsy," Politico, March 4, 2016, https://www.politico.com/story/2016/03/donald-trump-gop-party-reform-220222.

145. Ibid.

146. Ryan Teague Beckwith, "Read Mitt Romney's Speech about Donald Trump," *Time*, March 3, 2016, http://time.com/4246596/donald-trump-mitt-romney-utah-speech/.

147. *Time* Staff, "Here's Donald Trump's Presidential Announcement Speech," *Time*, June 16, 2015, http://time.com/3923128/donald-trump-announcement-speech/.

148. Ibid.

149. American University School of Communication, "Ana Navarro Condemns Trump As a 'Bigot' Who 'Does Not Represent Republican Values,'" October 10, 2016, video, 4:00, https://youtu.be/cM3pPs4Cbno.

150. Ibid.

151. Jonathan Swan, "Republican Strategist Ana Navarro Says She's Voting for Clinton," *The Hill*, November 7, 2016, http://thehill.com/blogs/ballot-box/presidential-races/304747-republican-strategist-ana-navarro-says-shes-voting-for.

152. "Trump's Executive Order: Who Does Travel Ban Affect?," BBC, February 10, 2017, http://www.bbc.com/news/world-us-canada-38781302.

153. Associated Press, "Ice Deportation Arrests Soar under Trump Administration, Drop in Border Arrests," NBC News, December 5, 2017, https://www.nbcnews.com/news/latino/ice-deportation-arrests-soar-under-trump-administration-drop-border-arrests-n826596.

154. Ibid.

155. Ibid.

156. Human Rights Watch, "The Deported: Immigrants Uprooted from the Country They Call Home" (December 5, 2017), https://www.hrw.org/report/2017/12/05/deported/immigrants-uprooted-country-they-call-home.

157. Samantha Raphelson, "Central American Immigrants Brace for End of Temporary Protected Status Program," National Public Radio, November 10, 2017, https://www.npr.org/2017/11/10/563333761/central-american-immigrants-brace-for-end-of-temporary-protected-status-program.

158. Peter Baker, "Trump Supports Plan to Cut Legal Immigration by Half," *New York Times*, August 2, 2017, https://www.nytimes.com/2017/08/02/us/politics/trump-immigration.html.

159. Ibid.

160. David Gelles et al., "Inside the C.E.O. Rebellion Against Trump's Advisory Councils," *New York Times*, August 16, 2017, https://www.nytimes.com/2017/08/16/business/trumps-council-ceos.html.

161. Peter Wehner, "Trump's Words Are Poison," Ethics and Public Policy Center, August 6, 2019, https://eppc.org/publications/trumps-words-are-poison/.

162. Elaine Kamarck and Christine Stenglein, "When Policy Is Cut Off from Reality: Donald Trump's Immigration Problem," *Brookings*, October 31, 2017, https://www.brookings.edu/research/when-policy-is-cut-off-from-reality-donald-trumps-immigration-problem/.

163. Ibid.

164. Ibid.

165. Rob Suls, "Less Than Half the Public Views Border Wall as an Important Goal for U.S. Immigration Policy," Pew Research Center, January 6, 2017, http://www.pewresearch.org/fact-tank/2017/01/06/less-than-half-the-public-views-border-wall-as-an-important-goal-for-us-immigration-policy/.

166. Ibid.

167. "Fox News Poll: May 24, 2017," Fox News Channel, https://www.foxnews.com/politics/fox-news-poll-may-24-2017.

168. Ryan Williams, interview with the author, September 29, 2016.

169. David Winston, WAMU Town Hall, American Forum, Washington, DC, October 2018.

170. Ibid.

171. Ibid.

172. "Family Separation under the Trump Administration—A Timeline," Southern Poverty Law Center, June 17, 2020, https://www.splcenter.org/news/2020/06/17/family-separation-under-trump-administration-timeline.

173. Politico Staff, "PHOTOS: Crisis at the Border," Politico, June 18, 2018, https://www.politico.com/gallery/2018/06/18/children-border-families-separated-002887?slide=0.

174. David Nakamura, "Trump Administration Announces End of Immigration Protection Program for 'Dreamers,'" Washington Post, September 5, 2017, https://www.washingtonpost.com/news/post-politics/wp/2017/09/05/trump-administration-announces-end-of-immigration-protection-program-for-dreamers/.

175. Ibid.

176. Scott Clement and David Nakamura, "Survey Finds Strong Support for 'Dreamers,'" Washington Post, September 25, 2017, https://www.washingtonpost.com/politics/survey-finds-strong-support-for-dreamers/2017/09/24/df3c885c-a16f-11e7-b14f-f41773cd5a14_story.html.

177. Nina Totenberg, "Supreme Court Rules for DREAMers, against Trump," National Public Radio, June 18, 2020, https://www.npr.org/2020/06/18/829858289/supreme-court-upholds-daca-in-blow-to-trump-administration.

178. Jennifer Merolla, S. Karthick Ramakrishnan, and Chris Haynes, "'Illegal,' 'Undocumented,' or 'Unauthorized': Equivalency Frames, Issue Frames, and Public Opinion on Immigration," Perspectives on Politics 11, no. 3 (2013): 789–807.

179. Ibid.

180. Jasmine Aguilera, "Why It's a Mistake to Simplify the 'Latino Vote,'" Time, November 10, 2020, https://time.com/5907525/latino-vote-2020-election/.

181. Esmeralda Bermudez (@BermudeWrites), "It's laughable that in 2020, this country still needs to be reminded, Sesame Street style, that Latinos are not a monolith & the Latino vote is a mirage. This misconception comes from how little u bother knowing us, how superficially u cover us & how absent we are in newsrooms," Twitter, November 3, 2020, 10:57 p.m., https://twitter.com/bermudezwrites/status/1323836686833344515.

182. Ibid.

183. Jennifer Medina, "The Macho Appeal of Donald Trump," New York Times, October 19, 2020, https://www.nytimes.com/2020/10/14/us/politics/trump-macho-appeal.html.

184. Ibid.

185. Patricia Mazzei, Glenn Thrush, and Giovanni Russonello, "Can Biden Regain Lost Ground with Latinos?," New York Times, November 3, 2020, https://www.nytimes.com/2020/11/03/us/politics/biden-latino-vote.html.

186. Ibid.

187. Lisa Lerer and Sydney Ember, "Kamala Harris Makes History as First Woman and Woman of Color as Vice President," New York Times, November 7, 2020, https://www.nytimes.com/2020/11/07/us/politics/kamala-harris.html.

188. Annie Linskey and Chelsea Janes, "Harris's Wooing of Black Activists Paved a Path to the Ticket," Washington Post, August 15, 2020, https://www.washingtonpost.com/politics/harriss-wooing-of-black-activists-paved-

a-path-to-the-ticket/2020/08/15/
d638b276-de70-11ea-b205-
ff838e15a9a6_story.html.

189. Ed O'Keefe, interview with the author, October 29, 2020.

190. Blake Montgomery, "James Mattis Blasts Trump for His Response to George Floyd Protests," *Daily Beast*, June 3, 2020, https://www.thedailybeast.com/trumps-former-defense-secretary-james-mattis-blasts-him-over-response-to-george-floyd-protests.

191. "National Voter Surveys: How Different Groups Voted," *New York Times*, November 3, 2020, https://www.nytimes.com/interactive/2020/11/03/us/elections/ap-polls-national.html.

192. Sam Fulwood, interview with the author, October 15, 2020.

Chapter 7

1. Steven L. Burg and Paul S. Shoup, *The War in Bosnia-Herzegovina: Ethnic Conflict and International Intervention* (Armonk, NY: M. E. Sharpe, 1999), 512.

2. CNN, "1994: Amanpour Questions Bill Clinton," April 4, 2012, video, 2:44, https://www.cnn.com/videos/world/2012/04/05/amanpour-clinton-bosnia-confrontation.cnn.

3. Christiane Amanpour, interview with the author, October 2001. This also comes from Jane Hall, "Breaking News," *More*, April 2001, 64, 68, 74.

4. Ibid.

5. CNN, "Man vs. Chinese Tank Tiananmen Square," June 3, 2013, video, 2:55, https://youtu.be/YeFzeNAHEhU.

6. See Johanna Neuman, *Lights, Camera, War: Is Media Technology Driving International Politics?* (New York: St. Martin's Press, 1996). Alex Selwyn-Holmes, "U.S Soldier Dragged through Mogadishu," *Iconic Photos* (blog), March 10, 2010, https://iconicphotos.wordpress.com/2010/03/10/u-s-marine-dragged-through-mogadishu/.

7. Noah Bonsey and Jeb Koogler, "Does the Path to Middle East Peace Stop in Doha?," *Columbia Journalism Review*, February 16, 2010, https://archives.cjr.org/campaign_desk/does_the_path_to_middle_east_p.php.

8. See W. Lance Bennett, "Toward a Theory of Press–State Relations in the United States," *Journal of Communication* 40, no. 2 (June 1990): 103–27.

9. Steven Livingston, "Clarifying the CNN Effect: An Examination of Media Effects According to Type of Military Intervention," *Shorenstein Center on Media, Politics and Public Policy*, Research Paper R-18, June 1997, https://shorensteincenter.org/wp-content/uploads/2012/03/r18_livingston.pdf.

10. Sean Aday, et al. "Watching from Afar: Media Consumption Patterns around the Arab Spring," *American Behavioral Scientist* 57, no. 7 (2013): 899–919.

11. Stuart N. Soroka, "Media, Public Opinion, and Foreign Policy," Harvard *International Journal of Press/Politics* 8, no. 1 (January 2003), http://www.degreesofdemocracy.net/Soroka(HIJPP).pdf.

12. Matthew A. Baum, "The Iraq Coalition of the Willing and (Politically) Able: Party Systems, the Press, and Public Influence on Foreign Policy," *American Journal of Political Science* 57, no. 2 (April 2013): 442–58.

13. Babak Bahador, "Did Pictures in the News Media Just Change U.S. Policy in Syria?," *Monkey Cage* (blog), *Washington Post*, April 10, 2017, https://www.washingtonpost.com/news/monkey-cage/wp/2017/04/10/did-media-images-just-change-u-s-policy-in-syria-three-lessons-from-kosovo/.

14. Doug Mataconis, "Was Obama's Syrian "Red Line" A Mistake?," *Outside the Beltway* (blog), April 26, 2013, https://www.outsidethebeltway

.com/was-obamas-syrian-red-line-a-mistake/.

15. See Lyse Doucet, "Syria & the CNN Effect: What Role Does the Media Play in Policy-Making?," Daedalus 147, no. 1 (Winter 2018).

16. Neuman, *Lights, Camera, War, 9.*

17. See Livingston, "Clarifying the CNN Effect."

18. Andrew Tyndall, interview with the author, July 17, 2020.

19. Anthony Leiserowitz et al., "Climate Change in the American Mind: April 2020," Yale Program on Climate Change Communication and George Mason University's Center for Climate Change Communication, April 2020, https://climatecommunication.yale .edu/wp-content/uploads/2020/05/ climate-change-american-mind-april-2020b.pdf.

20. "Year in Review 2014," Tyndall, interview, July 17, 2020. Report, http:// tyndallreport.com/yearinreview2014.

21. Andrew Tyndall, interview with the author, 2014.

22. "John Winthrop Dreams of a City on a Hill, 1630," American Yawp Reader, accessed July 22, 2020, https://www .americanyawp.com/reader/colliding-cultures/john-winthrop-dreams-of-a-city-on-a-hill-1630/.

23. See Sacvan Bercovitch, *The Puritan Origins of the American Self* (New Haven, CT: Yale University Press, 2011).

24. Donald E. Pease, "American Exceptionalism," in *American Literature* (New York: Oxford University Press, 2012).

25. Thomas Paine, *Rights of Man* (Mineola, NY: Dover Publications, 1999). https://www.abebooks.com/9780486 408934/Rights-Man-Dover-Thrift-Editions-0486408930/plp.

26. See Seymour Martin Lipset, *American Exceptionalism: A Double-Edged Sword* (New York: W. W. Norton & Company, 1996).

27. Wilber W. Caldwell, *American Narcissism: The Myth of National Superiority* (New York: Algora Publishing, 2006), 19.

28. See Godfrey Hodgson, *The Myth of American Exceptionalism* (Ann Arbor, MI: Sheridan Books, 2009).

29. Ron Elving, "With Latest Nativist Rhetoric, Trump Takes America Back to Where It Came From," National Public Radio, July 16, 2019, https://www .npr.org/2019/07/16/742000247/with-latest-nativist-rhetoric-trump-takes-america-back-to-where-it-came-from.

30. Bruce Drake and Carroll Doherty, "Key Findings on How Americans View the U.S. Role in the World," Pew Research Center, May 5, 2016, https://www.pewresearch .org/fact-tank/2016/05/05/key-find-ings-on-how-americans-view-the-u-s-role-in-the-world/.

31. Phil Stewart and Robin Emmott, "As Trump Confounds, Mattis Seen as Quiet Champion Among NATO Allies," Reuters, July 9, 2018, https://www.reuters.com/ article/us-nato-summit-mattis/ as-trump-confounds-mattis-seen-as-quiet-champion-among-nato-allies-idUSKBN1JZ26Y.

32. Richard Wike, Bruce Stokes, et al., "U.S. Image Suffers as Publics around World Question Trump's Leadership," Pew Research Center, June 26, 2017, https://www.pewresearch.org/ global/2017/06/26/u-s-image-suffers-as-publics-around-world-question-trumps-leadership/.

33. Ibid.

34. Richard Wike, Jacob Poushter, et al., "Trump Ratings Remain Low Around Globe, While Views of U.S. Stay Mostly Favorable," Pew Research Center, January 8, 2020, https://www .pewresearch.org/global/2020/01/08/ trump-ratings-remain-low-around-globe-while-views-of-u-s-stay-mostly-favorable/.

35. Christine Huang and Laura Silver, "U.S. Millennials Tend to Have Favorable Views of Foreign Countries and Institutions—Even as They Age," Pew Research Center, July 8, 2020, https://www.pewresearch.org/fact-tank/2020/07/08/u-s-millennials-tend-to-have-favorable-views-of-foreign-countries-and-institutions-even-as-they-age/.

36. Ibid.

37. Ibid.

38. Bethany Allen-Ebrahimian, "Timeline: The Early Days of China's Coronavirus Outbreak and Cover-Up," *Axios*, March 18, 2020, https://www.axios.com/timeline-the-early-days-of-chinas-coronavirus-outbreak-and-cover-up-ee65211a-afb6-4641-97b8-353718a5faab.html.

39. "COVID-19 Coronavirus Pandemic," Worldometer, accessed May 7, 2020, https://www.worldometers.info/coronavirus/#countries.

40. Ibid.

41. Sheryl Gay Stolberg and Eileen Sullivan, "As Trump Pushes to Reopen, Government Sees Virus Toll Nearly Doubling," *New York Times*, May 4, 2020, https://www.nytimes.com/2020/05/04/us/politics/trump-coronavirus-death-toll.html.

42. Nina Strochlic, "U.S. Coronavirus Deaths Now Surpass Fatalities in the Vietnam War," *National Geographic*, April 28, 2020, https://www.nationalgeographic.com/history/article/coronavirus-death-toll-vietnam-war-cvd. "COVID-19 United States Cases by County," accessed April 15, 2021, https://coronavirus.jhu.edu/us-map.

43. Heather Long and Andrew Van Dam, "U.S. Unemployment Rate Soars to 14.7 Percent, the Worst Since the Depression Era," *Washington Post*, May 8, 2020, https://www.washingtonpost.com/business/2020/05/08/april-2020-jobs-report/.

44. Ibid.

45. Joe Pinsker, "The Pandemic Will Cleave America in Two," *Atlantic*, April 10, 2020, https://www.theatlantic.com/family/archive/2020/04/two-pandemics-us-coronavirus-inequality/609622/.

46. Centers for Disease Control and Prevention, "REACH: CDC's Racial and Ethnic Approaches to Community Health Program," accessed May 11, 2020, https://www.cdc.gov/chronicdisease/resources/publications/factsheets/reach.htm.

47. Pinsker, "The Pandemic Will Cleave America in Two."

48. See the April 9, 2020, front page of the *New York Times* at https://static01.nyt.com/images/2020/04/08/nyt-frontpage/scannat.pdf.

49. Ben Poston, Tony Barboza, and Alejandra Reyes-Velarde, "Younger Blacks and Latinos Are Dying of COVID-at Higher Rates in California," *Los Angeles Times*, April 25, 2020, https://www.latimes.com/california/story/2020-04-25/coronavirus-takes-a-larger-toll-on-younger-african-americans-and-latinos-in-california.

50. John Eligon, Audra D. S. Burch, Dionne Searcey, and Richard A. Oppel Jr., "Black Americans Face Alarming Rates of Coronavirus Infection in Some States," *New York Times*, April 14, 2020, https://www.nytimes.com/2020/04/07/us/coronavirus-race.html.

51. Yasmeen Abutaleb, Anne Gearan, and John Wagner, "Top Health Officials War of Reopening's Perils," *Washington Post*, May 13, 2020, https://www.washingtonpost.com/national/coronavirus-warning-outbreaks-school/2020/05/12/17bf62d6-946a-11ea-82b4-c8db161ff6e5_story.html.

52. Linda Qiu, "Fact Check: President Trump's Repeated False Statements on Coronavirus—Underplaying Severity, Rewriting History, Blaming Others," *Chicago Tribune*, March 28, 2020, https://www.chicagotribune.com/coronavirus/ct-nw-nyt-fact-checking-

donald-trump-coronavirus-covid-19-20200328-jdzfeed5xngphefgyp-ou6spyra-story.html.

53. White House, "Remarks by President Trump at a USMCA Celebration with American Workers | Warren, MI," news release, January 30, 2020, https://www.whitehouse.gov/briefings-statements/remarks-president-trump-usmca-celebration-american-workers-warren-mi/.

54. White House, "Remarks by President Trump in Meeting with African American Leaders," news release, February 28, 2020, https://www.whitehouse.gov/briefings-statements/remarks-president-trump-meeting-african-american-leaders/.

55. Matthew J. Belvedere, "Trump Says He Trusts China's Xi on Coronavirus and the US Has It 'Totally Under Control,'" CNBC, January 22, 2020, https://www.cnbc.com/2020/01/22/trump-on-coronavirus-from-china-we-have-it-totally-under-control.html.

56. Linda Qiu, "Analyzing the Patterns in Trump's Falsehoods about Coronavirus," *New York Times*, March 27, 2020, https://www.nytimes.com/2020/03/27/us/politics/trump-coronavirus-factcheck.html.

57. Justin Wise, "Kudlow Claims Coronavirus Has Been Contained: 'It's Pretty Close to Air-Tight,'" *The Hill*, February 25, 2020, https://thehill.com/homenews/administration/484561-kudlow-claims-coronavirus-has-been-contained-its-pretty-close-to-air.

58. Ibid.

59. Qiu, "Analyzing the Patterns."

60. Lena H. Sun, "Top White House Official in Charge of Pandemic Response Exits Abruptly," *Washington Post*, May 10, 2018, https://www.washingtonpost.com/news/to-your-health/wp/2018/05/10/top-white-house-official-in-charge-of-pandemic-response-exits-abruptly/.

61. Toluse Olorunnipa, "Trump Tightens Grip on Coronavirus Information as He Pushes to Restart the Economy," *Washington Post*, May 7, 2020, https://www.washingtonpost.com/politics/trump-tightens-grip-on-coronavirus-information-as-he-pushes-to-restart-the-economy/2020/05/07/d4a05e42-9068-11ea-a9c0-73b93422d691_story.html.

62. Qiu, "Analyzing the Patterns."

63. David Frum, "This Is Trump's Fault," *Atlantic*, April 7, 2020, https://www.theatlantic.com/ideas/archive/2020/04/americans-are-paying-the-price-for-trumps-failures/609532/.

64. Tom McCarthy, "'It Will Disappear': The Disinformation Trump Spread about the Coronavirus—Timeline," *Guardian*, April 14, 2020, https://www.theguardian.com/us-news/2020/apr/14/trump-coronavirus-alerts-disinformation-timeline.

65. Robert Costa and Philip Rucker, "Woodward Book: Trump Says He Knew Coronavirus Was 'Deadly' and Worse Than the Flu While Intentionally Misleading Americans," *Washington Post*, September 9, 2020, https://www.washingtonpost.com/politics/bob-woodward-rage-book-trump/2020/09/09/0368fe3c-efd2-11ea-b4bc-3a2098fc73d4_story.html.

66. Adam Edelman, "'Life-and-Death Betrayal': Biden, Democrats Shred Trump Over Woodward Book Pandemic Revelations," NBC News, September 9, 2020, https://www.nbcnews.com/politics/2020-election/pelosi-democrats-shred-trump-over-woodward-book-pandemic-revelations-n1239673.

67. "Most Americans Say Trump Was Too Slow in Initial Response to Coronavirus Threat," Pew Research Center, April 16, 2020, https://www.people-press.org/2020/04/16/most-americans-say-trump-was-too-slow-in-

initial-response-to-coronavirus-threat/
pp_2020-04-16_trump-and-covid-
19_0-01/.

68. Ibid.

69. Tracy Conner, "Trump: Democrats' Coronavirus Criticism a 'New Hoax,'" *Daily Beast*, February 28, 2020, https://www.thedailybeast.com/trump-calls-democrats-coronavirus-criticism-a-new-hoax.

70. Nick Bilton, "Coronavirus Is Creating a Fake-News Nightmarescape," *Vanity Fair*, March 2, 2020, https://www.vanityfair.com/news/2020/03/corona-virus-is-creating-fake-news-nightmar-escape-social-media.

71. Donald J. Trump (@realDonaldTrump), "I never said the pandemic was a Hoax! Who would say such a thing? I said that the Do Nothing Democrats, together with their Mainstream Media partners, are the Hoax. They have been called out & embarrassed on this, even admitting they were wrong, but continue to spread the lie!," Twitter, April 25, 2020, 6:23 p.m., https://twitter.com/realdonaldtrump/status/1254174221481246721.

72. Bill McCarthy, "The President Who Cried Hoax? Experts Weigh in on Trump's Use of the Word," *PolitiFact*, April 1, 2020, https://www.politifact.com/article/2020/apr/01/president-who-cried-hoax-experts-weigh-trumps-use-/.

73. Ibid.

74. Oliver Darcy, "How Fox News Misled Viewers about the Coronavirus," CNN, March 12, 2020, https://www.cnn.com/2020/03/12/media/fox-news-coronavirus/index.html.

75. Aaron Rupar, "Hannity Claims He's 'Never Called the Virus a Hoax' 9 Days after Decrying Democrats' New Hoax,'" *Vox*, March 20, 2020, https://www.vox.com/2020/3/20/21186727/hannity-coronavirus-coverage-fox-news. Also,

see the video at Aaron Rupar (@atrupar), "HANNITY, March 9: 'This scaring the living hell out of people—I see it, again, as like, let's bludgeon Trump with this new hoax.' HANNITY, March 18: 'By the way, this program has always taken the coronavirus seriously. We've never called the virus a hoax,'" Twitter, March 19, 2020, 10:03 a.m., https://twitter.com/atrupar/status/1240640020714848257.

76. Oliver Darcy, "New Polls Show Effect of Right-Wing Media's Dismissive and Conspiratorial Coronavirus Coverage," CNN, March 18, 2020, https://www.cnn.com/2020/03/18/media/pew-study-coronavirus-media-coverage/index.html.

77. Justin McCarthy, "U.S. Coronavirus Concerns Surge, Government Trust Slides," *Gallup Blog*, March 16, 2020, https://news.gallup.com/poll/295505/coronavirus-worries-surge.aspx.

78. Amy Mitchell and J. Baxter Oliphant, "Americans Immersed in COVID-19 News; Most Think Media Are Doing Fairly Well Covering It," Pew Research Center, March 18, 2020, https://www.journalism.org/2020/03/18/americans-immersed-in-covid-19-news-most-think-media-are-doing-fairly-well-covering-it/.

79. Ibid.

80. Margaret Sullivan, "Surrounded by Experts, Trump Still Needed an Intervention by Tucker Carlson to Take Coronavirus Seriously," *Washington Post*, March 18, 2020, https://www.washingtonpost.com/lifestyle/media/surrounded-by-experts-trump-still-needed-an-intervention-by-tucker-carlson-to-take-coronavirus-seriously/2020/03/18/3cf67cb0-6922-11ea-9923-57073adce27c_story.html.

81. Journalism Professors, "Open Letter to the Murdochs," *Medium*, April 3,

2020, https://medium.com/@journalismprofs/open-letter-to-the-murdochs-9334e775a992.

82. Ibid.

83. Paul Bond, "Sean Hannity Defends Fox News After Journalism Professors Publish Critical Letter About Coronavirus Coverage," *Newsweek*, April 2, 2020, https://www.newsweek.com/sean-hannity-defends-fox-news-after-journalism-professors-publish-critical-letter-about-coronavirus-1495880.

84. Caleb Ecarma, "Fox News Is Preparing to Be Sued Over Coronavirus Misinformation," *Vanity Fair*, April 6, 2020, https://www.vanityfair.com/news/2020/04/fox-news-prepares-coronavirus-misinformation-lawsuits.

85. Kathleen Hall Jamieson and Dolores Albarracin, "The Relation Between Media Consumption and Misinformation at the Outset of the SARS-CoV-2 Pandemic in the US," *Harvard Kennedy School Misinformation Review*, April 20, 2020, https://misinforeview.hks.harvard.edu/article/the-relation-between-media-consumption-and-misinformation-at-the-outset-of-the-sars-cov-2-pandemic-in-the-us/.

86. Matthew Impelli, "Trump's Approval Rating Has Declined Most with Independents, Older Voters and Black Voters," *Newsweek*, May 13, 2020, https://www.newsweek.com/trumps-approval-rating-has-declined-most-independents-older-americans-black-voters-poll-finds-1503717.

87. Mara Liasson, "President Trump Changes His Reelection Pitch During the Coronavirus Crisis," National Public Radio, May 6, 2020, https://www.npr.org/2020/05/06/851631789/president-trump-changes-his-reelection-pitch-during-the-coronavirus-crisis. Also, David Smith, "Donald Trump Set to Fall Back on Xenophobia with Re-Election Plan in Tatters," *Guardian*, April 26, 2020, https://www.theguardian.com/us-news/2020/apr/26/donald-trump-xenophobia-re-election-campaign-2020.

88. Annie Karni, "Trump Re-Election Efforts Raise $212 Million for First Quarter of 2020," *New York Times*, April 27, 2020, https://www.nytimes.com/2020/04/13/us/politics/trump-fundraising-2020.html.

89. Shane Goldmacher, "Biden Faces a Cash Gap with Trump. He Has to Close It Virtually," *New York Times*, March 31, 2020, https://www.nytimes.com/2020/03/31/us/politics/biden-trump-campaign-fundraising.html.

90. Brian Schwartz, "Joe Biden Has Spent $500 Million on Ads This Year as He Seeks the Presidency," CNBC, October 9, 2020, https://www.cnbc.com/2020/10/09/joe-biden-hits-half-billion-dollar-mark-for-ads-in-trump-challenge.html.

91. Jeremy Page, Wenxin Fan, and Natasha Khan, "How It All Started: China's Early Coronavirus Missteps," *Wall Street Journal*, March 6, 2020, https://www.wsj.com/articles/how-it-all-started-chinas-early-coronavirus-missteps-11583508932.

92. Quint Forgey, "Trump on 'Chinese Virus' Label: 'It's Not Racist at All,'" *Politico*, March 18, 2020, https://www.politico.com/news/2020/03/18/trump-pandemic-drumbeat-coronavirus-135392.

93. Michael Martina and Trevor Hunnicutt, "Biden Says Trump Failed to Hold China Accountable on Coronavirus," Reuters, April 17, 2020, https://www.reuters.com/article/us-usa-election-china/biden-says-trump-failed-to-hold-china-accountable-on-coronavirus-idUSKBN21Z3DZ.

94. Ibid.
95. Jessica Xiao, "AAJA-HQ Commends Journalists Who Have Championed Coverage of AAPI Experiences during This Period of Increased Anti-Asian Incidents," Asian American Journalists Association, https://www.aaja.org/2021/03/16/aaja-hq-commends-journalists-who-have-championed-coverage-of-aapi-experiences-during-this-period-of-increased-anti-asian-incidents/.
96. John Schwartz, "Americans See Climate as a Concern, Even Amid Coronavirus Crisis," *New York Times*, May 19, 2020, https://www.nytimes.com/2020/05/19/climate/coronavirus-climate-change-survey.html.
97. Leiserowitz et al., "Climate Change in the American Mind."
98. Ibid.
99. Ibid.
100. Ibid.
101. Ibid.
102. Emily Holden, "The Media Is Failing on Climate Change—Here's How They Can Do Better Ahead of 2020," *Guardian*, April 30, 2019, https://www.theguardian.com/environment/2019/apr/30/what-will-it-take-for-the-media-to-focus-on-climate-change-in-the-2020-elections.
103. Katie Glueck and Lisa Friedman, "Biden Announces $2 Trillion Climate Plan," *New York Times*, July 14, 2020, https://www.nytimes.com/2020/07/14/us/politics/biden-climate-plan.html.
104. Ibid.
105. Ibid.
106. Andrew Tyndall, interview with the author, July 17, 2020.
107. Ibid.
108. Ibid.
109. Ibid.
110. See Committee to Protect Journalists at https://cpj.org/.
111. Andrew Kohut, "American International Engagement on the Rocks," Pew Research Center, July 11, 2013, http://www.pewglobal.org/2013/07/11/american-international-engagement-on-the-rocks/.
112. Christiane Amanpour, interview with the author, October 2001. This also comes from Hall, "Breaking News."
113. Ibid.
114. Anderson Cooper, interview with the author, October 19, 2013, Washington, DC.
115. Mark Landler, "For Obama, an Unexpected Legacy of Two Full Terms at War," *New York Times*, May 14, 2016, http://www.nytimes.com/2016/05/15/us/politics/obama-as-wartime-president-has-wrestled-with-protecting-nation-and-troops.html.
116. "Public Says U.S. Does Not Have Responsibility to Act in Syria," Pew Research Center, December 14, 2012, http://www.people-press.org/2012/12/14/public-says-u-s-does-not-have-responsibility-to-act-in-syria/.
117. Landler, "For Obama."
118. Mark Doyle, "Syria Most Dangerous Place in the World for Journalists," BBC News, August 20, 2014, http://www.bbc.com/news/world-middle-east-28865514.
119. Security Council, "Alarmed by Continuing Syria Crisis, Security Council Affirms Its Support for Special Envoy's Approach in Moving Political Solution Forward," United Nations, August 17, 2015, http://www.un.org/press/en/2015/sc12008.doc.htm.
120. Ban Ki-moon, "Crisis in Syria: Civil War, Global Threat," United Nations, June 25, 2014, http://www.un.org/sg/articles/articleFull.asp?TID=140&Type=Op-Ed&h=0.
121. AFP/Reuters, "Paris Attacks Death Toll Rises to 130," *RTÉ News*,

November 20, 2015, http://www.rte
.ie/news/2015/1120/747897-paris/.

122. Vivienne Walt, "ISIS Claims Responsibility for Paris Attacks as Arrests Are Made," *Time*, November 14, 2015, http://time.com/4112884/paris-attacks-isis-isil-france-francois-hollande/.

123. Maïa de La Baume, "French Planes Bomb ISIS Targets in Syria," *Politico*, November 15, 2015, http://www.politico.eu/article/french-planes-bomb-isis-targets-in-syria/.

124. Angelique Chrisafis, "Marine Le Pen's Front National Makes Political Gains after Paris Attacks," *Guardian*, December 1, 2015, http://www.theguardian.com/world/2015/dec/01/marine-le-pen-front-national-political-gains-paris-attacks.

125. Alicia Parlapiano et al., "Unraveling the Connections Among the Paris Attackers," *New York Times*, March 18, 2015, http://www.nytimes.com/interactive/2015/11/15/world/europe/manhunt-for-paris-attackers.html.

126. Author's monitoring of images on television and in print from coverage. Also, see Gregor Aisch et al., "Three Hours of Terror in Paris, Moment by Moment," *New York Times*, November 15, 2015, http://www.nytimes.com/interactive/2015/11/13/world/europe/paris-shooting-attacks.html.

127. "San Bernardino Shooting Updates," *Los Angeles Times*, December 9, 2015, http://www.latimes.com/local/lanow/la-me-ln-san-bernardino-shooting-live-updates-htmlstory.html.

128. Office of the Press Secretary, "Address to the Nation by the President," news release, December 6, 2015, https://www.whitehouse.gov/the-press-office/2015/12/06/address-nation-president.

129. Richard A. Serrano, "FBI Chief: San Bernardino Shooters Did Not Publicly Promote Jihad on Social Media," *Los Angeles Times*, December 16, 2015, http://www.latimes.com/nation/la-ln-fbi-san-bernardino-social-media-20151216-story.html.

130. Oren Dorell, "Muslims Report More Bias Cases across USA," *USA Today*, December 9, 2015, http://www.usatoday.com/story/news/2015/12/08/us-muslims-report-more-bias-cases-across-nation/76982412/.

131. Jenna Johnson, "Trump Calls for 'Total and Complete Shutdown of Muslims Entering the United States,'" *Washington Post*, December 7, 2015, https://www.washingtonpost.com/news/post-politics/wp/2015/12/07/donald-trump-calls-for-total-and-complete-shutdown-of-muslims-entering-the-united-states/.

132. Peter Cook, "Department of Defense Press Briefing by Pentagon Press Secretary Peter Cook in the Pentagon Briefing Room," news release, December 8, 2015, http://www.defense.gov/News/News-Transcripts/Transcript-View/Article/633414/department-of-defense-press-briefing-by-pentagon-press-secretary-peter-cook-in.

133. Seth G. Jones, Catrina Doxsee, and Nicholas Harrington, "The Escalating Terrorism Problem in the United States," Center for Strategic and International Studies, June 17, 2020, https://www.csis.org/analysis/escalating-terrorism-problem-united-states.

134. Frank Newport, "Gallup Review: U.S. Public Opinion on Terrorism," *Gallup Blog*, November 17, 2015, http://www.gallup.com/opinion/polling-matters/186665/gallup-review-public-opinion-terrorism.aspx.

135. Ibid.

136. David L. Altheide, *Creating Fear: News and the Construction of Crisis* (New York: Aldine de Gruyter, 2002), IX–X.

137. Ibid.

138. Barry Glassner, *The Culture of Fear: Why Americans Are Afraid of the Wrong Things* (New York: Basic Books, 2010). Also, Brigitte L. Nacos, Yaeli Bloch-Elkon, and Robert Y. Shapiro, *Selling Fear: Counterterrorism, the Media, and Public Opinion* (Chicago: University Chicago Press, 2011).

139. Ibid.

140. Zbigniew Brzezinski, "Terrorized by 'War on Terror,'" *Washington Post*, March 25, 2007, http://www.washingtonpost.com/wp-dyn/content/article/2007/03/23/AR2007032301613.html.

141. Zeke J. Miller and Alex Rogers, "GOP Ad Claims ISIS Plot to Attack U.S. Via 'Arizona's Backyard,'" *Time*, October 7, 2014, https://time.com/3478254/isis-nrcc-border-plot-gop-2014/.

142. "Almost All Adults Remember Exactly When They Heard about Sept. 11 Attacks," Pew Research Center, September 10, 2012, http://www.pewresearch.org/daily-number/almost-all-adults-remember-exactly-when-they-heard-about-sept-11-attacks/.

143. Ibid.

144. "United in Remembrance, Divided over Policies," Pew Research Center, September 1, 2011, http://www.people-press.org/2011/09/01/united-in-remembrance-divided-over-policies/.

145. Jonathan Rauch, "Be Not Afraid," *Atlantic*, March 2015, http://www.theatlantic.com/magazine/archive/2015/03/be-not-afraid/384965/.

146. Saifuddin Ahmed and Jorg Matthes, "Media Representation of Muslims and Islam From 2000 to 2015: A Meta-Analysis," *International Communication Gazette* 79, no. 3 (2017).

147. Gabriel Arana, "Islamophobic Media Coverage Is out of Control. It Needs to Stop," *Huffington Post*, November 19, 2015, http://www.huffingtonpost.com/entry/islamophobia-mainstream-media-paris-terrorist-attacks_us_564cb277e4b08c74b7339984.

148. Ibid.

149. Media Tenor, "Terror and Fear Shape the Image of Islam," news release, December 22, 2015, http://us.mediatenor.com/en/library/newsletters/798/terror-and-fear-shape-the-image-of-islam.

150. Ibid.

151. Office of the Press Secretary, "'Islam Is Peace' Says President," news release, September 17, 2001, https://georgewbush-whitehouse.archives.gov/news/releases/2001/09/20010917-11.html.

152. Ibid. Also, see Bridge Initiative Team, "New Study Analyzes Media Coverage of Islam over Time," Bridge Initiative, April 24, 2015, http://bridge.georgetown.edu/new-study-analyzes-media-coverage-of-islam-over-time/.

153. Erik Bleich and A. Maurits van der Veen, "Media Portrayals of Muslims: A Comparative Sentiment Analysis of American Newspapers, 1996–2015," *Politics, Groups, and Identities* (2018).

154. Ibid.

155. Akbar Ahmed, interview with the author, April 14, 2008, in "Islamophobia in the Media," WAMU. Also, see Akbar Ahmed, *Journey into Islam: The Crisis of Globalization* (Washington, DC: Brookings Institution Press, 2007).

156. Wesley Lowery, Kimberly Kindy, and Andrew Ba Tran, "In the United States, Right-Wing Violence Is on the Rise," *Washington Post*, November 25, 2018, https://www

.washingtonpost.com/national/in-the-united-states-right-wing-violence-is-on-the-rise/2018/11/25/61f7f24a-deb4-11e8-85df-7a6b4d25cfbb_story.html.

157. Eleanor Dearman, "Racism and the Aug. 3 Shooting: One Year Later, El Paso Reflects on the Hate behind the Attack," *El Paso Times*, August 1, 2020, https://www.elpasotimes.com/in-depth/news/2020/07/30/el-paso-walmart-shooting-community-reflect-racist-motive-behind-attack/5450331002/.

158. Ibid.

159. Jones, Doxsee, and Harrington, "The Escalating Terrorism Problem."

160. Ibid.

161. Zolan Kanno-Youngs, "Delayed Homeland Security Report Warns of 'Lethal' White Supremacy," *New York Times*, October 6, 2020, https://www.nytimes.com/2020/10/06/us/politics/homeland-security-white-supremacists-russia.html.

162. Ibid.

163. Dearman, "Racism and the Aug. 3 Shooting."

164. Louise Matsakis, "Pittsburgh Synagogue Shooting Suspect's Gab Posts Are Part of a Pattern," *Wired*, October 27, 2018, https://www.wired.com/story/pittsburgh-synagogue-shooting-gab-tree-of-life/.

165. Isabella Kwai, "White Supremacist Who Admitted Christchurch Killings Plans to Represent Himself," *New York Times*, August 26, 2020, https://www.nytimes.com/2020/07/13/world/australia/christchurch-mosque-killings-sentencing.html.

166. This timeline draws from Michael Massing's book, *Now They Tell Us: The American Press and Iraq* (New York: New York Review of Books, 2004). This article made the front page and is available at Michael R. Gordon and Judith Miller, "U.S. Says Hussein Intensifies Quest for A-Bomb Parts," *New York Times*, September 8, 2002, http://www.nytimes.com/2002/09/08/world/threats-responses-iraqis-us-says-hussein-intensifies-quest-for-bomb-parts.html.

167. Ibid.

168. Ibid.

169. Ibid.

170. Michael Massing, "Now They Tell Us," *New York Review of Books*, February 26, 2004, http://www.nybooks.com/articles/2004/02/26/now-they-tell-us/. Also, see Office of the Press Secretary, "Vice President Speaks at VFW 103rd National Convention," news release, August 26, 2002, https://georgewbush-whitehouse.archives.gov/news/releases/2002/08/20020826.html.

171. Wolf Blitzer, "Search for the 'Smoking Gun,'" CNN, January 10, 2003, http://www.cnn.com/2003/US/01/10/wbr.smoking.gun/.

172. "2nd Plenary Meeting," ed. United Nations General Assembly, September 12, 2002, https://documents-dds-ny.un.org/doc/UNDOC/GEN/N02/586/90/PDF/N0258690.pdf?OpenElement.

173. Miles O'Brien, "Ex-Inspector: Iraq Not Pursuing Nuclear Arms," CNN, September 8, 2002, http://www.cnn.com/2002/WORLD/meast/09/08/ritter.cnna/.

174. Todd S. Purdum and Patrick E. Tyler, "Top Republicans Break with Bush on Iraq Strategy," *New York Times*, August 16, 2002, http://www.nytimes.com/2002/08/16/world/top-republicans-break-with-bush-on-iraq-strategy.html.

175. Jonathan S. Landay, "Lack of Hard Evidence of Iraqi Weapons Worries Top U.S. Officials," McClatchy

DC, September 6, 2002, http://www
.mcclatchydc.com/news/special-
reports/iraq-intelligence/article
24433348.html.

176. Ibid.

177. Massing, "Now They Tell Us."

178. Ibid.

179. "From the Editors; the *Times* and Iraq," *New York Times*, May 26, 2004, http:// www.nytimes.com/2004/05/26/world/ from-the-editors-the-times-and-iraq .html.

180. Ibid.

181. For an account by a Bush administration counterterrorism official, see Richard A. Clarke, *Against All Enemies: Inside America's War on Terror* (New York: Free Press, 2004).

182. Linda J. Bilmes, "The Financial Legacy of Iraq and Afghanistan: How Wartime Spending Decisions Will Constrain Future National Security Budgets" (working paper, Harvard Kennedy School, Harvard University, Cambridge, MA, March 2013).

183. Jane Hall, "Commentary on Patriotism," *Harvard International Journal of Press/Politics* 7, no. 2 (2002).

184. This is based on the author's observation and research.

185. Steven Kull, "The Press and Public Misperceptions about the Iraq War," *Nieman Reports*, April 2004, http:// niemanreports.org/articles/the-press-and-public-misperceptions-about-the-iraq-war/.

186. Bill Moyers, "Buying the War," PBS, April 25, 2007, http://www.pbs .org/moyers/journal/btw/transcript1 .html.

187. Robert M. Entman, *Projections of Power: Framing News, Public Opinion, and U.S. Foreign Policy* (Chicago: University of Chicago Press, 2004).

188. Ibid.

189. Jonathan Landay, interview with the author, 2002.

190. Charles Silver, "Why We Fight: Frank Capra's WWII Propaganda Films," *Inside/Out* (blog) *Moma/Moma PS1*, June 7, 2011, http://www.moma.org/ explore/inside_out/2011/06/07/why-we-fight-frank-capras-wwii-propaganda-films/.

191. Connie Field, "The Life and Times of Rosie the Riveter" (1980).

192. Specifically, see page 134 in George H. Roeder Jr., *The Censored War*, 134. *American Visual Experience during World War Two* (New Haven, CT: Yale University, 1993).

193. Ibid.

194. MJ Bear and Jane Hall, "Summary Findings and Survey Results of Online Survey of Journalists and News Organizations in Iraq Regarding Issues of Self-Censorship in Iraq War Coverage," American University, March 17, 2005.

195. See Michael Arlen, *Living-Room War* (Syracuse, NY: Syracuse University Press, 1997).

196. Stanley Karnow, *Vietnam: A History*, 2nd ed. (New York: Penguin Books, 1997).

197. Daniel C. Hallin, *The "Uncensored War": The Media and Vietnam* (New York: Oxford University Press, 1986).

198. See David Halberstam, *The Powers That Be* (New York: Open Road Media, 2012).

199. CBS News and Associated Press, "Highlights of Some Cronkite Broadcasts," CBS News, July 17, 2009, http://www.cbsnews.com/news/highlights-of-some-cronkite-broadcasts/.

200. Karnow, *Vietnam: A History*.

201. Jed Duvall, interview with the author, 1999.

202. Bryan Whitman, interview with the author, February 24, 2004. Whitman was also interviewed for Jane Hall, "The Fire Next Time: Fighting the Next War," *Harvard International Journal of Press/Politics* 9, no. 3 (2004).

203. Robert Hodierne, interviews with the author, December 18, 2003, and February 18, 2004. See Hall, "The Fire Next Time."

204. Ibid.

205. John Donvan, interview with the author, December 11, 2003. Donvan was also interviewed for Hall, "The Fire Next Time."

206. Ibid.

207. Vago Muradian, interviews with the author, December 11, 2003, and February 19, 2004. Muradian was also interviewed for Hall, "The Fire Next Time."

208. Ibid.

209. Hodierne, interviews with the author, December 18, 2003, and February 18, 2004. Also, Hall, "The Fire Next Time."

210. Morley Safer, interview with the author, November 20, 2003. Safer was also interviewed for Hall, "The Fire Next Time."

Chapter 8

1. Kelly Dittmar, "Watching Election 2016 With a Gender Lens," PS: Political Science & Politics 49, no. 4 (October 2016).

2. Susan Page, "Why Are You Yelling? The Questions Female Candidates Still Face," USA Today, June 5, 2016, https://www.usatoday.com/story/news/politics/elections/2016/06/05/hillary-clinton-female-candidates-political-landscape-democrat-president/85343998/.

3. Ibid.

4. Megan Garber, "The Sexism Is Getting Sneakier," Atlantic, November 13, 2019, https://www.theatlantic.com/entertainment/archive/2019/11/elizabeth-warren-and-sneak-sexism/601876/.

5. David A. Fahrenthold, "Trump Recorded Having Extremely Lewd Conversation about Women in 2005," Washington Post, October 8, 2016, https://www.washingtonpost.com/politics/trump-recorded-having-extremely-lewd-conversation-about-women-in-2005/2016/10/07/3b9ce776-8cb4-11e6-bf8a-3d26847eeed4_story.html.

6. Dittmar, "Watching Election 2016."

7. Ibid.

8. Georgia Duerst-Lahti, "Reconceiving Theories of Power: Consequences of Masculinism in the Executive Branch," in The Other Elites: Women, Politics, and Power in the Executive Branch, ed. MaryAnne Borrelli and Janet M. Martin (Boulder, CO: Lynne Rienner Publishers, 1997).

9. Douglas Martin, "She Ended the Men's Club of National Politics," New York Times, March 26, 2011, http://www.nytimes.com/2011/03/27/us/politics/27geraldine-ferraro.html.

10. Lucina Di Meco, "#ShePersisted: Women, Politics & Power in the New Media World," (Wilson Center, Fall 2019), https://static1.squarespace.com/static/5dba105f102367021c44b63f/t/5dc431aac6bd4e7913c45f7d/1573138953986/191106+SHEPERSISTED_Final.pdf.

11. Alexander Frandsen and Aleszu Bajak, "Women on the 2020 Campaign Trail Are Being Treated More Negatively by the Media," Storybench, April 24, 2019, https://www.storybench.org/women-on-the-2020-campaign-trail-are-being-treated-more-negatively-by-the-media/.

12. Ibid.

13. Joanne Lipman, "Amy Klobuchar's 'Surge' Proves Media Still Has a 'Woman' Problem," USA Today, February 16, 2020, https://www.usatoday.com/story/opinion/2020/02/14/

amy-klobuchars-surge-shows-gender-inequality-sexism-media-men-majority-column/4754230002/.

14. Di Meco, "#ShePersisted."

15. Women in the World, "Hillary Clinton's Full Interview at the 2017 Women in the World Summit," April 6, 2017, video, 54:44, https://youtu.be/aI0iLIwfa2w.

16. Ibid.

17. Kathy Frankovic, "Elizabeth Warren Is Now Among Democratic Front Runners," *YouGov*, May 29, 2019, https://today.yougov.com/topics/politics/articles-reports/2019/05/29/elizabeth-warren-democratic-front-runner.

18. Annie Linskey and Amy B. Wang, "Elizabeth Warren's Exit Raises Questions about the Role of Women in U.S. Politics," *Washington Post*, March 5, 2020, https://www.washingtonpost.com/politics/sen-elizabeth-warren-ends-presidential-campaign/2020/03/05/98921986-4d33-11ea-9b5c-eac5b16dafaa_story.html.

19. Ibid.

20. Shane Goldmacher and Astead W. Herndon, "Elizabeth Warren, Once a Front-Runner, Drops Out of Presidential Race," *New York Times*, March 10, 2020, https://www.nytimes.com/2020/03/05/us/politics/elizabeth-warren-drops-out.html.

21. Marina Pitofsky, "Warren Says She Was Trying to End Bloomberg's Campaign with Debate Attacks," *The Hill*, March 6, 2020, https://thehill.com/homenews/campaign/486266-warren-says-she-was-trying-to-end-bloombergs-campaign-with-debate-attacks.

22. Goldmacher and Herndon, "Elizabeth Warren."

23. Michael Barbaro, featuring Astead W. Herndon, "The Field: What Happened to Elizabeth Warren?," *The Daily*, podcast audio, March 10, 2020, https://www.iheart.com/podcast/326-the-daily-28076606/episode/the-field-what-happened-to-elizabeth-58987124/.

24. Natalie Daher, "#ThankYouElizabeth: Warren Drops Out, and Tributes Come Pouring In," Now This, March 5, 2020, https://nowthisnews.com/politics/elizabeth-warren-drops-out-of-democratic-primary-tributes-pour-in.

25. Linskey and Wang, "Elizabeth Warren's Exit."

26. Molly Hensley-Clancy, "Staffers, Documents Show Amy Klobuchar's Wrath toward Her Aides," *BuzzFeed News*, February 8, 2019, https://www.buzzfeednews.com/article/mollyhensleyclancy/amy-klobuchar-staff-2020-election.

27. This is based on the author's observations.

28. Jodi Kantor and Tachel L. Swarns, "A New Twist in the Debate on Mothers," *New York Times*, September 1, 2008, https://www.nytimes.com/2008/09/02/us/politics/02mother.html.

29. Virginia García Beaudoux, "Five Ways the Media Hurts Female Politicians—and How Journalists Everywhere Can Do Better," *The Conversation*, January 18, 2017, https://theconversation.com/five-ways-the-media-hurts-female-politicians-and-how-journalists-everywhere-can-do-better-70771.

30. See Kathleen Hall Jamieson, *Beyond the Double Bind: Women and Leadership* (New York: Oxford University Press, 1995).

31. Ibid., 16.

32. Ibid., 25.

33. Ibid., 27.

34. Also, see Diana B. Carlin and Kelly L. Winfrey, "Have You Come a Long Way, Baby? Hillary Clinton, Sarah Palin, and Sexism in 2008 Campaign

Coverage," *Communication Studies* 60, no. 4 (July 28,2009) 326-343.

35. Sarah Gershon, "When Race, Gender, and the Media Intersect: Campaign News Coverage of Minority Congresswomen," *Journal of Women, Politics & Policy* 33, no. 2 (2012).

36. William Cummings, "Mia Love Slams Trump, Says GOP Paid Price for Not Letting Minorities 'Into Their Hearts,'" *USA Today*, November 27, 2018, https://www.usatoday.com/story/news/politics/elections/2018/11/26/mia-love-donald-trump-rebuke/2117629002/.

37. ABC News, "Barack Obama Tells Hillary Clinton She's 'Likeable Enough,'" video, October 12, 2015, 1:58, https://abcnews.go.com/Politics/video/barack-obama-tells-hillary-clinton-shes-likeable-34428886.

38. Celinda Lake, interview with the author, February 27, 2019.

39. Ibid.

40. Ryan Chiachiere, "Tucker Carlson on Clinton: '[W]Hen She Comes on Television, I Involuntarily Cross My Legs,'" *Media Matters for America*, July 18, 2007, https://www.mediamatters.org/research/2007/07/18/tucker-carlson-on-clinton-when-she-comes-on-tel/139362.

41. Ali Vitali, "Hillary Clinton Mask on Pole, Bullseye Poster Seen at Trump Rally," NBC News, October 22, 2016, https://www.nbcnews.com/card/hillary-clinton-mask-pole-bullseye-poster-seen-trump-rally-n671261.

42. Tessa Berenson, "Watch Donald Trump Call Hillary Clinton a 'Nasty Woman,'" *Time*, October 20, 2016, http://time.com/4537960/donald-trump-hillary-clinton-nasty-woman-debate/.

43. Barbara Lee Family Foundation, "Politics Is Personal: Keys to Likeability and Electability for Women" (April 2016), https://www.barbaraleefoundation.org/wp-content/uploads/BLFF-Likeability-Memo-FINAL.pdf.

44. Robin Givhan, "Condoleezza Rice's Commanding Clothes," *Washington Post*, February 25, 2005, http://www.washingtonpost.com/wp-dyn/articles/A51640-2005Feb24.html.

45. Ibid.

46. See Jane Hall, "Hillary and Liddy," *Media Studies Journal* 14, no. 1 (Winter 2000).

47. Brianna Ehley, "Clinton Dismisses Priebus' 'No Smile' Criticism," *Politico*, September 9, 2016, https://www.politico.com/story/2016/09/clinton-comments-no-smile-rnc-227879.

48. Sophia Tesfaye, "'Smile. You Just Had a Big Night': Joe Scarborough Responds to Hillary Clinton's Victorious Election Night in the Most Annoying Way Possible," *Salon*, March 16, 2016, https://www.salon.com/test/2016/03/16/smile_you_just_had_a_big_night_joe_scarborough_responds_to_hillary_clintons_victorious_election_night_in_the_most_annoying_way_possible/.

49. CNN, "Trump: Clinton Such a Nasty Woman," October 19, 2016, video, 0:43, https://youtu.be/Q2KOQfZ0Zd0.

50. Michael Kranish, "Dole Withdraws from Presidential Race," *Boston Globe*, October 21, 1999, A13.

51. Ibid.

52. Maureen Dowd, "Liberties; No Free War," *New York Times*, March 31, 1999, http://www.nytimes.com/1999/03/31/opinion/liberties-no-free-war.html. Also Arianna Huffington, "The Unbearable Lightness of Libby," Arianna Online, March 15, 1999.

53. This statement is based on the author's examination of news coverage of

Elizabeth Dole, Steve Forbes, George W. Bush, and John McCain in the race in 2000. See Hall, "Hillary and Liddy."

54. Caroline Heldman, Susan J. Carroll, and Stephanie Olson, "Gender Differences in Print Media Coverage of Presidential Candidates: Elizabeth Dole's Bid for the Republican Nomination," in Annual Meeting of the American Political Science Association (Washington, DC: Rutgers University, August 31–September 3, 2000).

55. Richard L. Berke, "As Political Spouse, Bob Dole Strays from Campaign Script," New York Times, May 17, 1999, A1.

56. David Von Drehle and Dan Balz, "Dole Enlists Husband to Raise Funds," Washington Post, September 25, 1999, A1.

57. Sean Aday and James Devitt, "Style Over Substance: Newspaper Coverage of Elizabeth Dole's Presidential Bid," The Harvard International Journal of Press/Politics 6, no. 2 (March 1, 2001).

58. Heldman, Carroll, and Olson, "Gender Differences."

59. This statement is based on the author's examination of coverage of the 2000 campaign.

60. Ibid.

61. Beth Fouhy, interview with the author, October 15, 1999, on "American Forum" at American University, Washington, DC. Also Hall, "Hillary and Liddy."

62. Eddie Mahe, interview with the author, October 15, 1999. Also, Hall, "Hillary and Liddy."

63. Richard L. Berke, interview with the author, September 9, 1999. Also Hall, "Hillary and Liddy."

64. Gallup News Service, "Majority of Americans Say More Women in Political Office Would Be Positive for the Country," Gallup Blog, January 4, 2001, http://news.gallup.com/poll/2143/

majority-americans-say-more-women-political-office-would-posi.aspx.

65. Ibid.

66. Richard L. Berke, interview with the author, September 7, 1999. Also Hall, "Hillary and Liddy."

67. World Economic Forum, "The Global Gender Gap Report 2016" (2016), http://www3.weforum.org/docs/GGGR16/WEF_Global_Gender_Gap_Report_2016.pdf. Also, see Uri Friedman, "Why It's So Hard for a Woman to Become President of the United States," Atlantic, November 12, 2016, https://www.theatlantic.com/international/archive/2016/11/clinton-woman-leader-world/506945/.

68. Laura Liswood, "Is 2008 the Year of the Woman President of the United States?" (presentation, Council of Women World Leaders, Aspen Institute, Washington, DC, July 20, 2005).

69. Ibid.

70. Pippa Norris, "Women Leaders Worldwide: A Splash of Color in the Photo Op," in Women, Media, and Politics, ed. Pippa Norris (New York: Oxford University Press, 1997) 149–166.

71. Ibid.

72. Laura Liswood, interview with the author, August 2005.

73. Liswood, "Is 2008 the Year of the Woman President of the United States?"

74. Eleanor Clift and Tom Brazaitis, Madam President: Shattering the Last Glass Ceiling (New York: Routledge, 2003), 90.

75. Ibid.

76. Eleanor Clift (remarks, Council of Women World Leaders, Aspen Institute, Washington, DC, July 20, 2005). Also, Eleanor Clift, interview with the author, July 2005.

77. Rodger Streitmatter, Mightier Than the Sword: How the News Media Have

Shaped American History (Boulder, CO: Westview Press, 1997), 37.

78. Ibid., 38.

79. For history of the women's suffrage movement, see Eleanor Flexner and Ellen Fitzpatrick, *Century of Struggle: The Woman's Rights Movement in the United States*, Third Revised ed. (Cambridge, MA: Belknap Press, 1996). Also, see Eleanor Clift, *Founding Sisters and the Nineteenth Amendment* (Hoboken, NJ: John Wiley & Sons, Inc., 2003). Also, see—as a companion book to a PBS documentary about Elizabeth Cady Stanton and Susan B. Anthony—Geoffrey C. Ward and Kenneth Burns, *Not for Ourselves Alone: The Story of Elizabeth Cady Stanton and Susan B. Anthony* (New York: Alfred A. Knopf, 1999).

80. "The Woman's Rights Convention— The Last Act of the Drama," *New York Herald*, September 12, 1852, 2 as cited in Streitmatter, *Mightier Than the Sword*, 41.

81. U.S. House of Representatives, "The Year of the Woman, 1992," https:// history.house.gov/Exhibitions-and-Publications/WIC/Historical-Essays/ Assembling-Amplifying-Ascending/ Women-Decade/.

82. Romesh Ratnesar, "Dianne Feinstein Goes Her Own Way," *Stanford Magazine*, November 10, 2017, https://stanfordmag.org/contents/ dianne-feinstein-goes-her-own-way.

83. Sen. Susan Collins (remarks, Kennedy Political Union, American University, Washington, DC, September 8, 2016).

84. Linskey and Wang, "Elizabeth Warren's Exit."

85. Center for American Women and Politics, Eagleton Institute of Politics, "Women in the U.S. Congress 2018," https://cawp.rutgers.edu/women-us-congress-2018.

86. Ibid.

87. Danny Lewis, "Victoria Woodhull Ran for President Before Women Had the Right to Vote," *Smithsonian*, May 10, 2016, https://www.smithsonianmag .com/smart-news/victoria-woodhull-ran-for-president-before-women-had-the-right-to-vote-180959038/. Also, see Ellen Fitzpatrick, *The Highest Glass Ceiling: Women's Quest for the American Presidency* (Cambridge, MA: Harvard University Press, 2016).

88. Biography.com, "Shirley Chisholm Biography," A&E Television Networks, https://www.biography.com/people/ shirley-chisholm-9247015. Also, see Shirley Chisholm, *Unbought and Unbossed* (United States: Take Root Media, 2010).

89. Jennifer L. Lawless and Richard L. Fox, *It Takes a Candidate: Why Women Don't Run for Office* (New York: Cambridge University Press, 2005), 13. Also, Jennifer L. Lawless and Richard L. Fox, *It Still Takes a Candidate: Why Women Don't Run for Office* (New York: Cambridge University Press, 2010).

90. Jennifer L. Lawless and Richard L. Fox, "Men Rule: The Continued Under-Representation of Women in U.S. Politics" (Washington, DC: Women & Politics Institute, School of Public Affairs, American University, January 2012), https://www.american.edu/spa/ wpi/upload/2012-men-rule-report-final-web.pdf, ii.

91. Ibid.

92. Ibid.

93. Karen Defilippi, interview with the author, September 10, 2020.

94. Dana Milbank, "A Thank-You for 18 Million Cracks in the Glass Ceiling," *Washington Post*, June 8, 2008, http:// www.washingtonpost.com/wp-dyn/ content/article/2008/06/07/ AR2008060701879.html.

95. See *Washington Post* and ABC News, "*Washington Post*-ABC News Poll September 19–22, 2016," *Washington Post*, September 28, 2016, https://www.washingtonpost.com/politics/polling/washington-postabc-news-poll-september-1922/2016/09/28/9fff3186-82d4-11e6-9578-558cc125c7ba_page.html.

96. Matt Zapotosky and Rosalind S. Helderman, "FBI Recommends No Criminal Charges in Clinton Email Probe," *Washington Post*, July 5, 2016, https://www.washingtonpost.com/world/national-security/fbi-chief-plans-remarks-to-media-amid-heightened-focus-on-clinton-email-probe/2016/07/05/a53513c4-42b9-11e6-bc99-7d269f8719b1_story.html.

97. Amy Chozick and Patrick Healy, "'This Changes Everything': Donald Trump Exults as Hillary Clinton's Team Scrambles," *New York Times*, October 28, 2016, https://www.nytimes.com/2016/10/29/us/politics/donald-trump-hillary-clinton.html.

98. CNN Library, "2016 Presidential Campaign Hacking Fast Facts," *CNN*, February 21, 2018, https://www.cnn.com/2016/12/26/us/2016-presidential-campaign-hacking-fast-facts/index.html.

99. Nate Silver, "The Comey Letter Probably Cost Clinton the Election," *FiveThirtyEight*, May 3, 2017, https://fivethirtyeight.com/features/the-comey-letter-probably-cost-clinton-the-election/.

100. Scott Clement and Emily Guskin, "Only 2 Points Separate Clinton, Trump in Latest Tracking Poll," *Washington Post*, October 29, 2016, https://www.washingtonpost.com/news/the-fix/wp/2016/10/29/linton-47-trump-45-in-post-abc-tracking-poll/.

101. Hillary Rodham Clinton, *What Happened* (New York: Simon & Schuster, 2017).

102. Chris Cillizza, "Hillary Clinton Just Delivered a Stunning Indictment of the 2016 Election—and Donald Trump," CNN, May 2, 2017, https://www.cnn.com/2017/05/02/politics/hillary-clinton-donald-trump/index.html.

103. Rebecca Traister, "Citizen Clinton," *NY Magazine*, May 29–June 11, 2017.

104. Ibid. Also, Gersh Kuntzman, "Hillary Clinton Shouldn't Be Writing a Book — She Should Be Drafting a Long Apology to America," *NY Daily News*, May 2, 2017, http://www.nydailynews.com/news/politics/hillary-clinton-book-apology-article-1.3130675.

105. Thomas E. Patterson, "News Coverage of the 2016 General Election: How the Press Failed the Voters," *Shorenstein Center, Harvard University*, December 7, 2016, https://shorensteincenter.org/news-coverage-2016-general-election/.

106. Jim Rutenberg, "RT, Sputnik and Russia's New Theory of War," *New York Times Magazine*, September 13, 2017, https://www.nytimes.com/2017/09/13/magazine/rt-sputnik-and-russias-new-theory-of-war.html. Also, Tom McCarthy, "How Russia Used Social Media to Divide Americans," *Guardian*, October 14, 2017, https://www.theguardian.com/us-news/2017/oct/14/russia-us-politics-social-media-facebook.

107. Duncan J. Watts and David M. Rothschild, "Don't Blame the Election on Fake News. Blame It on the Media," *Columbia Journalism Review*, December 5, 2017, https://www.cjr.org/analysis/fake-news-media-election-trump.php.

108. Ibid.

109. Andrew Dugan and Justin McCarthy, "Hillary Clinton's Favorable

Rating One of Her Worst," *Gallup Blog*, September 4, 2015, http://news.gallup.com/poll/185324/hillary-clinton-favorable-rating-one-worst.aspx.

110. Andrew Dugan, "Clinton's Status with Independents, GOP Comes Full Circle," *Gallup Blog*, August 4, 2015, http://news.gallup.com/opinion/polling-matters/184469/clinton-status-independents-gop-comes-full-circle.aspx. Also, *Washington Post* and ABC News, "*Washington Post*-ABC News Poll September 19–22, 2016."

111. Michael Kranish, "Hillary Clinton Regrets Her Iraq Vote. But Opting for Intervention Was a Pattern," *Washington Post*, September 15, 2016, https://www.washingtonpost.com/politics/hillary-clinton-regrets-her-iraq-vote-but-opting-for-intervention-was-a-pattern/2016/09/15/760c23d0-6645-11e6-96c0-37533479f3f5_story.html.

112. Nina Bahadur, "22 Sexist Things President Donald Trump Has Said about Women," *Self*, June 29, 2017, https://www.self.com/story/sexist-president-donald-trump-comments.

113. Aaron Blake, "Here Are the Megyn Kelly Questions That Donald Trump Is Still Sore about," *Washington Post*, January 26, 2016, https://www.washingtonpost.com/news/the-fix/wp/2016/01/26/here-are-the-megyn-kelly-questions-that-donald-trump-is-still-sore-about/.

114. Holly Yan, "Donald Trump's 'Blood' Comment about Megyn Kelly Draws Outrage," CNN, August 8, 2015, https://www.cnn.com/2015/08/08/politics/donald-trump-cnn-megyn-kelly-comment/index.html.

115. Ahiza Garcia, "Read Donald Trump's Tweets about Megyn Kelly and Fox's Response," CNN, March 19, 2016, http://money.cnn.com/2016/03/19/media/donald-trump-megyn-kelly-tweets-fox/index.html.

116. Megyn Kelly, *Settle for More* (New York: HarperCollins, 2016).

117. Garcia, "Read Donald Trump's Tweets."

118. Glenn Thrush and Maggie Haberman, "Trump Mocks Mika Brzezinski; Says She Was 'Bleeding Badly from a Face-Lift,'" *New York Times*, June 29, 2017, https://www.nytimes.com/2017/06/29/business/media/trump-mika-brzezinski-facelift.html.

119. Ibid.

120. Paul Solotaroff, "Trump Seriously: On the Trail with the GOP's Tough Guy," *Rolling Stone*, September 9, 2015, https://www.rollingstone.com/politics/news/trump-seriously-20150909.

121. *Variety* Staff, "Carly Fiorina Gets Huge Applause Responding to Trump's 'Face' Attack (Watch)," *Variety*, September 16, 2015, http://variety.com/2015/tv/news/carly-fiorina-gets-huge-applause-responding-to-trumps-face-attack-watch-1201595583/.

122. Ibid.

123. Katie Zezima, "Carly Fiorina Swipes at Trump: 'Look at This Face,'" *Washington Post*, September 11, 2015, https://www.washingtonpost.com/news/post-politics/wp/2015/09/11/carly-fiorina-swipes-at-trump-look-at-this-face/.

124. Fahrenthold, "Trump Recorded Having Extremely Lewd Conversation."

125. Ibid.

126. Ibid.

127. Ibid.

128. Jill Filipovic, "Our President Has Always Degraded Women—and We've Always Let Him," *Time*, December 5, 2017, http://time.com/5047771/donald-trump-comments-billy-bush/.

129. Karen Tumulty and Philip Rucker, "Shouting Match Erupts between Clinton and Trump Aides," *Washington Post*, December 1, 2016, https://www.washingtonpost.com/politics/shouting-match-erupts-

between-clinton-and-trump-aides/2016/12/01/7ac4398e-b7ea-11e6-b8df-600bd9d38a02_story.html.

130. Carly Wayne, Nicholas Valentino, and Marzia Oceno, "How Sexism Drives Support for Donald Trump," *Monkey Cage* (blog), *Washington Post*, October 23, 2016, https://www.washingtonpost.com/news/monkey-cage/wp/2016/10/23/how-sexism-drives-support-for-donald-trump/.

131. Chris Cillizza, "President-Elect Donald Trump's Cataclysmic, History-Making Upset," *Washington Post*, November 9, 2016, https://www.washingtonpost.com/news/the-fix/wp/2016/11/09/how-donald-trump-pulled-off-an-upset-of-cataclysmic-historic-proportions/.

132. Global Strategy Group and Garin Hart Yang, "Post-Election Research: Persuadable and Drop-Off Voters" (Priorities USA, April 2017), https://www.washingtonpost.com/r/2010-2019/WashingtonPost/2017/05/01/Editorial-Opinion/Graphics/Post-election_Research_Deck.pdf.

133. Stanley Greenberg, "The Democrats' 'Working-Class Problem,'" *American Prospect*, June 1, 2017, http://prospect.org/article/democrats%E2%80%99-%E2%80%98working-class-problem%E2%80%99.

134. Alec Tyson and Shiva Maniam, "Behind Trump's Victory: Divisions by Race, Gender, Education," Pew Research Center, November 9, 2016, https://www.pewresearch.org/fact-tank/2016/11/09/behind-trumps-victory-divisions-by-race-gender-education/.

135. Ibid.

136. Kelly Dittmar, "No, Women Didn't Abandon Clinton, nor Did She Fail to Win Their Support." *Medium*, November 11, 2016, https://medium.com/@kelly.dittmar/no-women-didnt-abandon-clinton-nor-did-she-fail-to-win-their-support-77d41e631fbd.

137. Lynn Vavreck, "The Ways That the 2016 Election Was Perfectly Normal," *Upshot* (blog), *New York Times*, May 1, 2017, https://www.nytimes.com/2017/05/01/upshot/the-ways-that-the-2016-election-was-perfectly-normal.html.

138. See John Sides, Michael Tesler, and Lynn Vavreck, *Identity Crisis: The 2016 Presidential Campaign and the Battle for the Meaning of America* (Princeton, NJ: Princeton University Press, 2018).

139. Heidi M. Przybyla and Fredreka Schouten, "At 2.6 Million Strong, Women's Marches Crush Expectations," *USA Today*, January 22, 2017, https://www.usatoday.com/story/news/politics/2017/01/21/womens-march-aims-start-movement-trump-inauguration/96864158/.

140. See, for example, Jim Rutenberg, "A Long-Delayed Reckoning of the Cost of Silence on Abuse," *New York Times*, October 22, 2017, https://www.nytimes.com/2017/10/22/business/media/a-long-delayed-reckoning-of-the-cost-of-silence-on-abuse.html. Also, see Jim Rutenberg, "A Failure of the Network News Star System," *New York Times*, November 29, 2017, https://www.nytimes.com/2017/11/29/business/media/matt-lauer-sexual-misconduct.html.

141. Aisha Harris, "She Founded Me Too. Now She Wants to Move Past the Trauma," *New York Times*, October 15, 2018, https://www.nytimes.com/2018/10/15/arts/tarana-burke-metoo-anniversary.html.

142. See Charlotte Alter, "A Year Ago, They Marched. Now a Record Number of Women Are Running for Office," *Time*, January 18, 2018, http://time

.com/5107499/record-number-of-women-are-running-for-office/.

143. John Gramlich, "10 Things We Learned about Gender Issues in the U.S. In 2017," Pew Research Center, December 28, 2017, http://www.pewresearch.org/fact-tank/2017/12/28/10-things-we-learned-about-gender-issues-in-the-u-s-in-2017/.

144. Daniella Diaz and Sunlen Serfaty, "Tammy Duckworth Gives Birth, First US Senator to Do So While in Office," CNN, April 9, 2018, https://www.cnn.com/2018/04/09/politics/tammy-duckworth-gives-birth-baby-girl/index.html.

145. Li Zhou, "A Historic New Congress Will Be Sworn in Today," *Vox*, January 3, 2019, https://www.vox.com/2018/12/6/18119733/congress-diversity-women-election-good-news.

146. Malliga Och and Shauna Shames, "Year of the Woman in Congress Leaves out Republicans," United Press International, January 2, 2019, https://www.upi.com/Year-of-the-Woman-in-Congress-leaves-out-Republicans/4671546435464/.

147. Ibid.

148. Center for American Women and Politics, Eagleton Institute of Politics, "Results: Women Candidates in the 2018 Elections," news release, November 29, 2018, https://www.cawp.rutgers.edu/sites/default/files/resources/results_release_5bletterhead5d_1.pdf.

149. Karen Defilippi, interview with the author, September 10, 2020.

150. Caroline Kitchener, "How the Republican Party Fixed Its Gender Crisis," *The Lily*, November 5, 2020, https://www.thelily.com/how-the-republican-party-fixed-its-gender-crisis/.

151. Katherine Tully-McManus, "Record Number of House GOP Women Just One of Many 'Firsts' for 117th Congress," *Roll Call*, November 12, 2020, https://www.rollcall.com/2020/11/12/record-number-of-house-gop-women-just-one-of-many-firsts-for-117th-congress/.

152. Center for American Women and Politics, Eagleton Institute of Politics, "Results: Women Candidates in the 2020 Elections," news release, November 4, 2020, https://cawp.rutgers.edu/election-analysis/results-women-candidates-2020-elections.

153. *Gender on the Ballot* Team, "Reminder: Only 9 States Currently Have a Woman Governor," *Gender on the Ballot*, April 30, 2020, https://www.genderontheballot.org/reminder-only-9-states-currently-have-a-woman-governor/.

154. Lisa Lerer and Susan Chira, "'There's a Real Tension.' Democrats Puzzle Over Whether a Woman Will Beat Trump," *New York Times*, January 5, 2019, https://www.nytimes.com/2019/01/05/us/politics/women-candidates-president-2020.html.

155. Linda Hirshman, "The Electability Trap," *Washington Post*, February 12, 2019, https://www.washingtonpost.com/news/posteverything/wp/2019/02/12/feature/will-americans-vote-for-a-woman-obsessing-over-the-question-makes-it-less-likely/.

156. Annie Linskey and David Weigel, "Before You Run Against Trump, You Have to Run Against Hillary (If You're a Woman)," *Washington Post*, January 3, 2019, https://www.washingtonpost.com/politics/before-you-run-against-trump-you-have-to-run-against-hillary-if-youre-a-woman/2019/01/03/

f552fc0c-0ec9-11e9-831f-3aa2c-2be4cbd_story.html.

157. Joe Biden, "I Have Fought for the Democratic Party My Whole Career," *Medium*, November 5, 2019, https://medium.com/@JoeBiden/i-have-fought-for-the-democratic-party-my-whole-career-2ca4a2dac271.

158. Megan Garber, "America Punished Elizabeth Warren for Her Competence," *Atlantic*, March 5, 2020, https://www.theatlantic.com/culture/archive/2020/03/america-punished-elizabeth-warren-her-competence/607531/.

159. Ibid.

160. Maggie Astor, "Kamala Harris and the 'Double Bind' of Racism and Sexism," *New York Times*, October 9, 2020. https://www.nytimes.com/2020/10/09/us/politics/kamala-harris-racism-sexism.html.

161. Tom Tapp, "Tucker Carlson Repeatedly Mispronounces Kamala Harris's Name on Fox News, Is Unrepentant When Corrected," *Deadline*, August 11, 2020, https://deadline.com/2020/08/tucker-carlson-mispronounces-kamala-harris-name-1203010936/.

162. Ewan Palmer, "Everything Rush Limbaugh Has Said About Kamala Harris," *Newsweek*, August 17, 2020, https://www.newsweek.com/rush-limbaugh-kamala-harris-radio-show-1525554.

163. Bianca Quilantan and David Cohen, "Trump Tells Dem Congresswomen: Go Back Where You Came From," *Politico*, July 14, 2019, https://www.politico.com/story/2019/07/14/trump-congress-go-back-where-they-came-from-1415692.

164. Annie Karni and Jeremy W. Peters, "Her Voice? Her Name? G.O.P.'s Raw Personal Attacks on Kamala Harris," *New York Times*, August 12, 2020, https://www.nytimes.com/2020/08/12/us/politics/kamala-harris-gop-attacks.html.

165. Karen Tumulty, Kate Woodsome, and Sergio Pecanha, "How Sexist, Racist Attacks on Kamala Harris Have Spread Online —A Case Study," *Washington Post*, October 7, 2020, https://www.washingtonpost.com/opinions/2020/10/07/kamala-harris-sexist-racist-attacks-spread-online/.

Annotated Media Resources

This guide is designed to assist you in researching and studying politics and the media. It includes the following:

- Primary sources for researching and analyzing media coverage of politics
- Secondary sources for scholarship on political communication issues
- Sites for researching political ads, polling, and public opinion on issues in politics and the media
- Links to political parties, advocacy and lobbying groups, and other political organizations
- Other useful links for further understanding the topic

Advocacy and Lobbying

- AARP: https://www.aarp.org/
- American-Arab Anti-Discrimination Committee: https://www.adc.org
- The American Federation of Labor and Congress of Industrial Organizations (AFL-CIO): https://aflcio.org
- American Friends Service Committee (AFSC): https://www.afsc.org
- American Petroleum Institute (API): https://www.api.org
- Americans for Tax Reform: https://www.atr.org
- Capital Area Immigrants' Rights Coalition (CAIR): https://www.caircoalition.org
- Christian Coalition of America: http://cc.org
- Concerned Women for America: https://concernedwomen.org
- Conservative Political Action Conference (CPAC): https://cpac.conservative.org
- Council on American-Islamic Relations (CAIR): https://www.cair.com
- Council for the National Interest: https://councilforthenationalinterest.org

- GLAAD: https://www.glaad.org

- NAACP (National Association for the Advancement of Colored People): https:/naacp.org

- National Association of Manufacturers (NAM): https://www.nam.org

- National Council of Churches: https://nationalcouncilofchurches.us

- National Education Association: https://www.nea.org

- National Rifle Association (NRA): https://home.nra.org

- National Trial Lawyers: https://thenationaltriallawyers.org

- Natural Resources Defense Council (NRDC): https://www.nrdc.org

- People's Action: https://peoplesaction.org

- Pharmaceutical Research and Manufacturers of America (PhRMA): https://www.phrma.org

- Planned Parenthood: https://www.plannedparenthood.org

- Service Employees International Union (SEIU): https://www.seiu.org

- Sierra Club: https://www.sierraclub.org

- UnidosUS: https://www.unidosus.org

- United States Public Interest Research Group (U.S. PIRG): https://uspirg.org

- U.S. Chamber of Commerce: https://www.uschamber.com

Campaign Finance, Sources of Funding and Overall Expenditures

- Campaign Media Analysis Group (Kantar Media): https://www.kantarmedia.com/us/our-solutions/advertising-monitoring-and-evaluation/political-ad-monitoring

- Center for Public Integrity: https://publicintegrity.org

- Federal Election Commission (FEC): https://www.fec.gov

- National Institute on Money in Politics: https://www.followthemoney.org

- Center for Responsive Politics: OpenSecrets.org: http://www.opensecrets.org

- Sunlight Foundation: https://sunlightfoundation.com

Comedy in Politics

- *The Daily Show with Trevor Noah* (Comedy Central): http://www
  .cc.com/shows/the-daily-show-with-trevor-noah

- *Last Week Tonight with John Oliver* (HBO): https://www.hbo.com/
  last-week-tonight-with-john-oliver

- *The Late Show with Stephen Colbert* (CBS): https://www.cbs.com/
  shows/the-late-show-with-stephen-colbert/

- *The Onion*: https://www.theonion.com

- *Saturday Night Live* (NBC): https://www.nbc.com/saturday-night-
  live

- *The Tonight Show Starring Jimmy Fallon* (NBC): https://www.nbc
  .com/the-tonight-show

Communication Policy, Editorial Integrity, and Civic Media

- Editorial Integrity for Public Media: https://publicmediaintegrity.org

- Media & Communications Policy: https://www.mediacompolicy
  .org

- Save the Internet (Free Press): https://www.freepress.net/issues/
  free-open-internet/net-neutrality

- Youth and Media Policy Working Group Initiative (Harvard
  University): https://cyber.harvard.edu/research/youthandmedia/
  policy

Databases for Further Academic Research

- ShadowTV: http://www.shadowtv.com/ shadowtv.com.

- CQ Press: Voting and Elections Collection: http://library.cqpress
  .com/elections/

- Dow Jones: Factiva: https://professional.dowjones.com/factiva/

- EBSCO: Communication Abstracts: https://www.ebsco.com/
  products/research-databases/communication-abstracts

- Internet Archive: TV News: https://archive.org/details/tv

- LexisNexis: https://www.lexisnexis.com/en-us/home.page

- Political MoneyLine: http://www.politicalmoneyline.com

- PressReader: https://www.pressreader.com/catalog

- ProQuest: https://www.proquest.com
- SAGE Journals: *International Political Science Abstracts*: https://journals.sagepub.com/home/iab

Fact-Checking Claims in Political Media

- FactCheck.org: https://www.factcheck.org
- Fact Checker (*Washington Post*): https://www.washingtonpost.com/news/fact-checker/
- Poynter Institute: https://www.poynter.org/media-news/fact-checking/
- PR Watch (Center for Media and Democracy): https://www.prwatch.org/

History of Presidential Campaigns and Campaign Commercials

- Library of Congress Web Archive: https://www.loc.gov/web-archives/collections
- Living Room Candidate: www.livingroomcandidate.org
- Paley Center for Media: https://www.paleycenter.org
- Political Communication Lab: http://pcl.stanford.edu/campaigns/
- Television Archive: http://www.televisionarchive.org
- Vanderbilt Television News Archive: https://tvnews.vanderbilt.edu

Media Studies

- American Journalism Review: https://ajr.org
- Berkman Klein Center for Internet & Society at Harvard University: https://cyber.harvard.edu
- *Columbia Journalism Review*: https://www.cjr.org
- *Nieman Reports*: https://niemanreports.org
- Pew Research Center Journalism & Media: https://www.journalism.org
- Pew Research Center Internet & Technology: https://www.pewresearch.org/internet
- Poynter Institute: https://www.poynter.org

- PressThink: https://pressthink.org
- Shorenstein Center on Media, Politics and Public Policy: https://shorensteincenter.org

Museums, Exhibits, and Special Collections

- Newseum (closed in 2019 but still has materials from its collection online): https://www.newseum.org

News Sources

- Broadcast Networks, Cable TV Networks, and Their Websites
  o ABC News: https://abcnews.go.com
  o CBS News: https://www.cbsnews.com
  o CNN: https://www.cnn.com
  o C-SPAN: https://www.c-span.org
  o Fox News Channel: https://www.foxnews.com
  o MSNBC: https://www.msnbc.com
  o National Public Radio (NPR): https://www.npr.org
  o NBC News: https://www.nbcnews.com

- International News Sources
  o Al Jazeera: https://www.aljazeera.com
  o BBC News: https://www.bbc.com/news
  o *The Economist*: https://www.economist.com
  o European Journalism Centre: https://ejc.net
  o *Financial Times*: https://www.ft.com
  o *The Guardian*: https://www.theguardian.com/us

- Political News Online
  o AP Newsroom: https://newsroom.ap.org
  o *Daily Beast*: https://www.thedailybeast.com
  o *HuffPost*: https://www.huffpost.com
  o *Politico*: https://www.politico.com
  o *Vox*: https://www.vox.com/

- National Newspaper Websites
  o *Los Angeles Times*: https://www.latimes.com
  o *New York Times*: https://www.nytimes.com
  o *USA Today*: https://www.usatoday.com
  o *Wall Street Journal*: https://www.wsj.com
  o *Washington Post*: https://www.washingtonpost.com

Open Government

- Open the Government: https://www.openthegovernment.org
- Participatory Politics Foundation: http://www.participatorypolitics.org

Opinion Magazines

- *Mother Jones* (Progressive): https://www.motherjones.com
- *The Nation* (Liberal): https://www.thenation.com
- *National Review* (Conservative): https://www.nationalreview.com
- *Reason* (Libertarian): https://reason.com

Political Action Committees

- Open Secrets: Behind the Candidates: Campaign Committees and Outside Groups: https://www.opensecrets.org/pres16/outside-groups
- Open Secrets: Super PACs: https://www.opensecrets.org/pacs/superpacs.php

Political Parties and Organizations

- Executive
  o Democratic National Committee: https://democrats.org
  o The Green Party of the United States: https://www.gp.org
  o Libertarian National Committee: https://www.lp.org
  o Constitution Party: http://www.constitutionparty.com
  o Republican National Committee: https://www.gop.com
  o Tea Party: https://www.teaparty.org
  o Voto Latino: https://votolatino.org
  o Young Americans for Freedom: http://students.yaf.org/young-americans-for-freedom

- Congressional
  o Congressional Asian Pacific American Caucus - https://capac-chu.house.gov
  o Congressional Black Caucus: https://cbc.house.gov
  o Congressional Hispanic Caucus: https://chci.org
  o Democratic Congressional Campaign Committee: https://dccc.org
  o Green Party Caucuses: https://www.gp.org/caucuses

- House Democratic Caucus: https://www.dems.gov
- House Freedom Caucus: https://www.facebook.com/freedomcaucus
- House Republican Conference: https://www.gop.gov
- National Republican Congressional Committee: https://www.nrcc.org
- Republican Liberty Caucus: https://rlc.org
- Senate Republican Conference: https://www.republican.senate.gov/public
- Tea Party Caucus: https://web.archive.org/web/20141205195335/http:/teapartycaucus-bachmann.house.gov
- Senate Democratic Caucus: https://www.democrats.senate.gov

Polls and Polling

- *FiveThirtyEight* (ABC News): https://fivethirtyeight.com/politics/

- Gallup: https://www.gallup.com

- *Monkey Cage* (*Washington Post*): https://www.washingtonpost.com/news/monkey-cage/

- Pew Research Center: https://www.pewresearch.org

- *RealClearPolitics*: https://www.realclearpolitics.com

- *The Upshot* (*New York Times*): https://www.nytimes.com/section/upshot

Professional Organizations in Media

- News Leaders Association: https://members.newsleaders.org

- Online News Association: https://journalists.org

- Radio Television Digital News Association: https://www.rtdna.org

Technology in Politics

- Access Info Europe: https://www.access-info.org

- TechPresident: https://techpresident.com

Think Tanks

- American Enterprise Institute: https://www.aei.org

- Brookings Institution: https://www.brookings.edu

- Cato Institute: https://www.cato.org

- Center for American Progress: https://www.americanprogress.org
- Heritage Foundation: https://www.heritage.org
- Hoover Institution: https://www.hoover.org
- New America: https://www.newamerica.org

Women in Media and Politics

- Center for American Women and Politics (Rutgers University): https://cawp.rutgers.edu
- Independent Women's Forum: https://www.iwf.org
- National Organization for Women: https://now.org
- WMC SheSource: https://www.womensmediacenter.com/shesource/
- Women & Politics Institute (American University): https://www.american.edu/spa/wpi/
- The Women's Media Center: https://www.womensmediacenter.com

Young People and Voting/Civic Engagement

- Center for Information & Research on Civic Learning and Engagement (CIRCLE) at Tufts University: https://circle.tufts.edu
- Institute of Politics at Harvard Kennedy School: https://iop.harvard.edu
- Rock the Vote: https://www.rockthevote.org

Index

ABC News, 18–20, 50, 60, 98, 103, 105, 153, 185, 194, 231
Abramowitz, A. I., 146–147
Abrams, F., 152
Abramson, J., 159
Access Hollywood, 1–2, 145, 251, 274
Ad makers, 67, 73
Advertisements, campaign, individual, 75–92
  "Break In" ad, Trump ad against Biden, 2020 campaign, 92
  "Celeb," McCain ad against Obama, 2008 campaign, 86
  "Daisy" ad, 79
  "Deplorables," Trump ad against Clinton, 2016, 89
  "Don't Let Hillary Leave You Defenseless," Trump ad against Clinton, 2016 presidential, 89
  "Eisenhower Answers America," 76, 77
  "Getting Started," Hillary Clinton ad, 2016, 88
  "Make 'Em Squeal" ad, Joni Ernst, 2914, 75–76
  "Mirrors" and "Role Models," Clinton ads against Trump, 2016, 89
  "Morning in America," Reagan, 78
  "Mourning in America 2020," 92
  Ron DeSantis "bedtime story" pro-Trump ad, 90
  "Soul of America," Biden ad 2020, 91–92
  Swift boats, case-study, 80–85
  "Texas Reloaded" ad, 93
  "The Courage to Change," Alexandria Ocasio-Cortez ad, 2018, 90
  "torrent" of ads, 92
  "Vote Together," Sanders ad, 2016, 87
  "Willie Horton," 79–81, 129.
  2008 presidential election, 85–86
  2016 presidential election, 87–89
  2018 Congressional midterm elections, 90–91
  2020 presidential election, 91–93
  See also Political advertising
  "3 a.m.," Clinton ad against Obama, 2008, 85
Affordable Care Act, 55, 57, 69, 138, 172, 197
Afghanistan war, 14, 232, 243–244, 247

Agenda-building, 46–47
  defined, 46
  modern-day examples, 46–47
Agenda-setting, 42–43
  defined, 42
  civil rights legislation as example, 43–44
  congressional hearings as example, 45
  role of elites, 45–46
  examples in major media today, 44–45
  need for orientation, 42
  on social media, 48–49
  Association technique, 77–78
Reverse agenda-setting, 47–48
  defined, 47
  modern-day examples, 48
  See also Priming
Ahmed, Akbar, interview, 239
Ailes, Roger, interview, 129; also 30, 80, 128, 276
  attacks on media, 129
  firing, 276
  founding of Fox News Channel, 30, 128
  Horton ad, 80
Air Wars (West), 70
Al-Assad, B., 214, 234
Alberta, T., 145
Albright, J., 166
Alcindor, Yamiche, interview, 154
Alden Global Capital, 27
Alien and Sedition Acts of 1798, 13
Al Jazeera, 213–214, 250
Alphabet Inc., 25–26 (table)
"Alternative facts," 11, 152
Altheide, D., 236
Amanpour, Christiane, interview, 213, 233; also, 126, 156, 216, 233
America Held Hostage, 50
American Carnage: On the Front Lines of the Republican Civil War and the Rise of President Trump (Alberta), 145
American exceptionalism, 216–217
  global public opinion, role of U.S., 218–219
American Exceptionalism: A Double-Edged Sword (Lipset), 217
American federal election campaigns, advertising, 67
American National Election Studies, 5
American Political Science Association, 17
American Society of News Editors, 26, 126

Annenberg Public Policy Center, 56, 72, 81
"Arab Spring," 31, 213
Aristotle, 67, 73
Arizona Republic, 41, 178
Army Times, 247
The Arsenio Hall Show, 171
Asian American and Pacific Islander
    (AAPI), 227, 269
Asian American Journalists Association, 227
Asian Americans, 227, 269
    Chinese Exclusion Act, 199
    anti-AAPI bias and rise in hate crimes, 227
    Donald Trump's false rhetoric linking
        coronavirus to Asian Americans, 227
Asian American Twitter, 49
Atlantic magazine, 221, 248, 251
AT&T, 20, 21–22 (table)
Audio, power of senses, 63
Auletta, K., 149
Ayatollah Khomeini, 50

Bachmann, M., 62
Baldwin, Tammy, 269
Ball, M., 59
Barack Obama, 150–151 See also Barack
    Obama and 2008, 2012 Presidential
    elections
Barbara Lee Family Foundation, 261
Baron, Martin, interview 28; also, 12
Ba Tran, A., 239–240
Baum, M., 174, 214
Benkler, Y., 169
Bennett, J. G., 267–268
Bennett, W. L., 113
Bentsen, L., 105
Berke, Richard, interview, 264–265
Beyond the Double Bind: Women and Leadership
    (Jamieson), 258
Bezos, J., 28
Bias, operational and cultural in
    news-gathering, 17, 97, 104–116
    perceptions of liberal, 16–18, 102, 112,
        113, 128
    perceptions of corporate, 16, 17, 48, 102,
        112, 113, 149
Bias toward immediacy, 96, 97–98
    conflict and narrow debate, 104–106
    establishment candidates, 110–113
    false equivalences, case-study, climate
        change, 121–125
    horse-race coverage, 109–110
    immediacy, early days, 97–98
    insiderism, 106–109

internet, 98–100
media and technology, history of,
    100–101(table)
media narratives, 115–119
objectivity in journalism, 120–125
official sources, 113–115
radio news, 98
social media, 99–103
telegraph, 97–98
Biden, Joe, 6–9, 53, 72, 85, 91–92,105–106,
    109, 136, 154, 169, 172, 175, 190, 197,
    209–211, 223, 226–227, 229–230
    electability factor, 8
    political advertising by, 72
    presidential debates, 105
    2020 presidential election and, 6–9, 53,
        72, 91–92, 169, 209–211, 223,
        226–227, 229–230, 256, 257, 280
Big Three broadcast networks, 18–19
Bimber, B., 98, 158
Birx, D., 222, 227
#BlackLivesMatter, 147, 183, 186–191
Black Voters, role in 2020 presidential
    election, 209–210
    study of, 190–191
    See also George Floyd, Michael Brown, Tray-
        von Martin, Eric Garner, Sandra Bland
Bland, Sandra, 188
Black Twitter, 49, 191
Bleich, E., 239
Bloomberg, M., 8, 72, 257
Boas, P., 178
Bok, S., 236–237
Boling, D., 142–143
Bolton, J., 156
Bond, Julian, interview, 43–44, 186
Booker, C., 7, 163
Boston Globe, 28, 118
Braun, C. M., 255 (table), 269
Brazaitis, T., 266
"Break In" ad, 92
Briffault, R., 70
Brown, Michael, 114, 188, 190–191
Brulle, R., 125
Brzezinski, Z., 237
Buchanan, P., 104, 106
Bucy, E. P., 58
Bush, George Herbert Walker, 75, 105,
    116, 129
    political ads, 79–80
Bush, George W., 14, 50–51, 59, 80, 81, 83,
    117–119, 195, 199, 201, 241–244, 262,
    264, 273

presidency and media, 149–150
"war on terror," 237
Bush, Jeb., 4, 105, 141, 172, 203
political advertising by, 72
Bush, Laura, 52
Butler, P., 188–189
Buttigieg, Mayor Pete, 7, 8, 105–106,
136, 164
BuzzFeed, 165

Cahill, M. B., 84
Card, A., 149
Carlin, D. B., 259
Carlson, T., 30, 130, 225, 260, 281
Carney, J., 52, 151
Carpini, M. X. D., 173
"Carpool Karaoke," 52, 171, 172
Carr, D., 27
Carter, Jimmy, 49–50, 78, 237
Cascading activation model, 245
Case studies
Building "The Wall" and framing
immigration, 205–208
Climate change, media coverage, 121–125
Elizabeth Dole's 2000 Presidential
campaign, 262–265
Framing and Counter-Framing Obamacare,
55–57
Media and Iraq war, 241–245
Media and Politics Research Tool Kit,
33–37 and 356–363 from annotated
resource pages in References sections
Role of late-night comedy shows, 171–176.
Swift boat campaign, 80–85
Castro, Julian, 7, 209
CBS News, 18–19, 20, 57, 98, 100 (table),
126, 211, 231 (table), 246, 249
*The Censored War: American Visual Experience
During World War II* (Roeder), 245–246
Center for American Women and Politics,
251, 279
statistics, 277–279
Center for Responsive Politics, 66, 68, 124
Center for Strategic and International Studies,
236, 240
Chauvin, D., 182
Cheney, Dick, 59, 241
Cheney, Liz, 59
Cheney, Mary, 59
Chisholm, S., 255 (table), 269
Citizens United v. Federal Election Commission,
66, 67, 140
Civic engagement, 28–29

Civil rights legislation, as example of agenda-
setting, 43–44
Civil rights movement, 18, 43–44, 183,
185–186
Clark, M. D., 190
Clear Channel Communications, 25
Clift, Eleanor, interview, 266–267
Climate change, 228–230
case study, 121–125
environmental legislation, 122
false objectivity, 123
fossil fuel industry, 124, 215, 229
funds on, 124–125
global warming, 121–124, 228
"hoax," 230
in 2020 presidential campaign, 229–230
public opinion and coverage, 122–123,
228–229
scientists and, 122
Climate Change Communication, 122,
228–229
"Climate skeptics," 121, 229
Clinton. Bill, 50, 55, 75, 112, 114, 135, 149,
151, 171, 189, 213, 258, 266, 270, 273
impeachment and Monica Lewinsky
scandal, public opinion, 50
"Clinton fatigue," 119
Clinton, Hillary, xiii, 1, 3, 5, 7, 53, 58, 66,
69, 71–72, 85, 89, 91, 111–113, 119,
254, 255, 256, 258, 259, 269, 275, 280
advertisements, campaigns, 85, 88, 91
and, 92
critiquing media coverage of, in 2016, 1–3,
272–273
double-bind and, 258–259
email server, mishandling of and media
coverage, 4, 88, 271–273
likeability factor, 260–262
presidential debates, 104–105
2008 and 2016 presidential campaigns,
270–273
2016 Presidential Election, 1–5, 87, 89,
104, 111–113, 140–141, 156, 158,
160, 166, 184, 191, 194, 254, 256
(table)
Clyburn, J., 8, 209
CNN, 12, 20, 30, 98, 107, 108, 113, 121,
123, 124, 128, 129, 138, 145, 151, 153,
154, 201, 212, 213, 216, 225, 232, 238,
242, 244
CNN effect, 213–215
founding, 101 (table)
insiderism, 107–108

international news, 213–216, 232, 233,
See also Chapter, 7
Iraq War, case study, 241–245
Code words, 54, 73, 79
distortion, political ads, 73–75
stereotyping and, 79–80
"Cognitive misers," 49
Cohen, B., 42
Cohen, E., 234
Cohen, J., 113
Cohen, R., 144
Cold War frame, 53, 217
Collins, Susan, 69, 138–140, 268
presentation on polarization and
Congressional gridlock, 138–140
Colorado Civil Rights Commission, 60
Columbia Journalism Review article,
112, 117
Columbia Journalism Review magazine, 63
Colvin, M., 234
Comcast Corporation, 22 (table)
Comey, J., 156, 161, 271–273
Committee to Protect Journalists (CPJ),
150, 232
Common Sense Media survey, 102
Communications Act of 1934, 19
Confirmation bias, 59, 164
Conflict and narrow debate, bias toward,
104–106
political talk shows, 104
presidential debates, 104–106
Congress, 138–139
campaign spending, public attitudes about,
140–144
covering Congress vs. presidency,
147–148
gun control legislation, 139–140
hyperpartisanship and gridlock in,
138–140
high cost of running for office, 140–143
polarization, 17, 137–140
nationalizing of local races, 144, 146
Trump and Republican party,
145–147
2016 presidential campaign, spending on,
142 (table)
Consumer advertisers, 73
Consumer Financial Protection Bureau,
8, 256–257
Conway, K., 11, 152
Cook Political Report, 8
Cooper, Anderson, interview, p. 233; also,
114, 162, 216

Corden, J., 52, 171, 172
Corker, B., 146
Coronavirus pandemic, xii, 8, 9, 29, 38,92, 115,
130, 137, 146, 152, 154, 169, 182, 211,
215, 219–226 Campaign and, 8–9, 225
Centers for Disease Control, 222
conservative media and, 223–226
Fox News Channel, role of, 38, 220,
223–226
international versus domestic, 219
knowledge of viewers, per cable network,
225–226
local and national news, 29
public opinion, Trump response, 224
racial, ethnic and economic disparities,
182, 221, 250
U.S. deaths in relation to U.S. war deaths,
220 (figure) public health data, 221
U.S. economy shut down, 220
Trump's response, 8–9, 222–223,
224 (figure)
2020 presidential election and, 8–9,
220–228
Council on American-Islamic Relations
(CAIR), 238
Counter-framing Obamacare, 55–57
Couric, K., 126, 175
Credibility, public opinion on media,
15–16, 102
Crenshaw, D., 93
Critiques and self-critiques of media in 2016
election, 177–178
Cronkite, W., 246–247
Crossfire, 104, 106
CrowdTangle, 103
Crowley, J., 90, 91
Cruz, Ted., 105, 116, 164
*The Culture of Fear: Why Americans Are Afraid
of the Wrong Things* (Glassner), 236
Cunningham, B., 120
Cybersecurity and Infrastructure Security
Agency, 170

DACA (Deferred Action for Childhood
Arrivals), 207–208
Daily Beast, 108
The Daily Show with Jon Stewart, 173–174
The Daily Show with Trevor Noah, 176
"Daisy" ad, 79
Dam, A. V., 220
"Dark-money" groups, 68
Darman, R., 57–58
Davis, R., 102

Davis, T., 144
Dean, Howard, interview, 63, 107
Dearing, J., 46
Defense & Aerospace Report, 248
Defilippi, Karen, interview, 270
DeGeneres, E., 60, 271, 272
Democratic primary campaign, 3? not only one,
    58, 142, 260
Derakhshan, H., 167
Deregulation of media, 19–26
Demographics, U.S., changing, 5, 200,
    203, 212
DeSantis, R., 90
Digital activism, 186–190
Digital media jobs, 27
Dionne, E. J., 104
Dittmar, K., 251–252
Diversity in media, 125–126
Doctor, K., 27
Doherty, C., 18
Dole, Elizabeth, 254, 255 (table)
    Case-study, 2000 presidential campaign,
        262–265
Domenech, B., 15
Donvan, John, interview, 247–248
Double bind for women in politics, 254,
    258–259
Downie, L., 150
DREAM Act (Development, Relief, and
    Education for Alien Minors Act), 207, 208
Duckworth, T., 277–278
Duerst-Lahti, G., 252
Dukakis, M., 79, 81, 194
Dunaway, J., 49

Eckford, E., 185
Economics of news, 18–19
Edwards. John, 116
"Eisenhower Answers America," TV ad, 76
Eisenhower, D. D., 77, 78
The Elements of Journalism (Kovach and
    Rosenstiel), 96, 120
Elites, role of in agenda-setting,
    45–46
The Ellen DeGeneres Show, 171
Ellsberg, D., 14
Entman, R., 53, 245
Episodic nature of news coverage, 40–42
Ernst, Joni, 75–76
Esquire magazine, 139
Establishment candidates, bias toward,
    110–113

Clinton's announcement, 111
    media coverage of Bernie Sanders, 112–113
    Sanders interview, 110–112
Evanega, S., 169
evangelical voters, 145, 146, 209
Eyes on the Prize documentary series, 186

Facebook, Inc., 25 (table)
Facebook, 2, 19, 26, 45, 48, 49, 56, 72,
    98–100, 102, 137, 187–188, 241
Face the Nation, 114, 126
FactCheck.org, 56, 72, 168
Fact-checking organizations, 56, 72, 168
Fairness & Accuracy in Reporting (FAIR),
    113, 244
"Fake news", Trump attacks on news
    organizations as, xiii, 11, 127, 138,
    151–154, 178
    See also First Amendment
Fake news/disinformation, 164–168
    coronavirus pandemic, 169, 226
    Facebook, 2016 presidential election,
        165–167
    FactCheck.org, 168
    Information Disorder, 167
    Instagram, 2016 presidential campaign,
        165–167
    Twitter, 2020, presidential election, role of,
        169–170
    spotting, 168–171
    2020 presidential campaign and election,
        role of, 165–167, 169, 170–171
Fallon, J., 172
Far-right terrorist attacks, 239–241
    Iraq War, case study, 241–245
Fauci, A., 222, 227
Fazio, L., 164
Federal Emergency Management Agency
    (FEMA), 114
Feeding the Beast (Walsh), 150
Feezell, J. T., 49
Feinstein, D., 266, 268
Feminist Twitter, 49
Ferraro, Geraldine, 9, 104, 210, 252,
    255 (table), 267
Fineman, H., 117
Fiorina, Carly, 1, 160, 254, 256 (table), 274
First Amendment, xii, 11, 13–16, 60, 67,
    100 (table), 155
    Freedom Forum survey, 15
Flake, J., 146, 147
Fletcher, M., 194

Floyd, George, death and protests, xiii, 9, 147, 152, 182–183, 188–190, 198, 211–212, 232

Flynn, M., 156

"Follow the money," 66

Ford, C. B., 145

Fowler, E. F., 69

Fox and Friends, 176

Fox Business Channel, 225

Fox Corporation, 23 (table)

Fox News Channel, 1, 4, 6, 9, 12, 16, 30, 31, 38, 56, 57, 101 (table), 102, 103, 107, 108, 112, 123, 128–129, 177, 187, 223–226, 227, 229, 238, 251, 260, 273, 276, 280–281
  agenda-building, 47
  "Building Wall" case study, 205–208
  climate change, case-study, 121–125, 229
  coronavirus pandemic and, 38, 220, 223–226
    knowledge of viewers, per cable network, 225–226
  founding, 101 (table)
  growth of, 30
  importance of cable news, 30, 31
  insiderism, news immediacy, 106
  trust and accountability, 129–130
  viewers' loyalty to as exclusive news source, 38, 47, 127–128

"Fox News story," 47

Fox, R. L., 269–270

Fouhy, Beth, interview, 264

Framing, 53–61, 193, 200
  defined, 55
  Cold War frame, 217
  case study, framing and counter-framing Obamacare, 55–57
  case study, framing building "the Wall" and immigration, 205–208
  framing language and issue frames, 54–55
  reframing same-sex marriage and, 59–61
  psychology of, 53
  power of sound, "Dean scream," 63
  visual, 61–62

Franklin, E., 69

Franz, M., 69

Freedom Forum survey, 15

Freedom of Information Act (FOIA), 14

Freedom of the Press Foundation, 48

Freedom to Marry, 59

Freelon, D., 190

"Frontline," 41–42

Frost, M., 144

Frum, D., 222

Full Frontal with Samantha Bee, 176

Fulwood III, Sam, interview, 196, 211

Gabbard, Tulsi, 7, 252, 256 (table)

Gabler, N., 40

Gallup polling, 50–51
  coronavirus pandemic, knowledge of per cable network, 225–226
  terrorists attack, 236
  media credibility and trust, 15, 126, 127
  same-sex marriage, 60
  Trump approval rating during impeachment, 7
  health care, 57
  woman as US president, 264–265

Gannett, 24 (table), 27

Gans, H. J., 113

Garber, M., 251, 280

Garner, Eric, 188, 191

Garza, A., 187

GateHouse Media, 27

Geer, J., 73

Gender, 251–257
  "ambitious" as negative for women, 260
  Gendered treatment of women in politics, defined and examples, from media coverage, 251–252
  See also Hillary Clinton and 2008 and 2016 Presidential Campaigns
  Kamala Harris, nomination of, 280–281
  'likeability' factor, 260–262
  case-study, Elizabeth Dole in 2000, 262–265
  gender dynamics in running for president, 254
  in 2016 presidential campaign, 254
  in 2020 presidential campaign, 279–280
  in voting and women candidates, 278–279
  Elizabeth Warren's campaign in 2020, 9, 256–257
  women in office, 255–256 (table)
  See also Women in Politics, Hillary Clinton and individual candidates and campaigns

Gergen, D., 149

Gershon, S., 259

Gillibrand, Kirsten, 7, 173, 252, 256, 280

Gillum, Andrew, 90, 107

Gingrich, N., 107, 159

Givhan, R., 261

Glassner, B., 236
Global financial crisis, 51
Global health crises, 215–216
Global public opinion, 216–218
Global Terrorism Database, 239–240
Global warming, climate change, 121–124,
    228–229
Goldmacher, S., 257
Goldwater, Barry, 79
Good Morning America, 173
Gore, Al, 117
    Media narrative in Gore-Bush 2000
        presidential campaign, 117–119
Gorn, E., 186
Grabe, M., 58
Granholm, J., 107
*The Great Alignment: Race, Party
    Transformation, and the Rise of Donald
    Trump* (Abramowitz), 146
"The Great Communicator," 58, 137, 149
Great Recession, 51, 197
Greenwald, G., 150
Grimes, A. L., 74
Groundhog Day, 139
Guess, A., 130
Gun control legislation, 139–140
Gun violence, 55, 139–140, 187–188

Haberman, M., 157
Hacker, J. S., 143
Hagel, C., 242
Halberstam, D., 246
Haley, N., 196
Hallin, D., 246
Hamby, C., 131
Hamby, P., 116, 161–162
Hannity, S., 30, 102, 130, 225, 237
Hardball, 106, 113, 118
Harris, J. F., 116
Harris, Kamala, xiii, 7, 9, 72, 106, 164, 168,
    172, 173, 175, 209–211, 252, 256
    (table), 259, 280–281
    "birtherism," 281
    intersectionality, 281
    nomination of, 7, 9, 280–281
    Trump's comment, 281
    as vice president, 209–211
Harris, T., 75
Hashtag, social media, 190–191
Hayes, D., 29
Hendrickson, C., 29
Hendricks, S., 112
Herndon, A., 257

Hindman, M., 46
Hodgson, G., 217
Hodierne, Robert, interview, 247–248
Hofstadter, R., 217
Holt, L., 161
Horse-race coverage, bias toward, 109–110
Horton, W., 79
Howard Stern Show, 273
Huckabee, M., 107, 116, 142 (table)
Huffington, A., 262
Humanitarian crises, 230–232
    "CNN effect," 213–215
    international news, importance of, 232–233
    media coverage by news organizations, 232
    Syrian civil war and, 233–234
    twenty top stories of 2019, 231 (table)
Humphrey, H., 43, 158
"Hunger for human awareness," news, 96
Hurd, W., 164

*Identity Crisis: The 2016 Presidential Campaign
    and the Battle for the Meaning of America*
    (Sides, Tesler and Vavreck), 5, 276
Identity politics, 4–6, 184, 275–276
IHeartMedia, 25
*Image Bite Politics: News and the Visual Framing
    of Elections* (Elizabeth and Bucy), 58
Immigration 199–208
    case-study, "Building 'the Wall' and framing
        Dreamers, 205–208
    framing immigrants in coverage and
        politics, 200–201
    George W. Bush, attempts to pass
        immigration reform, 199–200
    interview with Maria Elena Salinas,
        201–202
    Latino voters and vote in 2020, 208–209
    media coverage, impact of, 200
    Republican party and, pre-Trump,
        202–203
    Trump anti-immigrant rhetoric, 1, 5, 55,
        88, 203, 206
    Trump policies on, 203–208
    policy in U.S., historically, 199–200
Impact of political ads, 70–71
Impeachment, 6–7, 48, 50
"Imperial presidency," 147
Information disorder, 167
Inglehart, R. F., 5
Ingraham, L., 102, 130, 225, 237
Insiderism, bias toward, 106–109
    in media and politics, 106–108
    politics as insiders' game, 108–109

Instagram, 25 (table), 101 (table), 102,
    161–163, 165–166
  fake news/disinformation by Russian
      government, 2016 presidential
      campaign, 165–167
  See also fake/news disinformation
  use by 2020 presidential candidates and
      Rep. Alexandria Ocasio-Cortez
Internal Revenue Service, 71
International news, 213–216, 230, 233
Internet, xii, 10–11, 19, 25, 31, 38, 46, 47, 63,
    87, 96, 98–99, 101–102, 138, 164, 165,
    167, 194, 215, 235, 276
  redefinining immediacy, 98–99
  democratizing information, 31
  fake news/disincormation in 2016 and
      2020 campaigns, 102, 127, 129,
      151–152, 164–167
  history of, 100–101 (table)
  political elites, 46
  debate over regulation? 19–20
Internet giants, 25–26 (table)
Internet Research Agency (IRA), 166, 167
Iraq War, case study, 241–245
  cascading activation model, 245
  congressional debate, 243
  case-study, media failures in coverage of
      weapons of mass destruction, 242–245
Islamic State terrorist group (ISIS), 54, 74,
    235, 238
Issue frames, 54–55
*It's Even Worse Than It Looks: How the
    American Constitutional System Collided
    with the New Politics of Extremism* (Mann
    and Ornstein), 17
*It Takes a Candidate: Why Women Don't Run for
    Office* (Lawless and Fox), 269
Iyengar, S., 44, 45, 49, 64

Jamieson, K. H., 74, 82, 258, 259
Jarvis, Jeff, 99
Jefferson, T., 13, 199
Jet magazine, 186
Johnson, L., 14, 44, 79, 185, 246
Jolly, D., 142

Kahn-Cullors, P., 187, 188
Kahneman, D., 53, 54
Kamarck, E., 205–206
Kane, P., 111
Kantar data, 69
Kaplan, L., 168
Karpf, D., 31

Kasich, J., 107
Kavanagh, M., 224
Kavanaugh, B., 68, 139, 145, 148
Kelly, M., 1, 107, 251, 273–274
Kendi, X. I., 192
Kennedy. J., 51
Kennedy, J. F., 14, 44, 51, 58, 185, 237, 246
Kennicott, P., 62
Kerry, J., 74, 80–81, 83–85
Kessler, G., 72
Ki-moon, B., 234
Kinder, D. R., 44, 49, 64
Kindy, K., 239–240
King, Rodney, 187
King, Martin Luther, 43, 78, 185–186
Kislyak, S., 156
Klein, J., 108
Klobuchar, Amy, 7, 8, 105–106, 136, 252,
    256 (table), 258
Knight Foundation, 11
Koch-affiliated groups, 68, 125
Koch, C., 68
Kohut, A., 233
Koppel, T., 50
Kovach, B., 96, 120
Krauthammer, C., 108
Krebs, C., 170
Kristof, N., 254
Kudlow, L., 222
Kumar, M. J., 151
Kuntzman, G., 272
Kurtz, H., 119
Kuznia, R., 42

Ladd, J. M., 17
LaFree, G., 240
Lake, Celinda, interview, 260
Lakshmanan, Indira, interview, 16, 129–130
Landay, Jonathan, 242; interview, 245
Landrieu, M., 114
Larry King Live, 172
Last Week Tonight with John Oliver show,
    174, 176
Late Late Show, 52
Late Late Show with James Corden, 172
Late-night comedy, case study, 171–176
Late Night, 171, 172
Late Show with David Letterman, 174
Late Show with Stephen Colbert, 172, 173, 176
Latino voters and vote in 2020, 208–209
Lawless, J. L., 29, 269–270
Lee, Tien-Tsung, 17
"Legacy" media, 47, 173, 272

LGBTQ, 59–60, 203, 277
  See also same-sex marriage, framing, case study, public opinion, 61 (table)
Leiserowitz, A., 122, 228–229
Lemon, D., 153, 273
Lewandowski, C., 107, 108
Lewis, J., 185
Life magazine, 51, 245
Lights, Camera, War! (Neuman), 215
Limbaugh, R., 84, 102, 225, 227, 229
Lincoln Memorial, 62, 185
Lipman, J., 253
Lippmann, W., 39–40
Lipset, S. M., 217
Liptak, A., 60, 155–156
Liswood, Laura, interview, 265, 266
Local news crisis, 26–29
Local TV news, 29, 126, 128
Local TV stations, 19, 23 (table)
Long, H., 220
Lopez, I. H., 5
Los Angeles Police Department (LAPD), 187
Los Angeles Times, 27, 28, 41, 123, 177, 201, 221,223, 232
  circulation gains for, 28
Lowe, J., 51
Lowery, W., 189, 239–240

Madam President (Clift and Brazaitis), 266
Maddow, R., 6, 30, 47
Mahe, Eddie, interview, 264
Maibach, E., 229
"Make 'Em Squeal" ad, 75–76
Malcolm, E., 270
Manchin, J., 140
Mann, T., 17
Martin, Trayvon, 48, 187–188, 191, 196
Massing, M., 241, 243
Matthews, C., 106, 113, 157
McAdam, D., 184
McCain, John., 51, 81, 85, 116, 119, 138, 139, 145, 146, 194, 195, 262–264
  advertisements, campaigns, 85–86
McCallum, M., 30
McCarty, N., 17–18
McCaskill, C., 68, 107
McClatchy newspapers, 27
McCombs, M., 42–43, 44
McConnell, M., 74, 148
McCurry, Mike, interview, 154–155
McIlwain, C. D., 190
The McLaughlin Group show, 104
McLaughlin, J., 104

McLuhan, M., 31
Media analysis tool kit, 33
  annotated resource pages, 356–363
  how to do case study, 34–35
  research and analysis, 36–37
  topics, 36
Media and technology history, 100–101 (table)
Media archaeologists, 39
Media-centered politics, 10–11
  deregulation of media, 19–26
  economics of news, 18–19
  Federal Communications Commission, 19, 129
  First Amendment, xii, 11, 13–16, 60, 67, 155
  media bias, perceptions of, 16–18
  "media primary," 10, 32, 112
  objectivity in journalism, 120–125
  ownership of media, 20–24 (table)
  News deserts, 28–29
  political polarization and, 16–18
  public opinion, 15–16
  U.S. voter participation, 10
Media credibility and trust, 15, 126, 127
Media-effects theory, 39–42
  defined, 39
  examples from news coverage, 41, 42,
  Plato's cave-dwellers, public as, 39–40
Media-military relationship, 246–248
Media narratives, bias toward, 115–119
  access counts, 119
  coverage of Al Gore and George W. Bush, 117–118
  policy speeches and public, 115
  2004 presidential campaign, 116
  presidential candidates, coverage of, 116
  2008 presidential race, 116
  reporters, 119
  "straight-news" stories, 117
MediaQuant, 2
Media roles, xvi, 10, 11, 13, 15, 32, 39, 43, 98, 214
  agenda-setting theory, 42–43
  bias toward immediacy, 97
  cable news, importance of, 30–31
  civic engagement, 28–29
  coronavirus pandemic and, 29
  Internet and democratizing information, 31
  local news, 28–29
  newspapers, 26–27
Meet the Press, 106, 108, 114, 115, 154, 241
Meir, G., 266

Messaging and mobilizing, social media, 158
    Ocasio-Cortez's, 161–163
    2020 presidential campaign, 163–164
    Trump's, 160–161
    Twitter, 158–159
'Messaging war,' 56
#MeToo movement, 45, 186, 276
Mexican immigration, 1, 5, 203, 204, 206
Mightier Than the Sword: How the News Media Have Shaped American History (Streitmatter), 267
Mills, D., 52
Mink, P. T., 269
Misinformation. *See* Fake news/disinformation
Mitchell, A., 259
Mondale, W., 78, 105, 252
Monica Lewinsky scandal, 50, 154
"Morning in America" ad, 77–78
Mother Jones magazine, 74
"Mourning in America 2020," ad 92
Moyers, B., 76, 79
MSNBC, 6, 12, 30, 31, 107, 113, 154, 157
    agenda-building, 47
    founding 101 (table)
Mueller, R., 47
Muradian, Vago, interview, 248
Muslims, 138, 235–236, 238–239, 277
    Trump anti-Muslim rhetoric and policies, 236
    See Islamaphobia in media and politics
Murdoch, L., 226
Murdoch, R., 30, 128, 226
Murray, P., 268
Murrow, Edward R, 100 (figure)
The Myth of Digital Democracy (Hindman), 46

Nacos, B., 236–237
Nagourney, A., 11, 191–192, 195
Narratives. *See* Media narratives, bias toward
National Amusements, 20–21 (table)
National broadcast TV networks, 19
National Journal, 108, 138
National Public Radio (NPR), 6, 18, 108, 191, 168–169
National Rifle Association (NRA), 89, 140
National Security Agency (NSA), 15, 150
The Nature and Origins of Mass Opinion (Zaller), 45–46
Nature of news, 39–40, 97
Navarro, Ana, 108, 144; interview, 203–204
NBC News, 3, 18–19, 20, 98, 107, 115, 128, 185, 201, 231 (table)
Negative ads, 68, 79, 141

Nelson, S., 186
Neuman, J., 215
"New Eden," 216
Newport, F., 236
News Corp, 23 (table)
News deserts, 28–29
Newspapers, 26–28
    decline in local journalism, 28–29
    deregulation of ownership, 26–27
    online, 26
News peg, 41
News That Matters: Television & American Opinion (Iyengar and Kinder), 44
Newsweek magazine, 62, 117
The News with Brian Williams, 117
New Yorker, 45, 149
New York Herald, 267
New York Times, 4, 11, 12, 14, 27, 28, 41, 45, 111, 115, 117, 118, 120, 121, 123, 128, 129, 151, 153, 156, 177, 215, 223, 232, 241–243, 246, 258, 272, 276
    agenda-setting, 45
    circulation gains for, 10, 28
    history, 100–101 (table)
    Iraq War coverage, case-study, 215, 241–243
    #MeToo investigation, 45, 276
    Pentagon Papers case, 14
    Russia investigation, 161
    Trump, attacks on, 12, 121, 129, 151, 161
    Swift boat ad campaign, 81
New York Times Co. v. Sullivan, 14
New York Times Co. v. United States, 14
1917 Espionage Act, 150
1968 Democratic National Convention in Chicago, 158
Nixon, Richard, 14, 16, 43, 50, 101 (table), 104, 128, 147, 150, 152, 158, 229
Nobel Prize in Economics Sciences, 53
Noonan, P., 58, 149
Norris, P., 5, 266
Northeastern University School of Journalism, 253
Novak, J., 109
Now They Tell Us: The American Press and Iraq (Massing), 241, 243
Nyhan, B., 130

Obama, Barack, 2, 11, 13, 51, 52, 55, 57, 60, 61–62, 69, 74, 85, 86, 139, 140, 150–151, 158, 172, 191–197, 207, 214, 233–234

digital media, use of, 158
election, 69, 85–86, 191–193
framing as "the Other," 193–194
health-care reform, 55–57
"Islamic extremism," 237
immigration policy 197, 207
political advertising and, 69, 85–86
presidential debates, 104
reelection, 86, 107, 197
See also 2008 and 2012 presidential
        campaigns and elections and Obama
        Presidency
Obamacare, 55–57, 138–139
"Obama coalition," 195
Obama, Michelle, 52, 197, 281
Obama Presidency, 150–151, 191–193
    discussion of race, 195–196
    framing as "the Other," 193–195
    immigration policy, 197
    public opinion on racial discrimination,
        2016, 197–198
    See also Syrian War
Objectivity in journalism, 120–125
Ocasio-Cortez, Alexandria, 90–91, 131, 148,
        161–162, 281
Occupy Wall Street movement, 110, 112
Official sources, bias toward, 113–115
    criticisms of journalists, 113–114
    government officials interviews, 114
    Meet the Press, 115
    Sunday shows, 115
O'Keefe, Ed, interview, 148, 211
OpenSecrets.org, 71
Operational and cultural media biases,
        16–17
Orientation, need for, 42
Orlando Sentinel, 90
Ornstein, N., 17
O'Rourke, B., 116, 163, 164, 258
Out of Order (Patterson), 10
Owens, D., 102, 160–161
Ownership of media, 18, 20–24 (table)
    Alphabet Inc., 25–26 (table)
    AT&T, 21–22 (table)
    Comcast Corporation, 22 (table)
    Facebook, Inc., 25
    Fox Corporation, 23 (table)
    Gannett, 24 (table)
    music, 25
    National Amusements, 20–21 (table)
    News Corp, 23 (table)
    newspapers and local TV stations,
        23–24 (table)

Sinclair Broadcast Group, 24 (table)
Tegna, 24 (table)
The Walt Disney Company, 21 (table)

Paine, T., 216
Palin, S., 56, 85, 107, 175, 258, 259
The Partisan Divide: Congress in Crisis (Frost
        and Cohen), 144
Partisan media, 15–16, 44, 127
Party conventions, 157–158
Pasco, J., 189
Patient Protection and Affordable Care Act, 55
Patterson, Thomas E., 4, 10, 177
PBS NewsHour, 126, 154
Pease, D. E., 216
Pelosi, Nancy, 148, 255 (table), 268, 278
Pence, Mike, 9, 145, 281
Pentagon Papers case, 14, 152
Perkins, T., 145
Perot, R., 75, 172
Persuasive techniques, political ads and
        political communication, 66–67, 73–85
    and cross-list individual ads or say
    See also ads, political individual—
        association technique, 77–78
    classical rhetoric, logos, pathos and ethos, 73
    Biden "Soul of America" ad, 91–92
    code words and distortion, 73–75
    disassociation technique, 74
    juxtaposition and visual and auditory
        linking, 74
    false inferences, 67, 74, 82
    Heroism and "Plain-folks" technique,
        "Eisenhower Answers America,"
        ad, 76
    Willie Horton ad and racist appeals, 79–80
    Running against Washington: "Make 'Em
        Squeal" ad, 75–76
    "Morning in America" ad, positive
        messaging and association technique,
        77–78
    "Daisy" ad and provoking fear, 79
    Swift boat ad campaign, case-study,
        80–85
    False equivalences, 4, 97, 120
    climate-change case study, 121–125
Pew Research Center, 15, 17, 18, 35, 55,
        59, 71, 72, 102, 118, 127, 174, 206,
        233, 237
Pew polls
    American exceptionalism,
        generational, 219
    campaign spending, 71–72

confidence in media, 127–128
Fox News Channel viewers and
    coronavirus information, 225
"Building the Wall" and framing
    immigration, case-study, 205–208
fakenews, 102
party identification in evaluating
    media, 15
health care, 55, 59–60
global public opinion on Trump and
    policies, 218
social media, 11
polarization, 13, 227
Trump impact on political discourse, 103
2012 Presidential campaign, 72
global warming, 122
recall of 9/11 events, 237
polarization, 18, 127
Trump response to coronavirus pandemic,
    223–224 (figure)
same-sex marriage, 59–60
terrorist attacks of 9/11, 237
Gallup polling, 50–51
public opinion on:
American exceptionalism, generational,
    218, 219 (table)
campaign spending, 71, 72 (figure)
confidence in media, 127–128
Fox News Channel viewers and
    coronavirus information, 225
"Building the Wall" and framing
    immigration, case, study, 205–208
fake news, 102
party identification in evaluating media, 15
health care, 55
global public opinion on Trump and
    policies, 218
social media, 11, 102
polarization, 13, 227
Trump impact on political discourse, 103
2012 Presidential campaign, 72
global warming, 122
recall of 9/11 events, 237
Trump response to coronavirus pandemic,
    223–224 (figure)
same-sex marriage, 59–60
terrorist attacks of 9/11, 237
Philadelphia Inquirer, 242
Photographs, priming personal presidential
    traits, 51–52
Pierson, P., 143
Pinckney, C., 196
Pinsker, J., 221

Police shootings, fatal, 189, 196–198
American federal election campaigns, 67
Citizens United v. FEC decision, 66, 67
"dark-money" groups, 68
free media coverage of, 2016 presidential
    campaign, 3 (table)
fund-raising pressures on candidates,
    140–142
history of on TV, 76
impact on democracy, 66–72
impact of individual ads, 70–71
in campaigns, 66, 85–93
negative ads, rise of, 68
public opinion on money in politics, 71
spending on, 67–73, 143 (table)
super PACs, 67–68
voters learning from ads, 70
See also Advertisements, Persuasive
    Techniques and individual
    Presidential campaigns
The Political Brain (Westen), 78, 79
Polarization, political, 12, 16–18, 29, 30, 44,
    104, 127, 129, 227
Political consultants, 112, 141, 142 (table)
Politico, 45, 108, 116, 150–151, 168,
    203, 280
PolitiFact, 72, 223–224
Poole, K., 17
POV, 41
Power of senses, 61–63
sound, 63
symbols, debate over, 62
Presidency and media, 148–152
Bill Clinton, 50, 55, 75, 114, 135,
    149, 151, 171, 189, 213, 258, 266,
    270, 273
George W. Bush, 50, 81, 149–150, 237
impeachment and Monica Lewinsky
    scandal, public opinion, 50
Joe Biden, 9, 91–92 See also Joe
    Biden and 2020 presidential
    campaign
Richard Nixon, 14, 16, 43, 50, 101 (table),
    104, 128, 147, 150, 152, 158, 229
debate over, 62
Ronald Reagan, 19, 149–150
Trump, "Fake news", Trump attacks on
    news organizations as, 11, 129,
    151–154, 178
See also First Amendment and Donald
    Trump
Party conventions, changes in coverage,
    157, 158

White House briefings, changes in, 154–155

Mike McCurry, former press secretary, interview, 154–155

Presidential campaigns, priming, 50–51

Presidential debates, 104–106

Priming theory, 49–50
  defined, 49
  personal presidential traits, 51–52
  presidential campaigns, 50–51
  presidential spouses, 52–53
  See also Agenda-setting

Project for Excellence in Journalism, 56–57, 118

Provoking fear, political ads, 79

"Proxy war," 234

Public Broadcasting Service (PBS), 18, 42, 126, 186

Public opinion on—
  Gallup polling, 50–51
  coronavirus pandemic, knowledge of per cable network, 225–226
  terrorists attack, 236
  media credibility and trust, 15, 126, 127
  same-sex marriage, 60
  Trump approval rating during impeachment, 7
  health care, 57
  woman as US president, 264–265

Public Opinion (Lippmann), 39, 63

Pulitzer Prize awards, 28, 42, 189

Putin, V., 166

Qiu, L., 222

Quayle, D., 105

"The Queen of Rage," 62

Race in media and politics, 182–191
  anti-AAPI bias and rise in hate crimes, 227
  Asian Americans, 227, 269
  Asian American Twitter, 49
  #BlackLivesMatter, 183, 186–190
  Black Voters, role in 2020 presidential election, 209–210
  Breonna Taylor, 182, 189, 190, 198
  Chinese Exclusion Act, 199
  civil rights movement, 18, 43–44, 98, 100 (table), 185–186
  "defund the police," 92, 190, 211
  digital activism, 186–190
  Donald Trump's false rhetoric linking coronavirus to Asian Americans, 227
  Emmett Till, 185–186

Eric Deggans on media coverage in crisis, 191

Framing Obama as "the Other," 193–195

George Floyd's death and protests, 182–183, 189, 190

gun violence, 187–188

Julian Bond, interview on civil-rights movement and media, 43–44, 186

Kamala Harris, historic nomination and election, 209–210, 280–281

Obama presidency and, 191–192

Obama discussion of race, 195–197

Obama election and reelection, 191–192, 194, 195, 197

Police shootings, fatal, 189, 196–198

public opinion on racial discrimination, 197–198

Racial discrimination, public opinion on, 197–198

Rev. Wright and 2012 campaign, 86, 194–195

Study of social media and #BlackLives Matter, 190, 191

Sam Fulwood III, interview on race in media and politics, 196, 211

See also Barack Obama and Obama Presidency

Trump appeal to white voters, 1, 147, 184, 276

"Willie Horton" ad and racist appeals, 79, 129, 194

white supremacy, rise of, 205, 240–241

The Rachel Maddow Show, 6

Radio news, immediacy, 98, 100 (table)

Rage (Woodward), 223

Ramshaw, E., 177

Reagan, Ronald, 19, 49–50, 51–52, 57–58, 105, 137
  advertisements, 78, 88
  presidency and media, 149–150

Reeves, R., 76, 77

Regan, T., 225

Republic (Plato), 39–40

Republican National Convention, 157–158

Republican party and Donald Trump future of Republican party immigration, 202–203

Republican revolution, 149

Restless searchlight, 40

Reverse agenda-setting, 47–48

Rice, C., 242, 261

Ridout, T., 69, 89

Rights of Man (1792) (Paine), 216

Ritter, S., 242
Roeder, G. H., 245–246
Rogers, E. M., 46
Romney, Mitt, 7, 69, 73, 74, 86, 104, 145, 156, 159, 206
Roosevelt, F. D., 61
Roosevelt, T., 75
Rosenstiel, T., 96, 109, 120
Rosenthal, H., 17
Rothschild, D. M., 272
Roth, Y., 169
Rove, K., 107
Rubio, M., 88, 105, 115–116, 145
Rucker, P., 111
Rumsfeld, D., 242
Russert, T., 106
Ryan, Paul, 2, 145, 274

Safer, Morley, interview, 249
Salant, Richard, interview, 10
Salinas, Maria Elena, interview, 201–202
Same-sex marriage, reframing, 59–61
    Colorado Civil Rights Commission, 60
    groups supporting, 61 (table)
    media and, 59–60
    public opinion on, 59–60
Sanders, Bernie Sen., 3, 7–9, 16, 48, 71, 87, 162, 256–257
    campaign finance reform, 71–72
    interview, 110, 111
    critiquing media coverage of, 112–113
    2016 campaign, 71, 87, 88, 142, 144, 191, 243, 271, 273
    2020 campaign, 48, 113, 163–164, 168, 172, 175, 209
Saturday Night Live, 171, 174–175
Scarborough, J., 261, 272, 274
Schiff, A., 6, 7, 170
Schlesinger, A., 147
Schmidt, S., 108
Schroeder, P., 251
Schudson, M., 113–114, 120
Schwartz, T., 79
Scott, T., 6
Senate impeachment trial, 6–7
Senate Intelligence Committee, 166
Senate Judiciary Committee, 268
Senses, power of, 61–63
Sessions, J., 156
Shafer, J., 110
Shapiro, B., 103
Shaw, D., 42–43, 44
Sheingate, A., 141

Shipp, E. R., 118
Sides, J., 5
Silverman, C., 165
Sinclair Broadcast Group, 24–25, 24 (table)
Slate, 110
Snowden, E., 150
Social media 48–49, 99, 102, 158–164
    agenda-setting and reverse agenda-setting and, 48–49
    Fake News/Disinformation in 2016 presidential campaign, 102, 164–167
    in 2020 Presidential Campaign, 163–164, 168–170
    messaging and mobilizing, 158
    news immediacy, 99–103
    Obama and, 151, 158
    Ocasio-Cortez and, 161–163
    See also Facebook
    See also Instagram
    Twitter, Trump's use of, 47, 99, 161–162, 168–170
    Twitter, impact of, 99, 102, 158–159
    YouTube, 99, 102
The Sociology of News (Schudson), 120
Solomon, M., 59
Sorenson, T., 58
Sound, power of, 63
Souza, P., 52
Spicer, S., 11, 155
Stahl, L., 57–58, 149
Stamped from the Beginning (Kendi), 192
Steele, M., 107
Stein, J., 254
Stein, S., 30
Stelter, B., 25, 152
Stephens, M., 96
Stephenson, A., 77
Stereotyping, political ads, 73, 79–80
Straight-Talk Express, 119
Streitmatter, R., 267
Student Nonviolent Coordinating Committee (SNCC), 44, 186
Sullivan, M., 1, 131, 151
Super PACs, 66, 67–68, 140–141
Swift boat ad campaign, 80–85
    impact of, 83–85
    techniques of, 82–83

Tampa Bay Times, 72
Tani, M., 30
Tapper, Jake, interview, 157; also, 145, 274

Tax cuts, 9, 53
Tea Party movement, 56, 110, 186, 200
Tegna, 24 (table)
Telegraph, news immediacy, 97–98
Television's/government's, news coverage, 41
Terrorism, 50–51, 217, 235–236
    Terrorist attacks and media coverage,
        235, 236
    American Muslim groups, 235
    far-right domestic terrorism, 239–241
    fear frame, 236–238
    Islamic State terrorist group (ISIS), 74,
        235, 237
    Islamophobia in media and politics,
        238–239
    Public opinion on, 217–218
    9/11 terrorist attacks, public opinion on,
        236, 237–239, 244
    War in Iraq, case-study, 241–245
Tesler, M., 5, 276
"Texas Reloaded" ad, 93
Texas Tribune, 177
Thatcher, M., 266
"Miscast institution," 10
Thinking, Fast and Slow (Kahneman), 54
This Week show, 114, 126
Time magazine, 60, 61, 119, 151, 263
Times-Picayune, 27
Todd, Chuck, interview, 115, 152, 154
Tometi, O., 187
The Tonight Show, 171, 172
Tonight Show with Jay Leno, 174
The Tonight Show with Jimmy Fallon, 172
Toomey, P., 140
Tow Center for Digital Journalism, 166
Traister, R., 272
Trust and accountability in media, 96, 126–130
Trump, Donald, 1, 2, 5, 6, 92–93, 129,
        144–146, 151–152
    ads, 90–92, 167–170
    agenda-setting on social media, 47–48
    appeal to white voters, 1, 147, 184, 275
    approval rating, impeachment, 6, 7,
        146, 226
    Asian Americans, comments on, 227
    attacks on journalists and news media, 12,
        153–156
    "birtherism," 193, 194
    Black voters and, 209–210
    #BlackLivesMatter movement, comments
        on, 147, 210, 211
    "Building the Wall" and framing
        immigration, case study—205–208

comments about women, 1–2, 89, 257,
        259, 261, 262, 273–275, 280–281
Coronavirus pandemic pandemic response,
        8–9, 219–220, 222–223, 224 (figure)
"dog-whistle" politics, 5, 9
election fraud, false claims, 168–170
environment and, 229, 230
evangelical voters and, 145, 209
False claims about 2020 election results,
        169–171
"Fake news", Trump attacks on news
        organizations as, 11, 127, 129,
        151–154, 178
fake news/disinformation in 2016 and
        2020 campaigns, 165–167, 178
foreign policy, 217, 235–236
Fourth of July concert, use of
        symbols, 62, 63
free media, 1, 3 (figure), 69, 88
public opinion on pandemic response,
        223, 224 (figure)
George Floyd, death and protests,
        comments on, 147, 182, 184,
        190, 211
global public opinion on policies, 218
See also coronavirus and 2020 presidential
        campaign,
See also First Amendment
See also Identity politics
public opinion on Trump impact on social
        discourse, 103 (figure)
social media, use of, 48, 99, 160–161,
        168–170
immigration policies and race, 203–208
immigration rhetoric and policies,
        203–208
immigrants, 1–2, 5
impeachment, 6–7, 156, 231 (table)
journalists and, 120–121, 153–154
late-night comedy TV, 172, 174–176
Latino vote and voters, appeal to in 2020
        presidential election, 209–210
"Make America Great Again," 5, 88
Muslims, comments on and policies, 204,
        235, 236
news organizations, attacks on, 11, 12,
        151–155
Pence and, 9, 145
political advertising by, 69, 72
Presidency, 6, 12, 15, 47, 48, 55, 72, 89,
        115, 121, 130, 131, 133, 136, 137,
        148, 151–152, 157, 156, 169, 205,
        215, 238

presidency and media, 151–154
presidential debates, 104–105
2016 Presidential Election, 3–4, 87,
    88, 104, 105, 109, 113, 129, 142,
    144, 165, 166, 177, 270, 270–271,
    271–273
2020 Presidential campaign, 7, 9, 72,
    91–93, 148, 163, 167, 168–170, 209,
    226–227, 229–230
2020 Presidential Election, 7, 9, 72,
    91–93, 148, 163, 167, 168–170, 209,
    226–227, 229–230
Republican party and, 145–147
supporters' trust in media, polling,
    129–130
seniors and, 92
Twitter, use of, 47, 99, 161–162, 168
visual images and, 62
"War in Iraq," case-study, 241-245
white supremacists, comments, 205,
    240–241
2018 Congressional midterm election, 90,
    276–279
Trump: The Art of the Deal, 90
Tumulty, Karen, interview, 115
Turner, T., 30, 98
Tversky. A., 53, 54
Twitter, 2, 4, 7, 47, 48, 49, 98–99, 102,
    109, 129, 137, 158–159, 161–162,
    169–170
news immediacy, 99, 102–103
#BlackLivesMatter movement, study of,
    190–192
Asian American Twitter, 49
Black Twitter, 49, 191
Feminist Twitter, 49
Trump, use of, 12, 48, 99, 102, 109, 129,
    158–159, 160–161
Tyndall, Andrew, interview, 215, 216,
    231, 232
Tyndall Report, 3, 215

The Uncensored War (Hallin), 246
USA Today, 27, 62, 68, 153
USA Today Network, 41
U.S. News & World Report, 150
U.S. Supreme Court cases, 14, 60, 67, 208

Van Dam, A., 220
VandeHei, J., 116
Van der Veen, A. M., 239
Vavreck, L., 5, 70, 276
Vega, Cecilia, 153–154

Vietnam War, 246, 247, 249
The View, 52, 171
Visual and auditory linking ads, 74
Visual framing, 57–59
Voting, participation and nonvoters, 10, 11, 29
    gender gap, 278–279
Vox, 41

Wallace, G., 9, 43, 147
Wall Street Journal, 4, 27, 28, 41, 108, 123,
    156, 177, 239
agenda-setting, 45
circulation gains for, 28
ownership, 23 (table)
Swift boat ad campaign, 81
Walsh, Ken, interview, 150, 153
The Walt Disney Company, 21 (table)
Walter, A., 8
Wang, A. B., 257
Wardle, C., 167
Warren, Elizabeth, 7, 8, 9, 72, 163, 164, 168,
    174, 209, 251, 252, 280
    presidential campaign in 2020, 256–257
Warren, M., 139
War reporting, 245–249
future of, 248–249
World War II, 245, 246
Vietnam War, 14, 80, 101 (table), 246–249
See also "Pentagon papers" case
Afghanistan War, Washington Post,
    investigation, 14, 243
dissent in, 243, 245–246
media-military relationship, 246–248
nature of war, changes in, 248–249
wartime censorship and propaganda,
    245, 246
Washington Post, 1, 4, 12, 14, 27, 28, 41, 108,
    120, 123, 145, 153, 158, 177, 215,
    243, 274
agenda-setting, 45
circulation gains for, 10, 28
fatal police shootings investigation,
    189–190
#MeToo investigation, 45, 276
National Security Agency surveillance
    investigation, 150
Pentagon Papers case, 14
Swift boat ad campaign, 81
Iraq War, case-study, 242–243
Trump, attacks on, 12, 108, 129, 145, 151,
    153, 156, 161
Watergate investigation, 16,
    100–101 (chart), 112

Watchdog role of media, 13
Watts, D. J., 272
Weapons of mass destruction (WMDs), 84,
    150, 215, 241–242
Weaver, D. H., 16, 43
Weinstein. H., 45
Wesleyan Media Project, 66, 68
West, D. M., 70, 74, 86
Westen, D., 78, 79
White House changes, press briefing,
    154–157
White House photos, 51–52, 51 (figure)
White supremacy, rise of, 196, 205, 240, 241
Whitman, Bryan, interview, 247
Why Americans Hate Politics
    (Dionne), 104
*Why Americans Hate the Media and How It
    Matters* (Ladd), 17
Williams, B. A., 173
Williams, Ryan, interview, 159, 206
Williamson, M., 7, 252
"Willie Horton" ad, 79, 81, 129, 194
Willnat, L., 16
Winfrey, K. L., 259
Winston, David, interview, 84, 85, 207
Winthrop, J., 216
Women in politics, 251–255, 258–259
    Women in office, history of, 255–256 (table),
        267–269
    2018 congressional midterm elections, 6,
        252, 268, 276–278
    EMILY's List, 270
    history of, milestones, 255–256 (table)
    Seneca Falls Convention, 267
    underrepresentation of women in political
        office, 269–270
    women of color in Congress, 269
    women senators, 268
    "Year of the Woman" in Congress, 252,
        254, 268, 276–278
    case-study, Elizabeth Dole's 2000
        presidential campaign, 262–265
    barriers to running for office, 269–270
    "double bind", 254, 258–259
    "likeability" factor, 260–262
    See also Hillary Clinton and 2008 and
        2016 presidential campaigns
    See also Sarah Palin, Carly Fiorina and
        Michelle Bachmann
    See also Elizabeth Warren and 2020
        campaign

See also Kamala Harris and 2020 campaign
2018 and 2020 Congressional elections,
    Results, 6, 267–269
    Gains by Republican women in
        2020, 279
    See also Alexandria Ocasio-Cortez 2018
        congressional midterm elections and,
        268–269, 276–278, 277 (statistics on
        women elected)
    Sexist coverage and impact, 257, 258
Women leaders in U.S., 254, 265–266
    barriers to women running for office,
        265–267, 269, 270
    gender gap in voting, 278–279
    identity politics and voters in 2016, 275–276
    #MeToo Movement, 276–278
    underrepresentation of, 269–270
    women's suffrage, 267–269
    See also Hillary Clinton, Elizabeth Warren,
        Amy Klobuchar, Tulsi Gabbard,
        Kirsten Gillibrand, Kamala Harris
    See also Donald Trump
    See also Gender
    "Year of the Woman" in Congress, 252,
        254, 268, 276–278
Woodhull, V., 255 (table), 269
Woodward, B., 223
Wright, J., 86, 194

"Year of the Woman" in Congress, 252, 254,
    268, 276–278
YouGov, 225
YouTube, 25 (table), 35, 47, 99, 101,
    102, 138

Zaller, J., 45–46
Zinni, A. C., 62
Zirinsky, S., 126
Zuckerberg, M., 101 (table), 165
Zucker, J., 107
2008 presidential election, 85–86
    advertisements in campaigns, 85–86
    See also Hillary Clinton, Barack Obama,
        Bernie Sanders, John McCain &
        Sarah Palin
2012 presidential election
    advertisements in campaigns, 69, 86
    See also Barack Obama, Mitt Romney
2016 presidential election, 1–6, 87–89
    advertisements in campaigns, 87–89
    fake news/disinformation, 164–168

gun violence and, 140
identity politics, 4–6, 184, 275
impeachment, 6–7
political advertising, 69, 71
voting and polling data, 5
white supremacists, comments on, 240
See also Hillary Clinton, Donald Trump
    and Bernie Sanders individual and
    2016 presidential campaign
See also Women in politics and media
2016 Republican primary debates, 104–105
2018 congressional midterm elections, 69,
    90–91, 207, 252, 268
See also Year of the Woman
advertisements in campaigns, 90–91
2020 presidential campaign, 7–8, 163–164,
    167, 229–230,
Climate change, 229–230
Coronavirus pandemic, 8–9, 226–227

Gender, role of in, 279–280
See also Women in Politics
See also Black Voters, role in 2020
    presidential election, 209–210
See also Latino vote and voters in 2020
See also Joe Biden, Donald Trump,
    Hillary Clinton, Bernie Sanders,
    Elizabeth Warren, Kamala Harris,
    Pete Buttigieg, Amy Klobuchar, Cory
    Booker, Marianne Williamson, Tulsi
    Gabbard
2020 congressional elections 66, 252
2020 presidential election, 7–8, 91–93
advertisements in campaigns, 91–93
Biden campaign, 7–8, 91–92, 210,
    226–227
Identity politics, role of 4, 163, 256–257
Trump and, 92–93
Veterans and, 93